MIMESIS

MIMESIS

THE REPRESENTATION OF REALITY IN WESTERN LITERATURE

BY ERICH AUERBACH

TRANSLATED FROM THE GERMAN
BY WILLARD R. TRASK

Introduction by Edward W. Said

PRINCETON UNIVERSITY PRESS
PRINCETON AND OXFORD

Princeton University Press, 41 William Street, Princeton, New Jersey 08540
In the United Kingdom: Princeton University Press, 6 Oxford Street,
Woodstock, Oxfordshire OX20 1TW

press.princeton.edu

Written in Istanbul between May 1942 and April 1945. First published in Berne,
Switzerland, 1946, by A. Francke Ltd. Co.

First printing, 1953
Fiftieth anniversary printing, 2003
First Princeton Classics edition, 2013

Library of Congress Control Number 2013936719
ISBN 978-0-691-16022-1

British Library Cataloging-in-Publication Data is available

Printed on acid-free paper. ∞

Printed in the United States of America

10 9 8 7 6 5 4 3 2 1

Had we but world enough and time . . .

—ANDREW MARVELL

CONTENTS

INTRODUCTION TO THE FIFTIETH-ANNIVERSARY EDITION

by Edward W. Said

> . . . human beings are not born once and
> for all on the day their mothers give birth to them,
> but that life obliges them to give birth to themselves.
> —Gabriel García Márquez

THE influence and enduring reputation of books of criticism are, for the critics who write them and hope to be read for more than one season, dispiritingly short. Since World War Two the sheer volume of books appearing in English has risen to huge numbers, thus further ensuring if not ephemerality, then a relatively short life and hardly any influence at all. Books of criticism have usually come in waves associated with academic trends, most of which are quickly replaced by successive shifts in taste, fashion, or genuine intellectual discovery. Thus only a small number of books seem perennially present and, by comparison with the vast majority of their counterparts, to have an amazing staying power. Certainly this is true of Erich Auerbach's magisterial *Mimesis: The Representation of Reality in Western Literature*, published by Princeton University Press exactly fifty years ago in a satisfyingly readable English translation by Willard R. Trask.

As one can immediately judge by its subtitle, Auerbach's book is by far the largest in scope and ambition out of all the other important critical works of the past half century. Its range covers literary masterpieces from Homer and the Old Testament right through to Virginia Woolf and Marcel Proust, although as Auerbach says apologetically at the end of the book, for reasons of space he had to leave out a great deal of medieval literature as well as some crucial modern writers like Pascal and Baudelaire. He was to treat the former in his last, posthumously published book, *Literary Language and Its Public in Late Latin Antiquity and in the Middle Ages*, the latter in various journals and a collection of his essays, *Scenes from the Drama of European Literature*. In all these works Auerbach preserves the same essayistic style of criticism, beginning each chapter with a long quotation from a specific work cited in the original language, followed immediately by a serviceable translation (German in the original *Mimesis*, first published in Bern in 1946; English in most of his subsequent work), out of which a detailed *explication de texte* unfolds at a leisurely and ruminative pace; this in turns develops into a set of memorable comments about the relationship between the rhetorical style of the passage and its socio-political context, a feat that Auerbach manages with a minimum of fuss and with virtually no learned references. He explains in the concluding chapter of *Mimesis* that, even had he wanted to, he could not have made use of the available scholarly resources, first of all because he was in wartime Istanbul when the book was written and no Western research libraries were accessible for him to consult, second because had he been able to use references from the extremely voluminous secondary literature, the material would have swamped him and he would never have written the book. Thus along with the primary texts that he had with him, Auerbach relied mainly on memory and what seems like an infallible interpretive skill for elucidating relationships between books and the world they belonged to.

Even in English translation, the hallmark of Auerbach's style is an unruffled, at times even lofty and supremely calm, tone conveying a combination of quiet erudition allied with an overridingly patient and loving confidence in his mission as scholar and philologist. But who was he, and what sort of background and training did he have that enabled him to produce such work of truly outstanding influence and longevity? By the time *Mimesis* appeared in English he was already sixty-one, the son of a German Jewish family residing in Berlin, the city of his birth in 1892. By all accounts he received a classic Prussian education, graduating from that city's renowned Französisches Gymnasium, an elite high school where the German and Franco-Latin traditions were brought together in a very special way. He received a doctorate in law from the University of Heidelberg in 1913, and then served in the German army during World War One, after which he abandoned law and earned a doctorate in Romance languages at the University of Greifswald. Geoffrey Green, author of an important book on Auerbach, has speculated that "the violence and horrors" of the war experience may have caused the change in career from legal to literary pursuits, from "the vast, stolid legal institutions of society . . . to [an investigation of] the distant, shifting patterns of philological studies" (*Literary Criticism and the Structures of History, Erich Auerbach and Leo Spitzer,* Lincoln, University of Nebraska Press, 1982, pp. 20-21).

Between 1923 and 1929, Auerbach held a position at Berlin's Prussian State Library. It was then that he strengthened his grasp of the philological vocation and produced two major pieces of work, a German translation of Giambattista Vico's *The New Science* and a seminal monograph on Dante entitled *Dante als Dichter der irdischen Welt* (when the book appeared in English in 1961 as *Dante, Poet of the Secular World*, the crucial word *irdischen*, or "earthly," was only partially rendered by the considerably less concrete "secular"). Auerbach's life-long preoccupation with these two Italian authors underscores the specific and concrete character of his attention, so unlike that of contemporary critics, who prefer what is implicit to what the text actually says.

In the first place, Auerbach's work is anchored in the tradition of Romance philology, interestingly the study of those literatures deriving from Latin but ideologically unintelligible without the Christian doctrine of Incarnation (and hence of the Roman Church) as well as its secular underpinning in the Holy Roman Empire. An additional factor was the development out of Latin of the various demotic languages, from Provençal to French, Italian, Spanish, etc. Far from being the dry-as-dust academic study of word origins, philology for Auerbach and eminent contemporaries of his, like Karl Vossler, Leo Spitzer, and Ernst Robert Curtius, was in effect immersion in all the available written documents in one or several Romance languages, from numismatics to epigraphy, from stylistics to archival research, from rhetoric and law to an all-embracing working idea of literature that included chronicles, epics, sermons, drama, stories, and essays. Inherently comparative, Romance philology in the early twentieth century derived its main procedural ideas from a principally German tradition of interpretation that begins with the Homeric criticism of Friederich August Wolf (1759-1824), continues through Herman Schleiermacher's biblical criticism, includes some of the most important works of Nietzsche (who was a classical philologist by profession), and culminates in the often laboriously articulated philosophy of Wilhelm Dilthey.

Dilthey argued that the world of written texts (of which the aesthetic masterwork was the central pillar) belonged to the realm of lived experience (*Erlebnis*), which the interpreter attempted to recover through a combination of erudition and a subjective intuition (*eingefühlen*) of what the inner spirit (*Geist*) of the work was. His ideas about knowledge rest on an initial distinction between the world of nature (and of natural sciences) and the world of spiritual objects, the basis of whose knowledge he classified as a mixture of objective and subjective elements (*Geisteswissenschaft*), or knowledge of the products of mind or spirit. Whereas there is no real English or American equivalent for it (although the study of culture is a rough approximation), *Geisteswissenschaft* is a recognized academic sphere in German-speaking countries. In his later essay, "Epilegomena to *Mimesis*" (1953; translated from the German for the first time in this edition), Auerbach says explicitly that his work "arose from the themes and methods of German intellectual history and philology; it would be conceivable in no other tradition than in that of German romanticism and Hegel" (571).

While it is possible to appreciate Auerbach's *Mimesis* for its fine, absorbing explication of individual, sometimes obscure texts, one needs to disentangle its various antecedents and components, many of which are quite unfamiliar to modern readers but which Auerbach sometimes refers to in passing and always takes for granted in the course of his book. Auerbach's life-long interest in the eighteenth-century Neapolitan professor of Latin eloquence and jurisprudence Giambattista Vico is absolutely central to his work as critic and philologist. In the posthumously published 1745 third edition of his magnum opus *The New Science*, Vico formulated a revolutionary discovery of astonishing power and brilliance. Quite on his own, and as a reaction to Cartesian abstractions about ahistorical and contextless clear and distinct ideas, Vico argues that human beings are historical creatures in that they make history, or what he called "the world of the nations."

Understanding or interpreting history is therefore possible only because "men made it," since we can know only what we have made (just as only God knows nature because he alone made it). Knowledge of the past that comes to us in textual form, Vico says, can only be properly understood from the point of view of the maker of that past, which, in the case of ancient writers such as Homer, is primitive, barbaric, poetic. (In Vico's private lexicon the word "poetic" means primitive and barbaric because early human beings could not think rationally.) Examining the Homeric epics from the perspective of when and by whom they were composed, Vico refutes generations of interpreters who had assumed that because Homer was revered for his great epics he must also have been a wise sage like Plato, Socrates, or Bacon. Instead Vico demonstrates that in its wildness and willfulness Homer's mind was poetic, and his poetry barbaric, not wise or philosophic, that is, full of illogical fantasy, gods who were anything but godlike, and men like Achilles and Patrocles, who were most uncourtly and extremely petulant.

This primitive mentality was Vico's great discovery, whose influence on European romanticism and its cult of the imagination was profound. Vico also formulated a theory of historical coherence that showed how each period shared in its language, art, metaphysics, logic, science, law, and religion features that were common and appropriate to their appearance: primitive times produce primitive knowledge that is a projection of the barbaric mind—fantastic images of gods based on fear, guilt, and terror—and this in turn gives rise to institutions such as marriage and the burial of the dead that preserve the human race and give it a sustained history. The poetic age of giants and barbarians is succeeded by the age of heroes, and that slowly evolves into the age of men. Thus human history and society are created through a laborious process of unfolding, development, contradiction, and, most interestingly, representation. Each age has its own method, or optic, for seeing and then articulating reality: thus Plato develops his thought *after* (and not during) the period of violently concrete poetic images through which Homer spoke. The age of poetry gives way to a time when a greater degree of abstraction and rational discursivity become dominant.

All these developments occur as a cycle that goes from primitive to advanced and degenerate epochs, then back to primitive, Vico says, according to the modifications of the human mind, which makes and then can re-examine its own history from the point of view of the maker. That is the main methodological point for Vico as well as for Auerbach. In order to be able to understand a humanistic text, one must try to do so as if one is the author of that text, living the author's reality, undergoing the kind of life experiences intrinsic to his or her life, and so forth, all by that combination of erudition and sympathy that is the hallmark of philological hermeneutics. Thus the line between actual events and the modifications of one's own reflective mind is blurred in Vico, as it is in the numerous authors who were influenced by him, like James Joyce. But this perhaps tragic shortcoming of human knowledge and history is one of the unresolved contradictions pertaining to humanism itself, in which the role of thought in reconstructing the past can neither be excluded nor squared with what is "real." Hence the phrase, "the representation of reality" in the subtitle to *Mimesis* and the vacillations in the book between learning and personal insight.

By the early part of the nineteenth century Vico's work had become tremendously influential to European historians, poets, novelists, and philologists, from Michelet and Coleridge to Marx and, later, Joyce. Auerbach's fascination with Vico's historicism (sometimes called "historism") underwrote his hermeneutical philology and allowed him thus to read texts such as those by Augustine or Dante from the point of view of the author, whose relationship to his age was an organic and integral one, a kind of self-making within the context of the specific dynamics of society at a very precise moment in its development. Moreover, the relationship between the reader-critic and the text is transformed from a one-way interrogation of the historical text by an altogether alien mind at a much later time, into a sympathetic dialogue of two spirits across ages and cultures who are able to communicate with each other as friendly, respectful spirits trying to understand each other.

Now it is quite obvious that such an approach requires a great deal of erudition, although it is also clear that for the German Romance philologists of the early twentieth century with their formidable training in languages, history, literature, law, theology, and general culture, mere erudition was not enough. Obviously you could not do the basic reading if you had not mastered Latin, Greek, Hebrew, Provençal, Italian, French, and Spanish in addition to German and English. Nor could you if you did not know the traditions, main canonical authors, politics, institutions, and cultures of the time, as well as, of course, all of their interconnected arts. A philologist's training had to take many years, although in Auerbach's case he gives one the attractive impression that he was in no hurry to get on with it. He landed his first academic teaching job with a chair at the University of Marburg in 1929; this was the result of his Dante book, which in some ways, I think, is his most exciting and intense work. But in addition to learning and study, the heart of the hermeneutical enterprise was, for the scholar, to develop over the years a very particular kind of sympathy toward texts from different periods and different cultures. For a German whose specialty was Romance literature this sympathy took on an almost ideological cast, given that there had been a long period of historical enmity between Prussia and France, the most powerful and competitive of its neighbors and antagonists. As a specialist in Romance languages, the German scholar had a choice either to enlist on behalf of Prussian nationalism (as Auerbach did as a soldier during the First World War) and to study "the enemy" with skill and insight as a part of the continuing war effort or, as was the case with the postwar Auerbach and some of his peers, to overcome bellicosity and what we now call "the clash of civilizations" with a welcoming, hospitable attitude of humanistic knowledge designed to realign warring cultures in a relationship of mutuality and reciprocity.

The other part of the German Romance philologist's commitment to French, Italian, and Spanish generally and to French in particular is specifically literary. The historical trajectory that is the spine of *Mimesis* is the passage from the separation of styles in classical antiquity, to their mingling in the New Testament, their first great climax in Dante's *Divine Comedy*, and their ultimate apotheosis in the French realistic authors of the nineteenth century—Stendhal, Balzac, Flaubert, and then Proust. The representation of reality is Auerbach's theme, so he had to make a judgment as to where and in what literature it was most ably represented. In the "Epilegomena" he explains that "in most periods the Romance literatures are more representative of Europe than are, for example, the German. In the twelfth and thirteenth centuries France took unquestionably the leading role; in the fourteenth and fifteenth centuries Italy took it over; it fell again to France in the seventeenth, remained there also during the greater part of the eighteenth, partly still in the nineteenth, and precisely for the origin and development of modern realism (just as for painting)" (570). I think Auerbach scants the substantial English contribution in all this, perhaps a blind spot in his vision. Auerbach goes on to affirm that these judgments derive not from aversion to German culture but rather from a sense of regret that German literature "expressed . . . certain limitations of outlook in . . . the nineteenth century" (571). As we shall soon see, he does not specify what those were as he had done in the body of *Mimesis*, but adds that "for pleasure and relaxation" he still prefers reading Goethe, Stifter, and Keller rather than the French authors he studies, going once as far as saying after a remarkable analysis of Baudelaire that he did not like him at all (571).

For English readers today who associate Germany principally with horrendous crimes against humanity and with National Socialism (which Auerbach circumspectly alludes to several times in *Mimesis*), the tradition of hermeneutical philology embodied by Auerbach as a Romance specialist identifies two just as authentic aspects of classical German culture: its methodological generosity and, what might seem like a contradiction, its extraordinary attention to the minute, local detail of other cultures and languages. The great progenitor and clarifier of this extremely catholic, indeed almost altruistic, attitude is Goethe, who in the decade after 1810 became fascinated with Islam generally and with Persian poetry in particular. This was the period when he composed his finest and most intimate love poetry, the *West-Ostlicher Diwan* (1819), finding in the work of the great Persian poet Hafiz and in the verses of the Koran not only a new lyric inspiration allowing him to express a reawakened sense of physical love but, as he said in a letter to his good friend Zelter, a discovery of how, in the absolute submission to God, he felt himself to be oscillating between two worlds, his own and that of the Muslim believer who was miles, even worlds away from European Weimar. During the 1820s those earlier thoughts carried him toward a conviction that national literatures had been superseded by what he called *Weltliteratur*, or world literature, a universalist conception of all the literatures of the world seen together as forming a majestic symphonic whole.

For many modern scholars—including myself—Goethe's grandly utopian vision is considered to be the foundation of what was to become the field of comparative literature, whose underlying and perhaps unrealizable rationale was this vast synthesis of the world's literary production transcending borders and languages but not in any way effacing their individuality and historical concreteness. In 1951, Auerbach wrote an autumnal, reflective essay entitled "Philology and *Weltliteratur*" with a somewhat pessimistic tone because he felt that with the greater specialization of knowledge and expertise after the Second World War, the dissolution of the educational and professional institutions in which he had been trained, and the emergence of "new" non-European literatures and languages, the Goethean ideal might have become invalid or untenable. But for most of his working life as a Romance philologist he was a man with a mission, a European (and Eurocentric) mission it is true, but something he deeply believed in for its emphasis on the unity of human history, the possibility of understanding inimical and perhaps even hostile others despite the bellicosity of modern cultures and nationalisms, and the optimism with which one could enter into the inner life of a distant author or historical epoch even with a healthy awareness of one's limitations of perspective and insufficiency of knowledge.

Such noble intentions were insufficient, however, to save his career after 1933. In 1935, he was forced to quit his position in Marburg, a victim of Nazi racial laws and of an atmosphere of increasingly jingoistic mass culture presided over by intolerance and hatred. A few months later he was offered a position teaching Romance literatures at the Istanbul State University, where some years before Leo Spitzer had also taught. It was while he was in Istanbul, Auerbach tells us in the concluding pages of *Mimesis*, that he wrote and finished the book, which then appeared in Switzerland one year after the war's end. And even though the book is in many ways a calm affirmation of the unity and dignity of European literature in all its multiplicity and dynamism, it is also a book of countercurrents, ironies, and even contradictions that need to be taken into account for it to be read and understood properly. This rigorously fastidious attention to particulars, to details, to individuality is why *Mimesis* is not principally a book providing readers with usable ideas, which in the case of concepts like Renaissance, baroque, romanticism, and so on, are not exact but unscientific, as well as finally unusable. "Our precision [as philologists]," he says, "relates to the particular. The progress of the historical arts in the last two centuries consists above all, apart from the opening up of new material and in a great refinement of methods in individual research, in a perspectival formation of judgment, which makes it possible to accord the various epochs and cultures their own presuppositions and views, to strive to the utmost toward the discovery of those, and to dismiss as unhistorical and dilettantish every absolute assessment of the phenomena that is brought in from outside" (573).

Thus for all its redoubtable learning and authority *Mimesis* is also a personal book, disciplined yes, but not autocratic, and not pedantic. Consider, first of all, that even though *Mimesis* is the product of an extraordinarily thorough education and is steeped in an unparalleled inwardness and familiarity with European culture, it is an exile's book, written by a German cut off from his roots and his native environment. Auerbach seems not to have wavered, however, in his loyalty to his Prussian upbringing or to his feeling that he always expected to return to Germany. "I am a Prussian and of the Jewish faith," he wrote of himself in 1921, and despite his later diasporic existence he never seemed to have doubted where he really belonged. American friends and colleagues report that until his final illness and death in 1957, he was looking for some way to return to Germany. Nevertheless, after all those years in Istanbul he undertook a new postwar career in the United States, spending time at the Institute for Advanced Study in Princeton and as a professor at Pennsylvania State University, before he went to Yale as Sterling Professor of Romance Philology in 1956.

Auerbach's Jewishness is something one can only speculate about since, in his usually reticent way, he does not refer to it directly in *Mimesis*. One assumes, for instance, that the various intermittent and moving comments throughout the book about mass modernity and its relationship with, among others, the disruptive power of the nineteenth-century French realistic writers (the Goncourts, Balzac, and Flaubert) as well as "the tremendous crisis" it caused, are meant to suggest the menacing world and how that world affects the transformation of reality and consequently of style (the development of the *sermo humilis* due to the figure of Jesus). It is not hard to detect a combination of pride and distance as he describes the emergence of Christianity in the ancient world as the product of prodigious missionary work undertaken by the apostle Paul, a diasporic Jew converted to Christ. The parallel with his own situation as a non-Christian explaining Christianity's achievement is evident, but so too is the irony that, in so doing, he travels from his roots still further. Most of all, however, in Auerbach's searingly powerful and strangely intimate characterization of the great Christian Thomist poet Dante—who emerges from the pages of *Mimesis* as *the* seminal figure in Western literature—the reader is inevitably led to the paradox of a Prussian Jewish scholar in Turkish, Muslim, non-European exile handling (perhaps even juggling) charged, and in many ways irreconcilable, sets of antinomies that, though ordered more benignly than their mutual antagonism suggests, never lose their opposition to each other. Auerbach is a firm believer in the dynamic transformations as well as the deep sedimentations of history: yes, Judaism made Christianity possible through Paul, but Judaism remains, and it remains different from Christianity. So too, he says in a melancholy passage in *Mimesis*, will collective passions remain the same whether in Roman times or under National Socialism. What makes these meditations so poignant is an autumnal but unmistakably authentic sense of humanistic mission that is both tragic and hopeful. I shall return to these matters later.

I think it is quite proper to highlight some of the more personal aspects of *Mimesis* because in many ways it is, and should be read as, an unconventional book. Of course it has the manifest gravity of the Important Book, but as I noted above, it is by no means a formulaic one, despite the relative simplicity of its main theses about literary style in Western literature. In classical literature, Auerbach says, high style was used for nobles and gods who could be treated tragically; low style was principally for comic and mundane subjects, perhaps even for idyllic ones, but the idea of everyday human or worldly life as something to be represented through a style proper to it is not generally available before Christianity. Tacitus, for example, was simply not interested in talking about or representing the everyday, excellent historian though he was. If we go back to Homer, as Auerbach does in the celebrated and much-anthologized first chapter of *Mimesis*, the style is paratactic, that is, it deals with reality as a line of "externalized, uniformly illuminated phenomena, at a definite time and in a definite place, connected together without lacunae in a perpetual foreground [which technically speaking is parataxis, words and phrases added on rather than subordinated to each other]; thoughts and feelings completely expressed; events taking place in leisurely fashion and with very little of suspense" (11). So as he analyzes the return to Ithaca by Odysseus, Auerbach notes how the author simply narrates his greeting and recognition by the old nurse Euryclea, who knows him by the childhood scar he bears the moment she washes his feet: past and present are on an equal footing, there is no suspense, and one has the impression that nothing is held back, despite the inherent precariousness of the episode, what with Penelope's interloping suitors hanging about, waiting to kill her returning husband.

On the other hand, Auerbach's consideration of the Abraham and Isaac story in the Old Testament beautifully demonstrates how it "is like a silent progress through the indeterminate and the contingent, a holding of the breath . . . the overwhelming suspense is present. . . . The personages speak in the Bible story too; but their speech does not serve, as does speech in Homer, to manifest, to externalize thoughts—on the contrary, it serves to indicate thoughts which remain unexpressed. . . . [There is an] externalization of only so much of the phenomena as is necessary for the purpose of the narrative, all else left in obscurity; the decisive points of the narrative alone are emphasized, what lies beneath is nonexistent; time and place are undefined and call for interpretation; thoughts and feelings remain unexpressed, are only suggested by silence and the fragmentary speeches; the whole is permeated with the most unrelieved suspense and directed toward a single goal (and to that extent far more of a unity), remains mysterious and 'fraught with background'" (11-12). Moreover these contrasts can be seen in representations of human beings, in Homer of heroes "who wake every morning as if it were the first day of their lives," whereas the Old Testament figures, including God, are heavy with the implication of extending into the depths of time, space, and consciousness, hence of character, and therefore require a much more concentrated, intense act of attention from the reader.

A great part of Auerbach's charm as a critic is that, far from seeming heavy-handed and pedantic, he exudes a sense of searching and discovery, the joys and uncertainties of which he shares unassumingly with his reader. Lowry Nelson Jr., a younger colleague of his at Yale, wrote aptly in a memorial note of the self-instructing quality of Auerbach's work: "He was his own best teacher and learner. That process goes on in one's head, and one can become publicly aware of it to the extent of reproducing some of its primeval dramatic unfolding. The point is *how* you arrive, by what dangers, mistakes, fortuitous encounters, sleeps or slips of mind, by what insights achieved through great expense of time and passion and to what hard-won formulations in the face of history. . . . Auerbach had the ability to start with a single text without being coy, to expound it with a freshness that might pass for naiveté, to avoid making mere thematic or arbitrary connections, and yet to begin to weave ample fabrics from a single loom" ("Erich Auerbach: Memoir of a Scholar," *Yale Review*, Vol. 69, No. 2, Winter 1980, p. 318). As the 1953 "Epilegomena" demonstrates, however, Auerbach was adamant (if not also fierce) in rebutting criticisms of his claims; there is an especially tart exchange with his polymathic Romance colleague Curtius that shows the two formidable scholars slugging it out rather belligerently.

It is not an exaggeration to say that, like Vico, Auerbach was at heart an autodidact, guided in his diverse explorations by a handful of deeply conceived and complex themes with which he wove his ample fabric, which was not seamless or effortlessly spun out. In *Mimesis*, he resolutely sticks to his practice of working from disconnected fragments: each of the book's chapters is marked not only by a new author who bears little overt relationship to earlier ones, but also by a new beginning, in terms of the author's perspective and stylistic outlook, so to speak. The "representation" of reality is taken by Auerbach to mean an active dramatic presentation of how each author actually realizes, brings characters to life, and clarifies his or her own world; this of course explains why in reading the book we are compelled by the sense of disclosure that Auerbach affords us as he in turn re-realizes and interprets and, in his unassuming way, even seems to be staging the transmutation of a coarse reality into language and new life.

One major theme turns up already in the first chapter—the notion of incarnation—a centrally Christian idea, of course, whose prehistory in Western literature Auerbach ingeniously locates in the contrast between Homer and the Old Testament. The difference between Homer's Odysseus and Abraham is that the former is immediately present and requires no interpretation, no recourse either to allegory or to complicated explanations. Diametrically opposed is the figure of Abraham, who incarnates "doctrine and promise" and is steeped in them. These are "inseparable from" him and "for that very reason they are fraught with 'background' and [are] mysterious, containing a second, concealed meaning" (15). And this second meaning can only be recovered by a very particular act of interpretation, which, in the main piece of work Auerbach produced in Istanbul before he published *Mimesis* in 1946, he described as figural interpretation. (I refer here to Auerbach's long and rather technical essay "Figura," published in 1944 and now available in *Scenes from the Drama of European Literature: Six Essays* [Meridian Books, Inc., 1959; rept. Peter Smith, 1973]).

Here is another instance where Auerbach seems to be negotiating between the Jewish and European (hence Christian) components of his identity. Basically, figural interpretation develops as early Christian thinkers such as Tertullian and Augustine felt impelled to reconcile the Old with the New Testament. Both parts of the Bible were the word of God, but how were they related, how could they be read, as it were, together, given the quite considerable difference between the old Judaic dispensation and the new message emanating from the Christian Incarnation?

The solution arrived at, according to Auerbach, is the notion that the Old Testament prophetically prefigures the New Testament, which in turn can be read as a figural and, he adds, carnal (hence incarnate, real, worldly) realization or interpretation of the Old Testament. The first event or figure is "real and historical announcing something else that is also real and historical" (*Drama of European Literature*, 29). At last we begin to see, like interpretation itself, how history does not only move forward but also backward, in each oscillation between eras managing to accomplish a greater realism, a more substantial "thickness" (to use a term from current anthropological description), a higher degree of truth.

In Christianity, the core doctrine is that of the mysterious Logos, the Word made flesh, God made into a man, and therefore, literally, incarnation; but how much more fulfilling is the new idea that pre-Christian times can be read as a shadowy figure (*figura*) of what actually was to come? Auerbach quotes a sixth-century cleric as saying, "'that figure [a character or episode in the Old Testament that prophesies something comparable in the New Testament], without which not a letter of the Old Testament exists, now at length endures to better purpose in the New'; and from just about the same time [Auerbach continues] a passage in the writings of Bishop Avitus of Vienne . . . in which he speaks of the Last Judgment; just as God in killing the first-born in Egypt spared the houses daubed with blood, so may He recognize and spare the faithful by the sign of the Eucharist: *tu cognosce tuam salvanda in plebe figuram* ('recognize thine own figure in the people that are to be saved')" (*Drama of European Literature*, 46-47).

One last and quite difficult aspect of *figura* needs pointing out here. Auerbach contends that the very concept of *figura* also functions as a middle term between the literal-historical dimension and, for the Christian author, the world of truth, *veritas*. So rather than only convey an inert meaning for an episode or character in the past, in its second and more interesting sense *figura* is the intellectual and spiritual energy that does the actual connecting between past and present, history and Christian truth, which is so essential to interpretation. "In this connection," Auerbach claims, "*figura* is roughly equivalent to *spiritus* or *intellectus spiritalis*, sometimes replaced by *figuralitas*" (*Drama of European Literature*, 47). Thus for all the complexity of his argument and the minuteness of the often arcane evidence he presents, Auerbach, I believe, is bringing us back to what is an essentially Christian doctrine for believers but also a crucial element of *human* intellectual power and will. In this he follows Vico, who looks at the whole of human history and says, "mind made all this," an affirmation that audaciously reaffirms but also to some degree undercuts the religious dimension that gives credit to the Divine.

Auerbach's own vacillation between, on the one hand, his extraordinarily erudite and sensitive care for the intricacies of Christian symbolism and doctrine, his resolute secularism, and perhaps also his own Jewish background and, on the other, his unwavering focus on the earthly, the historical, the worldly gives *Mimesis* a fruitful inner tension. Certainly it is the finest description we have of the millennial effects of Christianity on literary representation. But *Mimesis* also glorifies as much as it animates with singular force and individualistic genius, most overtly in the chapters on verbal virtuosity in Dante, Rabelais, and Shakespeare. As we shall see in a moment, their creativity vies with God's in setting the human in a timeless as well as temporal setting. Typically, however, Auerbach chooses to express such ideas as an integral part of his unfolding interpretive quest in the book: he therefore does not take time out to explain his ideas methodologically but lets them emerge from the very history of the representation of reality as *it* begins to gather density and scope. Remember that, as his point of departure for analysis (which in a later essay he referred to and discussed as the *Ansatzpunkt*), Auerbach always comes back to the text and to the stylistic means used by the author to represent reality. This excavation of semantic meaning is most virtuosically evident in the essay "Figura" and in such brilliant shorter studies as his fertile examination of single phrases like *la cour et la ville*, which contain a whole library of meanings that illuminate seventeenth-century French society and culture.

Three seminal moments in the trajectory of *Mimesis* should now be identified in some detail. One is to be found in the book's second chapter, "Fortunata," whose starting point is a passage by the Roman author Petronius, followed by another by Tacitus. Both men treat their subjects from a one-sided point of view, that of writers concerned with maintaining the rigid social order of high and low classes. The wealthy and the important personages get all the attention, whereas the commoners or vulgar people are relegated to the fate of the unimportant and the vulgar. After having illustrated the insufficiencies of this classical separation of styles into high and low, Auerbach develops a wonderful contrast with that agonizing nocturnal moment in the Gospel of St. Mark when, standing in the courtyard of the High Priest's palace peopled with servant girls and soldiers, Simon Peter denies his relationship to the imprisoned Jesus. One particularly eloquent passage from *Mimesis* deserves quotation:

> It is apparent at first glance that the rule of differentiated styles cannot possibly apply in this case. The incident, entirely realistic both in regard to locale and *dramatis personae*—note particularly their low social station—is replete with problem and tragedy. Peter is no mere accessory figure serving as *illustratio*, like the soldiers Vibulenus and Percennius [in Tacitus], who are represented as mere scoundrels and swindlers. He is the image of man in the highest and deepest and most tragic sense. Of course this mingling of styles is not dictated by an artistic purpose. On the contrary, it was rooted from the beginning in the character of Jewish-Christian literature; it was graphically and harshly dramatized through God's incarnation in a human being of the humblest social station, through his existence on earth amid humble everyday people and conditions, and through his Passion which, judged by earthly standards, was ignominious; and it naturally came to have . . . a most decisive bearing upon man's conception of the tragic and the sublime. Peter, whose personal account may be assumed to have been the basis of the story, was a fisherman from Galilee, of humblest background and humblest education. . . . From the humdrum existence of his daily life, Peter is called to the most tremendous role. Here, like everything else to do with Jesus' arrest, his appearance on the stage—viewed in the world-historical continuity of the Roman Empire—is nothing but a provincial incident, an insignificant local occurrence, noted by none but those directly involved. Yet how tremendous it is, viewed in relation to the life a fisherman from the Sea of Galilee normally lives . . . (41-42).

Auerbach then goes on unhurriedly to detail the "pendulation" or swings in Peter's soul between sublimity and fear, faith and doubt, courage and defeat in order to show that those experiences are radically incompatible with "the sublime style of classical antique literature." This still leaves the question of why such a passage moves us, given that in classical literature it would appear only as farce or comedy. "Because it portrays something which neither the poets nor the historians of antiquity ever set out to portray: the birth of a spiritual movement in the depths of the common people, from within the everyday occurrences of contemporary life, which thus assumes an importance it could never have assumed in antique literature. What we witness is the awakening of 'a new heart and a new spirit.' All this applies not only to Peter's denial but also to every other occurrence which is related in the New Testament" (42-43). What Auerbach enables us to see here is "a world which on the one hand is entirely real, average, identifiable as to place, time, and circumstances, but which on the other hand is shaken in its very foundations, is transforming and renewing itself before our eyes" (43).

Christianity shatters the classical balance between high and low styles, just as Jesus' life destroys the separation between the sublime and the everyday. What is set in motion, as a result, is the search for a new literary pact between writer and reader, a new synthesis or mingling between style and interpretation that will be adequate to the disturbing volatility of worldly events in the much grander setting opened up by Christ's historical presence. To this end, St. Augustine's enormous accomplishment, linked as he was to the classical world by education, was to have been the first to realize that classical antiquity had been superseded by a different world requiring a new *sermo humilis*, or as Auerbach puts it, "a low style, such as would properly only be applicable to comedy, but which now reaches out far beyond its original domain, and encroaches upon the deepest and the highest, the sublime and the eternal" (72). The problem then becomes how to relate the discursive, sequential events of human history to each other within the new figural dispensation that has triumphed conclusively over its predecessor, and then to find a language adequate to such a task, once, after the fall of the Roman Empire, Latin was no longer the *lingua franca* of Europe.

Auerbach's choice of Dante to represent the second seminal moment in Western literary history is made to seem breathtakingly appropriate. Read slowly and reflectively, chapter 8 of *Mimesis*, "Farinata and Cavalcante," is one of the great moments in modern critical literature, a masterly, almost vertiginous embodiment of Auerbach's own ideas about Dante: that the *Divine Comedy* synthesized the timeless and the historical because of Dante's genius, and that Dante's use of the demotic (or vulgar) Italian language in a sense enabled the creation of what we have come to call literature. I will not try to summarize Auerbach's analysis of a passage from the tenth canto of the *Inferno* in which Dante the pilgrim and his guide Virgil are accosted by two Florentines who knew Dante from Florence but who are now committed to the Inferno, and whose internecine squabbles between the city's Guelph and Ghibelline factions carry on into the afterworld: readers should experience this dazzling analysis for themselves. Auerbach notes that the seventy lines he focuses on are incredibly packed, containing no less than four separate scenes, as well as more varied material than any other so far discussed in *Mimesis*. What particularly compels the reader is that Dante's Italian in the poem is, as Auerbach puts it assertively, "a well-nigh incomprehensible miracle," used by the poet "to discover the world anew" (182-183).

There is, first of all, its combination of "sublimity and triviality which, measured by the standards of antiquity, is monstrous." Then there is its immense forcefulness, its "repulsive and often disgusting greatness," according to Goethe, whereby the poet uses the vernacular to represent "the antagonism of the two traditions . . . that of antiquity . . . and that of the Christian era. . . . Dante's powerful temperament, which is conscious of both because its aspiration toward the tradition of antiquity does not imply for it the possibility of abandoning the other; nowhere does mingling of styles come so close to violation of all style" (184-185). Then there is its abundance of material and styles, all of it treated in what Dante claimed was "the common everyday language of the people," (186) which allowed a realism that brought forth descriptions of the classical, the biblical, and everyday worlds "not displayed within a single action, but instead an abundance of actions in the most diverse tonalities [which] follow one another in quick succession" (189). And finally, Dante manages to achieve through his style a combination of past, present, and future, since the two Florentine men who rise out of their flaming tombs to accost Dante so peremptorily are in fact dead but seem to live on somehow in what Hegel called a "changeless existence" remarkably devoid neither of history nor of memory and facticity. Having been judged for their sins and placed inside their burning encasement inside the kingdom of the damned, Farinata and Cavalcante are seen by us at a moment when we have "left the earthly sphere behind; we are in an eternal place, and yet we encounter concrete appearance and concrete occurrence there. This differs from what appears and occurs on earth, yet it is evidently connected with it in a necessary and strictly determined relation" (191).

The result is "a tremendous concentration [in Dante's style and vision]. We behold an intensified image of the essence of their being, fixed for all eternity in gigantic dimensions, behold it in a purity and distinctness which could never for one moment have been possible during their lives on earth" (192). What fascinates Auerbach is the mounting tension within Dante's poem, as eternally condemned sinners press their cases and aspire to the realization of their ambitions even as they remain fixed in the place assigned to them by Divine Judgment. Hence, the sense of futility and sublimity exuded simultaneously by the Inferno's "earthly historicity," which is always pointed in the end toward the white rose of the "Paradiso." So then "the beyond is eternal and yet phenomenal. . . . [I]t is changeless and of all time and yet full of history" (197). For Auerbach, therefore, Dante's great poem exemplifies the figural approach, the past realized in the present, the present prefiguring as well as acting like a sort of eternal redemption, the whole thing witnessed by Dante the pilgrim, whose artistic genius compresses human drama into an aspect of the divine.

The refinement of Auerbach's own writing about Dante is truly exhilarating to read, not just because of his complex, paradox-filled insights, but as he nears the end of the chapter, because of their Nietzschean audacity, often venturing toward the unsayable and the inexpressible, beyond normal or for that matter even divinely set limits. Having established the systematic nature of Dante's universe (framed by Aquinas' theocratic cosmology), Auerbach offers the thought that for all of its investment in the eternal and immutable, the *Divine Comedy* is even more successful in representing reality as basically human. In that vast work of art "the image of man eclipses the image of God," and despite Dante's Christian conviction that the world is made coherent by a systematic universal order, "the indestructibility of the whole historical and individual man turns *against* that order, makes it subservient to its own purposes, and obscures it" (202). Auerbach's great predecessor Vico had flirted with the idea that the human mind creates the divine, not the other way around, but living under the Church's umbrella in eighteenth-century Naples, Vico wrapped his defiant proposition in all sorts of formulae that seemed to preserve history for Divine Providence, and not for human creativity and ingenuity. Auerbach's choice of Dante for advancing the radically humanistic thesis carefully works through the great poet's Catholic ontology as a phase transcended by the Christian epic's realism, which is shown to be "ontogenetic," that is, "we are given to see, in the realm of timeless being, the history of man's inner life and unfolding" (202).

Yet Dante's Christian and post-Christian achievement could not have been realized had it not been for his immersion in what he inherited from classical culture—the capacity to draw human figures clearly, dramatically, and forcefully. In Auerbach's view, Western literature after Dante draws on his example but is rarely as intensely convincing in its variety, its dramatic realism, and stark universality as he was. Successive chapters of *Mimesis* treat medieval and early Renaissance texts as departures from the Dantean norm, some of them like Montaigne in his *Essais* stressing personal experience at the expense of the symphonic whole, others such as the works of Shakespeare and Rabelais brimming over with a linguistic verve and resourcefulness that overwhelms realistic representation in the interests of language itself. Characters like Falstaff or Pantagruel are realistically drawn to a certain degree, but what is as interesting to the reader as their vividness are the unprecedented riotous effects of the author's style. It is not a contradiction to say that this could not have happened without the emergence of humanism, as well as the great geographical discoveries of the period: both have the effect of expanding the potential range of human action while also continuing to ground it in earthly situations. Auerbach says that Shakespeare's plays, for instance, adumbrate "a basic fabric of the world, perpetually weaving itself, renewing itself, and connected in all its parts, from which all this arises and which makes it impossible to isolate any one event or level of style. Dante's general, clearly delimited figurality, in which everything is resolved in the beyond, in God's ultimate kingdom, and in which all characters attain their full realization only in the beyond, is no more" (327).

From this point on, reality is completely historical, and it, rather than the Beyond, has to be read and understood according to laws that evolve slowly. Figural interpretation took for its point of origin the sacred word, or Logos, whose incarnation in the earthly world was made possible by the Christ-figure, a central point, as it were, for organizing experience and understanding history. With the eclipse of the divine that is presaged in Dante's poem, a new order slowly begins to assert itself, and so the second half of *Mimesis* painstakingly traces the growth of historicism, a multiperspectival, dynamic, and holistic way of representing history and reality. Let me quote him at length on the subject:

> Basically, the way in which we view human life and society is the same whether we are concerned with things of the past or things of the present. A change in our manner of viewing history will of necessity soon be transferred to our manner of viewing current conditions. When people realize

> that epochs and societies are not to be judged in terms of a pattern concept of what is desirable absolutely speaking but rather in every case in terms of their own premises; when people reckon among such premises not only natural factors like climate and soil but also the intellectual and historical factors; when, in other words, they come to develop a sense of historical dynamics, of the incomparability of historical phenomena and of their constant inner mobility; when they come to appreciate the vital unity of individual epochs, so that each epoch appears as a whole whose character is reflected in each of its manifestations; when, finally, they accept the conviction that the meaning of events cannot be grasped in abstract and general forms of cognition and that the material needed to understand it must not be sought exclusively in the upper strata of society and in major political events but also in art, economy, material and intellectual culture, in the depths of the workaday world and its men and women, because it is only there that one can grasp what is unique, what is animated by inner forces, and what, in both a more concrete and a more profound sense, is universally valid: then it is to be expected that those insights will also be transferred to the present and that, in consequence, the present too will be seen as incomparable and unique, as animated by inner forces and in a constant state of development; in other words, as a piece of history whose everyday depths and total inner structure lay claim to our interest both in their origins and in the direction taken by their development (443-444).

Auerbach never loses sight of his original ideas about the separation and mingling of styles—how, for instance, classicism in France returned to the vogue for antique models and the high style, and late-eighteenth-century German romanticism overturned those norms by way of a hostile reaction to them in works of sentiment and passion. And yet in a rare moment of severe judgment, Auerbach shows that, far from using the advantages of historicism to represent the complexity and social change that were overtaking contemporary reality, early-nineteenth-century German culture (with the exception of Marx) turned away from it out of a fear of the future, which to Germany seemed always to be barging in at the culture from the outside in forms such as revolution, civil unrest, and the overturning of tradition.

Goethe comes in for the harshest treatment, even though we know that Auerbach loved his poetry and read him with the greatest pleasure. I do not think it is reading too much into the somewhat judgmental tone of chapter 17 of *Mimesis* ("Miller the Musician") to recognize that in its stern condemnation of Goethe's dislike of upheaval and even of change itself, his interest in aristocratic culture, his deep-seated wish to be rid of the "revolutionary occurrences" taking place all over Europe, and his inability to understand the flow of popular history, Auerbach was discussing no mere failure of perception but a profound wrong turn in German culture as a whole that led to the horrors of the present. Perhaps Goethe is made to represent too much. But were it not for his withdrawal from the present and for what he otherwise might have done for bringing German culture into the dynamic present, Auerbach speculates that Germany might have been integrated "into the emerging new reality of Europe and the world might have been prepared more calmly, have been accomplished with fewer uncertainties and less violence" (451-452).

At the time these regretful and actually understated lines were being written in the early 1940s, Germany had unleashed a storm on Europe that swept all before it. Before that, the major German writers after Goethe were mired in regionalism and a marvelously traditional conception of life as a vocation. Realism, as an overall style, never emerged in Germany, and except for Fontane, there was very little in the language that had the gravity, universality, and synthetic power to represent modern reality until Thomas Mann's *Buddenbrooks* in 1901. There is a brief acknowledgment that Nietzsche and Jacob Burckhardt were more in touch with their own time, but neither of course was "concerned with the realistic portrayal of contemporary reality" (519). As against the chaotic irrationality ultimately represented by the anachronistic ethos of National Socialism, Auerbach therefore locates an alternative in the realism of mainly French prose fiction in which writers such as Stendhal, Flaubert, and Proust sought to unify the fragmented modern world—with its unfolding class struggle, its industrialization, and its economic expansion combined with moral discomfort—in the eccentric structures of the modernist novel. And these replace the correspondence between Eternity and History that had enabled Dante's vision, and which was now completely overtaken by the disruptive and dislocating currents of historical modernity.

The last few chapters of *Mimesis* thus seem to have a different tone than what goes before them. Auerbach is now discussing the history of his own time, not that of the medieval and Renaissance past, nor that of relatively distant cultures. Evolving slowly from acute observation of events and characters in the mid-nineteenth century, realism in France (and, though he talks about it much less, England) takes on the character of an aesthetic style capable of rendering sordidness and beauty with unadorned directness, although in the process master-technicians like Flaubert, unwilling to intervene in the rapidly changing world of social upheaval and revolutionary change, also formulated an ethic of disinterested observation. It is enough to be able to see and represent what is going on, although the practice of realism usually concerns figures from low or, at most, bourgeois life. How this then turns into the magnificent richness of Proust's work based on memory, or into the stream-of-consciousness techniques of Virginia Woolf and James Joyce, is a topic that makes for some of Auerbach's most impressive later pages, though once again we should remind ourselves that what Auerbach is also describing is how his own work as a philologist emerges from modernity and is indeed an integral part of the representation of reality. Thus the modern Romance philology exemplified by Auerbach acquires its special intellectual identity by a kind of conscious affiliation with the realistic literature of its own time: the uniquely French achievement of dealing with reality from more than a local standpoint, universally, and with a specifically European mission. *Mimesis* bears within its pages its own rich history of the analysis of evolving styles and perspectives.

To help one understand the cultural and personal significance of Auerbach's quest, I'd like to recall the laboriously complicated narrative structure of Mann's postwar novel *Dr. Faustus* (published after Auerbach's work), which, far more explicitly than *Mimesis*, is a story both of modern German catastrophe as well as the attempt to understand it. The terrible story of Adrien Leverkuhn, a prodigiously endowed composer who makes a pact with the devil to explore the furthest reaches of art and mind, is narrated by his much less gifted childhood friend and companion, Serenus Zeitblom. Whereas Adrien's wordless musical domain allows him to enter the irrational and the purely symbolic on his way down into terminal madness, Zeitblom, who is a humanist and scholar, tries to keep up with him, translating Adrien's musical journey into sequential prose, struggling to make sense of what defies ordinary comprehension. Mann suggests that both men represent the two aspects of modern German culture: one as embodied in Adrien's defiant life and his pathbreaking music, which takes him beyond ordinary sense into the irrational demonic; the other as delivered in Zeitblom's sometimes bumbling and awkward narrative, that of a closely connected friend witnessing that which he is powerless to stop or prevent.

The novel's fabric is actually made up of three strands. In addition to Adrien's story and Zeitblom's attempts to grapple with it (which include the story of Zeitblom's own life and career as scholarly humanist and teacher), there are frequent allusions to the course of the war, concluding with Germany's final defeat in 1945. That history is not referred to in *Mimesis*, nor of course is there anything in it like the drama and the cast of characters that animate Mann's great novel. But in its allusions to the failure of German literature to confront modern reality, and Auerbach's own effort in his book to represent an alternative history for Europe (Europe perceived through the means of stylistic analysis), *Mimesis* is also an attempt to rescue sense and meanings from the fragments of modernity with which, from his Turkish exile, Auerbach saw the downfall of Europe, and Germany in particular. Like Zeitblom, he affirms the recuperative and redemptive human project for which, in its patient philological unfolding, his book is the emblem, and again resembling Zeitblom, he understands that like a novelist, the scholar must reconstruct the history of his own time as part of a personal commitment to his field. Yet Auerbach specifically forswears the linear narrative style, which, despite its numerous interruptions and parentheses, works so powerfully for Zeitblom and his readers.

Thus in comparing himself to modern novelists such as Joyce and Woolf, who re-create a whole world out of random, usually unimportant moments, Auerbach explicitly rejects a rigid scheme, a relentless sequential movement, or fixed concepts as instruments of study. "As opposed to this," he says near the end, "I see the possibility of success and profit in a method which consists in letting myself be guided by a few motifs which I have worked out gradually and without a specific purpose . . . which have become familiar and vital to me in the course of my philological activity" (548). What gives him the confidence to surrender to those motifs without a specific purpose is the realization that no one person can possibly synthesize the whole of modern life, and second, that there is an abiding "order and . . . interpretation of life which arise from life itself: that is, those which grow up in the individuals themselves, which are to be discerned in their thoughts, their consciousness, and in a more concealed form in their words and actions. For there is always going on within us a process of formulation and interpretation whose subject matter is our own self" (549).

This testimonial to self-understanding is a deeply affecting one, I think. Several recognitions and affirmations are at play and even at odds within it, so to speak. One of course is staking something as ambitious as the history of Western representations of reality neither on a preexisting method nor a schematic time-frame, but on personal interest, learning, and practice alone. Second, this then suggests that interpreting literature is "a process of formulation and interpretation whose subject matter is our own self." Third, rather than producing a totally coherent, neatly inclusive view of the subject, there is "not one order and one interpretation, but many, which may either be those of different persons or of the same person at different times; so that overlapping, complementing, and contradiction yield something that we might call a synthesized cosmic view or at least a challenge to the reader's will to interpretive synthesis" (549).

Thus it all unmistakably comes down to a personal effort. Auerbach offers no system, no shortcut to what he puts before us as a history of the representation of reality in Western literature. From a contemporary standpoint there is something impossibly naive, if not outrageous, that hotly contested terms like "Western," "reality," and "representation"—each of which has recently brought forth literally acres of disputatious prose among critics and philosophers—are left to stand on their own, unadorned and unqualified. It is as if Auerbach was intent on exposing his personal explorations and, perforce, his fallibility to the perhaps scornful eye of critics who might deride his subjectivity. But the triumph of *Mimesis*, as well as its inevitable tragic flaw, is that the human mind studying literary representations of the historical world can only do so as all authors do—from the limited perspective of their own time and their own work. No more scientific a method or less subjective a gaze is possible, except that the great scholar can always buttress his vision with learning, dedication, and moral purpose. It is this combination, this mingling of styles out of which *Mimesis* emerges. And to my way of thinking, its humanistic example remains an unforgettable one, fifty years after its first appearance in English.

MIMESIS

The translations of Chapters 1, 11, and 18
have appeared in the *Partisan Review*, that of Chapter 8
in the *Kenyon Review*.

Grateful acknowledgment is made to
the Bollingen Foundation
for the grant made available for translating.

1

ODYSSEUS' SCAR

Readers of the *Odyssey* will remember the well-prepared and touching scene in book 19, when Odysseus has at last come home, the scene in which the old housekeeper Euryclea, who had been his nurse, recognizes him by a scar on his thigh. The stranger has won Penelope's good will; at his request she tells the housekeeper to wash his feet, which, in all old stories, is the first duty of hospitality toward a tired traveler. Euryclea busies herself fetching water and mixing cold with hot, meanwhile speaking sadly of her absent master, who is probably of the same age as the guest, and who perhaps, like the guest, is even now wandering somewhere, a stranger; and she remarks how astonishingly like him the guest looks. Meanwhile Odysseus, remembering his scar, moves back out of the light; he knows that, despite his efforts to hide his identity, Euryclea will now recognize him, but he wants at least to keep Penelope in ignorance. No sooner has the old woman touched the scar than, in her joyous surprise, she lets Odysseus' foot drop into the basin; the water spills over, she is about to cry out her joy; Odysseus restrains her with whispered threats and endearments; she recovers herself and conceals her emotion. Penelope, whose attention Athena's foresight had diverted from the incident, has observed nothing.

All this is scrupulously externalized and narrated in leisurely fashion. The two women express their feelings in copious direct discourse. Feelings though they are, with only a slight admixture of the most general considerations upon human destiny, the syntactical connection between part and part is perfectly clear, no contour is blurred. There is also room and time for orderly, perfectly well-articulated, uniformly illuminated descriptions of implements, ministrations, and gestures; even in the dramatic moment of recognition, Homer does not omit to tell the reader that it is with his right hand that Odysseus takes the old woman by the throat to keep her from speaking, at the same time that he draws her closer to him with his left. Clearly outlined, brightly and uniformly illuminated, men and things stand out in a realm where everything is visible; and not less clear—wholly expressed, orderly even in their ardor—are the feelings and thoughts of the persons involved.

In my account of the incident I have so far passed over a whole series of verses which interrupt it in the middle. There are more than seventy of these verses—while to the incident itself some forty are devoted before the interruption and some forty after it. The interruption, which comes just at the point when the housekeeper recognizes the scar—that is, at the moment of crisis—describes the origin of the scar, a hunting accident which occurred in Odysseus' boyhood, at a boar hunt, during the time of his visit to his grandfather Autolycus. This first affords an opportunity to inform the reader about Autolycus, his house, the precise degree of the kinship, his character, and, no less exhaustively than touchingly, his behavior after the birth of his grandson; then follows the visit of Odysseus, now grown to be a youth; the exchange of greetings, the banquet with which he is welcomed, sleep and waking, the early start for the hunt, the tracking of the beast, the struggle, Odysseus' being wounded by the boar's tusk, his recovery, his return to Ithaca, his parents' anxious questions—all is narrated, again with such a complete externalization of all the elements of the story and of their interconnections as to leave nothing in obscurity. Not until then does the narrator return to Penelope's chamber, not until then, the digression having run its course, does Euryclea, who had recognized the scar before the digression began, let Odysseus' foot fall back into the basin.

The first thought of a modern reader—that this is a device to increase suspense—is, if not wholly wrong, at least not the essential explanation of this Homeric procedure. For the element of suspense is very slight in the Homeric poems; nothing in their entire style is calculated to keep the reader or hearer breathless. The digressions are not meant to keep the reader in suspense, but rather to relax the tension. And this frequently occurs, as in the passage before us. The broadly narrated, charming, and subtly fashioned story of the hunt, with all its elegance and self-sufficiency, its wealth of idyllic pictures, seeks to win the reader over wholly to itself as long as he is hearing it, to make him forget what had just taken place during the foot-washing. But an episode that will increase suspense by retarding the action must be so constructed that it will not fill the present entirely, will not put the crisis, whose resolution is being awaited, entirely out of the reader's mind, and thereby destroy the mood of suspense; the crisis and the suspense must continue, must remain vibrant in the background. But Homer—and to this we shall have to return later—knows no background. What he narrates is for the time being the only present, and fills both the stage and the reader's mind completely. So it is with the passage before us. When the young Euryclea (vv. 401ff.) sets the infant Odysseus on his grandfather Autolycus' lap after the banquet, the aged Euryclea, who a few lines earlier had touched the wanderer's foot, has entirely vanished from the stage and from the reader's mind.

Goethe and Schiller, who, though not referring to this particular episode, exchanged letters in April 1797 on the subject of "the retarding element" in the Homeric poems in general, put it in direct opposition to the element of suspense—the latter word is not used, but is clearly implied when the "retarding" procedure is opposed, as something proper to epic, to tragic procedure (letters of April 19, 21, and 22). The "retarding element," the "going back and forth" by means of episodes, seems to me, too, in the Homeric poems, to be opposed to any tensional and suspensive striving toward a goal, and doubtless Schiller is right in regard to Homer when he says that what he gives us is "simply the quiet existence and operation of things in accordance with their natures"; Homer's goal is "already present in every point of his progress." But both Schiller and Goethe raise Homer's procedure to the level of a law for epic poetry in general, and Schiller's words quoted above are meant to be universally binding upon the epic poet, in contradistinction from the tragic. Yet in both modern and ancient times, there are important epic works which are composed throughout with no "retarding element" in this sense but, on the contrary, with suspense throughout, and which perpetually "rob us of our emotional freedom"—which power Schiller will grant only to the tragic poet. And besides it seems to me undemonstrable and improbable that this procedure of Homeric poetry was directed by aesthetic considerations or even by an aesthetic feeling of the sort postulated by Goethe and Schiller. The effect, to be sure, is precisely that which they describe, and is, furthermore, the actual source of the conception of epic which they themselves hold, and with them all writers decisively influenced by classical antiquity. But the true cause of the impression of "retardation" appears to me to lie elsewhere—namely, in the need of the Homeric style to leave nothing which it mentions half in darkness and unexternalized.

The excursus upon the origin of Odysseus' scar is not basically different from the many passages in which a newly introduced character, or even a newly appearing object or implement, though it be in the thick of a battle, is described as to its nature and origin; or in which, upon the appearance of a god, we are told where he last was, what he was doing there, and by what road he reached the scene; indeed, even the Homeric epithets seem to me in the final analysis to be traceable to the same need for an externalization of phenomena in terms perceptible to the senses. Here is the scar, which comes up in the course of the narrative; and Homer's feeling simply will not permit him to see it appear out of the darkness of an unilluminated past; it must be set in full light, and with it a portion of the hero's boyhood—just as, in the *Iliad*, when the first ship is already burning and the Myrmidons finally arm that they may hasten to help, there is still time not only for the wonderful simile of the wolf, not only for the order of the Myrmidon host, but also for a detailed account of the ancestry of several subordinate leaders (16, vv. 155ff.). To be sure, the aesthetic effect thus produced was soon noticed and thereafter consciously sought; but the more original cause must have lain in the basic impulse of the Homeric style: to represent phenomena in a fully externalized form, visible and palpable in all their parts, and completely fixed in their spatial and temporal relations. Nor do psychological processes receive any other treatment: here too nothing must remain hidden and unexpressed. With the utmost fullness, with an orderliness which even passion does not disturb, Homer's personages vent their inmost hearts in speech; what they do not say to others, they speak in their own minds, so that the reader is informed of it. Much that is terrible takes place in the Homeric poems, but it seldom takes place wordlessly: Polyphemus talks to Odysseus; Odysseus talks to the suitors when he begins to kill them; Hector and Achilles talk at length, before battle and after; and no speech is so filled with anger or scorn that the particles which express logical and grammatical connections are lacking or out of place. This last observation is true, of course, not only of speeches but of the presentation in general. The separate elements of a phenomenon are most clearly placed in relation to one another; a large number of conjunctions, adverbs, particles, and other syntactical tools, all clearly circumscribed and delicately differentiated in meaning, delimit persons, things, and portions of incidents in respect to one another, and at the same time bring them together in a continuous and ever flexible connection; like the separate phenomena themselves, their relationships—their temporal, local, causal, final, consecutive, comparative, concessive, antithetical, and conditional limitations—are brought to light in perfect fullness; so that a continuous rhythmic procession of phenomena passes by, and never is there a form left fragmentary or half-illuminated, never a lacuna, never a gap, never a glimpse of unplumbed depths.

And this procession of phenomena takes place in the foreground—that is, in a local and temporal present which is absolute. One might think that the many interpolations, the frequent moving back and forth, would create a sort of perspective in time and place; but the Homeric style never gives any such impression. The way in which any impression of perspective is avoided can be clearly observed in the procedure for introducing episodes, a syntactical construction with which every reader of Homer is familiar; it is used in the passage we are considering, but can also be found in cases when the episodes are much shorter. To the word scar (v. 393) there is first attached a relative clause ("which once long ago a boar . . ."), which enlarges into a voluminous syntactical parenthesis; into this an independent sentence unexpectedly intrudes (v. 396: "A god himself gave him . . ."), which quietly disentangles itself from syntactical subordination, until, with verse 399, an equally free syntactical treatment of the new content begins a new present which continues unchallenged until, with verse 467 ("The old woman now touched it . . ."), the scene which had been broken off is resumed. To be sure, in the case of such long episodes as the one we are considering, a purely syntactical connection with the principal theme would hardly have been possible; but a connection with it through perspective would have been all the easier had the content been arranged with that end in view; if, that is, the entire story of the scar had been presented as a recollection which awakens in Odysseus' mind at this particular moment. It would have been perfectly easy to do; the story of the scar had only to be inserted two verses earlier, at the first mention of the word scar, where the motifs "Odysseus" and "recollection" were already at hand. But any such subjectivistic-perspectivistic procedure, creating a foreground and background, resulting in the present lying open to the depths of the past, is entirely foreign to the Homeric style; the Homeric style knows only a foreground, only a uniformly illuminated, uniformly objective present. And so the excursus does not begin until two lines later, when Euryclea has discovered the scar—the possibility for a perspectivistic connection no longer exists, and the story of the wound becomes an independent and exclusive present.

The genius of the Homeric style becomes even more apparent when it is compared with an equally ancient and equally epic style from a different world of forms. I shall attempt this comparison with the account of the sacrifice of Isaac, a homogeneous narrative produced by the so-called Elohist. The King James version translates the opening as follows (Genesis 22: 1): "And it came to pass after these things, that God did tempt Abraham, and said to him, Abraham! and he said, Behold, here I am." Even this opening startles us when we come to it from Homer. Where are the two speakers? We are not told. The reader, however, knows that they are not normally to be found together in one place on earth, that one of them, God, in order to speak to Abraham, must come from somewhere, must enter the earthly realm from some unknown heights or depths. Whence does he come, whence does he call to Abraham? We are not told. He does not come, like Zeus or Poseidon, from the Aethiopians, where he has been enjoying a sacrificial feast. Nor are we told anything of his reasons for tempting Abraham so terribly. He has not, like Zeus, discussed them in set speeches with other gods gathered in council; nor have the deliberations in his own heart been presented to us; unexpected and mysterious, he enters the scene from some unknown height or depth and calls: Abraham! It will at once be said that this is to be explained by the particular concept of God which the Jews held and which was wholly different from that of the Greeks. True enough—but this constitutes no objection. For how is the Jewish concept of God to be explained? Even their earlier God of the desert was not fixed in form and content, and was alone; his lack of form, his lack of local habitation, his singleness, was in the end not only maintained but developed even further in competition with the comparatively far more manifest gods of the surrounding Near Eastern world. The concept of God held by the Jews is less a cause than a symptom of their manner of comprehending and representing things.

This becomes still clearer if we now turn to the other person in the dialogue, to Abraham. Where is he? We do not know. He says, indeed: Here I am—but the Hebrew word means only something like "behold me," and in any case is not meant to indicate the actual place where Abraham is, but a moral position in respect to God, who has called to him—Here am I awaiting thy command. Where he is actually, whether in Beersheba or elsewhere, whether indoors or in the open air, is not stated; it does not interest the narrator, the reader is not informed; and what Abraham was doing when God called to him is left in the same obscurity. To realize the difference, consider Hermes' visit to Calypso, for example, where command, journey, arrival and reception of the visitor, situation and occupation of the person visited, are set forth in many verses; and even on occasions when gods appear suddenly and briefly, whether to help one of their favorites or to deceive or destroy some mortal whom they hate, their bodily forms, and usually the manner of their coming and going, are given in detail. Here, however, God appears without bodily form (yet he "appears"), coming from some unspecified place—we only hear his voice, and that utters nothing but a name, a name without an adjective, without a descriptive epithet for the person spoken to, such as is the rule in every Homeric address; and of Abraham too nothing is made perceptible except the words in which he answers God: *Hinne-ni,* Behold me here—with which, to be sure, a most touching gesture expressive of obedience and readiness is suggested, but it is left to the reader to visualize it. Moreover the two speakers are not on the same level: if we conceive of Abraham in the foreground, where it might be possible to picture him as prostrate or kneeling or bowing with outspread arms or gazing upward, God is not there too: Abraham's words and gestures are directed toward the depths of the picture or upward, but in any case the undetermined, dark place from which the voice comes to him is not in the foreground.

After this opening, God gives his command, and the story itself begins: everyone knows it; it unrolls with no episodes in a few independent sentences whose syntactical connection is of the most rudimentary sort. In this atmosphere it is unthinkable that an implement, a landscape through which the travelers passed, the serving-men, or the ass, should be described, that their origin or descent or material or appearance or usefulness should be set forth in terms of praise; they do not even admit an adjective: they are serving-men, ass, wood, and knife, and nothing else, without an epithet; they are there to serve the end which God has commanded; what in other respects they were, are, or will be, remains in darkness. A journey is made, because God has designated the place where the sacrifice is to be performed; but we are told nothing about the journey except that it took three days, and even that we are told in a mysterious way: Abraham and his followers rose "early in the morning" and "went unto" the place of which God had told him; on the third day he lifted up his eyes and saw the place from afar. That gesture is the only gesture, is indeed the only occurrence during the whole journey, of which we are told; and though its motivation lies in the fact that the place is elevated, its uniqueness still heightens the impression that the journey took place through a vacuum; it is as if, while he traveled on, Abraham had looked neither to the right nor to the left, had suppressed any sign of life in his followers and himself save only their footfalls.

Thus the journey is like a silent progress through the indeterminate and the contingent, a holding of the breath, a process which has no present, which is inserted, like a blank duration, between what has passed and what lies ahead, and which yet is measured: three days! Three such days positively demand the symbolic interpretation which they later received. They began "early in the morning." But at what time on the third day did Abraham lift up his eyes and see his goal? The text says nothing on the subject. Obviously not "late in the evening," for it seems that there was still time enough to climb the mountain and make the sacrifice. So "early in the morning" is given, not as an indication of time, but for the sake of its ethical significance; it is intended to express the resolution, the promptness, the punctual obedience of the sorely tried Abraham. Bitter to him is the early morning in which he saddles his ass, calls his serving-men and his son Isaac, and sets out; but he obeys, he walks on until the third day, then lifts up his eyes and sees the place. Whence he comes, we do not know, but the goal is clearly stated: Jeruel in the land of Moriah. What place this is meant to indicate is not clear—"Moriah" especially may be a later correction of some other word. But in any case the goal was given, and in any case it is a matter of some sacred spot which was to receive a particular consecration by being connected with Abraham's sacrifice. Just as little as "early in the morning" serves as a temporal indication does "Jeruel in the land of Moriah" serve as a geographical indication; and in both cases alike, the complementary indication is not given, for we know as little of the hour at which Abraham lifted up his eyes as we do of the place from which he set forth—Jeruel is significant not so much as the goal of an earthly journey, in its geographical relation to other places, as through its special election, through its relation to God, who designated it as the scene of the act, and therefore it must be named.

In the narrative itself, a third chief character appears: Isaac. While God and Abraham, the serving-men, the ass, and the implements are simply named, without mention of any qualities or any other sort of definition, Isaac once receives an appositive; God says, "Take Isaac, thine only son, whom thou lovest." But this is not a characterization of Isaac as a person, apart from his relation to his father and apart from the story; he may be handsome or ugly, intelligent or stupid, tall or short, pleasant or unpleasant—we are not told. Only what we need to know about him as a personage in the action, here and now, is illuminated, so that it may become apparent how terrible Abraham's temptation is, and that God is fully aware of it. By this example of the contrary, we see the significance of the descriptive adjectives and digressions of the Homeric poems; with their indications of the earlier and as it were absolute existence of the persons described, they prevent the reader from concentrating exclusively on a present crisis; even when the most terrible things are occurring, they prevent the establishment of an overwhelming suspense. But here, in the story of Abraham's sacrifice, the overwhelming suspense is present; what Schiller makes the goal of the tragic poet—to rob us of our emotional freedom, to turn our intellectual and spiritual powers (Schiller says "our activity") in one direction, to concentrate them there—is effected in this Biblical narrative, which certainly deserves the epithet epic.

We find the same contrast if we compare the two uses of direct discourse. The personages speak in the Bible story too; but their speech does not serve, as does speech in Homer, to manifest, to externalize thoughts—on the contrary, it serves to indicate thoughts which remain unexpressed. God gives his command in direct discourse, but he leaves his motives and his purpose unexpressed; Abraham, receiving the command, says nothing and does what he has been told to do. The conversation between Abraham and Isaac on the way to the place of sacrifice is only an interruption of the heavy silence and makes it all the more burdensome. The two of them, Isaac carrying the wood and Abraham with fire and a knife, "went together." Hesitantly, Isaac ventures to ask about the ram, and Abraham gives the well-known answer. Then the text repeats: "So they went both of them together." Everything remains unexpressed.

It would be difficult, then, to imagine styles more contrasted than those of these two equally ancient and equally epic texts. On the one hand, externalized, uniformly illuminated phenomena, at a definite time and in a definite place, connected together without lacunae in a perpetual foreground; thoughts and feeling completely expressed; events taking place in leisurely fashion and with very little of suspense. On the other hand, the externalization of only so much of the phenomena as is necessary for the purpose of the narrative, all else left in obscurity; the decisive points of the narrative alone are emphasized, what lies between is nonexistent; time and place are undefined and call for interpretation; thoughts and feeling remain unexpressed, are only suggested by the silence and the fragmentary speeches; the whole, permeated with the most unrelieved suspense and directed toward a single goal (and to that extent far more of a unity), remains mysterious and "fraught with background."

I will discuss this term in some detail, lest it be misunderstood. I said above that the Homeric style was "of the foreground" because, despite much going back and forth, it yet causes what is momentarily being narrated to give the impression that it is the only present, pure and without perspective. A consideration of the Elohistic text teaches us that our term is capable of a broader and deeper application. It shows that even the separate personages can be represented as possessing "background"; God is always so represented in the Bible, for he is not comprehensible in his presence, as is Zeus; it is always only "something" of him that appears, he always extends into depths. But even the human beings in the Biblical stories have greater depths of time, fate, and consciousness than do the human beings in Homer; although they are nearly always caught up in an event engaging all their faculties, they are not so entirely immersed in its present that they do not remain continually conscious of what has happened to them earlier and elsewhere; their thoughts and feelings have more layers, are more entangled. Abraham's actions are explained not only by what is happening to him at the moment, nor yet only by his character (as Achilles' actions by his courage and his pride, and Odysseus' by his versatility and foresightedness), but by his previous history; he remembers, he is constantly conscious of, what God has promised him and what God has already accomplished for him—his soul is torn between desperate rebellion and hopeful expectation; his silent obedience is multilayered, has background. Such a problematic psychological situation as this is impossible for any of the Homeric heroes, whose destiny is clearly defined and who wake every morning as if it were the first day of their lives: their emotions, though strong, are simple and find expression instantly.

How fraught with background, in comparison, are characters like Saul and David! How entangled and stratified are such human relations as those between David and Absalom, between David and Joab! Any such "background" quality of the psychological situation as that which the story of Absalom's death and its sequel (II Samuel 18 and 19, by the so-called Jahvist) rather suggests than expresses, is unthinkable in Homer. Here we are confronted not merely with the psychological processes of characters whose depth of background is veritably abysmal, but with a purely geographical background too. For David is absent from the battlefield; but the influence of his will and his feelings continues to operate, they affect even Joab in his rebellion and disregard for the consequences of his actions; in the magnificent scene with the two messengers, both the physical and psychological background is fully manifest, though the latter is never expressed. With this, compare, for example, how Achilles, who sends Patroclus first to scout and then into battle, loses almost all "presentness" so long as he is not physically present. But the most important thing is the "multilayeredness" of the individual character; this is hardly to be met with in Homer, or at most in the form of a conscious hesitation between two possible courses of action; otherwise, in Homer, the complexity of the psychological life is shown only in the succession and alternation of emotions; whereas the Jewish writers are able to express the simultaneous existence of various layers of consciousness and the conflict between them.

The Homeric poems, then, though their intellectual, linguistic, and above all syntactical culture appears to be so much more highly developed, are yet comparatively simple in their picture of human beings; and no less so in their relation to the real life which they describe in general. Delight in physical existence is everything to them, and their highest aim is to make that delight perceptible to us. Between battles and passions, adventures and perils, they show us hunts, banquets, palaces and shepherds' cots, athletic contests and washing days—in order that we may see the heroes in their ordinary life, and seeing them so, may take pleasure in their manner of enjoying their savory present, a present which sends strong roots down into social usages, landscape, and daily life. And thus they bewitch us and ingratiate themselves to us until we live with them in the reality of their lives; so long as we are reading or hearing the poems, it does not matter whether we know that all this is only legend, "make-believe." The oft-repeated reproach that Homer is a liar takes nothing from his effectiveness, he does not need to base his story on historical reality, his reality is powerful enough in itself; it ensnares us, weaving its web around us, and that suffices him. And this "real" world into which we are lured, exists for itself, contains nothing but itself; the Homeric poems conceal nothing, they contain no teaching and no secret second meaning. Homer can be analyzed, as we have essayed to do here, but he cannot be interpreted. Later allegorizing trends have tried their arts of interpretation upon him, but to no avail. He resists any such treatment; the interpretations are forced and foreign, they do not crystallize into a unified doctrine. The general considerations which occasionally occur (in our episode, for example, v. 360: that in misfortune men age quickly) reveal a calm acceptance of the basic facts of human existence, but with no compulsion to brood over them, still less any passionate impulse either to rebel against them or to embrace them in an ecstasy of submission.

It is all very different in the Biblical stories. Their aim is not to bewitch the senses, and if nevertheless they produce lively sensory effects, it is only because the moral, religious, and psychological phenomena which are their sole concern are made concrete in the sensible matter of life. But their religious intent involves an absolute claim to historical truth. The story of Abraham and Isaac is not better established than the story of Odysseus, Penelope, and Euryclea; both are legendary. But the Biblical narrator, the Elohist, had to believe in the objective truth of the story of Abraham's sacrifice—the existence of the sacred ordinances of life rested upon the truth of this and similar stories. He had to believe in it passionately; or else (as many rationalistic interpreters believed and perhaps still believe) he had to be a conscious liar—no harmless liar like Homer, who lied to give pleasure, but a political liar with a definite end in view, lying in the interest of a claim to absolute authority.

To me, the rationalistic interpretation seems psychologically absurd; but even if we take it into consideration, the relation of the Elohist to the truth of his story still remains a far more passionate and definite one than is Homer's relation. The Biblical narrator was obliged to write exactly what his belief in the truth of the tradition (or, from the rationalistic standpoint, his interest in the truth of it) demanded of him—in either case, his freedom in creative or representative imagination was severely limited; his activity was perforce reduced to composing an effective version of the pious tradition. What he produced, then, was not primarily oriented toward "realism" (if he succeeded in being realistic, it was merely a means, not an end); it was oriented toward truth. Woe to the man who did not believe it! One can perfectly well entertain historical doubts on the subject of the Trojan War or of Odysseus' wanderings, and still, when reading Homer, feel precisely the effects he sought to produce; but without believing in Abraham's sacrifice, it is impossible to put the narrative of it to the use for which it was written. Indeed, we must go even further. The Bible's claim to truth is not only far more urgent than Homer's, it is tyrannical—it excludes all other claims. The world of the Scripture stories is not satisfied with claiming to be a historically true reality—it insists that it is the only real world, is destined for autocracy. All other scenes, issues, and ordinances have no right to appear independently of it, and it is promised that all of them, the history of all mankind, will be given their due place within its frame, will be subordinated to it. The Scripture stories do not, like Homer's, court our favor, they do not flatter us that they may please us and enchant us—they seek to subject us, and if we refuse to be subjected we are rebels.

Let no one object that this goes too far, that not the stories, but the religious doctrine, raises the claim to absolute authority; because the stories are not, like Homer's, simply narrated "reality." Doctrine and promise are incarnate in them and inseparable from them; for that very reason they are fraught with "background" and mysterious, containing a second, concealed meaning. In the story of Isaac, it is not only God's intervention at the beginning and the end, but even the factual and psychological elements which come between, that are mysterious, merely touched upon, fraught with background; and therefore they require subtle investigation and interpretation, they demand them. Since so much in the story is dark and incomplete, and since the reader knows that God is a hidden God, his effort to interpret it constantly finds something new to feed upon. Doctrine and the search for enlightenment are inextricably connected with the physical side of the narrative—the latter being more than simple "reality"; indeed they are in constant danger of losing their own reality, as very soon happened when interpretation reached such proportions that the real vanished.

If the text of the Biblical narrative, then, is so greatly in need of interpretation on the basis of its own content, its claim to absolute authority forces it still further in the same direction. Far from seeking, like Homer, merely to make us forget our own reality for a few hours, it seeks to overcome our reality: we are to fit our own life into its world, feel ourselves to be elements in its structure of universal history. This becomes increasingly difficult the further our historical environment is removed from that of the Biblical books; and if these nevertheless maintain their claim to absolute authority, it is inevitable that they themselves be adapted through interpretative transformation. This was for a long time comparatively easy; as late as the European Middle Ages it was possible to represent Biblical events as ordinary phenomena of contemporary life, the methods of interpretation themselves forming the basis for such a treatment. But when, through too great a change in environment and through the awakening of a critical consciousness, this becomes impossible, the Biblical claim to absolute authority is jeopardized; the method of interpretation is scorned and rejected, the Biblical stories become ancient legends, and the doctrine they had contained, now dissevered from them, becomes a disembodied image.

As a result of this claim to absolute authority, the method of interpretation spread to traditions other than the Jewish. The Homeric poems present a definite complex of events whose boundaries in space and time are clearly delimited; before it, beside it, and after it, other complexes of events, which do not depend upon it, can be conceived without conflict and without difficulty. The Old Testament, on the other hand, presents universal history: it begins with the beginning of time, with the creation of the world, and will end with the Last Days, the fulfilling of the Covenant, with which the world will come to an end. Everything else that happens in the world can only be conceived as an element in this sequence; into it everything that is known about the world, or at least everything that touches upon the history of the Jews, must be fitted as an ingredient of the divine plan; and as this too became possible only by interpreting the new material as it poured in, the need for interpretation reaches out beyond the original Jewish-Israelitish realm of reality—for example to Assyrian, Babylonian, Persian, and Roman history; interpretation in a determined direction becomes a general method of comprehending reality; the new and strange world which now comes into view and which, in the form in which it presents itself, proves to be wholly unutilizable within the Jewish religious frame, must be so interpreted that it can find a place there. But this process nearly always also reacts upon the frame, which requires enlarging and modifying. The most striking piece of interpretation of this sort occurred in the first century of the Christian era, in consequence of Paul's mission to the Gentiles: Paul and the Church Fathers reinterpreted the entire Jewish tradition as a succession of figures prognosticating the appearance of Christ, and assigned the Roman Empire its proper place in the divine plan of salvation. Thus while, on the one hand, the reality of the Old Testament presents itself as complete truth with a claim to sole authority, on the other hand that very claim forces it to a constant interpretative change in its own content; for millennia it undergoes an incessant and active development with the life of man in Europe.

The claim of the Old Testament stories to represent universal history, their insistent relation—a relation constantly redefined by conflicts—to a single and hidden God, who yet shows himself and who guides universal history by promise and exaction, gives these stories an entirely different perspective from any the Homeric poems can possess. As a composition, the Old Testament is incomparably less unified than the Homeric poems, it is more obviously pieced together —but the various components all belong to one concept of universal history and its interpretation. If certain elements survived which did not immediately fit in, interpretation took care of them; and so the reader is at every moment aware of the universal religio-historical perspective which gives the individual stories their general meaning and purpose. The greater the separateness and horizontal disconnection of the stories and groups of stories in relation to one another, compared with the *Iliad* and the *Odyssey*, the stronger is their general vertical connection, which holds them all together and which is entirely lacking in Homer. Each of the great figures of the Old Testament, from Adam to the prophets, embodies a moment of this vertical connection. God chose and formed these men to the end of embodying his essence and will—yet choice and formation do not coincide, for the latter proceeds gradually, historically, during the earthly life of him upon whom the choice has fallen. How the process is accomplished, what terrible trials such a formation inflicts, can be seen from our story of Abraham's sacrifice. Herein lies the reason why the great figures of the Old Testament are so much more fully developed, so much more fraught with their own biographical past, so much more distinct as individuals, than are the Homeric heroes. Achilles and Odysseus are splendidly described in many well-ordered words, epithets cling to them, their emotions are constantly displayed in their words and deeds—but they have no development, and their life-histories are clearly set forth once and for all. So little are the Homeric heroes presented as developing or having developed, that most of them—Nestor, Agamemnon, Achilles—appear to be of an age fixed from the very first. Even Odysseus, in whose case the long lapse of time and the many events which occurred offer so much opportunity for biographical development, shows almost nothing of it. Odysseus on his return is exactly the same as he was when he left Ithaca two decades earlier. But what a road, what a fate, lie between the Jacob who cheated his father out of his blessing and the old man whose favorite son has been torn to pieces by a wild beast!—between David the harp player, persecuted by his lord's jealousy, and the old king, surrounded by violent intrigues, whom Abishag the Shunnamite warmed in his bed, and he knew her not! The old man, of whom we know how he has become what he is, is more of an individual than the young man; for it is only during the course of an eventful life that men are differentiated into full individuality; and it is this history of a personality which the Old Testament presents to us as the formation undergone by those whom God has chosen to be examples. Fraught with their development, sometimes even aged to the verge of dissolution, they show a distinct stamp of individuality entirely foreign to the Homeric heroes. Time can touch the latter only outwardly, and even that change is brought to our observation as little as possible; whereas the stern hand of God is ever upon the Old Testament figures; he has not only made them once and for all and chosen them, but he continues to work upon them, bends them and kneads them, and, without destroying them in essence, produces from them forms which their youth gave no grounds for anticipating. The objection that the biographical element of the Old Testament often springs from the combination of several legendary personages does not apply; for this combination is a part of the development of the text. And how much wider is the pendulum swing of their lives than that of the Homeric heroes! For they are bearers of the divine will, and yet they are fallible, subject to misfortune and humiliation—and in the midst of misfortune and in their humiliation their acts and words reveal the transcendent majesty of God. There is hardly one of them who does not, like Adam, undergo the deepest humiliation—and hardly one who is not deemed worthy of God's personal intervention and personal inspiration. Humiliation and elevation go far deeper and far higher than in Homer, and they belong basically together. The poor beggar Odysseus is only masquerading, but Adam is really cast down, Jacob really a refugee, Joseph really in the pit and then a slave to be bought and sold. But their greatness, rising out of humiliation, is almost superhuman and an image of God's greatness. The reader clearly feels how the extent of the pendulum's swing is connected with the intensity of the personal history—precisely the most extreme circumstances, in which we are immeasurably forsaken and in despair, or immeasurably joyous and exalted, give us, if we survive them, a personal stamp which is recognized as the product of a rich existence, a rich development. And very often, indeed generally, this element of development gives the Old Testament stories a historical character, even when the subject is purely legendary and traditional.

Homer remains within the legendary with all his material, whereas the material of the Old Testament comes closer and closer to history as the narrative proceeds; in the stories of David the historical report predominates. Here too, much that is legendary still remains, as for example the story of David and Goliath; but much—and the most essential—consists in things which the narrators knew from their own experience or from firsthand testimony. Now the difference between legend and history is in most cases easily perceived by a reasonably experienced reader. It is a difficult matter, requiring careful historical and philological training, to distinguish the true from the synthetic or the biased in a historical presentation; but it is easy to separate the historical from the legendary in general. Their structure is different. Even where the legendary does not immediately betray itself by elements of the miraculous, by the repetition of well-known standard motives, typical patterns and themes, through neglect of clear details of time and place, and the like, it is generally quickly recognizable by its composition. It runs far too smoothly. All cross-currents, all friction, all that is casual, secondary to the main events and themes, everything unresolved, truncated, and uncertain, which confuses the clear progress of the action and the simple orientation of the actors, has disappeared. The historical event which we witness, or learn from the testimony of those who witnessed it, runs much more variously, contradictorily, and confusedly; not until it has produced results in a definite domain are we able, with their help, to classify it to a certain extent; and how often the order to which we think we have attained becomes doubtful again, how often we ask ourselves if the data before us have not led us to a far too simple classification of the original events! Legend arranges its material in a simple and straightforward way; it detaches it from its contemporary historical context, so that the latter will not confuse it; it knows only clearly outlined men who act from few and simple motives and the continuity of whose feelings and actions remains uninterrupted. In the legends of martyrs, for example, a stiff-necked and fanatical persecutor stands over against an equally stiff-necked and fanatical victim; and a situation so complicated—that is to say, so real and historical—as that in which the "persecutor" Pliny finds himself in his celebrated letter to Trajan on the subject of the Christians, is unfit for legend. And that is still a comparatively simple case. Let the reader think of the history which we are ourselves witnessing; anyone who, for example, evaluates the behavior of individual men and groups of men at the time of the rise of National Socialism in Germany, or the behavior of individual peoples and states before and during the last war, will feel how difficult it is to represent historical themes in general, and how unfit they are for legend; the historical comprises a great number of contradictory motives in each individual, a hesitation and ambiguous groping on the part of groups; only seldom (as in the last war) does a more or less plain situation, comparatively simple to describe, arise, and even such a situation is subject to division below the surface, is indeed almost constantly in danger of losing its simplicity; and the motives of all the interested parties are so complex that the slogans of propaganda can be composed only through the crudest simplification—with the result that friend and foe alike can often employ the same ones. To write history is so difficult that most historians are forced to make concessions to the technique of legend.

It is clear that a large part of the life of David as given in the Bible contains history and not legend. In Absalom's rebellion, for example, or in the scenes from David's last days, the contradictions and crossing of motives both in individuals and in the general action have become so concrete that it is impossible to doubt the historicity of the information conveyed. Now the men who composed the historical parts are often the same who edited the older legends too; their peculiar religious concept of man in history, which we have attempted to describe above, in no way led them to a legendary simplification of events; and so it is only natural that, in the legendary passages of the Old Testament, historical structure is frequently discernible—of course, not in the sense that the traditions are examined as to their credibility according to the methods of scientific criticism; but simply to the extent that the tendency to a smoothing down and harmonizing of events, to a simplification of motives, to a static definition of characters which avoids conflict, vacillation, and development, such as are natural to legendary structure, does not predominate in the Old Testament world of legend. Abraham, Jacob, or even Moses produces a more concrete, direct, and historical impression than the figures of the Homeric world —not because they are better described in terms of sense (the contrary is the case) but because the confused, contradictory multiplicity of events, the psychological and factual cross-purposes, which true history reveals, have not disappeared in the representation but still remain clearly perceptible. In the stories of David, the legendary, which only later scientific criticism makes recognizable as such, imperceptibly passes into the historical; and even in the legendary, the problem of the classification and interpretation of human history is already passionately apprehended—a problem which later shatters the framework of historical composition and completely overruns it with prophecy; thus the Old Testament, in so far as it is concerned with human events, ranges through all three domains: legend, historical reporting, and interpretative historical theology.

Connected with the matters just discussed is the fact that the Greek text seems more limited and more static in respect to the circle of personages involved in the action and to their political activity. In the recognition scene with which we began, there appears, aside from Odysseus and Penelope, the housekeeper Euryclea, a slave whom Odysseus' father Laertes had bought long before. She, like the swineherd Eumaeus, has spent her life in the service of Laertes' family; like Eumaeus, she is closely connected with their fate, she loves them and shares their interests and feelings. But she has no life of her own, no feelings of her own; she has only the life and feelings of her master. Eumaeus too, though he still remembers that he was born a freeman and indeed of a noble house (he was stolen as a boy), has, not only in fact but also in his own feeling, no longer a life of his own, he is entirely involved in the life of his masters. Yet these two characters are the only ones whom Homer brings to life who do not belong to the ruling class. Thus we become conscious of the fact that in the Homeric poems life is enacted only among the ruling class—others appear only in the role of servants to that class. The ruling class is still so strongly patriarchal, and still itself so involved in the daily activities of domestic life, that one is sometimes likely to forget their rank. But they are unmistakably a sort of feudal aristocracy, whose men divide their lives between war, hunting, marketplace councils, and feasting, while the women supervise the maids in the house. As a social picture, this world is completely stable; wars take place only between different groups of the ruling class; nothing ever pushes up from below. In the early stories of the Old Testament the patriarchal condition is dominant too, but since the people involved are individual nomadic or half-nomadic tribal leaders, the social picture gives a much less stable impression; class distinctions are not felt. As soon as the people completely emerges—that is, after the exodus from Egypt—its activity is always discernible, it is often in ferment, it frequently intervenes in events not only as a whole but also in separate groups and through the medium of separate individuals who come forward; the origins of prophecy seem to lie in the irrepressible politico-religious spontaneity of the people. We receive the impression that the movements emerging from the depths of the people of Israel-Judah must have been of a wholly different nature from those even of the later ancient democracies—of a different nature and far more elemental.

With the more profound historicity and the more profound social activity of the Old Testament text, there is connected yet another important distinction from Homer: namely, that a different conception of the elevated style and of the sublime is to be found here. Homer, of course, is not afraid to let the realism of daily life enter into the sublime and tragic; our episode of the scar is an example, we see how the quietly depicted, domestic scene of the foot-washing is incorporated into the pathetic and sublime action of Odysseus' homecoming. From the rule of the separation of styles which was later almost universally accepted and which specified that the realistic depiction of daily life was incompatible with the sublime and had a place only in comedy or, carefully stylized, in idyl—from any such rule Homer is still far removed. And yet he is closer to it than is the Old Testament. For the great and sublime events in the Homeric poems take place far more exclusively and unmistakably among the members of a ruling class; and these are far more untouched in their heroic elevation than are the Old Testament figures, who can fall much lower in dignity (consider, for example, Adam, Noah, David, Job); and finally, domestic realism, the representation of daily life, remains in Homer in the peaceful realm of the idyllic, whereas, from the very first, in the Old Testament stories, the sublime, tragic, and problematic take shape precisely in the domestic and commonplace: scenes such as those between Cain and Abel, between Noah and his sons, between Abraham, Sarah, and Hagar, between Rebekah, Jacob, and Esau, and so on, are inconceivable in the Homeric style. The entirely different ways of developing conflicts are enough to account for this. In the Old Testament stories the peace of daily life in the house, in the fields, and among the flocks, is undermined by jealousy over election and the promise of a blessing, and complications arise which would be utterly incomprehensible to the Homeric heroes. The latter must have palpable and clearly expressible reasons for their conflicts and enmities, and these work themselves out in free battles; whereas, with the former, the perpetually smouldering jealousy and the connection between the domestic and the spiritual, between the paternal blessing and the divine blessing, lead to daily life being permeated with the stuff of conflict, often with poison. The sublime influence of God here reaches so deeply into the everyday that the two realms of the sublime and the everyday are not only actually unseparated but basically inseparable.

We have compared these two texts, and, with them, the two kinds of style they embody, in order to reach a starting point for an investigation into the literary representation of reality in European culture. The two styles, in their opposition, represent basic types: on the one hand fully externalized description, uniform illumination, uninterrupted connection, free expression, all events in the foreground, displaying unmistakable meanings, few elements of historical development and of psychological perspective; on the other hand, certain parts brought into high relief, others left obscure, abruptness, suggestive influence of the unexpressed, "background" quality, multiplicity of meanings and the need for interpretation, universal-historical claims, development of the concept of the historically becoming, and preoccupation with the problematic.

Homer's realism is, of course, not to be equated with classical-antique realism in general; for the separation of styles, which did not develop until later, permitted no such leisurely and externalized description of everyday happenings; in tragedy especially there was no room for it; furthermore, Greek culture very soon encountered the phenomena of historical becoming and of the "multilayeredness" of the human problem, and dealt with them in its fashion; in Roman realism, finally, new and native concepts are added. We shall go into these later changes in the antique representation of reality when the occasion arises; on the whole, despite them, the basic tendencies of the Homeric style, which we have attempted to work out, remained effective and determinant down into late antiquity.

Since we are using the two styles, the Homeric and the Old Testament, as starting points, we have taken them as finished products, as they appear in the texts; we have disregarded everything that pertains to their origins, and thus have left untouched the question whether their peculiarities were theirs from the beginning or are to be referred wholly or in part to foreign influences. Within the limits of our purpose, a consideration of this question is not necessary; for it is in their full development, which they reached in early times, that the two styles exercised their determining influence upon the representation of reality in European literature.

2

FORTUNATA

Non potui amplius quicquam gustare, sed conversus ad eum, ut quam plurima exciperem, longe accersere fabulas coepi sciscitarique, quae esset mulier illa, quae huc atque illuc discurreret. Uxor, inquit, Trimalchionis, Fortunata appellatur, quae nummos modio metitur. Et modo, modo quid fuit? Ignoscet mihi genius tuus, noluisses de manu illius panem accipere. Nunc, nec quid nec quare, in caelum abiit et Trimalchionis topanta est. Ad summam, mero meridie si dixerit illi tenebras esse, credet. Ipse nescit quid habeat, adeo saplutus est; sed haec lupatria providet omnia et ubi non putes. Est sicca, sobria, bonorum consiliorum, est tamen malae linguae, pica pulvinaris. Quem amat, amat; quem non amat, non amat. Ipse Trimalchio fundos habet qua milvi volant, nummorum nummos. Argentum in ostiarii illius cella plus iacet quam quisquam in fortunis habet. Familia vero babae babae, non mehercules puto decumam partem esse quae dominum suum noverit. Ad summam, quemvis ex istis babaecalis in rutae folium coniciet. Nec est quod putes illum quicquam emere. Omnia domi nascuntur: lana, credrae, piper, lacte gallinaceum si quaesieris, invenies. Ad summam, parum illi bona lana nascebatur; arietes a Tarento emit, et eos culavit in gregem . . . Vides tot culcitras: nulla non aut cochyliatum aut coccineum tomentum habet. Tanta est animi beatitudo. Reliquos autem collibertos eius cave contemnas; valde succossi sunt. Vides illum qui in imo imus recumbit; hodie sua octingenta possidet. De nihilo crevit. Modo solebat collo suo ligna portare. Sed quomodo dicunt—ego nihil scio, sed audivi—quom Incuboni pilleum rapuisset, thesaurum invenit. Ego nemini invideo, si quid deus dedit. Est tamen subalapo et non vult sibi male. Itaque proxime casam hoc titulo proscripsit: C. Pompeius Diogenes ex Calendis Iuliis cenaculum locat; ipse enim domum emit. Quid ille qui libertini loco iacet, quam bene se habuit! Non impropero illi. Sestertium suum vidit decies, sed male vacillavit. Non puto illum capillos liberos habere. . . .

This passage is taken from Petronius' romance, of which only one episode—the banquet at the house of the wealthy freedman Trimalchio—is extant in full. Our sample is chapter 37 and part of chapter 38. During dinner, the narrator, Encolpius, asks his neighbor who the woman is who keeps running back and forth through the hall. The following translation of the answer he receives attempts to do justice to its style:

> That's Trimalchio's wife. Fortunata they call her. She measures money by the bushel. Yet not so long ago, not so long ago, what was she? I hope you won't mind my putting it that way, but you wouldn't have accepted a piece of bread from her hands. Now she sits on top of the world and is Trimalchio's one and only. If she tells him at high noon it's dark, he'll agree. He can't keep track of what he owns; he's so filthy rich. But that bitch looks out for everything, even where you'd least expect it. She doesn't drink; she's level-headed; her advice is good. But she has a nasty tongue and gossips like a magpie once she gets settled on her cushion. When she likes a person, she really likes him. When she hates one, she certainly hates him. Trimalchio's estates reach as far as a falcon flies. And some money he has! There's more silver in his porter's lodge than any one man's whole estate. And the number of slaves he's got! O my God, I don't think one out of ten knows his master even by sight. Believe me, he could stick any of these louts here in his pocket. And don't you think he ever has to buy anything. Everything is produced on the premises: wool, wax, pepper, everything; if you asked for chicken milk, I'm sure they'd have it. Once, you know, he didn't produce enough high-grade wool. So he bought rams from Tarentum and had them mount his sheep . . . Look at these cushions. Every single one has purple or scarlet stuffing. Not bad to put a man's mind at ease. But his fellow freedmen are not to be despised either. They aren't badly off. Look at the one sitting all the way back there. Today he is worth eight hundred thousand, and when he started out he had nothing. Not so long ago he carried wood around on his back. But they say—of course I don't know, except that I have heard people talk about it—they say he stole a goblin's magic cap and then found a treasure. Well I won't begrudge a fellow what God has given him. Still, he has just been freed and is planning to do a lot for himself. The other day he put a notice on his place: "C. Pompeius Diogenes offers this dwelling for rent

> as of July 1st because he is buying a house." That one there sitting with the freedmen—he used to have a nicely feathered nest too. I don't want to say anything against him. He had a cool million. But somehow he slipped badly, and now I don't think even the hair on his head doesn't have a lien on it. . . .[1]

The answer, which goes on in the same style for some time longer, turns out, then, to be fairly circumstantial. Not only the woman about whom Encolpius inquires, but the host and some of the guests are also described. In addition, the speaker portrays himself: his language, and the standards of value which he applies, give a clear idea of his personality. His language is the ordinary, rather mushy jargon of an uneducated city businessman, full of clichés (*nummos modio metitur, ignoscet mihi genius tuus, noluisses de manu illius panem accipere, in caelum abiit, topanta est, ad summam*—nearly all of his expressions would have to be transcribed); and it comes out in that lusty tone of voice which expresses lively but trivial feelings: astonishment, wonder, protestation, indifference, pomposity. In short, in their linguistic form the *tam dulces fabulae* (sweet bits of small talk), as they are presently called, reveal themselves unmistakably as what they are, namely, vulgar chatter, although a considerable portion of their content may be true. At the same time too, they reveal what the man who utters them is—namely, one who fits perfectly into the milieu he is describing. His standards of value provide further evidence of the fact. For obviously, under all that he says, lie three convictions: that wealth is the greatest good, and the more of it the better (*tanta est animi beatitudo*); that the good things of life are simply a superfluity of articles of the best quality and the opportunity to enjoy them in the most vulgar manner possible; and that, in this sense, everyone quite naturally acts for his own material advantage. Yet withal he himself is doubtless only a small or middling man, who looks upon the truly rich with honest awe. Thus the good fellow describes not only Fortunata, Trimalchio, and their guests, but without being aware of it, himself. Although, as we see, he has a rather one-sided viewpoint and speaks more from emotion and association than from logic, he yet speaks circumstantially and, as it were, plastically; he is completely frank and goes into everything that bears on his subject. He leaves nothing obscure; he talks himself out. As in Homer, a clear and equal light floods the persons and things with which he deals; like Homer,

[1] The translator has profited by an English version of this passage contributed by Professors Oates and Raubitchek of Princeton University.

he has leisure enough to make his presentation explicit; what he says can have but one meaning, nothing is left mysteriously in the background, everything is expressed.

Of course, there are important differences from Homer's manner. In the first place, the presentation, explicit though it be, is entirely subjective, for what is set before us is not Trimalchio's circle as objective reality, but as a subjective image, as it exists in the mind of the speaker, who himself, however, belongs to the circle. Petronius does not say: This is so. Instead, he lets an "I," who is identical neither with himself nor yet with the feigned narrator Encolpius, turn the spotlight of his perception on the company at table—a highly artful procedure in perspective, a sort of twofold mirroring, which I dare not say is unique in antique literature as it has come down to us, but which is most unusual there. In outward form this procedure is certainly nothing new, for of course throughout antique literature characters speak of their experiences and impressions. But nowhere, except in this passage from Petronius, do we have, on the one hand, the most intense subjectivity, which is even heightened by individuality of language, and, on the other hand, an objective intent—for the aim is an objective description of the company at table, including the speaker, through a subjective procedure. This procedure leads to a more meaningful and more concrete illusion of life. Inasmuch as the guest describes a company to which he himself belongs both by inner convictions and outward circumstances, the viewpoint is transferred to a point within the picture, the picture thus gains in depth, and the light which illuminates it seems to come from within it. Modern writers, Proust for example, work in exactly the same way, only more consistently within the realm of the tragic and problematic—a matter which we shall soon take up. Petronius' procedure is thus in the highest degree artistic, and marks him, if he had no forerunners, as a creative genius: the company at table is measured by its own standards; merely expressing these standards passes judgment upon them, and in addition the vulgarity of these parvenus is brilliantly illuminated by the mere fact that such things can be said of them at their own table. There are germs of such a technique elsewhere in the satirical literature of antiquity. But I know of no other example so well considered and so well carried out.

Another important difference from Homeric procedure is the following: In his description, the guest considers it particularly important to stress what all these people formerly were, in contrast to what they now are. *Et modo, modo quid fuit,* he says with reference to Fortunata; *de nihilo crevit,* and *quam bene se habuit,* referring to two fellow guests. Homer too, as we remarked earlier, likes to bring in the lineage, station, and previous history of his characters. But the facts he gives are of a very different nature. They do not lead us to a situation of change, to something in process; on the contrary, they lead us to a fixed point from which we can take our bearings. His Greek audiences are schooled in mythology and genealogy; Homer undertakes to give them the family-tree of the character in question as a means of placing him. Just so, in modern times, a newcomer into an exclusive aristocratic or bourgeois society can be placed by information concerning his paternal and maternal relatives. Thus, rather than an impression of historical change, Homer evokes the illusion of an unchanging, a basically stable social order, in comparison with which the succession of individuals and changes in personal fortunes appear unimportant. But our guest (and in this, as in everything that he says, his feelings are those of the type he represents) has in mind actual historical change, the ups and downs of fortune. For him, the world is in ceaseless motion, nothing is certain, and wealth and social position are highly unstable. His sense of historical reality is one-sided, since it is centered entirely upon the possession of wealth, but it is genuine. (The other guests too perpetually refer to the instability of life.) The acquisition and loss of worldly goods is what interests him in life, and is what has taught him and his fellows to distrust all stability. Yesterday you were still a slave, a porter, a catamite—yesterday you could still be whipped, sold, deported—today you are suddenly a rich landowner, a speculator, enjoying prodigious luxury—and tomorrow it may be all over. Naturally, he asks: *et modo, modo quid fuit?* It is not, or not only, his envy and jealousy speaking—basically he is doubtless a kindly man; it is his most real and most profound interest.

Now, it is well known that the instability of fortune occupies an important place in antique literature and that antique philosophical ethics often takes the same concept as a starting point. But strangely enough, elsewhere it but rarely conveys the impression of a living historical reality. It appears either in tragedy, as a fate without precedent, far outside the common course of things; or in comedy, as the result of a wholly extraordinary concatenation of events. Whether the subject be King Oedipus, whom the long-prophesied curse finds and casts into the utmost wretchedness; or the poor girl or the slave who, turning out to be children of rich parents, given up for lost after a shipwreck or a kidnapping, can marry as their hearts desire—in both cases, something extraordinary happens, something especially arranged, something which is outside the usual course of events, and which affects only one person or a few people, while the rest of the world appears to remain apart from it and indeed to witness the extraordinary event from a spectator's viewpoint. In the mimetic literary art of antiquity, the instability of fortune almost always appears as a fate which strikes from without and affects only a limited area, not as a fate which results from the inner processes of the real, historical world. And though, to be sure, proverbial literature and the gnomic maxims of popular philosophy conceive of change of fortune as coming to all men in all conditions, they express the idea only theoretically. Sententious reflections upon the instability of earthly happiness are heard often enough at Trimalchio's banquet; and, on the other hand, in the guest's reference to a goblin (*incubo*), there lingers something of the tendency to ascribe changes of fortune to specific interventions from without. But in Petronius' book the highly practical and mundane, or what we may call the intrahistorical, concept of the instability of fortune, predominates; the account which Trimalchio gives of his rise to wealth is entirely practical and mundane, and there are similar passages elsewhere. In the passage before us, however, it is the very similarity of the cases cited, the fact that they are so similar as to constitute a series, which more especially conveys the impression of an intrahistorical process. This is no matter of one person, or a few people, being stricken by a fate without precedent, far outside the common course of things, while the rest of the world remains calm. On the contrary, merely in the guest's narrative, four persons are mentioned who are all in the same boat, all engaged in the same turbulent pursuit of unstable Fortune. Though each of them individually has his private destiny, their destinies are all similar; their lot, for all its turbulence, is the common lot, common and vulgar. And behind the four persons who are described, we see the entire company, every member of which, we surmise, has a similar destiny which can be described in similar terms. Behind them again, we see in imagination a whole world of similar lives, and finally find ourselves contemplating an extremely animated historico-economic picture of the perpetual ups and downs of a mob of fortune-hunters scrambling after wealth and stupid pleasures. It is easy to understand that a society of businessmen of the humblest origins is particularly suitable material for a representation of this nature, for conveying this view of things. Such a society most clearly reflects the ups and downs of existence, because there is nothing to hold the balance for it; its members have neither inward tradition nor outer stability; they are nothing without money. In all of antique literature there is hardly a passage which, in this sense, so strongly exhibits intrahistorical movement as the passage before us.

And now we come to the third and possibly most important difference from the Homeric style, the most significant peculiarity of Petronius' Banquet: it is closer to our modern conception of a realistic presentation than anything else that has come down to us from antiquity; and this not so much because of the common vulgarity of its subject matter but above all because of its precise and completely unschematized fixation of the social milieu. The guests gathered at Trimalchio's party are southern Italian freedmen-parvenus of the first century; they hold the views of such people and speak their language almost without literary stylization. The like can hardly be found anywhere else. Comedy indicates the social milieu much more abstractly and schematically, much less specifically as to time and place; it hardly exhibits the rudiments of individualized speech in its characters. Satire, to be sure, contains much that tends in our direction, but the presentation is never so broad, it is moralistic and concerned with branding some specific vice or ridiculous trait. The romance, finally, *fabula milesiaca*, the genre which doubtless includes Petronius' work, is—in the other specimens and fragments that have come down to us—so crammed with magic, adventure, and mythology, so overburdened with erotic detail, that it cannot possibly be considered an imitation of everyday life as it existed at the time—quite apart from the unrealistic and rhetorical stylization of its language. A broad and truly workaday style of presentation is most nearly approximated by certain products of Alexandrian literature, for instance the two women at the festival of Adonis, by Theocritus, or the brothelkeeper bringing suit, by Herondas. But both these pieces, which are in verse, are more playful in their realistic portrayal of sociological background data, and also more linguistically stylized, than Petronius. Petronius' literary ambition, like that of the realists of modern times, is to imitate a random, everyday, contemporary milieu with its sociological background, and to have his characters speak their jargon without recourse to any form of stylization. Thus he reached the ultimate limit of the advance of realism in antiquity. Whether he was the first and only writer to embark upon such a venture, whether and how far the Roman mime had blazed the trail for him, are questions which need not be taken up in this context.

Now if Petronius marks the ultimate limit to which realism attained in antiquity, his work will accordingly serve to show what that realism could not or would not do. The Banquet is a purely comic work. The individual characters, as well as the connecting narrative, are consciously and consistently kept on the lowest level of style both in diction and treatment. And this necessarily implies that everything problematic, everything psychologically or sociologically suggestive of serious, let alone tragic, complications must be excluded, for its excessive weight would break the style. Let us pause here for a moment and think of the nineteenth-century realists, of Balzac or Flaubert, of Tolstoi or Dostoevski. Old Grandet (in *Eugénie Grandet*) or Fedor Pavlovich Karamazov are not mere caricatures, as Trimalchio is, but terrible realities which must be taken wholly seriously; they are involved in tragic complications, and notwithstanding their grotesqueness, are themselves tragic. In modern literature the technique of imitation can evolve a serious, problematic, and tragic conception of any character regardless of type and social standing, of any occurrence regardless of whether it be legendary, broadly political, or narrowly domestic; and in most cases it actually does so. Precisely that is completely impossible in antiquity. There are, it is true, some transitional forms in bucolic and amatory poetry, but on the whole the rule of the separation of styles, touched upon in the first chapter of this study, remains inviolate. Everything commonly realistic, everything pertaining to everyday life, must not be treated on any level except the comic, which admits no problematic probing. As a result the boundaries of realism are narrow. And if we take the word realism a little more strictly, we are forced to conclude that there could be no serious literary treatment of everyday occupations and social classes—merchants, artisans, peasants, slaves—of everyday scenes and places—home, shop, field, store—of everyday customs and institutions—marriage, children, work, earning a living—in short, of the people and its life. Linked with this is the fact that the realists of antiquity do not make clear the social forces underlying the facts and conditions which they present. This could only be done in the realm of the serio-problematic. But since the characters do not leave the realm of the comic, their relation to the social whole is either a matter of clever adaptation or of grotesquely blameworthy isolation. In the latter case, the realistically portrayed individual is always in the wrong in his conflict with the social whole, which is represented as a given fact, an institution unalterably established in the background of the action and requiring no explanation in regard either to its origin or to its effects. This too has altered in modern times. In the realistic literature of antiquity, the existence of society poses no historical problem; it may at best pose a problem in ethics, but even then the ethical question is more concerned with the individual members of society than with the social whole. No matter how many persons may be branded as given to vice or as ridiculous, criticism of vices and excesses poses the problem as one for the individual; consequently, social criticism never leads to a definition of the motive forces within society.

Hence, behind the bustle which Petronius sets before us, we sense nothing which might help us understand the action in terms of its economic and political context; and the historical movement, of which we spoke above, is here only a surface movement. Of course this observation is not intended to suggest that Petronius ought to have worked an essay in national economy into his Banquet. He need not even have gone as far as Balzac who, in the novel mentioned above, *Eugénie Grandet,* described the growth of Grandet's fortune in a manner which reflects all of French history from the Revolution to the Restoration. An entirely unsystematic but continuous and conscious connection with the events and conditions of the time would have been enough. A modern Petronius would link a portrait of a profiteer to the inflation after the First World War, let us say, or to some other well-known crisis. Thackeray, although his method of elaboration remains ethical rather than historical, already links his great novel to the background of the Napoleonic and post-Napoleonic era. Nothing of the sort is found in Petronius. When the subject is the price of food stuffs (chapter 44), or other aspects of urban life (chapters 44, 45 and *passim*), or the history of the guests' lives and fortunes (the passage quoted and especially chapters 57 and 75f.), he will not even allude to a specific place, a definite time, a particular political and economic situation. True enough, we can easily determine that the place is a town in Southern Italy, the time that of the early emperors; the modern historian can use these indications as sociological raw material, and Petronius' contemporaries of course knew all this, possibly in greater detail than we do—but the author himself attributes no importance whatever to the contemporary-historical aspect of his work. Had he done so, that is, had he established a link between his individual events or relationships and specific political and economic situations of the early imperial period, a distinct historical background would have been provided for the reader, which he could supplement with his own knowledge; and the result would have been a historical third dimension in comparison with which Petronius' perspective, of which we spoke above, must appear but a two-dimensional surface; and we could use the term "historical movement" strictly and not merely in a comparative sense. But that would have violated the style within which Petronius undertook to remain; it would not have been possible without an idea which he could not conceive, that is, the idea of historical "forces." As things are, the kinesis—however animated—is limited to the picture itself; back of it, nothing moves, the world is static. We are clearly dealing with a period sketch, a portrait of a time; but the time is presented as though it had always existed unchanged as it does at present in this place, with masters bequeathing large slices of their wealth to slaves who do their sexual bidding, with enormously profitable deals within the reach of merchants, and so forth. The historicity of all these things, the fact that they are determined by an era, is not in itself of interest to Petronius or his contemporary readers. But we moderns note the fact and our historians of economics base their conclusions upon it.

Here we encounter a difficult question of principle which cannot be circumvented. If the literature of antiquity was unable to represent everyday life seriously, that is, in full appreciation of its problems and with an eye for its historical background; if it could represent it only in the low style, comically or at best idyllically, statically and ahistorically, the implication is that these things mark the limits not only of the realism of antiquity but of its historical consciousness as well. For it is precisely in the intellectual and economic conditions of everyday life that those forces are revealed which underlie historical movements; these, whether military, diplomatic, or related to the inner constitution of the state, are only the product, the final result, of variations in the depths of everyday life.

In this connection we may examine a specimen of antique historiography. I have selected a text which is not too far removed in time from the Banquet, and indeed one which represents a revolutionary movement from the depths, the beginning of the revolt of the Germanic legions after the death of Augustus, in Tacitus' *Annals*, Book 1, chapters 16f. It reads as follows:

Hic rerum urbanarum status erat, cum Pannonicas legiones seditio incessit, nullis novis causis, nisi quod mutatus princeps licentiam turbarum et ex civili bello spem praemiorum ostendebat. Castris aestivis tres simul legiones habebantur, praesidente Iunio Blaeso, qui fine Augusti et initiis Tiberii auditis ob iustitium aut gaudium intermiserat solita munia. Eo principio lascivire miles, discordare, pessimi cuiusque sermonibus praebere aures, denique luxum et otium cupere, disciplinam et laborem aspernari. Erat in castris Percennius quidam, dux olim theatralium operarum, dein gregarius miles, procax lingua et miscere coetus histrionali studio doctus. Is imperitos animos et, quaenam post Augustum militiae condicio, ambigentes impellere paulatim nocturnis conloquiis aut flexo in vesperam die et dilapsis melioribus deterrimum quemque congregare. Postremo promptis iam et aliis seditionis ministris, velut contionabundus interrogabat, cur paucis centurionibus, paucioribus tribunis in modum servorum oboedirent. Quando ausuros exposcere remedia, nisi novum et adhuc nutantem principem precibus vel armis adirent? Satis per tot annos ignavia peccatum, quod tricena aut quadragena stipendia senes et plerique truncato ex vulneribus corpore tolerent. Ne dimissis quidem finem esse militiae, sed aput vexillum tendentes alio vocabulo eosdem labores perferre. Ac si quis tot casus vita superaverit, trahi adhuc diversas in terras, ubi per nomen agrorum uligines paludum vel inculta montium accipiant. Enimvero militiam ipsam gravem, infructuosam: denis in diem assibus animam et corpus aestimari: hinc vestem arma tentoria, hinc saevitiam centurionum et vacationes munerum redimi. At Hercule verbera et vulnera, duram hiemem, exercitas aestates, bellum atrox aut sterilem pacem sempiterna. Nec aliud levamentum, quam si certis sub legibus militia iniretur: ut singulos denarios mererent, sextus decumus stipendii annus finem adferret; ne ultra sub vexillis tenerentur, sed isdem in castris praemium pecunia solveretur. An praetorias cohortes, quae binos denarios acceperint, quae post sedecim annos penatibus suis reddantur, plus periculorum suscipere? Non obtrectari a se urbanas excubias; sibi tamen aput horridas gentes e contuberniis hostem aspice.—Adstrepebat vulgus, diversis incitamentis, hi verberum notas, illi canitiem, plurimi detrita tegmina et nudum corpus exprobrantes. . . .

(Thus stood affairs at Rome, when a sedition made its appearance in the legions in Pannonia, without any fresh grounds, save that the accession of a new prince promised impunity to tumult, and held out the hope of advantages to be derived from a civil war. Three legions occupied a summer camp together, commanded by Junius Blaesus, who, upon notice of the death of Augustus and accession of Tiberius, had granted the soldiers a recess from their wonted duties for some days, as a time either of public mourning or festivity. From this beginning they waxed wanton and quarrelsome, lent their ears to the discourses of every profligate, and at last they longed for a life of dissipation and idleness, and spurned all military discipline and labor. In the camp was one Percennius, formerly a busy leader of theatrical factions, after that a common soldier, of a petulant tongue, and from his experience in theatrical party zeal, well qualified to stir up the bad passions of a crowd. Upon minds uninformed, and agitated with doubts as to what might be the condition of military service now that Augustus was dead, he wrought gradually by confabulations by night, or when day verged towards its close; and when all the better-disposed had retired to their respective quarters, he would congregate all the most depraved about him.

Lastly, when now also other ministers of sedition were at hand to second his designs, in imitation of a general solemnly haranguing his men, he asked them—"Why did they obey, like slaves, a few centurions and fewer tribunes? When would they be bold enough to demand redress, unless they approached the prince, yet a novice, and tottering on his throne, either with entreaties or arms? Enough had they erred in remaining passive through so many years, since decrepit with age and maimed with wounds, after a course of service of thirty or forty years, they were still doomed to carry arms; nor even to those who were discharged was there any end of service, but they were still kept to the colors, and under another name endured the same hardships. And if any of them survived so many dangers, still were they dragged into countries far remote, where, under the name of lands, they are presented with swampy fens, or mountain wastes. But surely, burdensome and ungainful of itself was the occupation of war;—ten asses a day the poor price of their persons and lives; out of this they must buy clothes, and tents, and arms,—out of this the cruelty of centurions must be redeemed, and occasional exemptions from duty; but, by Hercules, stripes, wounds, hard winters and laborious summers, bloody wars and barren peace, were miseries eternally to be endured; nor remained there other remedy than to enter the service upon certain conditions, as that their pay should be a denarius a day, sixteen years be the utmost term of serving; beyond that period to be no longer obliged to follow the colors, but have their reward in money, paid them in the camp where they earned it. Did the praetorian guards, who had double pay,—they who after sixteen years' service were sent home, undergo more dangers? This was not said in disparagement of the city guards; their own lot, however, was, serving among uncivilized nations, to have the enemy in view from their tents."

The general body received this harangue with shouts of applause, but stimulated by various motives,—some showing, in all the bitterness of reproach, the marks of stripes, others their hoary heads, many their tattered vestments and naked bodies.) *The Works of Tacitus*. The Oxford Translation. London: Bell. 1888.

At first sight it may seem that this passage does give really serious expression to a movement of the submerged, that it does painstakingly present the practical everyday motives, the underlying economic factors, and the actual events marking the inception of the movement. The grievances of the soldiers discussed in Percennius' speech—excessive length of service, hardships, insufficient pay, inadequate old-age provision, corruption, envy of the easier life of metropolitan troops—are presented vividly and graphically in a manner not frequently encountered even in modern historians. Tacitus is a great artist. Under his hands things come strikingly alive. The modern historian, we must imagine, would proceed more theoretically (one might say, more bookishly); on this occasion he would not have had Percennius speak; he would have presented a factually objective, well-documented study of pay-scales and welfare provisions, or he might have referred to such a study elsewhere in his own or in some colleague's publications. He would have gone on to discuss the justification of the soldier's demands; he would have given a brief review of the government's past and future policies in the matter, and so forth. All this Tacitus does not do; and the modern historian of antiquity, in order to apply his characteristic methodology, has to reorganize the material which the antique chroniclers have to offer, and to supplement it by inscriptions, excavators' findings, and various other types of indirect evidence.

Tacitus presents the soldiers' grievances and demands, which cast a light upon the facts of their everyday situation, as utterances of the ringleader Percennius; he sees no reason to discuss them, to inquire whether and how far they were justified, to explain how the Roman soldier's lot had changed since the days of the Republic, and the like. All this, he considers, is not worth treating, and it is evident that he could rely on his readers' not missing anything of the kind either. But this is not all. The factual information he gives on the causes of the revolt—information presented in the form of a ringleader's speech and not discussed further—he invalidates in advance by stating at the outset his own view of the real causes of the revolt in purely ethical terms: *nullis novis causis, nisi quod mutatus princeps licentiam turbarum et ex civili bello spem praemiorum ostendebat.* It would be difficult to put it more contemptuously. In his view, the whole thing is merely a matter of mob effrontery and lack of discipline. The blame is placed on the interruption of the usual schedule of duties (they are idle and therefore they shout, says Pharaoh of the Jews). We must be careful not to read into the word *novis* the admission that older grievances are justified. Nothing could be further from Tacitus' view. Time and again he dwells upon the point that only the worst elements are ready to rebel; and as for the leader Percennius, the former chief claqueur, boasting his *histrionale studium* and playing the general, Tacitus feels only the most profound contempt for him.

So it becomes manifest that Tacitus' vivid recital of the soldiers' grievances and demands is by no means based upon an understanding of those demands. This fact might naturally be explained as the result of Tacitus' characteristic attitude of aristocratic conservatism; to his mind, a rebellious legion is nothing but a lawless mob; a common soldier in the role of a mutinous ringleader defies classification in terms of constitutional law, especially since even during the revolutionary epoch of Roman history the most radical rebels could not attain their goal except by submitting to the established order of a civil service career. It may moreover be assumed that Tacitus viewed with alarm the growing power of the military; during the civil wars it had increased to threatening proportions, as later it came to undermine the very structure of the state. But this explanation is not enough. For Tacitus not only lacks understanding, he actually has no interest whatever in the facts underlying the soldiers' demands. He does not argue against their demands in objective terms; he will not take the trouble to prove that they are not justified; a few purely ethical considerations (*licentia, spes praemiorum, pessimus quisque, inexperti animi*) are quite enough to reject them in advance. Had other views existed in his time, views contrary to his own and based on a more clearly sociological and historical interpretation of human actions, Tacitus would have had to take a stand in regard to the problems thus raised—precisely as during the more recent decades of our own period even the most conservative politician still felt obliged to consider the problems raised by his socialist opponents' conception of politics, or at any rate to discuss them polemically, which often implied an elaborate preoccupation with them. Tacitus felt no such obligation, for no such opponents could exist. Historiography in depth—that is, methodical research into the historical growth of social as well as intellectual movements—is a thing unknown to antiquity. This fact has often been alluded to by modern students. So Norden writes in his *Antike Kunstprosa* (2, 647): "We must bear in mind that the historians of antiquity did not attain, and indeed did not seek to attain, a presentation of general, world-moving ideas." And Rostovtzeff in his *Social and Economic History of the Roman Empire* (p. 88): "The historians were not interested in the economic life of the Empire." These two statements, chosen at random, may at first sight appear to have little to do with each other, but what they express goes back to the same peculiarity of the ancients' way of viewing things; it does not see forces, it sees vices and virtues, successes and mistakes. Its formulation of problems is not concerned with historical developments either intellectual or material, but with ethical judgments. But this is most intimately connected with the prevailing view which is manifested in the stylistic differentiation between the tragic-problematic and realism. Both are based upon an aristocratic reluctance to become involved with growth processes in the depths, for these processes are felt to be both vulgar and orgiastically lawless.

An ethically oriented historiography, which also on the whole proceeds in strict chronological order, is bound to use an unchangeable system of categories and hence cannot produce synthetic-dynamic concepts of the kind we are accustomed to employ today. Concepts like "industrial capitalism" or "absenteeism," which are syntheses of characteristic data, applicable especially to specific epochs, and, on the other hand, concepts like Renaissance, Enlightenment, Romanticism, which first of all designate epochs but are also syntheses of characteristic data, sometimes applicable to epochs other than those originally designated by them, are designed to cover phenomena in motion; such phenomena are traced from their first sporadic appearance, then as they occur with progressive density, and finally as they abate and change and vanish; and an essential aspect of all these concepts is the fact that their growth and transformation—that is, an idea of evolution—is contained in them, is conceived as part of their content. On the contrary, the ethical and even the political concepts of antiquity (aristocracy, democracy, etc.) are fixed, aprioristic model concepts. All the modern authorities in the field, from Vico down to Rostovtzeff, have endeavored to dissolve these, to trace the formulation which lies concealed behind them, and which our thought can grasp, a formulation which we can only achieve by collecting and rearranging the characteristic data. As I open Rostovtzeff's work to check the quotation above, my eyes fall on this sentence: "The question, however, arises, How are we to account for the existence of comparatively large numbers of proletarians in Italy?" Such a sentence, such a question, is unthinkable in an author of classical antiquity. It reaches back behind any foreground movements and seeks the changes of significance to them in processes of historical growth which no antique author observed, still less reduced to system and coherence. When we read Thucydides we get, aside from a continuous account of foreground events, nothing but considerations which are statically aprioristic and ethical in content, on such matters as human nature or fate, and which, though it is true that they are sometimes applied to specific situations, are of an absolute validity in themselves.

Let us return to our passage from Tacitus. If he was not at all interested in the soldiers' demands and never intended to discuss them objectively, why does he express them so graphically in Percennius' speech? The reasons are purely aesthetic. The grand style of historiography requires grandiloquent speeches, which as a rule are fictitious. Their function is graphic dramatization (*illustratio*) of a given occurrence, or at times the presentation of great political or moral ideas; in either case they are intended as the rhetorical bravura pieces of the presentation. The writer is permitted a certain sympathetic entering into the thoughts of the supposed speaker, and even a certain realism. Essentially, however, such speeches are products of a specific stylistic tradition cultivated in the schools for rhetors. The composition of speeches which one person or another might have delivered on one or another great historical occasion was a favorite exercise. Tacitus is a master of his craft, and his speeches are not sheer display; they are really imbued with the character and the situation of the persons supposed to have delivered them; but they too are primarily rhetoric. Percennius does not speak his own language; he speaks Tacitean, that is, he speaks with extreme terseness, as a master of disposition, and highly rhetorically. Undoubtedly his words—though given as indirect discourse—vibrate with the actual excitement of mutinous soldiers and their leader. Yet even if we assume that Percennius was a gifted demagogue, such brevity, incisiveness, and order are not possible in a rebellious propaganda speech, and of soldiers' slang there is not the slightest trace. The same is true of the soldier Vibulenus' words in chapter 22. In the very next chapter they are discounted as lies. They are certainly profoundly moving, but they nevertheless represent the highest degree of rhetorical stylization. Though anaphora, here repeatedly employed (*quis fratri meo vitam, quis fratrem mihi reddit*), may have been frequent in popular usage, it still remains a rhetorical manifestation of the elevated style and has nothing to do with soldiers' language. And this is the second distinctive characteristic of antique historiography: it is rhetorical. The combination of ethical and rhetorical preoccupations gives it a high degree of order, clarity, and dramatic impact. In the case of the Romans there is further a broad and comprehensive view of the extensive stage on which the political and military events occur. Beyond these characteristics, the greatest writers possess a realistic knowledge of the human heart which, though it is soberly based on experience, is never mean. At times we even find traces of an ontogenetic derivation of individual characters, as for example in Sallust's portrait of Catiline and especially in Tacitus' portrait of Tiberius. But this is the limit which cannot be passed. The ethical and rhetorical approach are incompatible with a conception in which reality is a development of forces. Antique historiography gives us neither social history nor economic history nor cultural history. These can only be inferred indirectly from the data presented. However vast the difference between the two passages here considered—the talk of the dinner guest in Petronius and the Pannonian mutiny in Tacitus—both reveal the limits of antique realism and thus of antique historical consciousness.

It will be assumed that, to find a counter example in which these limits are extended, I should have to take a modern text. Yet here again I have at my disposal documents of Jewish-Christian literature which are approximately contemporaneous with Petronius and Tacitus. I choose the story of Peter's denial and I follow Mark's version of it—the differences in the Synoptists are, in any case, quite insignificant.

After the arrest of Jesus—he alone has been arrested, while his entourage has been allowed to escape—Peter, keeping at a safe distance, follows the armed men who take Jesus away. He has been bold enough to enter the court of the High Priest's palace and there, feigning the curiosity of an uninvolved spectator, he stands by the fire among the servants. In doing so he has displayed greater courage than the others. For, since he was a member of the prisoner's inner circle, the risk of his being recognized was very great. And in fact, as he stands there by the fire, a servant girl tells him to his face that he is one of Jesus' group. He denies this and tries unobtrusively to withdraw from the vicinity of the fire. It seems, however, that the girl has kept an eye on him; she follows him to the outer court and repeats her accusation, so that several bystanders hear it. He repeats his denial, but now his Galilean accent has been noticed and the situation begins to look dangerous for him. We are not told how he managed to get away. It is not likely that his third asseveration was given greater credence than the first two. Perhaps something happened to draw the crowd's attention away from him; or perhaps an order had been issued not to molest the prisoner's followers so long as they offered no resistance, and so it may have seemed enough to tell the suspect to move on.

It is apparent at first glance that the rule of differentiated styles cannot possibly apply in this case. The incident, entirely realistic both in regard to locale and *dramatis personae*—note particularly their low social station—is replete with problem and tragedy. Peter is no mere accessory figure serving as *illustratio*, like the soldiers Vibulenus and Percennius, who are represented as mere scoundrels and swindlers. He is the image of man in the highest and deepest and most tragic sense. Of course this mingling of styles is not dictated by an artistic purpose. On the contrary, it was rooted from the beginning in the character of Jewish-Christian literature; it was graphically and harshly dramatized through God's incarnation in a human being of the humblest social station, through his existence on earth amid humble everyday people and conditions, and through his Passion which, judged by earthly standards, was ignominious; and it naturally came to have—in view of the wide diffusion and strong effect of that literature in later ages—a most decisive bearing upon man's conception of the tragic and the sublime. Peter, whose personal account may be assumed to have been the basis of the story, was a fisherman from Galilee, of humblest background and humblest education. The other participants in the night scene in the court of the High Priest's palace are servant girls and soldiers. From the humdrum existence of his daily life, Peter is called to the most tremendous role. Here, like everything else to do with Jesus' arrest, his appearance on the stage—viewed in the world-historical continuity of the Roman Empire—is nothing but a provincial incident, an insignificant local occurrence, noted by none but those directly involved. Yet how tremendous it is, viewed in relation to the life a fisherman from the Sea of Galilee normally lives, and what enormous "pendulation" (Harnack in discussing the denial scene once used the term *Pendelausschlag*) is going on in him! He has left his home and his work; he has followed his master to Jerusalem; he has been the first to recognize him as the Messiah; when the catastrophe came, he was more courageous than the others; not only was he among those who tried to resist but even when the miracle which he had doubtless expected failed to occur, he once again attempted to follow Jesus as he had followed him before. It is but an attempt, halfhearted and timid, motivated perhaps by a confused hope that the miracle by which the Messiah would crush his enemies might still take place. But since his attempt to follow Jesus is a halfhearted, doubt-ridden venture, furtive and full of fear, he falls deeper than all the others, who at least had no occasion to deny Jesus explicitly. Because his faith was deep, but not deep enough, the worst happened to him that can happen to one whom faith had inspired but a short time before: he trembles for his miserable life. And it is entirely credible that this terrifying inner experience should have brought about another swing of the pendulum—this time in the opposite direction and far stronger. Despair and remorse following his desperate failure prepared him for the visions which contributed decisively to the constitution of Christianity. It is only through this experience that the significance of Christ's coming and Passion is revealed to him.

A tragic figure from such a background, a hero of such weakness, who yet derives the highest force from his very weakness, such a to and fro of the pendulum, is incompatible with the sublime style of classical antique literature. But the nature and the scene of the conflict also fall entirely outside the domain of classical antiquity. Viewed superficially, the thing is a police action and its consequences; it takes place entirely among everyday men and women of the common people; anything of the sort could be thought of in antique terms only as farce or comedy. Yet why is it neither of these? Why does it arouse in us the most serious and most significant sympathy? Because it portrays something which neither the poets nor the historians of antiquity ever set out to portray: the birth of a spiritual movement in the depths of the common people, from within the everyday occurrences of contemporary life, which thus assumes an importance it could never have assumed in antique literature. What we witness is the awakening of "a new heart and a new spirit." All this applies not only to Peter's denial but also to every other occurrence which is related in the New Testament. Every one of them is concerned with the same question, the same conflict with which every human being is basically confronted and which therefore remains infinite and eternally pending. It sets man's whole world astir—whereas the entanglements of fate and passion which Greco-Roman antiquity knows, always directly concern simply the individual, the one person involved in them. It is only by virtue of the most general relations, that is, by virtue of the fact that we too are human beings and thus are subject to fate and passion, that we experience "fear and pity." But Peter and the other characters in the New Testament are caught in a universal movement of the depths which at first remains almost entirely below the surface and only very gradually—the Acts of the Apostles show the beginnings of this development—emerges into the foreground of history, but which even now, from the beginning, lays claim to being limitless and the direct concern of everybody, and which absorbs all merely personal conflicts into itself. What we see here is a world which on the one hand is entirely real, average, identifiable as to place, time, and circumstances, but which on the other hand is shaken in its very foundations, is transforming and renewing itself before our eyes. For the New Testament authors who are their contemporaries, these occurrences on the plane of everyday life assume the importance of world-revolutionary events, as later on they will for everyone. They reveal their identity as a movement, a historically active dynamism, through the fact that time and again the impact of Jesus' teachings, personality, and fate upon this and that individual is described. While the aims upon which the movement is centered can as yet be neither clearly grasped nor expressed (it is after all one of its essential characteristics that it does not lend itself to simple definitions and explanations), its effects are already described in numerous examples of its driving dynamism, its surging hither and thither among the people—something which, as pure fact, no Greek or Roman writer would ever have thought of treating in comparably elaborate detail. A Greek or Roman writer describes a popular movement only as reaction to a specific practical complex of events—as Thucydides for instance describes the Athenians' attitude toward the project of an expedition to Sicily; the movement is characterized as a whole—as approving, disapproving, undecided, or perhaps tumultuous—just as the observer sees it, looking, as it were, from above; but it could not possibly occur that reactions so various among so many individuals of the common people should be made a major subject of literary treatment. What considerable portions of the Gospels and the Acts of the Apostles describe, what Paul's Epistles also often reflect, is unmistakably the beginning of a deep subsurface movement, the unfolding of historical forces. For this, it is essential that great numbers of random persons should make their appearance; for it is not possible to bring to life such historical forces in their surging action except by reference to numerous random persons—the term random being here employed to designate people from all classes, occupations, walks of life, people, that is, who owe their place in the account exclusively to the fact that the historical movement engulfs them as it were accidentally, so that they are obliged to react to it in one way or another.

It goes without saying that the stylistic convention of antiquity fails here, for the reaction of the casually involved person can only be presented with the highest seriousness. The random fisherman or publican or rich youth, the random Samaritan or adulteress, come from their random everyday circumstances to be immediately confronted with the personality of Jesus; and the reaction of an individual in such a moment is necessarily a matter of profound seriousness, and very often tragic. The antique stylistic rule according to which realistic imitation, the description of random everyday life, could only be comic (or at best idyllic), is therefore incompatible with the representation of historical forces as soon as such a representation undertakes to render things concretely; for this procedure entails entering into the random everyday depths of popular life, as well as readiness to take seriously whatever is encountered there; and inversely the rule of style can operate only in cases where the writer abandons any attempt to make historical forces concrete or feels no need to do so. It goes without saying that, in the New Testament writings, any raising of historical forces to the level of consciousness is totally "unscientific": it clings to the concrete and fails to progress to a systematization of experience in new concepts. Yet there is to be observed a spontaneous generation of categories which apply to epochs as well as to states of the inner life and which are much more pliable and dynamic than the categories of Greco-Roman historians. For example, there is the distinction of eras, the era of law or of sin and the era of grace, faith, and justice; there are the concepts of "love," "power," "spirit," and the like; and even such abstract and static concepts as that of justice have assumed a dialectic mobility (Romans 3: 21ff.) which renews them completely. Connected with this is everything concerned with inner rebirth and change—the words sin, death, justice, and so on, coming to express not merely action, event, and quality, but phases of an intrahistorical transformation. To be sure, in all this we must not forget that the transformation is here one whose course progresses to somewhere outside of history, to the end of time or to the coincidence of all times, in other words upward, and does not, like the scientific concepts of evolutionary history, remain on the horizontal plane of historical events. That is a decisive difference; and yet, whatever kind of movement it may be which the New Testament writings introduced into phenomenal observation, the essential point is this: the deep subsurface layers, which were static for the observers of classical antiquity, began to move.

In this view of things there is no room for ethical and rhetorical standards in the sense of the ancients. An occurrence like Peter's denial cannot be fitted into a system of judgments which operates with static categories, if for no other reason than the tremendous "pendulation" in the heart of one specific individual; and with the advent of an attitude which seeks justification not in works but in faith, the ethicism of the ancients has lost its supreme rank. And in regard to rhetoric the situation is the same. Surely, the New Testament writings are extremely effective; the tradition of the prophets and the Psalms is alive in them, and in some of them—those written by authors of more or less pronounced Hellenistic culture—we can trace the use of Greek figures of speech. But the spirit of rhetoric—a spirit which classified subjects in *genera*, and invested every subject with a specific form of style as the one garment becoming it in virtue of its nature—could not extend its dominion to them for the simple reason that their subject would not fit into any of the known genres. A scene like Peter's denial fits into no antique genre. It is too serious for comedy, too contemporary and everyday for tragedy, politically too insignificant for history—and the form which was given it is one of such immediacy that its like does not exist in the literature of antiquity. This can be judged by a symptom which at first glance may seem insignificant: the use of direct discourse. The maid says: And thou also wast with Jesus of Nazareth! He answers: I know not, neither understand I what thou sayest. Then the maid says to the bystanders: This is one of them.

And, Peter repeating his denial, the bystanders speak up: Surely thou art one of them, for thou art a Galilean by thy speech!—I do not believe that there is a single passage in an antique historian where direct discourse is employed in this fashion in a brief, direct dialogue. Dialogues with few participants are rare in their writings; at best they appear in anecdotal biography, and there the function they serve is almost always to lead up to famous pregnant retorts, whose importance lies not in their realistically concrete content but in their rhetorical and ethical impact—the sort of thing which later on, in the theory of the thirteenth-century Italian novella, was called a *bel parlare*. The celebrated anecdotes of Croesus and Solon may serve as examples. Generally speaking, direct discourse is restricted in the antique historians to great continuous speeches delivered in the Senate or before a popular assembly or a gathering of soldiers, in which connection the reader may remember what we said above in regard to Percennius' speech. But here—in the scene of Peter's denial—the dramatic tension of the moment when the actors stand face to face has been given a salience and immediacy compared with which the dialogue (stichomythy) of antique tragedy appears highly stylized. Comedy, satire, and the like may not properly be adduced for purposes of comparison; but in them too one would have to look hard to find anything of similar immediacy. In the Gospels, however, one encounters numerous face-to-face dialogues. I hope that this symptom, the use of direct discourse in living dialogue, suffices to characterize, for our purposes, the relation of the writings of the New Testament to classical rhetoric, so that I need not go further into the general problem, which has often been discussed. (I refer to Norden's book on the art of prose in antiquity, mentioned above.)

In the last analysis the differences in style between the writings of antiquity and early Christianity are conditioned by the fact that they were composed from a different point of view and for different people. Different as Petronius and Tacitus may be in a great many respects, they have the same viewpoint—they look down from above. Tacitus writes from a vantage point which surveys the fullness of events and transactions; he classifies and judges them as a man of the highest rank and the highest culture. That he does not fall into the dry and unvisualized, is due not only to his genius but to the incomparably successful cultivation of the visual, of the sensory, throughout antiquity. But the audience of his equals for whom he wrote demanded that the visual and sensory element respect the limits of what a long tradition had settled as good taste—in which connection we may note that there are to be found in him symptoms of a change in taste, a change in the direction of greater stress on the somber and gruesome, but this is a point we shall have to take up again in a different context. Petronius too looks from above at the world he depicts. His book is a product of the highest culture, and he expects his readers to have such a high level of social and literary culture that they will perceive, without doubt or hesitation, every shade of social blundering and of vulgarity in language and taste. However coarse and grotesque the subject matter may be, its treatment reveals no trace of the crude humor of a popular farce. Scenes like that of the dinner guest's reply or the quarrel between Trimalchio and Fortunata exhibit, it is true, the basest and commonest ideas, but they do so with such refined cross-purposes, with such an array of sociological and psychological presuppositions, as no popular audience could tolerate. And the vulgarity of language is not designed to arouse laughter in a large crowd but is rather a piquant condiment for the palate of a social and literary elite accustomed to viewing things from above with epicurean composure. It may perhaps be compared with the small talk of the hotel manager Aimé and similar characters in Proust's novel of Things Past; but such comparisons with works of modern realism are never quite to the point, because the latter contain far more in the way of serious problems. So Petronius too writes from above, for the class of the highly cultured—a class which at the time of the early emperors may have been quite large but which melted away later. On the other hand, the story of Peter's denial, and generally almost the entire body of New Testament writings, is written from within the emergent growths and directly for everyman. Here we have neither survey and rational disposition, nor artistic purpose. The visual and sensory as it appears here is no conscious imitation and hence is rarely completely realized. It appears because it is attached to the events which are to be related, because it is revealed in the demeanor and speech of profoundly stirred individuals and no effort need be devoted to the task of elaborating it. Even Tacitus, with his conscious endeavor to condense and summarize, describes human individuals in their outer appearance and inner existence, gives detailed portrayals of given situations. The author of the Gospel according to Saint Mark has no viewpoint which would permit him to present a factual, objective portrait of, let us say, the character of Peter. He is at the core of what goes on; he observes and relates only what matters in relation to Christ's presence and mission; and in the present case it does not even occur to him to tell us how the incident ended, that is, how Peter got away. Tacitus and Petronius endeavor to give us a sensory impression, the former of historical occurrences, the latter of a specific stratum of society, and in doing so they respect the limits of a specific aesthetic tradition. The author of the Gospel according to Saint Mark has no such purpose and knows no such tradition. Without any effort on his part, as it were, and purely through the inner movement of what he relates, the story becomes visually concrete. And the story speaks to everybody; everybody is urged and indeed required to take sides for or against it. Even ignoring it implies taking sides. To be sure, for a time its effectiveness was hampered by practical obstacles. For a time the language as well as the religious and social premises of the message restricted it to Jewish circles. Yet the negative reaction which it aroused in Jerusalem, both among the Jewish leaders and among the majority of the people, forced the movement to embark upon the tremendous venture of missionary work among the Gentiles, which was characteristically begun by a member of the Jewish diaspora, the Apostle Paul. With that, an adaptation of the message to the preconceptions of a far wider audience, its detachment from the special preconceptions of the Jewish world, became a necessity and was effected by a method rooted in Jewish tradition but now applied with incomparably greater boldness, the method of revisional interpretation. The Old Testament was played down as popular history and as the code of the Jewish people and assumed the appearance of a series of "figures," that is of prophetic announcements and anticipations of the coming of Jesus and the concomitant events. We have briefly discussed these matters in our first chapter. The total content of the sacred writings was placed in an exegetic context which often removed the thing told very far from its sensory base, in that the reader or listener was forced to turn his attention away from the sensory occurrence and toward its meaning. This implied the danger that the visual element of the occurrences might succumb under the dense texture of meanings. Let one example stand for many: It is a visually dramatic occurrence that God made Eve, the first woman, from Adam's rib while Adam lay asleep; so too is it that a soldier pierced Jesus' side, as he hung dead on the cross, so that blood and water flowed out. But when these two occurrences are exegetically interrelated in the doctrine that Adam's sleep is a figure of Christ's death-sleep; that, as from the wound in Adam's side mankind's primordial mother after the flesh, Eve, was born, so from the wound in Christ's side was born the mother of all men after the spirit, the Church (blood and water are sacramental symbols)—then the sensory occurrence pales before the power of the figural meaning. What is perceived by the hearer or reader or even, in the plastic and graphic arts, by the spectator, is weak as a sensory impression, and all one's interest is directed toward the context of meanings. In comparison, the Greco-Roman specimens of realistic presentation are, though less serious and fraught with problems and far more limited in their conception of historical movement, nevertheless perfectly integrated in their sensory substance. They do not know the antagonism between sensory appearance and meaning, an antagonism which permeates the early, and indeed the whole, Christian view of reality.

3

THE ARREST OF PETER VALVOMERES

Ammianus Marcellinus, an officer of high rank and historian, of the fourth century A.D., the extant portions of whose work describe the events between 350 and 380, reports, in chapter 7 of his book 15, a mob riot in Rome. The text runs as follows:

> Dum has exitiorum communium clades suscitat turba feralis, urbem aeternam Leontius regens, multa spectati judicis documenta praebebat, in audiendo celer, in disceptando justissimus, natura benevolus, licet autoritatis causa servandae acer quibusdam videbatur, et inclinatior ad amandum. Prima igitur causa seditionis in eum concitandae vilissima fuit et levis. Philocomum enim aurigam rapi praeceptum, secuta plebs omnis velut defensura proprium pignus, terribili impetu praefectum incessebat ut timidum: sed ille stabilis et erectus, immissis adparitoribus, correptos aliquot vexatosque tormentis, nec strepente ullo nec obsistente, insulari poena multavit. Diebusque paucis secutis, cum itidem plebs excita calore quo consuevit, vini causando inopiam, ad Septemzodium convenisset, celebrem locum, ubi operis ambitiosi Nymphaeum Marcus condidit imperator, illuc de industria pergens praefectus, ab omni toga adparitioneque rogabatur enixius ne in multitudinem se arrogantem immitteret et minacem, ex commotione pristina saevientem: difficilisque ad pavorem recte tetendit, adeo ut eum obsequentium pars desereret, licet in periculum festinantem abruptum. Insidens itaque vehiculo, cum speciosa fiducia contuebatur acribus oculis tumultuantium undique cuneorum veluti serpentium vultus: perpessusque multa dici probrosa, agnitum quendam inter alios eminentem, vasti corporis rutilique capilli, interrogavit an ipse esset Petrus Valvomeres, ut audierat, cognomento; eumque, cum esse sono respondisset objurgatorio, ut seditiosorum antesignanum olim sibi compertum, reclamantibus multis, post terga manibus vinctis suspendi praecepit. Quo viso sublimi tribuliumque adjumentum nequicquam implorante, vulgus omne paulo ante confertum per varia urbis membra diffusum ita evanuit, ut turbarum acerrimus con-

citor tamquam in judiciali secreto exaratis lateribus ad Picenum ejiceretur; ubi postea ausus eripere virginis non obscurae pudorem, Patruini consularis sententia supplicio est capitali addictus.

The following translation attempts to preserve the strangely baroque style of the original:

While that carrion crew was causing these catastrophes of general destruction, Leontius, governor of the Eternal City, gave many evidences of being an excellent judge—speedy in hearings, most just in decisions, by nature benevolent, though he seemed to some to be severe in the matter of maintaining his authority and over-inclined toward sensual love. Now the first cause of a rebellion breaking out against him was of the basest and slightest. For Philocomus, the charioteer, having been ordered to be arrested, the whole mob following him, as if defending the most precious treasure, set upon the prefect with dreadful tumult, to intimidate him; but he, firm and erect, ordering the police to intervene, had some seized and flogged and, while not a man murmured or resisted, sentenced them to deportation. A few days later, when the mob, again roused to its usual heat, alleging the scarcity of wine, congregated at the Septemzodium—a much frequented place, where the emperor Marcus had erected the ostentatious edifice of the Nymphaeum; there the prefect, purposely proceeding thither, was earnestly entreated by all his officials and attendants not to risk himself among the arrogant and threatening multitude, still angry from their earlier riot; he, being hard to frighten, went straight on, so that some of his following deserted him, though he was hastening into imminent danger. And so, sitting in his carriage, with an imposing confidence, he gazed with piercing eyes into the faces of the packed crowd raging all about like serpents; he steadfastly endured many shameful words; then recognizing one who was conspicuous among the rest by his great stature and red hair, he asked him if he was not Peter, surnamed Valvomeres, as he had heard; and when the man replied in blustering tones that he was, he ordered him, as a leader of the rioters long known to him, over the protests of very many, to be strung up [for a flogging] with his hands tied behind his back. When he was seen aloft, vainly imploring the help of his cronies, the whole mob, which had only a little before thronged together, now diffused through the various arteries of the city and vanished, so that this most fervid inciter of mobs, having had his sides harrowed open as if in a secret judgment chamber, was transported to Picenum; where later, having dared to rape a girl of not unillustrious family, he was sentenced by the consul Patruinus and underwent capital punishment.

Much of what we said in the preceding chapter concerning Tacitus' description of the soldiers' revolt applies to the present passage as well; indeed, it comes out even more strikingly here. Ammianus is still less inclined than Tacitus to concern himself with objective problems and to give a thorough analysis of the causes leading up to the riot, or of the condition of the Roman populace. Nothing, it seems to him, except their stupid effrontery is behind the Roman mob's unrest. It is quite possible that he is right in his attitude. The metropolitan masses had for centuries been spoiled by every government, they had been trained to idleness, and cannot have amounted to much. Yet a modern historian would have taken up the question of how such a state of affairs had come about, he would have discussed the problem of the mob's corruption, or at the very least have touched upon it. But this does not interest Ammianus at all; and in this attitude he goes much further than Tacitus. The latter acknowledges, after all, that there is a rational and coherently framed set of demands which the soldiers put forward and in regard to which the commanders in the field and the authorities have to take a stand. The parties negotiate; there is an objective and even a human relationship between them. This is apparent for instance in Blaesus' speech at the end of chapter 18 or in the scene of Agrippina's departure in chapter 41. However fickle and superstitious the soldiers may be in Tacitus' description, he never hesitates to admit that they are human beings of a definite culture and with a definite sense of honor. In Ammianus' scene, on the other hand, there is no objectively rational relationship whatever between the authorities and the rebels, let alone a human relationship based on mutual respect. There is only a physical relation based on magic and brute force. On one side there is a pure mass of bodies, stupid and full of effrontery, like a crowd of juvenile delinquents, and on the other imposing authority, fearlessness, instant decision, flogging. And as soon as the mob sees that one of their number is treated as all of them apparently deserve to be, they lose heart and vanish from the scene. Ammianus supplies as little information as Tacitus about the life these people lead—even less, for he has nothing corresponding to

Percennius' address. He gives nothing from which we might deduce any human contact. He does not make the populace talk (he barely mentions one nickname, Valvomeres, like Tacitus' *Cedo alteram*); instead, he clothes the whole incident in the somber splendor of his rhetoric, which is as distant from popular style as possible. Yet the incident is so treated that it produces a strongly sensory impression—to such an extent, in fact, that many readers will find it unpleasantly realistic. Ammianus has oriented it entirely toward gestures: the compact crowd set against the imposing prefect as he domineers over them. This element of the sensory and the gestural is prepared for from the first—through the choice of words and similes, to which we shall return later on—and reaches its climax in the scene at the Septemzodium when Leontius, sitting in his carriage with flashing eyes, confronts the "snakily" hissing mob like an animal tamer, unmoved as they rapidly vanish. A riot, a solitary man trying to quell it by the power of his eyes, then stepping in—some harsh words, a ringleader's muscular body raised high, finally a flogging. Then all is quiet, and, by way of conclusion, we get a rape and the subsequent capital punishment.

A comparison with Tacitus serves to show how much stronger the magical and the sensory has become at the expense of the human and the objectively rational. From the end of the first century of the Imperial Age something sultry and oppressive appears, a darkening of the atmosphere of life. It is unmistakable in Seneca, and the somber tone of Tacitus' historical writing has often been noted. But here in Ammianus we find that the process has reached the stage of a magical and sensory dehumanization. That the sensory vividness of the events should profit from this paralysis of the human is indeed notable. It might be objected that I have compared Tacitus' scene with a mob riot, not with a soldiers' rebellion. But in that case, there is only one scene which could enter into consideration, the soldiers' uprising at the beginning of book 20. To me, that scene is highly suspicious; it seems to deal, not with a spontaneous reaction on the part of the soldiers but with a planned mass demonstration in which the instincts of the soldiery are skilfully exploited in a way we know only too well from contemporary history. Such a passage could not be used for my purposes, and so I had to take the popular uprising in Rome. But the characteristics of Ammianus' style, which we discovered at first sight in this passage, are to be found all through his work. Everywhere human emotion and rationality yield to the magically and somberly sensory, to the graphic and the gestural. Certainly, Tacitus' Tiberius is somber enough, but he still retains a great deal of intrinsic humanity and dignity. In Ammianus nothing survives but the magical, the grotesque, and, with them, the rhetorically horripilating; we are astonished to see what a genius in this direction has come to flower in a practical, active, serious-minded, high-ranking officer. How powerful must have been the atmosphere which developed such talents in men of this rank and way of life (Ammianus apparently spent a large part of his life in arduous campaigns)! Read for instance Gallus' death journey (14, 11), or the journey of Julian's dead body (21, 16), or Procopius' proclamation as emperor (26, 6): "So there he stood, like a rotting corpse, like a man risen from the grave, without a mantle [because imperial purple could nowhere be found], his tunic embroidered in gold like an attendant at court, from the waist down dressed like a school boy . . . ; in his right hand he bore a lance, with his left hand he waved a piece of purple cloth . . . you might have thought that a splendidly decorated figure from the painting on a stage curtain or some grotesque part in a comedy had suddenly come to life . . . in servile flattery he addressed the wire-pullers of his elevation and promised them tremendous spoils and offices. . . . When he had mounted the tribunal and all were filled with amazement, keeping a gloomy silence, he thought—as he had previously feared—that his last hour had arrived; he trembled so that for a long time he could not speak. Finally he began, in a halting voice, to say a few words like a man about to die, justifying his action by his relationship with the imperial family. . . ." Again it is the gestural, the graphically imaged, which predominates. A whole gallery of gruesomely grotesque and extremely sensory-graphic portraits can be culled from Ammianus' work: the Emperor Constantius who never turns his head, never blows his nose, never spits, *tamquam figmentum hominis* (16, 10 and 21, 16); Julian, the great conqueror of the Alemanni, with the goatee, who is always scratching his head, thrusting out his narrow chest to make it look broader, and taking steps much too long for his short figure (17, 11 and 21, 14); the pleased-looking Jovian, whose body is so big around (*vasta proceritate et ardua*) that after his unexpected election to the imperial throne, in the middle of a campaign, there is trouble in finding imperial garments to fit him, and who, very soon after his election, at the age of thirty-three, dies an unexplained death (25, 10); the somber, melancholy conspirator Procopius, always looking down, who, scion of an illustrious family, hides among the scum of the people when he is unjustifiably suspected, and who, like many another character in Ammianus, tries to make himself emperor only because he sees no other way of saving his life—in which, to be sure, he does not succeed (26, 6-9); the secretary Leo, later chief of the imperial chancellery, "a Pannonian and a grave-robber, snorting forth cruelty from the grinning jaws of a wild beast" (*efflantem ferino rictu crudelitatem*) (28, 1); the soothsayer or "mathematician" Heliodorus, a professional informer who has had an incredibly successful career: he is now a gourmet, abundantly provided with money for his whores; he promenades his somber face through the city, where everyone fears him; he frequents houses of prostitution openly and eagerly (he is officer of the imperial bedchamber, *cubiculariis officiis praepositus*) and proclaims that the pleasures of the beloved father of the country will yet ruin many more subjects; the horrible irony of the words brings to mind Tacitus' *Tiberiolus meus* (*Ann.* 6, 5) but is even more disgusting; when Heliodorus dies suddenly, the entire court is obliged to attend his solemn funeral, bareheaded, barefoot, hands folded (29, 2); the Emperor Valentinian, a remarkable and handsome prince, although with somber and squinting eyes; in a dark mood he orders a groom's hand to be cut off because he was awkward in helping him mount a shying horse (30, 9); the Emperor Valens, campaigner against the Goths, swarthy, with one eye covered by a white film, with his rather protruding belly and crooked legs (31, 14). It would not be hard to prolong this list of portraits and supplement it with incidents and vignettes of manners of a nature no less grotesquely gruesome. And the background of it all is this: the persons treated live between a frenzy of bloodshed and mortal terror. Grotesque and sadistic, spectral and superstitious, lusting for power yet constantly trying to conceal the chattering of their teeth—so do we see the men of Ammianus' ruling class and their world. His strange sense of humor might also be mentioned—read for instance the description of the nobles whose pride makes them refuse the customary kiss of salutation, *osculanda capita in modum taurorum minacium obliquantes* [what a gesture!], *adulatoribus offerunt genua suavianda vel manus, id illis sufficere ad beate vivendum existimantes: et abundare omni cultu humanitatis peregrinum putantes, cuius forte etiam gratia sunt obligati, interrogatum quibus thermis utatur aut aquis, aut ad quam successerit domum* (28, 4: like threatening bulls they turn aside their heads, where they should be kissed, and offer their flatterers their knees to kiss or their hands, thinking that quite enough to ensure them a happy life; and they believe that a stranger is given an abundance of all the duties of courtesy, even though the great man may perhaps be under obligation to him, if he is asked what hot baths or waters he uses, or at what house he has been put up); or his remark on the dogmatic conflicts in the Christian Church: "Throngs of bishops hastened hither and thither to the synods as they call them, and while each sought to impose upon the other his own interpretation of the faith, they achieved nothing but a complete break-down of the overburdened means of transportation" (21, 16). In this humor there is always an element of bitterness, of the grotesque, very often of something grotesquely gruesome and inhumanly convulsive. Ammianus' world is somber: it is full of superstition, blood frenzy, exhaustion, fear of death, and grim and magically rigid gestures; and to counterbalance all this there is nothing but the equally somber and pathetic determination to accomplish an ever more difficult, ever more desperate task: to protect the Empire, threatened from without and crumbling from within. This determination gives the strongest among the actors on Ammianus' stage a rigid, convulsive superhumanity with no possibility of relaxation, expressed for example in the *moriar stando* which he attributes to Julian: *ut imperatorem decet, ego solus confecto tantorum munerum cursu moriar stando, contempturus animam, quam mihi febricula eripiet una* (24, 17).

Ammianus, as we hope we have shown, possesses a very strong sensory power of expression. If his Latin were not so hard to understand and so untranslatable, he might well be one of the most influential authors of antique literature. Yet his procedure is by no means imitative in the sense that he builds up his characters before our eyes and ears, out of their own premises, and lets them, as it were, think, feel, act, and speak out of their own nature; he does not let them speak their own natural language at all; he definitely belongs to the tradition of the antique historians in the elevated style, who look down from above and judge by moral standards, and who never make conscious and intentional use of the technique of realistic imitation because they scorn it as fit only for the low comic style. The particular form of this tradition, which seems to have been especially favored in late Roman times (it is already embodied in Sallust, but especially in Tacitus), is very strongly stoic in temper; it delights in choosing exceptionally somber subjects, which reveal a high degree of moral corruption, and then sharply contrasting them with its ideal concept of original simplicity, purity, and virtue. This is the pattern which Ammianus obviously wants to follow, as appears from many passages of his work in which he cites deeds and sayings of earlier times in moralistic contrast. But from the very beginning we sense—and, in Ammianus, the impression becomes unmistakable—that in this tradition the material increasingly masters the stylistic intent, until it finally overwhelms it and forces the style, with its pretension to reserve and refinement, to adapt itself to the content, so that diction and syntax, torn between the somber realism of the content and the unrealistically refined tendency of the style, begin to change and become inharmonious, overburdened, and harsh. The diction grows mannered; the constructions begin, as it were, to writhe and twist. The equable elegance is disturbed; the refined reserve gives way to a somber pomp; and, against its will as it were, the style renders a greater sensoriness than would originally have been compatible with *gravitas*, yet *gravitas* itself is by no means lost, but on the contrary is heightened. The elevated style becomes hyperpathetic and gruesome, becomes pictorial and sensory.

The first traces of this development are to be found in Sallust. An important contribution in this direction came from Seneca, who, though he does not belong to the tradition of Roman historiography, exercised a strong general influence. In Tacitus the somberness and weightiness of the historical style, reinforced by the somberness of the events he reports, is charged with sensory perception. Time and again it is there, evoked by the suggestive power of horrible happenings —but only to be quickly repressed again by the refined and pointed brevity of the style, which will not allow such outbursts to prevail (one example among many: the execution of Sejanus' children, *Ann.* 5, 9). In Ammianus the sensory, the perceivable, runs riot; it has forced its way into the elevated style, not by vulgarizing it popularly or comically but by exaggerating it beyond all bounds. With glittering words and pompously distorted constructions language begins to depict the distorted, gory, and spectral reality of the age.

Instead of the calm, refined vocabulary which briefly states the sensory or merely alludes to it moralistically, we have a gestural and pictorial vocabulary. For example in the description of the Roman riots, instead of an ethical expression of imperturbability, we have *stabilis, erectus, cum speciosa fiducia intuebatur acribus oculis*; instead of *iter non intermisit* we have *recte tetendit*; whipping is referred to in the pompously periphrastic yet sensory *latera exarare*; a like effect is produced by *pudorem eripere*; and where Tacitus says, for example, *accusatorum maior in dies et infestior vis grassabatur* (*Ann.* 4, 66), we here read: *dum has exitiorum communium clades suscitat turba feralis.* All these and many like examples show that this mannerism, this so-called turgidity, is not simply a product of the desire to be different but that it also, indeed above all, serves sensory vividness. We are forced to picture the scene. Then too there are the numerous comparisons of men with animals (serpent and bull are favorites), or of human events with events on the stage or in the realm of the dead. The choice of words is studied throughout, but in complete contrast to classical practice, which saw the choice and the studied in refined periphrases of sensory phenomena and allowed no one but the poet to depict them (though he too had to keep aloof from life in its present realities, if he wanted to avoid the low style of satire or comedy)—in complete contrast to all this, the studied in the elevated style of historiography now serves to depict things occurring in the present. Yet the depiction is not really imitative; the morally judging historian is still there, discoursing in the elevated style and avoiding the lowlands of imitative realism; only now he regularly uses the most glaring colors.

Ammianus' syntax gives rise to the same observations as his diction. Even though much in it may be explained by the striving for rhythmical cola and the strong Grecization of his style (cf. Norden, *Antike Kunstprosa,* 646ff.), enough remains which can be accounted for satisfactorily only by our present approach. His placing of nouns, especially of subject nominatives, his broadly construed use of appositive adjectives and participles, and his tendency to use word order to define and separate his clusters of appositions, all testify to his endeavor at all times to suggest a monumental, striking, and usually gestural perception. Note for example his elaboration of the subjects *turba feralis, Leontius regens, ille, Marcus imperator, praefectus, acerrimus concitor*; of the objects *urbem aeternam, Philocomum aurigam, multitudinem, vultus, agnitum quendam, eumque*; his wealth of appositions—Jespersen would call them "extra-positions"—and of quasi-appositional forms, each set out as independently as possible. With Leontius go *regens, celer, justissimus, benevolus,* then—given different syntactic treatment—*acer,* and, finally, *inclinatior ad amandum*; with *causa* go *vilissima* and *levis* in artful differentiation; with *plebs,* likewise differentiated, *secuta* and *defensura proprium pignus*; with *ille* go *stabilis* and *erectus*; with *multitudinem,* first *arrogantem* and then—set off from it and against each other—*minacem* and *saevientem*;

then follow—referring to the Prefect, continuing *pergens*, and strongly emphasized—*difficilis ad pavorem, insidens vehiculo, perpessus; agnitum quemdam* is taken up by *eminentem, vasti corporis, rutili capilli*, and later on *sublimi* and *implorante*; and the very name, *Petrus Valvomeres*, is introduced as an apposition with extreme emphasis. Other descriptively vivid elements of the sentence are likewise emphasized—as *ut timidum, nec strepente ullo nec obsistente, operis ambitiosi, enixius*, etc.; and the same impression is heightened when we look at longer word groups. *Urbem aeternam Leontius regens*, followed by a string of appositions, is intentionally monumental; so is *Marcus condidit imperator*; both dramatic and monumental (as image and gesture) is the opening clause, *insidens itaque vehiculo*; completely pictorial the anticipation by *contuebatur acribus oculis* of the showily animated and sonorous object, *tumultuantium undique cuneorum veluti serpentium vultus*; as is the *inter alios eminentem, vasti corporis, rutilique capilli* which rolls out after the colorless *agnitum quendam*. Tacitus would hardly have written a sentence like *Quo viso sublimi tribuliumque adiumentum nequidquam implorante*, with its inordinate weight of appositions, for the relation of *quo viso* to the compound apposition (the second member of which is itself overburdened) is completely unclassical. But how graphic it is! It makes us see Peter's convulsive struggle; we hear him howl.

Judged by classical standards, the style, both in diction and syntax, is overrefined and exaggeratedly sensory; its effects are powerful but distorted. Its effects are as distorted as the reality it represents. Ammianus' world is very often a caricature of the normal human environment in which we live; very often it is like a bad dream. This is not simply because horrible things happen in it—treason, torture, persecution, denunciations: such things are prevalent in almost all times and places, and the periods when life is somewhat more tolerable are not too frequent. What makes Ammianus' world so oppressive is the lack of any sort of counterbalance. For if it is true that man is capable of everything horrible, it is also true that the horrible always engenders counterforces and that in most epochs of atrocious occurrences the great vital forces of the human soul reveal themselves: love and sacrifice, heroism in the service of conviction, and the ceaseless search for possibilities of a purer existence. Nothing of the sort is to be found in Ammianus. Striking only in the sensory, resigned and as it were paralyzed despite its stubborn rhetorical passion, his manner of writing history nowhere displays anything redeeming, nowhere anything that points to a better future, nowhere a figure or an act about which stirs the refreshing atmosphere of a greater freedom, a greater humanity. It had begun, of course, in Tacitus, though by no means to the same extent. And the cause of it is doubtless the hopelessly defensive situation in which antique civilization found itself more and more deeply enmeshed. No longer able to generate new hope and new life from within, it had to restrict itself to measures which at best could only check decline and preserve the status quo; but these measures too grow more and more senile, their execution more and more arduous. All this is known, and I need not discuss it. But I should like to add that in Christianity itself—though Ammianus would not seem to be unfriendly in his attitude toward it—he sees nothing that might force a way through the prevailing futureless darkness.

It is clear that Ammianus' manner of presentation signifies the complete coming of age of something in the making since Seneca and Tacitus—that is, a highly rhetorical style in which the gruesomely sensory has gained a large place; a somber and highly rhetorical realism which is totally alien to classical antiquity. Such a mixture of rhetorical devices of the most refined sort with a glaring and boldly distorted realism can be studied at a much earlier period and on much lower levels of style: in Apuleius for instance, of whose style Eduard Norden—in his work on the art of prose in antiquity, to which we have more than once referred—offers a brilliant analysis. The level of style in a Milesian tale is naturally quite different from that of a historical work. But despite all its playful, amorous, and often silly frivolity, the *Metamorphoses* exhibits not only a similar mixture of rhetoric and realism, but also (though Norden failed to point it out) the same predilection for a haunting and gruesome distortion of reality. I have in mind not only the numerous metamorphoses and ghost stories, all of which border upon the gruesome and grotesque, but also many other things—the quality of the eroticism, for instance. With an extreme emphasis on desire, which all the spices of rhetorico-realistic art are employed to arouse in the reader too, there is a complete absence of human warmth and intimacy. There is always an admixture of something spectrally sadistic; desire is mixed with fear and horror; though to be sure there is a good deal of silliness too. And this runs through the entire book: it is full of fear, lust, and silliness. If the feeling of the silliness of the whole thing were not, at least for a modern reader, so pronounced, one might be tempted to think of certain recent writers—Kafka for example—whose world of gruesome distortion suggests the consistency of insanity. Let me elucidate what I have in mind by an apparently insignificant passage from the *Metamorphoses*. It occurs at the end of the first book (1, 24) and relates a purchase which the narrator Lucius makes in the market of a foreign (Thessalian) town. It runs as follows:

> . . . rebus meis in cubiculo conditis, pergens ipse ad balneas, ut prius aliquid nobis cibatui prospicerem, forum cuppedinis peto; inque eo piscatum opiparem expositum video. Et percontato pretio, quod centum nummis indicaret, aspernatus viginti denariis praestinavi. Inde me commodum egredientem continuatur Pythias, condiscipulus apud Athenas Atticas meus; qui me post aliquantum temporis amanter agnitum invadit, amplexusque et comiter deosculatus, Mi Luci, ait, sat pol diu est quod intervisimus te, at hercules exinde cum a Clytio magistro digressi sumus. Quae autem tibi causa peregrinationis huius? Crastino die scies, inquam. Sed quid istud? Voti gaudeo. Nam et lixas et virgas et habitum prorsus magistratui congruentem in te video. Annonam curamus, ait, et aedilem gerimus; et si quid obsonare cupis, utique commodabimus. Abnuebam, quippe qui iam cenae affatim piscatum prospexeramus. Sed enim Pythias, visa sportula succussisque in aspectum planiorem piscibus: At has quisquilias quanti parasti? Vix, inquam, piscatori extorsimus accipere viginti denarios. Quo audito statim arrepta dextra postliminio me in forum cuppedinis reducens: Et a quo, inquit, istorum nugamenta haec comparasti? Demonstro seniculum; in angulo sedebat. Quem confestim pro aedilitatis imperio voce asperrima increpans: Iam iam, inquit, nec amicis quidem nostris vel omnino ullis hospitibus parcitis, qui tam magnis pretiis pisces frivolos indicatis et florem Thessalicae regionis ad instar solitudinis et scopuli edulium caritate deducitis! Sed non impune. Iam enim faxo scias, quemadmodum sub meo imperio mali debeant coerceri. Et profusa in medium sportula iubet officialem suum insuper pisces inscendere ac pedibus suis totos obterere. Qua contentus morum severitudine meus Pythias, ac mihi ut abirem suadens: Sufficit mihi, o Luci, inquit, seniculi tanta haec contumelia. His actis consternatus ac prorsus obstupidus ad balneas me refero, prudentis condiscipuli valido consilio et nummis simul privatus et cena. . . .

(When my things were arranged in the room, I decided to go to the baths, but first I went to the market place to buy some food for supper. I there saw very good fish for sale, asked the price, and got it down from a hundred to twenty denarii. I was just about to leave when Pythias, a fellow student of mine from Athens, happened to pass by. After some hesitation he finally recognized me, came toward me with a great display of affection, kissed me, and said: "My dear Lucius, how long since I've seen you! I believe not since we left our teacher Clytius! But what are you doing here?" "You shall learn that tomorrow," I said. "But what does this mean? I must congratulate you; I see these servants and verges and yourself in the dress of a magistrate." "I am the aedile in charge of the market place," he said. "If there is anything you want to buy, I shall be delighted to help you." I declined and said that I had already bought enough fish for supper. But Pythias saw my basket, shook the fish to have a better look, and said: "And what did you pay for this stuff?" "With quite some trouble," I said, "I got the man to let me have them for twenty denarii." He took me by the hand and led me back to the market. "And from which of these dealers did you buy this stuff?" he asked. I pointed to a little old man sitting in a corner. At once, by reason of his power of office, he began giving him a piece of his mind. "So," he said, "this is how you treat my friends, to say nothing of other strangers! Selling such cheap fish for such a high price! By your excessive prices you transform this flowering city of Thessaly into a barren rock which no one cares to visit. But this must not pass unpunished. No—I shall show you how evil-doers are disciplined under my administration." Then he threw the contents of my basket on the ground and ordered one of his servants to step on the fish and grind his heels into them. Delighted with his severity, Pythias advised me to make myself scarce and said: "My dear Lucius, that was quite a disgrace for the old man; I think I shall let it go at that." Amazed if not stupefied by these occurrences, I went on to the baths. Through the energetic intervention of my smart fellow student I had lost both my money and my supper.)

No doubt there have been and are readers who simply laugh over this story and consider it a farce, a mere joke. But I do not believe that is quite enough. The behavior of Lucius' long-lost friend, of whom we are told nothing except that they had just been reunited, is either wilfully malicious (which he had no reason to be) or insane (but there is no reference to his not being quite right in his mind). We cannot avoid the impression of a half silly, half spectral distortion of ordinary, average occurrences in human life. The friend has been delighted by the unexpected encounter; he has offered his services and actually insisted on being of help. Yet without the slightest concern for the consequences of his action, he robs Lucius of his supper and his money. As for the fishmonger's punishment, there is no such thing; he still has his money. And if I am not mistaken, Pythias urges Lucius to leave the market place, because the dealers will not sell him anything after such an incident and might actually attempt to wreak vengeance upon him. The whole affair, with all its silliness, is carefully calculated to fool Lucius and play him a mean trick—but for what purpose and to what end? Is it silliness, is it malice, is it insanity? The silliness of it cannot prevent the reader from feeling bewildered and disturbed. And what a strangely unpleasant, foul, and somehow sadistic idea—that of the fish being trodden to pulp on the pavement of the market place by order of the law!

The same invasion of a glaringly pictorial realism into the elevated style, which we found in Ammianus, and which progressively undermines the classical separation of styles, obtains among the Christian authors too. In the Judaeo-Christian tradition, as we have previously pointed out, there was no separating the elevated style from realism; and on the other side, the influence of classical rhetoric upon the Church Fathers—a very strong influence, as we know, especially since many of the Fathers were highly educated men, thoroughly trained in philosophy and rhetoric—began to exert itself only when the undermining process just mentioned had gone quite far, not only in respect to the separation of styles but also in respect to stylistic harmony and restraint in general. Hence, in the Fathers too, we not infrequently encounter a mixture of rhetorical pomp and a glaring depiction of reality. Jerome in particular goes to extremes in these respects. His satirical caricatures, which far outdo Horace and Juvenal, are strongly pictorial; even more so are certain passages in which, without enjoining the slightest regard for convention and decency upon himself, he sets forth ascetic maxims which go into the least details of eating and drinking, of bodily care (or rather carelessness), and of sexual chastity. What extremes of vividness in the gruesome his epideictic style can attain, may be seen from a passage in his letters (66, 5; Pat. lat. 22, 641), which may be the most effective but it is by no means the only one of its kind. A woman of noble lineage, Paulina, has died and her surviving husband, Pammachius, has decided to give his wealth to the poor and become a monk. The eulogistic and hortatory epistle which Jerome writes on this occasion contains the following paragraph:

> Ardentes gemmae, quibus ante collum et facies ornabantur, egentium ventres saturant. Vestes sericae, et aurum in fila lentescens, in mollia lanarum vestimenta mutata sunt, quibus repellatur frigus, non quibus nudetur ambitio. Deliciarum quondam supellectilem virtus insumit. Ille caecus extendens manum, et saepe ubi nemo est clamitans, heres Paulinae, coheres Pammachii est. Illum truncum pedibus, et toto corpore se trahentem, tenerae puellae sustentant manus. Fores quae prius salutantium turbas vomebant, nunc a miseris obsidentur. Alius tumenti aqualiculo mortem parturit; alius elinguis et mutus, et ne hoc quidem habens unde roget, magis rogat dum rogare non potest. Ilic debilitatus a parvo non sibi mendicat stipem; ille putrefactus morbo regio supravivit cadaveri suo.
>
> Non mihi si linguae centum sint, oraque centum,
> Omnia poenarum percurrere nomina possim. (Aen. vi, 625, 627)
>
> Hoc exercitu comitatus incedit, in his Christum confovet, horum sordibus dealbatur. Munerarius pauperum et egentium candidatus sic festinat ad coelum. Ceteri mariti super tumulos conjugum spargunt violas, rosas, lilia, floresque purpureos, et dolorem pectoris his officiis consolantur. Pammachius noster sanctam favillam ossaque veneranda eleemosynae balsamis rigat. . . .
>
> (The shining gems which once adorned her neck and her face serve to make full the stomachs of the needy. The silken robes and interwoven threads of gold have been transformed into soft woollen clothes which are a cover against the cold, not an uncovering of vanity. What was once an instrument of luxury is employed by virtue. That blind man there who often extends his hand and calls out where no one is, becomes Paulina's heir, Pammachius' coheir. That other man with mutilated feet, who drags himself along with his entire body, is supported by a tender girl's hands. The gates, once spewing forth groups of adulating visitors, are now besieged by the poor. The one there with his swollen belly is pregnant with his own death. Another, tongueless and mute, has not even that with which he might implore, and implores the more persuasively because he cannot implore. This one, sickly from childhood, no longer needs to beg [?] for his alms; that one, decomposed by disease [jaundice?], survives his

own corpse. "Not, if a hundred tongues were mine and a hundred mouths, could I enumerate the names of all their sufferings." Accompanied by this host he advances. In them he cares for Christ. In their squalor he is washed white. Thus the treasurer of the poor, the *candidatus* [i.e., both the loving wooer and one who wears a white toga] of the indigent hurries toward heaven. Other husbands scatter on their wives' graves violets, roses, lilies, and purple flowers and by these offerings console the grief of their hearts. Our Pammachius sprinkles the balsam of mercy upon the sacred ashes and the venerable bones. . . .)

The procession of the sick folk and beggars is of course based on the Bible both in content and feeling. The Book of Job, together with the healings of the sick and the ethics of sacrifice and humility in the New Testament, form the basis for such a display of physical horrors. At a very early period, devoted self-sacrifice for the benefit of those suffering from repulsive diseases (*spirans cadaver*, Jerome says elsewhere), and especially physical contact with them while attending to their needs, were considered among the most important characteristics indicative of Christian humility and aspiration toward saintliness. But it is clear that the rhetorical devices of late antiquity likewise contributed their share to the glaring effect of our passage—and I am inclined to think that it is the lion's share. The showy pictorial style of this rhetoric is apparent from the very beginning in the contrasting expressions of the greatest luxury and the most pitiful misery, where the opposite poles of style are consciously displayed: *ardentes gemmae* over against *egentium ventres*! The same pictorial style is apparent in the play with verbal and conceptual antithesis (*lanarum vestimenta quibus repellatur frigus* over against *vestes sericae*, etc. *quibus nudetur ambitio—ubi nemo est clamitans—ne hoc quidem habens unde roget*, etc.—*supravivit cadaveri suo—sordibus dealbatur*—and so forth), in the preference given to showy adjectives and images, the emotive use of anaphora (*hoc, his, horum*). Of course, Jerome differs from his contemporary Ammianus in that the fire of his display (*ardentes gemmae*) is fed by love and enthusiasm—the lyrical flight of the concluding sentences, with Pammachius soaring heavenward and bedewing the ashes of his beloved with the balsam of charity is magnificent, doubly effective after the procession of the sick; and the flowers which Pammachius does not strew, but which are enumerated one by one, contribute their fragrance. It is a marvelous piece, a delight for lovers of what later on came to be called Baroque; and Ammianus, with his much more rigid and intrinsically frozen splendor, has nothing to compare with it. Yet even Jerome's hope, which enables him to rise to such moving lyrical heights, has no reference whatever to this world. His propaganda, directed entirely toward an ideal of ascetic virginity, is opposed to generation and intent upon the annihilation of the earthly. It is only with difficulty and halfheartedly that he allows the resistance, which had then just set in, to extract partial concessions from him. His is a somber fire too; in him too, the contrast between the pictorial splendor of the language and the somberly suicidal ethos, the immersion in horror, in distortion of life and hostility to life, is often almost unbearable. He is not the last to clothe such asceticism and murderous hatred of the world in an extravagantly pictorial style; that remains a Christian tradition. But in him the effect is all the more lugubrious because there is a complete lack of the opposing voices of delight in the world, which make themselves heard in all later forms of the Baroque, even in the most profoundly ecstatic devotion. It seems that declining antiquity, somberly and desperately on the defensive, could no longer produce such voices.

However, even in the Fathers there are texts which reveal a completely different, a much more dramatically militant attitude toward the realities of their time—and, with it, a completely different, a much less baroque form of expression, much more under the influence of the classical tradition. The following text, which I shall use to illustrate this, is chapter 8 of book 6 of Augustine's *Confessions*. The person referred to is Alypius, a friend of Augustine's earlier years and one of his disciples. The person addressed (*tu*) is God.

> Non sane relinquens incantatam sibi a parentibus terrenam viam, Romam praecesserat, ut ius disceret; et ibi gladiatorii spectaculi hiatu incredibili et incredibiliter abreptus est. Cum enim aversaretur et detestaretur talia, quidam eius amici et condiscipuli, cum forte de prandio redeuntibus per viam obvius esset, recusantem vehementer et resistentem familiari violentia duxerunt in amphitheatrum, crudelium et funestorum ludorum diebus, haec dicentem: si corpus meum in illum locum trahitis, et ibi constituitis, numquid et animum et oculos meos in illa spectacula potestis intendere? Adero itaque absens, ac sic et vos et illa superabo. Quibus auditis illi nihilo segnius eum adduxerunt secum, idipsum forte explorare cupientes, utrum posset efficere. Quo ubi ventum est,

et sedibus, quibus potuerunt, locati sunt, fervebant omnia imanissimis voluptatibus. Ille autem clausis foribus oculorum interdixit animo, ne in tanta mala procederet, atque utinam et aures obturavisset. Nam quodam pugnae casu, cum clamor ingens totius populi vehementer eum pulsasset, curiositate victus et quasi paratus quicquid illud esset etiam visu contemnere et vincere, aperuit oculos; et percussus est graviore vulnere in anima, quam ille in corpore, quem cernere concupivit, ceciditque miserabilius, quam ille quo cadente factus est clamor: qui per eius aures intravit, et reseravit eius lumina, ut esset, qùa feriretur et deiiceretur, audax adhuc potius quam fortis animus; et eo infirmior, quod de se etiam praesumpserat quod debuit tibi. Ut enim vidit illum sanguinem, immanitatem simul ebibit, et non se avertit, sed fixit adspectum, et hauriebat furias, et nesciebat; et delectabatur scelere certaminis, et cruenta voluptate inebriabatur. Et non erat iam ille qui venerat, sed unus de turba ad quam venerat, et verus eorum socius a quibus adductus erat. Quid plura? Spectavit, clamavit, exarsit, abstulit inde secum insaniam qua stimularetur redire: non tantum cum illis a quibus prius abstractus est, sed etiam prae illis, et alios trahens. Et inde tamen manu validissima et misericordissima eruisti eum tu, et docuisti eum non sui habere, sed tui fiduciam; sed longe postea.

(He, not relinquishing that worldly way which his parents had bewitched him to pursue, had gone before me to Rome, to study law, and there he was carried away in an extraordinary manner with an incredible eagerness after the gladiatorial shows. For, being utterly opposed to and detesting such spectacles, he was one day met by chance by divers of his acquaintance and fellow-students returning from dinner, and they with a friendly violence drew him, vehemently objecting and resisting, into the amphitheater, on a day of these cruel and deadly shows, he thus protesting: "Though you drag my body to that place, and there place me, can you force me to give my mind and lend my eyes to these shows? Thus shall I be absent while present, and so shall overcome both you and them." They hearing this, dragged him on nevertheless, desirous, perchance, to see whether he could do as he said. When they had arrived thither, and had taken their places as they could, the whole place became excited with the inhuman sports. But he, shutting up the doors of his eyes, forbade his mind to roam abroad after such naughtiness; and would that he had shut his ears also! For, upon the fall of one in the fight, a mighty cry from the whole audience stirring him strongly, he, overcome by curiosity, and prepared as it were to despite and rise superior to it, no matter what it were, opened his eyes, and was struck with a deeper wound in his soul than the other, whom he desired to see, was in his body; and he fell more miserably than he on whose fall that mighty clamor was raised, which entered through his ears, and unlocked his eyes, to make way for the striking and beating down of his soul, which was bold rather than valiant hitherto; and so much the weaker in that it presumed on itself, which ought to have depended on Thee. For, directly he saw that blood, he therewith imbibed a sort of savageness; nor did he turn away, but fixed his eye, drinking in madness unconsciously, and was delighted with the guilty contest, and drunken with the bloody pastime. Nor was he now the same he came in, but was one of the throng he came unto, and a true companion of those who had brought him thither. Why need I say more? He looked, shouted, was excited, carried away with him the madness which would stimulate him to return, not only with those who first enticed him, but also before them, yea, and to draw in others. And from all this didst Thou, with a most powerful and most merciful hand, pluck him, and taughtest him not to repose confidence in himself, but in Thee—but not until long after.) *The Confessions of St. Augustine.* Translated by J. C. Pilkington. Citadel Press. 1943.

Here too the forces of the time are at work: sadism, frenetic bloodlust, and the triumph of magic and sense over reason and ethics. But there is a struggle going on. The enemy is known, and the soul's counterforces are mobilized to meet him. In this case the enemy appears in the guise of a bloodlust produced by mass suggestion and affecting all the senses at once. When the defense blocks his way through the eyes, he forces his way in through the ears and so obliges the eyes to open too. The defense is still confident of its inmost fortress, the strength of its inner determination, its conscious will to refuse. But this inmost consciousness does not hold out for even an instant; it collapses immediately, and the pent-up forces which a great exertion of will has so far pressed into the service of the defense go over to the enemy. Let us try to see what this means. Against the increasing dominance of the mob, against irrational and immoderate lust, against the spell of magical powers, enlightened classical culture possessed the weapon of individualistic, aristocratic, moderate, and rational self-discipline. The various systems of ethics all agreed that a well-bred, self-aware, and self-reliant individual could through his own resources keep from intemperance and that, against his will, it could find no foothold in him. The doctrine of the Manichaeans too, from which Alypius' position was not very far removed at the time, relies on man's ability to recognize good and evil. So Alypius is not overly concerned when he is dragged *familiari violentia* into the amphitheater. He trusts in his closed eyes and his determined will. But his proud individualistic self-reliance is overwhelmed in no time. And it is not merely a random Alypius whose pride, nay whose inmost being, is thus crushed; it is the entire rational individualistic culture of classical antiquity: Plato and Aristotle, the Stoa and Epicurus. A burning lust has swept them away, in one powerful assault: *et non erat iam ille qui venerat, sed unus de turba ad quam venerat.* The individual, the man of noble self-reliance, the man who chooses for himself, despiser of excesses, has become one of the mass. And not only that: the very powers which enabled him to remain aloof from mass suggestion longer and with greater determination than others, the very energy which has until now made it possible for him to lead a proud life of his own—these same forces he now puts at the disposal of the mass and its instinctive urges; not only has he been seduced, he turns seducer. What he has despised, he now loves. He raves not only *with* the others but *before* them all: *non tantum cum illis, sed prae illis, et alios trahens.* As is only too natural in a young man of great and passionate vitality, he does not gradually concede a little, he rushes to the opposite extreme. The about-face is complete. And such an about-face from one extreme to the very opposite is also characteristically Christian. Like Peter in the denial scene (and inversely Paul on his way to Damascus), he falls the more deeply the higher he stood before. And, like Peter, he will rise again. For his defeat is not final. When God has taught him to rely on Him instead of on himself—and his very defeat is the first step toward that knowledge—he will triumph. For in the fight against magical intoxication, Christianity commands other weapons than those of the rational and individualistic ideal of antique culture; it is, after all, itself a movement from the depths, from the depths of the multitude as from the depths of immediate emotion; it can fight the enemy with his own weapons. Its magic is no less a magic than is bloodlust, and it is stronger because it is a more ordered, a more human magic, filled with more hope.

Such a text, however much it too may reveal of the somber traits of contemporary reality, is of a wholly different character from the work of Ammianus and the passage from Jerome quoted above. What distinguishes it at first glance from the other texts is the ardor of the dramatic human struggle it represents. Alypius is alive and fights. In comparison, not only Ammianus' characters but Pammachius too, in Jerome's letter, are static shadows which reveal nothing of a life within. This is the crucial characteristic which sets Augustine wholly outside the style of his age, so far as it is known to me: he feels and directly presents human life, and it lives before our eyes. The rhetorical devices, which he never disdains to use, either in this text or elsewhere, are closer on the whole, I believe, to the manner of the older, classical, Ciceronian writers than what we have found in Ammianus and Jerome. The extremely dramatic *spectavit, clamavit, exarsit, abstulit inde,* etc. reminds us of the figure in the second Catilinarian oration, *abiit, excessit, evasit, erupit,* to which, by the way, its genuinely meaningful crescendo and the ensuing transition to the factual make it vastly superior. Elsewhere too—especially in the second half of the text—there are a large number of figures of speech, antitheses, and clauses in parallel. The rhetorical element makes a more classical impression than in Ammianus or Jerome; yet it is clear—and unmistakably so even at a single glance—that we are not dealing with a classical text. The tone has something urgently impulsive, something human and dramatic, and the form exhibits a predominance of parataxes. Both of these characteristics, either considered individually or in their joint effect, are manifestly unclassical. If, for example, we examine the sentence, *nam quodam pugnae casu,* etc., which contains a whole series of hypotactically introduced members, we find that its climax is a movement which is at once dramatic and paratactic: *aperuit oculos, et percussus est,* etc.; and as we try to trace the impression back, we are reminded of certain Biblical passages, which in the mirror of the Vulgate become: *Dixitque Deus: fiat lux, et facta est lux*; or: *ad te clamaverunt, et salvi facti sunt; in te speraverunt, et non sunt confusi* (Ps. 22: 6); or *Flavit spiritus tuus, et operuit eos mare* (Exod. 15: 10); or: *aperuit Dominus os asinae, et locuta est* (Num. 22: 28). In all of these instances there is, instead of the causal or at least temporal hypotaxis which we should expect in classical Latin (whether with *cum* or *postquam,* whether with an ablative absolute or a participial construction) a parataxis with *et*; and this procedure, far from weakening the interdependence of the two events, brings it out most emphatically; just as in English it is more dramatically effective to say: He opened his eyes and was struck . . . than: When he opened his eyes, or: Upon opening his eyes, he was struck . . .

This observation upon the climax of the sentence, *aperuit oculos, et percussus est*, is but a symptom of a much more general state of affairs: Augustine certainly uses the classical periodic style and the corresponding figures (consciously so, as appears from his explanations in book 4 of his *De doctrina christiana*), but he does not allow it to dominate him. The urgently impulsive element in his character makes it impossible for him to accommodate himself to the comparatively cool and rational procedure of the classical, and specifically of the Roman, style, which looks at and organizes things from above. How frequently, especially in the case of a dramatic development, he puts clauses one beside the other, can be observed throughout our text: *Trahitis, et ibi constituitis; adero ac superabo; interdixit, atque utinam obturavisset; aperuit, et percussus est, ceciditque; intravit et reseravit; ebibit, et non se avertit, sed fixit, et nesciebat, et delectabatur, et inebriabatur, et non erat iam ille*. This would be impossible in classical Latin. It is unquestionably the Biblical form of parataxis—just as the content (the dramatization of an inner event, an inner about-face) is avowedly Christian. *Et non erat iam ille qui venerat, sed unus de turba ad quam venerat*: this is a sentence which in form as in content is unimaginable as a product of classical antiquity; it is Christian and, more specifically, Augustinian; for no one ever more passionately pursued and investigated the phenomenon of conflicting and united inner forces, the alternation of antithesis and synthesis in their relations and effects. And he did so not only in practical contexts (as in our case) but also in connection with purely theoretical problems, which under his hands become drama. His treatise on the Trinity is the most impressive illustration of this; but anyone who wishes to discover, from a brief though characteristic passage, how much of a problem Augustine sees in growth and development and yet how clear they are to his mind, may read the first sentences of *The Confessions* (1, 8) where the transition from childhood to adolescence is discussed; such a passage would be unthinkable before Augustine. Parataxis serves Augustine to express the impulsive and dramatic, most often in matters concerned with the inner life; on the other hand, he has almost no trace of what is the primary preoccupation of Ammianus and other authors of the period, even including the Christians among them: the vivid sensory depiction of outward events, especially of the magical, the morbid, and the horrible. In our text there is ample opportunity for vividness, but it is taken care of in a few effective but entirely general terms.

Yet here too the inner, tragic, and problematic event is embedded in concrete contemporary reality. The age of separate realms of style is over. Among pagan authors too, as we have seen, the depiction of reality made its way into the elevated style. And in a much purer form (which begins, and then but occasionally, to be distorted only when it comes into contact with the epideictic style of late antiquity) the principle of mixed styles makes its way into the writings of the Fathers from the Judaeo-Christian tradition. The true heart of the Christian doctrine—Incarnation and Passion—was, as we have previously noted (p. 41ff.), totally incompatible with the principle of the separation of styles. Christ had not come as a hero and king but as a human being of the lowest social station. His first disciples were fishermen and artisans; he moved in the everyday milieu of the humble folk of Palestine; he talked with publicans and fallen women, the poor and the sick and children. Nevertheless, all that he did and said was of the highest and deepest dignity, more significant than anything else in the world. The style in which it was presented possessed little if any rhetorical culture in the antique sense; it was *sermo piscatorius* and yet it was extremely moving and much more impressive than the most sublime rhetorico-tragical literary work. And the most moving account of all was the Passion. That the King of Kings was treated as a low criminal, that he was mocked, spat upon, whipped, and nailed to the cross—that story no sooner comes to dominate the consciousness of the people than it completely destroys the aesthetics of the separation of styles; it engenders a new elevated style, which does not scorn everyday life and which is ready to absorb the sensorily realistic, even the ugly, the undignified, the physically base. Or—if anyone prefers to have it the other way around—a new *sermo humilis* is born, a low style, such as would properly only be applicable to comedy, but which now reaches out far beyond its original domain, and encroaches upon the deepest and the highest, the sublime and the eternal. I have discussed these connections elsewhere ("Sermo humilis," *Romanische Forschungen*, Frankfurt am Main, vol. 63, 1952) and pointed out the special role played by Augustine. Equally at home in the world of classical rhetoric and in that of the Judaeo-Christian tradition, he may well have been the first to become conscious of the problem of the stylistic contrast between the two worlds; he formulated the problem very impressively in his treatise *De doctrina christiana* (4, 18) in connection with the cup of cold water mentioned in Matthew 10: 42.

The Christian mixture of styles is not especially noticeable at this early period (in the Middle Ages it can be seen much more clearly), because the Fathers do not often take occasion to concern themselves with current reality or to practice the imitation of it. They are no poets or novelists and, on the whole, no historians of their present. They are preoccupied with theological activities, especially apologetics and polemics, and these fill their writings. Passages like those here quoted from Jerome and Augustine, which depict current reality, are not very frequent. All the more frequently, however, do we find the Fathers pursuing the interpretation of reality—interpretation above all of Scripture, but also of large historical contexts, especially Roman history, for the purpose of bringing them into harmony with the Judaeo-Christian view of history. The method employed is almost exclusively that of figures, which has repeatedly been referred to in this book (pp. 16 and 48f.) and the significance and influence of which I have tried to some degree to clarify elsewhere ("Figura," *Arch. Roman.* 22, 436). Figural interpretation "establishes a connection between two events or persons in such a way that the first signifies not only itself but also the second, while the second involves or fulfills the first. The two poles of a figure are separated in time, but both, being real events or persons, are within temporality. They are both contained in the flowing stream which is historical life, and only the comprehension, the *intellectus spiritualis*, of their interdependence is a spiritual act." In practice we almost always find an interpretation of the Old Testament, whose episodes are interpreted as figures or phenomenal prophecies of the events of the New Testament. One example is to be found on pages 48f. above, and a large number of examples, with commentary, are given in the essay just mentioned.

This type of interpretation obviously introduces an entirely new and alien element into the antique conception of history. For example, if an occurrence like the sacrifice of Isaac is interpreted as prefiguring the sacrifice of Christ, so that in the former the latter is as it were announced and promised, and the latter "fulfills" (the technical term is *figuram implere*) the former, then a connection is established between two events which are linked neither temporally nor causally—a connection which it is impossible to establish by reason in the horizontal dimension (if I may be permitted to use this term for a temporal extension). It can be established only if both occurrences are vertically linked to Divine Providence, which alone is able to devise such a plan of history and supply the key to its understanding. The horizontal, that is the temporal and causal, connection of occurrences is dissolved; the here and now is no longer a mere link in an earthly chain of events, it is simultaneously something which has always been, and which will be fulfilled in the future; and strictly, in the eyes of God, it is something eternal, something omni-temporal, something already consummated in the realm of fragmentary earthly event. This conception of history is magnificent in its homogeneity, but it was completely alien to the mentality of classical antiquity, it annihilated that mentality down to the very structure of its language, at least of its literary language, which—with all its ingenious and nicely shaded conjunctions, its wealth of devices for syntactic arrangement, its carefully elaborated system of tenses—became wholly superfluous as soon as earthly relations of place, time, and cause had ceased to matter, as soon as a vertical connection, ascending from all that happens, converging in God, alone became significant. Wherever the two conceptions met, there was of necessity a conflict and an attempt to compromise—between, on the one hand, a presentation which carefully interrelated the elements of history, which respected temporal and causal sequence, remained within the domain of the earthly foreground, and, on the other hand, a fragmentary, discrete presentation, constantly seeking an interpretation from above.

The more cultivated in the antique sense of the term, the more deeply imbued with antique culture the writers of the patristic period were, the more imperatively did they feel the need for casting the content of Christianity in a mold which should be not a mere translation but an assimilation to their own tradition of perception and expression. Here again Augustine is an example; large portions of his *Civitas Dei*, especially books 15 to 18 where he treats of the progress (*procursus*) of the City of God on earth, show his constant endeavor to complement the figural-vertical interpretation by a representation of intrahistorical chains of events. As an example, any chapter in which he comments on a Biblical story may be read—for instance 16, 12. Here there is a discussion of the house of Terah, Abraham's father (that is, of Genesis 11: 26), which Augustine supplements by other Biblical passages, e.g., Joshua 24: 2. The subject of the chapter is Judaeo-Christian and so is the interpretation; the whole stands under the sign of the *civitas Dei* which, prefigured since Adam, is now fulfilled in Christ. The period of Terah and Abraham is interpreted as a link in the divine plan of salvation, as one of the stations in the figural sequence of preliminary, fragmentary, prophetic prototypes of the *civitas Dei,* and in this sense it is compared with the distant period of Noah. But, within this frame, there is visible a constant endeavor to fill in the lacunae of the Biblical account, to supplement it by other passages from the Bible and by original considerations, to establish a continuous connection of events, and in general to give the highest measure of rational plausibility to an intrinsically irrational interpretation. Almost everything which Augustine himself adds to the Biblical account serves to explain the historical situation in rational terms and to reconcile the figural interpretation with the conception of an uninterrupted historical sequence of events. The element of classical antiquity which asserts itself here is also apparent in the language—is, indeed, more apparent there than anywhere else; the periods, it is true, seem to be hastily constructed and make no impression of great art (there are too many relatives); but with their abundant display of connectives, their precise gradation of temporal, comparative, and concessive hypotaxes, their participial constructions, they still form a most striking contrast to the Biblical passage cited, with its parataxis and its lack of connectives. This contrast between text and Biblical citation is very frequently to be observed in the Fathers and almost always in Augustine. For the Latin translation of the Bible had preserved the paratactic character of the original. In such a passage as this from the *Civitas Dei,* one clearly recognizes the struggle in which the two worlds were engaged in matters of language as well as in matters of fact. It is a struggle which might well have led to a far-reaching rationalization and syntactic organization of the Judaeo-Christian tradition. It might have, but it did not. The antique mentality was already too shaken. And so the most important and most influential piece of literary work, the translation of the Bible, could only imitate the paratactic style of the original, thus meeting the prevailing trend in the popular language halfway, while the literary language declined; finally came the invasion of the Germanic peoples, who, despite their humble respect for antique culture, were unable to absorb its rationality and its refined syntactic texture.

Thus the figural interpretation of history emerged unqualifiedly victorious. Yet it was no fully adequate substitute for the lost comprehension of rational, continuous, earthly connections between things, for it could not be applied to any random occurrence, although of course there was no dearth of attempts to submit everything that happened to an interpretation directly from above. Such attempts were bound to founder upon the multiplicity of events and the unfathomableness of the divine councils. And so vast regions of event remained without any principle by which they might be classified and comprehended—especially after the fall of the Roman Empire, which, through the concept of the state which it exemplified, had at least oriented the interpretation of political occurrences. There remained passive observation, resigned acceptance, or active exploitation of whatever chanced to occur in the world of practical events—raw material which was absorbed in its rawest form. It was a very long time before the potentialities in Christian thought (mixture of styles, comprehensive penetration of the processes of existence), reinforced by the sensuality of new peoples, could manifest their vigor.

4

SICHARIUS AND CHRAMNESINDUS

The following story is found in Gregory of Tours' *History of the Franks* (7, 47 and 9, 19):

> Gravia tunc inter Toronicos cives bella civilia surrexerunt. Nam Sicharius, Johannis quondam filius, dum ad natalis dominici solemnia apud Montalomagensem vicum cum Austrighysilo reliquosque pagensis celebraret, presbiter loci misit puerum ad aliquorum hominum invitacionem, ut ad domum eius bibendi gracia venire deberint. Veniente vero puero, unus ex his qui invitabantur, extracto gladio, eum ferire non metuit. Qui statim cecidit et mortuos est. Quod cum Sicharius audisset, qui amicitias cum presbitero retinebat, quod scilicet puer eius fuerit interfectus, arrepta arma ad eclesiam petit, Austrighyselum opperiens. Ille autem hec audiens, adprehenso armorum aparatu, contra eum diregit. Mixtisque omnibus, cum se pars utraque conliderit, Sicharius inter clericos ereptus ad villam suam effugit, relictis in domo presbiteri cum argento et vestimentis quatuor pueris sauciatis. Quo fugiente, Austrighiselus iterum inruens, interfectis pueris aurum argentumque cum reliquis rebus abstulit. Dehinc cum in iudicio civium convenissent, et preceptum esset ut Austrighiselus, qui homicida erat et, interfectis pueris, res sine audienciam diripuerat, censura legali condempnaretur. Inito placito, paucis infra diebus Sicharius audiens quod res, quas Austrighiselus deripuerat, cum Aunone et filio adque eius fratre Eberulfo retinerentur, postposito placito, coniunctus Audino, mota sedicione, cum armatis viris inruit super eos nocte, elisumque hospicium, in quo dormiebant, patrem cum fratre et filio interemit, resque eorum cum pecoribus, interfectisque servis, abduxit. Quod nos audientes, vehimenter ex hoc molesti, adiuncto iudice, legacionem ad eos mittemus, ut in nostra presencia venientes, accepta racione, cum pace discederent, ne iurgium in amplius pulularet. Quibus venientibus coniunctisque civibus, ego aio: "Nolite, o viri, in sceleribus proficere, ne malum longius extendatur. Perdedimus enim eclesie filius; metuemus nunc, ne et alius in hac intencione careamus.

Estote, queso, pacifici; et qui malum gessit, stante caritate, conponat, ut sitis filii pacifici, qui digni sitis regno Dei, ipso Domino tribuente, percipere. Sic enim ipse ait: Beati pacifici, quoniam filii Dei vocabuntur. Ecce enim, etsi illi, qui noxe subditur, minor est facultas, argento eclesie redemitur; interim anima viri non pereat." Et hec dicens, optuli argentum eclesie; sed pars Chramnesindi, qui mortem patris fratresque et patrui requerebat, accepere noluit. His discedentibus, Sicharius iter, ut ad regem ambularet, preparat, et ob hoc Pectavum ad uxorem cernendam proficiscitur. Cumque servum, ut exerceret opera, commoneret elevatamque virgam ictibus verberaret, ille, extracto baltei gladio, dominum sauciare non metuit. Quo in terram ruente, currentes amici adprehensum servum crudeliter cesum, truncatis manibus et pedibus, patibolo damnaverunt. Interim sonus in Toronicum exiit, Sicharium fuisse defunctum. Cum autem hec Chramnesindus audisset, commonitis parentibus et amicis, ad domum eius properat. Quibus spoliatis, interemptis nonnullis servorum, domus omnes tam Sicharii quam reliquorum, qui participes huius ville erant, incendio concremavit, abducens secum pecora vel quecumque movere potuit. Tunc partes a iudice ad civitatem deducte, causas proprias prolocuntur; inventumque est a iudicibus, ut, qui nollens accepere prius conposicionem domus incendiis tradedit, medietatem precii, quod ei fuerat iudicatum, amitteret—et hoc contra legis actum, ut tantum pacifici redderentur—alia vero medietatem conposiciones Sicharius reddered. Tunc datum ab eclesia argentum, que iudicaverunt accepta securitate conposuit, datis sibi partes invicem sacramentis, ut nullo umquam tempore contra alteram pars alia musitaret. Et sic altercacio terminum fecit.

(9, 19) Bellum vero illud, quod inter cives Toronicus superius diximus terminatum, in rediviva rursum insania surgit. Nam Sicharius, cum post interfectionem parentum Cramsindi magnam cum eo amiciciam patravissed, et in tantum se caritate mutua diligerent, ut plerumque simul cibum caperent, ac in uno pariter stratu recumberent, quandam die cenam sub nocturno tempore preparat Chramsindus, invitans Sicharium ad epulum suum. Quo veniente, resident pariter ad convivium. Cumque Sicharius crapulatus a vino multa iactaret in Cramsindo, ad extremum dixisse fertur: "Magnas mihi debes referre grates, o dulcissime frater, eo quod interficerem parentes tuos, de quibus accepta composicione, aurum argentumque superabundat in domum tuam, et nudus essis et egens, nisi hec te causa paululum roborassit." Hec ille audiens, amare suscepit animo dicta Sichari, dixitque in corde suo: "Nisi ulciscar interitum parentum meorum, amitteri nomen viri debeo et mulier infirma vocare." Et statim extinctis luminaribus, caput Sichari seca dividit. Qui parvolam in ipso vitae terminum vocem emittens, cecidit et mortuus est. Pueri vero, qui cum eo venerant, dilabuntur. Cramsindus exanimum corpus nudatum vestibus adpendit in sepis stipite, ascensisque aequitibus eius, ad regem petiit. . . .

(Serious local fighting arose at that time between inhabitants of the region of Tours. For Sicharius, son of the late John, celebrated the feast of the Nativity of Our Lord at the village of Manthelan with Austrighiselus and the other neighbors. And the priest of the place sent a boy over to invite some of the men to come to his house for a drink. When the boy got there, one of those he invited drew his sword and did not refrain from striking at him. He fell down and was dead. Sicharius was friendly with the priest, and when he heard that one of his boys had been murdered, he took his arms and went to the church to wait for Austrighiselus. The latter heard about this and armed himself also and went to meet him. When they had all mingled in fighting and both parties suffered harm, Sicharius got away unnoticed under the protection of the clergy and made for his homestead leaving behind at the priest's place his silver, his clothes, and four of his servants who had been wounded. After he had fled, Austrighiselus broke into the building, killed the servants, and took away with him the gold, silver, and other things. When they appeared later before the people's court, the decision was that Austrighiselus was to be sentenced to the legal penalty for manslaughter and because, after killing the servants, he had taken the things without waiting for a hearing. Having accepted these arrangements, Sicharius heard a few days later that the things Austrighiselus had taken from him were stored at the place of Auno and his son and brother Eberulf, and forgetting about the arrangements, he joined with Audinus, broke the peace, and surprised them at night with armed men. He invaded the house where they were asleep, killed father, brother, and son, and having done away with the servants took all their belongings and their cattle. When we heard this, we grew greatly perturbed; we took up the matter with the judge and sent out a message to them: they should appear before us, present their case, and separate in peace so that the feud would not spread farther. When they came and the citizenry had assembled, I spoke to them saying: "Desist, you men, from committing such offenses and let not the evil extend farther. Already have we lost sons of the Church and are concerned lest we might lose more in this contention. Be peaceable, I beg you; and he who has committed evil, let him atone for it for charity's sake, that you may be children of peace, worthy to receive the Kingdom of God through the Lord's grace. For he says: Blessed are the peacemakers: for they shall be called the children of God. And if he who is the guilty one should be too poor he shall be redeemed by money of the Church so that the soul of that man may not perish." Thus speaking I offered them money of the Church. But Chramnesindus' party, wishing to avenge the death of his father, brother, and uncle, did not want to accept. Thus they departed, and Sicharius got ready for a journey to go to see the king. He therefore turned toward the region of Poitiers in order to visit his wife. When he urged on a servant to do his work and raised his cane and beat him, the latter drew his sword which he carried in his belt and had no qualms about wounding his master. As Sicharius fell to the ground, his friends came running, seized the servant, treated him cruelly, cut off his hands and feet and strung him up on the gallows. Meanwhile the rumor spread at Tours that Sicharius was dead. When Chramnesindus heard this he summoned his relatives and friends and rushed to Sicharius' house. When he had plundered it, killing a few servants in the process, he set all the houses on fire, both those which belonged to Sicharius and all the others, which belonged to men who made part of that village, and took with him the cattle and everything that could be moved. Then the parties were summoned before the judge in the city and pleaded their causes, and the judges found that he who had previously refused to accept the indemnity and had set the houses on fire should lose half the wergild previously adjudged to him—this was really against the law and was done only in order to calm them—while Sicharius was to pay the other half. Then the Church paid out the money. The indemnity was settled in accordance with the verdict, the parties were reconciled and swore each to the other that they would never again rise in arms against one another. Thus the quarrel came to an end.

The fighting among the citizens of Tours, which was ended as we have related above, broke out again with renewed fury. After slaying Chramnesindus' kinsmen, Sicharius had become very friendly with him, and they loved each other so dearly that they often ate together and slept together in one bed. Once Chramnesindus made ready a dinner towards night and invited Sicharius. He came and they sat down together for dinner. Sicharius got drunk with wine and made many boasts to Chramnesindus, and at last he is supposed to have said: "O brother, you are greatly indebted to me for killing your kinsmen, for you were paid for them, and now there is gold and silver in your house a-plenty. You would be poor and living a life of misery if I had not set you up a little." Chramnesindus heard Sicharius' words with bitterness in his soul and he spoke within his heart: "If I do not avenge the death of my kinsmen, I shall not be worthy of the name of man and ought to be called a weak woman." And immediately he put out the lights and split Sicharius' head with his blade. Sicharius uttered in the last moment of his life a little cry, fell down, and was dead. The servants that had come with him escaped. Chramnesindus stripped the garments from the dead body and hung it on a picket of the fence; then he mounted his horse and hastened to the king. . . .)

I imagine that the first impression this passage makes on a reader is that here an occurrence sufficiently confused in itself is very obscurely narrated. Even if one is not put off by the irregular orthography and inflections, one will still have some difficulty in getting a really clear idea of the facts involved. "At that time grave civil disturbances broke out among the inhabitants of Tours. For . . ." The cause of the disturbances should now follow; but what follows—dependent on *nam*—is some account of earlier events; in a village where many people had gathered to celebrate Christmas, the village priest sent out a servant to invite some of them to come and drink with him. But that is certainly not the cause of the disturbances at Tours. We are reminded of the narrative method which is frequent in spoken conversation, especially among uneducated or hasty or careless speakers. Something like: "Last night I was late getting away from the office. Because Smith had come to see the boss, and they were inside talking about the X business. And just before five, the boss comes and says: 'Say, Jones, couldn't you get these things itemized in a hurry, so we can give Mr. Smith all the material right now?' " And so on. Neither the priest's invitation nor Smith's presence in the boss's office represents the immediate cause for the outbreak of disturbances or Jones's being late leaving the office; they represent merely the first part of a complex of facts which the speaker is unable to organize syntactically. He intends now to state the cause of the result anticipated in the first independent sentence, but the amount of data requisite for the purpose confuses him. He has neither the energy to dispose all of it in a single construction through the aid of a system of dependent clauses, nor the foresight to recognize the difficulty and get around it by a synoptic introductory statement, as for instance, "It happened like this." As it stands, the *nam* is neither exact nor justified—precisely as in the similarly conceived sentence which comes later: *nam Sicharius cum post interfectionem*, etc., for there again the value of *nam* is not that it introduces the cause of the renewed outbreak of disturbances, it only brings in the first part of a complex of facts. And in both cases the impression of disorder is considerably increased by a change in the grammatical subject. In both cases the sentence starts out with Sicharius as the subject (both times Gregory evidently thinks of him as the chief character), and in both cases he is later forced to insert the subject of that portion of the complex of facts which represents all that he is capable of getting into a single construction. As a result, the sentences turn out to be grammatical monsters. True enough, the commentators (Bonnet; and Löfsted in his commentary on the *Peregrinatio Aetheriae*) have informed us that *nam* in Vulgar Latin, like many of the once extremely clear and precise connectives of Latin, has lost its original value, that it is no longer causal but merely indicates a colorless continuation or transition. But this state of affairs has by no means been reached in our two passages from Gregory. On the contrary, Gregory still senses the causal value; he employs it, but in a confused and imprecise manner. It may be that such instances can show us how *nam* came to be weakened as a causal particle by being so often used laxly—here the weakening process is still going on, it is not yet complete. It is remarkable that such procedures, which would seem to occur at all times in the spoken language, here make their way into the literary language of a man like Gregory of Tours, the scion of a high-ranking family and a noteworthy character in his time and his country.

Let us proceed. The servant presenting the invitation is killed "by one of those who were invited." Why? We are not told. That the killer must have been Austrighiselus or one of his group, we can only infer from what follows, for Sicharius wants to take revenge on him for the deed; but it is not stated. Further, the abrupt introduction of the various buildings—the church, the priest's house—and the words *inter clericos ereptus* give only a very confused notion of the events. We miss the aid of clarifying connectives. In exchange, other things seem exaggeratedly detailed. Why does not Gregory say simply: one of the guests killed the servant? He says: . . . *extracto gladio, eum ferire non metuit. Qui statim cecidit et mortuos est.* What a detailed treatment of an incident which, after all, is important only through its consequences! To motivate it would seem to have been more important than to tell us that the servant fell before he died! In the very next sentence, he is afraid that the reader may already have lost the connection, for he considers it necessary to add, *quod scilicet puer eius fuerit interfectus*—which only a reader of very limited capacity can have so soon forgotten! On the other hand, with his *Austrighiselum opperiens* he expects the same reader to have a considerable power of combination, for he has failed to tell us that Austrighiselus is in any way related to the killing—or for that matter that the entire party is not assembled in one place, as one could hardly fail to suppose. So the text goes on. The sentence which deals with first legal proceedings has no principal verb at all (*Dehinc cum in iudicio*); the following sentence is made a monster by its superimposed participial constructions, which follow no grammatical system whatever: *inito placito, postposito placito, coniunctus Audino, mota sedicione, elisumque hospicium.* Both the translation and the historical and legal interpretation of the two sentences are extremely difficult (as a matter of fact, the entire juridical procedure was the occasion for a much-discussed controversy between Gabriel Monod and Fustel de Coulanges, *Revue historique*, 31, 1886, and *Revue des questions historiques*, 41, 1887); this is due not merely to the ambiguity of the word *placitum* but also to the general lack of orderly arrangement in the rhetorical structure. And this again reveals that Gregory is not capable of arranging the occurrences themselves in an orderly fashion.

Austrighiselus disappears without the reader's being told what became of him; new characters are unexpectedly introduced, and it is only occasionally and incompletely that we learn how they are related to the events; the speech which Gregory makes to calm the excitement is also incomprehensible without some power of combination in the reader, for who is *illi qui noxe subditur*, and who the *vir* whose soul must not perish? On the other hand, a story like that of Sicharius' trip to Poitiers and of his being wounded by a servant—an incident whose bearing on the whole action is at best that it is the basis for the false rumor of his death—is presented in great detail. When we come to the second legal action or settlement procedure, we have once again to make a special effort to understand what party and what money are being referred to. And through the whole first part (which is from book 7), though there are numerous and often extremely clumsy subordinate constructions (the effort to write periodically is unmistakable), there is not a single clearly causal or concessive conjunction with the exception of *quoniam* in the Bible quotation, and *etsi*, the meaning of which is not quite clear to me, but it would seem to be rather conditional (=*si*) than causal or concessive. The second part (from book 9) does not make quite the same impression, because it very soon concentrates upon a single scene, so that the problem is less one of order than of visual directness. But here again the sentence *Nam Sicharius* which contains the exposition and which we discussed above, is a veritable monstrosity.

It goes without saying that a classical author would have arranged the material much more clearly—provided that he had treated it at all. For if we ask ourselves how Caesar or Livy or Tacitus or even Ammianus would have told this story, it immediately becomes obvious that they would never have told it. For them and their public, such a story would not have had the slightest interest. Who are Austrighiselus, Sicharius, and Chramnesindus? Not even tribal princes, and during the heyday of the Empire their bloody brawls would probably not even have elicited a special report to Rome from the provincial governor. This observation shows how narrow Gregory's horizon really is, how little perspective he has with which to view a large, coherent whole, how little he is in a position to organize his subject matter in accordance with the points of view which had once obtained. The Empire is no longer in existence. Gregory is no longer situated in a place where all the news from the *orbis terrarum* is received, sorted, and arranged according to its significance for the state. He has neither the news sources which were once available nor the attitude which once determined the manner in which the news was reported. He hardly surveys all of Gaul. A large part of his work, doubtless the most valuable, consists of what he himself witnessed in his own diocese or of what was reported to him from the neighboring territory. His material is essentially limited to what has been brought before his eyes. He has no political point of view in the old sense; if he may be said to have any at all, it is the interest of the Church; but there again his perspective is restricted; he does not conceive of the Church as a whole in such a way that his work forcibly conveys that whole; everything is locally restricted, both in substance and in thought. On the other hand, in contrast to his antique predecessors, whose work was often based on indirect and previously processed reports, most of the things Gregory relates in his *History of the Franks* he either saw himself or learned at first-hand from people involved in them. This is in keeping with his natural bent. For he is directly interested in what people are doing. They interest him as they move about him, irrespective of political considerations in a wider context. So far as it is present, he treats even politics anecdotally and humanly. Thus his work assumes a character much closer to personal memoirs than the work of any Roman historian. (We need hardly point out that Caesar's case is completely different.)

An earlier antique author, then, would not have treated this story at all. If it had been indispensable for the understanding of a more general political complex, he would have disposed of it in three lines. In cases where a series of acts of violence assume political importance in themselves—Jugurtha and his cousins in Sallust might serve as an example—the whole system of political motives, rationalized to the last detail and heightened by rhetoric, is set forth beforehand. Dramatic incidents without political interest are at best briefly alluded to, as for example in the case of the words *occultans sese tugurio muliebris ancillae* in connection with the murder of Hiempsal (*Jugurtha* 12). Gregory, on the other hand, tries hard, sometimes clumsily and prolixly but often with great success, to make the proceedings vividly visible. ". . . the priest of the village sent a servant to invite certain people to come to his house and drink. When the servant arrived, one of those who were invited drew his sword and had no qualms about wounding him. He fell to the ground and was dead." That is visually vivid narration, even though of a very simple sort. There could be no other reason for mentioning that the servant arrived or that he fell to the ground. It is the same with the vengeful attack upon Austrighiselus. Topographically the report is not very clear, but we sense the author's endeavor to give visual vividness to the successive phases of the occurrence. The same thing is true of Sicharius' argument with his servant, which has no bearing whatever upon the progress of the action. But in our text the most peculiar and striking illustration of Gregory's concern for visual vividness is the murder of Sicharius. How the two, of whom one had killed the other's next of kin not very long before, made friends and became so intimate and inseparable that they ate and slept together, how once again Chramnesindus invites Sicharius to feast with him, how Sicharius, talking wildly in his drunkenness, provokes the other to take vengeance for everything at once, and finally the murder itself—all this has such a visual vividness, and testifies to such an endeavor to imitate the occurrence directly, as Roman historiography never sought to achieve (even Ammianus' showy pictorial style is not imitative) and as can hardly be found anywhere in all the serious literature of antiquity. Furthermore, it is magnificent psychologically, an extremely arresting scene between two individuals, and filled with the strange atmosphere of the Merovingian period: the sudden and undisguised brutality which blots out every memory of the past and every thought of the future, and, on the other hand, the slight effect of Christian morality which, even though presented in its most primitive form, cannot penetrate these brutish souls—all this comes out in sharp relief in the scene. The plausible hypothesis that Chramnesindus had consciously lured Sicharius into a trap—that on his side the friendship was sheer hypocrisy designed to lull his enemy into security—Gregory does not even take into consideration. And he is probably right, for he knew the people among whom he lived. Besides, we read of equally unthinking acts everywhere in his work. It seems indeed that the two had honestly become such close friends that, their consciousness being alive only to the passing moment, it never occurred to them how unnatural and dangerous such a friendship really was. A few tactless drunken words seem to have brought the memory back to the surface, to have rekindled the forgotten hatred, so that the murder was the decision of a moment. This is all the more probable since Chramnesindus—as we learn from the following passage—found himself in a difficult situation in consequence of his act, for Sicharius had a powerful protectress in Queen Fredegunde; if Chramnesindus had taken time to think matters through, he might have acted differently. Gregory relates the whole incident without personal commentary, purely dramatically, shifting the tense and writing in the present as soon as he nears the decisive moment. Then he gives us direct discourse, not only for the bullying of the drunken Sicharius but also for what goes on inside Chramnesindus. Both these pieces of direct discourse are direct imitations of what was actually spoken and felt, free from all rhetorical editing. Sicharius' words sound as though they had been translated into Gregory's clumsy Latin from the vernacular in which they were spoken ("so they say," *dixisse fertur*). One might reconstruct the speech in current vernacular roughly as follows: "Brother, you ought to be grateful to me for killing your people. You pocketed the indemnity, and now you're a rich man. You wouldn't have a shirt to your back if this little business hadn't helped you out." And Chramnesindus' reaction is expressed in an unvoiced monologue which, for all its awkwardness, is sufficiently striking: "I ought to renounce the name of a man and be called a helpless woman, if I do not take revenge for the death of my people." And immediately the lights go out, Sicharius is killed, his death rattle is not forgotten, and once again we read *cecidit et mortuus est*; Gregory refuses to do without the falling body.

A scene, then, which no antique historian would have considered worth representing, Gregory relates in the most graphic manner; and it would seem to have been its very graphicness which made him want to represent it. If, for example, we read the story of the flight of the hostage Attalus (3, 15; it furnished the subject of Grillparzer's *Weh dem der lügt*), we come upon the scene where the fugitives hide from their mounted pursuers behind a bramble. The horsemen halt just in front of it: *dixitque unus, dum equi urinam proiecerint* . . . (and one of them said, while the horses staled . . .). What classical author would have given such a detail! We see how Gregory, to make his report come alive, invents such things spontaneously, out of the compulsion of his own imagination—after all, he was not present! What he related he tried to make visual, palpable, perceptible through all the senses. In this he is also served by the most distinctive characteristic of his style: the numerous brief pieces of direct discourse, which he uses wherever he has an opportunity. Any story that he can, he thus makes into a scene. We have already referred to the role which direct discourse plays in classical historiography (pp. 39 and 46). It is used there almost exclusively for set speeches in a rhetorical vein. The emotion and drama in them is purely rhetorical. They organize and regulate the facts but do not make them concrete. Gregory on the other hand gives us dialogues and similar brief utterances by his personages—words which break out in a moment and change the moment into a scene. I cannot here enumerate the long series of scenes in which he has one or two people speak in his clumsy Latin, which often gets in the way, which seems too eager to sound literary, but through which time and again the concrete vigor of the vernacular penetrates. But let me mention at least a few examples (of which the murder scene just mentioned already furnishes one). In the story of Attalus the conversation between the cook and his master (*rogo ut facias mihi prandium quod admirentur et dicant quia in domu regia melius non aspeximus*, 3, 15—I want you to fix up a dinner for me that will really surprise them and make them say they never saw a better, not even at the King's house; *ibid.*, the conversation at night between the cook and his son-in-law); in the struggle over the bishopric of Clermont, the threats with which the presbyter Cato assails the archdeacon Cautinus (*Ego te removebo, ego te humiliabo, ego tibi multas neces impendi praecipiam*, 4, 7—I'll kick you out, I'll make you eat dirt, I'll have you put to death by inches); the argument between King Chilperic and Gregory over the Trinity (anger and scorn in the King's answers, for instance, *manifestum est mihi in hac causa Hilarium Eusebiumque validos inimicos habere*—I obviously have some very powerful opponents in this matter, like Hilary and Eusebius —or *sapientioribus a te hoc pandam qui mihi consentiant*, 5, 44—I'll put this matter to wiser men than you and they will agree with me); Fredegundis at Bishop Praetextatus' sickbed, with the entire preceding and following scene (8, 31); Bishop Bertramnus of Bordeaux's answer concerning his sister (*requirat nunc eam revocetque quo voluerit, me obvium non habebit*, 9, 33—Let him look for her and take her wherever he wants to; I won't object); the violent argument between Princess Rigundis and her mother (9, 34); Guntchram Boso and the Bishop of Trier (9, 10); and as a particularly arresting example, the downfall of Mundericus, when, toward the end, where Mundericus is led through the gates of his castle by the traitor Aregyselus, the moment of suspense before the murder is set in sharp dramatic relief by a few words in direct discourse: *Quid adspicitis tam intenti, populi? An numquid non vidistis prius Mundericum?*—Why are you staring at us like that, you people? Haven't you ever seen Mundericus before? (3, 14).

In all these conversations and exclamations, brief, spontaneous passages between human beings are dramatized in a most concrete fashion: eye to eye, statement answering statement, the actors face one another breathing and alive—a procedure which can hardly be found in antique historiography; even the dialogue of the classical stage is shaped more rationally and more rhetorically. The spontaneous and brief dialogue does, however, occur in the Bible—compare what we said on the subject above, p. 45. Undoubtedly the rhythm and the atmosphere of the Bible, especially of the New Testament, are always present in Gregory's mind and help to determine his style. And they release forces which are already present in Gregory and his epoch. For everywhere in his History the spoken language of the people unmistakably makes its presence felt; though the time when it can be written is still far away, it keeps echoing through Gregory's consciousness. Gregory's literary Latin not only is decadent grammatically and syntactically, it is used in his work to an end for which, originally or at least in its heyday, it seemed little suited—that is, to imitate concrete reality. For the literary Latin, and especially the literary prose, of the golden age is an almost excessively organizing language, in which the material and sensory side of the facts is rather viewed and ordered from above than vividly presented in its materiality and sensoriness. Together with the rhetorical tradition, the legal and administrative genius of the Romans contributes to this. In the Roman prose of the golden age there is a predominant tendency simply to report matters of fact, if possible only to suggest them in very general terms, to allude to them, to keep aloof from them—and, on the other hand, to put all the precision and vigor of expression into syntactical connections, with the result that the style acquires as it were a strategic character, with extremely clear articulations, whereas the subject matter, the stuff of reality, which lies between them, though it is mastered, is not exploited in its sensory potentialities. (This is so even in Cicero's letters, and at times most emphatically; as an example one might read the famous apologia in the letter to P. Lentulus Spinther, ad fam. 1, 9, especially §21.) The tools of syntactical connection thus reach the height of subtlety, exactness, and diversity—an observation which applies not only to conjunctions and other devices of subordination, but also to the use of tenses, word order, antithesis, and numerous other rhetorical devices, which are likewise made to serve the same end of exact, subtle, yet pliable and richly shaded disposition. This wealth of articulations and dispositional devices makes possible a great variety of subjective exposition, amazingly facilitates reasoning on the facts, and leaves the writer a freedom—not again attained in such a measure until long afterward—to suppress certain facts and to suggest doubtful details without assuming explicit responsibility.

Gregory's language, on the other hand, is but imperfectly equipped to organize facts; as soon as a complex of events ceases to be very simple, he is no longer able to present it as a coherent whole. His language organizes badly or not at all. But it lives in the concrete side of events, it speaks with and in the people who figure in them. And it can give forceful and varied expression to their pleasure, their pain, their scorn and anger, or whatever other passions may chance to be raging in them (whereas the judgments Gregory occasionally passes on his characters are on the whole summary and devoid of finesse; for example 9, 19, toward the end, concerning Sicharius). How much more direct his sensory participation in events is than that of any classical author, we can learn from a comparison with the most realistic of them all, Petronius. Petronius copies the language of his parvenu freedmen, he makes them speak their corrupt and repugnant jargon as a much more conscious and exact imitator than Gregory; but it is obvious that he applies this style as a rhetorical device and that he would write a report or a history quite differently. He is a gentleman of rank and culture, presenting a farce to his equals, with every *raffinement*. He is consciously dealing in a comic art form, and if he so chooses he can write in many other veins as well. But Gregory has nothing to hand except his grammatically confused, syntactically impoverished, and almost sophomoric Latin; he has no stops to pull, as he has no public he might impress with an unfamiliar excitant, a new variant of style. But he does have the concrete events which take place around him; he witnesses them or he hears them "hot from the oven," and in a vernacular which, though we may be unable to form a completely clear idea of it, is obviously always present to his ear as the raw material of his story while he labors to translate it back into his semi-literary Latin. What he relates is his own and his only world. He has no other, and he lives in it.

Furthermore, the pattern of the events he has to report meets his style halfway. Compared with what earlier Roman historians had to report, they are all local events and they take place among people whose instincts and passions were violent and whose rational deliberations were crude and primitive. True enough, Gregory's work gives us a very imperfect idea of the connections of political events; but, reading it, we almost smell the atmosphere of the first century of Frankish rule in Gaul. There is a progressive and terrible brutalization. The point is not simply that unqualified force comes to the fore in every local district, so that the central governments are no longer alone in its possession, but also that intrigue and policy have lost all formality, have become wholly primitive and coarse. Such concealment and circumlocution in human intercourse as are characteristic of every higher culture—politeness, rhetorical euphemism, indirect approach, social appearances, legal formalities even in the pursuit of a political or commercial robbery, and so on—fall into abeyance, or, where some vestiges of them remain, survive at best as crude caricatures. Lusts and passions lose every concealing form; they show themselves in the raw and with palpable immediacy. This brutal life becomes a sensible object; to him who would describe it, it presents itself as devoid of order and difficult to order, but tangible, earthy, alive. Gregory was a bishop—it was his duty to develop Christian ethical attitudes; his office was a practical and demanding one, in which the cure of souls might at any moment be combined with political and economic questions. In the preceding epoch the center of gravity of the Church's activity had still been the consolidation of Christian dogma, a task in which subtlety and intellectuality had often been displayed to excess. In the sixth century that activity, at least in the West, was concentrated upon practical and organizational matters. This shift is vividly exemplified by Gregory. He lays no claim to rhetorical training; he has no interest in dogmatic controversies; for him the decisions of the Church Councils are fixed and beyond dispute. But there is room in his heart for everything that can impress the people—legends of the saints, relics, and miracles to feed the imagination, protection against violence and oppression, simple moral lessons made palatable by promises of future rewards. The people among whom he lived understood nothing about dogma and had but a very crude idea of the mysteries of the faith. They had lusts and material interests, mitigated by fear of one another and of supernatural forces.

Gregory seems to have been just the right man for these conditions. He was little more than thirty years old when he became Bishop of Tours. If we may judge the man by the writer, he must have been spirited and courageous, and certainly he was not easily disconcerted by anything he saw. He is one of the first examples of that actively practical sense of reality which we so often have occasion to admire in the Catholic church and which, developing early, made Christian dogma into something that would function in the realm of life on earth. Nothing human is foreign to Gregory. His lights search every depth. He calls things by their right names, yet manages to preserve his dignity and a certain unctuousness of tone. Nor does he in any sense refuse to employ secular in conjunction with spiritual means. He understands that the Church must be rich and powerful if she is to achieve lasting moral ends in this world, and that he who would make a lasting conquest of men's hearts must bind them to himself by practical interests too. Furthermore, the Church was forced into the domain of practical activity in many ways—by the giving and receiving of alms, by her role in mediating disputes, by the administration of her rapidly increasing land-holdings, and by all sorts of political involvements. In a higher and less immediately practical sense, Christianity had been realistic from the beginning. We have already discussed how Christ's life among the lower classes and the simultaneous sublimity and shamefulness of his Passion shattered the classical conception of the tragic and the sublime. But the Church's realism, as it appears, perhaps for the first time, in literary form in Gregory, goes still further, into practical activity in the practical world, is nourished by everyday experience, and has its feet on the ground. Gregory is professionally in contact with all the people and conditions he writes about; he is professionally interested in individual ethical phenomena; they are the ever-present field of his activity. From his activity in the pursuit of his duties he acquires his ability to observe and the desire to write down what he observes; and his very personal gift for the concrete evolved naturally from his office. In his case any aesthetic separation of the realms of the sublime and tragic on the one hand and of the everyday and real on the other is of course out of the question. A churchman, practically concerned with the life of men, cannot separate these realms. He encounters human tragedy every day in the mixed, random material of life.

To be sure, his talent and his temperament take this Bishop Gregory far beyond the realm of what is strictly concerned with his cure of souls and the practical problems of the Church. Half unconsciously he becomes a writer, a molder of things, laying hold of what is alive. Not every priest could have done that; yet at that period no one could have done it who was not a priest. Here lies the difference between the Christian and the original Roman conquest: the agents of Christianity do not simply organize an administration from above, leaving everything else to its natural development; they are duty bound to take an interest in the specific detail of everyday incidents; Christianization is directly concerned with and concerns the individual person and the individual event. It seems, furthermore, that Gregory was conscious of the significance and even of the specific character of his writings. For although he often apologizes for having the temerity to write despite his inadequate literary training (which is, by the way, a traditional rhetorical formula), he yet in one instance (9, 31) adds a solemn request to posterity not to alter his text in any way: *ut numquam libros hos aboleri faciatis aut rescribi, quasi quaedam eligentes et quaedam praetermittentes, sed ita omnia vobiscum integra inlibataque permaneant sicut a nobis relicta sunt.* And he makes the same point still more clearly in the following lines, which are an allusion to the rhetoric of the schools, whose further development in medieval Latin they seem to anticipate: "If you, priest of God, whoever you may be [so he addresses posterity] are so learned [here he enumerates every discipline and every branch of literary knowledge] that you find my style boorish [*ut tibi stilus noster sit rusticus*], I yet implore you, do not destroy what I have written." Today when Gregory, even as a stylist, seems to many of us more valuable than the majority of the most polished humanists, one cannot read such an apostrophe without emotion. In another passage he makes his mother appear to him in a dream and urge him to write, and then, when he objects that he is lacking in literary culture, answer him: *Et nescis, quia nobiscum propter intelligentiam populorum magis, sicut tu loqui potens es, habetur praeclarum?* (Do you not know that we hold the way you are able to write in higher esteem, because the people can understand it?) And so he falls to work courageously, to quench the thirst of the people: *sed quid timeo rusticitatem meam, cum dominus Redemptor et deus noster ad distruendam mundanae sapientiae vanitatem non oratores sed piscatores, nec philosophos sed rusticos praelegit?* (But why should I be ashamed of my lack of culture, if our Lord and Redeemer, to destroy the vanity of worldly wisdom, chose not orators but fishermen, not philosophers but peasants?) This entire passage, with the vision of his mother in a dream, does not occur in the *History of the Franks* but in the preface to the *Life of Saint Martin* and is directly related to the saint's miracles. But it can be applied without hesitation to everything Gregory ever wrote: in all his work he writes for general, immediate, sensory-concrete comprehension, in keeping with his talent, his temperament, and his office: *sicut tu loqui potens es.*

His style is wholly different from that of the authors of late antiquity, even the Christians among them. A complete change has taken place since the days of Ammianus and Augustine. Of course, as has often been observed, it is a decadence, a decline in culture and verbal disposition; but it is not only that. It is a reawakening of the directly sensible. Both style and treatment of content had become rigid in late antiquity. An excess of rhetorical devices, and the somber atmosphere which enveloped the events of the time, give the authors of late antiquity, from Tacitus and Seneca to Ammianus, a something that is labored, artificial, overstrained. With Gregory the rigidity is dissolved. He has many horrible things to relate; treason, violence, manslaughter are everyday occurrences; but the simple and practical vivacity with which he reports them prevents the formation of that oppressive atmosphere which we find in the late Roman writers and which even the Christian writers can hardly escape. When Gregory writes, the catastrophe has occurred, the Empire has fallen, its organization has collapsed, the culture of antiquity has been destroyed. But the tension is over. And it is more freely and directly, no longer haunted by insoluble tasks, no longer burdened by unrealizable pretensions, that Gregory's soul faces living reality, ready to apprehend it as such and to work in it practically. Let us look once again at the sentence with which Ammianus begins the narrative which we discussed in the preceding chapter: *Dum has exitiorum communium clades*, etc. Such a sentence surveys and masters a many-faceted situation, as well as supplying in addition a clear connection between what came first and what followed. But how labored it is and how rigid! Is it not a relief to turn from it to Gregory's beginning: *Gravia tunc inter Toronicos bella civilia surrexerunt . . . ?* To be sure, his *tunc* is only a loose and vague connective, and the language as a whole is unpolished, for *bella civilia* is certainly not the proper term for the disorderly brawls and thefts and killings which he has in mind. But things come to Gregory directly; he no longer needs to force them into the straitjacket of the elevated style; they grow or even run wild, no longer laced into the apparatus of the Diocletian-Constantinian reform, which brought only a new rule, being too late to bring a new life. Sensory reality, which, in Ammianus, where it was burdened by the fetters of tyrannical rules and the periodic style, could show itself only spectrally and metaphorically, can unfold freely in Gregory. A vestige of the old tyranny remains in his ambition to write literary Latin at all costs. The vernacular is not yet a usable literary vehicle; it obviously cannot yet satisfy the most modest requirements of literary expression. But it exists as a language which is spoken, which is used to deal with everyday reality, and as such it can be sensed through Gregory's Latin.

His style reveals to us a first early trace of the reawakening sensory apprehension of things and events, and this trace is all the more valuable to us because so few texts that can be used for our investigation have survived from his period and indeed from the entire second half of the first millennium.

5

ROLAND AGAINST GANELON

LVIII Tresvait la noit e apert la clere albe . . .
Par mi cel host (sonent menut cil graisle).
Li emperere mult fierement chevalchet.
"Seignurs barons," dist li emperere Carles,
"Veez les porz e les destreiz passages:
Kar me jugez ki ert en la rereguarde."
Guenes respunt: "Rollant, cist miens fillastre:
N'avez baron de si grant vasselage."
Quant l'ot li reis, fierement le reguardet,
Si li ad dit: "Vos estes vifs diables.
El cors vos est entree mortel rage.
E ki serat devant mei en l'ansguarde?"
Guenes respunt: "Oger de Denemarche:
N'avez baron ki mielz de lui la facet."

LIX Li quens Rollant, quant il s'oït juger,
Dunc ad parled a lei de chevaler:
"Sire parastre, mult vos dei aveir cher:
La rereguarde avez sur mei jugiet!
N'i perdrat Carles, li reis ki France tient,
Men escientre palefreid ne destrer,
Ne mul ne mule que deiet chevalcher,
Ne n'i perdrat ne runcin ne sumer
Que as espees ne seit einz eslegiet."
Guenes respunt: "Veir dites, jol sai bien."

LX Quant ot Rollant qu'il ert en la rereguarde,
Ireement parlat a sun parastre:
"Ahi! culvert, malvais hom de put aire,
Quias le guant me caïst en la place,
Cume fist a tei le bastun devant Carle?"

LXI "Dreiz emperere," dist Rollant le baron,
"Dunez mei l'arc que vos tenez el poign.

Men escientre nel me reproverunt
Que il me chedet cum fist a Guenelun
De sa main destre, quant reçut le bastun."
Li empereres en tint sun chef enbrunc,
Si duist sa barbe e detoerst sun gernun,
Ne poet muer que des oilz ne plurt.

LXII Anpres iço i est Neimes venud,
Meillor vassal n'out en la curt de lui,
E dist al rei: "Ben l'avez entendut;
Li quens Rollant, il est mult irascut.
La rereguarde est jugee sur lui:
N'avez baron ki jamais la remut.
Dunez li l'arc que vos avez tendut,
Si li truvez ki trés bien li aiut!"
Li reis li dunet e Rollant l'a reçut.

(LVIII 737 Night goes and bright dawn appears . . .
. . . .
Proudly the Emperor rides on horseback.
"Lords Barons," says Emperor Charles,
"See those gaps and those narrow passages;
Now decide for me who shall be in the rearguard."
Ganelon answers: "Roland, my stepson:
You have no baron of such great prowess."
When the King hears this, he looks at him fiercely,
And thus he spoke to him: "You are a living devil.
Into your body mortal rage has entered.
And who will be before me in the vanguard?"
Ganelon answers: "Ogier the Dane:
You have no baron who would do it better than he."

LIX Count Roland, when he hears himself chosen,
Then spoke as befits a knight:
"Sir stepfather, I must hold you very dear:
The rearguard you have adjudged to me!
Thereby shall Charles, the king who holds France, lose,
If I know rightly, neither palfrey nor charger,

Neither mule nor hinny which he is to ride,
Nor shall he lose thereby either hack or sumpter
Which has not first been fought for with sword."
Ganelon answers: "You speak true, I know it well."

LX When Roland hears that he will be in the rearguard,
Angrily he spoke to his stepfather:
"Ah! wretch, bad man of stinking birth,
Did you think the glove would drop from my hand in this place
As the staff did for you before Charles?"

LXI "Just Emperor," said Roland the baron,
"Give me the bow which you hold in your clenched hand.
If I know rightly, none shall reproach me
That it dropped from my hand as it did for Ganelon,
From his right hand, when he received the staff."
The Emperor kept his head bowed,
Stroked his beard and twisted his mustache,
He cannot keep his eyes from weeping.

LXII After this Naimes came there,
There was no better vassal than he at court,
And he said to the King: "Well have you heard it;
Count Roland, he is very angry.
The rearguard is allotted to him:
You have no baron who could (would?) change this.
Give him the bow which you have drawn,
And find him some to help him very well!"
The King gives it to him, and Roland received it.)

These lines are from the Oxford manuscript of the *Chanson de Roland*. They relate the appointment of Roland to a dangerous post, that of commander of the rearguard of the Frankish army, which is on its way back through the Pyrenees after the campaign in Spain. The choice is made at the suggestion of Roland's stepfather Ganelon. The manner of it corresponds to an earlier episode, the choice of Ganelon for the post of Charles's emissary to Marsilius, King of the Saracens, at the suggestion of Roland (ll. 274ff.). Both occurrences are rooted in an old enmity between the two barons, who are at odds over matters of money and property and seek to destroy one another (l. 3758). Any emissary to Marsilius, it was known from earlier experiences, was in great danger of losing his life. The events of Ganelon's mission showed that it would have cost him too his life, if he had not proposed to the Saracen King the treacherous bargain which at the same time would satisfy his own hatred and thirst for revenge: he promises the King that he will deliver into his hands the rearguard of the Frankish army, with Roland and his twelve closest friends, the douzepers, whom he represents (rightly) to be the war party at the Frankish court. He has now come back to the Frankish camp with Marsilius' insincere offer of peace and submission. The return of the army to France has begun. And Ganelon, to carry out the plan he has agreed upon with Marsilius, still has to arrange that Roland shall be appointed to the rearguard. This takes place in the lines quoted above.

The occurrence is related in five strophes (*laisses*). The first contains Ganelon's proposal and Charles's immediate reaction. The second, third, and fourth are concerned with Roland's attitude toward the proposal. The fifth takes up Naimes's intervention and the final appointment of Roland by the Emperor. The first laisse begins with an introduction of three lines, three paratactically juxtaposed principal clauses which describe the early-morning departure of the army (the subject immediately preceding was the past night and a dream of the Emperor's). Next comes the scene of the proposal, which is given in the form of a double exchange of speech and rejoinder: demand that a choice be made, reply (with proposal), counterquestion, and counterreply. Both pairs of speeches are fitted into the simplest stereotyped frame (*dist, respunt, dit, respunt*). After the first pair, they are interrupted by line 745, the only one containing a brief temporal hypotaxis. Everything else is in the form of principal clauses, juxtaposed and opposed like blocks, with a paratactic independence still further emphasized by mention of the speaking subject each time (especially striking, 740, *li emperere Carles*, although he is also the subject of the preceding sentence). Let us now examine the individual speeches. Charles's demand contains a causal train of reasoning: since we are to traverse a difficult terrain, choose for me. . . . But in keeping with the Emperor's proudly confident demeanor (*mult fierement*), it is presented paratactically in two principal clauses, a demonstrative clause (see the difficult terrain) and an imperative clause. In answer —like a gauntlet flung down—comes Ganelon's proposal, again a parataxis, with three members: first the name, then a reference, filled with triumphant revenge, to the kinship (*cist miens fillastre,* as a reminiscence of the corresponding *mis parastre,* l. 277, and l. 287, *ço set hom ben que jo sui tis parastres*), and finally the supporting argument with its conventional praise, no doubt uttered in a tone of scornful irony. After this we have the brief dramatic pause with Charles's fierce look. His reply—likewise purely paratactic in form—begins with violent expressions which show that he sees through Ganelon's plan, but also, as is later confirmed by Naimes, that he has in his power no effective means of rejecting the proposal. Perhaps we may interpret his concluding question as a sort of counterattack: I need Roland for the vanguard! If this interpretation is correct, Ganelon at any rate disposes of the counterattack at once, and the identity of structure between his second speech and his first emphasizes the slashing abruptness of his demeanor. His position is apparently very strong, and he is quite certain of victory. In syntax too, this laisse answers blow with blow.

To this keenness and finality of statement there is a certain contrast in the fact that many things in the scene are not particularly clear. We can hardly be expected to assume that the Emperor is bound by the proposal of a single one of his barons. In fact, in similar cases elsewhere (for example in the previous case of Ganelon's appointment, ll. 278-9 and 321-2; see also l. 243), explicit mention is made of the assent of the entire army. It may be conjectured that in the present instance the same assent is given without its being mentioned, or that the Emperor knows that there can be no doubt that it would be given. But even so, even if our text conceals a portion of the tradition—the fact that Roland has enemies among the Franks, who would be glad to see him given a dangerous assignment and removed from the Emperor's entourage, possibly for fear his influence might reverse the decision to end the war—even so it is puzzling that the Emperor should have failed to make arrangements beforehand for a solution agreeable to him, so that his call for a choice puts him in a position from which he knows no escape. He must after all be aware of what currents of thought prevail among his men, and in addition he has been warned by a dream. This connects with another enigma: how well does he see through Ganelon, how well does he know beforehand what is going to happen? We cannot assume that he is informed of Ganelon's plan in all its details. But if he is not, his reaction to the proposal (*vos estes vifs diables,* etc.) seems exaggerated. The Emperor's entire position is unclear; and despite all the authoritative definiteness which he manifests from time to time, he seems as it were somnambulistically paralyzed. The important and symbolic position—almost that of a Prince of God—in which he appears as the head of all Christendom and as the paragon of knightly perfection, is in strange contrast to his impotence. Although he hesitates, although he even sheds tears, although he foresees the impending disaster to some not clearly definable extent, he cannot prevent it. He is dependent upon his barons, and among them there is none who can change the situation at all (or should we say, who will? That depends on how we interpret line 779). In the same way, later on, at Ganelon's trial, he would be obliged to leave his nephew Roland's death unavenged were it not that, finally, a single knight is prepared to defend his cause. It is possible to find various explanations for all this: for example, the weakness of the central power in the feudal order of society, a weakness which, though it had hardly developed by Charlemagne's time, was certainly prevalent later, at the time when the *Chanson de Roland* originated; then, too, semireligious, semilegendary concepts of the kind found with many royal figures in the courtly romance, concepts which, to the personification of the great Emperor, add an admixture of passive, martyrlike, and somnambulistically paralyzed traits. Furthermore, his relation to Ganelon seems to contain elements of the Christ-Judas pattern.

The poem itself in any case gives no analyses or explanations whatever of the mysterious aspects of this and other events. We have to contribute them ourselves, and they rather detract from our aesthetic appreciation. The poet explains nothing; and yet the things which happen are stated with a paratactic bluntness which says that everything must happen as it does happen, it could not be otherwise, and there is no need for explanatory connectives. This, as the reader knows, refers not only to the events but also to the views and principles which form the basis of the actions of the persons concerned. The knightly will to fight, the concept of honor, the mutual loyalty of brothers in arms, the community of the clan, the Christian dogma, the allocation of right and wrong to Christians and infidels, are probably the most important of these views. They are few in number. They give a narrow picture in which only one stratum of society appears, and even that stratum in a greatly simplified form. They are posited without argument as pure theses: these are the facts. No argument, no explanatory discussion whatever is called for when, for example, the statement is made: *paien unt tort et chrestiens unt dreit* (l. 1015: heathens are wrong and Christians are right), although the life of the infidel knights

—except for the names of their gods—seems hardly different from that of the Christians. Often, it is true, they are referred to as depraved and horrible, at times in fantastic and symbolic ways, but they are knights too, and the structure of their society seems to be exactly the same as that of Christian society. The parallel extends to minor details and thus serves to render the narrowness of the representation of life still more striking. The Christianity of the Christians is simply a stipulation. It exhausts itself in the creed and the liturgic formulas that go with it. Furthermore it is, in a very extreme sense, made to serve the knightly will to fight and political expansion. The penance laid upon the Franks when they pray and receive absolution before going into battle is to fight hard; whoever falls in the fight is a martyr and can surely expect a place in Paradise. Conversions by force which involve the killing of those who offer resistance are works with which God is well pleased. This attitude, astonishing as a Christian attitude and non-existent as such in earlier times, is not based, here in the *Chanson de Roland*, on a given historical situation, as it was in Spain, whence it would seem to have stemmed. Nor is any other explanation of it given. That is the way it is—a paratactic situation made up of theses which, extremely narrow as they are, are yet full of contradictions.

Let us go on to the second part of the scene—Roland's reaction. It is the theme of three laisses. In the first two Roland addresses Ganelon, in the third the Emperor. His speeches contain three motifs of various strength and variously crossed: (1) a tremendously assertive and ferocious pride, (2) hatred for Ganelon, and (3), much weaker, devotion to the Emperor and the desire to serve him. (1) and (2) are crossed in such a way that (1) appears first, with great force, but even here is already imbued with (2) and (3). Roland loves danger and seeks it; he cannot be frightened. Furthermore he sets great value upon his prestige. He refuses to grant Ganelon the briefest moment of triumph. And so his first consideration is to point out emphatically, for all to hear, that he, unlike Ganelon in a comparable situation, has not lost his composure. Hence his expression of gratitude to Ganelon, which in view of the enmity between them—well known to all present—can have only an effect of irony and scorn. Hence too the enumeration of the various mounts and beasts of burden not one of which will he abandon without fight—a powerful, demonstrative, and very successful assertion of his pride and courage which even Ganelon is obliged to recognize, although in doing so he may well have his own thoughts in the back of his mind, for it is precisely Roland's intrepid self-confidence on which he relies in his plan to destroy him. But in any case, Ganelon's momentary triumph is spoiled. For, once Roland has made his attitude sufficiently known, he can give the reins to his hatred and contempt, which now assume the form of a scornful triumph on his part: you see, you scoundrel, I do not conduct myself as you did that time; and even when he stands before Charles to receive the bow, his expression of ready obedience, formulated so as to reveal impatience, is once again interspersed with his scornful and triumphant comparison between his behavior and Ganelon's.

The whole scene—Roland's display of self-confidence, followed by his sustained, repetitive, and triumphant outburst of hatred and scorn—is spread out over three laisses, and since the first two are addressed to Ganelon, with very similar opening phrases, distinguished only by the adverbial modifiers—the first time *a lei de chevaler*, the second time *ireement*—since furthermore a superficial and purely rational examination seems to show their contents to be incongruous—the first appearing friendly and the second angry—numerous editors and critics have doubted the authenticity of the text and have cut out one of the two laisses, usually the second. That this cannot be right was pointed out by Bédier in his commentary (Paris, Piazza, 1927, p. 151), and this—as the foregoing analysis may serve to indicate—is my view too. The second laisse presupposes the first. The attitude revealed in the first laisse, which stands in sharp contrast to Ganelon's attitude in that earlier scene, supplies the justification for the triumphant hatred of the second. I should like to corroborate this result by another, a stylistic, consideration. This kind of repeated resumption of the same situation in consecutive laisses, in a manner which at first leaves the reader in doubt as to whether he is confronted with a new scene or a complementary treatment of the first, is very frequent in the *Chanson de Roland* (as well as elsewhere in the *chansons de geste*). There are other instances where such resumptions occasion surprising shifts, as is the case in the passage here under discussion. In laisses 40, 41, and 42, the question which King Marsilius repeats three times in almost identical terms—i.e., when will Charles, who after all is getting on in years, tire of war—is answered by Ganelon in three different ways, of which the first gives not the least inkling of what the others will be. In his first answer Ganelon speaks exclusively in praise of Charles, and it is only in the second and third that he names Roland and his companions as warmongers, thus taking his first step toward treason;

in the following laisse, 43, he at last speaks plainly, and Charles is no longer referred to in friendly terms. Even before this, Ganelon's attitude in Marsilius' presence is not to be understood in purely rational terms. He displays such hostility and haughtiness that his purpose seems to be to irritate the king at all costs, and negotiation and treason appear to be out of the question. In other instances (laisses 5 and 6, 79 to 81, 83 to 86, 129 and 130, 133 to 135, 137 to 139, 146 and 147, etc.) there is no real contradiction between the content of one laisse and that of another, but here too one and the same point of departure is frequently used to push ahead in different directions or over different distances. When in laisse 80 Oliver climbs to the top of a hill and from there sees the approaching Saracen army, he summons Roland and talks to him of Ganelon's treason. In laisse 81, which also begins with Oliver's climbing the hill, no mention is made of Roland, but Oliver comes down as quickly as possible to report back to the Franks. In laisses 83 to 85, where Oliver thrice asks Roland to blow his horn and thrice receives the same negative reply, the function of the repetition is to make the scene more intense; as, in the *Chanson de Roland* generally, both the urgent-intense and the manifold-simultaneous are represented by the repetition and addition of many, and frequently of artfully varied, individual occurrences. The series of knights who assume a place in the action, as well as the series of battle scenes, are instances of this procedure. Laisses 129 to 131, where Roland himself proposes to blow his horn (prepared in laisse 128 and extremely artful in the expression of Roland's self-conscious regret), correspond to the earlier scene although the actors have exchanged roles. This time it is Oliver who thrice replies in the negative. His three answers are constructed with considerable psychological finesse. The first, with concealed irony, repeats Roland's own counterarguments but suddenly changes to a spontaneous outburst of sympathy (or admiration) at the sight of Roland's blood-stained arms. The second again begins ironically, and concludes in an outburst of anger. It is not until we reach the third that we have Oliver's reproaches and his grief formulated in an orderly manner. In the three laisses of the horn signal—133 to 135, presumably involving a threefold blowing of the horn—the effect which the horn produces upon the Franks is developed differently each time. Taken together, to be sure, the three effects represent a development too, that is, from surprise and confusion to a complete realization of the state of affairs (which Ganelon endeavors to prevent), but this development is not evenly progressive but spastic, now gaining, now losing ground, like generation or birth.

Varied repetition of the same theme is a technique stemming from medieval Latin poetics, which in turn draws it from antique rhetoric. This fact has recently been pointed out once again by Faral and E. R. Curtius. But neither the form nor the stylistic effect of the "regressions" in the *Chanson de Roland* can thus be explained or even described. It would seem that the series of similar events and the resumption of previous statements are phenomena related in character to the parataxis of sentence structure. Whether one comprehensive representation is replaced by a reiterative enumeration of individual scenes similar in form and progress; whether one intense action is replaced by a repetition of the same action, beginning at the same starting point time and again; or whether finally, instead of a process of complex and periodic development, we have repeated returns to the starting point, each one proceeding to elaborate a different element or motif: in all cases rationally organized condensations are avoided in favor of a halting, spasmodic, juxtapositive, and pro- and retrogressive method in which causal, modal, and even temporal relations are obscured. (In the very first laisse of the poem, the last line, *nes poet guarder que mals ne l'i ateignet*, looks very far into the future.) Time and again there is a new start; every resumption is complete in itself and independent; the next is simply juxtaposed to it, and the relation between the two is often left hanging. This too is a type of epic retardation in Goethe's and Schiller's sense (cf. above, pp. 4f.), but it is not managed through interpolations and episodes but through progression and retrogression within the principal action itself. This procedure is very markedly epic; it is even recitationally epic, for a listener arriving in the course of the recitation receives a coherent impression. At the same time it is a technique of subdividing the course of events into numerous rigid little divisions, mutually delimited by the use of stereotyped phrases.

Roland's three speeches are not as brief as the Emperor's and Ganelon's in the first laisse, but they too have no periodic flow. The long sentence of laisse 59 is merely an enumeration with repeated breaks. In all three laisses the subordinate clauses are of the simplest type; they are independent to a very high degree. Anything like flow of discourse does not arise. The rhythm of the *Chanson de Roland* is never flowing, as is that of the antique epic. Every line marks a new start, every stanza represents a new approach. This impression, already produced by the prevailing parataxis, is increased by the generally clumsy and ungrammatical handling of connections whenever a rare attempt is made to use somewhat more complex hypotaxes. Another factor is the assonant strophic pattern, which gives every line the appearance of an independent unit while the entire strophe appears to be a bundle of independent parts, as though sticks or spears of equal length and with similar points were bundled together. Consider for example Ganelon's speech in support of accepting Marsilius' offer of peace (ll. 220ff.), which contains a long sentence:

> Quant ço vos mandet li reis Marsiliun
> Qu'il devendrat jointes ses mains tis hum
> E tute Espaigne tendrat par vostre dun,
> Puis recevrat la lei que nus tenum,
> Ki ço vos lodet que cest plait degetuns,
> Ne li chalt, sire, de quel mort nus muriuns.

(If this is the message King Marsilius sends, that he will become—his hands folded—your vassal, and will hold all of Spain in fief to you, then will take the faith which we hold, he who recommends to you that we reject this proposal, to him it does not matter, Sire, what kind of death we die.)

The principal clause (*ne li chalt* . . .) comes at the end. But the beginning of the period does not consider what the pattern of the main clause is going to be and consequently—after the content of Marsilius' message has been stated—a shift in construction proves necessary. The *quant*-clause with its subordinate statements of the content (*que* . . . *e* . . . *puis* . . .)—which itself loses sight of its structure before it is half finished (*puis recevrat* . . . already begins breaking away from the anchorage in *que*)—remains an anacoluthon, and the emphatically anticipated *ki*-clause starts a new pattern. But in addition to this type of sentence structure, which is hypotactic in external appearance but in reality quite paratactic, there is also the subdivision in meaning according to the individual lines, the sharp incisions marked by the assonance in *u*, and the somewhat less emphatic but clearly noticeable caesuras in the middle of the line, which in all cases indicate units of meaning as well. No indeed—periodicity and flow of discourse are not among the characteristics of this style. It is admirably homogeneous, for the attitudes of the personages are so strongly molded and limited by the narrow range of the established order in which they move, that their thoughts, feelings, and passions can find room in such lines. The copious and connected argumentation of which Homer's heroes are so fond is wholly outside of their ken; and by the same token they are without any free-flowing, dynamic, and impulsive movement in expression. The words which the Emperor Charles utters when he hears the call of the horn (ll. 1768-9),

> Ce dist li reis: "Jo oi le corn Rollant.
> Unc nel sunast se ne fust cumbatant"

(This said the King: "I hear Roland's horn. Never would he sound it if he were not fighting.")

have often been compared with the corresponding lines in Vigny's poem "Le Cor,"

> Malheur! C'est mon neveu! malheur! car si Roland
> Appelle à son secours, ce doit être en mourant,

which is extremely informative in the present connection. But it is not necessary to adduce a romantic parallel; the same purpose can be served by classical and later European texts from periods preceding Romanticism. Consider Roland's death prayer (ll. 2384ff.) or the formally quite similar prayer uttered by the Emperor before the battle against Baligant (ll. 3100ff.). These follow liturgical models and consequently display a comparatively prolonged sweep in their syntax. Roland's prayer reads:

> 2384 Veire Paterne, ki unkes ne mentis,
> Seint Lazaron de mort resurrexis
> E Daniel des leons guaresis,
> Guaris de mei l'anme de tuz perilz
> Pur les pecchez que en ma vie fis!

(True Father, who never lied, who resurrected Saint Lazarus from the dead, and saved Daniel from the lions, save my soul from all dangers on account of the sins which I committed in my life!)

and the Emperor's:

> 3100 Veire Paterne, hoi cest jor me defend,
> Ki guaresis Jonas tut veirement
> De la baleine ki en sun cors l'aveit,
> E esparignas le rei de Niniven
> E Daniel del merveillus turment

Enz en la fosse des leons o fut enz,
Les .III. enfanz tut en un fou ardant!
La tue amurs me seit hoi en present!
Par ta mercit, se te plaist, me cunsent
Que mun nevold poisse venger Rollant!

(True Father, help me now on this day, Thou who didst Jonas truly save from the whale which had him in its belly, and spared the King of Nineveh, and Daniel from the terrible torture in the lions' den wherein he was, and the three men from the burning oven: let Thy love be with me today. Through Thy mercy, if it please Thee, grant me that I may avenge my nephew Roland.)

In this rigidly stereotyped use of the figures of redemption (figures which, as the literature of mysticism shows, can be employed in a very differently dynamic fashion), as well as in the almost static and reiterative manner of the apostrophizing supplication, there is, to be sure, a strong element of emotion, but there is also the narrow definitiveness of a spatially limited and perfectly unambiguous view of God, the universe, and fate. If we confront this with any prayer from the *Iliad*—I choose at random 305ff.,

πότνι' Ἀθηναίη ἐρυσίπτολι, δῖα θεάων,
ἆξον δὴ ἔγχος Διομήδεος ἠδὲ καὶ αὐτὸν
πρηνέα δὸς πεσέειν Σκαιῶν προπάροιθε πυλάων

(Mighty Athena, protectress of the city, sublime goddess, turn Diomedes' lance and make him fall headlong before the Skaean gates!)

with a violent upsurge in the movement of imploration (*ἠδὲ καὶ αὐτὸν πρηνέα δὸς πεσέειν*)—we discover how much greater possibilities for freely flowing, urgent, and imploring movements are to be found in Homer, and that his world, though certainly limited, yet has a much less rigid structure. The significant feature here is obviously not the run-on lines (which are frequent in antique versification) but the broad sweep of the richly nuanced sentence movement. This can equally well be displayed in rhymed verse without enjambment, whether the lines are short or long. And it appears quite early in Old French, as early as the twelfth century, in the octosyllabic rhymes of courtly romance or in shorter rhymed tales. If one compares the octosyllabic line of an old heroic epic, the fragment of *Gormund et Isembard*, which sounds like a series of detached and sharply marked bugle calls (*criant l'enseigne al rei baron,/ la Loovis, le fiz Charlun*), with the fluent, sometimes verbose, sometimes lyrical octosyllabic line of the courtly romance, one will quickly grasp the difference between rigid and fluent-connective syntax. And very soon indeed widely sweeping rhetorical movement appears in the courtly style. The following lines are from the *Folie Tristan* (after Bartsch, *Chrestomathie de l'ancien Français*, 12ᵉ éd., pièce 24):

> 31 en ki me purreie fier,
> quant Ysolt ne me deingne amer,
> quant Ysolt a si vil me tient
> k'ore de mei ne li suvient?

(In whom can I have confidence, if Ysolt deigns not to love me, if Ysolt considers me so despicable that she does not now remember me?)

This is an urgent movement of grief in the form of a rhetorical question with two similarly constructed subordinate clauses of which the second is broader in scope, while the whole passage displays ascending rhythm. In pattern, it is reminiscent of, though much simpler than, the famous lines in Racine's *Bérénice* (4, 5):

> Dans un mois, dans un an, comment souffrirons-nous,
> Seigneur, que tant de mers me séparent de vous:
> Que le jour recommence et que le jour finisse,
> Sans que jamais Titus puisse voir Bérénice,
> Sans que, de tout le jour, je puisse voir Titus?

Let us briefly complete the analysis of our text. At the end of laisse 61 the Emperor still hesitates to hand the bow to Roland, who stands before him, and thus definitely to give him the order. He bows his head, he strokes his beard, he weeps. The intervention of Naimes, which concludes the scene, is again entirely paratactic in structure. The modal connections implied in his remarks are not grammatically expressed. Otherwise the passage would have to read: "You have heard how angry Roland is because his name has been suggested for the rearguard. But since there is no baron who could (or: would?) fill his place, give him the bow, but at least make certain that his support is strong enough." The beautiful concluding line is also paratactic.

In the classical languages paratactic constructions belong to the low style; they are oral rather than written, comic and realistic rather than elevated. But here parataxis belongs to the elevated style. This is a new form of the elevated style, not dependent on periodic structure and rhetorical figures but on the power of juxtaposed and independent verbal blocks. An elevated style operating with paratactic elements is not, in itself, something new in Europe. The style of the Bible has this characteristic (cf. our first chapter). Here we may recall the discussion concerning the sublime character of the sentence *dixitque Deus: fiat lux, et facta est lux* (Genesis 1: 3) which Boileau and Huet carried on in the seventeenth century in connection with the essay *On the Sublime* attributed to Longinus. The sublime in this sentence from Genesis is not contained in a magnificent display of rolling periods nor in the splendor of abundant figures of speech but in the impressive brevity which is in such contrast to the immense content and which for that very reason has a note of obscurity which fills the listener with a shuddering awe. It is precisely the absence of causal connectives, the naked statement of what happens—the statement which replaces deduction and comprehension by an amazed beholding that does not even seek to comprehend—which gives the sentence its grandeur. But the case of the *chanson de geste* is completely different. The subject here is not the awesome riddle of creation and the Creator, not the creature man's relationship to one and the other. The subject of the *Chanson de Roland* is narrow, and for the men who figure in it nothing of fundamental significance is problematic. All the categories of this life and the next are unambiguous, immutable, fixed in rigid formulations. To be sure, rational comprehension has no direct access to them, but that is an observation which we ourselves make; the poem and its contemporary audience felt no such concern. They live safely and confidently in the rigid and narrow established order within which the duties of life, their distribution according to estates (cf. the division of labor between knights and monks, ll. 1877ff.), the character of supernatural forces, and mankind's relationship thereto are regulated in the simplest way. Within this frame there are abundant and delicate emotions; there is also a certain motley variegation in external phenomena; but the frame is so restricted and rigid that properly problematic situations, let alone tragedy, can hardly arise. There are no conflicts which deserve to be called tragic.

The early Germanic epic texts which have come down to us also exhibit paratactic construction; here too the warrior ethics of a nobility dominates, with its strict definitions of honor, justice, and ordeal by battle. And yet the final impression is quite different. The verbal blocks are more loosely juxtaposed, the space about the occurrences and the heaven above them are incomparably wider, destiny is more enigmatic, and the structure of society is not so rigidly established. The mere fact that the most famous Germanic epics, from the *Hildebrandslied* to the *Nibelungenlied*, derive their historical setting from the wild and spacious epoch of the tribal migrations rather than from the solidly established structure of the age of feudalism, gives them greater breadth and freedom. The Germanic themes of the age of the migrations did not reach Gallo-Roman territory, or at least they could not strike root there. And Christianity has almost no significance at all for the Germanic heroic epic. Free and immediate forces, still unsubdued by settled forms, are stronger in it, and the human roots—so at least it seems to me—go deeper. We cannot say of the Germanic poems of the heroic epic cycle, as we said of the *Chanson de Roland*, that the problematic and tragic element is lacking in them. Hildebrand is more directly human and tragic than Roland, and how much more deeply motivated are the conflicts in the *Nibelungenlied* than the hatred between Roland and Ganelon!

Yet we do encounter the same restricted and definitely established cosmos when we take up an early Romance religious text. We have several of these which precede the *Chanson de Roland* chronologically. The most important is the *Chanson d'Alexis*, a saint's legend, which crystallized in the eleventh century in an Old French form still extant in several manuscripts. According to the legend, Alexius was the late-born only son of a noble Roman family. He was carefully educated, entered the emperor's service, and in accordance with his father's wishes was to marry a virgin of equal rank. He obeyed, but on the bridal night he left his wife without having touched her and lived for seventeen years as a poor beggar in a strange land (Edessa in northeastern Syria, the modern Turkish Urfa), that he might serve only God. Leaving his refuge to escape being revered as a saint, he was driven back to Rome by a storm. There he passed another seventeen years, still unrecognized and living as a despised beggar under the steps of his father's house, unmoved by the sorrow of his parents and his wife, whose laments he often heard without revealing his identity. Not until after his death was he finally and miraculously recognized and thenceforth revered as a saint. The attitudes reflected in this text are different entirely from those of the *Chanson de Roland*. But it exhibits the same paratactic and rigid style, the same narrowness, indisputability, and fixity of all categories. Everything is settled, white or black, good or bad, and never requires further search or justification. Temptation is there, to be sure, but there is no realm of problem. On the one hand there is serving God, forsaking the world and seeking eternal bliss—on the other, natural life in the world, which leads to "great sorrow." There are no other levels of consciousness, and external reality—the many additional phenomena which have their place in the universe and which ought somehow to constitute the frame for the occurrences of the narrative—is submitted to such reduction that nothing survives but an insubstantial background for the life of the saint. About him are grouped, accompanying his activities with appropriate pantomime, his father, mother, and bride. A few other characters required by the action appear, but they are even more shadowy. Everything else is completely schematized, both sociologically and geographically speaking. This is the more surprising since the scene seems to embrace the extent and variety of the entire Roman Empire. Nothing remains of West and East but churches, voices from on high, praying multitudes—nothing but the ever identical environment of the life of a saint; even as in the *Chanson de Roland*, the same social structure—that of feudalism—and the same ethos is dominant throughout, among both pagans and Christians. But here this is much more pronounced. The world has become very small and narrow; and in it everything revolves rigidly and immutably about a single question, which has been answered in advance and which it is man's duty to answer rightly. He knows what road he must follow, or better, there is but one road open to him, there is no other. He knows too that he will reach a fork in the road, and that then he must turn right although the tempter will try to entice him to turn left. Everything else has vanished, the whole sweeping infinity of the outer and inner worlds, with its innumerable possibilities, configurations, and strata.

This, without doubt, is not Germanic; nor is it, I believe, Christian; at least it is not the necessary and original version of Christianity. For Christianity, the product of a variety of premises, and coming to grips with a variety of realities, has proved itself—before and after this period—incomparably more elastic, more rich, and more complexly stratified. This narrowness can hardly be original at all; it contains too many and too various inherited elements for that; it is not narrowness, it is a narrowing process. It is the process of rigidification and reduction which late antiquity underwent and which has figured in our earlier chapters. To be sure, a significant part is played in it by the simplified reduced form which Christianity assumed in its clash with exhausted or barbaric peoples.

In the Old French *Chanson d'Alexis* the scene of the bridal night, which is one of the high points of the poem, reads as follows (stanzas 11 to 15, text after Bartsch, *Chrestomathie*, 12ᵉ éd.):

11 Quant li jorz passet ed il fut anoitiet,
ço dist li pedre: "filz, quer t'en va colchier,
avuec ta spouse, al comant Deu del ciel."
ne volst li enfes son pedre corrocier,
vait en la chambre o sa gentil moillier.

12 Com vit le lit, esguardat la pulcele,
donc li remembret de son seignour celeste
que plus ad chier que tote rien terrestre;
"e! Deus," dist il, "si forz pechiez m'apresset!
s'or ne m'en fui, molt criem que ne t'en perde."

13 Quant en la chambre furent tuit soul remes,
danz Alexis la prist ad apeler:
la mortel vide li prist molt a blasmer,
de la celeste li mostrat veritet;
mais lui ert tart qued il s'en fust tornez.

14 "Oz mei, pulcele, celui tien ad espous
Qui nos redemst de son sanc precious.
en icest siecle nen at parfite amour:
la vide est fraile, n'i at durable onour;
ceste ledece revert a grant tristour."

15 Quant sa raison li at tote mostrede,
donc li comandet les renges de sa spede,
ed un anel dont il l'out esposede.
donc en ist fors de la chambre son pedre;
en mie nuit s'en fuit de la contrede.

(When the day was passed and night had come, thus spake his father: "Son, now go to bed, with your spouse, as the God of Heaven commands." The son did not want to anger his father; he goes into the chamber with his gentle wife.

When he saw the bed, he looked at the maiden, then he remembers his Heavenly Lord whom he holds more dear than any earthly thing; "Ah, God!" said he, "how strongly sin presses upon me! If I flee not now, much I fear that I shall thereby lose Thee."

When they were left all alone in the chamber, Master Alexis began to speak to her: mortal life he began to chide to her, of heavenly life he showed her the truth; but much he wished that he were gone from there.

"Hear me, maiden, take Him for spouse who redeemed us with his precious blood. In this world there is no perfect love: life is frail, there is no lasting honor in it; this joy becomes great sorrow."

When he had set forth all his mind to her, he gives her the thong of his sword and a ring with which he had married her. Then he went out of the chamber in his father's house; in the middle of the night he fled from the country.)

However different the tenor of the two poems may be, the stylistic resemblance to the *Chanson de Roland* is very striking. In both, the paratactic principle goes far beyond mere technique of sentence structure. In both we have the same repeated returning to fresh starts, the same spasmodic progression and retrogression, the same independence of the individual occurrences and their constituent parts. Stanza 13 recapitulates the situation at the beginning of stanza 12, but carries the action further and in a different direction. Stanza 14 repeats, concretely and in direct discourse, the statement made in stanza 13 (of which, however, the last line had already gone further). Instead of the construction, "When they were alone in the room, he remembered . . . , and said 'Listen . . . ' ", we have the following arrangement: 1. "When he was in the room, he remembered . . ." 2. "When they were in the room, he said that . . . ." (indirect discourse) 3. "Listen, (he said) . . ." Each of the stanzas presents a complete and autonomous scene. The impression of a unified, progressive event whose advance binds together the various elements is much weaker than the impression of a juxtaposition of three very similar but separate scenes. One may generalize on the basis of this impression: the *Chanson d'Alexis* is a string of autonomous, loosely interrelated events, a series of mutually quite independent scenes from the life of a saint, each of which contains an expressive yet simple gesture. The father ordering Alexis to join his bride in the chamber; Alexis at the bedside, speaking to his bride; Alexis at Edessa distributing his worldly goods to the poor; Alexis the beggar; the servants sent out after him but failing to recognize him and giving him an alms; the mother's lament; the conversation between mother and bride; and so forth. It is a cycle of scenes. Each one of these occurrences contains one decisive gesture with only a loose temporal or causal connection with those that follow or precede. Many of them (the mother's lament, for example) are subdivided into several similar and individually independent pictures. Every picture has as it were a frame of its own. Each stands by itself in the sense that nothing new or unexpected happens in it and that it contains no propulsive force which demands the next. And the intervals are empty. But it is with no dark and profound emptiness, in which much befalls and much is prepared, in which we hold our breath in trembling expectation, the emptiness sometimes conjured up in the style of the Bible, with its intervals which make us ponder. Instead, it is a colorless duration without relief or substance, sometimes only a moment, sometimes seventeen years, sometimes wholly indefinable.

The course of events is thus resolved into a series of pictures; it is, as it were, parceled out. The *Chanson de Roland* taken as a whole is more compressed; the coherence is clearer; the individual picture sometimes displays more movement. But the representational technique (and this means more than mere technical procedure, it includes the idea of structure which poet and audience apply to the narrated event) is still exactly the same: it strings independent pictures together like beads. The intervals in the *Chanson de Roland* are not always so very empty and flat; landscape sometimes intrudes; we see or hear armies riding through valleys and mountain passes—yet the occurrences are still strung together in such a fashion that, time and again, completely independent and self-contained scenes result. The number of the characters who maintain the action is very small in the *Chanson de Roland* too; all the others—although they are far more varied than in the Alexis—seem mere types. Those participating in the action of the individual scenes are fixed to the spot; it is but rarely that a newcomer joins their number; and when that occurs (Naimes or Turpin acting as mediators), there is a sharp break. The variously altering relationship between a large number of persons, with the consequent involvements and element of adventure so characteristic of epic elsewhere, is here completely lacking. So much the stronger is the element of impressive gestures, both in the Alexis and the Roland. The urge to establish connections and pursue developments is feeble. Even within an individual scene, the development, if any, is halting and laborious.

But the gestures of the scenic moment are simply and plastically impressive in the highest degree.

This impressiveness of gestures and attitudes is obviously the purpose of the technique under consideration when it divides the course of events into a mosaic of parceled pictures. The scenic moment with its gestures is given such power that it assumes the stature of a moral model. The various phases of the story of the hero or the traitor or the saint are concretized in gestures to such an extent that the pictured scenes, in the impression they produce, closely approach the character of symbols or figures, even in cases where it is not possible to trace any symbolic or figural signification. But very often such a signification can be traced: in the *Chanson de Roland* it is present in the person of Charlemagne, in the description of many characteristics of the pagan knights, and of course in the prayers. As for the *Chanson d'Alexis*, E. R. Curtius' excellent interpretation (*Zeitschrift für romanische Philologie*, 56, 113ff., especially pp. 122 and 124) conclusively supports the idea of a figural fulfillment in the beyond. This figural tradition played no small part in discrediting the horizontal, historical connections between events and in encouraging rigidification of all categories. Thus the prayers cited above exhibit the figures of redemption completely rigidified. The parceling of the events of the Old Testament, which are interpreted figurally in isolation from their historic context, has become a formula. The figures—as on the sarcophagi of late antiquity—are placed side by side paratactically. They no longer have any reality, they have only signification. With respect to the events of this world, a similar tendency prevails: to remove them from their horizontal context, to isolate the individual fragments, to force them into a fixed frame, and, within it, to make them impressive gesturally, so that they appear as exemplary, as models, as significant, and to leave all "the rest" in abeyance. It is easy to see that such a procedure permits but a small, extremely narrow portion of reality to assume visual plasticity, that portion which the crystallized idioms of the established categories are able to convey. But small as it may be, it does assume visual plasticity, and this shows that the high point of the process of rigidification has been passed. It is precisely in the isolated pictures that the germs of a revival are to be found.

The Latin text which may be assumed to have been the source for the French *Chanson d'Alexis* (it will be found in the *Acta Sanctorum* of July 17; it is here cited after Förster-Koschwitz, *Altfranzösisches Übungsbuch*, sixth edition, 1921, pp. 299ff.) is perhaps not much older than the French version, for the legend, which originated in Syria, can be traced in the West only at a comparatively late date. But it exhibits the form of the saint's legend of late antiquity much more purely. Its treatment of the bridal night deviates from the Old French version in a highly characteristic fashion:

> Vespere autem facto dixit Euphemianus filio suo; "Intra, fili, in cubiculum et visita sponsam tuam." Ut autem intravit, coepit nobilissimus juvenis et in Christo sapientissimus instruere sponsam suam et plura ei sacramenta disserere, deinde tradidit ei annulum suum aureum et rendam, id est caput baltei, quo cingebatur, involuta in prandeo et purpureo sudario, dixitque ei: "Suscipe haec et conserva, usque dum Domino placuerit, et Dominus sit inter nos." Post haec accepit de substantia sua et discessit ad mare. . . .
>
> (When it was evening, Euphemianus said to his son: "Go into the bedroom, son, and visit your wife." But when he entered, the noble youth began most sagely to teach his wife of Christ and to explain to her many holy things, then he gave her his golden ring and the thong of his sword wrapped in a purple cloth of silk and spoke to her: "Take these and keep them as long as it pleases the Lord, and the Lord be between us." After that he took some of his wealth and went down to the sea.)

It will have been noticed that the Latin text is likewise almost wholly paratactic. But it does not exploit the possibilities of parataxis; it has not come to know them. It has leveled and flattened the whole scene to complete uniformity. The narration proceeds without any ups and downs, without change of tone, "monotonously": so that not only the frame but even the picture within it remains motionless, is rigid and without dynamism. The inner struggle which the temptation brings about in Alexis' soul and for which the Old French version has the simplest and most beautiful expression, is not even mentioned. There seems to be no temptation at all. And the great movement of Alexis' words in direct discourse to his bride (*Oz mei, pulcele* . . .)—one of the strongest movements of the entire Old French poem, in which Alexis rises to his full stature and which is the first outbreaking of his real nature—is evidently something the French poet created out of the pale Latin words of his source. The flight too first becomes dramatic in the French text. The Latin version is much smoother and more uniformly progressive; but the human movement is weak, is barely alluded to, as if the story had to do with a ghost and not a living being. The same impression continues as one reads on. A really human formulation can be found only in the vernacular version. New in it (and we mention only the most important points) are the mother's lament in the deserted room and, later, the saint's inner struggle when the storm drives him back to Rome. Here Alexius hesitates before taking upon himself the most difficult trial of all, which is to live as an unknown beggar in his father's house, where day after day he sees his nearest relatives mourning for him. He wishes that the cup might pass from him; yet he accepts it. The Latin text knows no hesitation and no inner struggle, here as in the scene of the bridal night. Alexis goes to his father's house because he does not want the burden to fall on anyone else.

It was vernacular poetry—our comparison of these two texts seems to show—which first imparted relief to the individual pictures, so that their characters took on life and human fullness. This life, to be sure, is restricted by the rigidity and narrowness of the categories, which persist unalterably, and it fails all too easily for lack of progressive movement; but it is precisely through the resistance offered by the frame of rigid categories that it acquires impressiveness and force. It was the vernacular poets who first saw man as a living being and found the form in which parataxis possesses poetic power. Instead of a thin, monotonous trickle of juxtapositions, we now have the laisse form, with its abrupt advances and regressions and its abundance of energetic new beginnings, which is a new elevated style. If the life which this stylistic procedure can seize upon is narrowly restricted and without diversity, it is nevertheless a full life, a life of human emotion, a powerful life, a great relief after the pale, intangible style of the late antique legend. The vernacular poets also knew how to exploit direct discourse in terms of tone and gesture. We have already referred to Alexis' address to his bride and to his mother's lament. In addition we may mention the words in which, after his return to Rome, the saint asks his father for food and shelter. In the French version they have a concrete and direct appeal to which the Latin text could not possibly attain. The French passage reads:

> Eufemiiens, bels sire, riches om,
> quer me herberge por Deu en ta maison;
> soz ton degret me fai un grabaton
> empor ton fil dont tu as tel dolour;
> toz sui enfers, sim pais por soue amour. . . .

(Euphemianus, noble lord, wealthy man, may it please thee to give me shelter in thy house for the sake of God. Under thy stairs arrange a sickbed for me, for thy son's sake through whom thou hast such great sorrow. I am very ill; so feed me for the sake of thy love to him. . . .)

and the Latin parallel:

Serve Dei, respice in me et fac mecum misericordiam, quia pauper sum et peregrinus, et jube me suscipi in domo tua, ut pascar de micis mensae tuae et Deus benedicat annos tuos et ei quem habes in peregre misereatur.

(Servant of God, look at me and be charitable to me, for I am poor and a stranger; and give orders that I be received in thy house, so that I may feed upon the crumbs from thy table, and may God bless thy years and have mercy on him whom you have wandering far from home.)

We observed earlier that it would be a mistake simply to make Christianity responsible for the rigidity and narrowness which appear in the late antique legend and from which the vernacular texts are able to emancipate themselves only gradually. In our earlier chapters we attempted to show that the first effect of the Judaeo-Christian manner of dealing with the events in the world of reality led to anything but rigidity and narrowness. The hiddenness of God and finally his *parousia*, his incarnation in the common form of an ordinary life, these concepts—we tried to show—brought about a dynamic movement in the basic conception of life, a swing of the pendulum in the realms of morals and sociology, which went far beyond the classic-antique norm for the imitation of real life and living growth. Even the Church Fathers, Augustine in particular, have not by any means come down to us as schematized figures pursuing a rigidly preordained course, and Augustine's friend, Alypius, whose inner upheaval at the gladiatorial games we discussed in an earlier passage, comes fully alive as he struggles, is defeated, and finally recovers. Rigid, narrow, and unproblematic schematization is originally completely alien to the Christian concept of reality. It is true, to be sure, that the rigidifying process is furthered to a considerable degree by the figural interpretation of real events, which, as Christianity became established and spread, grew increasingly influential and which, in its treatment of actual events, dissolved their content of reality, leaving them only their content of meaning. As dogma was established, as the Church's task became more and more a matter of organization, its problem that of winning over peoples completely unprepared and unacquainted with Christian principles, figural interpretation must inevitably become a simple and rigid scheme. But the problem of the process of rigidification as a whole goes deeper; it is linked to the decline of the culture of antiquity. It is not Christianity which brought about the process of rigidification, but rather Christianity was drawn into it. With the collapse of the Western Roman Empire and the principle of order which it embodied—a principle which had itself been long characterized by certain senile traits of calcification—the inner coherence of the *orbis terrarum* disintegrated too, and a new world could only be rebuilt from its parceled fragments. During the process, the politically and psychologically crude ethos of the newly emerging peoples everywhere clashed with the surviving institutions of Rome, the vestiges of antique culture, which retained a tremendous prestige despite decline and rigidification. It was a clash of the very young and the age old, and at first the very young was paralyzed, until it had managed to come to terms with the vestiges of tradition, until it had filled them with its own life and brought them to a new florescence. The process of rigidification was naturally least pronounced in countries where the culture of late antiquity had never played a dominant role, that is, in the countries at the center of the Germanic world; it was considerably more pronounced in the Romance countries, where a real clash occurred, and perhaps it is no accident that France —where the Germanic influence was stronger than in any other Romance country—was the first to begin emancipating itself from that influence.

It appears to me that the first elevated style of the European Middle Ages arose at the moment when the single event is filled with life. That is why this style is so rich in individual scenes of great effectiveness, scenes in which only a very few characters confront one another, in which the gestures and speeches of a brief occurrence come out in sharp relief. The characters, facing one another at close quarters, without much room for movement, nevertheless stand there as individuals clearly set off from one another. What is said of them never degenerates into mere talk; it always remains a solemn statement in which every address, every phrase, and indeed every word, has a value of its own, separate and emphatic, with no trace of softness and no relaxed flow. Confronting the reality of life, this style is neither able nor willing to deal with its breadths or depths. It is limited in time, place, and social milieu. It simplifies the events of the past by stylizing and idealizing them. The feeling it seeks to arouse in its auditor is admiration and amazement for a distant world, whose instincts and ideals, though they certainly remain his own, yet evolve in such uncompromising purity and freedom, in comparison with the friction and resistance of real life, as his practical existence could not possibly attain. Human movements and great, towering exemplary figures appear with striking effect; his own life is not there at all. To be sure, in the very tone of the *Chanson de Roland* there is a great deal of contemporaneity. It does not begin with an announcement which removes the events to a distant past ("Long ago it came to pass . . . Of olden days I will sing . . .") but with a strongly immediate note, as though Charles, our great Emperor, were almost still a living man. The naive transfer of events three centuries past into the ethos of feudal society of the early crusading period, the exploitation of the subject matter in the interest of ecclesiastic and feudal propaganda, give the poem a quality of living presentness. Something like a nascent national consciousness is even perceptible in it. When we read—to choose a simple illustration—the line in which Roland tries to organize the imminent attack of the Frankish knights (1165):

Seignurs barons, suef, le pas tenant!

we hear the echo of a common scene of contemporary feudal cavalry maneuvers. But these are isolated instances. Class limitation, idealization, simplification, and the shimmering veil of legend prevail.

The style of the French heroic epic is an elevated style in which the structural concept of reality is still extremely rigid and which succeeds in representing only a narrow portion of objective life circumscribed by distance in time, simplification of perspective, and class limitations. I shall be saying nothing new, but merely reformulating what I have said many times, if I add that in this style the separation of the realm of the heroic and sublime from that of the practical and everyday is a matter of course. Strata other than that at the top of the feudal system simply do not appear. The economic bases of society are not even mentioned. This is carried much further than in the heroic epic of the early Germanic and Middle High German periods and is also in striking contrast to the heroic epic of Spain, which begins to appear but little later. Yet the *chanson de geste*, and the *Chanson de Roland* in particular, was popular. It is true that these poems deal exclusively with the exploits of the upper stratum of feudal society, but there is no doubt that they address the common people as well. The explanation may be that despite the marked material and juridic differences between the various strata of the lay population they were as yet essentially on the same intellectual level; that, indeed, the ideals men cherished were still uniform, or at least that secular ideals other than those of knighthood and heroism were not ready to be put into practice and into words. That the *chanson de geste* was a force and an influence on all levels of society is shown by the fact that about the end of the eleventh century the clergy—whose attitude toward vernacular lay literature had not theretofore been benevolent—began to exploit the heroic epic for their own purpose. The fact that these themes survived for centuries, that they were recast in ever new versions and quickly sank to the level of country-fair entertainment, proves their enduring popularity among the lower classes. For audiences of the eleventh, twelfth, and thirteenth centuries the heroic epic was history; in it the historical tradition of earlier ages was alive. No other tradition existed, at least none accessible to those audiences. It is only about the year 1200 that the first vernacular chronicles are composed, but they do not relate the past, they are eye-witness accounts of contemporary events, and even so they are strongly influenced by the epic style. And indeed, the heroic epic *is* history, at least insofar as it recalls actual historical conditions—however much it may distort and simplify them—and insofar as its characters always perform a historico-political function. This historico-political element is abandoned by the courtly novel, which consequently has a completely new relationship to the objective world of reality.

6

THE KNIGHT SETS FORTH

NEAR the beginning of Chrétien de Troyes' *Yvain,* a courtly romance of the second half of the twelfth century, one of the knights of King Arthur's court relates an adventure which once befell him. His narrative begins as follows:

Il avint, pres a de set anz
Que je seus come païsanz
Aloie querant avantures,
Armez de totes armeüres
Si come chevaliers doit estre,
Et trovai un chemin a destre
Parmi une forest espesse.
Mout i ot voie felenesse,
De ronces et d'espines plainne;
A quelqu'enui, a quelque painne
Ting cele voie et cel santier.
A bien pres tot le jor antier
m'an alai chevauchant einsi
Tant que de la forest issi,
Et ce fu an Broceliande.
De la forest an une lande
Antrai et vi une bretesche
A demie liue galesche;
Si tant i ot, plus n'i ot pas.
Celle part ving plus que le pas
Et vi le baille et le fossé
Tot anviron parfont et lé,
Et sor le pont an piez estoit
Cil cui la forteresce estoit,
Sor son poing un ostor mué.
Ne l'oi mie bien salué,
Quant il me vint a l'estrier prandre,
Si me comanda a desçandre.
Je desçandi; il n'i ot el,

Que mestier avoie d'ostel;
Et il me dist tot maintenant
Plus de çant foiz an un tenant,
Que beneoite fust la voie,
Par ou leanz venuz estoie.
A tant an la cort an antrames,
Le pont et la porte passames.
Anmi la cort au vavassor,
Cui Des doint et joie et enor
Tant come il fist moi cele nuit,
Pandoit une table; je cuit
Qu'il n'i avoit ne fer ne fust
Ne rien qui de cuivre ne fust.
Sor cele table d'un martel,
Qui panduz iere a un postel,
Feri li vavassors trois cos.
Cil qui amont ierent anclos
Oïrent la voiz et le son,
S'issirent fors de la meison
Et vindrent an la cort aval.
Li un seisirent mon cheval,
Que li buens vavassors tenoit.
Et je vis que vers moi venoit
Une pucele bele et jante.
An li esgarder mis m'antante:
Ele fu longue et gresle et droite.
De moi desarmer fu adroite;
Qu'ele le fist et bien et bel.
Puis m'afubla un cort mantel,
Ver d'escarlate peonace,
Et tuit nos guerpirent la place,
Que avuec moi ne avuec li
Ne remest nus, ce m'abeli;
Que plus n'i queroie veoir.
Et ele me mena seoir
El plus bel praelet del monde
Clos de bas mur a la reonde.
La la trovai si afeitiee,
Si bien parlant et anseigniee,
De tel sanblant et de tel estre,

Que mout m'i delitoit a estre,
Ne ja mes por nul estovoir
Ne m'an queïsse removoir.
Mes tant me fist la nuit de guerre
Li vavassors, qu'il me vint querre,
Quant de soper fu tans et ore.
N'i poi plus feire de demore,
Si fis lues son comandemant.
Del soper vos dirai briemant,
Qu'il fu del tot a ma devise,
Des que devant moi fu assise
La pucele qui s'i assist.
Apres soper itant me dist
Li vavassors, qu'il ne savoit
Le terme, puis que il avoit
Herbergié chevalier errant,
Qui avanture alast querant,
S'an avoit il maint herbergié.
Apres ce me pria que gié
Par son ostel m'an revenisse
An guerredon, se je poïsse.
Et je li dis: "Volantiers, sire!"
Que honte fust de l'escondire.
Petit por mon oste feïsse,
Se cest don li escondeïsse,
Mout fu bien la nuit ostelez,
Et mes chevaus fu anselez
Lues que l'an pot le jor veoir;
Car j'an oi mout proiié le soir;
Si fu bien feite ma proiiere.
Mon buen oste et sa fille chiere
Au saint Esperit comandai,
A trestoz congié demandai,
Si m'an alai lues que je poi. . . .

(It happened seven years ago that, lonely as a countryman, I was making my way in search of adventures, fully armed as a knight should be, when I came upon a road leading off to the right into a thick forest. The road there was very bad, full of briars and thorns. In spite of the trouble and inconvenience, I followed the road and path. Almost the entire day I went thus riding until I emerged from the forest of Broceliande. Out from the forest I passed into the open country where I saw a wooden tower at the distance of half a Welsh league: it may have been so far, but it was not any more. Proceeding faster than a walk, I drew near and saw the palisade and moat all round it, deep and wide, and standing upon the bridge, with a moulted falcon upon his wrist, I saw the master of the castle. I had no sooner saluted him than he came forward to hold my stirrup and invited me to dismount. I did so, for it was useless to deny that I was in need of a lodging-place. Then he told me more than a hundred times at once that blessed was the road by which I had come thither. Meanwhile, we crossed the bridge, and passing through the gate, found ourselves in the courtyard. In the middle of the courtyard of this vavasor, to whom may God repay such joy and honour as he bestowed upon me that night, there hung a gong not of iron or wood, I trow, but all of copper. Upon this gong the vavasor struck three times with a hammer which hung on a post close by. Those who were upstairs in the house, upon hearing his voice and the sound, came out into the yard below. Some took my horse which the good vavasor was holding; and I saw coming toward me a very fair and gentle maid. On looking at her narrowly I saw she was tall and slim and straight. Skilful she was in disarming me, which she did gently and with address; then, when she had robed me in a short mantle of scarlet stuff spotted with a peacock's plumes, all the others left us there, so that she and I remained alone. This pleased me well, for I needed naught else to look upon. Then she took me to sit down in the prettiest little field, shut in by a wall all round about. There I found her so elegant, so fair of speech and so well informed, of such pleasing manners and character, that it was a delight to be there, and I could have wished never to be compelled to move. But as ill luck would have it, when night came on, and the time for supper had arrived, the vavasor came to look for me. No more delay was possible, so I complied with his request. Of the supper I will only say that it was all after my heart, seeing that the damsel took her seat at the table just in front of me. After the supper the vavasor admitted to me that, though he had lodged many an errant knight, he knew not how long it had been since he had welcomed one in search of adventure. Then, as a favour, he begged of me to return by way of his residence, if I could make it possible. So I said to him: "Right gladly, sire!" for a refusal would have been impolite, and that was the least I could do for such a host. That night, indeed, I was well lodged, and as soon as the morning light appeared, I found my steed ready saddled, as I had requested the night before; thus my request was carried out. My kind host and his dear daughter I commended to the Holy Spirit, and, after taking leave of all, I got away as soon as possible.) *Arthurian Romances by Chrétien de Troyes.* Translated by W. Wistar Comfort. New York: E. P. Dutton & Company.

Continuing his narrative, the knight, whose name is Calogrenant, tells how he encounters a herd of bulls and how the herdsman, a grotesquely ugly and gigantic *vilain,* tells him of a magic spring not far away. It flows under a beautiful tree. A golden vessel hangs nearby, and when water from the spring is poured from the vessel over an emerald tablet which lies beside it, such a terrible storm arises in the forest that no one has ever lived through it. Calogrenant attempts the adventure. He withstands the storm and then enjoys the sunny calm which follows, enlivened by the song of many birds. But then a knight appears who, reproaching him with the damage the storm has caused to his property, defeats him, so that he has to return to his host on foot and weaponless. He is again very well received and is assured that he is indeed the first to have escaped from the adventure unscathed. Calogrenant's story makes a great impression on the knights at Arthur's court. The King decides to ride to the magic spring himself, with a large following. However, one of the knights, Calogrenant's cousin Yvain, gets there before him, defeats and kills the knight of the spring, and, by means which are partly miraculous and partly very natural, wins the love of his widow.

Although only some seventy years separate this text from the preceding one, and although here too we are dealing with an epic work of the feudal age, a first glance suffices to show a complete change in stylistic movement. The narrative flows; it is light and almost easy. It is in no hurry to get on, but its progress is steady. Its parts are connected without any gaps. Here too, to be sure, there are no strictly organized periods; the advance from one part of the story to the next is loose and follows no set plan; nor are the values of the conjunctions yet clearly established—*que* especially has to fulfill far too many functions, so that many causal connections (e.g. ll. 231, 235, or 237) remain somewhat vague. But this does not harm the narrative continuity; on the contrary, the loose connections make for a very natural narrative style, and the rhyme—handled very freely and independently of the sense structure—never breaks in obtrusively. It permits the poet an occasional line of padding or a detailed circumlocution (e.g. l. 193 or ll. 211-216), which merge smoothly into the style and actually increase the impression of naive, fresh, and easy breadth. How much more elastic and mobile this language is than that of the *chanson de geste*, how much more adroitly it prattles on, conveying narrative movements which, though still naive enough, already have far freer play in their variety, can be observed in almost every sentence. Let us take lines 241 to 246 as an example: *La la trovai si afeitiee, si bien parlant et anseigniee, de tel sanblant et de tel estre, que mout m'i delitoit a estre, ne ja mes por nul estovoir ne m'an queïsse removoir.* The sentence, linked by *la* to the preceding one, is a consecutive period. The ascending section has three steps, the third step contains an antithetically constructed summary (*sanblant-estre*) which reveals a high degree of analytical skill (already a matter of course) in the judgment of character. The descending section is bipartite, and the parts are carefully set off against each other: the first—stating the fact of delight—in the indicative mood; the second—hypothetical—in the subjunctive. Nothing so subtle in structure, and merging with the narrative as a whole so smoothly and without apparent effort, is likely to have occurred in vernacular literatures before the courtly romance. I take this opportunity to observe that in the slow growth of a hypotactically richer and more periodic syntax, a leading role seems to have been played (down to the time of Dante) by consecutive constructions (the sentence quoted on page 100 from the *Folie Tristan* also culminates in a consecutive movement). While other types of modal connection were still comparatively undeveloped, this one flourished and developed characteristic functions of expression which were later lost; the subject has recently been discussed in an interesting study by A. G. Hatcher (*Revue des Études Indo-européennes*, 2, 30).

Calogrenant tells King Arthur's Round Table that, seven years earlier, he had ridden away alone in quest of adventure, armed as befits a knight, and he had come upon a road leading to the right, straight through a dense forest. Here we stop and wonder. To the right? That is a strange indication of locality when, as in this case, it is used absolutely. In terms of terrestrial topography it makes sense only when used relatively. Hence it must here have an ethical signification. Apparently it is the "right way" which Calogrenant discovered. And that is confirmed immediately, for the road is arduous, as right ways are wont to be; all day long it leads through a dense forest full of brambles and thickets, and at night it reaches the right goal: a castle where Calogrenant is received with delight, as though he were a long-awaited guest. It is only at night, it seems, as he rides out of the forest, that he discovers where he is: on a heath in Broceliande. Broceliande in Armorica, on the continent, is a fairyland well known in Breton legend, with a magic spring and an enchanted forest. How Calogrenant —who presumably started out from King Arthur's court on the Island of Britain—managed to get to continental Brittany is not explained. We hear nothing of a crossing of the sea, as we hear nothing of it later (ll. 760ff.) in Yvain's case, who in turn undoubtedly sets out from Carduel in Wales although his journey to the "right road" in Broceliande is described in vague and legendary terms. No sooner does Calogrenant discover where he is, than he sees a hospitable castle. On the bridge stands the lord of the castle, with a hunting falcon on his fist, welcoming him with a delight which goes far beyond the expression of ready hospitality, and which once again assures us that we have been hearing about a "right way": *et il me dist tot maintenant plus de çant fois an un tenant, que beneoite fust la voie, par ou leanz venuz estoie.* The subsequent phases of his welcome follow the knightly ceremonial whose graceful forms seem to have long been established; striking three times upon a copper plate, the host summons his servants; the traveler's horse is led away; a beautiful maiden appears, who is the daughter of the lord of the castle; it is her duty to relieve the guest of his armor, to replace it by a comfortable and beautiful coat, and then, alone with him in a charming garden, to keep him pleasant company until supper is ready. After the meal the lord of the castle informs his guest that he has been receiving knights errant in pursuit of adventure for a very long time; he urges him to visit the castle again on his way back; strangely enough he tells him nothing about the adventure of the spring, although he knows about it and although he is well aware that the dangers which await his guest there will in all probability prevent his contemplated return. But that seems to be quite as it should be; at any rate it in no wise reduces the meed of praise which Calogrenant and, later, Yvain bestow upon their host's hospitality and knightly virtues. So Calogrenant rides away in the morning, and it is not until he meets the satyrlike *vilain* that he hears of the magic spring. This *vilain* of course has no idea of what *avanture* is—how could he, not being a knight?—but he knows the magic qualities of the spring, and he makes no secret of his knowledge.

Obviously we are now deep in fairy tale and magic. The right road through the forest full of brambles, the castle which seems to have sprung out of the ground, the nature of the hero's reception, the beautiful maiden, the strange silence of the lord of the castle, the satyr, the magic spring—it is all in the atmosphere of fairy tale. And the indications of time are as reminiscent of fairy tale as the indications of place. Calogrenant has kept quiet about his adventure for seven years. Seven is a fairy-tale number, and the seven years mentioned at the beginning of the *Chanson de Roland* likewise impart a touch of the legendary: seven years—*set anz tuz pleins*—is the time the Emperor Charles had spent in Spain. However, in the *Chanson de Roland* they are really "full" years; they are *tuz pleins,* because the Emperor used them to subdue the entire land down to the sea and to take all its castles and cities except Saragossa. In the seven years between Calogrenant's adventure at the spring and the time of his narration, on the other hand, nothing seems to have happened or at least we are told nothing about it. When Yvain sets off on the same adventure he finds everything exactly as Calogrenant had described it: the lord of the castle, the maiden, the bulls with their horribly ugly giant of a herdsman, the magic spring, and the knight who defends it. Nothing has changed; the seven years have passed without leaving a trace, just as time usually does in a fairy tale. The landscape is the enchanted landscape of fairy tale; we are surrounded by mystery, by secret murmurings and whispers. All the numerous castles and palaces, the battles and adventures, of the courtly romances—especially of the Breton cycle—are things of fairyland: each time they appear before us as though sprung from the ground; their geographical relation to the known world, their sociological and economic foundations, remain unexplained. Even their ethical or symbolic significance can rarely be ascertained with anything approaching certainty. Has the adventure at the spring any hidden meaning? It is evidently one of those which the Knights of the Round Table are bound to undergo, yet an ethical justification for the combat with the knight of the magic spring is nowhere given. In other episodes of the courtly romances it is sometimes possible to make out symbolic, mythological, or religious motifs; for instance, the journey to the underworld in *Lancelot,* the motif of liberation and redemption in numerous instances, and especially the theme of Christian grace in the Grail legend—but it is rarely possible to define the meaning precisely, at least so long as the courtly romance remains true to type. It is from Breton folklore that the courtly romance took its elements of mystery, of something sprung from the soil, concealing its roots, and inaccessible to rational explanation; it incorporated them and made use of them in its elaboration of the knightly ideal; the *matière de Bretagne* apparently proved to be the most suitable medium for the cultivation of that ideal—more suitable even than the stuff of antiquity, which was taken up at about the same time but which soon lost ground.

A self-portrayal of feudal knighthood with its mores and ideals is the fundamental purpose of the courtly romance. Nor are its exterior forms of life neglected—they are portrayed in leisurely fashion, and on these occasions the portrayal abandons the nebulous distance of fairy tale and gives salient pictures of contemporary conditions. Other episodes in courtly romance convey much more colorful and detailed pictures of this sort than our passage does; but even our passage permits us to observe the essential features which indicate its realistic character. The lord of the castle with his falcon; the summoning of the servants by striking a copper plate; the beautiful young mistress of the castle, relieving the visitor of his armor, wrapping him in a comfortable cloak, and entertaining him most pleasantly until supper is served—all these are graceful vignettes of established custom, one might say of a ritual which shows us courtly society in its setting of highly developed conventionality. The setting is as fixed and isolating, as distinct from the mores of other strata of society, as is that of the *chanson de geste*, but it is much more refined and elegant. Women play an important part in it; the mannerly ease and comfort of the social life of a cultured class have been attained. And indeed it has assumed a nature which is long to remain one of the most distinctive characteristics of French taste: graceful amenity with almost an excess of subtlety. The scene with the young lady of the castle—her appearance, his way of looking at her, the removal of his armor, the conversation in the meadow—though it is not a particularly developed example, yet sufficiently conveys the impression of that delicately graceful, limpid and smiling, fresh and elegantly naive coquetry of which Chrétien in particular is a past master. Genre scenes of this sort are found in French literature very early—in the *chansons de toile* and once even in the *Chanson de Roland*, in the laisse which tells of Margariz of Seville (ll. 955ff.); but their full development was a contribution of courtly society, and Chrétien's great charm especially is in no small measure due to his gift for carrying on this tone in the most varied fashion. We find the style in its greatest brilliance where the subject matter is the dalliance of true love. Between these scenes of dalliance come antithetical reasonings over the emotions involved, seemingly naive yet of accomplished artistry and grace. The most celebrated example occurs at the beginning of the *Cligès*, where the budding love between Alixandre and Soredamors—with its initial reticence and mutual hide-and-seek and the ultimate welling up of emotions—is represented in a series of enchanting scenes and analytical soliloquies.

The grace and attractiveness of this style—whose charm is freshness and whose danger is silly coquetry, trifling, and coldness—can hardly be found in such purity anywhere in the literature of antiquity. Chrétien did not learn it from Ovid; it is a creation of the French Middle Ages. It must be noted, furthermore, that this style is by no means restricted to love episodes. In Chrétien, and also in the later romance of adventure and the shorter verse narrative, the entire portrayal of life within feudal society is tuned to the same note, not only in the twelfth but also in the thirteenth century. In charmingly graceful, delicately painted, and crystalline verses, knightly society offers its own presentment; thousands of little scenes and pictures describe its habits, its views, and its social tone for us. There is a great deal of brilliance, of realistic flavor, of psychological refinement, and also a great deal of humor in these pictures. It is a much richer, more varied, and more comprehensive world than the world of the *chansons de geste*, although it too is only the world of a single class. At times indeed Chrétien seems to break through this class confinement, as in the workroom of the three hundred women in the Chastel de Pesme Avanture (*Yvain*, 5107ff.) or in the description of the wealthy town whose citizens (*quemune*) attempt to storm the castle where Gauvain is quartered (*Perceval*, 5710ff.)—but such episodes are after all only a colorful setting for the life of the knight. Courtly realism offers a very rich and pungent picture of the life of a single class, a social stratum which remains aloof from the other strata of contemporary society, allowing them to appear as accessories, sometimes colorful but more usually comic or grotesque; so that the distinction in terms of class between the important, the meaningful, and the sublime on the one hand and the low-grotesque-comic on the other, remains strictly intact in regard to subject matter. The former realm is open only to members of the feudal class. Yet a real separation of styles is not in question here, for the simple reason that the courtly romance does not know an "elevated style," that is, a distinction between levels of expression. The easy-going, adroit, and elastic rhymed octosyllable effortlessly adapts itself to any subject and any level of emotion or thought. Did it not elsewhere serve the most varied ends, from farce to saint's legend? When it treats very serious or terrible themes, it is apt—at least to our way of feeling—to fall into a certain touching naïveté and childishness. And indeed, there is the courage of a child in the freshness of outlook which undertook—with the sole tool of a literary language so young that it had no ballast of theory, had not yet emerged from the confusion of dialectical forms—to master a life which had, after all, attained a considerable degree of differentiation. The problem of levels of style is not consciously conceived in the vernaculars until much later, that is, from the time of Dante.

But an even stronger limitation than that in terms of class results for the realism of the courtly romance from its legendary, fairy-tale atmosphere. It is this which makes all the colorful and vivid pictures of contemporary reality seem, as it were, to have sprung from the ground: the ground of legend and fairy tale, so that—as we said before—they are entirely without any basis in political reality. The geographical, economic, and social conditions on which they depend are never explained. They descend directly from fairy tale and adventure. The strikingly realistic workroom in *Yvain*, which I mentioned earlier, and in which we even find discussions of such things as working conditions and workers' compensation, was not established because of concrete economic conditions but because the young king of the Island of Maidens had fallen into the hands of two evil gnomelike brothers and ransomed himself by promising that once a year he would deliver to them thirty of his maidens to perform labor. The fairy-tale atmosphere is the true element of the courtly romance, which after all is not only interested in portraying external living conditions in the feudal society of the closing years of the twelfth century but also and especially in expressing its ideals. And with that we reach the very core of courtly romance, insofar as its particular ethos came to be important in the history of the literary treatment of reality.

Calogrenant sets out without mission or office; he seeks adventure, that is, perilous encounters by which he can prove his mettle. There is nothing like this in the *chanson de geste*. There a knight who sets off has an office and a place in a politico-historical context. It is doubtless simplified and distorted in the manner of legend, but it is maintained insofar as the characters who take part in the action have a function in the real world—for instance, the defense of Charles's realm against the infidels, their conquest and conversion, and so forth. Such are the political and historical purposes served by the feudal ethos, the warriors' ethos which the knights profess. Calogrenant, on the other hand, has no political or historical task, nor has any other knight of Arthur's court. Here the feudal ethos serves no political function; it serves no practical reality at all; it has become absolute. It no longer has any purpose but that of self-realization. This changes its nature completely. Even the term which we find for it in the *Chanson de Roland* most frequently and in the most general acceptation—the term *vasselage*—seems gradually to drop out of fashion. Chrétien uses it three times in *Erec*, in *Cligès* and *Lancelot* it occurs in one passage each, and after that not at all. The new term which he now prefers is *corteisie*, a word whose long and significant history supplies the most complete interpretation of the ideal concept of class and man in Europe. In the *Chanson de Roland* this word does not yet occur. Only the adjective *curteis* appears three times, twice in reference to Olivier in the combination *li proz e li curteis*. It would seem that *corteisie* achieved its synthetic meaning only in the age of chivalry or courtly culture, which indeed derives the latter name from it. The values expressed in it—refinement of the laws of combat, courteous social intercourse, service of women—have undergone a striking process of change and sublimation in comparison with the *chanson de geste* and are all directed toward a personal and absolute ideal—absolute both in reference to ideal realization and in reference to the absence of any earthly and practical purpose. The personal element in the courtly virtues is not simply a gift of nature; nor is it acquired by birth; to implant them now requires, besides birth, proper training too, as preserving them requires the unforced will to renew them by constant and tireless practice and proving.

The means by which they are proved and preserved is adventure, *avanture*, a very characteristic form of activity developed by courtly culture. Of course, fanciful depiction of the miracles and dangers awaiting those whom their destiny takes beyond the confines of the familiar world into distant and unexplored regions had long been known, as well as no less imaginative ideas and narratives about the mysterious perils which also threaten man within the geographically familiar world, from the influence of gods, spirits, demons, and other magic powers; so too the fearless hero who, by strength, virtue, cunning, and the help of God, overcomes such dangers and frees others from them was known long before the age of courtly culture. But that an entire class, in the heyday of its contemporary flowering, should regard the surmounting of such perils as its true mission—in the ideal conception of things as its exclusive mission; that the most various legendary traditions, especially but not only those of the Breton cycle, are taken over by it for the purpose of producing a chivalrous world of magic especially designed for the purpose, in which fantastic encounters and perils present themselves to the knight as if from the end of an assembly-line—this state of affairs is a new creation of the courtly romance. Although these perilous encounters called *avantures* now have no experiential basis whatever, although it is impossible to fit them into any actual or practically conceivable political system, although they commonly crop up without any rational connection, one after the other, in a long series, we must be careful not to be misled by the modern value of the term adventure, to think of them as purely "accidental." When we moderns speak of adventure, we mean something unstable, peripheral, disordered, or, as Simmel once put it, a something that stands outside the real meaning of existence. All this is precisely what the word does not mean in the courtly romance. On the contrary, trial through adventure is the real meaning of the knight's ideal existence. That the very essence of the knight's ideal of manhood is called forth by adventure, E. Eberwein undertook to show some years since with reference to the *Lais* of Marie de France (*Zur Deutung mittelalterlicher Existenz*, Bonn and Cologne, 1933, pp. 27ff.). It can also be demonstrated on the basis of the courtly romance.

Calogrenant seeks the right way and finds it, as we said before. It is the right way into adventure, and this very seeking and finding of it shows him to be one of the chosen, a true knight of King Arthur's Round Table. As a true knight worthy of adventure, he is received by his host—who is also a knight—with delight and with blessings for having found the right way. Host and guest both belong to one social group, a sort of order, admission into which is through a ceremonial election and all members of which are bound to help one another. The host's real calling, the only meaning of his living where he does, seems to be that he should offer knightly hospitality to knights in quest of adventure. But the help he gives his guest is made mysterious by his silence in regard to what lies ahead for Calogrenant. Apparently this secretiveness is one of his knightly duties, quite in contrast to the *vilain*, who withholds nothing of what he knows. What the *vilain* does know are the material circumstances of the adventure; but what "adventure" is, he does not know, for he is without knightly culture. Calogrenant, then, is a true knight, one of the elect. But there are many degrees of election. Not he, but only Yvain, proves capable of sustaining the adventure. The degrees of election, and specific election for a specific adventure, are sometimes more clearly emphasized in the *Lancelot* and the *Perceval* than in the *Yvain*; but the motif is unmistakable wherever we have to do with courtly literature. The series of adventures is thus raised to the status of a fated and graduated test of election; it becomes the basis of a doctrine of personal perfection through a development dictated by fate, a doctrine which was later to break through the class barriers of courtly culture. We must not overlook the fact, it is true, that, contemporaneously with courtly culture, there was another movement which gave expression to this graduated proving of election, as well as to the theory of love, with much greater rigor and clarity—namely, Victorine and Cistercian mysticism. This movement was not restricted to one class, and it did not require adventure.

The world of knightly proving is a world of adventure. It not only contains a practically uninterrupted series of adventures; more specifically, it contains nothing but the requisites of adventure. Nothing is found in it which is not either accessory or preparatory to an adventure. It is a world specifically created and designed to give the knight opportunity to prove himself. The scene of Calogrenant's departure shows this most clearly. He rides on all day and encounters nothing but the castle prepared to receive him. Nothing is said about all the practical conditions and circumstances necessary to render the existence of such a castle in absolute solitude both possible and compatible with ordinary experience. Such idealization takes us very far from the imitation of reality. In the courtly romance the functional, the historically real aspects of class are passed over. Though it offers a great many culturally significant details concerning the customs of social intercourse and external social forms and conventions in general, we can get no penetrating view of contemporary reality from it, even in respect to the knightly class. Where it depicts reality, it depicts merely the colorful surface, and where it is not superficial, it has other subjects and other ends than contemporary reality. Yet it does contain a class ethics which as such claimed and indeed attained acceptance and validity in this real and earthly world. For it has a great power of attraction which, if I mistake not, is due especially to two characteristics which distinguish it: it is absolute, raised above all earthly contingencies, and it gives those who submit to its dictates the feeling that they belong to a community of the elect, a circle of solidarity (the term comes from Hellmut Ritter, the Orientalist) set apart from the common herd. The ethics of feudalism, the ideal conception of the perfect knight, thus attained a very considerable and very long-lived influence. Concepts associated with it—courage, honor, loyalty, mutual respect, refined manners, service to women—continued to cast their spell on the contemporaries of completely changed cultural periods. Social strata of later urban and bourgeois provenance adopted this ideal, although it is not only class-conditioned and exclusive but also completely devoid of reality. As soon as it transcends the sphere of mere conventions of intercourse and has to do with the practical business of the world, it proves inadequate and needs to be supplemented, often in a manner most unpleasantly in contrast to it. But precisely because it is so removed from reality, it could—as an ideal—adapt itself to any and every situation, at least as long as there were ruling classes at all.

So it came to pass that the knightly ideal survived all the catastrophes which befell feudalism in the course of the centuries. It survived even Cervantes' *Don Quixote,* in which the problem was interpreted in the most thorough manner. Don Quixote's first setting forth, with his arrival at nightfall at an inn which he takes to be a castle, is a perfect parody of Calogrenant's journey—precisely because the world which Don Quixote encounters is not one especially prepared for the proving of a knight but is a random, everyday, real world. By his detailed description of the circumstances of his hero's life, Cervantes makes it perfectly clear, at the very beginning of his book, where the root of Don Quixote's confusion lies: he is the victim of a social order in which he belongs to a class that has no function. He belongs to this class; he cannot emancipate himself from it; but as a mere member of it, without wealth and without high connections, he has no role and no mission. He feels his life running meaninglessly out, as though he were paralyzed. Only upon such a man, whose life is hardly better than a peasant's but who is educated and who is neither able nor permitted to labor as a peasant does, could romances of chivalry have such an unbalancing effect. His setting forth is a flight from a situation which is unbearable and which he has borne far too long. He wants to enforce his claim to the function proper to the class to which he belongs. It goes without saying that, three and a half centuries earlier, and in France, the situation is completely different. Feudal knighthood is still of crucial importance in military matters. The growth of an urban bourgeoisie and the growth of absolutism with its trend toward centralization are still in their earliest stages. But if Calogrenant had really set off on his quest as he describes it, he would even then have encountered things very different from those he reports. At the time of the second and third crusades, in the world of Henry II or Louis VII or Philip Augustus, things were hardly managed as they are in courtly romances. The courtly romance is not reality shaped and set forth by art, but an escape into fable and fairy tale. From the very beginning, at the height of its cultural florescence, this ruling class adopted an ethos and an ideal which concealed its real function. And it proceeded to describe its own life in extrahistorical terms, as an absolute aesthetic configuration without practical purpose. Certainly, one explanation of so strange a phenomenon lies in the surging imagination of that great century, in its spontaneous and soaring flight beyond reality into the absolute. But this explanation is too general to be adequate, especially since the courtly epic offers not only adventure and absolute idealization but also graceful manners and pompous ceremonies. One feels tempted to suggest that the long functional crisis of the feudal class had already begun to make itself felt—even at the time of the flowering of courtly literature. Chrétien de Troyes, who lived first in Champagne where, precisely during his lifetime, the great commercial fairs began to assume outstanding continental importance, then in Flanders where the burghers attained economic and political significance earlier than elsewhere north of the Alps, may well have begun to sense that the feudal class was no longer the only ruling class.

The widespread and long-enduring flowering of the courtly-chivalric romance exerted a significant and, more precisely, a restrictive influence upon literary realism, even before the antique doctrine of different levels of style began to be influential in the same restrictive direction. Finally the two were merged in the idea of an elevated style, as it gradually developed during the Renaissance. In a later chapter we shall return to this point. Here we shall discuss only the various influences which—as characteristics of the knightly ideal—were a hindrance to the full apprehension of reality as given. In this connection, as previously noted, we are not yet concerned with style in the strict sense. An elevated style of poetic expression had not yet been produced by the courtly epic. On the contrary, it did not even employ the elements of sublimity present in the paratactic form of the heroic epic. Its style is rather pleasantly narrative than sublime; it is suitable for any kind of subject matter. The later trend toward a linguistic separation of styles goes back entirely to the influence of antiquity, and not to that of courtly chivalry. Restrictions in terms of subject matter, however, are all the stronger.

They are class-determined. Only members of the chivalric-courtly society are worthy of adventure, hence they alone can undergo serious and significant experiences. Those outside this class cannot appear except as accessories, and even then generally in merely comic, grotesque, or despicable roles. This state of affairs is less apparent in antiquity and in the older heroic epic than here, where we are dealing with a conscious exclusiveness within a group characterized by class solidarity. Now it is true that before very long there were tendencies at work which sought to base the solidarity of the group not on descent but on personal factors, on noble behavior and refined manners. The beginning of this can already be discerned in the most important examples of the courtly epic itself, for in them the picture of the knightly individual, with increasing emphasis on inner values, is based on personal election and personal formation. Later, when—in Italy especially—social strata of urban background took over the courtly ideal and refashioned it, the concept of nobility became ever more personal, and as such it was actually often contrasted polemically with the other concept of nobility based solely on lineage. But all this did not render the ideal less exclusive. It continued to apply to a class of the elect, which at times indeed seemed to constitute a secret society. In the process, social, political, educational, mystical, and class motifs were interwoven in the most varied way. But the most important point is that this emphasis on inner values by no means brought a closer approach to earthly realities. On the contrary: in part at least it was precisely the emphasis laid on the inner values of the knightly ideal which caused the connection with the real things of this earth to become ever more fictitious and devoid of practical purpose. The relation of the courtly ideal to reality is determined by the fictitiousness and lack of practical purpose which, as we hope we have sufficiently shown, characterize it from the very first. Courtly culture gives rise to the idea, which long remained a factor of considerable importance in Europe, that nobility, greatness, and intrinsic values have nothing in common with everyday reality—an attitude of much greater emotional power and of much stronger hold on the minds of men than the classical forms of a turning away from reality, as we find them for example in the ethics of Stoicism. To be sure, antiquity offers one form of turning away from reality even more compelling in its hold on men's minds, and that is Platonism. There have been repeated attempts to show that Platonic elements were a contributing factor in the development of the courtly ideal. In later times Platonism and the courtly ideal complemented each other perfectly. The most famous illustration of this is probably Count Castiglione's *Il Cortegiano*. Yet the specific form which turning away from reality received from courtly culture—with the characteristic establishment of an illusory world of class (or half class, half personal) tests and ordeals—is still, despite its superficial Platonic varnish, a highly autonomous and essentially a medieval phenomenon.

All this has a bearing on the particular choice of subjects which characterizes the courtly epic—it is a choice which long exercised a decisive influence upon European literature. Only two themes are considered worthy of a knight: feats of arms, and love. Ariosto, who evolved from this illusory world a world of serene illusion, expressed the point perfectly in his opening lines:

> Le donne, i cavalier, l'arme, gli amori,
> Le cortesie, l'audaci imprese io canto . . .

Except feats of arms and love, nothing can occur in the courtly world —and even these two are of a special sort: they are not occurrences or emotions which can be absent for a time; they are permanently connected with the person of the perfect knight, they are part of his definition, so that he cannot for one moment be without adventure in arms nor for one moment without amorous entanglement. If he could, he would lose himself and no longer be a knight. Once again it is in the serene metamorphosis or the parody, Ariosto or Cervantes, that this fictitious form of life finds its clearest interpretation. As for feats of arms, I have nothing more to add. The reader will understand why, following Ariosto, I have chosen this term rather than "war," for they are feats accomplished at random, in one place as well as another, which do not fit into any politically purposive pattern. As for courtly love, which is one of the most frequently treated themes of medieval literary history, I need also say only what is relevant to my purpose. The first thing to bear in mind is that the classical form of it, if I may use the expression, which instantly comes to mind when courtly love is mentioned—the beloved as the mistress whose favor the knight strives to deserve through valorous deeds and perfect, even slavish, devotion—is by no means the only, or even the predominant form of love to be found during the heyday of the courtly epic. We need but remember Tristan and Iseut, Erec and Enide, Alixandre and Soredamors, Perceval and Blancheflor, Aucassin and Nicolete—none of these examples taken at random from among the most famous pairs of lovers entirely fits into the conventional schema and some of them do not fit into it at all. As a matter of fact, the courtly epic displays at first glance an abundance of quite different, extremely concrete love stories, thoroughly impregnated with reality. Sometimes they permit the reader completely to forget the fictitiousness of the world in which they take place. The Platonizing schema of the unattainable, vainly wooed mistress who inspires the hero from afar—a schema stemming from Provençal poetry and reaching its perfection in the Italian "new style"—does not predominate in the courtly epic at first. Then too, although the descriptions of the amorous state, the conversations between the lovers, the portrayal of their beauty, and whatever else forms an essential part of the setting for these episodes of love, reveal —especially in Chrétien—a great deal of gracefully sensuous art, they yet have hardly any hyperbolic *galanterie*. For that, a very different level of style is required than what the courtly epic affords. The fictitious and unreal character of the love stories is as yet hardly a matter of the stories themselves. It rather lies in their function within the total structure of the poem. Love in the courtly romances is already not infrequently the immediate occasion for deeds of valor. There is nothing surprising in this if we consider the complete absence of practical motivation through a political and historical context. Love, being an essential and obligatory ingredient of knightly perfection, functions as a substitute for other possibilities of motivation which are here lacking. This implies, in general outline, the fictitious order of events in which the most significant actions are performed primarily for the sake of a lady's favor; it also implies the superior rank assigned to love as a poetic theme which came to be so important for European literature. The literature of the ancients did not rank love very high on the whole. It is a predominant subject neither in tragedy nor in the great epic. Its central position in courtly culture moulded the slowly emerging elevated style of the European vernaculars. Love became a theme for the elevated style (as Dante confirms in *De Vulgari Eloquentia*, 2, 2) and was often its most important theme. This was accomplished by a process of sublimation of love which led to mysticism or gallantry. And in both cases it led far from the concrete realities of this world. To this sublimation of love, the Provençals and the Italian "new style" contributed more decisively than did the courtly epic. But it too played a significant part in the elevated rank ascribed to love, for it introduced it into the realm of heroism and class principles and merged it with them.

So the result of our interpretation and the considerations which have accompanied it is that courtly culture was decidedly unfavorable to the development of a literary art which should apprehend reality in its full breadth and depth. Yet there were other forces at work in the twelfth and thirteenth centuries which were able to nourish and further such a development.

7

ADAM AND EVE

. . . Adam vero veniet ad Evam, moleste ferens quod cum ea locutus sit Diabolus, et dicet ei:

Di moi, muiller, que te querroit
Li mal Satan? que te voleit?
Eva — Il me parla de nostre honor.
Adam — Ne creire ja le traïtor!
Il est traïtre, bien le sai.
Eva — Et tu coment?
Adam — Car l'esaiai!
Eva — De ço que chalt me del veer?
Il te fera changer saver.
Adam — Nel fera pas, car nel crerai
De nule rien tant que l'asai.
Nel laisser mais venir sor toi
Car il est mult de pute foi.
Il volt traïr ja son seignor,
E soi poser al des halzor.
Tel paltonier qui ço ad fait
Ne voil vers vus ait nul retrait.

Tunc serpens artificiose compositus ascendet juxta stipitem arboris vetite. Cui Eva propius adhibebit aurem, quasi ipsius ascultans consilium. Dehinc accipiet Eva pomum, porriget Ade. Ipse vero nondum eum accipiet, et Eva dicet ei:

Manjue, Adam, ne sez que est;
Pernum ço bien que nus est prest.
Adam — Est il tant bon?
Eva — Tu le saveras;
Nel poez saver sin gusteras.
Adam — J'en duit!
Eva — Fai le!
Adam — Nen frai pas.
Eva — Del demorer fai tu que las.

Adam Et jo le prendrai.
Eva Manjue, ten!
Par ço saveras e mal e bien.
Jo en manjerai premirement.
Adam E jo aprés.
Eva Seurement.

Tunc commedet Eva partem pomi, et dicet Ade:

Gusté en ai. Deus! quele savor!
Unc ne tastai d'itel dolçor,
D'itel savor est ceste pome!
Adam De quel?
Eva D'itel nen gusta home.
Or sunt mes oil tant cler veant,
Jo semble Deu le tuit puissant.
Quanque fu, quanque doit estre
Sai jo trestut, bien en sui maistre.
Manjue, Adam, ne faz demore;
Tu le prendras en mult bon'ore.

Tunc accipiet Adam pomum de manu Eve, dicens:

Jo t'en crerrai, tu es ma per.
Eva Manjue, nen poez doter.

Tunc commedat Adam partem pomi. . . .

(Then Adam shall go to Eve, vexed because the Devil has talked to her, and shall say to her:

Tell me, woman, what did the evil Satan want from you? What was he looking for?
Eve He spoke about our weal.
Adam Don't you believe that traitor. He is a traitor, I well know.
Eve But how do you know?
Adam I have tried it out.
Eve Why should I care about that and not see him again? He will make you change your mind.
Adam He won't, for I won't believe him in anything I have not tried out. Don't let him come near you again, for he is a fellow of very bad faith. He wanted to betray his

Lord and set himself in His height. I don't want a scoundrel who has done that to have anything to do with you.

Then a skilfully fashioned serpent shall climb up along the trunk of the tree. Eve shall turn her ear toward it as though listening to its advice. Then Eve shall take the apple and offer it to Adam. He shall not yet accept it, and Eve shall say to him:

Eat, Adam, you don't know what it is. Let us take this good thing which is ready for us.

Adam Is it so good?

Eve You will find out. You cannot find out if you do not taste it.

Adam I am afraid of it.

Eve Do it.

Adam I won't do it.

Eve You hesitate because you are cowardly.

Adam So I shall take it.

Eve Eat, I tell you! By it you shall know evil and good. I will eat first.

Adam And I afterwards.

Eve Certainly.

Here Eve shall eat a piece of the apple and say to Adam:

I have tasted it. God, what a savor! Never have I tasted such sweetness. Of such savor is this apple!

Adam Of what savor?

Eve No man ever tasted the like. Now my eyes are so clear-sighted, I seem like God, the Almighty. All that was, all that will be, I know entirely and am master of it. Eat, Adam, do not hesitate. You will take it in a fortunate hour.

Then Adam shall take the apple from the hand of Eve and shall say:

I shall believe you. You are my equal.

Eve Eat, you have nothing to fear.

Then Adam shall eat part of the apple. . . .)

This piece of dialogue occurs in the *Mystère d'Adam,* a Christmas play from the latter part of the twelfth century, which is extant in a single manuscript. Very little has come down to us from the earliest period of the liturgical drama (or the drama that grew out of the liturgy) in the vernacular, and of that little, the *Mystère d'Adam* is one of the oldest specimens. The Fall, which occupies the greater part of it (after which there is still room for the murder of Abel and the procession of the prophets announcing Christ's coming), begins with an unsuccessful attempt by the Devil to lead Adam astray. The Devil then approaches Eve, and this time has better luck. Immediately afterward, he runs off (to Hell), but as he does so, Adam gets a glimpse of him. The scene reprinted above begins after his disappearance. No such scene in the form of a dialogue occurs in Genesis, nor does any preceding attempt on the Devil's part to lead Adam astray. In dialogue form, Genesis gives only the scene between Eve and the serpent, which, according to a very old tradition, is identical with the Devil (see Rev. 12: 9); the passage that follows is entirely narrative: *vidit igitur mulier quod bonum esset lignum ad vescendum, et pulchrum oculis, aspectuque delectabile; et tulit de fructu illius, et comedit; deditque viro suo, qui comedit.* It is from these last words that our scene developed.

It is divided into two parts. The first contains a conversation between Adam and Eve concerning the desirability of dealing with the Devil; here the apple is not mentioned. In the second, Eve takes the apple from the tree and tempts Adam into eating of it. The two parts are separated by the intervention of the serpent—the *serpens artificiose compositus*—which whispers something into Eve's ear. What it is we are not told, but we can imagine it, for immediately afterward Eve reaches for the apple, offers it to the reluctant Adam, and utters what will be her principal motif, often repeated: *Manjue, Adam*! Thus she breaks off the first conversation, concerning dealing with the Devil, before it is finished; she does not reply to Adam's last speech, but brings about a completely new situation, a *fait accompli* which cannot but surprise Adam the more since so far there has been no mention of the apple in his conversation with her. She appears to be acting upon the serpent's advice and this also explains the serpent's intervention at this precise juncture: for to win Eve over to itself and for its purpose would no longer be necessary; that had already been accomplished in the preceding scene between Eve and the Devil, which had concluded with Eve's decision to taste the apple and give Adam some of it too. The serpent's intervention in the middle of the conversation between Adam and Eve can serve no other purpose than to give Eve a directive which is needed at this precise moment: namely, that she should break off the discussion, which from the Devil's point of view was becoming dangerous and useless, and should instead proceed to action. But the reason the discussion is dangerous and useless from the Devil's viewpoint is the evident fact that it fails to convince Adam, while there is even a risk that Eve herself may again begin to hesitate.

Now let us examine the first part of the scene, that is, the conversation concerning the desirability of dealing with the Devil. Adam calls his wife to account as a French farmer or burgher might have done when, upon returning home, he saw something that he did not like: his wife talking to a fellow with whom he has already had unpleasant experiences and with whom he does not want to have anything to do. Woman, *muiller*, he says to her, what was that fellow doing around here? What did he want with you? Eve answers in a way that is meant to impress him: "He talked of how we could better ourselves!" (for "weal, advantage, betterment" would seem to be the sense of *honor* here; even in the *chansons de geste* the word has a strongly materialistic value). "Don't you believe him," says Adam emphatically, "he is a traitor, I know all about him!" Eve knows all about him too, but it has never occurred to her that such a thing could be called treason. There is no moral consciousness in her as there is in Adam; in its place she has a naive, childishly hardy, and unreflectingly sinful curiosity. Adam's clear appraisal and condemnation of the Devil and his schemes disconcerts her. She falls back on an insincere and impertinent but embarrassed question, the sort of question which has been asked a thousand times in similar situations by naive, impetuous people who are governed by their instincts: "How do you know?" The question does her no good. Adam is too sure of his ground. "I have found out by experience!" These words cannot be Eve's, as a textual critic has recently assumed (we shall have more to say about this); for only Adam has consciously had such an experience, and it is the tone of *his* voice which we hear in this energetic reply. Eve on the other hand has in nowise interpreted her conversation with the Devil as an experience of his treachery; her playful curiosity failed to grasp the ethical problem. Even now she does not grasp it, for she does not want to. She has made up her mind to give the other side (the Devil) a try for once. But she senses that she cannot contradict Adam seriously when he says that the Devil is a traitor. So she abandons the course she had taken with the question "How do you know?", and instead comes out—half frightened and half brazen—with her real thoughts: "Why should that prevent me from seeing him. He will change your mind for you too!" (*changer saver* refers to *bien le sai*, the knowledge of the Devil's treachery which only Adam has). But this was a wrong move, for now Adam grows seriously angry: "He won't do that, because I shall never trust him!" And with the authority of a man who knows himself master of his house and fully in the right as to the facts, he now clearly states the reasons for his view and forbids Eve to have any dealings with the Devil ("with a scoundrel who did a thing like that you can have nothing to do"), for he remembers the part which God bade him play in relation to the woman: *Tu la governe par raison* (l. 21). At this point the Devil senses that his plan is miscarrying and so he intervenes.

I have discussed this passage in detail because the text of the manuscript is somewhat confused in respect to the distribution of lines between the two speakers and especially because S. Etienne (*Romania*, 1922, pp. 592-595) proposed a reading for lines 280-287 which was adopted in Chamard's edition (Paris, 1925) but which I do not find convincing. It is as follows:

Adam Ne creire ja le traitor!
Il est traitre.
Eva Bien le sai.
Adam Et tu coment?
Eva Car l'asaiai.
De ço que chalt me del veer?
Adam Il te ferra changer saver.
Eva Nel fera pas, car nel crerai
De nule rien tant que l'asai.
Adam Nel laisser mais. . . .

I consider this impossible. The very different tone of the two characters is completely confused. It is not possible for Eve to say *bien le sai*, nor for Adam to ask how she knows, nor for Eve to refer to her previous experience. And to expunge Adam's emphatic answer "the Devil will never succeed in that" from the conversation by interpreting it as a reassuring remark which Eve offers to calm Adam's apprehensions, strikes me as completely misguided. In support of his proposal, Etienne contends that Eve's answer, *de ço que chalt me del veer?* to Adam's assertion, "I know from experience" (as the earlier editors, and I too, have understood it), would be *d'une maladresse inconcevable*; she would be admitting to Adam that she was in league with the Devil:

ayant ainsi convaincu Adam de sa complicité avec le tentateur elle réussirait dès la scène suivante à le persuader d'accepter d'elle ce qu'il avait refusé de son compère! This, Etienne insists, would be against all verisimilitude, as it would be that Eve should say: Satan will make you change your mind—for *Satan n'intervient plus,* and after all it is Eve who leads Adam astray! It is evident that Etienne conceives of Eve as an extremely skillful and diplomatic person, whose object is to soothe Adam and make him forget the tempter Satan against whom he is prejudiced, or at least to make him understand that she does not blindly rely on Satan but intends to wait and see whether his promises come true.

Such speeches are hardly calculated to soothe Adam, and the fact that Satan does not reappear is in no way an argument against Eve's remarking that he may make Adam change his mind. Aside from these minor flaws, Etienne's view proves that he has failed to understand the significance of the serpent's intervention and the tremendous effect produced on Adam by Eve's compliance with the serpent's advice (that is, her picking the apple from the tree), although these points furnish the key to the entire scene. Why does the serpent intervene? Because it senses that things are going badly for it. Eve, in fact, is clumsy, very clumsy, even though her clumsiness is not hard to understand. For without the Devil's special help she is but a weak—though curious and hence sinful—creature, far inferior to her husband and easily guided by him. That is how God created her from Adam's rib. And God explicitly ordered Adam to guide her, and Eve to obey and serve him. Confronted with Adam, Eve is fearful, submissive, self-conscious. She feels she cannot cope with his clear and reasonable and manly will. The serpent alone changes all this. It upsets the order of things established by God, it makes the woman the man's master, and so leads both to ruin.

The serpent accomplishes this by advising Eve to break off the theoretical discussion and to confront Adam with a wholly unexpected *fait accompli.* Earlier, when the Devil had talked to Eve, he had given her the directive: *primes le pren, Adam le done!* (take it—the apple —first, then give it to Adam). It is of this directive that the serpent now reminds her. Adam must not be approached where he is strong but where he is weak. He is a good man, a French peasant or burgher. In the normal course of life he is reliable and sure of himself. He knows what he is supposed to do and what not. God's orders were clear, and his honest decency is rooted in this unambiguous certainty which guards him against dubious entanglements. He also knows that he has his wife under his thumb. He is not afraid of her occasional whims, which he regards as childish and not at all dangerous. Suddenly something unprecedented happens, something that upsets his whole system of life. The woman who a moment ago was chattering away with childish thoughtlessness, without rhyme or reason, whom but a moment ago he had caught up sharp with a few determined words which permitted no rejoinder—the same woman suddenly displays a will of her own, completely independent of his will; she reveals it through an act which to him seems a monstrous portent. She picks the apple from the tree as though it were the easiest and most natural thing in the world to do, and then presses him hard with her *manjue, Adam!* four times repeated. His horrified refusal, which the Latin stage direction expresses in the words *Ipse autem nondum eum accipiet,* cannot possibly be exaggerated. But his earlier calm assurance has vanished completely. The shock has been too severe; the roles are exchanged; Eve is master of the situation. The few words which he still manages to stammer out show that he is in a state of utter confusion. He vacillates between fear and desire—not actually a desire for the apple but rather a desire to prove and assert himself: is he, as a man, to be afraid of doing what the woman has just successfully done? And when he finally overcomes his fear and takes the apple, he does it with a most touching movement of feeling: what his wife does, he will do too; he will trust her: *jo t'en crerrai, tu es ma per. Perniciose misericors,* as Bernard of Clairvaux once described it (Pat. Lat. 183, 460). Here we see how wrongly Etienne formulates the situation (see above), when he thinks it surprising that Eve, as the Devil's ally, should succeed in leading Adam astray although the Devil himself could not do so. Actually no one but she could succeed here (with the Devil's help), for only she is connected with Adam in so special a relationship that her actions affect him spontaneously and deeply. She is *sa per,* the Devil is not—quite apart from the fact that an essential element in Adam's seduction is the *fait accompli* of the apple picked from the tree and offered to him, and that the apple had to be picked by a human being, not by the Devil. Now, while in this second part of the scene Adam appears to be disconcerted and confused, Eve—to use the language of sport—is in great form. The Devil has taught her how to get the better of her man; he has showed her where her strength is greater than his: in unconsidered action, in her lack of any innate moral sense, so that she transgresses the restriction with the foolhardiness of a child as soon as the man loses his hold (*sa discipline*) upon her (l. 36). There she stands, seductive, the apple in her hand, and plays with poor, confused, uprooted Adam. Urging him, holding out promises, ridiculing his fears, she leads him on, and finally she has an inspired idea: she will take the first bite herself! And so she does. And then, when, praising the flavor and the effect of the fruit ecstatically, she approaches him once again with her *manjue, Adam,* there is no escape left for him. He takes the apple, with the touching phrase we quoted above. Again she says, for the last time, "Come, eat it! Don't be afraid!" And it is all over.

The episode which is here presented to us in dramatic form is the starting point of the Christian drama of redemption, and hence is a subject of the utmost importance and the utmost sublimity from the point of view of the author and his audience. However, the presentation aims to be popular. The ancient and sublime occurrence is to become immediate and present; it is to be a current event which could happen any time, which every listener can imagine and is familiar with; it is to strike deep roots in the mind and the emotions of any random French contemporary. Adam talks and acts in a manner any member of the audience is accustomed to from his own or his neighbor's house; things would go exactly the same way in any townsman's home or on any farm where an upright but not very brillant husband was tempted into a foolish and fateful act by his vain and ambitious wife who had been deceived by an unscrupulous swindler. The dialogue between Adam and Eve—this first man-woman dialogue of universal historical import—is turned into a scene of simplest everyday reality. Sublime as it is, it becomes a scene in simple, low style.

In antique theory, the sublime and elevated style was called *sermo gravis* or *sublimis*; the low style was *sermo remissus* or *humilis*; the two had to be kept strictly separated. In the world of Christianity, on the other hand, the two are merged, especially in Christ's Incarnation and Passion, which realize and combine *sublimitas* and *humilitas* in overwhelming measure.

This is a very old Christian motif (see above, especially pp. 72f.). It comes to life again in the theological and particularly the mystic literature of the twelfth century. In Bernard of Clairvaux and the Victorines it occurs frequently, with both *humilitas* and *sublimitas* being employed, in relation to Christ as well as absolutely, in antithetic contrast. *Humilitas virtutum magistra, singularis filia summi regis* (says Bernard, *Epist.* 469, 2, Pat. Lat. 182, 674), *a summo coelo cum coelorum domino descendens. . . . Sola est humilitas quae virtutes beatificat et perennat, quae vim facit regno coelorum* (Matt. 11: 12), *quae dominum majestatis humiliavit usque ad mortem, mortem autem crucis* (Phil. 2: 8). *Verbum enim Dei in sublimi constitutum ut ad nos descenderet, prior humilitas invitavit.*

> (Humility is the mistress of the virtues, the excellent daughter of the highest King, descending from the highest heaven with the Lord of the heavens. . . . It is humility alone which makes the virtues blessed and everlasting, which forces the kingdom of heaven, which humbled the Lord of Majesty unto death, even the death of the cross. For that the Word of God, dwelling in the Sublime, should descend to us, was first prompted by humility.)

In his sermons too the antithesis *humilitas-sublimitas* appears time and again: both in reference to Christ's Incarnation, when he exclaims, prompted by Luke 3: 23, "being (as was supposed) the son of Joseph," *O humilitas virtus Christi! o humilitatis sublimitas! quantum confundis superbiam nostrae vanitatis!* (*In epiph. Domini sermo*, 1, 7; Pat. Lat. 183, 146), as also in regard to the Passion and Christ's mission in general, considered as an object of emulation: *Propterea, dilectissimi, perseverate in disciplina quam suscepistis, ut per humilitatem ad sublimitatem ascendatis, quia haec est via et non est alia praeter ipsam. Qui aliter vadit, cadit potius quam ascendit, quia sola est humilitas quae exaltat, sola quae ducit ad vitam. Christus enim, cum per naturam divinitatis non haberet quo cresceret vel ascenderet, quia ultra deum nihil est, per descensum quomodo cresceret invenit, veniens incarnari, pati, mori, ne moreremur in aeternum. . . .* (*In ascens. Dom.* 2, 6; Pat. Lat. 183, 304.)

> (Therefore, dearly beloved, persevere in the discipline which you have taken upon you, so that by humility you may ascend to sublimity, for this is the way and there is none other. Who walks otherwise falls rather than rises, for it is humility alone which exalts, humility alone which leads to life. For Christ, having, by his divine nature, nowhither to grow or to ascend, because beyond God there is nothing, found by descending a way to grow, coming to be made flesh, to suffer, to die, that we should not die in eternity. . . .)

But the most beautiful passage of this kind—and at the same time one that is most characteristic of the style of Bernard the mystic—may well be the following, from his commentary on the Song of Songs: O *humilitas, o sublimitas! Et tabernaculum Cedar* (Cant. 1: 5), *et sanctuarium Dei; et terrenum habitaculum, et coeleste palatium; et domus lutea, et aula regia; et corpus mortis, et templum lucis; et despectio denique superbis, et sponsa Christi.* Nigra est, sed formosa, filiae Jerusalem (Cant. 1: 5-6): *quam etsi labor et dolor longi exilii decolorat, species tamen coelestis exornat, exornant pelles Salomonis* (Cant. 1: 5). *Si horretis nigram, miremini et formosam; si despicitis humilem, sublimem suspicite. Hoc ipsum quam cautum, quam plenum consilii, plenum discretionis et congruentiae est, quod in sponsa dejectio ista, et ista celsitudo secundum tempus quidem eo moderamine sibi pariter contemperantur, ut inter mundi huius varietates et sublimitas erigat humilem, ne deficiat in adversis; et sublimem humilitas reprimat, ne evanescat in prosperis? Pulchre omnino ambae res, cum ad invicem contrariae sint, sponsae tamen pariter cooperantur in bonum, subserviunt in salutem.*

(O humility, O sublimity! [Thou art] the tents of Kedar, and the sanctuary of God; an earthly habitation, and a heavenly palace; a house of clay, and a kingly court; a body of death, and a temple of light; lastly, a scorn to the proud, and the bride of Christ. *She is black but comely, O daughters of Jerusalem*: though the toil and pain of a long exile discolor her, yet a heavenly beauty adorns her, the curtains of Solomon adorn her. If you shudder at her blackness, admire too her beauty; if you despise her humbleness, behold her sublimity. How provident it is, how full of discretion and congruence, that this very degradation and this very exaltation of the bride compensate each other in this temporal world, so that amid its many changes sublimity raises up the humble man so that he does not fail in adversity, and humility restrains the proud man so that he does not grow vain in prosperity! Most beautiful, then, are they both, forasmuch as, though they are contraries, they work together alike for the good of the bride and serve her salvation.)

These significant passages are concerned with the thing itself, not with its literary treatment. *Sublimitas* and *humilitas* are here wholly ethico-theological categories, not aesthetico-stylistic ones. Yet in this latter sense too, that is in terms of style, the antithetical fusion of the two was emphasized, so early as the patristic period, as a characteristic of Holy Scripture—especially by Augustine (see above, pp. 72f.). The point of departure was the Scripture text that God had hidden these things from the wise and prudent and revealed them unto babes (Matt. 11: 25; Luke 10: 21), as well as the fact that Christ had chosen fishermen and publicans and such humble people as his first disciples (see also I Cor. 1: 26ff.) rather than men of rank or learning. But the question of style became really acute when the spread of Christianity exposed Holy Scripture, and Christian literature in general, to the aesthetic criticism of highly educated pagans. They were horrified at the claim that the highest truths were contained in writings composed in a language to their minds impossibly uncivilized and in total ignorance of the stylistic categories. This criticism did not go unheeded, and the Fathers were generally far more concerned with the traditional standards of classical style than were the earliest Christian documents. But the same criticism also opened their eyes to the true and distinctive greatness of Holy Scripture—namely, that it had created an entirely new kind of sublimity, in which the everyday and the low were included, not excluded, so that, in style as in content, it directly connected the lowest with the highest. With this yet another train of thought was associated, based on the occult character of many passages in the Bible and the great difficulty in interpreting them: while on the one hand Scripture speaks very simply, as if to children, on the other hand it contains secrets and riddles which are revealed to very few; but even these passages are not written in a pretentious and erudite style, so that they can be understood only by the highly educated, proud in their knowledge, they can be understood by all who are humble and filled with faith. Augustine—who described his own advance to a comprehension of Holy Scripture in his *Confessions* (especially 3, 5 and 6, 5)—expresses this in a letter to Volusianus (137, 18) in the following terms: *ea vero quae (sacra scriptura) in mysteriis occultat, nec ipsa eloquio superbo erigit, quo non audeat accedere mens tardiuscula et inerudita quasi pauper ad divitem; sed invitat omnes humili sermone, quos non solum manifesta pascat, sed etiam secreta exerceat veritate, hoc in promptis quod in reconditis habens.* Or in the first chapter of *De trinitate: Sacra scriptura parvulis congruens nullius generis rerum verba vitavit* [clearly an allusion to the antique separation of styles], *ex quibus quasi gradatim ad divina atque sublimia noster intellectus velut nutritus assurgeret.* Among the numerous similar passages in Augustine which vary this theme in many ways, I will mention one more, because it describes the type of comprehension which is open to the humble and simple. It occurs in the

Enarrationes in Psalmos and refers to the words, *suscipiens mansuetos Dominus,* in Psalm 146: *Conticescant humanae voces, requiescant humanae cogitationes; ad incomprehensibilia non se extendant quasi comprehensuri, sed tamquam participaturi*—a passage in which we see a most beautiful fusion of mystic elements and the concretely sensuous desire to share in possession (in opposition, of course, to the "proud" intellectual arrogance of those who insist on understanding). Peter Lombard, the *Magister sententiarum,* virtually copied the passage in his commentary on the Psalms, composed about the middle of the twelfth century. And the complete transformation into mysticism is to be found in Bernard, who bases comprehension entirely upon meditation on Christ's life and Passion: *Beati qui noverunt gustu felicis experientiae, quam dulciter, quam mirabiliter in oratione et meditatione scripturas dignetur Dominus revelare* (*in feria* 2 *Paschatis sermo,* 20).

Several thoughts in complex interdependence are expressed in these passages: that Holy Scripture favors those whose hearts are simple and filled with faith; that such a heart is a prerequisite to "sharing" in it, for sharing and not a purely rational understanding is what it seeks to offer; that the occult and obscure elements it contains are likewise not couched in an "elevated style" (*eloquio superbo*) but in simple words, so that anyone can ascend *quasi gradatim* from the simple to the sublime and divine, or, as Augustine puts it in the *Confessions,* that one must read it as a child would: *verum tamen illa erat, quae cresceret cum parvulis.* And the idea that it differs in all these respects from the great secular writers of antiquity is likewise one that survived all through the Middle Ages. As late as the second half of the fourteenth century, Benvenuto da Imola, commenting on the line in Dante in which Beatrice's manner of speaking is described (*Inf.* 2, 56: *e comminciommi a dir soave e piana*), writes: *et bene dicit, quia sermo divinus est suavis et planus, non altus et superbus sicut sermo Virgilii et poetarum*—although Beatrice as a mouthpiece of divine wisdom has to say much that is dark and difficult.

The medieval Christian drama falls perfectly within this tradition. Being a living representation of Biblical episodes as contained, with their innately dramatic elements, in the liturgy, it opens its arms invitingly to receive the simple and untutored and to lead them from the concrete, the everyday, to the hidden and the true—precisely as did that great plastic art of the medieval churches which, according to E. Mâle's well-known theory, is supposed to have received decisive stimuli from the mysteries, that is, from the religious drama. The purpose of the liturgical or more generally the Christian theater is attested from a very early period. In the tenth century Saint Ethelwold, Bishop of Winchester, describes a dramatized Easter ceremony used by some priests *ad fidem indocti vulgi ac neofitorum corroborandam* and recommends it as worthy of imitation (quoted after E. K. Chambers, *The Mediaeval Stage,* 2, 308). And in the twelfth century Suger of Saint-Denis puts it more profoundly and more generally in his frequently-quoted verse: *Mens hebes ad verum per materialia surgit.*

Let us now return to our text, the scene between Adam and Eve. It speaks *humili sermone* to the simple and pure in spirit. It situates the sublime event within their everyday lives, so that it is spontaneously present to them. Yet it does not forget that the subject is a sublime one; it leads from the simplest reality directly to the highest, most secret, and divine truth. The *Mystère d'Adam* is introduced by a liturgical reading of Scripture from Genesis, with lector and responding chorus. Then come the dramatized events of the Fall, with God Himself appearing among the dramatis personae. The story is carried on to the murder of Abel. And the conclusion of the whole is a procession of the Old Testament prophets announcing the coming of Christ. The scenes which render everyday contemporary life (the finest are the one between the Devil and Eve and the one here under discussion—two masterly pieces of incomparable purity, truly peers of the most perfect sculptures in Chartres, Reims, Paris, or Amiens) are, then, fitted into a Biblical and world-historical frame by whose spirit they are pervaded. And the spirit of the frame which encompasses them is the spirit of the figural interpretation of history. This implies that every occurrence, in all its everyday reality, is simultaneously a part in a world-historical context through which each part is related to every other, and thus is likewise to be regarded as being of all times or above all time. Let us begin with God Himself, who appears after the creation of the world and man to lead Adam and Eve into Paradise and make his will known to them. He is called *figura.* This term can be interpreted as referring simply to the priest who was to act—that is to say, be the figure for—the part and whom one hesitated to call Deus as one called the other actors Adam, Eve, etc. But a truly figural interpretation here seems likelier; for although God's role in what actually takes place in the *Mystère d'Adam* is merely that of the lawgiver and the judge who punishes transgression, yet the redeeming

Saviour is already figurally present in him. The stage direction announcing his appearance reads as follows: *Tunc veniet Salvator indutus dalmatica, et statuantur choram eo Adam et Eva. . . . Et stent ambo coram Figura. . . .* God, then, is first called *Salvator* and only afterward *Figura,* which would seem to justify the explanation: *figura salvatoris.* This supratemporal figural conception is taken up again later on. When Adam has eaten of the apple, he is immediately overcome by the most profound remorse. He breaks out into desperate self-accusations, which finally turn against Eve too, and which conclude as follows:

Par ton conseil sui mis a mal,
De grant haltesce sui mis a val.
N'en serrai trait por home né,
Si Deu nen est de majesté.
Que di jo, las? por quoi le nomai?
Il me aidera? Corocé l'ai.
Ne me ferat ja nul aïe,
For le filz qu' istra de Marie.
Ne sai de nus prendre conroi,
Quant a Deu ne portames foi.
Or en soit tot a Deu plaisir!
N'i ad conseil que del morir.

(Through your advice I have been brought to evil, from a great height I have fallen into great depth. I shall not be raised from it by man born of woman, unless it be God in His Majesty. What am I saying, alas? Why did I name Him? He help me? I have angered Him. No one will help me now except the Son who will come forth from Mary. To no one can I turn for protection, since in God we kept no faith. Now then let everything be according to God's will! There is no council but to die.)

From this text—especially from the phrase, *for le filz qu' istra de Marie*—it is clear that Adam has advance knowledge of all of Christian world history, or at least of Christ's coming and the redemption from that original sin which he, Adam, has just committed. In the very depth of his despair he already knows of the grace which will be fulfilled in its time. That grace—albeit a thing of the future, and even of a specific historically identifiable part of the future—is nevertheless included in the present knowledge of any and all times. For in God there is no distinction of times since for him everything is a simultaneous present, so that—as Augustine once put it—he does not possess foreknowledge but simply knowledge. One must, then, be very much on one's guard against taking such violations of chronology, where the future seems to reach back into the present, as nothing more than evidence of a kind of medieval naïveté. Naturally, such an interpretation is not wrong, for what these violations of chronology afford is in fact an extremely simplified overall view adapted to the simplest comprehension—but this simultaneous overall view is at the same time the expression of a unique, exalted, and hidden truth, the very truth of the figural structure of universal history. Everything in the dramatic play which grew out of the liturgy during the Middle Ages is part of one—and always of the same—context: of one great drama whose beginning is God's creation of the world, whose climax is Christ's Incarnation and Passion, and whose expected conclusion will be Christ's second coming and the Last Judgment. The intervals between the poles of the action are filled partly by figuration, partly by imitation, of Christ. Before his appearance there are the characters and events of the Old Testament—of the age of the Law—in which the coming of the Saviour is figurally revealed; this is the meaning of the procession of prophets. After Christ's Incarnation and Passion there are the saints, intent upon following in his footsteps, and Christianity in general—Christ's promised bride—awaiting the return of the Bridegroom. In principle, this great drama contains everything that occurs in world history. In it all the heights and depths of human conduct and all the heights and depths of stylistic expression find their morally or aesthetically established right to exist; and hence there is no basis for a separation of the sublime from the low and everyday, for they are indissolubly connected in Christ's very life and suffering. Nor is there any basis for concern with the unities of time, place, or action, for there is but one place—the world; and but one action—man's fall and redemption. To be sure, the entire course of world history is not represented each time. In the early periods we have only separate fragments, most frequently Easter and Christmas plays which arose from the liturgy. But the whole is always borne in mind and figurally represented. From the fourteenth century on, the full cycle appears in the mystery plays.

The everyday and real is thus an essential element of medieval Christian art and especially of the Christian drama. In contrast to the feudal literature of the courtly romance, which leads away from the reality of the life of its class into a world of heroic fable and adventure, here there is a movement in the opposite direction, from distant legend and its figural interpretation into everyday contemporary reality. In our text the realistic is still within the frame of the actualization of domestic episodes, of a conversation between the wife and the flattering seducer and another between husband and wife. There are as yet no coarsely realistic or farcical elements; at most the scurrying about of the devils (*interea Demones discurrant per plateas, gestum facientes competentem*) may have given occasion for some crude jokes. But later it is different: realism of a coarser grain begins to thrive, and varieties of mixed style, of the blunt juxtaposition of Passion and crude farce, develop, which to us appear strange and unseemly. When this development actually began cannot be clearly ascertained. But it was probably much earlier than the surviving dramatic texts make it appear. For complaints about the growing coarseness of the liturgical plays (not to be confused with their outright condemnation: that is another problem, which cannot be taken up in our context) occur as early as the twelfth century—for example in Herrad of Landsberg. It is most likely that a good deal of this sort of thing was already in evidence at that period, for, in general, it is the period of a reawakening popular realism. The subliterary survival of the tradition of the antique mime and the more conscious, more strongly critical, and more forceful observation of life, which, beginning with the twelfth century, seems to have set in among the lower classes too, led at that time to a flourishing development of the popular farce, whose spirit may well be assumed to have soon found its way into the religious drama as well. The audience was exactly the same; and it seems that even the lower clergy often shared the taste of the people in these matters. In any case, the extant documents of Christian dramatic literature indicate that the realistic and in particular the grotesque and farcical element became increasingly current, that it reached a climax in the fifteenth century, and thus afforded a sufficiency of arguments to the ultimately successful attacks of the countermovement which, inspired by humanist taste and (from Wycliffe on) by the sterner attitudes of the Reformation, considered the Christian mysteries tasteless and unseemly.

The popular farce does not enter into our discussion because its realism remains within the limits of the purely comic and unproblematic. But we shall list certain scenes from the mysteries which initiated a particularly striking development of realism. To begin with, there is the nativity in the stable at Bethlehem, with ox and ass and sometimes also midwives and godmothers (together with the appropriate dialogue) and occasionally the most outspoken episodes involving Joseph and the maids. Then the announcement to the shepherds, the arrival of the Three Kings, and the slaughter of the children are given realistic trappings. Still more striking and, to later taste, still more unseemly, are the outspoken scenes connected with the Passion: the crude and sometimes farcical conversations between the soldiers while Christ is crowned with thorns, is scourged, carries the cross, and finally even during the crucifixion itself (throwing dice for the clothes, the scene with Longinus, etc.). Among the episodes connected with the Resurrection there is especially the visit of the three Marys to the shop of the chandler (*unguentarius*) to buy ointments for the body of Christ, and the running and racing of the disciples to reach the sepulchre (according to John 20: 3, 4); the former is turned into a marketplace scene, the latter into a frolicsome free-for-all. The representation of Mary Magdalene in her sinful days is sometimes detailed and precise, and in the procession of the prophets there are also a few figures which give occasion for grotesque scenes (Balaam and the ass!). Our list is quite incomplete. There are conversations between workmen (at the building of the Tower of Babel for instance), who discuss their trades and the bad times. There are noisy and boisterous scenes at inns, and farcical jokes and dirty stories in plenty. All this finally leads to abuse and disorder, and it may rightly be said that the colorful world of contemporary life occupies an ever-increasing place. Yet it is misleading to speak of a progressive secularization of the Christian passion play, as is generally done. For the *saeculum* is included in this drama as a matter of principle and from the beginning, and the question of more or less is not a question of principle. A real secularization does not take place until the frame is broken, until the secular action becomes independent; that is, when human actions outside of Christian world history, as determined by Fall, Passion, and Last Judgment, are represented in a serious vein; when, in addition to this manner of conceiving and representing human events, with its claim to be the only true and valid one, other ways of doing so become possible.

Then too the transfer—anachronistic to our way of feeling—of the events into a contemporary setting and into contemporary forms of life is equally unexceptionable. This again is something which, in the *Mystère d'Adam,* is only indicated to the extent that Adam and Eve speak like simple people of twelfth-century France (*tel paltonier qui ço ad fait*). Elsewhere and later, this is much more striking. In the fragment of a French Easter play which belongs to the beginning of the thirteenth century and which likewise survives in only one manuscript (I use the text in Förster-Koschwitz, *Altfranzösisches Übungsbuch*, 6th edition, 1921, pp. 214ff.), the subject matter is the scene with Joseph of Arimathaea and the scene with the blind Longinus who is healed by Christ's blood; here Pilate's soldiers are referred to as *chivalers* or addressed as *vaissal;* and the whole tone of social intercourse—in the conversations between Pilate and Joseph, for example, or between Joseph and Nicodemus—is quite unmistakably and touchingly the tone of thirteenth-century France. At the same time the figural "omnitemporalness" of the events works most harmoniously and effectively toward the end of embedding them in the familiar setting of popular everyday life. To be sure, some quite modest and naive attempts in the direction of a separation of styles are also to be found. They occur in the earliest liturgical drama, and indeed even in the sequence which is of such great importance as its precursor, the *Victimae paschali,* when the more dogmatic introductory verses are almost immediately followed by the dialogue: *Dic nobis Maria*. . . . Something corresponding is to be seen in the alternate use of Latin and Old French in several plays from the beginning of the twelfth century, as for example the *Sponsus* (*Romania* 22, 177ff.). Our *Mystère d'Adam* puts some particularly solemn passages into rhymed decasyllabic quatrains, which are weightier in tone than the octosyllabic rhymed couplets otherwise employed. From a much later period we have in the *Mystère du vieil Testament* some passages (quoted by Ferdinand Brunot in his *Histoire de la langue française,* 1, 526ff.) in which God and the angels speak a strongly Latinized French while workmen and thieves, and especially Balaam in conversation with his ass, express themselves in decidedly spicy colloquial language. But in all these cases the approximation is too close to give the impression of a real separation of styles. On the contrary their effect is to bring the two spheres together. This style-mingling approximation of the two spheres is not limited to Christian dramatic literature; it is found everywhere in Christian literature throughout the Middle Ages (in some countries, especially Spain, in later periods too), as soon as that literature is addressed to a wider circle. This must have been especially apparent in the realm of the popular sermon, of which, however, we possess a fair number of examples only from a very late period. In these the juxtaposition of a figural use of Scripture and of drastic realism appears in a way which impresses the taste of later ages as grotesque. In this connection the reader may consult E. Gilson's very informative essay "La Technique du sermon médiéval" (in the collection of his papers, *Les Idées et les Lettres*, Paris, 1932, pp. 93ff.).

At the beginning of the thirteenth century there appears in Italy a man who embodies, in exemplary fashion, the mixture we are discussing of *sublimitas* and *humilitas*, of ecstatically sublime immersion in God and humbly concrete everydayness—with a resulting irresolvable fusion of action and expression, of content and form. He is Saint Francis of Assisi. The core of his being and the impact of his life are centered upon the will to a radical and practical imitation of Christ. In Europe, after the age of the martyrs had ended, this had come to assume a predominantly mystico-contemplative form; he gave it a turn toward the practical, the everyday, the public, and the popular. Self-surrendering and meditative mystic though he himself was, the decisive thing for him and his companions was living among the people, living among the lowliest as the lowliest and most despised of them all: *sint minores et subditi omnibus.* He was no theologian, and his knowledge, though respectable in itself and ennobled by his poetic powers, was essentially popular, direct, and concretely accessible. His humility was not at all of the sort which fears public contacts or even public display. He forced his inner impulse into outer forms; his being and his life became public events; from the day when, to signify his relinquishment of the things of this world, he gave back his clothes to his upbraiding father before the eyes of the bishop and the whole town of Assisi, down to the day when, dying, he had himself laid naked on the naked earth so that, as Thomas of Celano put it (*Legenda secunda*, 214), in his last hour, when the archfiend might still rage, he could fight naked with a naked enemy (*ut hora illa extrema, in qua poterat adhuc hostis irasci, nudus luctaretur cum nudo*), everything he did was a scene. And his scenes were of such power that he carried away with him all who saw them or only heard of them. The great saint of the twelfth century, Bernard of Clairvaux, was also a fisher of men, and his eloquence was irresistible. He too was an enemy of human wisdom (*sapienta secundum carnem*), and yet how much more aristocratic, how much more rhetorically erudite is his style. I should like to show this by an example, and I choose two letters of similar content for the purpose. In his Epistle 322 (Pat. Lat. 182, 527-528) Bernard congratulates a young nobleman upon forsaking the world of his own free will and entering a monastery. Bernard praises his wisdom, which is from above; he thanks God for having given it to him; he encourages him and fortifies him against future trials by referring to the help of Christ:

> . . . Si tentationis sentis aculeos, exaltatum in ligno serpentem aeneum intuere (Num. 21, 8; Ioan. 3, 14); et suge non tam vulnera quam ubera Crucifixi. Ipse tibi erit in matrem, et tu eris ei in filium; nec pariter Crucifixum laedere aliquatenus poterunt clavi, quin per manus eius et pedes ad tuos usque perveniant. Sed inimici hominis domestici eius (Mich. 7, 6). Ipsi sunt qui non te diligunt, sed gaudium suum ex te. Alioquin audiant ex puero nostro: si diligeretis me, gauderetis utique, quia vado ad patrem (Ioan. 14, 28). "Si prostratus," ait beatus Hieronymus, "jaceat in limine pater, si nudato sinu, quibus te lactavit, ubera mater ostendat, si parvulus a colle pendeat nepos, per calcatum transi patrem, per calcatam transi matrem, et siccis oculis ad vexillum crucis evola. Summum pietatis est genus, in hac parte pro Christo esse crudelem." Phreneticorum lacrymis ne movearis, qui te plangunt de gehennae filio factum filium Dei. Heu! Quaenam miseris tam dira cupido (Verg. Aen. 6, 721)? Quis tam crudelis amor, quae tam iniqua dilectio? Corrumpunt bonos mores colloquia mala (I Cor. 15, 33). Propterea, quantum poteris, fili, confabulationem hospitum declinato, quae, dum aures implent, evacuant mentem. Disce orare Deum, disce levare cor cum manibus; disce oculos supplices in caelum erigere, et Patri misericordiarum miserabilem faciem repraesentare in omni necessitate tua. Impium est sentire de Deo, quod continere possit super te viscera sua, et avertere aurem a singultu tuo vel clamore. De caetero spiritualium patrum consiliis haud secus quam majestatis divinae praeceptis acquiescendum in omnibus esse memento. Hoc fac, et vives; hoc fac, et veniet super te benedictio, ut pro singulis quae reliquisti centuplum recipias, etiam in praesenti vita. Nec vero credas spiritui suadenti nimis id festinatum, et in maturiorem aetatem differendum fuisse. Ei potius crede qui dixit: Bonum est homini, cum portaverit iugum ab adolescentia sua. Sedebit solitarius, levavit enim se supra se (Thren. 3, 27/8). Bene vale, studeto perseverantiae, quae sola coronatur.

(If you feel the prickings of temptation, consider the brazen serpent raised on the wood; and suck not the wounds but rather the breasts of the Crucified. He shall be as a mother to you, and you as a son to Him; nor could the nails hurt the Crucified save as they passed through his hands and feet to yours. But a man's enemies are the men of his own house. They it is who love not you but their own joy that comes from you. Otherwise they would hear the words of our youth: If ye loved me ye would rejoice because I go unto the Father. "Did thy father," says St. Jerome, "lie prostrate on the threshold, did thy mother, her bosom bared, show thee the breasts at which she gave thee suck, did thy little nephew hang on thy neck, walk roughshod over thy father, walk roughshod over thy mother, and hasten dry-eyed to the banner of the cross. In such case the highest mercy is to be cruel for Christ." Be not moved by the tears of the fools who mourn because, from a son of Gehenna, you are become a son of God. Alas! What a mad desire these wretches have! What a cruel love! What an iniquitous delight! Evil communications corrupt good manners. Wherefore, as much as you are able, my son, avoid the conversation of your hosts, who, while they fill your ears, empty your mind. Learn to pray to God, learn to lift up your heart when you lift up your hands; learn to raise eyes of supplication to heaven, and in every need that befalls you, to show your pitiful face to the Father of pity. It is impious to think that God could close his heart to you and turn his ear from your sobs and cries. For the rest, remember in all things to follow the counsel of your spiritual father no less closely than the commandment of the Divine Majesty. Do this, and you shall live; do this, and blessing shall come upon you, so that for one thing you have given up you shall receive a hundred, even in this present life. Nor believe the counsel of him who would persuade you that this is overhasty and can be deferred until you have reached riper years. Rather believe him who said: It is good for a man that he bear the yoke in his youth. He sitteth alone, because he hath borne it upon him. Fare well, strive after perseverance, which alone gains the crown.)

This is certainly a living and inspiring text, and some of its thoughts and formulations—for instance, that of the relatives who do not love *you* but *gaudium suum ex te*, or the assurance that the hundredfold reward will come even in this life—are, if I am not mistaken, typically Bernardian. But how conscious the composition of the whole is; how many the prerequisites for understanding it, how many rhetorical devices it contains! To be sure, we must take into consideration that in Cistercian circles anyone would immediately catch the figural import of the allusions to Scripture (the brazen serpent as a figure of Christ; the blood from Christ's wounds as nourishing milk; participation in the torture of the cross, in the nails which pierce Christ's hands and feet, as the ecstatic consolation of love in the *unio passionalis*). This type of interpretation and of thinking must have struck root even among the common people, for all the sermons are full of it. But the abundance of Bible texts, the way they are pieced together, the quotation from Jerome and that from Virgil, give this personal letter a highly literary appearance; and in the use of rhetorical questions, of antitheses and anaphoras, Bernard is quite on a par with Jerome, from whom he quotes a highly characteristic passage (possibly even increasing its rhetorical polish). Let me enumerate the most striking antitheses and anaphoras. As for antitheses, we have: *non tam vulnera quam ubera; ipse tibi in matrem, tu ei in filium*; his and your hands and feet; *non te, sed gaudium suum ex te*; in the Jerome passage, *pietas—crudelis*; then, *filius gehennae, filius Dei; crudelis amor, iniqua dilectio; dum aures implent, evacuant mentem*. As for anaphoras, they begin in the Jerome passage, which in its way is magnificent: *si prostratus, si nudato, si parvulus—per calcatum, per calcatam, et siccis oculis* . . . ; then comes Bernard himself: *quis tam crudelis amor, quae* . . . ; *disce orare, disce levare, disce erigere; hoc fac et vives, hoc fac et veniet*. And in addition there are plays on words, like *patri misericordiarum miserabilem faciem repraesentare*.

And now let us hear Francis of Assisi. There are only two personal letters which can be ascribed to him with any certainty: one *ad quendam ministrum* of the year 1223, the other to the favorite disciple of his last years, Brother Leo (Pecorella) of Assisi. Thus both belong to the end of his life, for Francis died in 1225. I choose the first, which is concerned with a difference of opinion within the order in regard to the treatment of brothers who had committed a mortal sin, and I quote only the first, and more general, part of the letter (after the *Analekten zur Geschichte des Franciscus von Assisi*, edited by H. Boehmer, Tübingen and Leipzig, 1904, p. 28):

> Fratri N. ministro. Dominus te benedicat. Dico tibi sicut possum de facto anime tue, quod ea, que te impediunt amare Dominum Deum, et quicumque tibi impedimentum fecerint sive fratres sive alii, etiamsi te verberarent, omnia debes habere pro gratia. Et ita velis et non aliud. Et hoc sit tibi per veram obedien-

tiam Domini Dei et meam, quia firmiter scio, quod illa est vera obedientia. Et dilige eos, qui ista faciunt tibi, et non velis aliud de eis, nisi quantum Dominus dederit tibi. Et in hoc dilige eos et non velis quod [pro te? only in one of the six extant Mss.] sint meliores christiani. Et istud sit tibi plus quam heremitorium. Et in hoc volo cognoscere, si diligis Deum et me servum suum et tuum, si feceris istud, scilicet quod non sit aliquis frater in mundo, qui peccaverit, quantumcumque potuerit peccare, quod, postquam viderit occulos tuos, unquam recedat sine misericordia tua, si querit misericordiam, et si non quereret misericordiam, tu queras ab eo, si vult misericordiam. Et, si millies postea appareret coram occulis tuis, dilige eum plus quam me ad hoc, ut trahas eum ad Dominum, et semper miserearis talibus. . . .

(To Brother N., Minister [of the Order]. God bless you. I speak to you as best I can concerning your soul. All the things that would hinder you in your love of the Lord God, and all persons who obstruct your path—be they brethren or others—even if they beat you, you must consider it all a grace. And will it thus and not otherwise. And that you must consider your true obedience toward the Lord God and me, for I know for certain that it is the true obedience. And love those who do these things to you, and do not desire anything else from them but what God may give to you. And love them for this and do not desire that they be better Christians. And let this be more for you than the hermitage. And herein will I know whether you love God and me, his and your servant, in whether you do this, that is, if there be no brother in the world who, having sinned as much as he can sin, when he has come to see your countenance, shall ever go away from you without your charity if he seeks charity, and if he does not seek charity, that you try with him whether he wishes charity. And if afterwards he appears a thousand times before your countenance, love him more than you now love me, that you draw him toward the Lord, and always have charity for such. . . .)

In this passage we have no exegesis of Scripture and no figures of speech. The sentence structure is hurried, awkward, and uncalculated. All the sentences begin with *et*. But the person who writes these hurried lines is obviously so inspired by his theme, it fills him so completely, and the desire to communicate himself and to be understood is so overwhelming, that parataxis becomes a weapon of eloquence.

Like the ever-gathering waves of a strong surf, these *et*-constructions strike from the heart of the saint to that of the recipient, as is expressed at the very beginning in *sicut possum* and *de facto anime tue.* For the *sicut possum* expresses, together with humility (as best I can), the most complete dedication of powers, and *de facto anime tue* implies that the factual question under discussion carries with it the spiritual salvation of him who has to decide it. And that it is a matter "between me and you" is a point Francis does not lose sight of throughout the entire letter. He knows that the other loves and admires him, and he makes use of this love at every moment to draw him toward the right path (*ut trahat eum ad Dominum*): *et in hoc volo cognoscere si diligis Deum et me servum suum et tuum,* so he implores him. He commands him to love the backsliding sinner, even if he comes to see him a thousand times, more than "you love me at this moment." The contents of the letter is the doctrine, carried to its utmost limit, that evil must be neither avoided nor opposed. It is an exhortation—not to leave the world behind—but to mingle with its torment and to endure evil with passionate devotion. Indeed, he is to wish for nothing else: *et ita velis et non aliud.* And Francis reaches an extreme which begins to look almost suspicious from the viewpoint of moral theology when he writes: *et in hoc dilige eos et non velis quod sint meliores Christiani* —for is it permissible, for the sake of one's own trial through suffering, to repress the wish that one's fellow be a better Christian? Only through submission to evil is it possible, according to Francis' conviction, for the power of love and obedience to prove themselves: *quia firmiter scio quod illa est vera obedienta.* This is more than solitary meditation far from the world: *et istud sit tibi plus quam heremitorium.* The extreme character of this view is reflected in the language: in the numerous demonstratives which signify "precisely this and nothing else"; or in the clauses introduced by *quicumque, etiamsi, quantumcumque, et si millies,* all of which mean, "and even if . . ."

The wholly unliterary directness of expression, then, so closely related to the spoken language, supports a very radical content. To be sure, it is nothing new, for from the beginning suffering within the world and submission to evil are among the major Christian motifs; but the stresses are placed differently. Suffering and submission are no longer a passive form of martyrdom but an unremitting self-humiliation in the everyday course of things. While Bernard dealt with secular affairs as a great politician of the Church and withdrew from them into the solitude of contemplation to attain the experience of *imitatio Christi,* Francis considers secular affairs the proper setting for *imitatio,* although, to be sure, in his case secular affairs are not the great political events in which Bernard played a leading part, but the everyday doings of random persons, whether within the Order or out among the people. The entire structure of the mendicant orders, and especially that of the Franciscan organization, drove the friars into everyday public life, among the people, and even though it is certainly true that solitary meditation lost its great religious importance neither for Francis of Assisi nor for his successors, it yet could not rob the order of its pronouncedly popular character.

Now, the saint's public appearances, as we said above, are always impressive, graphic, and indeed scenic. The anecdotes which relate them are very numerous, and among them there are some which strike later taste as almost grotesque or even farcical; as when we are told that, celebrating Christmas in the stable at Greccio, with ox and ass and praesepium, both in singing and preaching he pronounced the word Bethlehem in imitation of a bleating lamb; or that after an illness in the course of which he had taken some choicer food, upon his return to Assisi he ordered one of the brothers to lead him through the town on a rope, as though he were a criminal, shouting: Behold the glutton who crammed his belly full of chicken behind your backs! But in their time and place such scenes did not produce a farcical effect. Their arrestingness, exaggeration, vividness did not appear shocking, but as a graphic, exemplary revelation of a saintly life, directly illuminating, comprehensible to all, and inspiring all to examine themselves in comparison and to share in the experience. Together with such arresting and persuasively effective scenes, there are other anecdotes which bear witness to great delicacy and gentleness and reveal a considerable, purely instinctive psychological gift. At crucial moments Francis always knows what is going on in others' hearts, and hence his intervention usually strikes the crucial spot; it arouses emotion, it staggers. Everywhere it is the startling and graphic directness of his character which produces such strong, such exemplary, and such unforgettable effects. Here I should like to quote one more anecdote which (although the occasion is comparatively insignificant and ordinary) gives an excellent description of one of his characteristic appearances. It is taken from the *Legenda secunda* by Thomas of Celano (*S. Francisci Assisiensis vita et miracula . . . auctore Fr. Thoma de Celano . . . recensuit* P. *Eduardus Alenconiensis.* Romae, 1906, pp. 217-218).

> Factum est quodam die Paschae, ut fratres in eremo Graecii mensam accuratius solito albis et vitreis praepararent. Descendens autem pater de cella venit ad mensam, conspicit alto sitam vaneque ornatam; sed ridenti mensae nequaquam arridet. Furtim et pedetentim retrahit gressum, capellum cuiusdam pauperis qui tunc aderat capiti suo imponit, et baculum gestans egreditur foras. Exspectat foris ad ostium donec incipiant fratres; siquidem soliti erant non exspectare ipsum, quando non veniret ad signum. Illis incipientibus manducare, clamat verus pauper ad ostium: Amore domini Dei, facite, inquit, eleemosynam isti peregrino pauperi et infirmo. Respondent fratres: Intra huc, homo, illius amore quem invocasti. Repente igitur ingreditur, et sese comedentibus offert. Sed quantum stuporem credis peregrinum civibus intulisse? Datur petenti scutella, et solo solus recumbens discum ponit in cinere. Modo sedeo, ait, ut frater Minor. . . .
>
> (It happened one Easter Day that the brothers at the hermitage of Greccio set the table more lavishly than usual with linen and glassware. When the father comes down from his cell to go to the table, he sees it with its vain decoration. But the pleasing table no way pleases him. Furtively and quietly he retraces his steps, puts on his head the hat of a pauper who happened to be there, takes his staff in his hand, and leaves the house. Outside he waits until the brothers begin, for they were accustomed not to wait for him when he did not come at the signal. When they begin their meal, this true pauper calls out at the door: For the love of God, give this poor sick pilgrim an alms. The brothers answer: Come in, man, for the love of Him whom you have invoked. So he quickly enters and appears before the diners. But what surprise do you think seized the household at sight of this stranger! At his request he is given a bowl, and alone he sits down on the floor and sets his plate in the ashes. "Now," he says, "I am seated like a Minorite. . . .")

The occasion, as I have said, is insignificant, but what an inspired scenic idea to take a pauper's hat and staff and go begging of beggars! We can well imagine the brothers' confusion and humiliation when he sits down in the ashes with his bowl and says: Now I am seated like a Minorite. . . .

The saint's manner of life and expression was taken over by the Order and produced a very peculiar atmosphere. In both the good and bad sense, it became extremely popular. The excess of drastic vigor of expression made of the friars the creators, and soon too the subject, of dramatic, witty, and frequently coarse and obscene anecdotes. The coarser realism of the later Middle Ages is often linked to the activity and appearances of the Franciscans. Their influence in this direction can be traced down to the Renaissance. This too was clearly demonstrated, a few years ago, in an essay by Etienne Gilson ("Rabelais franciscain," in the volume previously mentioned, *Les Idées et les Lettres*, pp. 197ff.). We shall have to return to this point in a later chapter. On the other hand, Franciscan power of expression led to a still more direct and intense representation of human events; it asserts itself in popular religious poetry, which, during the thirteenth century, under the influence of the Franciscan and other popular ecstatic movements, treated the Passion scene especially (Mary at the cross) as a livingly dramatic and human episode. The most famous piece, one that is included in many anthologies, is by Jacopone da Todi (b. 1230), a very expressive mystic and poet of the period immediately before Dante. In his later years he was a member of the Franciscan Order, specifically of its radical wing, the Spirituals. His Passion poem is in the form of a dialogue. The speakers are a messenger, the Virgin Mary, the "crowd," and finally Christ himself. I quote the beginning of it after E. Monaci's *Crestomazia italiana dei primi secoli* (Citta di Castello, 1912, p. 479):

Nunzio — Donna del paradiso
lo tuo figliolo è priso / Jesu Christo beato.
Accurre, donna e vide / che la gente l'allide,
credo che llo s'occide / tanto l'on flagellato.

Vergine — Como essere purria, / che non fe mai follia
Christo la spene mia, / hom l'avesse pilgliato?

Nunzio — Madonna, ell'è traduto, / Juda sì l'à venduto,
Trenta dinar n'à 'uto, / facto n'à gran mercato.

Vergine — Succurri, Magdalena; / jonta m'è adosso pena;
Christo figlio se mena / como m'è annuntiato.

Nunzio — Succurri, donna, ajuta, / ch'al tuo figlio se sputa
e la gente llo muta, / onlo dato a Pilato.

Vergine — O Pilato, non fare / l figlio mio tormentare;
ch'io te posso mostrare / como a torto è accusato.

Turba — Crucifì, crucifige / homo che si fa rege
secondo nostra lege / contradice al senato.

Vergine — Prego che m'entennate, / nel mio dolor pensate,
forsa mo ve mutate / da quel ch'ete parlato.
Nunzio — Tragon fuor li ladroni, / che sian sui compagnoni.
Turba — De spine si coroni, / ché rege s'è chiamato!
Vergine — O filglio, filglio, filglio! / filglio, amoroso gilglio,
filglio, chi dà consilglio / al cor mio angustiato?
O filglio, occhi jocundi, / filglio, co non respundi?
filglio, perché t'ascundi / dal pecto o se' lactato?
Nunzio — Madonna, ecco la croce / che la gente l'aduce,
ove la vera luce / dej' essere levato. . . .

(Messenger — Lady of Paradise,
Thy son is taken / Jesus Christ the blessed.
Hasten, Lady, and see / how the people maltreat him.
I think he will die, / so much have they flailed him.
Virgin — How could it be, / for never did wrong
Christ, my hope, / that they have taken him?
Messenger — Lady, he was betrayed, / Judas sold him,
Thirty denarii he got for it, / he made a great bargain of it.
Virgin — Help me, Magdalene; / misfortune has befallen me;
Christ my son is being led away / as has been told me.
Messenger — Help, Lady, assist us, / they spit at your son
and the people take him away, / they have handed him over to Pilate.
Virgin — O Pilate, do not do it, / do not torture my son;
for I can show you / how he is wrongly accused.
Crowd — Crucify, crucify / the man who makes himself king;
according to our law / he rebels against the Senate.
Virgin — I beg you, listen to me, / think of my pain,
Perhaps you will soon change / what you have said.
Messenger — They are bringing the thieves / who are to be his companions.
Crowd — Crown him with thorns, / him who has called himself king.
Virgin — O son, son, son! / son, beloved lily,
son, who will advise / my anguished heart?
O son, eyes of joy, / son, why do you not answer?
son, why do you hide / from the breast which gave you milk?

Messenger Lady, here is the cross / which the people bring
whereon the true light / is to be raised. . . .)

This text, like the Old French text discussed at the beginning of this chapter, presents a complete embedding of the sublime and sacred event in a reality which is simultaneously contemporary Italian and omnitemporal. Its popular character is apparent in the first place in matters of language, by which I mean not only the dialectal forms but also "popularity" of expression in the sociological sense (for example, *jonta m'è adosso pena,* in the mouth of the Holy Virgin). It is further shown in the freedom with which the Biblical episode is rendered, giving Mary a much more important and active part than even the Gospel according to Saint John does, so that the opportunity arises for dramatic development of her anxiety, her pain, and her mourning. Closely connected with this is the crowding together of scenes and characters, so that Mary can address Pilate directly and the picture yet admit the carrying in of the cross. Magdalene, who is called upon to help, and John, to whom Christ later entrusts his mother, appear together with Mary like a group of friends and neighbors. And finally the popular element also appears in the illogical anachronism of the conception—a subject which we discussed in detail in connection with the Old French treatment of the Fall. On the one hand Mary is an anxious and helplessly lamenting mother, who sees no way out, and falls back on pleading; on the other hand the messenger calls her *donna del paradiso,* and everything has been foretold to her.

In all these respects—that is, so far as the embedding of the action in the popular and everyday is concerned—the two texts, though about a century apart, are closely related. Yet it is apparent that there is also an important and fundamental stylistic difference between them. Jacopone's poem preserves but little of the enchanting and transparent candor of the Adam play. On the other hand, it is more intense, more direct, more tragic. This is not due to the difference in subject matter, to the fact that Jacopone's theme is the lament of a mother. Or rather, it is no coincidence that Italian religious folk poetry of the thirteenth century produces its most beautiful works in treatments of this scene. Such a free flow and indeed dramatic outburst of pain, anxiety, and pleading as is achieved in Jacopone's accumulated vocatives, imperatives, and urgent questions, would not, I believe, have been possible in the thirteenth century in any other European vernacular. It reveals a freedom from self-conscious restraint, a sweetly passionate abandonment to feeling, a release from all timidity in public expression, compared with which the earlier and most of the contemporary works of the Middle Ages seem awkward and impeded. Even Provençal, which almost from the beginning, from Guilhem de Peitieu on, possesses great freedom of expression, is outdone by such a text, if only because its repertoire contains no such great tragic theme. It would perhaps be rash to maintain that Italian literature owed this freedom of dramatic expression to Saint Francis, for it was doubtless implicit in the character of the people; but it cannot be denied that, a great poet, an instinctive master of the art of acting out his own being, he was the first to awaken the dramatic powers of Italian feeling and of the Italian language.

8

FARINATA AND CAVALCANTE

"O Tosco che per la città del foco
vivo ten vai così parlando onesto,
piacciati di restare in questo loco.
La tua loquela ti fa manifesto
di quella nobil patria natìo
a la qual forse fui troppo molesto."
Subitamente questo suono uscìo
d'una de l'arche; però m'accostai,
temendo, ut poco più al duca mio.
Ed el mi disse: "Volgiti: che fai?
Vedi là Farinata che s'è dritto:
da la cintola in su tutto 'l vedrai."
I'avea già il mio viso nel suo fitto;
ed el s'ergea col petto e con la fronte
com'avesse l'inferno in gran dispitto.
E l'animose man del duca e pronte
mi pinser tra le sepulture a lui,
dicendo: "Le parole tue sien conte."
Com'io al piè de la sua tomba fui,
guardommi un poco, e poi, quasi sdegnoso,
mi dimandò: "Chi fur li maggior tui?"
Io ch'era d'ubidir disideroso,
non gliel celai, ma tutto gliel'apersi;
ond' ei levò le ciglia un poco in soso.
Poi disse: "Fieramente furo avversi
a me e a miei primi e a mia parte,
sì che per due fiate li dispersi."
"S'ei fur cacciati, ei tornar d'ogni parte"
rispuosi lui "l'una e l'altra fiata;
ma i vostri non appreser ben quell'arte."
Allor surse a la vista scoperchiata
un' ombra lungo questa infino al mento:
credo che s'era in ginocchie levata.

Dintorno mi guardò, come talento
avesse di veder s'altri era meco;
e poi che il sospecciar fu tutto spento
piangendo disse: "Se per questo cieco
carcere vai per altezza d'ingegno,
mio figlio ov'è? perchè non è ei teco?"
E io a lui: "Da me stesso non vegno:
colui ch'attende là, per qui mi mena,
Forse cui Guido vestro ebbe a disdegno."
Le sue parole e 'l modo de la pena
m'avean di costui già letto il nome;
però fu la risposta così piena.
Di subito drizzato gridò: "Come
dicesti? elli ebbe? non viv'elli ancora?
non fiere li occhi suoi il dolce lome?"
Quando s'accorse d'alcuna dimora
ch'io facea dinanzi a la risposta
supin ricadde, e più non parve fora.
Ma quell'altro magnanimo a cui posta
restato m'era, non mutò aspetto,
nè mosse collo, nè piegò sua costa;
E, "Se," continuando al primo detto,
"elli han quell'arte," disse, "mal appresa,
ciò mi tormenta più che questo letto. . . ."

("O Tuscan! who through the city of fire goest alive, speaking thus decorously; may it please thee to stop in this place. Thy speech clearly shows thee a native of that noble country, which perhaps I vexed too much." Suddenly this sound issued from one of the chests: whereat in fear I drew a little closer to my Guide. And he said to me: "Turn thee round; what art thou doing? lo there Farinata! who has raised himself erect; from the girdle upward thou shalt see him all." Already I had fixed my look on his; and he rose upright with breast and countenance, as if he entertained great scorn of Hell; and the bold and ready hands of my Guide pushed me amongst the sepultures to him, saying: "Let thy words be numbered." When I was at the foot of his tomb, he looked at me a little; and then, almost contemptuously, he asked me: "Who were thy ancestors?" I, being desirous to obey, concealed it not; but opened the whole to him: whereupon he raised his brows a little; then he said: "Fiercely adverse were they to me, and to my progenitors, and to my party; so that twice I scattered them." "If they were driven forth, they returned from every quarter, both times," I answered him; "but yours have not rightly learnt that art." Then, beside him, there rose a shadow, visible to the chin; it had raised itself, I think, upon its knees. It looked around me, as if it had a wish to see whether someone were with me; but when all its expectation was quenched, it said, weeping: "If through this blind prison thou goest by height of genius, where is my son and why is he not with thee?" And I to him: "Of myself I come not: he, that waits yonder, leads me through this place; whom perhaps thy Guido held in disdain." Already his words and the manner of his punishment had read his name to me: hence my answer was so full. Rising instantly erect, he cried: "How saidst thou: he held? lives he not still? does not the sweet light strike his eyes?" When he perceived that I made some delay in answering, supine he fell again, and shewed himself no more. But that other, magnanimous, at whose desire I had stopped, changed not his aspect, nor moved his neck, nor bent his side. "And if," continuing his former words, he said, "they have learnt that art badly, it more torments me than this bed. . . .") *The Inferno of Dante Alighieri.* English version by Dr. J. A. Carlyle. "Temple Classics" edition. J. M. Dent, 1922.

This episode from the tenth canto of the *Inferno* begins with Virgil and Dante walking along a secret pathway among flaming chests whose lids stand open. Virgil explains that they are the tombs of heretics and atheists, and promises Dante fulfillment of his hinted wish to communicate with one of the spirits there confined. Dante is about to reply when he is taken aback by the sound of a voice which rises from one of the chests, beginning with the dark o-sounds of *O Tosco.* One of the condemned has raised himself erect in his chest and addresses them as they pass. Virgil tells Dante his name; it is Farinata degli Uberti, a Florentine, a Ghibelline party leader and captain, who died shortly before Dante's birth. Dante stations himself at the foot of the tomb; a conversation begins, only to be interrupted a few lines later (l. 52) as abruptly as the conversation between Dante and Virgil had been. This time again it is one of those condemned to the chests who interrupts, and Dante recognizes him immediately, by his situation and his words: he is Cavalcante de' Cavalcanti, the father of Dante's early friend, the poet Guido Cavalcanti. The scene which now takes place between Cavalcante and Dante is brief (only 21 lines). As soon as it comes to an end with Cavalcante's sinking back into his chest, Farinata resumes the interrupted conversation.

Within the brief space of about seventy lines we thus have a triple shift in the course of events; we have four scenes crowded together, each full of power and content. None is purely expository—not even the first, a comparatively calm conversation between Dante and Virgil, which I have not included in the passage given above. Here, it is true, the reader, and Dante too, are being acquainted with the new setting which is opening before them, i.e., the sixth circle of Hell; but the scene also contains its own independent theme, the psychological process in which the two speakers are involved. Contrasting most sharply with the theoretical calm and psychological delicacy of this prelude, there follows an exceedingly dramatic second scene, initiated by the sudden sound of Farinata's voice and the abrupt appearance of his body raising itself in its tomb, by Dante's alarm and Virgil's encouraging words and gestures. Here—erect and abrupt as his body—Farinata's moral stature is developed, larger than life as it were, and unaffected by death and the pains of Hell. He is still the same man he was in his lifetime. It is the Tuscan accents from Dante's lips which have made him rise and address the passing figure with proudly courteous dignity. When Dante turns toward him, Farinata first inquires into his ancestry, in order to learn with whom he is dealing, whether with a man of noble descent, whether with friend or foe. And when he hears that Dante belongs to a Guelph family, he says with stern satisfaction that he twice drove that hated party from the city. The fate of Florence and the Ghibellines is still uppermost in his mind. Dante replies that the expulsion of the Guelphs did not profit the Ghibellines in the long run, that in the end it was the latter who remained in exile; but he is interrupted by the emergence of Cavalcante, who has heard Dante's words and recognized him. His peering head comes into sight; it is attached to a much slighter body than Farinata's. He hopes to see his son with Dante, but when he looks in vain, he breaks into anxious questions which show that he too continues to have the same character and the same passions that he had in his lifetime, though they are very different from Farinata's: love of life on earth, belief in the autonomous greatness of the human mind, and above all love and admiration for his son Guido. As he asks his urgent questions, he is excited, almost beseeching, thus differentiating himself sharply from Farinata's imposing greatness and self-discipline; and when he infers (wrongly) from Dante's words that his son is no longer alive, he collapses; whereupon Farinata, unmoved and without reference to the intervening episode, replies to the last remark Dante had addressed to him, and what he says characterizes him completely: If, as you say, the banished Ghibellines have not succeeded in returning to the city, that is a greater torment to me than the bed on which I lie.

More is packed together in this passage than in any of the others we have so far discussed in this book; but there is not only more, the material is not only weightier and more dramatic within so short a space; it is also intrinsically much more varied. Here we have the relation not merely of one event but of three different events, the second of which—the Farinata scene—is interrupted and cut in two by the third. There is, then, no unity of action in the ordinary sense. Nor is this comparable with what we found in the scene from Homer discussed in our first chapter, where the reference to Odysseus' scar occasioned a lengthy, circumstantial, episodic narrative which carried us far from the original subject. In Dante's case the subject is changed abruptly and in rapid succession. Farinata's words interrupt Virgil's and Dante's conversation *subitamente*; the *allor surse* of line 52 cuts without transition through the Farinata scene, which is just as precipitately resumed by *ma quell'altro magnanimo*. The unity of the passage is dependent upon the setting, the physical and moral climate of the circle of heretics and atheists; and the rapid succession of independent episodes or mutually unrelated scenes is a concomitant of the structure of the Comedy as a whole. It presents the journey of an individual and his guide through a world whose inhabitants remain in whatever place is assigned to them. Despite this rapid succession of scenes, there is no question of any parataxis in Dante's style. Within every individual scene there is an abundance of syntactic connectives; and when—as in the present instance—the scenes are juxtaposed in sharp contours without transition, the confrontation is managed by means of artistically varied devices of expression which are rather changes of approach than parataxes. The scenes are not set stiffly side by side and in the same key—we are thinking of the Latin legend of Alexis (pp. 116f.) and even of the *Chanson de Roland*—they rise from the depths as particular forms of the momentarily prevailing tonality and stand in contrapuntal relation to one another.

To make this clearer we shall more closely examine the points at which the scene changes. Farinata interrupts the conversing pair with the words: O *Tosco, che per la città del foco vivo ten vai. . . .* This is an address, a vocative introduced by O, with a succeeding relative clause which, in comparison with the vocative, is decidedly weighty and substantial; and only then comes the request, which is again weighted down with reserved courtesy. We hear, not, "Tuscan, stop!" but "O Tuscan, who . . . , may it please thee to linger in this place." The construction, "O thou who" is extremely solemn and comes from the elevated style of the antique epic. Dante's ear remembers its cadence as it remembers so many other things in Virgil, Lucan, and Statius. I do not think the construction occurs before this in any medieval vernacular. But Dante uses it in his own way: with a strong adjuratory element—which is present in antiquity at most in prayers—and with so condensed a content in the relative clause as only he can manage. Farinata's feeling and attitude toward the passing pair are so dynamically epitomized in the three qualifiers, *per la città del foco ten vai, vivo, così parlando onesto,* that had the master Virgil really heard those words, he might well have been more dismayed than Dante in the poem; his own relative clauses after a vocative are perfectly beautiful and harmonious, to be sure, but never so concise and arresting. (See for example *Aeneid,* 1, 436: *o fortunati quibus iam moenia surgunt!* or, still more interesting because of its full rhetorical swell, 2, 638: *vos o quibus integer aevi / sanguis, ait, solidaeque suo stant robore vires, / vos agitate fugam.*) Note also how the antithesis "through the city of fire" and "alive" is expressed entirely, and therefore the more effectively, through the position of the word *vivo.*

After these three lines of address comes the tercet in which Farinata identifies himself as Dante's fellow countryman, and only then, after he has finished speaking, the statement: Suddenly this sound issued, etc., a statement which one would normally expect to find introducing a surprising event, but which here—where it follows the event—produces a comparatively quiet effect as a mere explanation of what is occurring. So that, in a recitation of the entire passage, these lines would have to be read more softly. There is no question, then, of any straightforward paratactic attaching of the Farinata scene to the conversation of the two travelers. On the one hand we must not forget the fact that Virgil vaguely announced it beforehand in the course of the conversation (lines 16 to 18); on the other hand, it is so strong, so violent, so overpowering an irruption of a different realm—in the local, ethical, psychological, and aesthetic senses—that its connection with what precedes is no mere juxtaposition but the vital relationship of counterpoint, of the sudden breaking in of something dimly foreboded. The events are not—as we put it in connection with the *Chanson de Roland* and the Legend of Alexis—divided into little parcels; they live together, despite their contrast and actually because of it.

The second change of scene is managed through the words *Allor surse,* in line 52. It seems simpler and less remarkable than the first. What, after all, is more normal than to introduce a sudden new occurrence with the words, "Then it befel . . ."? But if we ask ourselves where in pre-Dantean medieval vernacular literature we might find a comparable linguistic maneuver, interrupting the action in course by a dramatically incisive "then," we should, I think, have a long search before us. I for one know of none. *Allora* at the beginning of a sentence is naturally quite frequent in Italian literature before Dante. It occurs for instance in the stories of the *Novellino* but with much less force of meaning. Such sharp breaks are in keeping with neither the style nor the time-sense of pre-Dantean narrative, not even with those of the French epics, where *ez vos* or *atant ez vos* occurs in a similar though much weaker sense (for example, *Roland* 413 and elsewhere). That even extremely dramatic turnings of the tide of action were handled with stiff circumstantiality may be observed for example in Villehardouin when he relates the intervention of the Doge of Venice at the storming of Constantinople. When his men hesitate to land, the aged and blind Doge orders them upon pain of death to set him ashore first, with the flag of Saint Mark. This the chronicler introduces with the words: *or porres oir estrange proece.* This is just as though Dante, instead of *allora,* had said, "And then something quite extraordinary happened." The Old French *ez vos* may serve to point the way as we try to find the correct Latin term for this abruptly intervening "then." For it is not *tum* or *tunc*; in many cases it is rather *sed* or *iam.* But the real equivalent, which gives the full force, is *ecce,* or still better *et ecce.* This is found less frequently in the elevated style than in Plautus, in Cicero's letters, in Apuleius, etc., and especially in the Vulgate. When Abraham takes the knife to sacrifice his son Isaac, we read: *et ecce Angelus Domini de caelo clamavit, dicens: Abraham, Abraham.* I think this linguistic maneuver, which effects so sharp an interruption, is too harsh to stem from the elevated style of classical Latin; but it corresponds perfectly with the elevated style of the Bible. And furthermore, Dante uses the Biblical *et ecce* verbatim on another occasion where a state of affairs is interrupted by a sudden, though not quite so dramatic, occurrence (*Purg.*, 21, 7: *ed ecco, sì come ne scrive Luca . . . ci apparve . . .* after Luke 24: 13: *et ecce duo ex illis . . .*). I am not prepared to state as a certainty that Dante introduced the linguistic maneuver of this abruptly interrupting "then" into the elevated style and that it was a Biblical echo with him. But this much would seem to be certain: at the time Dante wrote, the dramatically arresting "then" was by no means as obvious and generally available as it is today; and he used it more radically than any other medieval writer before him.

But we must also consider the meaning and the sound of the word *surse*, which Dante uses in at least one other passage with telling effect to describe a sudden emergence (*Purg.* 6, 72-73: *e l'ombra tutta in se romita / surse vêr lui . . .*). The *allor surse* of line 52, then, has hardly less weight than the words of Farinata which bring in the first interruption; this *allor* is one of those paratactic forms which establish a dynamic relationship between the members they connect. The conversation with Farinata is interrupted—once he has heard part of it, Cavalcante cannot wait for it to end, he simply loses his self-control. And the part he plays—his peering expression, his whining words, and his precipitate despair when he sinks back—forms a sharp contrast with Farinata's weighty calm when he resumes speaking after the third shift (ll. 73ff.).

The third shift, *ma quell'altro magnanimo*, etc., is much less dramatic than the first two. It is calm, proud, and weighty. Farinata alone dominates the scene. But the contrast with what precedes is thus only the more striking. Dante calls Farinata *magnanimo*, employing an Aristotelian term which may have come to life in his vocabulary through its use by Thomas Aquinas or, more probably, by Brunetto Latini and which is applied in an earlier passage to Virgil. This is doubtless a conscious contrast to Cavalcante (*costui*); and the three identically constructed cola which express Farinata's aloofness (*non mutò aspetto, nè mosse collo, nè piegò sua costa*) are undoubtedly designed not only to describe Farinata himself but also to contrast his attitude with Cavalcante's. This is aurally apparent from the regularly constructed clauses which come to the listener while he is still conscious of the irregular and plaintively thronging questions of the other. (The wording of these questions, ll. 58 to 60 and 67 to 69, Dante may well have modeled after Andromache's appearance, *Aeneid*, 3, 310, that is, after a woman's lamentations.)

Abruptly, then, as these events succeed one another, this is no paratactic construction. The most vital continuity of movement vibrates through the entire passage. Dante has at his disposal an abundance of stylistic devices which no European vernacular before him could equal. And he does not use them singly; he connects them in an uninterrupted relationship. Virgil's encouraging words (ll. 31-33) consist exclusively of principal clauses without any formal connection by conjunctions. There is a short imperative, a short question, then another imperative with an object and an explanatory relative, and a future clause of adhortative import with an adverbial qualifier. But the quick succession, the concise formulation of the individual parts, and their mutual balance exhibit to perfection the natural vitality of spoken discourse: "Turn around! What are you doing? etc." Withal there are semantic connections of the most subtle kind. There is the ordinary causal relation (*però*), but in addition to it we have the connective *onde* hovering between temporal and causal value, and the hypothetically causal *forse che*, which some early commentators consider to be courteously softening. There are the most varied temporal, comparative, and graduated hypothetical connections, supported by the greatest possible elasticity of verbal inflections and verbal order. Note, for instance, the ease with which Dante keeps syntactic control of the scene of Cavalcante's appearance so that it runs smoothly on through three tercets to the end of his first speech (l. 60). The unity of the construction here rests upon three verbal pillars, *surse, guardò, disse.* The first supports the subject, the adverbial qualifiers, and, in addition, the explanatory parenthesis *credo che*; the second, *guardò*, carries the first lines of the second tercet with the as-if clause; while the third line of this same tercet points toward the *disse* and Cavalcante's direct discourse, which marks the climax of the whole movement from an initial forte through a decrescendo to a renewed crescendo beginning with line 57.

Should this analysis find any readers but little versed in medieval vernacular literature, they may well be surprised that I here emphasize and praise the extraordinary character of syntactic constructions which are today used by every halfway talented literary man and indeed by many who, though they write nothing but letters, have had a modicum of literary training. But if we start from his predecessors, Dante's language is a well-nigh incomprehensible miracle. There were great poets among them. But, compared with theirs, his style is so immeasurably richer in directness, vigor, and subtlety, he knows and uses such an immeasurably greater stock of forms, he expresses the most varied phenomena and subjects with such immeasurably superior assurance and firmness, that we come to the conclusion that this man used his language to discover the world anew. Very often it is possible to demonstrate or to conjecture where he acquired this or that device of expression; but his sources are so numerous, his ear hears them, his intellect uses them, so accurately, so simply, and yet so originally, that demonstrations and conjectures of this sort can only serve to increase our admiration for the power of his linguistic genius. A text such as the one we are considering may be approached at any point, and every point will yield a surprise, something unimaginable in the vernacular literatures at an earlier date. Let us take something as insignificant-looking as the clause, *da me stesso non vegno*. Is it conceivable that so short and yet complete a formulation of such a thought in particular, that so incisive a semantic organization in general, and a *da* used in this sense, should occur in the work of an earlier vernacular author? Dante uses *da* in this sense in several other passages (*Purg.*, 1, 52: *da me non venni*; also *Purg.*, 19, 143: *buona da sè*; and *Par.*, 2, 58: *ma dimmi quel che tu da te ne pensi*). The meaning "of one's own motion," "of one's own free will," "by oneself," would seem to have been a further development of the meaning "(coming) from." Guido Cavalcanti writes in the canzone *Donna mi prega*: [*Amore*] *non è vertute ma da quella vene*. It is of course not possible to claim that Dante created this new semantic turn, for even if no single passage of the sort could be found in earlier texts, that still might mean no more than that no such passage happens to be extant; and even if nothing of the sort was ever written before his time, it still may have been current in spoken language. Indeed, the latter possibility strikes me as likely, because a scholarly background would more naturally have suggested *per*. What is certain, however, is that in adopting or creating this short expression, Dante gave it a vigor and depth previously inconceivable—the effect, in our passage, being further enhanced by a twofold opposition: on the one hand to *per altezza d'ingegno* and on the other to *colui ch'attende là*, both rhetorical circumlocutions avoiding the real name, haughtily in one instance and respectfully in the other.

The *da me stesso* perhaps stems from the spoken language; and elsewhere too it may be observed that Dante by no means scorns colloquialisms. The *Volgiti: che fai?*, especially from Virgil's mouth and coming immediately after Farinata's solemnly composed apostrophe, has the ring of spontaneous and unstylized speech, of everyday conversation among ordinary speakers. The case is not very different with the harsh question *chi fur li maggior tui?* unadorned as it is with any of the graces of circumlocution, and with Cavalcante's *Come dicesti? elli ebbe?* etc. Reading further through this canto, we come, toward the end, upon the passage where Virgil asks, *perchè sei tu si smarrito?* (l. 125). All these quotations, detached from their context, could well be imagined in any ordinary conversation on the familiar level of style. Beside them we find formulations of the highest sublimity, which are also stylistically "sublime" in the antique sense. There is no doubt that the stylistic intent in general is to achieve the sublime. If this were not clear from Dante's explicit statements, we could sense it directly from every line of his work, however colloquial it may be. The weightiness, *gravitas*, of Dante's tone is maintained so consistently that there can never be any doubt as to what level of style we find ourselves upon. Nor is it possible to doubt that it was the poets of antiquity who gave Dante the model of the elevated style—which he was the first to adopt. He himself acknowledges in many passages, both in the Comedy and in the *De vulgari eloquentia,* how much he owes them in regard to the elevated style of the vernacular. It may well be that he does so in the very passage we are discussing, for the much-disputed line about Virgil "whom perhaps . . . Guido held in disdain" permits this interpretation among many others; almost all the early commentators took it in an aesthetic sense. Yet there is no denying that Dante's conception of the sublime differs essentially from that of his models, in respect to subject matter no less than to stylistic form. The themes which the Comedy introduces represent a mixture of sublimity and triviality which, measured by the standards of antiquity, is monstrous. Of the characters which appear in it, some belong to the recent past or even to the contemporary present and (despite *Par.*, 17, 136-138), not all of them are famous or carefully chosen. Quite often they are frankly represented in all the humble realism of their spheres of life. And in general, as every reader is aware, Dante knows no limits in describing with meticulous care and directness things which are humdrum, grotesque, or repulsive. Themes which cannot possibly be considered sublime in the antique sense turn out to be just that by virtue of his way of molding and ordering them. His mixture of stylistic levels has already been noted. One need but think of the line, "and let them scratch wherever they itch," which occurs in one of the most solemn passages of the *Paradiso* (17, 129), in order to appreciate all the immense difference between Dante and let us say Virgil.

Many important critics—and indeed whole epochs of classicistic taste—have felt ill at ease with Dante's closeness to the actual in the realm of the sublime—that is, as Goethe put it in his *Annals* for the year 1821, with his "repulsive and often disgusting greatness." This is not surprising. For nowhere could one find so clear an instance of the antagonism of the two traditions—that of antiquity, with the principle of the separation of styles, and that of the Christian era, with its mingling of styles—as in Dante's powerful temperament, which is conscious of both because its aspiration toward the tradition of antiquity does not imply for it the possibility of abandoning the other; nowhere does mingling of styles come so close to violation of all style. During the later phases of antiquity the educated saw in the Bible a violation of style. And the later Humanists could not but have precisely the same reaction to the work of their greatest predecessor, the man who was first to read the poets of antiquity again for the sake of their art and to assimilate their tone, the man who was the first to conceive the idea of the *volgare illustre*, the idea of great poetry in the vernacular, and to carry it out; no other reaction was possible for them, precisely because Dante had done all that. The mixture of styles in the literary works of the earlier Middle Ages, as for instance in the Christian drama, seemed pardonable because of their naïveté; those works could not lay claim to high poetic dignity; their popular purpose and popular character justified or at any rate excused their being what they were; they did not really enter the realm of things that need be taken into account and judged seriously. With Dante, however, it was impossible to speak of naïveté and the absence of higher claims. His numerous explicit statements, all his references to Virgil as his model, his invocations of the Muses, of Apollo, and of God, his tensely dramatic relationship to his own work—so clearly apparent from many passages—and finally and above all, the very tone of every line of the poem itself, bear witness to the fact that the claims he makes are of the highest order. It is not surprising that the tremendous phenomenon which the Comedy represents should have made later Humanists and men of humanistic training ill at ease.

In his theoretical utterances Dante himself betrays a certain indecision in regard to the question of the stylistic category in which the Comedy might fall. In his *De vulgari eloquentia*—a treatise on the *canzone*, which would still seem to be wholly uninfluenced by the Comedy—the demands which Dante makes upon the elevated and tragic style are very different from those with which, in the Comedy, he later complies—they are much narrower in respect to choice of subject matter, and much more puristic and concerned with separation of styles in respect to choice of forms and words. He was then under the influence of Provençal poetry and of the poetry of the Italian *stil nuovo*—both excessively artificial and intended for an initiated elite; and with these he connected the antique doctrine of the separation of styles which the medieval theorists of the art of rhetoric refused to let die. Dante never freed himself completely from these views; otherwise he could not have called his great work a comedy in clearest opposition to the term *alta tragedia* which he applied to Virgil's *Aeneid* (*Inf.*, 20, 113). He seems, then, not to claim the dignity of the elevated tragic style for his great poem. And here we must also consider the justification he adduces for his choice of the designation comedy in the tenth paragraph of his letter to Cangrande. There he says: Tragedy and comedy are distinguished firstly by the course of their action, which, in tragedy, progresses from a noble and quiet beginning to a terrible conclusion, and, in comedy, inversely from a bitter beginning to a happy conclusion; and secondly (a point of greater importance to us) by their style, their *modus loquendi: elate et sublime tragedia; comedia vero remisse et humiliter*; and so, he says, his poem must be called a comedy, on the one hand because of its unhappy beginning and happy conclusion, and on the other hand because of its *modus loquendi: remissus est modus et humilis, quia locutio vulgaris in qua et mulier-cule communicant.* At first one is inclined to assume that this is a reference to his use of the Italian language. In that case the style would be low simply because the Comedy is written in Italian and not in Latin. But it is difficult to attribute such an assertion to Dante, who defended the noble dignity of the vernacular in his *De vulgari eloquentia*, who was himself the founder of the elevated style in the vernacular through his *canzoni*, and who had finished the Comedy at the time when he wrote his letter to Cangrande. For these reasons several modern students have taken *locutio* to mean not language but style. In that case Dante merely wished to say that the style of his work was not that of an elevated Italian or—as he himself described it (*De vulg. el.*, 1, 17)—of the *vulgare illustre, cardinale, aulicum et curiale*, but of the common everyday language of the people.

In any event, here too he does not claim for his work the dignity of an elevated tragic style, it is at best an intermediate style; and even this he does not express very clearly but merely quotes the passage from Horace's *Ars poetica* (93ff.) where Horace says that comedy too sometimes makes use of tragic strains and vice versa. On the whole he classifies his work as being of the low style—although, shortly before, he had discussed its multiplicity of meanings (which certainly does not agree with the idea of the low style); and although he more than once describes that portion of it which he sends to Cangrande with his dedicatory letter, that is, the *Paradiso*, as *cantica sublimis*, and qualifies its materia as *admirabilis*. This uncertainty persists in the Comedy itself, but here the consciousness that both subject and form may claim the highest poetic dignity predominates. Within the poem itself he continues to call it a comedy, but we have already had occasion to enumerate the various points which indicate that he was fully conscious of its stylistic character and rank. Yet although he chooses Virgil as his guide, although he invokes Apollo and the Muses, he avoids ever referring to his poem as sublime in the antique sense. To express its particular kind of sublimity, he coins a special phrase: *il poema sacro, al quale ha posto mano e cielo e terra* (*Par.*, 25, 2-3). It is not easy to see how Dante, after having found this formula and after having completed the Comedy, could still have expressed himself upon its character with the pedantry exhibited in the passage from the letter to Cangrande just referred to. However, so great was the prestige of the classical tradition, obscured as it still was by pedantic schematization, so strong was the predilection for fixed theoretical classifications of a kind which we can but consider absurd, that such a possibility cannot be gainsaid after all. The contemporary or rather immediately succeeding commentators likewise took up the question of style in a purely pedantic vein. There were, to be sure, a few exceptions: Boccaccio for example, whose analysis, however, cannot satisfy us, since it avoids facing the question squarely; and especially the extremely vivid Benvenuto da Imola, who, having explained the threefold division of classical styles (the elevated tragic, the intermediate polemico-satiric, the low comic), continues as follows:

> Modo est hic attente notandum quod sicut in isto libro est omnis pars philosophiae ["every division of philosophy"], ut dictum est, ita est omnis pars poetriae. Unde si quis velit subtiliter investigare, hic est tragoedia, satyra et comoedia. Tragoedia quidem, quia describit gesta pontificum, principum, regum, baronum, et aliorum magnatum et nobilium, sicut patet in toto libro. Satyra, id est reprehensoria; reprehendit enim mirabiliter et audacter omnia genera viciorum, nec parcit dignitati, potestati

vel nobilitati alicuius. Ideo convenientius posset intitulari satyra quam tragoedia vel comoedia. Potest etiam dici quod sit comoedia, nam secundum Isidorum comoedia incipit a tristibus et terminatur ad laeta. Et ita liber iste incipit a tristi materia, scilicet ab Inferno, et terminatur ad laetam, scilicet ad Paradisum, sive ad divinam essentiam. Sed dices forsan, lector: cur vis mihi baptizare librum de novo, cum autor nominaverit ipsum Comoediam? Dico quod autor voluit vocare librum Comoediam a stylo infimo et vulgari, quia de rei veritate est humilis respectu litteralis [sic], quamvis in genere suo sit sublimis et excellens. . . . (*Benvenuti de Rambaldis de Imola Comentum super D. A. Comoediam . . . curante Jacobo Philippo Lacaita.* Tomus Primus, Florentiae, 1887, p. 19.)

(Now here it must be carefully noted that just as in this book there is every division of philosophy, as we said, so there is every division of poetry. So that, if one look narrowly, here is tragedy, satire, and comedy. Tragedy first, because it describes the deeds of pontiffs, princes, kings, barons, and other magnates and great lords, as appears throughout the whole book. Satire, that is reprehension; for it admirably and boldly reprehends all kinds of vice, without sparing anyone's dignity, power, or nobility. Hence it could be more properly entitled satire than tragedy or comedy. But it can also be said to be a comedy, for according to Isidore comedy begins with sad things and ends with joyous ones. And thus this book begins with a sad subject, that is with Hell, and ends with a joyous one, that is with Paradise, or the Divine Being. But perhaps, reader, you will say: Why do you want to rebaptize the book for me, when the author called it a Comedy? I say that the author wished to call it a comedy because of its low and vernacular style, and in fact, speaking literally, it is low in style, but in its kind it is sublime and exalted. . . .)

Benvenuto's temperament cuts right through the thicket of didactic theory: this book, he says, contains every kind of writing just as it does every kind of knowledge; and if its author called it a comedy because its style is low and popular, he was right in a literal sense, but in its way it is a sublime and great style.

The abundance of subjects treated in the Comedy suffices in itself to pose the problem of the elevated style in a wholly new way. For the Provençals and the poets of the "new style," there was but one great theme: courtly love. It is true that in his *De vulgari eloquentia* Dante enumerates three themes (*salus, venus, virtus,* i.e., deeds of valor, love, and virtue), yet in almost all the great *canzoni* the two others are subordinated to the theme of love or are clothed in an allegory of love. Even in the Comedy this pattern is preserved through the figure of Beatrice and the role assigned to her, yet here the pattern has a tremendous scope. The Comedy, among other things, is a didactic poem of encyclopedic dimensions, in which the physico-cosmological, the ethical, and the historico-political order of the universe is collectively presented; it is, further, a literary work which imitates reality and in which all imaginable spheres of reality appear: past and present, sublime grandeur and vile vulgarity, history and legend, tragic and comic occurrences, man and nature; finally, it is the story of Dante's—i.e., one single individual's—life and salvation, and thus a figure of the story of mankind's salvation in general. Its dramatis personae include figures from antique mythology, often (but not always) in the guise of fantastic demons; allegorical personifications and symbolic animals stemming from late antiquity and the Middle Ages; bearers of specific significations chosen from among the angels, the saints, and the blessed in the hierarchy of Christianity; Apollo, Lucifer, and Christ, Fortuna and Lady Poverty, Medusa as an emblem of the deeper circles of Hell, and Cato of Utica as the guardian of Purgatory. Yet, in respect to an attempt at the elevated style, all these things are not so new and problematic as is Dante's undisguised incursions into the realm of a real life neither selected nor preordained by aesthetic criteria. And indeed, it is this contact with real life which is responsible for all the verbal forms whose directness and rigor—almost unknown in the elevated style—offended classicistic taste. Furthermore, all this realism is not displayed within a single action, but instead an abundance of actions in the most diverse tonalities follow one another in quick succession.

And yet the unity of the poem is convincing. It is due to its all-inclusive subject, which is the *status animarum post mortem*. Reflecting God's definitive judgment, this *status* must needs represent a perfectly harmonious whole, considered both as a theoretical system and as a practical reality and hence also as an aesthetic entity; indeed it must needs express the unity of God's universal order in a purer and more immediate form than this earthly sphere or anything that takes place within it, for the beyond—even though it fail of perfection until Judgment Day—is not, at least not to the same extent as the earthly sphere, evolution, potentiality, and provisionality, but God's design in active fulfillment. The unified order of the beyond, as Dante presents it to us, can be most immediately grasped as a moral system in its distribution of souls among the three realms and their subdivisions. On the whole the system follows Aristotelian-Thomist ethics. It groups the sinners in Hell first according to the degree of their evil will, and within those categories according to the gravity of their misdeeds; the penitents in Purgatory according to the evil impulses of which they must purify themselves; and the blessed in Paradise according to the measure of their participation in the vision of God. This ethical system is, however, interwoven with other hierarchical systems of a physico-cosmological or historico-political order. The location of the Inferno, of the Mount of Purgatory, and of the circles of Paradise constitute a physical as well as an ethical picture of the universe. The doctrine of souls which underlies the ethical order is at once a physiological and a psychological anthropology; and there are many other ways in which the ethical and physical orders are basically connected. The same holds true for the historico-political order. The community of the blessed in the white rose of the Empyrean is at the same time also the goal of the historical process of salvation, which is both the guiding principle for all historico-political theories and the standard of judgment by which all historico-political events are measured. In the course of this poem this is constantly expressed, at times most circumstantially (as for instance in the symbolic occurrences on the summit of Purgatory, the Earthly Paradise); so that the three systems of order —the ethical, the physical, and the historico-political—always present and always demonstrable, appear as one single entity.

In order to show how the unity of the transcendental order operates as a unity of the elevated style, we return to our quoted text. Farinata's and Cavalcante's lives on earth are over; the vicissitudes of their destinies have ceased; their state is definitive and immutable except that it will be affected by one single change, their ultimate recovery of their physical bodies at the Resurrection on the Last Day. As we find them here, then, they are souls parted from their bodies. Dante does, however, give them a sort of phantom body, so that they can be seen and can communicate and suffer (cf., in this connection, *Purg.*, 3, 31ff.). Their only link to life on earth is memory. In addition they have—as Dante explains in the very canto with which we are concerned—a measure of knowledge of past and future which goes beyond the earthly norm. Their vision is hyperopic: they clearly see earthly events of the somewhat distant past or future, and hence can foretell the future, but they are blind to the earthly present. (This explains Dante's hesitation when Cavalcante asks him whether his son is still alive; Cavalcante's ignorance surprises him, the more so because other souls had prophesied future events to him.) Their own earthly lives, then, they still possess completely, through their memories, although those lives are ended. And although they are in a situation which differs from any imaginable situation on earth not only in practical terms (they lie in flaming tombs) but also in principle by virtue of their temporal and spatial immutability, the impression they produce is not that they are dead—though that is what they are—but alive.

Here we face the astounding paradox of what is called Dante's realism. Imitation of reality is imitation of the sensory experience of life on earth—among the most essential characteristics of which would seem to be its possessing a history, its changing and developing. Whatever degree of freedom the imitating artist may be granted in his work, he cannot be allowed to deprive reality of this characteristic, which is its very essence. But Dante's inhabitants of the three realms lead a "changeless existence." (Hegel uses the expression in his Lectures on Aesthetics in one of the most beautiful passages ever written on Dante.) Yet into this changeless existence Dante "plunges the living world of human action and endurance and more especially of individual deeds and destinies." Considering our text again, we ask how this may come about.

The existence of the two tomb-dwellers and the scene of it are certainly final and eternal, but they are not devoid of history. This Hell has been visited by Aeneas and Paul and even by Christ; now Dante and Virgil are traveling through it; it has landscapes, and its landscapes are peopled by infernal spirits; occurrences, events, and even transformations go on before our very eyes. In their phantom bodies the souls of the damned, in their eternal abodes, have phenomenal appearance, freedom to speak and gesture and even to move about within limits, and thus, within their changelessness, a limited freedom of change. We have left the earthly sphere behind; we are in an eternal place, and yet we encounter concrete appearance and concrete occurrence there. This differs from what appears and occurs on earth, yet is evidently connected with it in a necessary and strictly determined relation.

The reality of the appearances of Farinata and Cavalcante is perceived in the situation in which they are placed and in their utterances.

In their position as inhabitants of flaming tombs is expressed God's judgment upon the entire category of sinners to which they belong, upon heretics and infidels. But in their utterances, their individual character is manifest in all its force. This is especially striking with Farinata and Cavalcante because they are sinners of the same category and hence find themselves in the same situation. Yet as individuals of different personalities, of different lots in their former lives, and of different inclinations, they are most sharply contrasted. Their eternal and changeless fate is the same; but only in the sense that they have to suffer the same punishment, only in an objective sense. For they accept their fate in very different ways. Farinata wholly disregards his situation; Cavalcante, in his blind prison, mourns for the beauty of light; and each, in gesture and word, completely reveals the nature proper to each, which can be and is none other than that which each possessed in his life upon earth. And still more: from the fact that earthly life has ceased so that it cannot change or grow, whereas the passions and inclinations which animated it still persist without ever being released in action, there results as it were a tremendous concentration. We behold an intensified image of the essence of their being, fixed for all eternity in gigantic dimensions, behold it in a purity and distinctness which could never for one moment have been possible during their lives upon earth.

There can be no doubt that this too is part of the judgment which God has pronounced upon them; God has not only grouped the souls in categories and distributed them accordingly among the various divisions of the three realms; He has also given each soul a specific eternal situation, in that He has never destroyed an individual form but on the contrary has fixed it in his eternal judgment—nay more, not until He has pronounced that judgment has He fully perfected it and wholly revealed it to sight. Here in Hell Farinata is greater, stronger, and nobler than ever, for never in his life on earth had he had such an opportunity to prove his stout heart; and if his thoughts and desires center unchanged upon Florence and the Ghibellines, upon the successes and failures of his former endeavors, there can be no doubt that this persistence of his earthly being in all its grandeur and hopeless futility is part of the judgment God has pronounced upon him. The same hopeless futility in the continuance of his earthly being is displayed by Cavalcante; it is not likely that in the course of his earthly existence he ever felt his faith in the spirit of man, his love for the sweetness of light and for his son so profoundly, or expressed it so arrestingly, as now, when it is all in vain. We must also consider that, for the souls of the dead, Dante's journey represents their only chance in all eternity to speak to one from among the living. This is an aspect of the situation which impels many to express themselves with the utmost intensity and which brings into the changelessness of their eternal fate a moment of dramatic historicity. And finally, one more distinguishing characteristic of the situation in which the dwellers in Hell find themselves is their strangely restricted and expanded range of knowledge. They have forfeited the vision of God participated in to various degrees by all beings on earth, in Purgatory, and in Paradise; and with it they have lost all hope; they know the past and the future in the passing of time on earth and hence the hopeless futility of their personal existence, which they have retained without the prospect of its finally flowing into the divine community; and they are passionately interested in the present state of things on earth, which is hidden from them. (A striking case in point is, with Cavalcante and several others, the figure of Guido da Montefeltro in Canto 27. Speaking with difficulty through the flames which shoot from his head, he implores Virgil to stop and speak to him, in a long adjuration, permeated with memories and grief, which reaches its climax in the words of line 28: *dimmi se i Romagnuoli han pace o guerra!*)

Dante, then, took over earthly historicity into his beyond; his dead are cut off from the earthly present and its vicissitudes, but memory and the most intense interest in it stirs them so profoundly that the atmosphere of the beyond is charged with it. This is less pronounced on the Mount of Purgatory and in Paradise, because there the souls do not look back upon life on earth, as they do in Hell, but forward and up; as a result, the farther we ascend the more clearly is earthly existence seen together with its divine goal. But earthly existence remains always manifest, for it is always the basis of God's judgment and hence of the eternal condition of the soul; and this condition is everywhere not only a matter of being assigned to a specific subdivision of the penitent or blessed but is a conscious presentment of the soul's previous life on earth and of the specific place it duly occupies in the design of God's order. For it is precisely the absolute realization of a particular earthly personality in the place definitively assigned to it, which constitutes the Divine Judgment. And everywhere the souls of the dead have sufficient freedom to manifest their individual and particular nature—at times, it is true, only with considerable difficulty, for often their punishment or their penitence or even the clear light of their bliss makes it hard for them to appear and to express themselves; but then, overcoming the obstacle, self-expression breaks out only the more effectively.

These ideas are found in the passage from Hegel referred to above. Over twenty years ago I used them as the basis of a study of Dante's realism (*Dante als Dichter der irdischen Welt*, 1929). Since then I have been concerned with the question what conception of the structure of events, in other words what conception of history, is the foundation for Dante's realism, this realism projected into changeless eternity. It has been my hope that in the process I might learn something further and more exact about the basis of Dante's elevated style, for his elevated style consists precisely in integrating what is characteristically individual and at times horrible, ugly, grotesque, and vulgar with the dignity of God's judgment—a dignity which transcends the ultimate limits of our earthly conception of the sublime. Obviously Dante's conception of what happens, of history, is not identical with that commonly accepted in our modern world. Indeed he does not view it merely as an earthly process, a pattern of earthly events, but in constant connection with God's plan, toward the goal of which all earthly happenings tend. This is to be understood not only in the sense of human society as a whole approaching the end of the world and the advent of the millennium in a constant forward motion (with all history, then, directed horizontally, into the future); but also in the sense that every earthly event and every earthly phenomenon is at all times—independently of all forward motion—directly connected with God's plan; so that a multiplicity of vertical links establish an immediate relation between every earthly phenomenon and the plan of salvation conceived by Providence. For all of creation is a constant reduplication and emanation of the active love of God (*non è se non splendor di quella idea che partorisce amando il nostro Sire, Par.*, 13, 53-54), and this active love is timeless and affects all phenomena at all seasons. The goal of the process of salvation, the white rose in the Empyrean, the community of the elect in God's no longer veiled presence, is not only a certain hope for the future but is from all eternity perfect in God and prefigured for men, as is Christ in Adam. It is timelessly or at all times that Christ's triumph and Mary's coronation take place in Paradise; at all times the soul whose love has not been drawn toward a false goal goes unto Christ, its beloved, who wedded it with his blood.

In the Comedy there are numerous earthly phenomena whose theoretical relation to the divine plan of salvation is set forth in detail. From the point of view of modern readers the most astounding instance, and in political and historical terms at the same time the most important one, is the universal Roman monarchy. It is in Dante's view the concrete, earthly anticipation of the Kingdom of God. Aeneas' journey to the underworld is granted as a special grace in view of Rome's earthly and spiritual victory (*Inf.*, 2, 13ff.); from the beginning, Rome is destined to rule the world. Christ appears when the time is fulfilled, that is, when the inhabited world rests in peace in Augustus' hands. Brutus and Cassius, the murderers of Caesar, suffer beside Judas in the jaws of Lucifer. The third Caesar, Tiberius, is the legitimate judge of Christ incarnate and as such the avenger of original sin. Titus is the legitimate executor of the vengeance upon the Jews. The Roman eagle is the bird of God, and in one passage Paradise is called *quella Roma onde Cristo è Romano* (cf. *Par.*, 6; *Purg.*, 21, 82ff.; *Inf.*, 34, 61ff.; *Purg.*, 32, 102; etc., also numerous passages in the *Monarchia*). Furthermore, Virgil's role in the poem can only be understood on this premise. We are reminded of the figure of the earthly and heavenly Jerusalem, and indeed the whole concept is an example of figural thinking. Just as the Judaeo-Christian method of interpretation, consistently applied to the Old Testament by Paul and the Church Fathers, conceives of Adam as a figure of Christ, of Eve as a figure of the Church, just as generally speaking every event and every phenomenon referred to in the Old Testament is conceived as a figure which only the phenomena and events of Christ's Incarnation can completely realize or "fulfill" (to use the conventional expression), so the universal Roman Empire here appears as an earthly figure of heavenly fulfillment in the Kingdom of God.

In my essay "Figura" (referred to above, p. 73), I have shown—convincingly, I hope—that the Comedy is based on a figural view of things. In the case of three of its most important characters—Cato of Utica, Virgil, and Beatrice—I have attempted to demonstrate that their appearance in the other world is a fulfillment of their appearance on earth, their earthly appearance a figure of their appearance in the other world. I stressed the fact that a figural schema permits both its poles—the figure and its fulfillment—to retain the characteristics of concrete historical reality, in contradistinction to what obtains with symbolic or allegorical personifications, so that figure and fulfillment—although the one "signifies" the other—have a significance which is not incompatible with their being real. An event taken as a figure preserves its literal and historical meaning. It remains an event, does not become a mere sign. The Church Fathers, especially Tertullian, Jerome, and Augustine, had successfully defended figural realism, that is, the maintenance of the basic historical reality of figures, against all attempts at spiritually allegorical interpretation. Such attempts, which as it were undermine the reality of history and see in it only extra-historical signs and significations, survived from late antiquity and passed into the Middle Ages. Medieval symbolism and allegorism are often, as we know, excessively abstract, and many traces of this are to be found in the Comedy itself. But far more prevalent in the Christian life of the High Middle Ages is the figural realism which can be observed in full bloom in sermons, the plastic arts, and mystery plays (cf. the preceding chapter); and it is this figural realism which dominates Dante's view.

The world beyond—as we put it earlier—is God's design in active fulfillment. In relation to it, earthly phenomena are on the whole merely figural, potential, and requiring fulfillment. This also applies to the individual souls of the dead: it is only here, in the beyond, that they attain fulfillment and the true reality of their being. Their career on earth was only the figure of this fulfillment. In the fulfillment of their being they find punishment, penance, or reward. That man's existence on earth is provisional and must be complemented in the world beyond, is a concept in keeping with Thomist anthropology, if E. Gilson's observations on the subject are valid. He writes (*Le thomisme*, 3rd ed., Paris, 1927, p. 300): *une sorte de marge nous tient quelque peu en deçà de notre propre définition; aucun de nous ne réalise plénièrement l'essence humaine ni même la notion complète de sa propre individualité.* It is precisely this *notion complète de leur propre individualité* which the souls attain in Dante's beyond by virtue of God's judgment; and specifically, they attain it as an actual reality, which is in keeping with the figural view and the Aristotelian-Thomist concept of form. The relation of figure fulfilled, which the dead in Dante represent in reference to their own past on earth, is most readily demonstrable in those cases in which not only character and essential being, but also a signification apparent in the earthly figure, are fulfilled: as for example in the case of Cato of Utica, whose merely figural role as the guardian of earthly political freedom is fulfilled in the role he plays at the foot of the Mount of Purgatory as the guardian of the eternal freedom of the elect (*Purg.*, 1, 71ff.: *libertà va cercando*; cf. also *Archiv. Roman.*, 22, 478-481). In this instance the figural approach can explain the riddle of Cato's appearance in a place where we are astonished to find a pagan. Such a demonstration is not often possible. Yet the cases where it *is* possible suffice to let us see Dante's basic conception of the individual in this world and in the world beyond. The character and the function of a human being have a specified place in God's idea of order, as it is figured on earth and fulfilled in the beyond.

Both figure and fulfillment possess—as we have said—the character of actual historical events and phenomena. The fulfillment possesses it in greater and more intense measure, for it is, compared with the figure, *forma perfectior*. This explains the overwhelming realism of Dante's beyond. When we say, "This explains . . . ," we do not of course overlook the genius of the poet who was capable of such a creation. To put it in the words of the old commentators, who distinguish between *causa efficiens, materialis, formalis,* and *finalis* of the poem: *Causa efficiens in hoc opere, velut in domo facienda aedificator, est Dantes Allegherii de Florentia, gloriosus theologus, philosophus et poeta* (Pietro Alighieri; in a similar vein also Jacopo della Lana). But the particular way in which his realistic genius achieved form, we explain through the figural point of view. This enables us to understand that the beyond is eternal and yet phenomenal; that it is changeless and of all time and yet full of history. It also enables us to show in what way this realism in the beyond is distinguished from every type of purely earthly realism. In the beyond man is no longer involved in any earthly action or entanglement, as he must be in an earthly representation of human events. Rather, he is involved in an eternal situation which is the sum and the result of all his actions and which at the same time tells him what were the decisive aspects of his life and his character. Thus his memory is led along a path which, though for the inhabitants of Hell it is dreary and barren, is yet always the right path, the path which reveals what was decisive in the individual's life. In this condition the dead present themselves to the living Dante. The suspense inherent in the yet unrevealed future—an essential element in all earthly concerns and their artistic imitation, especially of a dramatic, serious, and problematic kind—has ceased. In the Comedy only Dante can feel this suspense. The many played-out dramas are combined in one great play, involving his own fate and that of all mankind; they are but exempla of the winning or losing of eternal bliss. But passions, torments, and joys have survived; they find expression in the situations, gestures, and utterances of the dead. With Dante as spectator, all the dramas are played over again in tremendously concentrated form—sometimes in a few lines, as in the case of Pia de' Tolomei (*Purg.*, 5, 130). And in them, seemingly scattered and fragmented, yet actually always as parts within a general plan, the history of Florence, of Italy, of the world, unfolds. Suspense and development, the distinguishing characteristics of earthly phenomena, are no more. Yet the waves of history do reach the shores of the world beyond: partly as memories of the earthly past; partly as interest in the earthly present; partly as concern for the earthly future; in all cases as a temporality figurally preserved in timeless eternity. Each of the dead interprets his condition in the beyond as the last act, forever being played out, of his earthly drama.

In the first canto of the poem Dante says to Virgil: "Thou alone art he to whom I owe the beautiful style which has done me honor." This is doubtless correct—and even more in respect to the Comedy than to his earlier works and *canzoni.* The motif of a journey to the underworld, a large number of individual motifs, many stylistic turns—for all these he is indebted to Virgil. Even the change in his theory of style from the time of his treatise *De vulgari eloquentia*—a change which took him from the merely lyrico-philosophical to the great epic and hence to full-dimensional representation of human events—cannot be accounted for by anything but the influence of classical models and in particular of Virgil. Of the writers we know, he was the first to have direct access to the poet Virgil. Virgil, much more than medieval theory, developed his feeling of style and his conception of the sublime. Through him he learned to break the all too narrow pattern of the Provençal and contemporary Italian *suprema constructio.* Yet as he approached the problem of his great work, which was to come into being under the sign of Virgil, it was the other, the more immediately present, the more living traditions which overwhelmed him. His great work proved to be in the mixed style and figural, and indeed in the mixed style as a result of the figural approach. It proved to be a comedy; it proved to be—also in terms of style—Christian. After all that we have said on the subject in the course of these interpretations, there can be no need for again explaining that (and why) conceiving all earthly occurrences through the medium of a mixed style—without aesthetic restriction in either subject matter or form—as an entity sublimely figural, is Christian in spirit and Christian in origin. Hence too the unity of the whole poem, in which a wealth of themes and actions is organized in a single universal pattern which embraces both heaven and earth: *il poema sacro, al quale ha posto mano e cielo e terra.* And, on the other hand, it was again Dante who first felt and realized the *gravitas* proper to the antique elevated style, and even surpassed it. Let him say what he will; let it be as vulgar, grotesque, horrible, or sneering as may be: the tone remains that of the elevated style. It is impossible to imagine that the realism of the Comedy could ever sink to the level of farce and serve the purposes of popular entertainment as the realism of the Christian drama so often does. Dante's level of tone is unthinkable in medieval epics before his time; and he learned it, as can be shown by many examples, from antique models. Before Dante, vernacular literature—especially that of Christian inspiration—is on the whole rather naive so far as questions of style are concerned, and that despite the influence of scholastic rhetoric—an influence which of late has been rather heavily emphasized. But Dante, although he takes his material from the most living and sometimes from the humblest vernacular, has lost this naive quality. He subdues every turn of expression to the gravity of his tone, and when he sings of the divine order of things, he solves his problem by using periodic articulations and devices of sentence structure which command gigantic masses of thought and concatenations of events; since antiquity nothing comparable had existed in literature (one example may stand for many: *Inf.*, 2, 13-36). Is Dante's style still a *sermo remissus et humilis*, as he calls it himself and as Christian style should be even in the sphere of the sublime? The question could perhaps be answered in the affirmative; the Fathers themselves did not scorn the conscious employment of the art of rhetoric, not even Augustine. The crux of the matter is what purpose and what attitude the artistic devices serve.

In our passage two of the damned are introduced in the elevated style. Their earthly character is preserved in full force in their places in the beyond. Farinata is as great and proud as ever, and Cavalcante loves the light of the world and his son Guido not less, but in his despair still more passionately, than he did on earth. So God had willed; and so these things stand in the figural realism of Christian tradition. Yet never before has this realism been carried so far; never before—scarcely even in antiquity—has so much art and so much expressive power been employed to produce an almost painfully immediate impression of the earthly reality of human beings. It was precisely the Christian idea of the indestructibility of the entire human individual which made this possible for Dante. And it was precisely by producing this effect with such power and so much realism that he opened the way for that aspiration toward autonomy which possesses all earthly existence. In the very heart of the other world, he created a world of earthly beings and passions so powerful that it breaks bounds and proclaims its independence. Figure surpasses fulfillment, or more properly: the fulfillment serves to bring out the figure in still more impressive relief. We cannot but admire Farinata and weep with Cavalcante. What actually moves us is not that God has damned them, but that the one is unbroken and the other mourns so heart-rendingly for his son and the sweetness of the light. Their horrible situation, their doom, serves only, as it were, as a means of heightening the effect of these completely earthly emotions. Yet it seems to me that the problem with which we are here concerned is not conceived broadly enough if, as has frequently been done, it is formulated exclusively in terms of Dante's admiration or sympathy for a number of individuals encountered in Hell. The essence of the matter, what we have in mind, is not restricted to Hell nor, on the other hand, to Dante's admiration or sympathy. All through the poem there are instances in which the effect of the earthly figure and its earthly destiny surpasses or is subserved by the effect produced by its eternal situation. Certainly, the noble souls among the damned, Francesca da Rimini, Farinata, Brunetto Latini, or Pier della Vigna, are also good examples in support of my view; but it seems to me that the emphasis is not where it belongs if only such instances are adduced, for a doctrine of salvation in which the eternal destiny depends upon grace and repentance can no more dispense with such figures in Hell than it can with virtuous pagans in Limbo. But as soon as we ask why Dante was the first who so strongly felt the tragic quality in such figures and expressed it with all the overwhelming power of genius, the field of speculation immediately broadens. For it is with the same power that Dante treats all earthly things of which he laid hold. Cavalcante is not great, and figures like Ciacco the glutton or the insanely irate Filippo Argenti he handles now with sympathetic contempt, now with disgust. Yet that does not prevent the portrayal of earthly passions in these instances from far surpassing, in their wholly individual fulfillment in the beyond, the portrayal of a collective punishment, nor the latter from frequently only heightening the effect of the former. This holds true even of the elect in Purgatory and Paradise. Casella singing one of Dante's *canzoni* and those who listen to him (*Purg.*, 2), Buonconte telling of his death and what became of his body (*Purg.*,

5), Statius kneeling before his master Virgil (*Purg.*, 21), the young King of Hungary, Carlo Martello of Anjou, who so charmingly expresses his friendship for Dante (*Par.*, 8), Dante's ancestor Cacciaguida, proud, old-fashioned, and full of the civic history of Florence (*Par.*, 15-17), even the Apostle Peter (*Par.*, 27), and how many others, open before us a world of earthly-historical life, of earthly deeds, endeavors, feelings, and passions, the like of which the earthly scene itself can hardly produce in such abundance and power. Certainly they are all set fast in God's order, certainly a great Christian poet has the right to preserve earthly humanity in the beyond, to preserve the figure in its fulfillment and to perfect the one and the other to the best of his capabilities. But Dante's great art carries the matter so far that the effect becomes earthly, and the listener is all too occupied by the figure in the fulfillment. The beyond becomes a stage for human beings and human passions. Think of the earlier figural forms of art—of the mysteries, of religious sculpture—which never, or at best most timidly, ventured beyond the immediate data supplied by the Bible, which embarked upon the imitation of reality and the individual only for the sake of a livelier dramatization of Biblical themes—think of these and contrast them with Dante who, within the figural pattern, brings to life the whole historical world and, within that, every single human being who crosses his path! To be sure, this is only what was demanded from the first by the Judaeo-Christian interpretation of the phenomenal; that interpretation claims universal validity. But the fullness of life which Dante incorporates into that interpretation is so rich and so strong that its manifestations force their way into the listener's soul independently of any interpretation. When we hear Cavalcante's outburst: *non fiere li occhi suoi il dolce lome?* or read the beautiful, gentle, and enchantingly feminine line which Pia de' Tolomei utters before she asks Dante to remember her on earth (*e riposato de la lunga via, Purg.*, 5, 131), we experience an emotion which is concerned with human beings and not directly with the divine order in which they have found their fulfillment. Their eternal position in the divine order is something of which we are only conscious as a setting whose irrevocability can but serve to heighten the effect of their humanity, preserved for us in all its force. The result is a direct experience of life which overwhelms everything else, a comprehension of human realities which spreads as widely and variously as it goes profoundly to the very roots of our emotions, an illumination of man's impulses and passions which leads us to share in them without restraint and indeed to admire their variety and their greatness.

And by virtue of this immediate and admiring sympathy with man, the principle, rooted in the divine order, of the indestructibility of the whole historical and individual man turns *against* that order, makes it subservient to its own purposes, and obscures it. The image of man eclipses the image of God. Dante's work made man's Christian-figural being a reality, and destroyed it in the very process of realizing it. The tremendous pattern was broken by the overwhelming power of the images it had to contain. The coarse disorderliness which resulted during the later Middle Ages from the farcical realism of the mystery plays is fraught with far less danger to the figural-Christian view of things than the elevated style of such a poet, in whose work men learn to see and know themselves. In this fulfillment, the figure becomes independent: even in Hell there are great souls, and certain souls in Purgatory can for a moment forget the path of purification for the sweetness of a poem, the work of human frailty. And because of the special conditions of man's self-fulfillment in the beyond, his human reality asserts itself even more strongly, concretely, and specifically than it does, for example, in antique literature. For this self-fulfillment, which comprises the individual's entire past—objectively as well as in memory—involves ontogenetic history, the history of an individual's personal growth; the resultant of that growth, it is true, lies before us as a finished product; but in many cases we are given a detailed portrayal of its several phases; it is never entirely withheld from us. More accurately than antique literature was ever able to present it, we are given to see, in the realm of timeless being, the history of man's inner life and unfolding.

9

FRATE ALBERTO

In a famous novella of the *Decameron* (4, 2), Boccaccio tells of a man from Imola whose vice and dishonesty had made him a social outcast in his native town, so that he preferred to leave it. He went to Venice, there became a Franciscan monk and even a priest, called himself Frate Alberto, and managed to attract so much attention by striking penances and pious acts and sermons that he was generally regarded as a godly and trustworthy man. Then one day he tells one of his penitents—a particularly stupid and conceited creature, the wife of a merchant away on a journey—that the angel Gabriel has fallen in love with her beauty and would like to visit her at night. He visits her himself as Gabriel and has his fun with her. This goes on for a while, but in the end it turns out badly. This is what happens:

> Pure avenne un giorno che, essendo madonna Lisetta con una sua comare, et insieme di bellezze quistionando, per porre la sua innanzi ad ogni altra, si come colei che poco sale aveva in zucca, disse: Se voi sapeste a cui la mia bellezza piace, in verità voi tacereste dell'altre. La comare vaga d'udire, si come colei che ben la conoscea, disse: Madonna, voi potreste dir vero, ma tuttavia non sappiendo chi questo si sia, altri non si rivolgerebbe così di leggiero. Allora la donna, che piccola levatura avea, disse: Comare, egli non si vuol dire, ma l'intendimento mio è l'agnolo Gabriello, il quale più che sè m'ama, si come la più bella donna, per quello che egli mi dica, che sia nel mondo o in maremma. La comare allora ebbe voglia di ridere, ma pur si tenne per farla più avanti parlare, e disse: In fè di Dio, madonna, se l'agnolo Gabriello è vostro intendimento, e dicevi questo, egli dee ben esser così; ma io non credeva che gli agnoli facesson queste cose. Disse la donna: Comare, voi siete errata; per le piaghe di Dio egli il fa meglio che mio marido; e dicemi che egli si fa anche colassù; ma perciocchè io gli paio più bella che niuna che ne sia in cielo, s'è egli innamorato di me, e viensene a star meco ben spesso: mo vedi vu? La comare partita da madonna Lisetta, le parve mille anni che ella fosse in parte ove ella potesse queste cose ridire; e

ragunatasi ad una festa con una gran brigata di donne, loro ordinatamente raccontò la novella. Queste donne il dissero a' mariti et ad altre donne; e quelle a quell' altre, e così in meno di due dì ne fu tutta ripiena Vinegia. Ma tra gli altri, a' quali questa cosa venne agli orecchi, furono i cognati di lei, li quali, senza alcuna cosa dirle, si posero in cuore di trovare questo agnolo, e di sapere se egli sapesse volare; e più notti stettero in posta. Avvenne che di questo fatto alcuna novelluzza ne venne a frate Alberto agli orecchi, il quale, per riprender la donna, una notte andatovi, appena spogliato s'era, che i cognati di lei, che veduto l'avean venire, furono all'uscio della sua camera per aprirlo. Il che frate Alberto sentendo, e avvisato ciò che era, levatosi, non avendo altro rifugio, aperse una finestra, la qual sopra il maggior canal rispondea, e quindi si gittò nell'aqua. Il fondo v'era grande, et egli sapeva ben notare, si che male alcun non si fece: e notato dall'altra parte del canale, in una casa, che aperta v'era, prestamente se n'entrò, pregando un buono uomo, che dentro v'era, che per l'amor di Dio gli scampasse la vita, sue favole dicendo, perchè quivi a quella ora et ignudo fosse. Il buono uomo mosso a pietà, convenendogli andare a far sue bisogne, nel suo letto il mise, e dissegli che quivi infino alla sua tornata si stesse; e dentro serratolo, andò a fare i fatti suoi. I cognati della donna entrati nella camera trovarono che l'agnolo Gabriello, quivi avendo lasciate l'ali, se n'era volato: di che quasi scornati, grandissima villania dissero alla donna, e lei ultimamente sconsolata lasciarono stare, et a casa lor tornarsi con gli arnesi dell'agnolo.

(However, it chanced one day that Madam Lisetta, being in dispute with a gossip of hers upon the question of female charms, to set her own above all others, said, like a woman who had little wit in her noddle, "An you but knew whom my beauty pleaseth, in truth you would hold your peace of other women." The other, longing to hear, said, as one who knew her well, "Madam, maybe you say sooth; but knowing not who this may be, one cannot turn about so lightly." Thereupon quoth Lisetta, who was eath enough to draw, "Gossip, it must go no farther; but he I mean is the angel Gabriel, who loveth me more than himself, as the fairest lady (for that which he telleth me) who is in the world or the Maremma." The other had a mind to laugh, but contained herself, so she might make Lisetta speak further, and said, "Faith, madam, an the angel Gabriel be your lover and tell you this, needs must it be so; but methought not the angels did these things." "Gossip," answered the lady, "you are mistaken; zounds, he doth what you wot of better than my husband and telleth me they do it also up yonder; but, for that I seem to him fairer than any she in heaven, he hath fallen in love with me and cometh full oft to lie with me; seestow now?" The gossip, to whom it seemed a thousand years till she would be whereas she might repeat these things, took her leave of Madam Lisetta and foregathering at an entertainment with a great company of ladies, orderly recounted to them the whole story. They told it again to their husbands and other ladies, and these to yet others, and so in less than two days Venice was all full of it. Among others to whose ears the thing came were Lisetta's brothers-in-law, who, without saying aught to her, bethought themselves to find the angel in question and see if he knew how to fly, and to this end they lay several nights in wait for him. As chance would have it, some inkling of the matter came to the ears of Fra Alberto, who accordingly repaired one night to the lady's house, to reprove her, but hardly had he put off his clothes ere her brothers-in-law, who had seen him come, were at the door of her chamber to open it. Fra Alberto, hearing this and guessing what was to do, started up and having no other resource, opened a window, which gave upon the Grand Canal, and cast himself thence into the water. The canal was deep there and he could swim well, so that he did himself no hurt, but made his way to the opposite bank and hastily entering a house that stood open there, besought a poor man, whom he found within, to save his life for the love of God, telling him a tale of his own fashion, to explain how he came there at that hour and naked. The good man was moved to pity and it behoving him to go do his occasions, he put him in his own bed and bade him abide there against his return; then, locking him in, he went about his affairs. Meanwhile, the lady's brothers-in-law entered her chamber and found that the angel Gabriel had flown, leaving his wings there; whereupon, seeing themselves baffled, they gave her all manner hard words and ultimately made off to their own house with the angel's trappings, leaving her disconsolate.) *The Decameron.* Giovanni Boccaccio. Translation by John Payne. The Macy Library edition.

As I have said, the story ends very badly for Frate Alberto. His host hears on the Rialto what happened that night at Madonna Lisetta's and infers who the man he took in is. He extorts a large sum of money from Frate Alberto and then betrays him nevertheless; and he does it in so disgusting a way that the frate becomes the object of a public scandal with moral and practical consequences from which he never recovers. We feel almost sorry for him, especially if we consider with what delight and indulgence Boccaccio relates the erotic escapades of other clerics no better than Frate Alberto (for instance 3, 4—the story of the monk Don Felice who induces his lady love's husband to perform a ridiculous penance which keeps him away from home nights; or 3, 8, the story of an abbot who takes the husband to Purgatory for a while and even makes him do penance there).

The passage reprinted above contains the crisis of the novella. It consists of Madonna Lisetta's conversation with her confidante and the consequences of their conversation: the strange rumor spreading through the town; the relatives hearing it and deciding to catch the angel; the nocturnal scene in which the frate escapes for the time being by boldly jumping into the canal. The conversation between the two women is psychologically and stylistically a masterly treatment of a vivid everyday scene. Both the confidante who, suppressing her laughter, voices some doubt with simulated politeness to get Lisetta to go on talking, as well as the heroine herself who, in her vaingloriousness, lets herself be lured even beyond the limits of her innate stupidity, impress us as true to life and natural. Yet the stylistic devices which Boccaccio employs are anything but purely popular. His prose, which has often been analyzed, reflects the schooling it received from antique models and the precepts of medieval rhetoric, and it displays all its arts. It summarizes complex situations in a single period and puts a shifting word order at the service of emphasizing what is important, of retarding or accelerating the tempo of the action, of rhythmic and melodic effect.

The introductory sentence itself is a rich period, and the two gerunds *essendo* and *quistionando*—one in initial, the other in final position, with a leisurely interval between them—are as well-calculated as the syntactic stress on *la sua* which concludes the first of two rhythmically quite similar cadences, the second of which ends with *ogni altra*. And when the actual conversation begins, our good Lisetta is so enthusiastic about herself that she fairly bursts into song: *se voi sapeste a cui la mia bellezza piace. . . .* Still more delightful is her second speech with its many brief and almost equisyllabic units in which the so-called *cursus velox* predominates. The most beautiful of them, *ma l'intendiménto mío / è l'ágnolo Gabriéllo*, is echoed in her confidante's reply, *se l'ágnolo Gabriéllo / è vóstro intendiménto*. In this second speech we find the first colloquialisms: *intendimento*, presumably of social rather than local color, can hardly have been in polite usage in this particular acceptation (roughly, *desiderium*, English "sweetheart"), nor yet the expression *nel mondo o in maremma* (which gives us another charming cadence). The more excited she grows, the more numerous are the colloquial and now even dialectal forms: the Venetian *marido* in the enchanting sentence which stresses the praises of Gabriel's erotic prowess by the adjurational formula, *per le piaghe di Dio*, and the climactic effect (again Venetian), *mo vedi vu*, whose note of vulgar triumph is the more humorous as, just before, she had again been singing sweetly, . . . *ma perciocchè io gli paio più bella che niuna che ne sia in cielo, s'è egli innamorato di me*. . . .

The next two periods comprise the spreading of the rumor throughout the town, in two stages. The first leads from *la comare* to the *brigata di donne*, the second from *queste donne* to *Vinegia*. Each has its own source of motion: the first in the confidante's impatience to unburden herself of her story, an impatience whose urgency and subsequent appeasement come out remarkably well in a corresponding movement of the verbs (*partita . . . le parve mille anni che ella fosse . . . dove potesse . . . e ragunatasi . . . ordinatamente raccontò*); the second, in the progressive expansion, paratactically expressed, of the field covered. From here on the narration becomes more rapid and more dramatic. The very next sentence reaches all the way from the moment when the relatives hear the rumor to their nocturnal ambush, although there is room in it for a few additional details of fact and psychological description. Yet it seems relatively empty and calm compared with the two which follow and in which the entire night scene in Lisetta's house, down to Frate Alberto's bold leap, takes its course in two periods which, however, together constitute but a single movement. This is done by interlacing hypotactic forms, with participial constructions (generally a favorite device with Boccaccio) playing the most important part. The first sentence begins quietly enough with the principal verb *avenne* and the corresponding subject clause *che . . . venne . . .*; but in the attached relative clause, *il quale* (a secondary subordinate clause, that is), the catastrophe bursts: . . . *andatovi, appena spogliato s'era, che i cognati . . . furono all' uscio*. And then comes a tempest of verb forms: *sentendo, e avvisato, levatosi, non avendo, aperse, e si gittò*. If only by reason of the brevity of the crowding units, the effect is one of extraordinary speed and dramatic precipitation. And for the same reason—despite the learned and classical origin of the stylistic devices employed—it is not at all literary; the tone is not that of written language but of oral narrative, the more so because the position of the verbs, and hence the length and tempo of the intervening sections of greater calm, is constantly varied in an artistically spontaneous fashion: *sentendo* and *avvisato* are placed close together, as are *levatosi* and *non avendo, aperse* soon follows, but the concluding *si gittò* appears only after the relative clause referring to the window. I do not quite see, by the way, why Boccaccio has the frate hear of the rumor which is going the rounds. So shrewd a knave would hardly put his head in such a trap, in order to give Lisetta a piece of his mind, if he were at all aware that there was any risk. The whole thing, it seems to me, would be more natural if he had no inkling that something was afoot. His quick and bold escape requires no special motivation in the form of a previously crystallized suspicion. Or did Boccaccio have some other reason for making the statement? I see none.

While the frate swims the canal, the narrative becomes momentarily quieter, more relaxed, slower: we have principal verbs, in an imperfect of description, arranged paratactically. But no sooner has he reached the other side than the verbs begin jostling each other again, especially when he enters the strange house: *prestamente se n'entrò, pregando . . . che per l'amor di Dio gli scampasse la vita, sue favole dicendo, perchè . . . fosse*. The intervals between verbs are likewise brief or urgent. Exceedingly condensed and hurried is *quivi a quella ora e ignudo*. Then the tide begins to ebb. The ensuing sentences are still packed full of factual information and hence with participial hypotaxes, but at least they are governed by the progressively more leisurely pace of principal clauses linked by "and": *mise, et dissegli, e andò. Entrati . . . trovarono che . . . se n'era volato* is still quite dramatic; but then comes the progressive relaxation of the paratactic series *dissero, e ultimamente lasciarono stare, e tornarsi*.

Of such artistry there is no trace in earlier narrative literature. First let us take a random example from the Old French genre of droll tales in verse, the greatest number of which were produced about a century before Boccaccio. I choose a passage from the fablel *Du prestre qui ot mere a force* (from Berlin Ms Hamilton 257, after the text by G.

Rohlfs, *Sechs altfranzösische Fablels*, Halle, 1925, p. 12). The theme is a priest who has a very mean, ugly, and stingy mother whom he keeps away from his house while he spoils his mistress, especially in the matter of clothes. The cantankerous old woman complains of this, and the priest answers:

"Tesiez", dist il, "vos estes sote;
De quoi me menez vos dangier,
Se du pein avez a mengier,
De mon potage et de mes pois;
Encor est ce desor mon pois,
Car vos m'avez dit mainte honte."
La vieille dit: "Rien ne vos monte
Que ie vodre d'ore en avant
Que vos me teigniez par covent
A grant honor com vostre mere."
Li prestre a dit: "Par seint pere,
James du mien ne mengera,
Or face au pis qu'ele porra
Ou au mieus tant com il li loist!"
"Si ferai, mes que bien vos poist",
Fet cele, "car ie m'en irai
A l'evesque et li conterai
Vostre errement et vostre vie,
Com vostre meschine est servie.
A mengier a ases et robes,
Et moi volez pestre de lobes;
De vostre avoir n'ai bien ne part."
A cest mot la vieille s'en part
Tote dolente et tot irée.
Droit a l'evesque en est allée.
A li s'en vient et si se claime
De son fiuz qui noient ne l'aime,
Ne plus que il feroit un chien,
Ne li veut il fere nul bien.
"De tot en tot tient sa meschine
Qu'il eime plus que sa cosine;
Cele a des robes a plenté."
Quant la vieille ot tot conté
A l'evesque ce que li pot,

Il li respont a un seul mot,
A tant ne li vot plus respondre,
Que il fera son fiz semondre,
Qu'il vieigne a court le jour nommé.
La vieille l'en a encliné,
Si s'en part sanz autre response.
Et l'evesque fist sa semonse
A son fil que il vieigne a court;
Il le voudra tenir si court,
S'il ne fet reson a sa mere.
Je criem trop que il le compere.
Quant le termes et le jor vint,
Que li evesques ses plet tint,
Mout i ot clers et autres genz,
Des proverres plus de deus cens.
La vieille ne s'est pas tue,
Droit a l'evesque en est venue
Si li reconte sa besoigne.
L'evesque dit qu'el ne s'esloigne,
Car tantost com ses fiz vendra,
Sache bien qu'il le soupendra
Et toudra tot son benefice. . . .

("Be still," he said, "you are silly! What are you complaining about, since you have bread to eat and my soup and my peas? And even that is a burden to me, for you keep saying nasty things to me." The old woman says: "That won't do you any good, for I want from now on that you bind yourself to honor me greatly as your mother." The priest said: "By the Holy Father, never again shall she eat of what I have. Let her do her worst, or her best, as she likes." "I shall, and more than will suit you," says the old woman, "for I am going to go to the bishop and tell him about your misdoing and your life, and how well your mistress is served. She has enough to eat and plenty of clothes, and me you want to feed on empty words. Of your wealth I have no part." With these words the old woman runs off, grieved and angry. Straight to the bishop she went. She gets to him and complains of her son who loves her no more than he would a dog and will do nothing for her. "He cares for his mistress above everything else and loves her more than his relatives. She has plenty of clothes."

When the old woman had told the bishop everything she could, he answers her in a word. For the moment he will not say more than that he will have her son summoned and he must come to court on the appointed day. The old woman bowed, and leaves without further reply. And the bishop issued his summons to her son that he must come to court. He means to rein him in short if he does not do what is right by his mother. I am very much afraid he is going to pay dearly for it. When the time and the day came on which the bishop held his court, there were many clerks and other people and more than two hundred priests. The old woman did not keep quiet. She went straight up to the bishop and told him her business. The bishop tells her not to leave, because as soon as her son arrives she should know that he will suspend him and take away his whole benefice. . . .)

The old woman misunderstands the word *soupendra.* She thinks her son is to be hanged. Now she regrets having accused him, and in her anxiety she points out the first priest who comes in, and claims that he is her son. To this uncomprehending victim the bishop administers such a tongue-lashing that the poor fellow has no chance to get in a word. The bishop orders him to take his old mother with him and henceforth to treat her decently, as a priest should. And woe to him if there should be any more complaints about his conduct! The bewildered priest takes the old woman with him on his horse. On his way home he meets the old woman's real son and tells him about his adventure, while the old woman makes signs to her son not to give himself away. The other priest ends his story by saying that he would gladly give forty pounds to anyone who would rid him of his unwanted burden. Fine, says the son, it's a bargain; give me the money, and I will relieve you of your old woman. And it was done.

Here too the part of the story reprinted begins with a realistic conversation, an everyday scene, the quarrel between mother and son, and here too the course of the conversation is a very lively crescendo. Just as, in the other case, Lisetta's confidante, by replying with ostensible amiability, gets Lisetta to talk on and on until her secret is out, so here the old woman, by her cantankerous complaints, irritates her son until he flies into a rage and threatens to cut off the supply of food he has been giving her, whereupon the mother, also beside herself with rage, runs off to the bishop. Although the dialect of the piece is hard to identify (Rohlfs considers that of the Ile de France likely), the tone of the conversation is far less stylized and more directly popular than in Boccaccio. It is invariably the common speech of the people (and the people includes the lower clergy): thoroughly paratactic, with lively questions and exclamations, full, and indeed overfull, of popular turns of expression. The narrator's tone is not essentially different from that of his characters. He too tells his story in the same simple tone, with the same sensory vividness, giving a graphic picture of the situation through the most unpretentious means and the most everyday words. The only stylization he permits himself is the verse form, rhymed octosyllabic couplets, which favors extremely simple and brief sentence patterns and as yet knows nothing of the rhythmic multiplicity of later narrative verse forms, such as those of Ariosto and Lafontaine. Thus the arrangement of the narrative which follows upon the dialogue is wholly artless, even though its freshness makes it delightful. In paratactic single file, without any effort to complicate or to unravel, without any compression of what is of secondary importance, without any change of tempo, the story runs or stumbles on. In order to bring in the joke about *soupendre,* the scene between the old woman and the bishop has to be repeated, and the bishop himself has to state his views no less than three times. No doubt these things and, more generally, the many details and lines of padding brought in to resolve difficulties of rhyme, give the narrative a pleasantly leisurely breadth. But its composition is crude and its character is purely popular, in the sense that the narrator himself belongs to the type of people he describes, and of course also to the people he addresses. His own horizon is socially and ethically as narrow as that of his personages and of the audience he wishes to set laughing by his story. Narrator, narrative, and audience belong to the same world, which is that of the common, uneducated people, without aesthetic or moral pretensions. In keeping with this is the characterization of the personages and of the way they act, a characterization which is certainly lively and graphic but also relatively crude and monochromatic. They are popular in the sense that they are characters with which everybody was familiar at the time: a boorish priest susceptible to every kind of worldly pleasure, and a cantankerous old woman. The minor characters are not described as specific individuals at all; we get only their behavior, which is determined by the situation.

In the case of Frate Alberto, on the other hand, we are told his previous history, which explains the very specific character of his malicious and witty shrewdness. Madonna Lisetta's stupidity and the silly pride she takes in her womanly charms are unique of their kind in this particular mixture. And the same holds true of the secondary characters. Lisetta's confidante, or the *buono uomo* in whose house Frate Alberto takes refuge, have a life and a character of their own which, to be sure, is only hastily indicated but which is clearly recognizable. We even get an inkling of what sort of people Madonna Lisetta's relatives are, for there is something sharply characteristic in the grim joke, *si posero in cuore di trovare questo agnolo e di sapere se egli sapesse volare.* The last few words approach the form which German criticism has recently come to call *erlebte Rede* (free indirect discourse). Then too the setting is much more clearly specified than in the fablel. The events of the latter may occur anywhere in rural France, and its dialectal peculiarities, even if they could be more accurately identified, would be quite accidental and devoid of importance. Boccaccio's tale is pronouncedly Venetian. It must also be borne in mind that the French fablel is quite generally restricted to a specific milieu of peasants and small townspeople, and that the variations in this milieu, insofar as they are observable at all, owe their existence exclusively to the accidental place of origin of the piece in question, whereas in Boccaccio's case we are dealing with an author who in addition to this Venetian setting chose numerous others for his tales: for example Naples in the novella about Andreuccio da Perugia (2, 5), Palermo in the one about Sabaetto (8, 10), Florence and its environs in a long series of droll tales. And what is true of the settings is equally true of the social atmosphere. Boccaccio surveys and describes, in the most concrete manner, all the social strata, all the classes and professions, of his time. The gulf between the art of the fablel and the art of Boccaccio by no means reveals itself only in matters of style. The characterization of the personages, the local and social setting, are at once far more sharply individualized and more extensive. Here is a man whose conscious grasp of the principles of art enables him to stand above his subject matter and to submerge himself in it only so far as he chooses, a man who shapes his stories according to his own creative will.

As for Italian narrative literature before Boccaccio, the specimens known to us from that period have rather the character of moralizing or witty anecdotes. Their stylistic devices as well as the orbit of their views and concepts are much too limited for an individualized representation of characters and settings. They often exhibit a certain brittle refinement of expression but in direct appeal to the senses they are by far inferior to the fablels. Here is an example:

> Uno s'andò a confessare al prete suo, ed intra l'altre cose disse: Io ho una mia cognata, e'l mio fratello è lontano; e quando io ritorno a casa, per grande domistichezza, ella mi si pone a sedere in grembo. Come debbo fare? Rispose il prete: A me il facesse ella, ch'io la ne pagherei bene! (From the *Novellino*, ed. Letterio di Francia, Torino, 1930. Novella 87, p. 146.)

> (A man went to his priest to confess and said to him, among other things: I have a sister-in-law, and my brother is away; and when I get home, in her great familiarity, she comes and sits on my lap. What shall I do? The priest answered: If she did that to me, I'd show her!)

In this little piece the whole emphasis is on the priest's ambiguous answer; everything else is mere preparation and is told straight forwardly, in rather flat parataxes, without any sort of graphically sensory visualization. Many stories of the *Novellino* are similarly brief anecdotes, whose subject is a witty remark. One of the book's subtitles is, accordingly, *Libro di Novelle e di bel parlar gentile*. There are some longer pieces as well; most of these are not droll tales but moralizing and didactic narratives. But the style is the same throughout: flatly paratactic, with the events strung together as though on a thread, without palpable breadth and without an environment for the characters to breathe in. The undeniable artistic sense of the *Novellino* is chiefly concerned with brief and striking formulations of the principal facts of the event being narrated. In this it follows the model of medieval collections of moral examples in Latin, the so-called *exempla*, and it surpasses them in organization, elegance, and freshness of expression. With sensory visualization it is hardly concerned, but it is clear that here, as with its Italian contemporaries, this limitation is a result of the linguistic and intellectual situation which prevailed at the time. The Italian vernacular was as yet too poor and lacking in suppleness, the horizon of concepts and judgments was as yet too narrow and restricted, to make possible a relaxed command of factual data and a sensory representation of multiplex phenomena. The entire available power of sensory visualization is concentrated upon a single climactic witticism, as, in our example, upon the priest's reply. If it is permissible to base a judgment upon a single case, that of Fra Salimbene de Adam, a Franciscan and the extremely gifted author of a Latin chronicle, it would seem that, at the end of the thirteenth century, Latin, as soon as a writer heavily interspersed it with Italian vulgarisms, as Salimbene did, could yield a much greater sensory force than written Italian. Salimbene's chronicle is full of anecdotes. One of these—which has been repeatedly quoted by others as well as by myself—I will cite at this point. It tells the story of a Franciscan named Detesalve, and runs as follows:

> Cum autem quadam die tempore yemali per civitatem Florentie ambularet, contigit, ut ex lapsu glatiei totaliter caderet. Videntes hoc Florentini, qui trufatores maximi sunt, ridere ceperunt. Quorum unus quesivit a fratre qui ceciderat, utrum plus vellet habere sub se? Cui frater respondit quod sic, scilicet interrogantis uxorem. Audientes hoc Florentini non habuerunt malum exemplum, sed commendaverunt fratrem dicentes: Benedicatur ipse, quia de nostris est!—Aliqui dixerunt quod alius Florentinus fuit, qui dixit hoc verbum, qui vocabatur frater Paulus Millemusce ex ordine Minorum. (Chronica, ad annum 1233; Monumenta Germaniae historica, Scriptores 32, 79.)

> (One day in winter when he was walking about in the city of Florence, it happened that he fell flat on the frozen ground. Seeing this, the Florentines, who are great jokers, began to laugh. One of them asked the friar who was lying there if he would not like to have something put under him. To which the friar answers Yes, the wife of him who asked. When they heard this, the Florentines did not take it amiss but praised the friar, saying: Good for him, he is one of us!—Some say that he who said this was another Florentine, named Paul Thousandflies, of the Minorite Order.)

Here too the point is a witty rejoinder, a *bel parlare*. But at the same time we have a real scene: a winter landscape, the monk who has slipped and lies there on the ground, the Florentines standing about making fun of him. The characterization of the participants is much livelier, and in addition to the climactic jest (*interrogantis uxorem*) there are other witticisms and vulgarisms (*utrum plus vellet habere sub se; benedicatur ipse quia de nostris est; frater Paulus Millemusce*; and before that *trufatores*) which are doubly amusing and savory by reason of their transparent Latin disguise. Sensory visualization and freedom of expression are here more fully developed than in the *Novellino*.

Yet whatever we choose from among the products of the earlier period—be it the crude, boorish sensory breadth of the fabliaux, or the threadbare, sensorily poor refinement of the *Novellino*, or Salimbene's lively, vividly graphic wit—none of it is comparable to Boccaccio. It is in him that the world of sensory phenomena is first mastered, is organized in accordance with a conscious artistic plan, caught and held in words. For the first time since antiquity, his *Decameron* fixes a specific level of style, on which the relation of actual occurrences in contemporary life can become polite entertainment; narrative no longer serves as a moral exemplum, no longer caters to the common people's simple desire to laugh; it serves as a pleasant diversion for a circle of well-bred young people of the upper classes, of ladies and gentlemen who delight in the sensual play of life and who possess sensitivity, taste, and judgment. It was to announce this purpose of his narrative art that Boccaccio created the frame in which he set it. The stylistic level of the *Decameron* is strongly reminiscent of the corresponding antique *genus*, the antique novel of love, the *fabula milesiaca*. This is not surprising, since the attitude of the author to his subject matter, and the social stratum for which the work is intended, correspond quite closely in the two periods, and since for Boccaccio too the concept of the writer's art was closely associated with that of rhetoric. As in the novels of antiquity, Boccaccio's literary art is based upon a rhetorical treatment of prose; as in them, the style sometimes borders on the poetic; he too sometimes gives conversation the form of well-ordered oratory. And the general impression of an "intermediate" or mixed style, in which realism and eroticism are linked to elegant verbal formulations, is quite similar in the two cases. Yet while the antique novel is a late form cast in languages which had long since produced their best, Boccaccio's stylistic endeavor finds itself confronted by a newly-born and as yet almost amorphous literary language. The rhetorical tradition—which, rigidified in medieval practice into an almost spectrally senile mechanism, had, so recently as the age of Dante, been still timidly and stiffly tried out on the Italian *volgare* by the first translators of ancient authors—in Boccaccio's hands suddenly becomes a miraculous tool which brings Italian art prose, the first literary prose of postclassical Europe, into existence at a single stroke. It comes into existence in the decade between his first youthful work and the *Decameron*. His particular gift of richly and sweetly moving prose rhythms, although a heritage from antiquity, he possessed almost from the beginning. It is already to be found in his earliest prose work, the *Filocolo,* and seems to have been a latent talent in him, which his first contact with antique authors brought out. What he lacked at first was moderation and judgment in using stylistic devices and in determining the level of style; sound relationship between subject matter and level of style had still to be achieved and become an instinctive possession. A first contact with the concept of an elevated style as practiced by the ancients—especially since the concept was still influenced by medieval notions—very easily led to what might be termed a chronic exaggeration of the stylistic level and an inordinate use of erudite embellishment. This resulted in an almost continuously stilted language, which, for that very reason, could not come close to its object and which, in such a form, was fit for almost nothing but decorative and oratorical purposes. To grasp the sensory reality of passing life was completely impossible to a language so excessively elevated.

In Boccaccio's case, to be sure, the situation was different from the beginning. His innate disposition was more spontaneously sensory, inclined toward creating charmingly flowing and elegant forms imbued with sensuality. From the beginning he was made for the intermediate rather than the elevated style, and his natural bent was strongly furthered by the atmosphere of the Angevin court at Naples where he spent his youth and where the playfully elegant late forms of the chivalric culture of Northern France had taken stronger hold than elsewhere in Italy. His early works are *rifacimenti* of French romances of chivalric love and adventure in the late courtly style; and in their manner, it seems to me, one can sense something characteristically French: the broader realism of his descriptions, the naive refinement and the delicate nuances of the lovers' play, the late feudal mundaneness of his social pictures, and the malice of his wit. Yet the more mature he grows, the stronger become the competing bourgeois and humanist factors and especially his mastery of what is robust and popular. In any case, in his youthful works the tendency toward rhetorical exaggeration—which represented a danger in Boccaccio's case too—plays a role only in his representation of sensual love, as do the excess of mythological erudition and of conventional allegorizing which prevail in some of them. Thus we may assert that despite his occasional attempts (as in the *Teseida*) to reach out for something more, he remains within the limits of the intermediate style—of the style which, combining the idyllic and the realistic, is designated for the representation of sensual love. It is in the intermediate, idyllic style that he wrote the last and by far the most beautiful of his youthful works, the *Ninfale fiesolano*; and the intermediate style serves too for the great book of the hundred novelle. In the determination of stylistic level it is unimportant which of his youthful works were written partly or wholly in verse and which in prose. The atmosphere is the same in them all.

Within the realm of the intermediate style, to be sure, the nuances in the *Decameron* are most varied, the realm is no narrow one. Yet even when a story approaches the tragic, tone and atmosphere remain tenderly sensual and avoid the grave and sublime; and in stories which employ far more crudely farcical motifs than our example, both language and manner of presentation remain aristocratic, inasmuch as both narrator and audience unmistakably stand far above the subject matter, and, viewing it from above with a critical eye, derive pleasure from it in a light and elegant fashion. It is precisely in the more popularly realistic and even the crudely farcical subjects that the peculiarity of the intermediate elegant style is most clearly to be recognized; for the artistic treatment of such stories indicates that there is a social class which, though it stands above the humble milieu of everyday life, yet takes delight in its vivid representation, and indeed a delight whose end is the individually human and concrete, not the socially stratified type. All the Calandrinos, Cipollas, and Pietros, the Peronellas, Caterinas, and Belcolores are, like Frate Alberto and Lisetta, individualized and living human beings in a totally different way from the villein or the shepherdess who were occasionally allowed to enter courtly poetry. They are actually much more alive and, in their characteristic form, more precise than the personages of the popular farce, as may be apparent from what we have indicated above, and this although the public they are meant to please belongs to an entirely different class. Quite evidently there was in Boccaccio's time a social class—high in rank, though not feudal but belonging to the urban aristocracy—which derived a well-bred pleasure from life's colorful reality wherever it happened to be manifested. It is true, the separation of the two realms is maintained to the extent that realistic pieces are usually set among the lower classes, the more tender and more nearly tragic pieces usually among the upper. But even this is not a rigidly observed rule, for the bourgeois and the sentimentally idyllic are apt to constitute borderline cases; and elsewhere too the same sort of mixture is not infrequent (e.g., the novella of Griselda, 10, 10).

The social prerequisites for the establishment of an intermediate style in the antique sense were fulfilled in Italy from the first half of the fourteenth century. In the towns an elevated stratum of patrician burghers had come to the fore; their mores, it is true, were still in many respects linked to the forms and ideas of the feudal courtly culture, but, as a result of the entirely different social structure, as well as under the influence of early humanist trends, they soon received a new stamp, becoming less bound up with class, and more strongly personal and realistic. Inner and outer perception broadened, threw off the fetters of class restriction, even invaded the realm of learning, thitherto the prerogative of clerical specialists, and gradually gave it the pleasant and winning form of personal culture in the service of social intercourse. The language, so recently a clumsy and inelastic tool, became supple, rich, nuanced, flourishing, and showed that it could accommodate itself to the requirements of a discriminating social life of refined sensuality. The literature of society acquired what it had not previously possessed: a world of reality and of the present. Now there is no doubt that this gain is strictly connected with the much more important gain on a higher stylistic level, Dante's conquest of a world, made a generation before. This connection we shall now attempt to analyze, and for that purpose we return to our text.

Its most conspicuous distinguishing characteristics, if we compare it with earlier narratives, are the assurance with which, in both perception and syntactical structure, it handles complex factual data, and the subtle skill with which it adapts the narrative tempo and level of tone to the inner and outer movement of the narrated events. This we have tried to show in detail above. The conversation between the two women, the spreading of the rumor through the town, and the dramatic night scene at Lisetta's house are made a clearly surveyable, coherent whole within which each part has its own independent, rich, and free motion. That Dante possesses the same ability to command a real situation of any number of constituent parts and varied nuances, that he possesses it to a degree which no other medieval author known to us can even distantly approach, I tried to show in the preceding chapter, using as my example the occurrences at the beginning of the tenth canto of the *Inferno*. The coherence of the whole, the shift in tone and rhythmic pulse between let us say the introductory conversation and the appearance of Farinata, or upon Cavalcante's sudden emergence and in his speeches, the sovereign mastery of the syntactic devices of language, I there analyzed as carefully as I know how. Dante's command over phenomena impresses us as much less adaptable but also as much more significant than the corresponding ability in Boccaccio. In itself the heavy beat of the tercets, with their rigid rhyme pattern, does not permit him as free and light a movement as Boccaccio allowed himself, but he would have scorned it in any case. Yet there is no mistaking the fact that Dante's work was the first to lay open the panorama of the common and multiplex world of human reality. Here, for the first time since classical antiquity, that world can be seen freely and from all sides, without class restriction, without limitation of the field of vision, in a view which may turn everywhere without obstruction, in a spirit which places all phenomena in a living order, and in a language which does justice both to the sensory aspect of phenomena and to their multiple and ordered interpenetration. Without the *Commedia* the *Decameron* could not have been written. No one will deny this, and it is also clear that Dante's rich world is transposed to a lower level of style in Boccaccio. This latter point is particularly striking if we compare two similar movements—for example, Lisetta's sentence, *Comare, egli non si vuol dire, ma l'intendimento mio è l'agnolo Gabriello,* in our text, and *Inferno* 18, 52, where Venedico Caccianimico says, *Mal volontier lo dico; / ma sforzami la tua chiara favella, / Che mi fa sovvenir del mondo antico.* It is of course not his gift of observation and his power of expression for which Boccaccio is indebted to Dante. These qualities he had by nature and they are very different from the corresponding qualities in Dante. Boccaccio's interest is centered on phenomena and emotions which Dante would not have deigned to touch. What he owes to Dante is the possibility of making such free use of his talent, of attaining the vantage point from which it is possible to survey the entire present world of phenomena, to grasp it in all its multiplicity, and to reproduce it in a pliable and expressive language. Dante's power, which could do justice to all the various human presences in his work, Farinata and Brunetto, Pia de' Tolomei and Sordello, Francis of Assisi and Cacciaguida, which could make them arise out of their own specific conditions and speak their own language—that power made it possible for Boccaccio to achieve the same results for Andreuccio and Frate Cipolla or his servant, for Ciappelletto and the baker Cisti, for Madonna Lisetta and Griselda. With this power of viewing the world synthetically there also goes a critical sense, firm yet elastic in perspective, which, without abstract moralizing, allots phenomena their specific, carefully nuanced moral value—a critical sense which, indeed, causes the moral value to shine out of the phenomena themselves.

In our story, after the relatives reach home *con gli arnesi del agnolo,* Boccaccio continues as follows: *In questo mezzo, fattosi il dì chiaro, essendo il buono uomo in sul Rialto, udì dire come l'agnolo Gabriello era la notte andato a giacere con Madonna Lisetta, e da cognati trovatovi, s'era per paura gittato nel canale, nè si sapeva che divenuto se ne fosse.*

> (Broad day come, the good man with whom Fra Alberto had taken refuge, being on the Rialto, heard how the angel Gabriel had gone that night to lie with Madam Lisetta and being surprised by her kinsmen, had cast himself for fear into the canal, nor was it known what was come of him.) Trans. John Payne.

The tone of seeming seriousness, which never mentions the fact that the Venetians on the Rialto are bursting with laughter, insinuates, without a word of moral, aesthetic, or any other kind of criticism, exactly how the occurrence is to be evaluated and what mood the Venetians are in. If instead Boccaccio had said that Frate Alberto's behavior was underhanded and Madonna Lisetta stupid and gullible, that the whole thing was ludicrous and absurd, and that the Venetians on the Rialto were greatly amused by it, this procedure would not only have been much clumsier but the moral atmosphere, which cannot be exhausted by any number of adjectives, would not have come out with anything like the force it now has. The stylistic device which Boccaccio employs was highly esteemed by the ancients, who called it "irony." Such a mediate and indirectly insinuating form of discourse presupposes a complex and multiple system of possible evaluations, as well as a sense of perspective which, together with the occurrence, suggests its effect. In comparison, Salimbene strikes us as decidedly naive when, in the anecdote quoted above, he inserts the sentence, *videntes hoc Florentini, qui trufatores maximi sunt, ridere ceperunt.* The note of malicious irony in our present passage from Boccaccio is his own. It does not occur in the *Commedia.* Dante is not malicious. But the breadth of view, the incisive rendering of a clearly defined, complex evaluation by means of indirect suggestion, the sense of perspective in binding up event with effect, are Dante's creation. He does not tell us who Cavalcante is, what he feels, and how his reactions are to be judged. He makes him appear and speak, and merely adds: *le sue parole e il modo de la pena m'avean di costui già letto il nome.* Long before we are given any details, Dante fixes the moral tone of the Brunetto episode (*Inf.*, 15):

Così adocchiato da cotal famiglia
  fui conosciuto da un che mi prese
  per lo lembo e gridò: Qual maraviglia!
E io, quando 'l suo braccio a me distese,
  ficcai li occhi per lo cotto aspetto,
  sì che 'l viso abbrucciato non difese
la conoscenza sua al mio intelletto;
  e chinando la mia a la sua faccia
  rispuosi: Siete voi qui, ser Brunetto?
E quelli: O figliuol mio. . . .

(Thus eyed by that family, I was recognized by one who took me by the skirt, and said: "What a wonder!" And I, when he stretched out his arm to me, fixed my eyes on his baked aspect, so that the scorching of his visage hindered not my mind from knowing him; and bending my face to his, I answered: "Are you here, Ser Brunetto?" And he: "O my son! . . .") Trans. Dr. J. A. Carlyle, "Temple Classics."

Without a single word of explanation he gives us the whole Pia de' Tolomei in her own words (*Purg.*, 5; see above, p. 201):

Deh, quando tu sarai tornato al mondo
  e riposato de la lunga via,
  (seguitò il terzo spirito al secondo),
ricorditi di me che son la Pia. . . .

("Pray, when thou shalt return to the world, and art rested from thy long journey," followed the third spirit after the second, "remember me, who am La Pia. . . .")

And from among the abundance of instances in which Dante illustrates the effects of phenomena, or even phenomena through their effects, I choose the famous simile of sheep coming out of the pen, by which he describes the slow dispelling of the amazement which fell upon the crowd in the Antipurgatorio at the sight of Virgil and Dante (*Purg.*, 3). Compared with such methods of characterization, which operate with the most exact perception of what is individual and the most varied and subtle means of expression, everything earlier seems narrow and crude and without any real order as soon as it attempts to come close to phenomena. Take for instance the lines in which the author of the previously quoted fablel describes his priest's old mother:

Qui avoit une vieille mere
Mout felonnesse et mout avere;
Bochue estoit, noire et hideuse
Et de touz biens contralieuse.
Tout li mont l'avoit contre cuer,
Li prestres meisme a nul fuer
Ne vosist pour sa desreson
Qu'el entrast ja en sa meson;
Trop ert parlant et de pute ere. . . .

(He had an old mother who was a horrible creature and very avaricious. Hunch-backed she was, and black and hideous and opposed to everything that was good. Everybody loathed her. Even the priest, because of her unreasonableness, would under no conditions let her come into his house. She was too much of a gossip and too disgusting. . . .)

This is by no means devoid of graphic elements, and the transition from a general characterization to effect upon the surroundings, and then the *meisme*-climax giving the son's attitude, represents a natural and vivid continuity. But everything is stated in the coarsest and crudest manner possible; there is no personal and no precise perception. The adjectives, on which, after all, the principal work of characterization must fall, seem to be sprinkled into the lines at random, as syllable count and rhyme happened to permit, in a hotchpotch of moral and physical characteristics. And of course the entire characterization is direct. To be sure, Dante by no means scorns direct characterization through adjectives, at times through adjectives of the widest content. But then the effect is something like this:

La mia sorella che tra bella e buona
non so qual fosse più. . . . (*Purg.*, 24, 13-14.)

(My sister, who, whether she were more fair or more good I know not. . . .)

Nor does Boccaccio scorn the direct method of characterization. At the very beginning of our text we find two popular phrases which serve to set forth Lisetta's stupidity directly and graphically: *che poco sale avea in zucca* and *che piccola levatura avea.* Reading the beginning of the novella, we find a whole collection of things similar in form and intent: *una giovane donna bamba e sciocca; sentiva dello scemo; donna mestola; donna zucca al vento, la quale era anzi che no un poco dolce di sale; madonna baderla; donna poco fila.* This little collection looks like a merry game Boccaccio is playing with his knowledge of amusing colloquial phrases and perhaps it also serves to describe the vivacious mood of the teller of the tale, Pampinea, whose purpose it is to divert the company, who have just been touched to tears by the preceding story. In any case, Boccaccio is very fond of this sort of play with a variety of phrases drawn from the vigorous and imaginative language of the common people. Consider for instance the way in which (in novella 10 of the sixth day) Frate Cipolla's servant, Guccio, is characterized, partly directly and partly by his master. It is a striking example of Boccaccio's characteristic mixture of popular elements and subtle malice, ending in one of the most beautifully extended periods that he ever wrote (*ma Guccio Imbratta il quale era,* etc.). In it the stylistic level shifts from a most enchanting lyrical movement (*più vago di stare in cucina che sopra i verdi rami l'usignolo*) through the coarsest realism (*grassa e grossa e piccola e mal fatta e con un paio di poppe che parevan due ceston da letame,* etc.) to something approaching horror (*non altramenti che si gitta l'avoltoio alla carogna*), yet all the parts form a whole by virtue of the author's malice, which glints through everywhere.

Without Dante such a wealth of nuances and perspectives would hardly have been possible. But of the figural-Christian conception which pervaded Dante's imitation of the earthly and human world and which gave it power and depth, no trace is to be found in Boccaccio's book. Boccaccio's characters live on earth and only on earth. He sees the abundance of phenomena directly as a rich world of earthly forms. He was justified in so doing, because he had not set out to compose a great, weighty, and sublime work. He has much better reason than Dante to call the style of his book *umilissimo e rimesso* (introduction to the fourth day), for he really writes for the entertainment of the unlearned, for the consolation and amusement of the *nobilissime donne,* who do not go to study at Rome or Athens or Bologna. With much wit and grace he defends himself in his conclusion against those who claim that it is unseemly for a weighty and serious man (*ad un uom pesato e grave*) to write a book with so many jests and fooleries:

> Io confesso d'essere pesato, e molte volte de' miei dì esser stato; e perciò, parlando a quelle che pesato non m'hanno, affermo che io non son grave, anzi son io si lieve che io sto a galla nell'acqua:

e considerato che le prediche fatte da' frati, per rimorder delle lor colpe gli uomini, il più oggi piene di motti e di ciance e di scede si veggono, estimai che quegli medesimi non stesser male nelle mie novelle, scritte per cacciar la malinconia delle femmine.

(I confess to being a man of weight and to have been often weighed in my time, wherefore, speaking to those ladies who have not weighed me, I declare that I am not heavy; nay, I am so light that I abide like a nutgall in water, and considering that the preachments made of friars, to rebuke men of their sins, are nowadays for the most part seen full of quips and cranks and jibes, I conceived that these latter would not sit amiss in my stories written to ease women of melancholy.) Trans. John Payne.

Boccaccio is probably on solid ground with his malicious little thrust at the preaching friars (to be found in almost exactly the same words, though on a quite different level of tone, in Dante, *Par.*, 29, 115). But he forgets or does not know that the vulgar and naive farcicality of the sermons is a form—already, it is true, a somewhat degenerate and disreputable form—of Christian-figural realism (see above, pp. 158-161). Nothing of the sort applies in his case. And the very thing which justifies him from his point of view ("if even the preachers joke and jape, why cannot I do the same in a book designed to amuse?") puts his venture, from the Christian-medieval point of view, in a dubious light. What a sermon, under the aegis of Christian figuralism, has a perfect right to do (exaggerations may go to objectionable extremes, but the right as a matter of principle cannot be denied), a secular author may not do—all the more because his work is not in the last analysis quite as light in weight as he claims; it is simply not naive and devoid of basic attitudes, as the popular farces are. If it were, then, from the Christian-medieval point of view, it could be regarded as a venial irregularity of the kind occasioned by man's instincts and his need for entertainment, as proof of his imperfection and weakness. But such is not the case with the *Decameron*. Boccaccio's book is of the intermediate style, and for all its frivolity and grace, it represents a very definite attitude, and one which is by no means Christian. What I have in mind is not so much Boccaccio's way of making fun of superstition and relics, nor even such blasphemies as the phrase *la resurrezion della carne* for a man's sexual erection (3, 10). Such things are part and parcel of the medieval repertoire of farce and need not necessarily be of fundamental importance—

although of course, once an anti-Christian or anti-ecclesiastical movement was under way, they acquired great propagandistic effectiveness. Rabelais, for example, unmistakably uses them as a weapon (a similarly blasphemous joke is to be found toward the end of chapter 60 of *Gargantua*, where words from the 24th Psalm, *ad te levavi*, are used in a corresponding sense, a fact which serves, however, to show once again how traditional, how much a part of the repertoire, this type of joke really was; for another example see *tiers livre*, 31, toward the end). The really important characteristic of the attitude reflected in the *Decameron*, the thing which is diametrically opposed to medieval-Christian ethics, is the doctrine of love and nature which, though it is usually presented in a light tone, is nevertheless quite certain of itself. The reasons why the modern revolt against Christian doctrines and forms of life could prove its practical power and its propagandistic efficacy so successfully in the realm of sexual morality are grounded in the early history and in the essential nature of Christianity. In that realm the conflict between the worldly will to life and the Christian sufferance of life became acute as soon as the former attained to self-consciousness. Doctrines of nature which praised the instinctive life of sex and demanded its emancipation had already played an important role in connection with the theological crisis at Paris in the seventies of the thirteenth century; they also found literary expression in the second part of the *Roman de la Rose*, by Jean de Meun. All this has no direct bearing on Boccaccio. He is not concerned with these theological controversies of many decades earlier. He is no half-scholastic pedagogue like Jean de Meun. His ethics of love is a recasting of courtly love, tuned several degrees lower in the scale of style, and concerned exclusively with the sensual and the real. That it is now earthly love which is in question is unmistakable. There is still a reflection of the magic of courtly love in some of the novelle in which Boccaccio expresses his attitude most clearly. Thus the story of Cimone (5, 1)—which, like the earlier *Ameto*, has education through love as its central theme—clearly shows that it is descended from the courtly epic. The doctrine that love is the mother of all virtues and of everything noble in man, that it imparts courage, self-reliance, and the ability to make sacrifices, that it develops intelligence and social accomplishments, is a heritage from courtly culture and the *stil nuovo*. Here, however, it is presented as a practical code of morals, valid for all classes. The beloved is no longer an inaccessible mistress or an incarnation of the divine idea, but the object of sexual desires. Even in details (though not quite consistently) a sort of ethics of love is discernible—for example, that it is permissible to employ any kind of treachery and deceit against a third person (the jealous rival, the parents, or whatever other powers hinder the designs of love) but not against the object of one's love. If Frate Alberto gets so little sympathy from Boccaccio, it is because he is a hypocrite and because he won Madonna Lisetta's love not honestly but by underhanded methods. The *Decameron* develops a distinct, thoroughly practical and secular ethical code rooted in the right to love, an ethics which in its very essence is anti-Christian. It is presented with much grace and without any strong claim to doctrinal validity. The book rarely abandons the stylistic level of light entertainment. Yet at times it does, when Boccaccio defends himself against attacks. This happens in the introduction to the fourth day when, addressing himself to the ladies, he writes:

> E, se mai con tutta la mia forza a dovervi in cosa alcuna compiacere mi disposi, ora più che mai mi vi disporrò; perciocchè io conosco che altra cosa dir non potrà alcun con ragione, se non che gli altri et io, che vi amiamo, naturalmente operiamo. Alle cui leggi, cioè della natura, voler contrastare, troppe gran forze bisognano, e spesse volte non solamente in vano, ma con grandissimo danno del faticante s'adoperano. Le quali forze io confesso che io non l'ho nè d'averle disidero in questo; e se io l'avessi, più tosto ad altrui le presterei, che io per me l'adoperassi. Per che tacciansi i morditori, e, se essi riscaldar non si possono, assiderati si vivano; e ne' lor diletti, anzi appetiti corrotti standosi, me nel mio, questa brieve vita, che posta n'è, lascino stare.

> (And if ever with all my might I vowed myself to seek to please you in aught, now more than ever shall I address myself thereto; for that I know none can with reason say otherwise than that I and others who love you do according to nature, whose laws to seek to gainstand demandeth overgreat strength, and oftentimes not only in vain, but to the exceeding hurt of whoso striveth to that end, is this strength employed. Such strength I confess I have not nor ever desired in this to have; and an I had it, I had liefer lend it to others than use it for myself. Wherefore, let the carpers be silent and an they avail not to warm themselves, let them live benumbed and abiding in their delights—or rather their

corrupt appetites,—leave me to abide in mine for this brief life that is appointed me.) Trans. John Payne

This, I believe, is one of the most aggressive and energetic passages Boccaccio ever wrote in defense of his ethics of love. The view he wishes to express cannot be understood; yet one cannot fail to see that it is without weight. Such a battle cannot seriously be fought with a few words on the irresistibility of nature and a couple of malicious allusions to the private vices of one's adversaries. Nor, indeed, did Boccaccio have any such intention. We treat him unfairly and judge by a wrong standard if we measure the order of life which speaks from his work by Dante's standard or by the works of the later and fully developed Renaissance. The figural unity of the secular world falls apart at the very moment when it attains—in Dante—complete sovereignty over earthly reality. Sovereignty over reality in its sensory multiplicity remained as a permanent conquest, but the order in which it was comprehended was now lost, and for a time there was nothing to take its place. This, as we said, must not be made a reproach against Boccaccio, but it must be registered as a historical fact which goes beyond him as a person. Early humanism, that is, lacks constructive ethical force when it is confronted with the reality of life; it again lowers realism to the intermediate, unproblematic, and non-tragic level of style which, in classical antiquity, was assigned to it as an extreme upper limit, and, as in the same period, makes the erotic its principal, and almost exclusive, theme. Now, however, this theme contains—what in antiquity there could be no question of its containing—an extremely promising germ of problem and conflict, a practical starting point for the incipient movement against the culture of medieval Christianity. But at first, and merely in itself, the erotic is not yet strong enough to treat reality problematically or even tragically. When Boccaccio undertakes to depict all the multiplex reality of contemporary life, he abandons the unity of the whole: he writes a book of novelle in which a great many things stand side by side, held together only by the common purpose of well-bred entertainment. Political, social, and historical problems which Dante's figuralism penetrated completely and fused into the most everyday reality, fall entirely by the wayside. What happens to erotic and metaphysical problems, and what level of style and human depth they attain in Boccaccio's work, can easily be ascertained from comparisons with Dante.

There are in the *Inferno* several passages in which damned souls challenge or mock or curse God. Good examples are the important scene in canto 14 in which Capaneus, one of the seven against Thebes, challenges God from amid the rain of fire and exclaims: *Qual io fui vivo, tal son morto*—or the scornful gesture of the robber of churches Vanni Fucci in canto 25, upon his recovery from the dreadful metamorphosis caused by the serpent's bite. In both cases the revolt is conscious and is in keeping with the history, character, and condition of the two condemned sinners. In Capaneus' case it is the unvanquished defiance of Promethean rebellion, an enmity to God which is superhuman; in Vanni Fucci it is wickedness immeasurably exaggerated by despair. Boccaccio's first novella (1, 1) tells the story of the vicious and fraudulent notary Ser Ciappelletto who falls mortally ill away from home, in the house of two Florentine usurers. His hosts know the evil life he has led and fear the worst for themselves if he should die in their house without confession and absolution. That he will be refused absolution if he makes a true confession, they have no doubt. To extricate his hosts from this difficult situation, the mortally ill old man deceives a naive confessor with a false and absurdly overpious confession in which he represents himself as a virginal, almost faultless paragon of all virtues, who is yet beset by exaggerated scruples. In this fashion he not only obtains absolution, but after his death his confessor's testimony gains him the reverence due to a saint. This sneering contempt for confession in the hour of death would seem to be a theme which could hardly be treated without the assumption of a basically anti-Christian attitude on the part of the penitent nor without the author's taking a stand—be it Christian and hence condemnatory, or anti-Christian and hence approving—in regard to the problem involved; but here it is merely auxiliary to working out two farcically comic scenes: the grotesque confession and the solemn interment of the supposed saint. The problem is hardly posed. Ser Ciappelletto decides upon his course of action quite lightly, merely in order to free his hosts from imminent danger by a last sly trick which shall be worthy of his past; the justification he alleges for it is so stupid and frivolous that it proves that he has never given a serious thought to God or his own life ("in the course of my life I have offended God so much that in the hour of death a little more or less won't matter"); and equally frivolous and exclusively concerned with what is momentarily expedient are the two Florentine masters of the house who, as they listen to the confession, do, it is true, say to each other: "What sort of man is he, who even now when he is old and ill and about to appear before the throne of the heavenly judge will not desist from his evil tricks but wishes to die as he has lived"—but who then, when they see that the end of assuring him a Christian burial has been gained, do not give the matter another thought. Now it is certainly true and quite in accordance with common experience that many people undertake the most momentous acts with no full conviction commensurate with such acts, simply in consequence of a momentary situation, force of habit, a fleeting impulse. Yet from the author who relates a matter of this kind, we still expect a comparative evaluation. And in fact Boccaccio does allow the narrator Panfilo to take a position in a few concluding words. But they are lame words, indecisive and without weight; they are neither atheistic nor decisively Christian, as the subject demands. There is no doubt, Boccaccio reports the monstrous adventure only for the sake of the comic effect of the two scenes mentioned above, and avoids any serious evaluation or taking of position.

In the story of Francesca da Rimini, Dante had given grandeur and reality in accordance with his way of being and his stage of development. Here, for the first time in the Middle Ages, is no *avanture*, no tale of enchantment; it is free from the charmingly witty coquetry and the class ceremonial of love which were characteristic of courtly culture; it is not hidden behind a veil of secret meaning, as in the *stil nuovo*. Instead it is a truly present action on the highest level of tone, equally immediate and real in terms of memories of an earthly destiny as in terms of an encounter in the beyond. In the love stories which Boccaccio tries to present tragically or nobly (they are mostly to be found among the novelle of the fourth day), the preponderant ingredients are the adventurous and the sentimental. At the same time the adventure is no longer, as it was in the heyday of the courtly epic, the trial and test of the chosen few, which as a fully assimilated element in the ideal conception of class had become an inner necessity (see above, pp. 134-136), but really only coincidence, the ever unexpected product of quickly and violently shifting events. The elaboration of the coincidental character of the adventure can even be demonstrated in novelle in which comparatively little occurs, as for instance the first of the fourth day, the story of Guiscardo and Ghismonda. Dante scorned to mention the conditions under which Francesca and Paolo were surprised by her husband; in treating such a theme he scorns every kind of finely wrought coincidence, and the scene which he describes—the lovers reading the book together—is the most ordinary thing in the world, of interest only through what it leads to. Boccaccio devotes a considerable portion of his text to the complicated and adventurous methods the lovers are forced to employ in order to meet undisturbed, and to the chance concatenation of events which leads to their discovery by the father, Tancredi. These are adventures like those in the courtly romance—for example the love story of Cligès and Fenice in Chrétien de Troyes' romance. But the fairy tale atmosphere of the courtly epic is gone, and the ethical concept of the knight's testing has become a general morality of nature and love, itself expressed in extremely sentimental forms. The sentimental, in turn, which is often bound up with physical objects (the heart of the beloved, the falcon), and to that extent is reminiscent of fairy tale motifs, is in the majority of cases tricked out with a superabundance of rhetoric—think, for example, of Ghismonda's long apology. All these novelle lack any decisive unity of style. They are too adventurous and too reminiscent of fairy tales to be real, too free from magic and too rhetorical to be fairy tales, and much too sentimental to be tragic. The novelle which aim at the tragic are not immediate and direct in the realm either of reality or of feeling. They are at best what is called touching.

It is precisely when Boccaccio tries to enter the realm of problem or tragedy that the vagueness and uncertainty of his early humanism becomes apparent. His realism—which is free, rich, and assured in its mastery of phenomena, which is completely natural within the limits of the intermediate style—becomes weak and superficial as soon as the problematic or the tragic is touched upon. In Dante's *Commedia* the Christian-figural interpretation had compassed human and tragic realism, and in the process had itself been destroyed. Yet that tragic realism had immediately been lost again. The worldliness of men like Boccaccio was still too insecure and unsupported to serve, after the fashion of Dante's figural interpretation, as a basis on which the world could be ordered, interpreted, and represented as a reality and as a whole.

10

MADAME DU CHASTEL

Antoine de la Sale, a Provençal knight of the late feudal type, soldier, court official, tutor of princes, authority on heraldry and tournaments, was born about 1390 and died after 1461. For the greater part of his life he was in the service of the Anjous, who fought until about 1440 for their Kingdom of Naples but who also held extensive possessions in France. He left them in 1448 to become the tutor of the sons of Louis de Luxembourg, Count of Saint-Pol, who played a significant part in the vicissitudinous relations between the French kings and the dukes of Burgundy. In his youth Antoine de la Sale took part in a Portuguese expedition to North Africa; he was often in Italy with the Anjous; he knew the courts of France and Burgundy. It seems that he began his writing career with compilations for his princely charges—an activity which may have revealed to him a talent and inclination for narrative. His best-known work is at once a pedagogical novel and a love story, *l'Hystoyre et plaisante Cronique du Petit Jehan de Saintré*, probably the most vivid literary document of the late feudal period in France. For a time other works were also ascribed to him: the *Quinze Joyes de Mariage* and the *Cent Nouvelles Nouvelles*, although neither shows any of his very distinctive and unmistakable characteristics. Recently—especially since W. Söderjhelm's book on the French novella of the fifteenth century (Paris, 1910)—most students seem inclined to reject these ascriptions.

He was some seventy years of age when he wrote a consolatory treatise for a lady who had lost her first child. This piece, *le Réconfort de Madame du Fresne*, was published by J. Nève in his book on Antoine de la Sale (Paris and Brussels, 1903, pp. 101-155). It begins with a very warmhearted introduction, which—in addition to pious exhortations—contains quotations from the Bible, Seneca, and Bernard of Clairvaux, as well as the folktale of the shroud and a passage in praise of a recently dead saint. Then follow two stories of brave mothers. Of these stories the first is by far the more important. It relates—although with numerous errors and mistaken identities—an episode from the Hundred Years' War.

The English under the Black Prince are besieging the fortress of

Brest. The commander of the fortress, the Seigneur du Chastel, is finally forced to conclude an agreement by the terms of which he is to surrender the fortress to the Black Prince at a specified date if no help arrives before then; as hostage he gives his only son, a boy of thirteen; upon these conditions the Black Prince grants a truce. Four days before the specified period runs out, a ship with provisions arrives at the port. There is great rejoicing, and the commander sends a herald to the Prince with the request that he return the hostage, since help has arrived. At the same time, in accordance with the customs of chivalry, he asks the Prince to help himself to whatever provisions he may wish. The Prince, angry at seeing the long-coveted prize, of which he had thought himself sure, escaping him, refuses to consider the arrival of provisions as help in the sense of the agreement, and demands that the fortress be surrendered on the specified day, otherwise the hostage will be forfeited. The various stages of this train of events are narrated very effectively, with precise, if somewhat too circumstantial descriptions of the ceremonious appearances of the heralds with their several messages. We are told how the Prince first sends a negative though not completely unambiguous answer; how the Seigneur du Chastel, filled with somber premonitions, summons his relatives and friends to counsel him; how at first they merely look at one another in silence; none wants to speak first; none is ready to believe that the Prince is serious; none has anything to advise if such should prove to be the case: *Toutteffoiz, conclurent que rendre la place, sans entier deshonneur, à loyalement conseillier, n'en veoient point la fachon.* Then we are told how during the night the commander's wife observes his trouble and finally gets the truth from him; how she swoons; how the day before the truce expires the Prince's heralds appear with a clear demand that the agreement be carried out; how they are received and dismissed with a ceremony and courtesy in sharp contrast with the hostile content of the words spoken; how the Seigneur du Chastel shows his friends and relatives a serene and determined countenance; and how, during the night, when he is alone with his wife, he breaks down and completely abandons himself to his despair. This is the climax of the narrative:

> Madame, qui de l'autre lez son très grand dueil faisoit, voyant perdre de son seigneur l'onneur ou son très bel et gracieux filz, que au dist de chascun, de l'aaije de XIII ans ne s'en trouvoit ung tel, doubta que son seigneur n'en preist la mort. Lors en son cuer

se appensa et en soy meismes dist: Helasse moy dollente! se il se muert, or as-tu bien tout perdu. Et en ce penssement elle l'appella. Mais il riens n'entendit. Alors elle, en s'escriant, lui dist: "Ha! Monseigneur, pour Dieu, aiez pitié de moy, vostre povre femme, qui sans nul service reprouchier, vous ay sy loyalment amé, servy et honnouré, vous à jointes mains priant que ne vueillez pas vous, nostre filz et moy perdre a ung seul cop ainssy." Et quant le sire entend de Madame son parler, à chief de pièce luy respondit: "Helasse, m'amye, et que est cecy? Où est le cuer qui plus ne amast la mort que vivre ainssi où je me voy en ce très dur party?" Alors, Madame, comme très saige et prudente, pour le resconfforter, tout-à-cop changa son cruel dueil en très vertueulx parler et lui dist: "Monseigneur, je ne diz pas que vous ne ayez raison, mais puisque ainssi est le voulloir de Dieu, il vuelt et commande que de tous les malvaiz partis le mains pire en soit prins." Alors, le seigneur lui dist: "Doncques, m'amye, conseilliez moy de tous deux le mains pire à vostre advis."—"A! Monseigneur, dist-elle, il y a bien grant choiz. Mais de ceste chose, à jointes mains vous supplie, pardonnez moy, car telles choses doivent partir des nobles cuers des vertueulx hommes et non pas des femelins cuers des femmes qui, par l'ordonnance de Dieu, sommes à vous, hommes, subgettes, especialement les espouseez et qui sont meres des enffants, ainssi que je vous suis et à nostre filz. Sy vous supplie, Monseigneur, que de ce la congnoissance ne s'estende point à moy." —"Ha, m'amye, dist-il, amour et devoir vuellent que de tous mes principaulx affaires, comme ung cuer selon Dieu en deux corps, vous en doye deppartir, ainssi que j'ay toujours fait, pour les biens que j'ay trouvez en vous. Car vous dictes qu'il y a bien choiz. Vous estes la mere et je suis vostre mary. Pourquoy vous prie à peu de parolles que le choiz m'en declairiez." Alors, la très desconffortee dame, pour obeir luy dit: "Monseigneur, puisque tant voullez que le chois vous en die"—alors renfforca la prudence de son cuer par la très grande amour que elle à lui avoit, et lui dist: "Monseigneur, quoy que je dye, il me soit pardonné; des deux consaulx que je vous vueil donner, Dieux avant, Nostre Dame et monseigneur saint Michiel, que soient en ma pensee et en mon parler. Dont le premier est que vous laissiez tous vos dueilz, vos desplaisirs et vos penssers, et ainssy feray-je. Et les remettons tous ès mains de nostre vray Dieu, qui fait tout pour le mieulx. Le IIme et derrain est que vous, Monseigneur, et chascun homme et femme vivant, savez que, selon droit de nature et experience des yeulx, est chose plus apparante que les enffans sont filz ou filles de leurs meres qui en leurs flans les ont portez et enffantez que ne sont de leurs maris, ne de ceulx à qui ont les donne. Laquelle chose, Monseigneur, je dis pour ce que ainssi nostre filz est plus apparant mon vray filz qu'il n'est le vostre, nonobstant que vous en soyez le vray pere naturel. Et de ce j'en appelle nostre vray Dieu à tesmoing au très espouventable jour du jugement. Et car pour ce il est mon vray filz, qui moult chier m'a cousté à porter l'espasse de IX mois en mes flans, dont en ay receu maintes dures angoisses et par mains jours, et puis comme morte à l'enffanter, lequel j'ay sy chierement nourry, amé et tenu chier jusques au jour et heure que il fut livré. Touttefoiz ores, pour toujours mais, je l'abandonne ès mains de Dieu et vueil que jamais il ne me soit plus riens, ainssi que se jamais je ne le avoye veu, ains liberalement de cuer et franchement, sans force, contrainte, ne viollence aucune, vous donne, cede et transporte toute la naturelle amour, l'affection et le droit que mere puelt et doit avoir à son seul et très amé filz. Et de ce j'en appelle à tesmoing le trestout vray et puissant Dieu, qui le nous a presté le espasse de XIII ans, pour la tincion et garde de vostre seul honneur, à tous jours mais perdu se aultrement est. Vous ne avez que ung honneur lequel après Dieu, sur femme, sur enffans et sur toutes choses devez plus amer. Et sy ne avez que ung seul filz. Or advisez duquel vous avez la plus grande perte. Et vrayement, Monseigneur, il y a grant choiz. Nous sommes assez en aaige pour en avoir, se à Dieu plaist; mais vostre honneur une foiz perdu, lasse, jamais plus ne le recouvrerez. Et quant mon conseil vous tendrez, les gens diront de vous, mort ou vif que soiez: C'est le preudomme et très loyal chevallier. Et pour ce, Monseigneur, sy très humblement que je scay, vous supplie, fetes comme moy, et en lui plus ne penssés que se ne l'euissiez jamaiz eu; ains vous resconffortez, et remerciez Dieu de tout, qui le vous a donné pour votre honneur rachetter."

Et quant le cappitaine oist Madame si haultement parler, avec un contemplatif souspir, remercia Jhesus-Crist, le très hault et puissant Dieu, quant du cuer de une femeline et piteuse creature partoient sy haultes et sy vertueuses parolles comme celles que Madame disoit, ayant ainssy du tout abandonné la grant amour de son seul et très aimé filz, et tout pour l'amour de lui. Lors en briefves parolles luy dist: "M'amye, tant que l'amour de mon cuer se puelt estendre, plus que oncques mais vous remercie du très hault et piteux don que m'avez maintenant fait. J'ay ores oy la guette du jour corner, et ja soit que ne dormissions à nuit, sy me fault-il lever; et vous aucum peu reposerez."—"Reposer, dist-elle, hellas, Monseigneur, je n'ay cuer, œul, ne membre sur mon corps qui en soit d'accord. Mais je me leveray et yrons à messe tous deux remerchier Nostre Seigneur de tout."

(Madame, who on the other side made great moan, seeing either her lord's honor lost or her beautiful and gracious son, whose equal at the age of thirteen, as everyone said, could not be found, feared that her lord might die of it. Then she thought in her heart and spoke within herself: "Alas, how wretched I am! If he dies, then you have lost everything." And in this thought she called to him. But he heard nothing. Then, raising her voice, she said to him: "Ah, my lord, for the sake of God, have pity upon me, your poor wife, who has loved and served and honored you loyally without complaint about any service, and who begs you with clasped hands, do not ruin thus at once yourself, your son, and me." And when the lord heard Madame's words, he finally answered her: "Alas, my dear, what is all this? Where is the heart that would not rather love death than live as I see myself, in these very dire straits?" Thereupon Madame, who was very wise and prudent, to comfort him, suddenly changed her bitter meaning to brave counsel and said to him: "My lord, I do not say that you are not right, but since such is God's will, he wills and commands that of all bad things the least evil be taken." Then the lord said to her: "Then, my dear, advise me which of the two is the less evil in your opinion."—"Oh, my lord," she said, "that is a hard choice. But of this, I beg you with clasped hands, relieve me, for such things must issue from the noble hearts of brave men and not from the female hearts of women who, by God's command, are subject to you men, especially wives and mothers of children as I am to you and our son. Therefore I implore you, my lord, that the decision of this be not given to me." —"Ah, my dear," he said, "love and duty require that in all my important affairs—as one heart in two bodies according to God—I should let you share as I have always done because of the good that I have found in you. Now you said that there is here a choice. You are the mother and I am your husband. Therefore I ask you that in few words you set forth the choice to me." Then the most disconsolate woman said, obeying: "My Lord, since you so wish that I tell you the choice,"—and here she strengthened the prudence of her heart by the great love she bore to him and said: "My lord, whatever I say, may it be forgiven me. Two counsels I would give you, and in them may first God and our Lady and my lord Saint Michael be present in my thought and speech. The first is that you leave all your mourning, your sorrow, and your thoughts, and so too shall I. And let us put them all in the hands of our true God who does all for the best. The second and last is that you, my lord, and every man and woman alive, know that by natural right and the experience of our eyes it is more apparent that children are sons and daughters of their mothers who have carried them in their loins and given birth to them than they are of their husbands or of any others (?) to whom they are given. And this I say, my lord, for thus it is more apparent that our son is my true son than that he is yours although you are his true natural father. And of this I call our true God to bear witness on the very terrible day of judgment. And for this then he is my true son, who cost me very dear to carry nine months in my loins while I suffered throughout many a day many a great anxiety, and to give birth to whom I almost died, whom I so dearly fed and loved and cherished down to the day and the hour when he was given over. But now and for ever more I abandon him into the hands of God and it is my will that he shall never more be anything to me, as though I had never seen him, but of my own free will, without force, constraint, or violence whatever, I give, cede, and transfer to you all the natural love, affection, and right which a mother can and must have for her only and dearly loved son. Of this I call to witness the most true and powerful God who lent him to us for the space of thirteen years, for the maintenance and safeguarding of your sole honor which will be lost for ever more if it is to be otherwise. You have but one honor which, after God, you must love more than wife, child, and all things. And likewise you have but one son. Consider now which would be the greater loss to you. And truly, my lord, here is a great choice. We are still of an age to have sons, if it pleases God. But your honor, once lost, alas, you can never recover. And if you follow my counsel, people will say of you, whether you are dead or alive: That is a man of honor and a very loyal knight. And therefore, my lord, as humbly as I know how, I beg you, do as I do, and think no more of him than if you had never had him. But take courage and thank God for everything, for He has given him to you to redeem your honor."

And when the commander heard Madame speak so valiantly, with a thoughtful sigh he thanked Jesus Christ, the most high and powerful God, that from the heart of a female and weak creature could come such high and virtuous words as those Madame spoke, having thus entirely abandoned the love of her only and most beloved son and all for the love of him. Then in brief words he said to her: "My dear, as far as the love of my heart can reach, more than ever I now thank you for the high and grievous gift you have now given me. I have just heard the watch sound daybreak, and although we have not slept this night, I must arise; but you rest a little."—"Rest," she said, "alas, my lord, I have neither heart nor eye nor limb to my body which agrees to that. But I shall rise and we shall go to mass together to thank Our Lord for everything.")

After this scene the narrative continues at great length. Again the Prince's heralds appear, to demand the surrender and threaten the boy's execution. They are dismissed. Then the commander decides to try a sortie to save the boy by force. At this point the narrative shifts to the enemy's camp, where the Prince has the boy led out to execution in chains and forces the Seigneur du Chastel's herald (whose name is also Chastel) to join the procession, despite his resistance. Then we are taken back inside the fortress and told how the commander's wife tries to make him give up the projected sortie and how she swoons, while the guards see the enemy's men returning from the execution, which means that it is too late for the sortie; how the commander has his wife put to bed and how he consoles her; and how the herald Chastel returns to the fortress and reports the events to the commander, repeating numerous details which had already been presented in another form. However, I will here quote the description of the boy's death as the herald tells it:

Mais l'enffant qui, au resconffort des gardes, cuidoit que on le menast vers le chastel, quand il vist que vers le mont Reont alloient, lors s'esbahist plus que oncques mais. Lors tant se prist à plourer et desconfforter, disant à Thomas, le chief des gardes: "Ha! Thomas, mon amy, vous me menez morir, vous me menez morir; hellas! vous me menez morir! Thomas, vous me menez morir! hellas! monsieur mon pere, je vois morir! hellas! madame ma mere, je vois morir, je vois morir! hellas, hellas, hellas, je vois morir, morir, morir, morir!" Dont en criant et en plourant, regardant devant et derrière et entour lui, à vostre coste d'arme que je portoye, lasse my! et il me vist, et quant il me vist, à haute voix s'escria, tant qu'il peust. Et lors me dist: "Ha! Chastel, mon amy, je voiz morir! hellas! mon ami, je voiz morir!" Et quant je ainssi le oys crier, alors, comme mort, à terre je cheys. Et convint, par l'ordonnance, que je fusse emporté après luy, et là, à force de gens, tant soustenu que il eust prins fin. Et quant il fust sur le mont descendu, là fust un frere qui, par belles parolles esperant en la grâce de Dieu, peu à peu le eust confessé et donné l'absolucion de ses menus pechiez. Et car il ne povoit prendre la mort en gré, lui convint tenir le chief, les bras et les jambes lyez, tant se estoit jusques aux os des fers les jambes eschiees, ainsi que depuis tout me fut dit. Et quand ceste sy très cruelle justice fut faitte, et à chief de piece que je fus de pasmoison revenu, lors je despouillay vostre coste d'armes, et sur son corps la mis. . . .

(But the child, who thought, after the guards' consoling words, that he was being taken toward the fortress, when he saw that they were going toward Mont Réont, was frightened more than ever. He now began to weep and despair and said to Thomas, the leader of the guards: "Oh, Thomas, my friend, you take me away to die, you take me away to die. Alas, you take me away to die, Thomas, you take me away to die. Alas, my lord father, I shall die. Alas, my lady mother, I shall die. I shall die! Alas, alas, alas, I shall die, die, die, die!" And crying thus and weeping, looking before and behind and around him, he saw me, woe unto me!, with your coat of arms which I wore, and when he saw me, he called aloud, as loud as he could. And he said to me: "Ah, Chastel, my friend, I shall die! Alas! My friend, I shall die!" And when I heard him cry thus, then like dead I fell to the ground. And according to orders I was carried after him and there by many men was held until he met his end. And when he was set down on the mount, there was there a friar who, by beautiful words of hope in the grace of God, little by little confessed him and absolved him from his little sins. And because he could not take death willingly, they had to hold his head and bind his arms and legs so that the legs were bruised by the iron down to the bones, as it was all told to me afterward. And when this very cruel sentence was executed and I had at last revived from my faint, I took off your coat of arms and put it on his body. . . .)

The herald concludes his report with the bitter words which passed between himself and the Prince when he asked for and received the boy's dead body. Then we are told how the Seigneur, having heard all this, speaks a prayer:

Beaux sires Dieux, qui le me avez jusques à aujourd'uy presté, vueillez en avoir l'âme et lui pardonner de ce que il a la mort mal prinse en gré, et à moi aussi, quant pour bien faire l'ay mis en ce party. Hellasse! povre mere, que diras-tu quant tu saras la piteuse mort de ton chier filz, combien que pour moy tu le avoyes de tous poins abandonné pour acquittier mon honneur. Et, beau sires Dieux, soiez en ma bouche pour l'en resconforter.

(Fair Lord God, who until this day hast lent him to me, deign now to receive his soul and forgive him that he took death unwillingly, and forgive me too that to do right I brought him to this pass. Alas, poor mother, what will you say when you learn the pitiful death of your beloved son, although for me you had given him up entirely to save my honor. Oh, fair Lord God, be in my mouth to comfort her for it.)

Then follows the solemn burial and the scene at table when, in the presence of a great gathering, the commander tells his wife of the boy's death, which he has so far kept from her. She remains calm. A few days later the Prince is obliged to raise the siege. The commander has an opportunity to launch a successful surprise attack, in which a considerable number of the enemy are taken prisoner. The twelve of highest rank, who offer large sums of ransom money, he causes to be hanged on a high gallows, which can be seen from far off. The others have their right eyes pierced and their right hands and right ears cut off; after which he sends them back:

Allez à vostre seigneur Herodes, et luy dittes de par vous grant mercis des autres yeulx, oreilles et poings senestres que je vous laisse, pour ce que il donna le corps mort et innocent de mon filz à Chastel mon herault.

(Go to your master Herod and thank him for your left eyes,

ears, and hands, which I let you keep because he gave the dead and innocent body of my son to Chastel, my herald.)

This text, which I have presented in somewhat greater detail (in part because its circumstantiality is one of its significant characteristics and in part because to most readers it is less readily accessible than those already discussed), is more than a century younger than Boccaccio's *Decameron.* But the impression it produces is incomparably more medieval and un-modern. This general impression is spontaneous and very strong. I shall try to clarify the various elements which produce it.

In regard to form, neither the structure of individual sentences nor the composition of the story as a whole displays any of the humanists' antiquity-inspired plasticity, versatility, clarity, and order. The sentences are not, it is true, predominantly paratactic in structure, but the hypotaxes are often clumsy, full of heavy emphasis, and at times unclear in their connectives. A sentence like this (from the wife's speech): *Et car pour ce il est mon vray filz, qui moult chier m'a cousté à porter l'espasse de IX mois en mes flans, dont en ay receu maintes dures angoisses et par maints jours, et puis comme morte à l'enffanter, lequel j'ay si chierement nourry, amé et tenu chier jusques au jour et heure que il fut livré*—exhibits in the sequence of its relative subordinations a certain lack of clarity as to what belongs with what. The words *et puis comme morte à l'enffanter* fall completely outside the syntactic order, although the entire passage is not at all intended as an emotionally disordered outburst but as a careful and solemn discourse. The elaborate solemnity, the pompous ceremony of this style are certainly, in the last analysis, based upon the rhetorical traditions of antiquity—but wholly upon its pedantic medieval transformation, not upon the humanistic renewal of its original character. This also accounts for the solemnly invocational accumulation of pleonastic or quasi-pleonastic expressions like *nourry, amé et tenu chier*, which occur constantly—for instance again in the very next sentence: *liberalement de cuer et franchement, sans force, contrainte ne viollence aucune, vous donne, cede et transporte toute la naturelle amour, l'affection et le droit. . . .* This is reminiscent of the pompous style of legal and diplomatic documents, and the numerous invocations of God, the Virgin, and the saints are perfectly in place in the same style. As in such solemn documents, the matter at issue is frequently introduced by an array of formulas, apostrophes, adverbial phrases, and sometimes even by a whole procession of preparatory clauses, so that it makes its appearance like a prince or king who is preceded by heralds, bodyguards, court officials, and flag-bearers. The night conversation offers a wealth of pertinent illustrations; and so do the scenes of the heralds arriving with their messages. And although in these latter instances the procedure necessarily results from the subject matter itself, it is impossible to miss the relish with which La Sale exploits it to the full whenever he sees an opportunity. When we read: *Monseigneur le cappitaine de ceste place, nous, comme officiers d'armes et personnes publicques, de par le prince de Galles, nostre très redoubté seigneur, ceste foiz pour toutes à vous nous mande, de par sa clemence de prince, vous signiffier, adviser et sommer . . .* , it is unmistakable that, even at a moment when he is deeply moved and horrified by the Prince's cruelty, La Sale derives supreme pleasure from getting this emphatic but syntactically confused display of class pomp down on paper. And there we have it in a nutshell; his language is a class language; and everything determined by class is non-humanist. The stable class-determined order of life, in which everything has and keeps its place and its form, is reflected in this solemn and circumstantial rhetoric, with its abundance of formulas, its superabundance of conventional gestures and invocations. Every person has a proper form of address. Madame du Chastel calls her husband *Monseigneur*, he says *m'amye* to her. Every person makes the gesture which befits his rank and the circumstances, as though in accordance with an eternal model established once and for all (*à jointes mains vous supplie*). When the Prince forces the commander's herald to witness the boy's execution (the scene is described twice), we hear this: . . . *alors, en genoulx et mains jointes je me mis et lui dis: "A! très redouté prince, pour Dieu, souffrez que la clarté de mes malheureux yeux ne portent pas à mon très dollent cuer la très piteuse nouvelle de la mort de l'innocent filz de mon maistre et seigneur; il souffist bien trop se ma langue, au rapport de mes oreilles, le fait à icelui monseigneur vrayement." Lors dist le prince: "Vous yrez, veuilliez ou non."* The tradition which we have here reentered is most strikingly to be felt in outstandingly solemn passages where, as we said, the matter at issue is surrounded by a defense in depth of solemnly introductory formulas. From such passages it becomes clear that we are dealing with formations of the late antique period of decadence, formations which, from the early Middle Ages onward, were absorbed and developed by class-determined cultures. In the vernaculars this tradition extends from the compact and magnificent rhetoric of the Strasbourg Oaths to the preambles of royal edicts (*Louis par la grâce de Dieu,* etc.). As for the structure of the narrative as a whole, it is hardly possible to speak of any conscious organization. The attempt to proceed chronologically leads to much confusion and repetition. And even though we may wish to make allowances because the author was an old man (there is something of senile circumstantiality in the style of the work), the same paratactic and slightly confused kind of composition is already to be found in the novel of little Jehan de Saintré, which was written some years earlier. It is the style of the chronicles, which enumerates events one after the other with frequent and somewhat abrupt shifts from one scene to another. The naive quality of this procedure is further emphasized by the formula with which every such shift is introduced: and now let us stop telling this and let us turn to that. . . . The mixture of heavily pompous language with the naïveté of enumeration in composition produces an impression of dragging and ponderous monotony in tempo which is not without its peculiar magnificence. It is a variety of the elevated style; but it is class-determined, it is nonhumanist, nonclassical, and entirely medieval.

The same impression of the class-determined medieval approach is also produced by the content of the story, and here I wish to point out especially how striking a thing it is to a modern reader that a political and military occurrence, which belongs in a historical context well known to us, is viewed exclusively as a problem in the ethos of class. Nothing is ever said about the actual importance of the fortress, about the unfortunate consequences which its fall would have for the cause of France and her king. On the contrary, the entire concern is with the knightly honor of the Seigneur du Chastel, with a pledged word and its interpretation, with the fealty of a vassal, with an oath, with personal responsibility. The commander once even offers to meet the Prince in knightly single combat to settle the differences of opinion which have arisen in regard to the interpretation of the agreement. Everything factual is smothered under a luxuriant growth of solemn knightly ceremony; but this does not preclude the prevalence of a brutal cruelty, which is not yet modern, purposeful, and as it were rationalized, but is still entirely personal and emotional. The execution of the boy is a completely senseless act of barbarism, and equally senseless is the commander's revenge upon more than a hundred innocent victims, who are hanged or mutilated—and who otherwise, but for the commander's personal lust for vengeance, would have been sent back for ransom. The impression all this makes is as if the political and military direction of war were still completely unrationalized, as if any effective control of operations did not exist, so that the measures taken depend largely upon the personal relations, the emotional reactions, and the concepts of knightly honor of the commanders who happen to be facing each other in any particular encounter. As a matter of fact, this may well have still been the case during the Hundred Years' War. Even much later, in the very period of full-fledged absolutism, there are still to be found—especially in military life, where the conventions of the knightly spirit were longest preserved—unmistakable traces of a relationship between friends and foes which is wholly of the personal and knightly type. Still, it is precisely during the fifteenth century, the time when La Sale lived, that a change begins to make itself felt. The political and military methods of knighthood meet with failure, its ethos shows signs of breaking down, and its functions begin to be more and more exclusively decorative. La Sale's novel of little Jehan de Saintré is eloquent though unintentional testimony to the ostentatious and parasitic senselessness of knightly feats of arms at this epoch. But of the impending change, La Sale refuses to take notice. He lives enveloped in a class-determined atmosphere with its distinctive conception of honor, its ceremonies, and its heraldic pomp. Even his learning, which is more strongly apparent in his other works than in the *Réconfort*, is a mosaic of moral quotations in the late scholastic spirit; it is specifically a scholastic compilation serving the ends of feudal and knightly class education.

La Sale, then, remains unaffected by the movement which led the great Italian authors of the fourteenth century to extend their domain over all of contemporary reality. His language and his art in general are class-determined; his horizon is narrow, although he has traveled so widely. Wherever he went, he saw many notable things, but all he ever noted in them was their courtly and knightly aspect. The *Réconfort* too is written in this spirit. But in the midst of its late feudal and already somewhat brittle stylistic pomp, there appears—as the text quoted above shows—a truly tragic occurrence of the highest dignity, which is narrated a little ceremoniously and circumstantially, it may be, but yet with great warmth and simplicity of feeling, as the subject deserves. In medieval literature there is hardly another instance of so simple, so extremely real, so exemplarily tragic a conflict, and I have often wondered why this beautiful passage is so little known. The conflict is completely unschematized; it has nothing to do with any of the traditional motifs of courtly literature. It involves a woman, but a mother and not a mistress. It is not romantically moving, like the story of Griselda, but a piece of practical, graspable reality. The background of knightly ceremonial does not interfere with its simple grandeur, for one is ready to grant without argument that a woman, especially in this era, conforms to prevailing conditions. Indeed, Madame du Chastel's submissiveness, her humility, her obedient bowing to her husband's will, show only the more impressively the sterling force and freedom of her nature as it awakes in a time of need. In the last analysis the conflict concerns her alone; for although he shows himself undecided and complains, there is no doubt as to what decision he must make. But it depends on her attitude whether and how he can withstand the shock. And in a quick and clear acceptance of the situation she regains control over herself through the argument: *se il se muert, or as-tu bien tout perdu.* And she forthwith resolves to extricate him from his useless self-torture, to show him the road she knows he must take, by taking it before him. As soon as she has succeeded in attracting his attention, she first gives him what he most urgently needs, that is, order in his thoughts, consciousness of the problem he must solve: there is a decision to be made between two evils, and he must choose the lesser. When, still helpless, he asks which is the lesser, she at first avoids answering the question: that, she says, is not to be decided by a frail woman but by a man's virtue and courage. She thus puts him under the necessity of as it were ordering her to express her views, which means that she reinstates him, albeit only outwardly, in his accustomed position of leadership and responsibility. By this very fact she has extricated him from the state of spineless querulousness which was undermining his strength and his self-respect. And then she sets the example he must follow. Children, she says, are more the children of their mothers, who carried them and gave birth to them and suckled them, than of their fathers. Our son is more my son than yours; and yet I now renounce all my love of him as though I had never had him; I sacrifice my love for him; for we can have other children, but if your honor is lost, it cannot be recovered. And if you follow my advice, people will praise you: *c'est le preudomme et très loyal chevalier.* . . . It is hard to decide what is most praiseworthy in this speech, its self-effacement or its self-control, its goodness or its clarity. That a woman under such a trial does not abandon herself to her grief but sees the situation clearly as it really is; that she understands there can be no question of surrendering the fortress and that hence the boy is lost in any case if the Prince is in earnest; that she manages by her intervention to restore her husband's inner poise, by her example to give him the courage to make a decision, and even, by her reference to the fame he will gain, to offer him some measure of consolation and most certainly to give him back the pride and self-respect which will make it easier for him to play the part assigned to him—all this has a simple beauty and grandeur which can vie with any classical text. Very beautiful too is the conclusion when, released from his tension, he can pray again, and thank her, and even ask her to rest a little longer: *Reposer, dist-elle, hellas, Monseigneur, je n'ay cuer, oeul, ne membre sur mon corps qui en soit d'accord. . . .*

It is apparent that the late-feudal epideictic style is able to produce a visual representation of such a genuinely tragic and genuinely real scene. However superficial this style may be in political and military matters, whose true relations and causal connections it no longer grasps, it stands the test in a perfectly simple, directly human action. This is the more remarkable since in our case the place of the action is extremely everyday and domestic, the personages are a married couple, talking over their troubles at night in bed. In the classical conception of the ancients this is no proper setting for a tragic action in the elevated style. Here the tragic, the grave, the problematic appears in the everyday life of a family. And although the people involved belong to the high nobility and are steeped in feudal forms and traditions, the situation in which we find them—in bed at night, not as lovers but as man and wife, grieving under dire stress, and intent upon helping one another—is of a kind that impresses us more as middle-class, or rather as generally human, than as feudal. Despite the solemn and ceremonious language, what takes place is very simple and very naive. A few simple thoughts and emotions appear, in harmony or in conflict. There is no question of any stylistic separation between the tragic and everyday realism. During its heyday, in the twelfth and thirteenth centuries, French courtly literature produced nothing so real and "creatural."[1] A married couple in bed—that might at least have occurred in a popular farce. And what can we say about the representation of the weeping and lamenting boy as he is led to his death! I shall not praise it. It is unnecessary, either for the reader or for the unfortunate father (to whom the herald's report is addressed), that the minute details of the occurrence should be depicted with so much sensory

[1] *Kreatürliches*. The word, a neologism of the 1920's, implies the suffering to which man is subject as a mortal creature. (Translator's note.)

evidence. The more striking is it that so large a measure of unconcealed creatural realism can be united with a tragic event in this style of heraldic ostentation. Everything is calculated to bring out in visual clarity the contrast between the innocence of the boy and the gruesome execution, between the protected life he has so far led and the merciless reality which suddenly breaks in on it: the pity of the guards, who have made friends with the boy during his brief detention as a hostage; his childish, uncomprehending outpouring of lamentation, twice heard, in which, saying the same words over and over, he clings to every present and absent source of help; his struggling against death to the very last moment, despite the consoling words of the monk who hears his confession, until his desperate resistance makes the fetters wear the flesh of his legs to the bone. . . . The Seigneur du Chastel is spared nothing, nor is the reader.

What we have observed here, this interplay between the epideictic style of knightly ceremony and a starkly creatural realism which does not shun but actually savors crass effects, is not a new discovery of ours. From the romantic period on, this combination has been an integral part of the current concept of the Middle Ages. More exact research has established that it was at the end of the Middle Ages—during the fourteenth and especially the fifteenth century—that the combination evolved and became strikingly and characteristically apparent. For more than thirty years now, we have had an excellent and widely-known study of this epoch, Huizinga's *The Waning of the Middle Ages*, in which the phenomenon is repeatedly analyzed in various contexts. What is common to the two elements and holds them together is certain factors in the sensory taste of the period: ponderousness and somberness, dragging tempo, strongly charged coloration. As a result its epideictic style often has a somewhat exaggerated sensory impressiveness; its realism often has a certain ponderousness of form and at the same time something directly creatural and fraught with tradition. Many realistic forms—the Dance of Death for example—have the character of processions or parades. The traditionalism of the serious, creatural realism of this period is explained by its origin. It stems from Christian figuralism and takes almost all its intellectual and artistic motifs from the Christian tradition. The suffering creature is present to it in the Passion of Christ, the portrayal of which becomes more and more brutal while its sensory and mystic power of suggestion grows stronger, or in the passions of the martyrs. Domestic intimacy and "serious" *intérieur* ("serious" in comparison with the *intérieur* of the farces) it derives from the Annunciation and other domestic scenes which were to be found in Scripture. In the fifteenth century the embedding of the events of the story of salvation in the contemporary daily life of the people had reached such a pitch, and their minutest details had become so penetrated with typology, that religious realism exhibits symptoms of excess and crude degeneracy. We have mentioned this fact in an earlier passage (pp. 158ff.); it has often been observed, very clearly and with great penetration by Huizinga for example, so that we need not go into it further. Yet in our context some other points must be made in regard to the realism of the closing Middle Ages. And the first is that the picture of man living in reality which the Christian mixture of styles had produced—that is, the creatural picture—begins likewise to appear outside of the Christian sphere in its more restricted sense. We find it in our narrative, which relates a feudal and military occurrence. Then we must point out that the representation of real contemporary life now turns with particular care and great art to the intimate, domestic, and everyday detail of family life. This too, as we have just observed, results from the Christian mixture of styles; it is a development for which the conceptual patterns are to be found in the motifs connected with the Virgin Mary's and Christ's birth. It exhibits, especially in the domain of the visual arts, far more allusions of a typological nature than was assumed until recently.

But the development was also furthered by the rise of the upper-bourgeois culture which made itself strongly felt toward the end of the Middle Ages especially in northern France and Burgundy. This culture was not, it is true, quite conscious of itself (it was a long time before the "third estate" was given a place in theory which corresponded with the actual situation); in its attitudes and its style of life it long remained, despite its considerable wealth and growing power, a lower rather than an upper bourgeoisie. But it supplied motifs for the mimetic arts, motifs which were precisely of the intimately domestic variety—both as picturesque *intérieur* and as representing domestic and economic conditions and problems. The domestic, intimate, and everyday aspects of personal life sometimes come through even in cases involving members of the feudal nobility or of the princely class. Here too we find that intimate occurrences are represented much more often, in greater detail, and more plainly than before—as is the case in our text and frequently also in the writings of the chroniclers (Froissart, Chastellain, etc.). Hence literature and art, despite their predilection for feudal and heraldic display, have on the whole a much more bourgeois character than was true in the earlier Middle Ages. And finally a third point must be stressed as being of essential importance for late medieval realism—the very point which induced me to employ in this chapter the new term "creatural." It is characteristic of Christian anthropology from its beginnings that it emphasizes man's subjection to suffering and transitoriness. This was a necessary concomitant of the idea of Christ's Passion as part of the story of salvation. Yet during the twelfth and thirteenth centuries the corresponding devaluation and denigration of earthly existence had not reached the extreme which characterizes the era here under discussion. During the earlier centuries of the Middle Ages the idea that life on earth has value and purpose was still very much alive. Human society had specific tasks to accomplish; it had to realize a specific ideal form on earth in order to prepare men for the Kingdom of God. Within the confines of the present study, Dante is an example of a man for whom (as for many of his contemporaries) secular planning and political endeavor on the part of individuals and human society at large was highly significant, ethically relevant, and decisive for eternal salvation. It may be that the social ideals of those early centuries had lost in power and prestige because events so stubbornly gave them the lie and that new developments were initiated which were in no way compatible with them. It may be that people did not know how to interpret and organize the new political and economic forms of life which were being initiated, or again that the will to a theoretical comprehension of practical earthly life was paralyzed by the various trends toward a popular ecstaticism, by the ever more emotionally realistic mysticism of the Passion, and the prevailing form of piety which was increasingly degenerating into superstition and fetishism. Certain it is that during the last centuries of the Middle Ages there are to be observed symptoms of fatigue and barrenness in constructive-theoretical thinking, especially insofar as it is concerned with the practical organization of life on earth, with the result that the "creatural" aspect of Christian anthropology—life's subjection to suffering and transitoriness—comes out in crass and unmitigated relief. The peculiar feature of this radically creatural picture of man, which is in particularly sharp contrast to the classico-humanistic picture, lies in the fact that it combines the highest respect for man's class insignia with no respect whatever for man himself as soon as he is divested of them. Beneath them there is nothing but the flesh, which age and illness will ravage until death and putrefaction destroy it. It is, if you like, a radical theory of the equality of all men, not in an active and political sense but as a direct devaluation of life which affects every man individually. Whatever he does and attempts is vain. Although his instincts oblige him to act and to cling to life on earth, that life has neither worth nor dignity. It is not in their relation to one another or even "before the law" that all men are equal; on the contrary: God has appointed that there be inequality between them in their lives on earth. But they are equal before death, before creatural decay, before God. True enough, even at this early period we find individual instances (in England especially of a very forceful kind) where politico-economic conclusions are drawn from this doctrine of equality. But by far the more prevailing attitude is that which, in the creatural character of man, reads only the fruitlessness and vanity of all earthly endeavor. For many in the countries north of the Alps, consciousness of their own predestined decay with that of all their works has a paralyzing effect upon intellectual endeavor insofar as its purpose is to make practical plans concerned with life on earth. All action aimed at the future of life in this world seems to them without value and without dignity, a mere play of instincts and passions. Their relation to earthly reality combines acceptance of its existing forms as an intensely expressive pageantry and radical unmasking of it as transitory and vain. The most extreme means are employed to elaborate this contrast between life and death, youth and age, health and sickness, idle and triumphant boastfulness in regard to one's earthly role and miserable and plaintive rebellion against inexorable destruction. These simple themes are subjected to ever new variations—morose or passionately complaining, pious or cynical or again both at once—and often with gripping power. Average everyday life, with its sensual pleasures, its sorrows, its decline with age and illness, its end, has seldom been so impressively represented as during this epoch; and stylistically these representations are of a character which is clearly differentiated not only from the realistic art of the ancients—which goes without saying—but also from that of the earlier Middle Ages.

We have from this period a number of literary representations of a night conversation between a married couple. Of those which I know, a particularly characteristic one is the scene from the first of the *Quinze Joyes de Mariage*, in which the wife wants a new dress. I quote it from the Bibliothèque elzévirienne edition (2nd ed., Paris, 1857, pp. 9ff.):

Lors regarde lieu et temps et heure de parler de la matière à son mary; et voulentiers elles devroient parler de leurs choses especialles là où leurs mariz sont plus subjets et doivent estre plus enclins pour octrier: c'est ou lit, ouquel le compagnon dont j'ay parlé veult atendre à ses délitz et plaisirs, et lui semble qu'il n'a aultre chouse à faire. Lors commence et dit ainsi la Dame: "Mon amy, lessez-moy, car je suis à grand mal-aise.—M'amie, dit-il, et de quoy?—Certes, fait-elle, je le doy bien estre, mais je ne vous en diray jà rien, car vous ne faites compte de chose que je vous dye.—M'amie, fait-il, dites-moy pour quoy vous me dites telles paroles?—Par Dieu, fait-elle, sire, il n'est jà mestier que je le vous dye: car c'est une chose, puis que je la vous auroye dite, vous n'en feriez compte, et il vous sembleroit que je le feisse pour autre chose.—Vrayement, fait-il, vous me le direz." Lors elle dit: "Puis qu'il vous plest, je le vous diray: Mon amy, fait-elle, vous savez que je fuz l'autre jour à telle feste, où vous m'envoiastes, qui ne me plaisoit gueres mais quand je fus là, je croy qu'il n'y avoit femme (tant fust-elle de petit estat) qui fust si mal abillée comme je estoye: combien que je ne le dy pas pour moy louer, mais, Dieu merci, je suis d'aussi bon lieu comme dame, damoiselle ou bourgeoise qui y fust; je m'en rapporte à ceulx qui scevent les lignes. Je ne le dy pas pour mon estat, car il ne m'en chaut comme je soye; mais je en ay honte pour l'amour de vous et de mes amis.—Avoy! dist-il, m'amie, quel estat avoient-elles à ceste feste?—Par ma foy, fait-elle, il n'y avoit si petite de l'estat dont je suis qui n'eust robe d'écarlate, ou de Malignes, ou de fin vert, fourrée de bon gris ou de menu-ver, à grands manches, et chaperon à l'avenant, à grant cruche, avecques un tessu de soye rouge ou vert, traynant jusques à terre, et tout fait à la nouvelle guise. Et avoie encor la robe de mes nopces, laquelle est bien usée et bien courte, pour ce que je suis creue depuis qu'elle fut faite; car je estoie encore jeune fille quand je vous fus donnée, et si suy desja si gastée, tant ay eu de peine, que je sembleroye bien estre mere de telle à qui je seroye bien fille. Et certes je avoye si grant honte quand je estoye entre elles, que je n'ousoie ne savoye faire contenance. Et encore me fit plus grand mal que la Dame de tel lieu, et la femme de tel, me disrent devant tous que c'estoit grand'honte que je n'estoye mielx abillée. Et par ma foy, elles n'ont garde de m'y trouver mès en pièce.—Avoy! m'amie, fait le proudomme, je vous diray: vous savez bien, m'amie, que nous avons assez affaire, et savez, m'amie, que quant nous entrames en nostre menage nous n'avions gueres de meubles, et nous a convenu achapter liz, couchez, chambres, et moult d'autres choses, et n'avons pas grant argent à present; et savez bien qu'il fault achapter deux beufs pour notre mestoier de tel lieu. Et encore chaist l'autre jour le pignon de nostre grange par faulte de couverture, qu'il faut reffaire la premiere chouse. Et si me fault aller à l'assise de tel lieu, pour le plait que j'ay de vostre terre mesme de tel lieu, dont je n'ay riens eu ou au moins bien petit, et m'y fault faire grand despence.—Haa! sire, je savoye bien que vous ne me sauriez aultre chose retraire que ma terre." Lors elle se tourne de l'aultre part, et dit: "Pour Dieu, lessés moi ester, car je n'en parleray ja mais.—Quoy dea, dit le proudomme, vous vous courroucez sans cause.—Non fais, sire, fait-elle: car si vous n'en avez rien eu, ou peu, je n'en puis mais. Car vous savez bien que j'estoye parlée de marier à tel, ou à tel, et en plus de vingt aultres lieux, qui ne demendoyent seullement que mon corps; et savez bien que vous alliez et veniez si souvent que je ne vouloie que vous; dont je fu bien mal de Monseigneur mon père, et suis encor, dont je me doy bien haïr; car je croy que je suy la plus maleurée femme qui fust oncques. Et je vous demande, sire, fait-elle, si les femmes de tel et de tel, qui me cuidèrent bien avoir, sont en tel estat comme je suy. Si ne sont-elles pas du lieu dont je suy. Par Sainct Jehan, mieulx vallent les robes que elles lessent à leurs chamberieres que celles que je porte aux dimanches. Ne je ne scey que c'est à dire dont il meurt tant de bonnes gens, dont c'est grand dommage: à Dieu plaise que je ne vive gueres! Au moins fussés vous quite de moy, et n'eussés plus de desplesir de moy.—Par ma foy, fait-il, m'amie, ce n'est pas bien dit, car il n'est chose que je ne feisse pour-vous; mais vous devez regarder à nostre fait: tournez vous vers moy, et je feray ce que vous vouldrez.—Pour Dieu, fait-elle, lessés moi ester, car, par ma foy, il ne m'en tient point. Pleust à Dieu qu'il ne vous en tenist jamès plus que il fait à moy; par ma foy vous ne me toucheriez jamès.—Non? fait-il.—Certes, fait-elle, non." Lors, pour l'essaier bien, ce lui semble, il lui dit: "Si je estoie trespassé, vous seriez tantoust mariée à ung aultre.—Seroye! fait-elle: ce seroit pour le plaisir que g'y ay eu! Par le sacrement Dieu, jamès bouche de homme ne toucheroit à la moye; et si je savoye que je deusse demourer après vous, je feroye chouse que je m'en iroye la premiere." Et commence à plorer. . . .

(Then she considers time and place and hour to talk of the matter to her husband. And prone they are to talk of their personal matters where their husbands are most submissive and inclined to grant; that is in bed where the companion I have mentioned wants to attend to his joys and pleasures, and he thinks there is nothing else for him to do. Then the lady begins and says: "My dear, leave me alone, for I am greatly troubled." "My dearest," says he, "but why?" "Indeed," says she, "I have good reason to be, but I will not tell you of it, for you pay no attention to anything I say." "My dear," says he, "tell me why you say such words to me?" "By God," says she, "it is useless to tell you; for it is a thing that, after I had told you about it, you would not bother about it, and you would think that I did it for another reason." "Now truly," says he, "you shall tell me." Then she says: "Since you wish it, I will tell you. My dear," says she, "you know that the other day I was at that party where you had sent me, although I didn't like it at all. But when I was there, I think there wasn't a woman, no matter how low in rank, who was dressed as poorly as I was. I don't say it to boast, but, thank God, I come from as good a place as any lady, damsel, or townswoman who was there. I appeal to those who know something about lineage. I don't say it for my sake, for it makes no difference to me how I look, but I am ashamed for your sake and the sake of my friends." "Indeed!" says he. "My dear, what did the women wear at that party?" "Faith," says she, "not one of any condition, not even the least, who did not have a dress of scarlet or Malines or fin vert trimmed with bon gris or menu-ver, with big sleeves and a hat to match . . . with a red or green veil down to the floor and quite in the newest style. But I still had my wedding dress which is all worn and much too short because I have grown since it was made. For I was still a young girl when I was married to you, and yet I am already so run down with all the worry I have had that I look like the mother of many a woman whose daughter I could be. And truly, I was so ashamed when I was among them that I lost heart and did not know how to behave. And it troubled me still more when Lady Soandso, and Soandso's wife, told me before all the others that it was a great shame that I was not better dressed. But I swear they won't lay eyes on me in that place again." "Come, come, my dear," says the good man, "I'll tell you: You know very well, my dear, that we have enough on our hands, and you know, my dear, that when we set up housekeeping we had hardly any furniture, and we had to buy beds, bedding, and many other things, and now we have not much cash. And you know well that we must buy a team of oxen for our tenant at Soandso. And the other day the gable of our barn came down because it was not roofed and that will have to be fixed the first thing. And then I have to go to court at Soandso because of the suit I have on account of your land in Soandso which has not brought me in a thing or at least very little, and that again will be a great expense." "Ah, I knew you would not think of anything to come back at me with but my land." Then she turns the other way and says: "For God's sake, leave me in peace, I won't ever mention it again." "Now, now," says the good man, "you get all excited without cause." "I do not," says she, "for if the land brought you nothing, or little, that isn't my fault. For you know very well that I could have married Soandso and Suchandsuch and twenty others, all of whom asked for nothing but my body. And you know that you came to the house so often that I finally wanted no one but you, and because of that I quarreled with my father, and we haven't made up yet, which is a heavy burden on my conscience. I think I am the most miserable woman who ever lived. And I ask you," she says, "if the wives of Soandso and Suchandsuch, who were so eager to get me, are in such a state as I. Yet they don't come from as good a family as I. By Saint John, the dresses they give their maids are better than my Sunday best. I don't know why so many good people die, which is a great pity; please God I shall not live much longer! At least then you would be rid of me and would have no further trouble from me." "Faith," says he, "my dear, you must not talk that way, for there is nothing I would not do for you. But you must consider our affairs. Turn around now, and I will do what you ask." "Oh God," says she, "leave me in peace, for I don't feel like it. Might it please God that you never felt any more like it than I do; faith, you would never touch me again." "Wouldn't I?" says he. "Certainly not," says she. Then, to put her to the test, as he thinks, he says to her: "If I were dead, you would soon be married to another." "Would I?" says she, "I suppose because of the fun I got from it! By God, never again would a man's mouth touch mine, and if I knew I had to live beyond your time, I would do something to pass on before you." And she falls to weeping. . . .)

This text, probably composed a few decades before the *Réconfort,* is obviously from an entirely different sphere of events and is consequently written on a level of style entirely different from that of the scene between the Seigneur du Chastel and his wife. In the latter, the issue is the life of an only child; in the *Quinze Joyes* it is a new dress. In the *Réconfort* there is true accord, a real partnership between man and wife; in the *Quinze Joyes* there is no trust between them, but each follows his own instincts, each observes the instincts of the other, not in order to understand them and meet them halfway but merely to exploit them for selfish purposes. The woman proceeds with great though childishly ingenuous skill; the man is cruder and less aware of what he is doing. But he too lacks the feeling which is an essential element in genuine love: the feeling for what can gladden the partner's heart. The way he reacts to her concern over clothes might well irritate a less foolish woman, however much he may be in the right so far as the facts go. Finally, in the story of the du Chastels, the wife is the heroine. In the *Quinze Joyes* she is too, but not through the greatness and purity of her heart but through the superiority of her deceitfulness and energy in the eternal struggle which marriage is represented to be. The level of style differs correspondingly: the *Quinze Joyes* lacks any claim to an elevated tone; the dialogue between man and wife does not seek to render anything but the tone of an everyday conversation, and it is only in the introductory statements that an element of moral didacticism is present, which, however, derives much more from practical psychology and concrete experience than is usual in medieval moralizing. The ceremonious and ostentatious elevation which constitutes the class character of the *Réconfort* is in marked contrast to the frankly intermediate, bourgeois forms of expression and behavior in the conversation on the subject of the new dress.

And yet the historical approach shows that here two kinds of style are coming together. We said above that feudal literature in its heyday has nothing to show which is comparable in realism and domestic intimacy with the scene between the Seigneur du Chastel and his wife. A tragic problem, presented in a conversation at night between husband and wife, is something so direct that the old-fashioned ostentatious ornateness of the class-determined language, rather than lessen the impression of the human and the creatural, touchingly enhances it. On the other hand the subject which is treated in our scene from the *Quinze Joyes*—a woman who, at night in bed, talks her husband into a new dress—is really material for farce. But here the theme is taken seriously; and not merely in its crudity and generality, by way of illustration and example, but in a concrete representation which is precise in its rendering of the nuances and details of the material and psychological situation. For although the author gave his work the form of a collection of exempla, it yet has nothing to do with the earlier, wholly unrealistic, purely didactic collections of exempla in the manner of the *Seven Wise Masters* or the *Disciplina Clericalis*; it is much too concrete for that. Nor has it anything to do with the farces; for that, it is much too serious. The little work, whose author is not known to us, is a very significant document in the history of the antecedents of modern realism. It renders everyday life or at least one of its most important spheres, that of marriage and family life, in all its sensory reality, and it takes this everyday subject seriously and indeed problematically. This seriousness, to be sure, is of a special type. In earlier times the misogynous and anticonnubial tendencies of clerical ethics had produced a kind of realistic literature which, with sullen and morose didacticism, enumerated all the miseries and dangers of marriage, family life, bringing up children, etc., tricking out its presentation with allegories and examples. These themes had been handled especially impressively, and at times most concretely, by Eustache Deschamps, who died at the beginning of the fifteenth century. From this tradition the author of the *Quinze Joyes* derived not only almost all the individual motifs of his work but also his half-moralizing, satirical, and more sullenly carping than tragically serious attitude toward his subject.

However, even Eustache Deschamps (see, for example, numbers 15, 17, 19, 38, or 40 of his *Miroir de Mariage*) never succeeded in evoking a real scene involving husband and wife in that emmeshing dual play of all levels of consciousness, which is what a marriage is. With him the elements of realism remain superficial, something in the style of what the nineteenth century called genre scenes. The motifs contained in the passage quoted above are almost all represented in Deschamps too. With him too the wife wants new clothes, appeals to the fact that others are better dressed although they do not come from families as good as hers. But the whole thing does not take place at night and in bed; it is not connected with the play of sexual relations, the motif of remarriage after the husband's death, or all the allusions to how the marriage came about and to the property which she brought with her and which so far has yielded hardly any revenue but instead has been the cause of costly litigation. Deschamps enumerates his motifs, at times vividly, more often all too prolixly. The author of the *Quinze Joyes* knows what marriage is, he knows the bad of it, and the good too, for in the *Quatorziesme Joye* (p. 116) he has the sentence: *car ilz sont deux en une chose, et nature y a ouvré tant par la douceur de sa forse, que si l'un avoit mal, l'autre le sentiroit.* He has the married couple really live together; he combines his motifs in such a way that the "*deux en une chose*" becomes palpable, chiefly, it is true, in its evil implications, as a situation which enables husband and wife to hurt each other deeply, as the eternal struggle of two creatures fettered to each other, as deceit and betrayal in their partnership. This gives his book a tragic character. It is not very lofty tragedy, nor is it unintermittent. The individual problems are too narrow and petty for that; above all, the character of the victim, that is, the husband, is not free enough. He has neither goodness nor dignity, neither humor nor self-control. He is nothing but a harassed paterfamilias, and his love of his wife is entirely egotistical, without any understanding of her individual nature. He thinks of himself simply as her proprietor and feels that his proprietary rights are constantly in danger. If, then, anyone prefers to eschew the word tragic, he must nevertheless acknowledge that the practical vicissitudes of a human being in his everyday existence have here been given a literary expression which did not exist earlier. And there is in fact a convergence of the stylistic levels of the *Réconfort*, which is written in the feudal tradition, and the *Quinze Joyes*, whose motifs are drawn from the farces and from popular clerical moralizing. There comes into being a level of style which considers the everyday scene of current life worthy of detailed and serious portrayal; which at times, reaching upward, attains the realm of tragedy, at times touches the realm of satire and moral didacticism below; which deals much more penetratingly than before with the immediacy of human existence, its physical actualities, its domestic aspects, everyday enjoyments, the decline of life, and its end; and which, in all this, has no fear of harsh effects.

The sensory present which is thus made manifest remains within the class-determined forms of the time yet nonetheless everywhere reveals itself as a general reality which binds all men together through their common creatural conditions of life (*la condition de l'homme*, as it would later be called). From as early as the fourteenth century, we find instances of this more immediate, more sensory, more detailed realism. They are numerous in Eustache Deschamps, and Froissart relates episodes involving questions of life and death with a sensory circumstantiality which is not so very different from the manner in which La Sale relates the death of the young du Chastel. When the six leading burghers of Calais, clad only in shirt and trousers, a rope around their necks, the key to the city in their hands, kneel before the English king, who wants to have them executed, we hear him gnash his teeth; the queen, who throws herself at his feet begging for grace for the prisoners, is in the last stages of pregnancy, and he, fearing that in her condition she may come to harm if he does not grant her request, does so with the words: "*Ha! dame, j'aimasse trop mieux que vous fussiez autre part que ci!*" (*Chroniques*, 1, 321). Still more marked in their detailed realism are the episodes of book 3 which treat of the death of young Gaston de Foix. Huizinga grants them "an almost tragic power." The subject is a family tragedy at a princely court in southern France, and it is reported in a series of extremely clear and graphic scenes, all the details of which are delineated. The terrible proceedings between father and son achieve complete directness in these sketches of courtly mores (the two princes gaming and fighting, the prince with his Italian greyhound at table, and so forth). During the fifteenth century realism becomes even more sensory, the colors become even more glaring. Yet the representation always remains within the bounds of medieval class-determination and of Christianity. The utmost perfection of a creatural realism which remains completely within the sensory and, for all its radicalism of emotion and expression, shows no trace of intellectually categorizing power, or even of revolutionary power, shows indeed no will whatever to make this world any different from what it is, is to be found in François Villon.

We are still—as is clearly to be seen precisely in Villon—dealing with the effects of the Christian mixture of styles. Without it, the type of realism we have called creatural would not be conceivable. But by now it has freed itself from serving the concept of a Christian universal order; indeed, it no longer serves any concept of order whatever. It is fully independent; it has become an end in itself. Once before in the course of this study we encountered a married couple: Adam and Eve in the *Mystère d'Adam*. In that instance the direct imitation of contemporary reality served a timeless and universal purpose, that is, the graphic portrayal of the story of salvation, and beyond this it did not go. Now too the link between here and there, between this world and eternal salvation, remains unsevered. "Creaturality" necessarily implies such a relation to the divine order; it is constantly referred to; furthermore, the fifteenth century is precisely the great epoch of the passion play, is under the influence of a mysticism which revels in creatural-realistic imagery. However, there has been a shift of emphasis, it now falls much more strongly upon life on earth. And this life on earth is contrasted far more strikingly and far more effectively with earthly decay and earthly death than with eternal salvation. Graphic portrayal is now much more immediately in the service of earthly events; it enters into their sensory content, it seeks their sap and their savor, it seeks the joy and torment which flow directly from life on earth itself. This realistic art has conquered an unlimited cycle of themes and much subtler means of expression. But its growth during this period is restricted to the sensory domain. While the old order declines, there is nothing in Franco-Burgundian realism to announce the rise of a new one. This realism is poor in ideas; it lacks constructive principles and even the will to attain them. It drains the reality of that which exists and, in its very existence, falls to decay; it drains it to the dregs, so that the senses, and the emotions aroused by them, get the flavor of immediate life; and, having done that, it seeks nothing further. Indeed, the sensory itself, for all the intensity of the expression, is narrow; its horizon is restricted. Not one of the writers of this cultural sphere surveys and masters the totality of the earthly reality of his time as did Dante or even Boccaccio. Each knows only his own sphere, and it is a narrow sphere even in the case of men who, like Antoine de la Sale, have traveled widely in the course of their lives. Only through a disposition, an active will, to give the world a form does the gift of understanding and rendering the phenomena of life acquire the power to transcend the narrow confines of one's own life. The death of the du Chastel boy or of Prince Gaston de Foix gives us nothing beyond the very concrete experience of youth, enmeshment, and excruciating death; when it is all over, the reader is left with nothing but a sensory, an almost physical, horror from the experience of life's transitoriness. Beyond that the writers give us nothing: no judgment which might have weight, no perspective, no conviction, no principles. Indeed, even their psychology, which is often extremely striking in its concern with the immediate and the particular (the conversation between man and wife in the *Quinze Joyes* may be recalled in this connection) is far more creatural than individual.

It is evident that these writers needed the sensory experience which their spheres of life afforded them, but that on the other hand they did not strive to go further because each such sphere provides sufficient material in the way of creatural contingency. Boccaccio was known in France—especially through the translation by Laurent de Premierfait (1414); and more or less contemporaneously with the *Réconfort*, a collection of stories after the model of the *Decameron* made its appearance in Burgundy, the *Cent Nouvelles Nouvelles* (edition by T. Wright, Paris, 1857-58). But what constitutes the very essence of Boccaccio is not imitated, indeed is apparently not even recognized. The *Cent Nouvelles* is a collection of robust stories which are served up at a gathering of men, and these men, although representing courtly and high feudal society and in part even the princely ruling class, feel perfectly at ease in the atmosphere of the popular farcical style. Nothing is left of Boccaccio's elegantly humanistic "intermediate style," of his doctrine of love, his service of women, of the human, critical, and embracing perspective of the *Decameron*, of the multiplicity of its scenes and its reports of life. It goes without saying that the language too, though flavorful and expressive, shows no sign of having been penetrated by humanism and is anything but literary. The prose of Alain Chartier, who had died two decades earlier, is much more refined and rhythmically studied. Among the stories there are not a few which treat motifs also represented in the *Decameron*. The motif of the angel Gabriel occurs (in the fourteenth nouvelle) in the variant of a hermit who, by the aid of a hollow stick which he passes through the wall of her house, conveys to a pious widow the "divine command" to bring him her daughter because from her union with the hermit will be born a child destined to ascend the Papal throne and to reform the Church. Mother and daughter obey the command; the hermit finally lets them wring a reluctant consent from him. But after he enjoys the daughter for a time, she becomes pregnant, and gives birth to a girl! The nouvelle is very crudely composed (the "divine" visitation and command are repeated three times; the girl and her mother go to see the hermit three times); the characterization of mother, daughter, and hermit, compared with that of Frate Alberto and Madonna Lisetta, is purely "creatural," that is to say, not at all without life, and indeed quite true to life, but without any individualization. As a sensory rendering of a comic incident the whole story is quite effective. There is much popular and colloquial humor in it (*la vieille, de joy emprise, cuidant Dieu tenir par les piez*), but it is incomparably cruder, narrower, and on a lower level of attitude and form than Boccaccio.

The realism of the Franco-Burgundian culture of the fifteenth century is, then, narrow and medieval. It has no new attitudes which might reshape the world of earthly realities and it is hardly aware that the medieval categories are losing their power. It hardly notices what decisive changes are taking place in the structure of life; and in breadth of vision, refinement of language, and formative power it is far inferior to what the Italian late medieval and early humanist flowering had produced a full century earlier in Dante and Boccaccio. In it, however, a deeper penetration of the sensory and the creatural asserted itself, and this Christian heritage it preserved and passed on to the Renaissance. In Italy, Boccaccio and the early humanists no longer felt this creatural seriousness in the experience of life. In France itself, and north of the Alps in general, every kind of serious realism was in danger of being choked to death by the vines of allegory. But the spontaneous vigor of the sensory was stronger, and thus the creatural realism of the Middle Ages came to be passed on to the sixteenth century. It supplied the Renaissance with a strongly counterbalancing factor against the forces working toward a separation of styles which grew out of the humanists' emulation of antiquity.

11

THE WORLD IN PANTAGRUEL'S MOUTH

In the thirty-second chapter of his second book (which, however, was the first written and published) Rabelais tells how Pantagruel's army, during the campaign against the people of the Almyrodes (the "Salties"), is surprised on the road by a downpour; how Pantagruel orders them to press close together—he can see above the clouds that it is only a brief shower, and meanwhile he will provide them with shelter. Whereupon he puts out his tongue (*seulement à demi*), and covers them as a hen covers her chicks. Only the writer himself (*je, qui vous fais ces tant veritables contes*), who had already taken cover elsewhere, and now emerges from it, finds no room left under the tongue-roof:

> Doncques, le mieulx que je peuz, montay par dessus, et cheminay bien deux lieues sus sa langue tant que entray dedans sa bouche. Mais, ô Dieux et Deesses, que veiz je là? Jupiter me confonde de sa fouldre trisulque si j'en mens. Je y cheminoys comme l'on faict en Sophie à Constantinoble, et y veiz de grans rochiers comme les mons des Dannoys, je croys que c'estoient ses dentz, et de grands prez, de grandes forestz, de fortes et grosses villes, non moins grandes que Lyon ou Poictiers. Le premier que y trouvay, ce fut un homme qui plantoit des choulx. Dont tout esbahy luy demanday: "Mon amy, que fais tu icy?—Je plante, dist-il, des choulx.—Et à quoy ny comment, dis-je?—Ha, Monsieur, dist-il, chascun ne peut avoir les couillons aussi pesant q'un mortier, et ne pouvons estre tous riches. Je gaigne ainsi ma vie, et les porte vendre au marché en la cité qui est icy derriere.—Jesus, dis-je, il y a icy un nouveau monde?—Certes, dist-il, il n'est mie nouveau, mais l'on dist bien que hors d'icy y a une terre neufve où ilz ont et soleil et lune et tout plein de belles besoignes; mais cestuy cy est plus ancien.—Voire mais, dis-je, comment a nom ceste ville où tu portes vendre tes choulx?—Elle a, dist il, nom Aspharage, et sont christians, gens de bien, et vous feront grande chere." Bref, je deliberay d'y aller. Or, en mon chemin, je trouvay un compaignon qui tendoit aux pigeons, auquel je demanday:

"Mon amy, d'ont vous viennent ces pigeons icy?—Cyre, dist il, ils viennent de l'aultre monde." Lors je pensay que, quand Pantagruel basloit, les pigeons à pleines volées entroyent dedans sa gorge, pensans que feust un colombier. Puis entray en la ville, laquelle je trouvay belle, bien forte et en bel air; mais à l'entrée les portiers me demanderent mon bulletin, de quoy je fuz fort esbahy, et leur demanday: "Messieurs, y a il icy dangier de peste?—O, Seigneur, dirent ilz, l'on se meurt icy auprès tant que le charriot court par les rues.—Vray Dieu, dis je, et où?" A quoy me dirent que c'estoit en Laryngues et Pharyngues, qui sont deux grosses villes telles que Rouen et Nantes, riches et bien marchandes, et la cause de la peste a esté pour une puante et infecte exhalation qui est sortie des abysmes des puis n'a gueres, dont ilz sont mors plus de vingt et deux cens soixante mille et seize personnes despuis huict jours. Lors je pensé et calculé, et trouvé que c'estoit une puante halaine qui estoit venue de l'estomach de Pantagruel alors qu'il mangea tant d'aillade, comme nous avons dict dessus. De là partant, passay entre les rochiers, qui estoient ses dentz, et feis tant que je montay sus une, et là trouvay les plus beaux lieux du monde, beaux grands jeux de paulme, belles galeries, belles praries, force vignes et une infinité de cassines à la mode italicque, par les champs pleins de delices, et là demouray bien quatre moys, et ne feis oncques telle chere pour lors. Puis descendis par les dentz du derrière pour venir aux baulièvres; mais en passant je fuz destroussé des brigans par une grande forest que est vers la partie des aureilles. Puis trouvay une petite bourgade à la devallée, j'ay oublié son nom, où je feiz encore meilleure chere que jamais, et gaignay quelque peu d'argent pour vivre. Sçavez-vous comment? A dormir; car l'on loue les gens à journée pour dormir, et gaignent cinq et six solz par jour; mais ceulx qui ronflent bien fort gaignent bien sept solz et demy. Et contois aux senateurs comment on m'avoit destroussé par la valée, lesquelz me dirent que pour tout vray les gens de delà estoient mal vivans et brigans de nature, à quoy je cogneu que, ainsi comme nous avons les contrées de deçà et delà les montz, aussi ont ilz decà et delà les dentz; mais il fait beaucoup meilleur deçà, et y a meilleur air. Là commençay penser qu'il est bien vray ce que l'on dit que la moytié du monde ne sçait comment l'autre vit, veu que nul avoit encores escrit de ce pais là, auquel sont plus de xxv royaulmes habitez, sans les desers le un gros bras de mer, mais j'en ay composé un grand livre intitulé l'Histoire des Gorgias, car ainsi les ay-je nommez parce qu'ilz demourent en la gorge de mon maistre Pantagruel. Finablement vouluz retourner, et passant par sa barbe, me gettay sus ses epaulles, et de là me devallé en terre et tumbé devant luy. Quand il me apperceut, il me demanda: "D'ont viens tu, Alcofrybas?—Je luy responds: De vostre gorge, Monsieur.—Et depuis quand y es tu, dist il?—Despuis, dis je, que vous alliez contre les Almyrodes. —Il y a, dist il, plus de six moys. Et de quoy vivois tu? Que beuvoys tu?—Je responds: Seigneur, de mesme vous, et des plus frians morceaulx qui passoient par vostre gorge j'en prenois le barraige.—Voire mais, dist il, où chioys tu?—En vostre gorge, Monsieur, dis-je.—Ha, ha, tu es gentil compaignon, dist il. Nous avons, avecques l'ayde de Dieu, conquesté tout le pays des Dipsodes; je te donne la chatellenie de Salmigondin.—Grand mercy, dis je, Monsieur. Vous me faictes du bien plus que n'ay deservy envers vous."

(Then, as well as I could, I got upon it, and went along full two leagues upon his tongue, and so long marched, that at last I came into his mouth. But, oh gods and goddesses, what did I see there! Jupiter confound me with his trisulk lightning if I lie! I walked there as they do in Sophie, at Constantinople, and saw there great rocks, like the mountains in Denmark—I believe that those were his teeth. I saw also fair meadows, large forests, great and strong cities, not a jot less than Lyons or Poictiers. The first person I met there was a man planting cabbages, whereat being very much amazed, I asked him, My friend, what dost thou make here? I plant cabbages, said he. But how, and wherewith, said I? Ha, Sir, said he, everyone cannot have his ballocks as heavy as a mortar, neither can we be all rich. Thus do I get my living, and carry them to the market to sell in the city which is here behind. Jesus! said I, is there here a new world? Sure, said he, it is never a jot new, but it is commonly reported, that, without this, there is a new earth, whereof the inhabitants enjoy the light of a sun and moon, and that it is full of very good commodities; but yet this is more ancient than that. Yea, but, said I, what is the name of that city, whither thou carriest thy cabbages to sell? It is called Aspharage, said he, and all the in-dwellers are Christians, very honest men, and will make you good cheer. To be brief, I resolved to go thither. Now, in my way, I met with a fellow that was lying in wait to catch pigeons, of whom I asked, My friend, from whence come these pigeons? Sir, said he, they come from the other world. Then I thought, that, when Pantagruel yawned, the pigeons went into his mouth in whole flocks, thinking that it had been a pigeon-house.

Then I went into the city, which I found fair, very strong, and seated in a good air; but at my entry the guard demanded of me my pass or ticket. Whereat I was much astonished, and asked them, My masters, is there any danger of the plague here? O Lord, said they, they die hard by here so fast, that the cart runs about the streets. Good God, said I, and where? Whereunto they answered, that it was in Larynx and Pharynx, which are two great cities, such as Rouen and Nantes, rich and of great trading. And the cause of the plague was by a stinking and infectious exhalation, which lately vapoured out of the depths of the wells, whereof there have died above two and twenty hundred and threescore thousand and sixteen persons within this seven-night. Then I considered, calculated, and found, that it was an unsavoury breathing, which came out of Pantagruel's stomach, when he did eat so much garlic, as we have aforesaid.

Parting from thence, I passed amongst the rocks, which were his teeth, and never left walking, till I got up on one of them; and there I found the pleasantest places in the world, great large tennis courts, fair galleries, sweet meadows, store of vines, and an infinite number of banqueting summer outhouses in the fields, after the Italian fashion, full of pleasure and delight, where I stayed full four months, and never made better cheer in my life as then. After that I went down by the hinder teeth to come to the chaps. But in the way I was robbed by thieves in a great forest, that is in the territory towards the ears. Then, going on downward, I fell upon a pretty petty village—truly I have forgot the name of it—where I was yet merrier than ever, and got some certain money to live by. Can you tell how? By sleeping. For there they hire men by the day to sleep, and they get by it fivepence or sixpence a day, but they that can snore hard get at least ninepence. How I had been robbed in the valley, I informed the senators, who told me, that, in very truth, the people of that side were bad livers, and naturally thievish, whereby I perceived well, that as we have with us countries be-hither and beyond the mountains, so have they there countries be-hither and beyond the teeth. But it is far better living on this side, and the air is purer. There I began to think, that it is very true, which is commonly said, that one half of the world knoweth not how the other half liveth; seeing none before myself had ever written of that country, wherein are above five and twenty kingdoms inhabited, besides deserts, and a great arm of the sea. Concerning which, I have composed a great book intituled The History of the Gorgians, for so I have named them because they dwell in the gorge of my master Pantagruel.

At last I was willing to return, and, passing by his beard, I cast myself upon his shoulders, and from thence slid down to the ground, and fell before him. As soon as I was perceived by him, he asked me, Whence comest thou, Alcofrybas? I answered him, Out of your mouth, my lord! And how long hast thou been there? said he. Since the time, said I, that you went against the Almyrodes. That is more than six months ago, said he. And wherewith didst thou live? What didst thou drink? I answered, My lord, of the same that you did, and of the daintiest morsels that passed through your throat I took toll. Yea, but, said he, where didst thou shite? In your throat, my lord, said I. Ha, ha, thou art a merry fellow, said he. We have with the help of God conquered all the land of the Dipsodes; I will give thee the Lairdship of Salmigondin. Grammercy, my lord, said I, you gratify me beyond all that I have deserved of you.) After Urquhart's translation. *Gargantua and Pantagruel.* Translated by Sir Thomas Urquhart and Peter le Motteux. New York: E. P. Dutton & Co. 1929.

Rabelais did not himself invent the theme of this comic adventure. In the chapbook of the Giant Gargantua (I use a reprint of a copy preserved in Dresden, from W. Weigand's edition of Regis' translation of Rabelais, 3rd ed., Berlin, 1923, Vol. 2, pp. 398ff.: cf. also note 7 in Abel Lefranc's critical edition, 4, 330), we are told how the 2,943 armed men who were to strangle Gargantua in his sleep wandered into his open mouth, mistaking the teeth for great cliffs, and how later, when he quenched his thirst after sleeping, all but three of them were drowned, the three saving themselves in a hollow tooth. In a later passage of the chapbook, Gargantua gives fifty prisoners temporary quarters in a hollow tooth; they even find an indoor tennis court there, a *jeu de paume*, to keep them amused. (Rabelais uses the hollow tooth in another passage, book 1, chapter 38, where Gargantua swallows six pilgrims and a head of lettuce.) Aside from these French sources, Rabelais has in mind, in connection with our passage, an antique author whom he highly esteemed, Lucian, who in his *True History* (1, 30ff.) tells of a sea monster which swallows a ship with all its crew; in its maw they find woods, mountains, and lakes, in which live various half-animal creatures as well as two human beings, father and son, who had been swallowed twenty-seven years earlier after a shipwreck; they too plant cabbages and have built a shrine to Poseidon. Rabelais, in his way, has combined these two prototypes, taking from the chapbook the giant's mouth, which despite its immense dimensions, has not entirely lost the characteristics of a mouth, and placing within it Lucian's picture of a landscape and a society. Indeed, he goes even further than Lucian (twenty-five kingdoms with large cities, whereas in Lucian it is only a matter of some thousand fabulous beings). But he is at little pains to reconcile the two themes: the presumable size of a mouth so densely populated bears no relation to the speed of the return journey; still less the fact that, after Alcofrybas gets back, the giant notices him and speaks to him; and least of all does the information Alcofrybas gives concerning his diet and defecations during his stay inside the mouth correspond with the highly developed agricultural and domestic life which he found there—whether he has simply forgotten it or is deliberately not mentioning it. Apparently the conversation with the giant, which closes the scene, serves no purpose but that of giving a comical characterization of the kind-hearted Pantagruel, who shows a lively interest in the bodily welfare of his friend, particularly in his being supplied with plenty of good drink, and who good-humoredly rewards his undaunted admission concerning his defecations with the gift of a chatelleny—although our honest Alcofrybas had, so to speak, found himself a cushy job for the duration of the war. The way in which the recipient of the gift expresses his thanks ("I have done nothing to deserve it") is in this case no mere form of speech but suits the circumstances perfectly.

Despite his recollections of literary prototypes, Rabelais has gone entirely his own way in constructing the world inside the giant's mouth. Alcofrybas finds no fabulous half-animal beings, no little handful of men painfully adapting themselves to their surroundings, but a fully developed society and economy, in which everything goes on just as it does at home in France. At first he is astonished that human beings live there at all; yet what surprises him most is that things are not somehow strange and different, but just like things in the world he knows. This begins with his very first encounter: he is not as amazed to find a man here (he has already seen the cities from a distance) as he is to find him quietly planting cabbages, as if they were both in Touraine. So he asks him, *tout esbahy*: Friend, what are you doing here? and receives a complacent, tongue-in-cheek answer such as he might well have got from a Tourangeau peasant, of the type which many of Rabelais' characters often represent themselves to be: *Je plante, dist-il, des choulx.*

It reminds me of a small boy's remark which I once overheard; he was using the telephone for the first time, so that his grandmother, who lived in another town, could hear his voice; asked, "And what are you doing, lad?" he answered, proudly and factually, "I'm telephoning." Here the case is slightly different: the peasant is not only naive and limited, he also has the rather reserved humor which is extremely French and particularly characteristic of Rabelais. He has a very good notion that the stranger is from that other world of which he has heard rumors; but he pretends to notice nothing, and answers the second question, which is also purely an exclamation of astonishment (approximately: But why? How come?), as naively as he had the first, with a juicy peasant figure of speech which signifies that he is not rich; he earns his living from his cabbages, which he sells in the neighboring city. Now at last the visitor begins to grasp the situation: Jesus, he exclaims, this is an entirely new world! No, it is not new, says the peasant, but people say there's a new land out there where they have a sun and moon and all sorts of fine things; but this land here is older.

The fellow talks of the "new world" as people in Touraine or anywhere in Western or Central Europe might have spoken of the then newly discovered lands, of America or India; but he is cunning enough to suspect that the stranger is an inhabitant of that other world, for he reassures him as to the people in the city: They are good Christians and will not treat you badly; assuming, and in this case he is right, that the designation "good Christians" will serve as a reassuring guarantee for the stranger too. In short, this inhabitant of the outskirts of Aspharage behaves just as his congener in Touraine would have done. So things go on, frequently interrupted by grotesque explanations, which likewise maintain no sort of proportion; for when Pantagruel opens his mouth, which contains so many kingdoms and cities, the dimensions of the opening ought not to be easily confused with a pigeon-house. But the theme "everything just as at home" persists unchanged. At the city gate, Alcofrybas is asked for his health certificate, because the plague is rampant in the great cities of the land;

this is a reference to the pestilence which raged in the cities of northern France during the years 1532 and 1533 (cf. A. Lefranc's Introduction to his critical edition, p. xxxi). The fine mountain landscape of the teeth is a picture of the Western European agricultural countryside, and the country houses are built in the Italian style, which was beginning to become the fashion in France too at that period. In the village where Alcofrybas passes the last days of his stay in Pantagruel's mouth, the situation, except for the grotesque method of earning money by sleeping, at five to six sous per diem, with an extra bonus for strong snorers (a recollection of the traditional Land of Cockaigne), is thoroughly European: When the senators condole with him for having been robbed on his way through the mountain forest, they give him to understand that the people "over yonder" are uncultured barbarians who do not know how to live. And he infers that in Pantagruel's maw there are countries on this side and on the other side of the teeth, as at home there are countries on this side and the other side of the mountains.

Whereas Lucian produces what is in all essentials a fantasy of travel and adventure, and the chapbook puts all the emphasis on the grotesqueness of enlarged dimensions, Rabelais maintains a constant interplay of different locales, different themes, and different levels of style. While Alcofrybas, the Abstractor of Quintessences, is making his journey of discovery through Pantagruel's mouth, Pantagruel and his army continue the war against the Almyrodes and Dipsodes; and in the journey of discovery itself, at least three different categories of experience alternate and intermingle. The frame is provided by the grotesque theme of gigantic dimensions, which is never for a moment left out of sight and is constantly recalled by ever new and absurd comic conceits; by the pigeons that fly into the giant's mouth when he yawns, by the explanation of the plague as the result of Pantagruel's eating garlic and the poisonous vapors which rise from his stomach afterward, by the transformation of the teeth into a mountain landscape, by the manner of the return journey, and by the closing conversation. Meanwhile there is developed an entirely different, entirely new, and, at the period, extremely current theme—the theme of the discovery of a new world, with all the astonishment, the widening horizons and change in the world picture, which follow upon such a discovery.

This is one of the great motifs of the Renaissance and of the two following centuries, one of the themes which served as levers toward political, religious, economic, and philosophical revolution. It constantly reappears—whether writers place an action in that still new and half-unknown world, because there they can construct a purer and more primitive milieu than the European, a device which provides an effective and at the same time a piquantly surreptitious method of criticizing things at home; or whether they introduce an inhabitant of those strange lands into the European world and let their criticism of the established order in Europe arise out of his naive astonishment and his general reaction to what he sees. In either case the theme has a revolutionary force which shakes the established order, sets it in a broader context, and thus makes it a relative thing. In our passage, Rabelais only lets the theme begin to sound, he does not develop it. Alcofrybas' astonishment when he sees the first inhabitant of the mouth belongs in this category of experiences, as does, above all, the reflection he makes at the end of his journey—Then it became clear to me how right people are when they say: One half the world does not know how the other half lives. Rabelais immediately buries the theme under grotesque jokes, so that in the episode as a whole it is not dominant. But we must not forget that Rabelais first called the country of his giants Utopia, a name which he borrowed from Thomas More's book, which had appeared sixteen years earlier, and that More—to whom, of all his contemporaries, Rabelais perhaps owed the most—was one of the first to use the theme of a distant country, in the reformistic manner described above, as an example. It is not only the name: the country of Gargantua and Pantagruel, with its political, religious, and educational forms, is not only called, it is Utopia; a distant, still hardly discovered land, lying, like More's Utopia, somewhere in the East, although to be sure it sometimes seems that it can be found in the heart of France. We shall return to this.

So much for the second of the themes contained in our passage; it cannot develop freely there, partly because the grotesque joking of the first theme perpetually thwarts it, partly because it is immediately intercepted and paralyzed by the third; the theme *tout comme chez nous*. The most astonishing and most absurd thing about this Gorgiasian world is precisely that it is not entirely different from ours but on the contrary resembles it in the minutest detail; it is superior to ours in that it knows of our world whereas we know nothing of it, but otherwise it is exactly like it. Thus Rabelais gives himself the opportunity of exchanging the roles—that is, of making the cabbage-planting peasant appear as a native European who receives the stranger from the other world with European naïveté; above all, he gives himself the possibility of developing a realistic scene of everyday life. This is the third theme, which is entirely incompatible with the two others (the grotesque farcicality of the giants, and the discovery of a new world) and which stands in deliberately absurd contrast to them. The whole machinery of huge dimensions and of the daring voyage of discovery seems, then, to have been set in motion only to bring us a peasant of Touraine engaged in planting cabbages.

Just as the locales and the themes change, so too do the styles. The predominant style is that which corresponds to the grotesque theme which serves as frame—the grotesque-comic and popular style, and in its most energetic form, in which the most forceful expressions appear. Beside it, and mingled with it, there is matter-of-fact narrative, philosophical ideas flash out, and amid all the grotesque machinery rises the terrible creatural picture of the plague, when the dead are taken from the city by cartloads. This sort of mixture of styles was not invented by Rabelais. He of course adapted it to his temperament and his purposes, but, paradoxically, it stems from late medieval preaching, in which the Christian tradition exaggerated the mixture of styles to the utmost (cf. p. 161f). These sermons are at once popular in the crudest way, creaturally realistic, and learned and edifying in their figural Biblical interpretation. From the spirit of late medieval preaching, and above all from the atmosphere which surrounded the popular (in both the good and bad senses) mendicant orders, the humanists adopted this mixture of styles, especially for their anti-ecclesiastical, polemical, and satirical writings. From the same spring, Rabelais, who had been a Franciscan in his youth, drew it "more pure" than anyone else. He had studied the mendicant form of life and form of expression at the source and had made it his own in his peculiar way; he can no longer do without it; much as he hated the mendicant orders, their flavorful and earthy style, graphic to the point of ludicrousness, was exactly suited to his temperament and his purpose, and no one ever got so much out of it as he. This filiation was pointed out, for the benefit of those to whom it had not earlier been obvious, by E. Gilson in his fine essay *Rabelais franciscain* (cf. p. 170); we shall later return to this question of style too.

The passage which we have been discussing is a comparatively simple one. The interplay of locales, themes, and stylistic levels in it is comparatively easy to observe, and to analyze it requires no circumstantial investigations. Other passages are far more complex—those, for example, in which Rabelais gives full vent to his erudition, his countless allusions to contemporary events and persons, and his hurricane word-formations. Our analysis has permitted us, with little effort, to recognize an essential principle of his manner of seeing and comprehending the world: the principle of the promiscuous intermingling of the categories of event, experience, and knowledge, as well as of dimensions and styles. Examples, both from the work as a whole and from sections of it, can be multiplied at will.

Abel Lefranc has shown that the events of book 1, especially the war against Picrochole, take place on the few square miles of the region which lies around La Devinière, an estate belonging to Rabelais' father's family; and even to one who does not or did not know this in detail, the place names and certain homely local happenings indicate a provincial and circumscribed setting. At the same time armies of hundreds of thousands appear, and giants, in whose hair cannon balls stick like lice, take part in the battles; arms and victuals are enumerated in quantities which a great kingdom could not have amassed in those days; the number of soldiers alone who enter the vineyard of the monastery of Seuillé and are there cut down by Frère Jean is given as 13,622, women and small children not included. The theme of gigantic dimensions serves Rabelais for perspectivistic effects of contrast, which upset the reader's balance in an insidiously humorous way; he is perpetually flung back and forth between provincially piquant and homely forms of existence, gigantic and grotesquely extra-normal events, and Utopian-humanitarian ideas; he is never permitted to come to rest on a familiar level of events. The forcefully realistic or obscene elements, too, are made to seethe like an intellectual whirlpool by the tempo of the presentation; and the ceaseless succession of allusions, the storms of laughter which such passages evoke, break through all the ideas of order and decency which prevailed at the time. If one reads such a short text as, for example, Frère Jean des Entommeures' exhortation in book 1, chapter 42, one finds two robust jokes in it. The first is in regard to a charm which protects against heavy artillery: Frère Jean does not merely say that he does not believe in it, he effortlessly changes the level of observation, places himself on that of the church, which enforces the belief as a condition of divine aid, and, from that point of view, says: the charm will not help me because I do not believe a word of it. The second joke is in regard to the effect of a monk's frock. Frère Jean begins with the threat that he will drape his frock over any man who shows himself a coward. Naturally one's first thought is that this is intended as a punishment and a disgrace; any man so clad would be forthwith dispossessed of the qualities of a proper man. But no, in a twinkling he changes the viewpoint: the frock is medicine for unmanly men; they become men as soon as they have it on; by this he means that the deprivation enforced by vows and the monastic life particularly increases the virile capacities both of courage and sexual potency; and he concludes his exhortation with the anecdote of the Sieur de Meurle's "feeble-reined" greyhound, which was wrapped in a monk's frock; from that moment no fox or hare escaped him and he served all the bitches in the neighborhood, though previously he had been among the *frigidis et maleficiatis* (this is the title of a decretal). Or again, read the long-winded account of the things which serve for wiping the posterior, to which the young Gargantua treats us in book 1, chapter 13: what a wealth of improvisation! We find poems and syllogisms, medicine, zoology, and botany, contemporary satire and costume lore. Finally the delight which the intestines share with the whole body when the act referred to is performed with the neck of a young, live, well-downed gosling, is connected with the bliss of the heroes and demi-gods in the Elysian Fields, and Grandgousier compares the wit which his son had displayed on the occasion with that of the young Alexander in Plutarch's well-known anecdote, which tells how he alone recognized the cause of a horse's wildness, namely its fear of its own shadow.

Let us consider a few selected passages from the later books. In book 3, chapter 31, the physician Rondibilis, consulted by Panurge in connection with his plan of marrying, sets forth the methods of allaying the all-too-powerful sex urge: first, immoderate wine-drinking; second, certain medicaments; third, steady physical labor; fourth, avid study. Each of these four methods is expounded for several pages, with a superabundance of medical and humanistic erudition through which enumerations, quotations, and anecdotes shower like rain. Fifthly, Rondibilis goes on, the sexual act itself. . . . Stop, says Panurge, that's what I was waiting for, that's the method for me, I leave the others to anyone who wants to use them. Yes, says Frère Jean, who has been listening, Brother Scyllino, Prior of Saint Victor's near Marseille, had a name for that method, he called it mortifying the flesh. . . . The whole thing is a mad farce, but Rabelais has filled it with his perpetual flow of changing ideas, his unfailing *trouvailles*, which purposely jumble together all the categories of style and knowledge.

It is the same with the grotesque defense of Judge Bridoye (chapters

39-42 of the same book), who carefully prepared his cases, postponed them again and again, and then decided them by a cast of the dice and who nevertheless for forty years pronounced nothing but wise and just judgments. In his speech, senile drivel is mixed with subtly ironic wisdom, the most wonderful anecdotes are told, the whole of legal terminology is poured out upon the reader in a grotesque cascade of words, every obvious or absurd opinion is supported by a welter of comical quotations from Roman Law and the glossarists; it is a fireworks display of wit, of juridical and human experience, of contemporary satire and contemporary manners and morals, an education in laughter, in rapid shifts between a multiplicity of viewpoints.

As a last example, let us take the scene on shipboard, when Panurge bargains with the sheepmonger Dindenault over a wether (book 4, chapters 6-8). This is perhaps the most effective scene between two characters in Rabelais. The owner of the flock of sheep, the merchant Dindenault from Saintonge, is a choleric and pompous person, but at the same time he is endowed with the crafty, idiomatic, and subtle wit which is natural to almost all of Rabelais' personages. At their very first encounter he has fooled the Eulenspiegel Panurge to the top of his bent; and, but for the intervention of the ship's captain and Pantagruel, they would have come to blows. Later, as they sit with the others drinking wine, apparently reconciled, Panurge again asks him to sell him one of his sheep. Then, for page after page, Dindenault cries up his wares. In the course of his speech, he reverts even more markedly to the insulting tone he had first taken with Panurge, whom, with a mixture of suspicion, impertinence, joviality, and condescension, he treats as a fool or a swindler wholly unworthy of such fine wares. Panurge, on the other hand, now remains calm and polite, merely repeating his request for a sheep. Finally, at the insistence of the bystanders, Dindenault names an exorbitant price. Panurge warns him that many a man has fared ill from trying to get rich too fast. Dindenault flies into a rage and begins cursing him. Very well, says Panurge . . . then counts out the money, chooses a fine fat wether, then, while Dindenault is still reviling him, suddenly throws the wether into the sea. The whole flock jump overboard after it. The despairing Dindenault tries in vain to hold them back. A powerful ram drags him overboard, and he drowns in the same posture in which Odysseus once fled from Polyphemus' cave. His shepherds and herdsmen are pulled overboard in the same fashion. Panurge picks up a long oar and pushes away those who are trying to swim back to the ship, meanwhile treating the drowning men to a splendid oration on the joys of eternity and the miseries of life in this world.

So the joke ends grimly, and even rather frighteningly, if one considers the intensity of the ever-cheerful Pantagruel's urge for vengeance. Yet it remains a joke, which Rabelais has, as usual, stuffed with the most various and grotesque erudition, this time on the subject of sheep—their wool, their hides, their intestines, their flesh, and all their other parts—and adorned, as usual, with mythology, medicine, and strange alchemical lore. Yet this time, the center of interest does not lie in the multifarious outpouring of the ideas which come to Dindenault in his praise of sheep, it lies in the copious portrait which he gives of his own character, and which accounts for the manner of his end. He is taken in and he perishes because he cannot adjust himself, cannot change himself, but instead, in his blind folly and vaingloriousness, runs straight forward, like Picrochole or the *écolier limousin*, his one-track mind incapable of registering his surroundings. It never occurs to him that Panurge may be sharper than himself, that he might sacrifice money for revenge. Thick-headedness, inability to adjust, one-track arrogance which blinds a man to the complexity of the real situation, are vices to Rabelais. This is the form of stupidity which he mocks and pursues.

Almost all the elements which are united in Rabelais' style are known from the later Middle Ages. The coarse jokes, the creatural concept of the human body, the lack of modesty and reserve in sexual matters, the mixture of such a realism with a satiric or didactic content, the immense fund of unwieldy and sometimes abstruse erudition, the employment of allegorical figures in the later books—all these and much else are to be found in the later Middle Ages. And one might be tempted to think that the only new thing in Rabelais is the degree to which he exaggerates them and the extraordinary way in which he mingles them. But this would be to miss the essence of the matter. The way in which these elements are exaggerated and intertwined produces an entirely new picture. Moreover, Rabelais' purpose, as is well known, is diametrically opposed to medieval ways of thinking: this gives even the individual elements a different meaning. Late medieval works are confined within a definite frame, socially, geographically, cosmologically, religiously, and ethically; they present but one aspect of things at a time; where they have to deal with a multiplicity of things and aspects, they attempt to force them into the definite frame of a general order. But Rabelais' entire effort is directed toward playing with things and with the multiplicity of their possible aspects; upon tempting the reader out of his customary and definite way of regarding things, by showing him phenomena in utter confusion; upon tempting him out into the great ocean of the world, in which he can swim freely, though it be at his own peril.

In my opinion, many critics miss the essential point when they make Rabelais' divorce from Christian dogma the decisive factor in interpreting him. True, he is no longer a believer, in the ecclesiastical sense; but he is very far from taking a stand upon some definite form of disbelief, like a rationalist of later times. Nor is it permissible to draw any too far-reaching conclusions from his satire on Christian subjects, for the Middle Ages already offer examples of this which are not essentially different from Rabelais' blasphemous joking. The revolutionary thing about his way of thinking is not his opposition to Christianity, but the freedom of vision, feeling, and thought which his perpetual playing with things produces, and which invites the reader to deal directly with the world and its wealth of phenomena. On one point, to be sure, Rabelais takes a stand, and it is a stand which is basically anti-Christian; for him, the man who follows his nature is good, and natural life, be it of men or things, is good: we should not even need the express confirmation of this conviction which he gives us in the constitution of his Abbey of Thélème, for it speaks from every line of his work. Connected with this conviction is the fact that his creatural treatment of mankind no longer has for its keynote, as does the corresponding realism of the declining Middle Ages, the wretchedness and perishableness of the body and of earthly things in general; in Rabelais, creatural realism has acquired a new meaning, diametrically opposed to medieval creatural realism—that of the vitalistic-dynamic triumph of the physical body and its functions. In Rabelais, there is no longer any Original Sin or any Last Judgment, and thus no metaphysical fear of death. As a part of nature, man rejoices in his breathing life, his bodily functions, and his intellectual powers, and, like nature's other creatures, he suffers natural dissolution. The breathing life of men and nature calls forth all Rabelais' love, his thirst for knowledge and his power of verbal representation. It makes him a poet—for he is a poet, and indeed a lyric poet, even though he lacks sentiment. It is triumphant earthly life which calls forth his realistic and super-realistic mimesis. And that is completely anti-Christian, just as it is so opposed to the range of ideas which the creatural realism of the later Middle Ages arouses in us, that it is precisely in the medieval traits of his style that his alienation from the Middle Ages is most strikingly displayed; their purpose and function have changed completely.

This rise of man to wholeness in the natural world, this triumph of the animal and the creatural, offers us the opportunity to remark in more detail how ambiguous and therefore subject to misconstruction is the word individualism, which is often, and certainly not unjustifiably, used in connection with the Renaissance. There is no doubt that, in Rabelais' view of the world, in which all possibilities are open, which plays with every aspect, man is freer in his thinking, in realizing his instincts and his wishes, than he was earlier. But is he therefore more individualistic? It is not easy to say. At least he is less closely confined to his own idiosyncrasy, he is more protean, more inclined to slip into someone else's shoes; and his general, super-individual traits, especially his animal and instinctive traits, are greatly emphasized. Rabelais has created very strongly marked and unmistakable characters, but he is not always inclined to keep them unmistakable; they begin to change, and suddenly another personage peers out of them, as the situation or the author's whim demands. What a change in Pantagruel and Panurge during the course of the work! And even at the given moment, Rabelais is not much concerned with the unity of a character, when he mingles complacent cunning, wit, and humanism, with an elementally pitiless cruelty which is perpetually flickering in the background. If we compare the grotesque underworld of book 2, chapter 30 (in which he turns his personages' earthly situations and characters topsy-turvey), with Dante's beyond, we see how summarily Rabelais deals with human individuality; he delights in tumbling it over. Actually the Christian unity of the cosmos, and the figural preservation of the earthly personality in the divine judgment, led to a very strong concept of the indestructible permanence of the individual (most strongly evident in Dante, but also to be seen elsewhere). And this was first endangered when Christian unity and Christian immortality no longer dominated the European concept of the universe.

The description of the underworld referred to above is also inspired by a dialogue of Lucian's (*Menippus seu Nekyomantia*), but Rabelais carries the joke much further—indeed, far beyond the limits of discretion and taste. His humanistic relation to antique literature is shown in his remarkable knowledge of the authors who furnish him with themes, quotations, anecdotes, examples, and comparisons; in his thought upon political, philosophical, and educational questions, which, like that of the other humanists, is under the influence of antique ideas; and particularly in his view of man, freed as it is from the Christian and stratified-social frame of reference which characterized the Middle Ages. Yet his indebtedness to antiquity does not imprison him within the confines of antique concepts; to him, antiquity means liberation and a broadening of horizons, not in any sense a new limitation or servitude; nothing is more foreign to him than the antique separation of styles, which in Italy even in his own time, and soon after in France, led to purism and "Classicism." In Rabelais there is no aesthetic standard; everything goes with everything. Ordinary reality is set within the most improbable fantasy, the coarsest jokes are filled with erudition, moral and philosophical enlightenment flows out of obscene expressions and stories. All this is far more characteristic of the later Middle Ages than of antiquity—at least in antiquity "laughing truth-telling" had never known such a wide swing of the pendulum to either side; for that, the late medieval mixture of styles was necessary. Yet Rabelais' style is not merely the Middle Ages monstrously exaggerated. When, like a late medieval preacher, he mingles a formless plethora of erudition with coarse vulgarity, the erudition no longer has the function of supporting some doctrine of dogma or ethics by authority—instead, it furthers the grotesque game which either makes the momentary subject matter seem ridiculous and nonsensical, or at least raises the question of how seriously Rabelais means what he is saying. His popular appeal too is different from that of the Middle Ages. Undoubtedly Rabelais appeals to the people, because an uneducated public—so far as it understands his language—can always be vastly amused by his stories. But those to whom his work is really addressed are members of an intellectual elite, not the people. The preachers addressed the people; their vivid sermons were intended for direct delivery. Rabelais' work was meant to be printed, in other words to be read. That, in the sixteenth century, still meant that it was addressed to a very small minority; and even in that small minority, he is not addressing the same stratum as that for which the chapbooks were intended.

Rabelais himself expressed his opinion on the level of style of his work, and in doing so he cited not a medieval but an antique example, namely Socrates. The text is one of the finest and ripest in his work, the Prologue to *Gargantua*, that is, to the first book, which, however, as we mentioned before, was not written and published until after the second. *Beuveurs tres illustres, et vous, Verolez très précieux—car à vous, non a aultres, sont dediez mes escriptz*—thus begins the celebrated text, which, in its polyphonic richness, in its announcement of the various themes of the work, can be compared to a musical overture. Few if any authors ever before addressed their readers in this fashion, and the Prologue becomes even more of a prodigy through the sudden appearance of a subject, which, after such a beginning, is the last thing one expects: *Alcibiades ou dialoge de Platon intitulé Le Bancquet, louant son precepteur Socrates, sans controverse prince des philosophes, entre aultres parolles le dict estre semblable es Silenes.* . . . For the platonizing mystics of the Renaissance, for the *libertins spirituels* in Italy, Germany, and France, Plato's *Symposium* was almost a sacred text; and it is something from the *Symposium* that he has a mind to tell the "illustrious drinkers and thrice-precious pockified blades," as Urquhart drolly translates it. With this very sentence he sets the tone, that of the most prodigious and unrestrained mixture of genres. There immediately follows an insolent and grotesque paraphrase of the passage in which Alcibiades compares Socrates with the figures of Silenus inside which there are little images of the gods; for, like the Sileni, he is outwardly repulsive, ridiculous, boorish, poor, awkward, a grotesque figure and a mere vulgar buffoon (this part of the comparison, which, in Plato, Alcibiades only briefly suggests, Rabelais sets forth at length); but within him there were the most wonderful treasures: superhuman insight, amazing virtue, unconquerable courage, invariable content, perfect firmness, incredible scorn for all those things for which men lie awake and run and bestir themselves and fight and travel. And what—Rabelais in effect goes on—did I mean to accomplish by this Prologue? That you, when you read all the pleasant titles of my writings (here follows a parade of grotesque book titles), will not suppose that there is nothing in them but jests and stuff for laughter and mockery. You must not so quickly draw conclusions from mere outward appearances. The habit does not make the monk. You must open the book and carefully consider what is in it; you will see that the contents are worth far more than the container promised, that the subjects are nowhere near so foolish as the title suggests. And even if, in the literal sense of the contents, you still find enough stuff for laughter of the sort that the title promises, you must not be satisfied with only that: you must probe deeper. Have you ever seen a dog that has found a marrow bone? Then you must have observed how devoutly he guards it, how fervently he seizes it, how prudently he approaches it, with what affection he breaks it open, how diligently he sucks it.

Why does he do all this, what does he expect as his reward for so much trouble? Only a little marrow. But indeed that little is the most precious and perfect nourishment. Like him, you must have a keen nose to smell these goodly, well-fattened books (*ces beaux livres de haulte gresse*), to perceive and value their contents; then, by sedulous reading and frequent meditation, you must break the bone and suck the marrow, which contains the substance—or the things which I intend by my Pythagorean symbols—in the sure hope that by so reading you will win intelligence and courage; for you will find in it a far finer taste and a more abstruse teaching, which will reveal deep secrets and terrible mysteries to you touching both our religion and our political and economic life.

In the closing sentences of the Prologue, to be sure, he turns all profound interpretation into comedy again; but there can be no doubt that, with his example of Socrates, his comparison of the reader to the dog who breaks open the bone, and his designating his work as *livres de haulte gresse,* he meant to indicate a purpose which lay close to his heart. The comparison of Socrates to the figures of Silenus (to which Xenophon also refers) appears to have made a great impression on the Renaissance (Erasmus includes it in his *Adagia,* and this is perhaps Rabelais' direct source). It offers a concept of Socrates' personality and style which seems to give the authority of the most impressive figure among the Greek philosophers to the mixture of genres which was a legacy of the Middle Ages. Montaigne too produces Socrates as his star witness for the same point at the beginning of the twelfth essay of his third book; the tone of the passage is quite different from Rabelais', but the subject under discussion is the same—the mixture of styles:

> Socrates faict mouvoir son ame d'un mouvement naturel et commun. Ainsi dict un païsan, ainsi dict une femme. Il n'a jamais en la bouche que cochers, menuisiers, savetiers et maçons. Ce sont inductions et similitudes tirées des plus vulgaires et cogneues actions des hommes: chacun l'entend. Sous une si vile forme nous n'eussions jamais choisi la noblesse et splendeur de ses conceptions admirables. . . .

> (Socrates makes his mind move with a natural and familiar motion. A peasant says this, a woman says that. He never speaks but of charioteers, joiners, cobblers and masons. His inductions and similes are drawn from the most common and best-known activi-

ties of men; everybody understands him. Under so humble a form we should never have recognized the nobility and splendour of his admirable ideas. . . .) Translated by E. J. Trechmann, Oxford University Press, 1927.

To what extent Montaigne or even Rabelais were justified in calling Socrates to witness when they declared their liking for a strong and popular style, may here be left out of consideration. It is enough for us that a "Socratic" style meant to them something free and untrammeled, something close to ordinary life, and indeed, for Rabelais, something close to buffoonery (*ridicule en son maintien, le nez pointu, le reguard d'un taureau, le visaige d'un fol . . . tousjours riant, tousjours beuvant d'autant à un chascun, tousjours se guabelant. . . .*), in which at the same time divine wisdom and perfect virtue are concealed. It is as much a style of life as a literary style; it is, as in Socrates (and in Montaigne too), the expression of the man. As a level of style, this mixture was particularly suitable for Rabelais. First, on purely practical grounds, it permitted him to touch upon things that shocked the reactionary authorities of his time, to display them in a twilight between jest and earnest, which, in case of need, made it easier for him to avoid full responsibility. Secondly, it was thoroughly consonant with his temperament—out of which, despite the earlier tradition, which was present in his mind, it arose as an absolutely characteristic phenomenon. And above all, it precisely served his purpose—namely, a fruitful irony which confuses the customary aspects and proportions of things, which makes the real appear in the super-real, wisdom in folly, rebellion in a cheerful and flavorful acceptance of life; which, through the play of possibilities, casts a dawning light on the possibility of freedom. I consider it a mistake to probe Rabelais' hidden meaning—that is, the marrow of the bone—for some definite and clearly outlined doctrine; the thing which lies concealed in his work, yet which is conveyed in a thousand ways, is an intellectual attitude, which he himself calls Pantagruelism; a grasp of life which comprehends the spiritual and the sensual simultaneously, which allows none of life's possibilities to escape. To describe it more in detail is not a wise undertaking—for one would immediately find oneself forced into competition with Rabelais. He himself is constantly describing it, and he can do it better than we can. I wish to add but one thing—namely, that the intoxication of his multifarious play never degenerates into formless ravings and thus into something inimical to life; wildly as the storm sometimes rages in his book, every line, every word, is strictly under control.

The riches of his style are not without their limits; the grotesque frame in itself excludes deep feeling and high tragedy; and it is not probable that he could have attained to them. Hence it might be doubted whether he has rightfully been given a place in our study, since what we are tracing is the combination of the everyday with tragic seriousness. Certainly, no one can deny him the former, since he constantly makes it appear in the setting of his super-real world, and, in describing it, becomes a poet. That, among many other things, he was a lyric poet, a polyphonic poet of realistic situations, has often been remarked and numerous passages have been quoted to demonstrate it—for example, the wonderful sentence at the end of book 1, chapter 4, which describes the dance on the lawn.

We shall not deny ourselves the pleasure of quoting at least one example of his lyrico-everyday polyphony, namely the poem of the sheep, which he slips into the brief moment between the bargaining scene and the unexpected throwing of the ram into the sea, while Dindenault, stupid and unsuspecting, is shamelessly belaboring Panurge with broad witticisms (end of book 4, chapter 7):

> Panurge, ayant payé le marchant, choisit de tout le troupeau un beau et grand mouton, et l'emportoit cryant et bellant, oyans tous les aultres et ensemblement bellans et regardans quelle part on menoit leur compaignon.
>
> (Panurge, having paid the merchant, chose out of all the flock a fine topping ram; and as he was hauling it along, crying out and bleating, all the rest, hearing and bleating in concert, stared to see whither their brother ram should be carried.) After Motteux's translation.

The short sentence, with its many participles, is a picture and a poem. Then tone and theme change:

> Ce pendant le marchant disoit à ses moutonniers: "O qu'il a bien sceu choisir, le challant! Il se y entend, le paillard! Vrayement, le bon vrayement, je le reservoys pour le seigneur de Cancale, comme bien congnoissant son naturel. Car, de sa nature, il est tout joyeulx et esbaudy quand il tient une espaule de mouton en main bien seante et advenente, comme une raquette gauschiere, et, avecques un cousteau bien tranchant, Dieu sçait comment il s'en escrime!"

(Meanwhile the merchant was saying to his shepherds: Ah! how well the knave could choose him out a ram; the whoreson has skill in cattle. Truly, aye really and truly, I reserved that very one for the Lord of Cancale, well knowing his disposition: for he is by nature overjoyed and all agog when he holds a good-sized handsome shoulder of mutton, like a left-handed racket, in one hand, with a good sharp carver in the other; God wot how he fences with it then!)

This presentation of the Sieur de Cancale's character provides an entirely different but no less striking picture, to the highest degree concrete and amusing, and at the same time fitting in perfectly, because the broad description of someone unknown to the entire audience, and of his relations with the speaker, clearly indicates Dindenault's crude and at the same time witty bumptiousness. Then the ram is thrown into the sea, and immediately the lyrical theme *criant et bellant* is heard again (beginning of chapter 8):

Soubdain, je ne sçay comment, le cas feut subit, je ne eus loisir le consyderer, Panurge, sans aultre chose dire, jette en pleine mer son mouton criant et bellant. Tous les aultres moutons, crians et bellans en pareille intonation, commencerent soy jecter et saulter en mer après, à la file. La foulle estoit à qui premier y saulteroit après leur compaignon. Possible n'estoit les en garder,

(On a sudden, you would wonder how the thing was so soon done; for my part I cannot tell you, for I had not leisure to mind it; Panurge, without any further tittle-tattle, throws you his ram overboard into the middle of the sea, crying and bleating. Upon this all the other sheep in the ship, crying and bleating in the same tone, made all the haste they could to leap and plunge into the sea after him, one behind t'other, and great was the throng who should leap in first after their leader. It was impossible to hinder them,)

And now a sudden excursion into grotesque erudition:

comme vous scavez estre du mouton le naturel, tous jours suyvre le premier, quelque part qu'il aille. Aussi le dict Aristoteles, lib. IX, de Histo. animal., estre le plus sot et inepte animant du monde.

(for you know that it is the nature of sheep always to follow the first, wheresoever it goes; which makes Aristotle, lib. 9 De

Hist. Animal., mark them for the most silly and foolish animals in the world.)

So much for the everyday. But the seriousness lies in the joy of discovery—pregnant with all possibilities, ready to try every experiment, whether in the realm of reality or super-reality—which was characteristic of his time, the first half of the century of the Renaissance, and which no one has so well translated into terms of the senses as Rabelais with the language which he created for his book. That is why it is possible to call his mixture of styles, his Socratic buffoonery, a high style. He himself found a charming phrase for the high style of his book, which is itself an example of that style. It is taken from the art of fattening stock, we have already quoted it above: *ces beaux livres de haulte gresse.*

12

L'HUMAINE CONDITION

Les autres forment l'homme: je le recite; et en représente un particulier bien mal formé, et lequel si j'avoy à façonner de nouveau, je ferois vrayment bien autre qu'il n'est. Meshuy, c'est fait. Or, les traits de ma peinture ne fourvoyent point, quoiqu'ils se changent et diversifient. Le monde n'est qu'une branloire perenne. Toutes choses y branlent sans cesse: la terre, les rochers du Caucase, les pyramides d'Aegypte, et du branle public et du leur. La constance mesme n'est autre chose qu'un branle plus languissant. Je ne puis asseurer mon object; il va trouble et chancelant, d'une yvresse naturelle. Je le prens en ce poinct, comme il est, en l'instant que je m'amuse à luy: je ne peinds pas l'estre, je peinds le passage; non un passage d'aage en autre, ou, comme dict le peuple, de sept en sept ans, mais de jour en jour, de minute en minute. Il faut accomoder mon histoire à l'heure; je pourray tantost changer, non de fortune seulement, mais aussi d'intention. C'est un contrerolle de divers et muables accidens, et d'imaginations irresolues, et, quand il y eschet, contraires; soit que je soys autre moy-mesmes, soit que je saisisse les subjects par autres circonstances et considérations. Tant y a que je me contredis bien à l'adventure, mais la verité, comme disoit Demades, je ne la contredis point. Si mon ame pouvoit prendre pied, je ne m'essaierois pas, je me resoudrois; elle est tousjours en apprentissage et en espreuve.

Je propose une vie basse et sans lustre: c'est tout un; on attache aussi bien toute la philosophie morale à une vie populaire et privée, que à une vie de plus riche estoffe: chaque homme porte la forme entière de l'humaine condition. Les autheurs se communiquent au peuple par quelque marque particuliere et estrangiere; moy le premier par mon estre universel, comme Michel de Montaigne, non comme grammairien, ou poete, ou jurisconsulte. Si le monde se plaint de quoy je parle trop de moy, je me plains de quoy il ne pense seulement pas à soy. Mais est-ce raison que, si particulier en usage, je pretende me rendre public en cognoissance? est-il aussi raison que je produise au monde, où la façon et l'art ont tant de credit et de commandement, des effets de nature et crus et simples, et d'une nature encore bien foiblette? est-ce pas faire une muraille sans pierre, ou chose semblable, que de bastir des livres sans science et sans art? Les fantasies de la musique sont conduictes par art, les miennes par sort. Au moins j'ay cecy selon la discipline, que jamais homme ne traicta subject qu'il entendist ne congneust mieux que je fay celuy que j'ay entrepris, et qu'en celuy-là je suis le plus sçavant homme qui vive; secondement, que jamais aucun ne penetra en sa matiere plus avant, ni en esplucha plus particulierement les membres et suites, et n'arriva plus exactement et plus plainement à la fin qu'il s'estoit proposé à sa besoingne. Pour la parfaire, je n'ay besoing d'y apporter que la fidelité: celle-là y est, la plus sincere et pure qui se trouve. Je dis vrai, non pas tout mon saoul, mais autant que je l'ose dire; et l'ose un peu plus en vieillissant; car il semble que la coustume concede à cet aage plus de liberté de bavasser et d'indiscretion à parler de soy. Il ne peut advenir icy, ce que je veoy advenir souvent, que l'artizan et sa besoigne se contrarient. . . . Un personnage sçavant n'est pas sçavant partout; mais le suffisant est partout suffisant, et à ignorer mesme; icy, nous allons conformément, et tout d'un train, mon livre et moy. Ailleurs, on peut recommander et accuser l'ouvrage, à part de l'ouvrier; icy, non; qui touche l'un, touche l'autre.

(Others form man; I describe him, and portray a particular, very ill-made one, who, if I had to fashion him anew, should indeed be very different from what he is. But now it is done. Now the features of my painting do not err, although they change and vary. The world is but a perennial see-saw. All things in it are incessantly on the swing, the earth, the rocks of the Caucasus, the Egyptian pyramids, both with the common movement and their own particular movement. Even fixedness is nothing but a more sluggish motion. I cannot fix my object; it is befogged, and reels with a natural intoxication. I seize it at this point, as it is at the moment when I beguile myself with it. I do not portray the thing in itself. I portray the passage; not a passing from one age to another, or, as the people put it, from seven years to seven years, but from day to day, from minute to minute. I must adapt my history to the moment. I may presently change, not only by chance, but also by intention. It is a record of diverse and changeable events, of undecided, and, when the occasion arises, contradictory ideas; whether it be that I am another self, or that I grasp a subject in different circumstances and see it from a different point of view. So it may be that I contradict myself, but, as Demades said, the truth I never contradict. If my mind could find a firm footing, I should not speak tentatively, I should decide; it is always in a state of apprenticeship, and on trial.

I am holding up to view a humble and lustreless life; that is all one. Moral philosophy, in any degree, may apply to an ordinary and secluded life as well as to one of richer stuff; every man carries within him the entire form of the human constitution. Authors communicate themselves to the world by some special and extrinsic mark; I am the first to do so by my general being, as Michel de Montaigne, not as a grammarian or a poet or a lawyer. If the world finds fault with me for speaking too much of myself, I find fault with the world for not even thinking of itself. But is it reasonable that I, who am so retired in actual life, should aspire to make myself known to the public? And is it reasonable that I should show up to the world, where artifice and ceremony enjoy so much credit and authority, the crude and simple results of nature, and of a nature besides very feeble? Is it not like making a wall without stone or a similar material, thus to build a book without learning or art? The ideas of music are guided by art, mine by chance. This I have at least in conformity with rules, that no man ever treated of a subject that he knew and understood better than I do this that I have taken up; and that in this I am the most learned man alive. Secondly, that no man ever penetrated more deeply into his matter, nor more minutely analyzed its parts and consequences, nor more fully and exactly reached the goal he had made it his business to set up. To accomplish it I need only bring fidelity to it; and that is here, as pure and sincere as may be found. I speak the truth, not enough to satisfy myself, but as much as I dare to speak. And I become a little more daring as I grow older; for it would seem that custom allows this age more freedom to prate, and more indiscretion in speaking of oneself. It cannot be the case here, as I often see elsewhere, that the craftsman and his work contradict each other. . . . A learned man is not learned in all things; but the accomplished man is accomplished in all things, even in ignorance. Here, my book and I go hand in hand together, and keep one pace. In other cases we may commend or censure the work apart from the workman; not so here. Who touches the one touches the other.) *The Essays of Montaigne*. Translated by E. J. Trechmann, Oxford University Press, 1927.

This is the beginning of chapter 2 of book 3 of Montaigne's *Essais*. In Villey's edition (Paris, Alcan, 1930), the pagination of which will be given in all our future references, the passage is found on page 39 of volume 3. It is one of those numerous passages in which Montaigne speaks of the subject matter of the essays, of his purpose of representing himself. He begins by emphasizing the fluctuations, the unstable and changeable nature of his material. Then he describes the procedure he employs in treating so fluctuating a subject. Finally he takes up the question of the usefulness of his venture. The train of reasoning in the first paragraph can easily be rendered in the form of a syllogism: I describe myself; I am a creature which constantly changes; ergo, the description too must conform to this and constantly change. We shall try to analyze how each member of the syllogism is expressed in the text.

"I describe myself." Montaigne does not say this directly. He brings it out through the contrast to "others" much more energetically and, as we shall see in a moment, in a more richly nuanced fashion than would have been possible by a mere statement. *Les autres forment l'homme, moy . . .* : here it becomes apparent that the contrast is twofold. The others shape, I relate (cf. a little further on: *je n'enseigne pas, je raconte*); the others shape "man," I relate "a man." This gives us two stages of the contrast: *forment—recite, l'homme—un particulier*. This *particulier* is himself; but that too he does not say directly but paraphrases it with his reticent, ironical, and slightly self-satisfied modesty. The paraphrase consists of three parts, of which the second has both a principal and a subordinate clause: *bien mal formé; si j'avoy . . . , je ferois . . . ; meshuy c'est fait*. The major premise of the syllogism, then, contains in its formulation at least three groups of ideas which build it up and interpret it in various forms of counter- or concurrent motion: 1. the others shape, I relate; 2. the others shape *man*, I tell of *one* man; 3. this one man (I) is "unfortunately" already formed. All this is gathered in one single rhythmic movement without the slightest possibility of confusion; and indeed almost completely without syntactic vincula, without conjunctions or quasi-conjunctional connectives. The coherence, the intellectual nexus established through the unity of meaning and the rhythm of the sentence, is adequate by itself. To make this point clearer, let me supply some syntactic vincula: (*Tandis que*) *les autres forment l'homme, je le recite;* (*encore faut-il ajouter que*) *je represente un particulier* (*; ce particulier, c'est moi-même qui suis, je le sais,*) *bien mal formé;* (*soyez sûrs que*) *si j'avais à le façonner de nouveau, je le ferais vrayment bien autre qu'il n'est.* (*Mais, malheureusement*) *meshuy c'est fait.* Of course my emendations are at best of approximate value. The nuances which Montaigne expresses by omitting them cannot be caught in full.

As for the minor premise (I am a creature subject to constant change), Montaigne does not express it at once. He leaves the logical continuity in the lurch and first introduces the conclusion, in the form of the surprising assertion: *Or, les traits de ma peinture ne fourvoyent pas, quoy qu'ils se changent et diversifient.* The word *or* indicates that the continuity has been interrupted for a new start. It serves at the same time to tone down the suddenness and surprisingness of the assertion. The word *quoique,* here sharply employed as a precise syntactic vinculum, brings the problem out in bold relief.

Now at last comes the minor premise, not directly but as the conclusion of a subordinate syllogism, which runs as follows: the world changes constantly; I am part of the world; ergo, I change constantly. The major premise is furnished with illustrations, and the way in which the world changes is analyzed as being twofold: all things undergo the general change and each its own in addition. Then follows a polyphonic movement introduced by the paradox about stability which is likewise but a form of slower fluctuation. Throughout this polyphonic movement, which takes up the entire remainder of the paragraph, the minor premise of the second syllogism, as self-evident, sounds but faintly. The two themes here intertwined are the minor premise and the conclusion of the main argument: I am a creature which constantly changes; ergo, I must make my description conform to this. Here Montaigne is at the center of the realm which is peculiarly his own: the play and counterplay between I and I, between Montaigne the author and Montaigne the theme; turns of expression equally rich in meaning and sound, and referring now to the one I, now to the other, most often to both, flow from his pen. We are left to choose which we prefer to consider the most precise, characteristic, and true and to admire the most; that on natural drunkenness, that on depicting change, the one on external change (*fortune*) and inner change (*intention*), the quotation from Demades, the contrast between *s'essayer* and *se résoudre* with the beautiful image, *si mon âme pouvait prendre pied.* For each one and for all together what Horace said of completely successful works holds true: *decies repetita placebit.*

I hope this breaking up of the paragraph into syllogisms will not be found too pedantic. It shows that the structure of the thought in this lively passage, so rich in unexpected departures, is precise and logical; that the many movements which add, discriminate, go deeper, or sometimes even retreat concessively, serve to present the idea, as it were, in its practical application; that, furthermore, the order is repeatedly broken, that some propositions are anticipated, that others are altogether omitted so that the reader must supply them. The reader must cooperate. He is drawn into the movement of the thought, but at every moment he is expected to pause, to check, to add something. Who *les autres* are he must surmise; who the *particulier* is, likewise. The clause with *or* seems to take him far afield, and only after a time does he gradually understand what it is driving at. Then, to be sure, the essential point is presented to him in a wealth of formulations which carry away his imagination; but even then in such a way that he must still exert himself, for each of the formulations is so individualized that it has to be digested. None fits into a ready-made pattern of thought or discourse.

Although the content of the paragraph is intellectual and even rigorously logical, although what we have here is a keen and original intellectual effort to probe the problem of self-analysis, the vitality of the will to expression is so strong that the style breaks through the limits of a purely theoretical disquisition. I suppose anyone who has read enough of Montaigne to feel at home in the essays must have had the same experience as I. I had been reading him for some time, and when I had finally acquired a certain familiarity with his manner, I thought I could hear him speak and see his gestures. This is an experience which one seldom has with earlier theoretical writers as strongly as with Montaigne, probably with none of them. He often omits conjunctions and other syntactic connectives, but he suggests them. He skips intermediate steps of reasoning, but replaces what is lacking by a kind of contact which arises spontaneously between steps not connected by strict logic. Between the clauses *la constance mesme n'est autre chose . . .* and the following *je ne puis asseurer mon object . . .*, a step is obviously missing, a clause which ought to state that I, the object I am studying, being a fragment of the world, must likewise be subject to the double change mentioned. Later on he says this in detail, but even here he has created the atmosphere which provisionally establishes the contact and yet leaves the reader actively intent. Occasionally he repeats ideas which he considers important over and over in ever-new formulations, each time working out a fresh viewpoint, a fresh characteristic, a fresh image, so that the idea radiates in all directions. All these are characteristics which we are much more used to finding in conversation—though only in the conversation of exceptionally thoughtful and articulate people—than in a printed work of theoretical content. We are inclined to think that this sort of effect requires vocal inflection, gesture, the warming up to one another which comes with an enjoyable conversation. But Montaigne, who is alone with himself, finds enough life and as it were bodily warmth in his ideas to be able to write as though he were speaking.

This is related to the manner in which he endeavors to apprehend his subject, himself—the very manner, that is, which he describes in our paragraph. It is a ceaseless listening to the changing voices which sound within him, and it varies in elevation between reticent, slightly self-satisfied irony and a very emphatic seriousness which fathoms the ultimate bases of existence. The irony he displays is again a mixture of several motifs: an extremely sincere disinclination to take human beings tragically (man is *un subject merveilleusement vain, divers et ondoyant*, 1, 1, p. 10: *autant ridicule que risible*, 1, 50, p. 582; *le badin de la farce*, 3, 9, p. 434); a faint note of proudly aristocratic contempt for the writer's craft (*si j'étais faiseur de livres*, 1, 20, p. 162, and again, 2, 37, p. 902); finally, and this is the most important point of all, an inclination to belittle his own particular approach. He calls his book *ce fagotage de tant de diverses pièces* (2, 37, p. 850), *cette fricassée que je barbouille icy* (3, 13, p. 590), and once he even compares it to an old man's feces: *ce sont icy . . . des excremens d'un vieil esprit, dur tantost, tantost lasche, et toujours indigeste* (3, 9, p. 324). He never tires of emphasizing the artless, personal, natural, and immediate character of his writing, as though it were something he must apologize for, and the irony of this form of modesty does not always come out as clearly and completely as it does in the second paragraph of our text, which we shall analyze below. So much, for the present, on Montaigne's irony. It gives his style an extremely delightful flavor, and a flavor perfectly suited to his subject; but the reader should beware of becoming too entangled by it. He means it seriously and emphatically when he says that his representation, however changeable and diverse it is, never goes astray and that though perhaps at times he contradicts himself, he never contradicts the truth. Such words mirror a very realistic conception of man based on experience and in particular on self-experience: the conception that man is a fluctuating creature subject to the changes which take place in his surroundings, his destiny, and his inner impulses. Thus Montaigne's apparently fanciful method, which obeys no preconceived plan but adapts itself elastically to the changes of his own being, is basically a strictly experimental method, the only method which conforms to such a subject. If one wishes to produce an exact and factual description of a constantly changing subject, one must follow its changes exactly and factually; one must describe the subject as one found it, under as many different experimental conditions as possible, for in this way one may hope to determine the limits of possible changes and thus finally arrive at a comprehensive picture.

It is this strict and, even in the modern sense, scientific method which Montaigne endeavors to maintain. Perhaps he would have objected to the pretentiously scientific-sounding word "method," but a method it is, and two modern critics—Villey (*Les Sources et l'Évolution des Essais de Montaigne*, 2nd edition, Paris, 1933, 2, 321) and Lanson (*Les Essais de Montaigne*, Paris, n.d., 265)—have applied the term to his activity, albeit not quite in the sense here envisaged. Montaigne has described his method with precision. In addition to our passage there are others worthy of note. Our paragraph makes it very clear that he is forced, and why he is forced, to adopt his procedure—he must adapt himself to his subject matter. It also explains the meaning of the title *Essais*, which might fittingly though not very gracefully be rendered as "Tests upon One's Self" or "Self-Try-Outs." Another passage (2, 37, p. 850) emphasizes the developmental principle which his procedure is intended to bring out and has an extremely characteristic conclusion which is by no means exclusively ironical: *Je veux representer le progrez de mes humeurs, et qu'on voye chaque piece en sa naissance. Je prendrois plaisir d'auoir commencé plus tost, et à recognoistre le train de mes mutations. . . . Je me suis envieilly de sept ou huict ans depuis que je commençay. Ce n'a pas esté sans quelque nouvel acquest. J'y ay pratiqué la colique, par la liberalité des ans: leur commerce et longue conversation ne se passe aysément sans quelque tel fruit. . . .* A still more significant passage (2, 6, pp. 93-94) states quite unironically and with that calm yet insistent earnestness which marks the upper limits of Montaigne's style—he never goes beyond this in stylistic elevation—how highly he thinks of his venture: *C'est une espineuse entreprinse, et plus qu'il ne semble, de suyvre une allure si vagabonde que celle de nostre esprit; de penetrer dans les profondeurs opaques de ses replis internes; de choisir et arrester tant de menus airs de ses agitations; et est un amusement nouveau et extraordinaire qui nous retire des occupations communes du monde, ouy, et des plus recommandées. Il y a plusieurs années que je n'ay que moy pour visée à mes pensées, que je ne contrerolle et estudie que moy; et si j'estudie autre chose, c'est pour soudain le coucher sur moy, ou en moy. . . .*

These sentences are also significant because they indicate what limits Montaigne had set to his undertaking, because they state not only what he intends to do but also what he intends not to do, that is, to investigate the outer world. That interests him only as the setting and occasion for his own movements. With this we come to another form of his deceptive and reserved irony: his frequent asseverations of his ignorance and irresponsibility in regard to everything related to the outer world, which he likes best to designate as *les choses: A peine respondroys-je à autruy de mes discours qui ne m'en responds pas à moy . . . ce sont icy mes fantasies, par lesquelles je ne tasche point à donner à connoistre les choses, mais moy. . . .* (2, 10, p. 152). These "things" are for him only a means of self-testing; they serve him only *à essayer ses facultés naturelles* (*ibid.*) and he does not feel it in any way his duty to take a responsible stand toward them. This too can best be stated in his own words: *De cent membres et visages qu'a chaque chose, j'en prens un. . . . J'y donne une poincte, non pas le plus largement, mais le plus profondément que je sçay . . . sans dessein, sans promesse, je ne suis pas tenu d'en faire bon, ny de m'y tenir moy mesme, sans varier quand il me plaist, et me rendre au doubte et à l'incertitude, et à ma maistresse forme qui est l'ignorance . . .* (1, 50, p. 578). This passage alone suffices to show what this ignorance amounts to. Concealed behind self-irony and modesty there is a very definite attitude which serves his major purpose and to which he adheres with the charmingly elastic tenacity which is his own. Elsewhere he reveals to us even more clearly what this ignorance, his *maistresse forme*, means to him. For he conceives of an *ignorance forte et genereuse* (3, 11, p. 493) and values it more highly than all factual knowledge because its acquisition requires greater wisdom than the acquisition of scientific knowledge. It is not only a means of clearing the way for him to the kind of knowledge which matters to him, that is, self-knowledge, but it also represents a direct way of reaching what is the ultimate goal of his quest, namely, right living: *le grand et glorieux chef d'œuvre de l'homme, c'est vivre à propos* (3, 13, p. 651). And in this animated personality there is such a complete surrender to nature and destiny, that he considers it useless to strive for a greater knowledge of them than they themselves grant us to experience: *Le plus simplement se commettre à nature, c'est s'y commettre le plus sagement. Oh! que c'est un doux et mol chevet, et sain, que l'ignorance et l'incuriosité, à reposer une teste bien faicte!* (3, 13, p. 580); and a little before that he says: . . . *je me laisse ignoramment et negligemment aller à la loy generale du monde; je la sçauray assez quand je la sentiray. . . .*

Deliberate ignorance and indifference in regard to "things" is part of his method; he seeks in them only himself. This one subject of his he tests by innumerable experiments undertaken on the spur of the moment; he illuminates it from every direction; he fairly encircles it. The result is not, however, a mass of unrelated snapshots, but a spontaneous apprehension of the unity of his person emerging from the multiplicity of his observations. In the end there is unity and truth; in the end it is his essential being which emerges from his portrayal of the changing. To track oneself down by such a method is in itself a way leading to self-possession: *l'entreprise se sent de la qualité de la chose qu'elle regarde; car c'est une bonne portion de l'effect, et consubstantielle* (1, 20, p. 148). At every moment of the continual process of change Montaigne possesses the coherence of his personality; and he knows it: *Il n'est personne, s'il s'escoute, qui ne descouvre en soy une forme sienne, une forme maistresse* (3, 2, p. 52); or, in another passage: *les plus fermes imaginations que j'aye, et generalles, sont celles qui, par maniere de dire, nasquirent avec moy; elles sont naturelles et toutes miennes* (2, 17, pp. 652-653). To be sure, this *forme sienne* cannot be put into a few precise words; it is much too varied and too real to be completely contained in a definition. Yet for Montaigne the truth is *one,* however multiple its manifestations; he may contradict himself, but not truth.

No less a part of Montaigne's method is the peculiar form of his Essays. They are neither an autobiography nor a diary. They are based on no artfully contrived plan and do not follow chronological order. They follow chance—*les fantasies de la musique sont conduictes par art, les miennes par sort.* Strictly speaking it is "things" after all which direct him—he moves among them, he lives in them; it is in things that he can always be found, for, with his very open eyes and his very impressionable mind, he stands in the midst of the world. But he does not follow its course in time—nor a method whose aim is to attain knowledge of one specific thing or of a group of things. He follows his own inner rhythm, which, though constantly induced and maintained by things, is not bound to them, but freely skips from one to another. He prefers *une alleure poetique, à sauts et à gambades* (3, 9, p. 421). Villey has shown (*Les Sources*, etc., 2, p. 3ff.) that the form of the Essays stems from the collections of exempla, quotations, and aphorisms which were a very popular genre in late antiquity and throughout the Middle Ages and which in the sixteenth century helped to spread humanistic material. Montaigne had begun in this vein. Originally his book was a collection of the fruit of his reading, with running commentary. This pattern was soon broken; commentary predominated over text, subject matter or point of departure was not only things read but also things lived—now his own experiences, now what he heard from others or what took place around him. But the principle of clinging to concrete things, to what happens, he never gave up, any more than he did his freedom not to tie himself to a fact-finding method or to the course of events in time. From things he takes the animation which saves him from abstract psychologizing and from empty probing within himself. But he guards himself against becoming subject to the law of any given thing, so that the rhythm of his own inner movement may not be muffled and finally lost. He praises this procedure very highly, especially in the ninth essay of book 3, from which we have quoted a few statements, and he cites Plato and other authors of antiquity as his models. His appeal to the authority of the many Platonic dialogues whose structure is apparently loose while their theme is not abstractly detached but embedded in the character and situation of the interlocutors, is doubtless not wholly unjustified; but it is beside the point. Montaigne is something new. The flavor of the personal, and indeed of a single individual, is present much more strikingly, and the manner of expression is much more spontaneous and closer to everyday spoken discourse, although no dialogue is involved. Then too, the description of the Socratic style in another passage in essay 12—we have referred to it in our chapter on Rabelais (p. 280)—exhibits a strongly Montaigne-colored Socrates. No philosopher of antiquity, not even Plato in his presentation of the discoursing Socrates, could write so directly out of the will of his own concrete existence, so juicily, so animally, and so spontaneously. And at bottom Montaigne knows this too. In a passage where he objects to his style being praised and asks the reader to concern himself only with subject matter and meaning (1, 40, p. 483), he goes on to say: *Si suis je trompé, si gueres d'autres donnent plus à prendre en la matiere; et comment que ce soit, mal ou bien, si nul escrivain l'a semée ny gueres plus materielle, ny au moins plus drue en son papier.*

The second portion of the text quoted at the beginning of this chapter discusses the question whether his undertaking is justified and useful. This is the question to which Pascal, we know, gave so emphatic a negative answer (*le sot projet qu'il a de se peindre!*). Again both arrangement and expression are full of reservedly ironic modesty. It seems as though he himself had not quite the courage to answer the question with a clear affirmative, as though he were trying to excuse himself and plead extenuating circumstances. This impression is deceptive. He has already decided the question in his first sentence, long before he actually formulates it; and what later sounds almost like an apology (*au moins j'ay* . . .), unexpectedly turns into a self-affirmation so determined, so basic, and so conscious of its own idiosyncrasy that the impression of modesty and apologetic attitude vanishes completely. The order in which he presents his ideas is as follows:

1. I depict a lowly and unillustrious life; but that is of no consequence; even the lowliest life contains the whole of things human.

2. In contrast to others I depict no specialized body of knowledge, no special skill, which I have acquired; I present myself, Montaigne, in my entire person, and I am the first to do so.

3. If you reproach me with talking too much about myself, I reply by reproaching you with not even thinking about yourselves.

4. Only now does he formulate the question: Is it not presumptuous to wish to bring so limited an individual case to general and public knowledge? Is it reasonable that I should offer to a world which is only prepared to appreciate form and art, so undigested and simple a product of nature, and, to make matters worse, so insignificant a product of nature?

5. Instead of an answer he now gives these "extenuating circumstances": a) no one has ever been so fully versed in his subject as I am in mine; b) no one has ever gone so deeply into his subject, so far into all its parts and ramifications; no one has ever carried out his purpose so exactly and so completely.

6. To achieve this I need nothing but unreserved sincerity and of that I have no lack. I am a little hampered by conventions; at times I should like to go somewhat further; but as I grow older I permit myself certain liberties which people are inclined to excuse in an old man.

7. In my case one thing at least cannot happen, as it does in the case of many a specialist: that man and work are not in accord; that one admires the work but finds the author a mediocrity in daily life—or vice versa. A man of learning is not learned in all fields; but a whole person is whole everywhere, including where he is ignorant. My book and I are one thing; he who speaks of the one speaks equally of the other.

This condensation shows the duplicity of his modesty; it shows it almost more clearly than the original text, because, being disconnected and dry, it lacks Montaigne's amiable flow of expression. But the original is definite enough. The contrast "I—the others," the malice toward specialists, and particularly the motifs "I am the first" and "no one has ever" cannot be missed and stand out more sharply at each re-reading of the passage. We will now discuss these seven points individually. This to be sure is a somewhat meager expedient, if only for the reason that the points intermingle and are hard to keep apart. But it is necessary if one desires to get out of the text everything that is in it.

The statement that he depicts a lowly and unillustrious life is grossly exaggerated. Montaigne was a great gentleman, respected and influential, and it was his own choice that he made only so moderate and reluctant a use of his political possibilities. But the device of exaggerated modesty, which he frequently employs, serves him to set the main idea in stronger relief: any random human destiny, *une vie populaire et privée*, is all he needs for his purpose. *La vie de Cesar*, he says elsewhere (3, 13, p. 580), *n'a point plus d'exemple que la nostre pour nous: et emperiere et populaire, c'est tousjours une vie que tous accidens humains regardent. Escoutons y seulement.* . . . And then follows the famous sentence upon the *humaine condition* which is realized in any and every human being. With this sentence he has evidently answered the question of the significance and use of his undertaking. If every man affords material and occasion enough for the development of the complete moral philosophy, then a precise and sincere self-analysis of any random individual is directly justified. Indeed, one may go a step further: it is necessary, because it is the only way—according to Montaigne—which the science of man as a moral being can take. The method of listening (*escoutons y*) can be applied with any degree of accuracy only to the experimenter's own person; it is in the last analysis a method of self-auscultation, of the observation of one's own inner movements. One cannot observe others with the same exactness: *Il n'y a que vous qui sçache si vous estes lasche et cruel ou loyal et devotieux; les autres ne vous voyent point, ils vous devinent par conjectures incertaines* . . . (3, 2, pp. 45-46). And one's own life, the life to whose movements one must listen, is always a random life, for it is simply one of the millions of variants of the possibilities of human existence in general. The obligatory basis of Montaigne's method is the random life one happens to have.

But then this random life of one's own must be taken as a whole. That is the portion of his declaration which we have listed above as point 2. It is a requirement one can easily understand. Every kind of specialization falsifies the moral picture; it presents us in but one of our roles; it consciously leaves in darkness broad reaches of our lives and destinies. From a book on Greek grammar or international law the author's personal existence cannot be known, or at best only in those rare cases where his temperament is so strong and idiosyncratic that it breaks through in any manifestation of his life. Montaigne's social and economic circumstances made it easy for him to develop and preserve his whole self. His needs were met halfway by his period, which had not yet fully developed for the upper classes of society the duty, the technique, and the ethos of specialized work, but on the contrary, under the influence of the oligarchic civilization of antiquity, strove for the most general and most human culture of the individual. Not one of his known contemporaries advanced in this direction so far as he did. Compared with him they are all specialists: theologians, philologists, philosophers, statesmen, physicians, poets, artists; they all present themselves to the world *par quelque marque particuliere et estrangiere*. Montaigne too, under the pressure of circumstances, was at times lawyer, soldier, politician; he was the mayor of Bordeaux for several years. But he did not give himself over to such activities; he merely lent himself for a time and subject to recall, and he promised those who laid tasks upon him *de les prendre en main, non pas au poulmon et au foye* (3, 10, p. 438). The method of using one's own random life in its totality as a point of departure for moral philosophy, for the examination of the *humaine condition*, is in pronounced contrast to all the methods which investigate a large number of individuals in accordance with some definite plan—with respect to their possessing or lacking certain traits, let us say, or to their behavior in certain situations. All such methods seem to Montaigne pedantic and empty abstractions. In them he cannot recognize man, that is, himself; they disguise and simplify and systematize so that the reality is lost. Montaigne limits himself to the detailed investigation and description of one single specimen, himself, and even in this investigation nothing is further from his method than isolating his subject in any manner, than detaching it from the accidental conditions and circumstances in which it is found at a particular moment, in order to arrive at its real, permanent, and absolute essence. Any such attempt to attain to the essence by isolating it from the momentary accidental contingencies would strike him as absurd because, to his mind, the essence is lost as soon as one detaches it from its momentary accidents. For this very reason he must renounce an ultimate definition of himself or of man, for such a definition would of necessity have to be abstract. He must limit himself to probing and reprobing himself, and renounce any *se résoudre*. But he is the kind of man for whom such a renunciation is not difficult, for he is convinced that the total object of cognition cannot be expressed. Furthermore his method, despite its seeming vagaries, is very strict in that it confines itself to pure observation. It undertakes no search into general causes. When Montaigne cites causes, they are of an immediate kind and themselves susceptible to observation. On this point there is a polemic passage which is timely even today: *Ils laissent là les choses et s'amusent à traicter les causes: plaisans causeurs! La cognoissance des causes appartient seulement à celuy qui a la conduite des choses, non à nous qui n'en avons que la souffrance, et qui en avons l'usage parfaictement plein selon notre nature, sans en penetrer l'origine et l'essence. . . . Ils commencent ordinairement ainsi: Comment est ce que cela se faict? Mais se faict il? faudroit il dire . . .* (3, 11, p. 485). We have intentionally refrained in all these remarks on Montaigne's method from bringing up the almost inescapably associated technical terms of those modern philosophical methods which are related to his by affinity or contrast. The informed reader will supply these technical terms. We avoid them because there is nowhere a complete congruence, and precise qualifications would take us too far afield.

We have as yet said nothing concerning a few words which Montaigne, in describing his method of depicting his own random life in its totality for the purpose of investigating the *humaine condition*, puts in a syntactically prominent position. They are the words *moy le premier* and they confront us with the questions: Does he mean this seriously, and is he right? The first question can be answered summarily. He does mean to be taken seriously, for he repeats the assertion in various places. The theme "no one has ever," which follows a little further on in our text, is only a variant of it, and another passage —part of which we have quoted above on page 292f.—the passage on the *amusement nouveau et extraordinaire . . . de penetrer dans les profondeurs de ses replis internes* is introduced in the following manner: *Nous n'avons nouvelles que de deux ou trois anciens qui ayent battu ce chemin; et si ne pouvons dire si c'est du tout en pareille maniere à cette-ci, n'en connoissant que leurs noms. Nul depuis ne s'est jeté sur leur trace* . . . (2, 6, p. 93). There is, then, no doubt that Montaigne, despite all his modesty and his ironical attitude toward himself, was serious in making this assertion. But is he right in it? Do we really have no comparable work from earlier times? I cannot help thinking of Augustine. Montaigne never mentions the *Confessions*, and Villey (*Les Sources*, 1, 75) assumes that he did not know them well. But it is not possible that he should not have been aware at least of the existence and the character of this famous book. Perhaps he rather shrank from the comparison; perhaps it is a perfectly genuine and unironical modesty that prevents him from establishing a relationship between himself and his method and the most important of the Fathers. And he is right when he says that it was not at all *en pareille maniere*. Both purpose and approach are very different. And yet there is no other earlier author from whom anything so basically important is preserved in Montaigne's method as the consistent and unreserved self-investigation of Augustine.

As for the third part of his statement (the rebuttal: you do not even think of yourselves), we may note that tacitly underlying it is the typically Montaignesque concept of "I myself." In the ordinary sense, the people here addressed do think a great deal of themselves, too much so indeed. They think of their interests, their desires, their worries, their information, their activities, their families, their friends. All this, for Montaigne, is not "themselves." All this is only a part of "I myself"; it can even lead—and generally it does lead—to an obscuration of the self and to the loss of it: that is to say, whenever the individual abandons himself so completely to one or to another or to several of these things that his present consciousness of his own existence in its entirety, that his full consciousness of a life distinctively his own, melts away in the process. The full consciousness of one's own life implies for Montaigne also full consciousness of one's own death. *Ils vont, ils viennent, ils trottent, ils dansent; de mort, nulles nouvelles* (1, 20, pp. 154-155).

Parts five and six of the statement—his doubt whether the publication of such a work is justified and the apologies he uses to meet that doubt—may be discussed together. The real answer to the question, he has given before. He poses it now only in order that he may once again bring out the unique characteristics of his undertaking, this time in a few excellently formulated antitheses (e.g. *particulier en usage* as against *public en cognoissance*, or *par art* as against *par sort*). The text is further significant because of the unexpected turn it takes from an apologetic formulation to a clear-cut admission of his awareness of his importance. This admission, introduced by the motif *jamais homme* or *jamais aucun*, reveals a new aspect of his method. To paraphrase: Never, he says, has any man been so fully master of his subject, nor pursued it so far into all its details and ramifications, nor accomplished his purpose so unqualifiedly. There may be a faint echo of self-irony in formulations like *en celuy-là je suis le plus sçavant homme qui vive*, yet these sentences are an amazingly frank and clear and emphatic underlining of the uniqueness of his book. They go beyond the previously discussed *moy le premier* inasmuch as they reveal Montaigne's conviction that no branch of learning and no form of knowledge could possibly be acquired with as much exactness and comprehensiveness as self-knowledge. For him Know Thyself is not only a pragmatic and moral precept but an epistemological precept too. This is also the reason why he is so little interested in the knowledge which the sciences of nature furnish and why he has no trust in it. Only things human and moral are able to fascinate him. Like Socrates he could say that the trees teach him nothing; only the people in the city can do that. Montaigne even gives this thought a polemic barb when he speaks of those who take pride in their knowledge of natural science: *Puisque ces gens là n'ont pas peu se resoudre de la cognoissance d'eux mesmes et de leur propre condition, qui est continuellement presente à leurs yeux, qui est dans eux . . . , comment les croirois je de la cause du flux et du reflux de la riviere du Nil?* (2, 17, p. 605). However, the primacy of self-knowledge acquires a positive epistemological significance only in regard to the moral study of man; for in his study of his own random life Montaigne's sole aim is an investigation of the *humaine condition* in general; and with that he reveals the heuristic principle which we constantly employ—consciously or unconsciously, reasonably or unreasonably—when we endeavor to understand and judge the acts of others, whether the acts of our close associates or more remote acts which belong in the realms of politics or history. We apply criteria to them which we have derived from our own lives and our own inner experience—so that our knowledge of men and of history depends upon the depth of our self-knowledge and the extent of our moral horizon.

Montaigne's interest in the lives of others was always most intense. To be sure, he cannot rid himself of a certain distrust for historians. He feels that they present human beings too exclusively in extraordinary and heroic situations and that they are only too ready to give fixed and consistent portraits of character: *les bons autheurs mesmes ont tort de s'opiniastrer à former de nous une constante et solide contexture* (2, 1, p. 9). He thinks it preposterous to derive a concept of the whole individual from one or several climactic episodes of a life; what he misses is a sufficient regard for the fluctuations and alterations in a man's inner state: *pour juger d'un homme, il faut suivre longuement et curieusement sa trace* (2, 1, p. 18). He wants to experience man's everyday, normal, and spontaneous conduct, and for that his own environment, which he can observe in personal experience, is just as valuable to him as the material of history: *moy . . . qui estime ce siècle comme un autre passé, j'allegue aussi volontiers un mien amy que Aulu Gelle et que Macrobe* . . . (3, 13, p. 595). Private and personal occurrences interest him as much as or possibly even more than matters of state, and it is not even necessary that they should really have happened: . . . *en l'estude que je traitte de noz mœurs et mouvemens, les temoignages fabuleux, pourvu qu'ils soient possibles, y servent comme les vrais: advenu ou non advenu, à Paris ou à Rome, à Jean ou à Pierre, c'est toujours un tour de l'humaine capacité* (1, 21, p. 194). All this concern with the experience of life in others passes through the filter of self-experience. We must not be misled by certain utterances of Montaigne's, as when he voices the warning that one should not judge others by oneself or deem impossible what one cannot imagine or what contradicts our own customs. This is referable only to people whose self-experience is too narrow and shallow, and the lesson one might draw from such utterances is simply a demand for greater elasticity and breadth in our inner consciousness. For Montaigne could give no other heuristic principle in the realm of historico-moral knowledge than self-experience, and there are several passages which describe his method from this point of view, for example the following: *Cette longue attention que j'employe à me considérer me dresse à juger aussi passablement des autres. . . . Pour m'estre, dès mon enfance, dressé à mirer ma vie dans celle d'autruy, j'ay acquis une complexion studieuse en cela* (3, 13, p. 585). *Mirer sa vie dans celle d'autrui*: in these words lies the complete method of an activity which sets itself the goal of understanding the actions or thoughts of others. Everything else, the compilation of sources and testimonies, the factual critique and sifting of the data of tradition, is only auxiliary and preparatory labor.

The sixth of the points we have distinguished in Montaigne's statement is concerned with his sincerity: it is all that he needs to carry out his purpose, and he possesses it. He says so himself, and it is true. He is eminently sincere in all that concerns himself, and he would gladly (as he says here and in several other passages in the Essays, and even in his preface) be a little franker still; but the conventions of social conduct impose some limitation upon him. His critics, however, have at most found fault with his excess of sincerity, never with a lack of it. He speaks about himself a great deal, and the reader becomes acquainted with all the details not only of his intellectual and spiritual life but also of his physical existence. A great deal of information about his most personal characteristics and habits, his illnesses, his food, and his sexual peculiarities, is scattered through the Essays. There is, to be sure, a certain element of self-satisfaction in all this. Montaigne is pleased with himself; he knows that he is in all respects a free, a richly gifted, a full, a remarkably well-rounded human being, and despite all his self-irony he cannot completely conceal this delight in his own person. But it is a calm and self-rooted consciousness of his individual self, free from pettiness, arrogance, insecurity, and coquetry. He is proud of his *forme toute sienne.* But his delight in himself is not the most important nor the most distinctive motif of his sincerity, which applies equally to mind and body. Sincerity is an essential part of his method of depicting his own random life in its entirety. Montaigne is convinced that, for such a portrayal, mind and body must not be separated; and calmly, without accompanying his self-portrayal by any convulsive gestures, he gave his conviction practical form, with an openness and reality such as hardly anyone before him and very few after him attained. He speaks in detail of his body and his physical existence, because it is an essential ingredient of his self, and he has managed to pervade his book with the corporeal savor of his personality without ever arousing a feeling of surfeit. His bodily functions, his illnesses, and his own physical death, of which he talks a great deal in order to accustom himself to the idea of death, are so intimately fused in their concrete sensory effects with the moral-intellectual content of his book that any attempt to separate them would be absurd.

Connected with this in turn is the dislike which, as we mentioned before, he entertains for the formal systems of moral philosophy. The things he holds against them—their abstraction, the tendency of their methodology to disguise the reality of life, and the turgidity of their terminology—can all be reduced in the last analysis to the fact that partly in theory and partly at least in pedagogical practice they separate mind and body and do not give the latter a chance to have its say. They all, according to Montaigne, have too high an opinion of man; they speak of him as if he were only mind and spirit, and so they falsify the reality of life: *Ces exquises subtilitez ne sont propres qu'au presche; ce sont discours qui nous veulent envoyer touts bastez en l'autre monde. La vie est un mouvement materiel et corporel, action imparfaicte de sa propre essence, et desreglée; je m'emploie à la servir selon elle* . . . (3, 9, pp. 409-410).

The passages in which he speaks of the unity of mind and body are very numerous and reflect many different aspects of his attitude. At times his ironical modesty predominates: . . . *moy, d'une condition mixte, grossier* . . . , *si simple que je me laisse tout lourdement aller aux plaisirs presents de la loy humaine et generale, intellectuellement sensibles, sensiblement intellectuels* (3, 13, p. 649). Another extremely interesting passage throws light on his attitude toward Platonism and at the same time toward antique moral philosophy in general: *Platon craint nostre engagement aspre à la douleur et à la volupté, d'autant que* (because) *il oblige et attache par trop l'âme au corps; moy plutost au rebours, d'autant qu'il l'en desprend et descloue* (1, 40, pp. 100-101). Because for Plato the body is an enemy of moderation, seducing the soul and carrying it away; for Montaigne the body is naturally endowed with *un juste et modéré tempérament envers la volupté et envers la douleur*, while *ce qui aiguise en nous la douleur et la volupté, c'est la poincte de nostre esprit.* In our connection, however, the most important passages on this point are those which reveal the Christian-creatural sources of his view. In the chapter *de la présomption* (2, 17, p. 615) he writes:

> Le corps a une grand' part à nostre estre, il y tient un grand rang; ainsi sa structure et composition sont de bien juste considération. Ceux qui veulent desprendre nos deux pièces principales, et les sequestrer l'un de l'autre, ils ont tort; au rebours, il les faut r'accupler et rejoindre; il faut ordonner à l'âme non de se tirer à quartier, de s'entretenir à part, de mespriser et abandonner le corps (aussi ne le sçauroit elle faire que par quelque sin-

gerie contrefaicte), mais de se r'allier à luy, de l'embrasser . . . , l'espouser en somme, et luy servir de mary, à ce que leurs effects ne paraissent pas divers et contraires, ains accordans et uniformes. Les Chrestiens ont une particuliere instruction de cette liaison; ils sçavent que la justice divine embrasse cette société et joincture du corps et de l'âme, jusques à rendre le corps capable des recompenses eternelles; et que Dieu regarde agir tout l'homme, et veut qu'entier il reçoive le chastiment, ou le loyer, selon ses merites.

And he closes with praise of the Aristotelian philosophy:

> La secte Peripatetique, de toutes sectes la plus sociable, attribue à la sagesse ce seul soing, de pourvoir et procurer en commun le bien de ces deux parties associées; et montre les autres sectes, pour ne s'estre assez attachez à la considération de ce meslange, s'estre partialisées, cette-cy pour le corps, cette autre pour l'âme, d'une pareille erreur; et avoir escarté leur subject, qui est l'homme; et leur guide, qu'ils advouent en general estre Nature.

Another similarly significant passage occurs at the end of book 3, in the concluding chapter *de l'expérience* (3, 13, p. 663):

> A quoy faire demembrons nous en divorce un bastiment tissu d'une si joincte et fraternelle correspondance? Au rebours, renouons le par mutuels offices; que l'esprit esveille et vivifie la pesanteur du corps, le corps arreste la legereté de l'esprit et la fixe. Qui velut summum bonum laudat animae naturam, et tamquam malum naturam carnis accusat, profecto et animam carnaliter appetit, et carnem carnaliter fugit; quoniam id vanitate sentit humana, non veritate divina [from Augustine, *De civitate Dei*, 14, 5]. Il n'y a piece indigne de notre soin, en ce present que Dieu nous a faict; nous en devons conte jusques à un poil; et n'est pas une commission par acquit (roughly: offhand) à l'homme de conduire l'homme selon sa condition; elle est expresse, naifve et très-principale, et nous l'a le Createur donnée serieusement et severement . . . [Those who would renounce their bodies] veulent se mettre hors d'eux, et eschapper à l'homme; c'est folie; au lieu de se transformer en anges, ils se transforment en bestes; au lieu de se hausser, ils s'abattent. Ces humeurs transcendentes m'effrayent. . . .

That Montaigne's unity of mind and body has its roots in Christian-creatural anthropology could be demonstrated even without these testimonies. It is the basis of his realistic introspection; without it the latter would be inconceivable. But such passages (we might also adduce 3, 5, p. 219, with an important remark on the asceticism of the saints) go to show how conscious he was of the connection. He appeals to the dogma of the resurrection of the flesh and Bible texts. In this specific connection he praises the Aristotelian philosophy, of which otherwise he does not think very highly (*Je ne recognois, chez Aristote, la plus part de mes mouvements ordinaires*). He cites one of the many passages where Augustine opposes the dualistic and spiritualistic tendencies of his time. He uses the contrast *ange-bête* which Pascal was to borrow from him. He might easily have added considerably to the number of Christian testimonies in support of his view. Above all he might have called upon the incarnation of the Word itself for support. He did not do so, although the idea undoubtedly occurred to him; in this connection it could not but force itself upon anyone brought up a Christian in Montaigne's day. He avoided the allusion, obviously intentionally, for it would automatically have given his statements the character of a profession of Christianity, which was far from what he had in mind. He likes to keep away from such ticklish subjects. But the question of his religious profession—which, by the way, I consider an idle question—has nothing to do with the observation that the roots of his realistic conception of man are to be found in the Christian-creatural tradition.

We now come to the last part of our text. It is concerned with the unity which in his case exists between the work and the author, in contrast to the specialists, who exhibit a fund of professional knowledge but loosely related to their person. He says the same thing, with some different nuances, in another passage (2, 18, p. 666): *Je n'ay pas plus faict mon livre que mon livre m'a faict: livre consubstantiel à son autheur, d'une occupation propre, membre de ma vie, non d'une occupation et fin tierce et estrangiere, comme tous autres livres.* Nothing need be added to that. But his malice against the erudite expert and against specialization requires some comment, with a view to determining the historical position of such utterances. The ideal of a non-specialized man, a man developed on all sides, reached humanism from both the theory and the example of antiquity, but the social structure of the sixteenth century did not permit its full realization. Furthermore, it was precisely the effort required by the rediscovery of the heritage of antiquity which brought into existence a new type of humanist expert and specialist. Rabelais may still have been convinced that perfect personal culture was necessarily identical with the mastery of all branches of knowledge, that universality, then, was the sum of all specialized erudition. Possibly his surrealistic program of education for Gargantua was meant to be taken seriously in this sense. In any case, it could not be achieved; and the scientific labor that had to be performed is now subjected, far more than in the Middle Ages, to a progressive specialization. In diametric contrast to this is the ideal of an all-around and uniformly perfected personality. This ideal was the more influential since it was not upheld by humanism alone; it was also supported by the late feudal idea of the perfect courtier, which was revived by absolutism and enriched by Platonizing tendencies. Then too, with the growth of wealth and the wider diffusion of elementary education, there was a great increase in the number of those —partly noblemen and partly members of the urban bourgeoisie—who, aspiring to participation in cultural life, required a form of knowledge which should not be specialized erudition. Thus there arose a nonprofessional, strongly social, and even fashionable form of general knowledge. It was, of course, not encyclopedic in range although it represents as it were an extract from all branches of knowledge, with a pronounced preference for the literary and for the aesthetic generally; humanism, indeed, was itself in a position to furnish most of the material. Thus arose the class of those who were later to be called "the educated." Since it was recruited from the socially and economically most influential circles, to whom good breeding and conduct in the fashionable sense, amiability in social intercourse, aptitude for human contact, and presence of mind meant more than any specialized competence; since in such circles, even when their origin was middle class, feudal and knightly value concepts were still dominant; since these were supported by the classicizing ideals of humanism insofar as the ruling classes of antiquity had also regarded preoccupation with art and science not as a professional matter but as *otium*, as an ornament indispensable for the man destined to the most general life and to political leadership: there soon resulted a sort of contempt for professional specialization. The scholar committed to a particular discipline and, in general, the individual committed to a particular profession or trade—the human individual who was fully absorbed in his specialized knowledge and revealed the fact in his behavior and in his conversation—was considered comic, inferior, and plebeian. This attitude attained its fullest development with the French absolutism of the seventeenth century, and we shall have to speak of it in greater detail hereafter, since it contributed to no small extent to the ideal of a separation of styles which dominates French classicism. For the more general a man's culture and the less it recognizes a specialized knowledge and a specialized activity, at least as a point of departure for a more general survey of things, the further removed from the sphere of the concrete, the lifelike, and the practical will be the type of all-around perfection striven after.

In this development—although it certainly would not have been to his liking—Montaigne has an important place. His *homme suffisant* who is *suffisant* always, *même à ignorer*, is doubtless a predecessor of that *honnête homme* who—like Molière's marquises—need not have learned anything in particular in order to judge everything with fashionable assurance. After all, Montaigne is the first author who wrote for the educated stratum just described; by the success of the Essays the educated public first revealed its existence. Montaigne does not write for a particular class, nor for a particular profession, nor for "the people," nor for Christians; he writes for no party; he does not consider himself a poet; he writes the first work of lay introspection, and lo!, there were people—men and women—who felt that they were spoken to. Some of the humanist translators—especially Amyot, whom Montaigne praises for it—had prepared the way. Yet as an independent writer, Montaigne is the first. And so it is only natural that his ideas of personal culture are those adapted to that first stratum of educated people who were still eminently aristocratic and not yet obliged to do specialized work. To be sure, in his case this does not imply that his own culture and way of life became abstract, void of reality, remote from random everyday events, and "style-separating." Precisely the opposite is true. His fortunate and richly gifted nature required no practical duties and no intellectual activity within a specialized subject in order to remain close to reality. From one instant to the next, as it were, it specialized in something else; every instant it probed another impression and did so with a concreteness which the century of the *honnête homme* would certainly have considered unseemly. Or we might say: he specialized in his own self, in his random personal existence as a whole. Thus his *homme suffisant* is after all not as yet the *honnête homme;* he is "a whole man." Furthermore, Montaigne lived at a time when absolutism, with its leveling effect and consequent standardization of the form of life of the *honnête homme,* was not yet fully developed. This is the reason why, though Montaigne occupies an important place in the prehistory of this form of life, he is still outside of it.

The text we have analyzed is a good point of departure for a conscious comprehension of the largest possible number of the themes and attitudes in Montaigne's undertaking, the portrayal of his own random personal life as a whole. He displays himself in complete seriousness, in order to illuminate the general conditions of human existence. He displays himself embedded in the random contingencies of his life and deals indiscriminately with the fluctuating movements of his consciousness, and it is precisely his random indiscriminateness that constitutes his method. He speaks of a thousand things and one easily leads to another. Whether he relates an anecdote, discusses his daily occupations, ponders a moral precept of antiquity, or anticipatorily savors the sensation of his own death, he hardly changes his tone; it is all the same to him. And the tone he uses is on the whole that of a lively but unexcited and very richly nuanced conversation. We can hardly call it a monologue for we constantly get the impression that he is talking to someone. We almost always sense an element of irony, often a very strong one, yet it does not in the least interfere with the spontaneous sincerity which radiates from every line. He is never grandiose or rhetorical; the dignity of his subject matter never makes him renounce an earthy popular turn of expression or an image taken from everyday life. The upper limit of his style is, as we noted above, the earnestness which prevails almost throughout our text, particularly in the second paragraph. It makes itself felt here—as it frequently does elsewhere—through boldly contrasted and usually antithetic clauses together with distinct and striking formulations. Yet sometimes there is an almost poetic movement too, as in the passage from 2, 6 which we quoted above on page 292f. The *profondeurs opaques* are almost lyrical, yet he immediately interrupts the long poetic rhythm by the energetic and conversational *ouy*. A really elevated tone is foreign to him, he wants none of it; he is made to be completely at ease on a level of tone which he himself characterizes as *stile comique et privé* (1, 40, p. 485). This is unmistakably an allusion to the realistic style of antique comedy, the *sermo pedester* or *humilis*, and similar allusions occur in large numbers. But the content he presents is in no sense comic; it is the *humaine condition* with all its burdens, pitfalls, and problems, with all its essential insecurity, with all the creatural bonds which confine it. Animal existence, and the death which is inseparable from it, appear in frightening palpability, in gruesome suggestiveness.

No doubt such a creatural realism would be inconceivable without the preparatory Christian conception of man, especially in the form it took during the later Middle Ages. And Montaigne is aware of this too. He is aware that his extremely concrete linking of mind and body is related to Christian views of man. But it is also true that his creatural realism has broken through the Christian frame within which it arose. Life on earth is no longer the figure of the life beyond; he can no longer permit himself to scorn and neglect the here for the sake of a there. Life on earth is the only one he has. He wants to savor it to the last drop: *car enfin c'est nostre estre, c'est nostre tout* (2, 3, p. 47). To live here is his purpose and his art, and the way he wants this to be understood is very simple but in no sense trivial. It entails first of all emancipating oneself from everything that might waste or hinder the enjoyment of life, that might divert the living man's attention from himself. For *c'est chose tendre que la vie, et aysée à troubler* (3, 9, p. 334). It is necessary to keep oneself free, to preserve oneself for one's own life, to withdraw from the all-too binding obligations of the world's affairs, not to tie oneself down to this, that, or the other: *la plus grande chose du monde c'est de sçavoir estre à soy* (1, 39, pp. 464-465). All this is serious and fundamental enough; it is much too high for the *sermo humilis* as understood in antique theory, and yet it could not be expressed in an elevated rhetorical style, without any concrete portrayal of the everyday; the mixture of styles is creatural and Christian. But the attitude is no longer Christian and medieval. One hesitates to call it antique either; for that, it is too rooted in the realm of the concrete. And still another point must here be considered. Montaigne's emancipation from the Christian conceptual schema did not—despite his exact knowledge and continuous study of antique culture—simply put him back among the ideas and conditions among which men of his sort had lived in the days of Cicero or Plutarch. His newly acquired freedom was much more exciting, much more of the historical moment, directly connected with the feeling of insecurity. The disconcerting abundance of phenomena which now claimed the attention of men seemed overwhelming. The world—both outer world and inner world—seemed immense, boundless, incomprehensible. The need to orient oneself in it seemed hard to satisfy and yet urgent. True enough, among all the important and at times as it were more than life-sized personages of his century, Montaigne is the calmest. He has enough of substance and elasticity in himself, he possesses a natural moderation, and has little need of security since it always reestablishes itself spontaneously within him. He is further helped by his resignedly negative attitude toward the study of nature, his unswerving aspiration toward nothing but his own self. However, his book manifests the excitement which sprang from the sudden and tremendous enrichment of the world picture and from the presentiment of the yet untapped possibilities the world contained. And—still more significant—among all his contemporaries he had the clearest conception of the problem of man's self-orientation; that is, the task of making oneself at home in existence without fixed points of support. In him for the first time, man's life—the random personal life as a whole—becomes problematic in the modern sense. That is all one dares to say. His irony, his dislike of big words, his calm way of being profoundly at ease with himself, prevent him from pushing on beyond the limits of the problematic and into the realm of the tragic, which is already unmistakably apparent in let us say the work of Michelangelo and which, during the generation following Montaigne's, is to break through in literary form in several places in Europe. It has often been said that the tragic was unknown to the Christian Middle Ages. It might be more exact to put it that for the Middle Ages the tragic was contained in the tragedy of Christ. (The expression "tragedy of Christ," is no modern license. It finds support in Boethius and in Honorius Augustodunensis.) But now the tragic appears as the highly personal tragedy of the individual, and moreover, compared with antiquity, as far less restricted by traditional ideas of the limits of fate, the cosmos, natural forces, political forms, and man's inner being. We said before that the tragic is not yet to be found in Montaigne's work; he shuns it. He is too dispassionate, too unrhetorical, too ironic, and indeed too easy-going, if this term can be used in a dignified sense. He conceives himself too calmly, despite all his probing into his own insecurity. Whether this is a weakness or a strength is a question I shall not try to answer. In any case, this peculiar equilibrium of his being prevents the tragic, the possibility of which is inherent in his image of man, from coming to expression in his work.

13

THE WEARY PRINCE

Prince Henry: Before God, I am exceeding weary.

Poins: Is it come to that? I had thought weariness durst not have attached one of so high blood.

Prince Henry: Faith, it does me; though it discolours the complexion of my greatness to acknowledge it. Does it not show vilely in me to desire small beer?

Poins: Why, a prince should not be so loosely studied as to remember so weak a composition.

Prince Henry: Belike, then, my appetite was not princely got; for, by my troth, I do now remember the poor creature, small beer. But, indeed, these humble considerations make me out of love with my greatness. What a disgrace is it to me to remember thy name? or to know thy face to-morrow? or to take note how many silk stockings thou hast; viz., these, and those that were thy peach-coloured ones? or to bear the inventory of thy shirts, as, one for superfluity, and one other for use? . . .

This is a conversation between Prince Henry (subsequently King Henry) and one of the boon companions of his youthful frolics. It occurs in Shakespeare's *Henry IV*, part 2, at the beginning of the second scene of act 2. The comic disapproval of the fact that a person of such high rank should be subject to weariness and the desire for small beer, that his mind should be obliged so much as to notice the existence of so lowly a creature as Poins and even to remember the inventory of his clothes, is a satire on the trend—no longer negligible in Shakespeare's day—toward a strict separation between the sublime and the realm of everyday realities. Attempts in this direction were inspired by the example of antiquity, especially by Seneca, and were spread by the humanist imitators of antique drama in Italy, France, and in England itself. But they had not yet met with complete success. However important the influence of antiquity may have been on Shakespeare, it could not mislead him, nor yet other dramatists of the Elizabethan period, into this separation of styles. The medieval-Christian and at the same time popular-English tradition which opposed such a development was still too strong. At a much later period, more than a century and a half after his death, Shakespeare's work became the ideal and the example for all movements of revolt against the strict separation of styles in French classicism. Let us try to determine what the mixture of styles in his work signifies.

The motif is introduced by Poins, and then immediately taken up by the Prince in a humorous vein with an undertone of rhetorical preciosity which serves to emphasize the contrasts: "it discolours the complexion of my greatness" versus "small beer." Goaded on by Poins's second reply, the Prince playfully develops the theme: "small beer" now becomes a wretched creature that has sneaked into the noble recesses of his consciousness against all law and order, as it were. Now other "humble considerations" occur to him and put him out of conceit with his own greatness. From among them, with wittily charming impertinence, he falls upon the very Poins who stands before him: is it not a shame to me, he argues, that I should remember your name, your face, and even the inventory of your clothes?

A large number of the elements of mixed style are mentioned or alluded to in these few lines: the element of physical creaturalness, that of lowly everyday objects, and that of the mixture of classes involving persons of high and low rank; there is also a marked mixture of high and low expressions in the diction, there is even use of one of the classical terms which characterize the low style, the word "humble." All this is abundantly represented in Shakespeare's tragic works. Examples of the portrayal of the physical-creatural are numerous: Hamlet is fat and short of breath (according to another reading he is not fat but hot); Caesar faints from the stench of the mob acclaiming him; Cassio in *Othello* is drunk; hunger and thirst, cold and heat affect tragic characters too; they suffer from the inclemencies of the weather and the ravages of illness: in Ophelia's case insanity is represented with such realistic psychology that the resulting stylistic effect is completely different from what we find in Euripides' *Herakles* for example; and death, which can be depicted on the level of the pure sublime, here often has its medieval and creatural appearance (skeletons, the smell of decomposition, etc.). Nowhere is there an attempt to avoid mentioning everyday utensils or, in general, to avoid the concrete portrayal of the everyday processes of life; these things have a much larger place than they do in antique tragedy, although there too, even before Euripides, they were not so completely taboo as with the classicists of the sixteenth and seventeenth centuries.

More important than this is the mixture of characters and the consequent mixture of tragic and comic elements. To be sure, all the characters whom Shakespeare treats in the sublime and tragic manner are of high rank. He does not, as the Middle Ages did, conceive of "everyman" as tragic. He is also more consciously aristocratic than Montaigne. In his work the *humaine condition* is reflected very differently in the different classes, not only in practical terms but also from the point of view of aesthetic dignity. His tragic heroes are kings, princes, commanders, noblemen, and the great figures of Roman history. A borderline case is Shylock. To be sure, in terms of his class, he is not a common everyday figure; he is a pariah; but his class is low. The slight action of the *Merchant of Venice*, with its fairy-tale motifs, is almost too heavily burdened by the weight and problematic implications of his character, and many actors who have undertaken the part have tried to concentrate the entire interest of the play upon him and to make him a tragic hero. His character is a temptation to tragic overemphasis: his hatred has the deepest and most human motivation, is much more deeply based than the wickedness of Richard III; it becomes significant through its power and tenacity. In addition, Shylock formulates it in phrases which echo great humanitarian ideas, especially those which most deeply moved and influenced later centuries. The most famous of these formulations is the answer which he gives the doge at the beginning of the great court scene (4, 1) when, alone against all the others, he defends his rigid and pitiless legal viewpoint: Why do you not treat your slaves as your equals? You will answer: The slaves are ours: so do I answer you. At this and many other moments there is something about him of somber and at the same time truly human greatness. And in general he does not lack problematic depth, impressiveness of character, power and passion, and strength of expression. And yet in the end Shakespeare drops these tragic elements with heedless Olympian serenity. In earlier scenes he had already put a strong emphasis on ludicrous and grotesque traits in Shylock's character, notably his miserliness and his somewhat senile fear; and in the scene with Tubal (end of 3, 1), where he alternately laments the loss of the valuables which Jessica has taken with her and rejoices over Antonio's ruin, Shylock is frankly a figure from farce. In the end Shakespeare dismisses him, without greatness, as a circumvented fiend, just as he found him in his sources, and after his departure he adds a whole act of poetical fairy-tale sport and amorous dalliance, while Shylock is forgotten and abandoned. There is no doubt, then, that the actors are wrong who have tried to make Shylock a tragic hero. Such a conception is at odds with the economy of the play as a whole. Shylock has less greatness by far than Marlowe's gruesome Jew of Malta and that despite the fact that Shakespeare saw and stated the human problem of his Jew much more deeply. For him Shylock, both in terms of class and aesthetically, is a low figure, unworthy of tragic treatment, whose tragic involvement is conjured up for a moment, but is only an added spice in the triumph of a higher, nobler, freer, and also more aristocratic humanity. Our Prince has the same views. Far be it from him to respect Poins as his equal, although he is the best among the characters in the Falstaff group, although he possesses both wit and valor. What arrogance there is in the words he addresses to him only a few lines before the passage quoted above: ". . . I could tell to thee —as to one it pleases me, for fault of a better, to call my friend. . . ." The manner in which Shakespeare elsewhere treats the middle and lower classes we shall take up in due course. In any case, he never renders them tragically. His conception of the sublime and tragic is altogether aristocratic.

But if we disregard this class restriction, Shakespeare's mixing of styles in the portrayal of his characters is very pronounced. In most of the plays which have a generally tragic tenor there is an extremely close interweaving of the tragic and the comic, the sublime and the low. This effect is brought about by the joint use of several methods. Tragic actions in which public or other tragic events occur, alternate with humorous popular and rowdy scenes which are now closely, now somewhat more loosely connected with the principal action. Or again in the tragic scenes themselves, and with the tragic heroes, there appear fools and other humorous types who accompany, interrupt, and—each in his own way—comment upon what the heroes do, suffer, and say. Finally, not a few of Shakespeare's tragic characters have their own innate tendency to break the stylistic tenor in a humorous, realistic, or bitterly grotesque fashion. There are numerous examples of the three procedures, and very frequently two of these methods, or even all three, are used in conjunction. For the first—the alternation of tragic and comic scenes in a tragedy—we may cite the populace scenes in the Roman plays, or the Falstaff episodes in the histories, or the grave-digger scene in *Hamlet*. The last named example verges on the tragic and, because of Hamlet's own appearance in it, might almost be used as an illustration of the second or even the third procedure. The most famous example of the second procedure—sublime and tragic personages accompanied by comic commentators—is the fool in *King Lear*; but much more in the same genre can be found not only in *Lear* but also in *Hamlet, Romeo and Juliet,* and elsewhere. Still more decisive for the stylistic character of Shakespeare's tragedy is the third procedure, the mixture of styles in the tragic personage himself. In Shylock's case—where, to be sure, Shakespeare in the end decided in favor of an interpretation in terms of the comic and the low—we have already observed the shifting back and forth between the tragic and the comic within one character. But the same phenomenon, in variously proportioned mixtures, is also to be found in characters who are treated as unqualifiedly tragic. Even Romeo's sudden falling in love with Juliet, for example, is almost fit for a comedy, and an almost unconscious development takes the characters in this play of love from childlike beginnings to a tragic climax. Gloucester's successful wooing of Lady Anne at the bier of Henry VI (*King Richard III*, 1, 2), has something darkly grotesque; Cleopatra is childish and moody; even Caesar is undecided, superstitious, and his rhetorical pride is almost comically exaggerated. There is much more of this nature. Hamlet and Lear especially furnish the most significant examples. Hamlet's half real, half pretended insanity rages, within a single scene and even a single speech, through all levels of style. He jumps from the obscene to the lyrical or sublime, from the ironically incongruous to dark and profound meditation, from humiliating scorn leveled at others and himself to the solemn assumption of the right to judge and proud self-assertion. Lear's rich, forceful, and emotional arbitrariness has in its incomparable sublimity elements that strike us as painfully senile and theatrical. The speeches of his faithful fool themselves tear at his mantle of sublimity; but more incisive are the stylistic ruptures which lie in his own nature: his excesses of emotion, his impotent and helpless outbursts of anger, his inclination to indulge in bitterly grotesque histrionics. In the fourth scene of act 2 he falls on his knees before his wicked daughter Regan, who has hurt and is still hurting him most grievously, in order to act out as it were the step he is expected to take (that is, to ask Goneril, his other daughter, to forgive him). This is an extreme and theatrical gesture of bitterly grotesque self-humiliation. He is always ready to exaggerate; he wants to force heaven and earth to witness the extremes of his humiliation and to hear his complaints. Such gestures seem immeasurably shocking in an old man of eighty, in a great king. And yet they do not in the least detract from his dignity and greatness. His nature is so unconditionally royal that humiliation only brings it out more strongly. Shakespeare makes him speak the famous words "aye, every inch a king," himself, from the depth of his insanity, grotesquely accoutered, a madman playing the king for a moment. Yet we do not laugh, we weep, and not only in pity but at the same time in admiration for such greatness, which seems only the greater and more indestructible in its brittle creaturality.

Let these examples suffice. Their purpose is merely to remind the reader of these generally known facts and to present them in an arrangement that accords with our particular problem. Shakespeare mixes the sublime and the low, the tragic and the comic in an inexhaustible abundance of proportions. And the picture is further enriched if we also consider the fabulous and fantastic comedies in which there are also occasional overtones of the tragic. Among the tragedies there is none in which a single level of style is maintained from beginning to end. Even in *Macbeth* we have the grotesque scene with the porter (2, 1).

In the course of the sixteenth century the conscious distinction of the categories of tragic and comic in human destiny had come to the fore again. A similar distinction was not, it is true, entirely unknown during the Middle Ages, but in those earlier centuries the conception of the tragic could not develop unimpeded. This is not entirely due—as a matter of fact it is not due at all—to the fact that the tragic works of antiquity were unknown, that antique theory had been forgotten or misundersood. Facts of this nature could not have interfered with the independent development of the tragic. The reason is rather that the Christian figural view of human life was opposed to a development of the tragic. However serious the events of earthly existence might be, high above them stood the towering and all-embracing dignity of a single event, the appearance of Christ, and everything tragic was but figure or reflection of a single complex of events, into which it necessarily flowed at last: the complex of the Fall, of Christ's birth and passion, and of the Last Judgment. This implies a transposition of the center of gravity from life on earth into a life beyond, with the result that no tragedy ever reached its conclusion here below. To be sure, we had occasion earlier, especially in the chapter on Dante, to point out that this by no means signifies a devaluation of life on earth or of human individuality; but it did bring with it a blunting of tragic climaxes here on earth and a transposition of catharsis into the other world.

Then, in the course of the sixteenth century, the Christian-figural schema lost its hold in almost all parts of Europe. The issue into the beyond, although it was totally abandoned only in rare instances, lost in certainty and unmistakability. And at the same time antique models (first Seneca, then the Greeks also) and antique theory reappeared, unclouded. The powerful influence of the authors of antiquity greatly furthered the development of the tragic. It was, however, unavoidable that this influence should at times have been at odds with the new forces which, arising from contemporary conditions and the autochthonous culture, were driving toward the tragic.

The dramatic occurrences of human life were seen by antiquity predominantly in the form of a change of fortune breaking in upon man from without and from above. In Elizabethan tragedy on the other hand—the first specifically modern form of tragedy—the hero's individual character plays a much greater part in shaping his destiny. This is, I believe, the prevailing view, and on the whole it appears to me to be correct. But it needs to be qualified and supplemented. In the introduction to an edition of Shakespeare which I have before me (*The Complete Works of W.S.*, London and Glasgow, n.d., Introduction by St. John Ervine, p. xii) I find it expressed in the following terms: "And here we come on the great difference between the Greek and the Elizabethan drama: the tragedy in the Greek plays is an arranged one in which the characters have no decisive part. Theirs but to do and die. But the tragedy in the Elizabethan plays comes straight from the heart of the people themselves. Hamlet is Hamlet, not because a capricious god has compelled him to move to a tragic end, but because there is a unique essence in him which makes him incapable of behaving in any other way than he does." And the critic continues by emphasizing Hamlet's freedom of action, which allows him to doubt and hesitate before he comes to a decision—a freedom of action which Oedipus and Orestes do not possess. In this form the contrast is formulated too absolutely. It is not possible to deny Euripides' Medea a "unique essence" and even freedom of action or to overlook the fact that she has moments of indecision when she fights her own gruesome passion. Indeed, even Sophocles, that almost model representative of classical antiquity, shows at the beginning of his *Antigone*, in the conversation between the two sisters, an example of two persons who find themselves in exactly the same situation but who decide—without any pressure of fate and purely in accordance with their own particular characters—in favor of different courses of conduct. Yet the English critic's basic idea is sound: in Elizabethan tragedy and specifically in Shakespeare, the hero's character is depicted in greater and more varied detail than in antique tragedy, and participates more actively in shaping the individual's fate. But it is also possible to describe the difference in another way: one might say that the idea of destiny in Elizabethan tragedy is both more broadly conceived and more closely linked to the individual character than it is in antique tragedy. In the latter, fate means nothing but the given tragic complex, the present network of events in which a particular person is enmeshed at a particular moment. To whatever else may have happened to him during his life, so long as it is not part of the prehistory of the present conflict, to what we call his "milieu," little attention is given, and apart from age, sex, social status, and references to his general type of temperament, we learn nothing about his normal existence. The essence of his personality is revealed and evolves exclusively within the particular tragic action; everything else is omitted. All this is based upon the way in which antique drama arose and on its technical requirements. Freedom of movement, which it reached only very slowly, is much less, even in Euripides, than in the modern drama. In particular, the above-mentioned strict limitation to the given tragic conflict is based upon the fact that the subjects of antique tragedy are almost exclusively taken from the national mythology, in a few cases from national history. These were sacred subjects and the events and personages involved were known to the audience. The "milieu" too was known, and furthermore it was almost always approximately the same. Hence there was no reason to describe its special character and special atmosphere. Euripides challenged the tradition by introducing new interpretations, both of action and character, into the traditional material. But this can hardly be compared with the multiplicity of subject matter, the freedom of invention and presentation which distinguish the Elizabethan and the modern drama generally. What with the great variety of subject matter and the considerable freedom of movement of the Elizabethan theater, we are in each instance given the particular atmosphere, the situation, and the prehistory of the characters. The course of events on the stage is not rigidly restricted to the course of events of the tragic conflict but covers conversations, scenes, characters, which the action as such does not necessarily require. Thus we are given a great deal of "supplementary information" about the principal personages; we are enabled to form an idea of their normal lives and particular characters apart from the complication in which they are caught at the moment. Thus fate here means much more than the given conflict. In antique tragedy it is almost always possible to make a clear distinction between the natural character of a personage and the fate which befalls him at the moment. In Elizabethan tragedy we are in most cases confronted not with purely natural character but with character already formed by birth, situation in life, and prehistory (that is, by fate)—character in which fate has already had a great share before it fulfils itself in the form of a specified tragic conflict. The latter is often only the occasion which releases a tragic situation prepared long before. This is particularly apparent in the cases of Shylock and Lear. What happens to them individually, is individually predestined for them; it fits the specific character of Shylock or of Lear, and this character is not only the natural character but one prepared by birth, situation, and prehistory, that is, by fate, for its unmistakable idiosyncrasy and for the tragic situation destined for it.

We have already mentioned one of the causes or at least premises of this far more broadly conceived presentation of human destiny: the theater of the Elizabethans offers a much more varied human world than did the antique theater. Its range of subject matter covers all lands and times and all the combinations of fancy. There are themes from English and Roman history, from the legendary past, from novelle and fairy tales. The places of the action are England, Scotland, France, Denmark, Italy, Spain, the islands of the Mediterranean, the Orient, ancient Greece, ancient Rome, ancient Egypt. The exotic appeal which Venice, Verona, and the like had for an English audience in the year 1600 is an element that was virtually—not to say completely—unknown to the theater of the ancients. A figure like Shylock's raises through its mere existence problems outside the sphere of the classical drama. Here we must point out that the sixteenth century had attained a comparatively high level of historical consciousness and historical perspective. For a similar development the antique theater had little occasion, because the range of its subject matter was too limited and because the antique audience did not regard any form of life and culture except its own either as equal in value or as worthy of artistic attention. During the Middle Ages all practical acquaintance with alien forms of life and culture was lost. Although two past cultures—the antique and the Judaeo-Christian—were of great importance within the frame of medieval civilization, and although both of them, especially the Judaeo-Christian, were often portrayed in literature and art, there was yet such a lack of historical consciousness and perspective that the events and characters of those distant epochs were simply transferred to the present forms and conditions of life: Caesar, Aeneas, Pilate became knights, Joseph of Arimathaea a burgher, and Adam a farmer, of twelfth or thirteenth century France, England, or Germany.

With the first dawn of humanism, there began to be a sense that the events of classical history and legend and also those of the Bible were not separated from the present simply by an extent of time but also by completely different conditions of life. Humanism with its program of renewal of antique forms of life and expression creates a historical perspective in depth such as no previous epoch known to us possessed: the humanists see antiquity in historical depth, and, against that background, the dark epochs of the intervening Middle Ages. It makes no difference what errors of conception and interpretation they may have been guilty of in detail—the vision in perspective was gained. From Dante on it is possible to detect traces of such a historical perspective; in the sixteenth century it grows more distinct and more widely known, and even though, as we shall see, the tendency to accept antiquity as an absolute model and to neglect everything pertaining to the intervening centuries threatened to expel historical perspective from men's consciousness again, it was never successful to the extent of reestablishing the autarchic life natural to antique culture or the historical naïveté of the twelfth and thirteenth centuries. In addition there is in the sixteenth century the effect of the great discoveries which abruptly widened the cultural and geographic horizon and hence also men's conception of possible forms of human life. The various European peoples came to regard themselves as national entities and hence grew conscious of their distinctive characteristics. Finally the schism in the Church contributed to differentiating various groups of people. In consequence the comparatively simple contrast of Greek or Roman versus barbarian or Christian versus heathen was replaced by a much more complex picture of human society. This did not happen all at once; it was prepared over a long period of time; but in the sixteenth century it progresses by leaps and bounds, adding enormously both to the breadth of perspective and to the number of individuals acquiring it. The world of realities in which men live is changed; it grows broader, richer in possibilities, limitless. And it changes correspondingly when it appears as the subject matter of artistic representation. The sphere of life represented in a particular instance is no longer the only one possible or a part of that only and clearly circumscribed one. Very often there is a switch from one sphere to another, and even in cases where this does not occur, we are able to discern as the basis of the representation a freer consciousness embracing an unlimited world. We have commented upon this in connection with Boccaccio and especially in connection with Rabelais; we could also have done so in connection with Montaigne. In Elizabethan tragedy and particularly in Shakespeare, perspective consciousness has become a matter of course, although it is neither very precise nor uniformly expressed. Shakespeare and the authors of his generation sometimes have erroneous ideas about foreign lands and cultures; they sometimes intentionally mingle contemporary scenes and allusions with a foreign theme, as for example the observations on the London stage in *Hamlet*. Quite often Shakespeare makes the setting of a play some fairyland only loosely connected with real times and places. But this too is only a playing upon the perspective view. Consciousness of the manifold conditions of human life is a fact with him, and he can take it for granted on the part of his audience.

Within a specific theme there is still another type of evidence of perspective consciousness. Shakespeare and many of his contemporaries are averse to completely detaching a turn of fortune which concerns a single person or a limited number of persons from its general context of events and presenting it on a single level of style, as the tragic poets of antiquity had done and wherein their sixteenth and seventeenth century imitators even outdid them at times. This isolating procedure, which is to be explained through the religious, mythological, and technical premises of the antique theater, is out of keeping with the concept of a magical and polyphonic cosmic coherence which arose during the Renaissance. Shakespeare's drama does not present isolated blows of fate, generally falling from above and involving but a few people in their effects, while the milieu is limited to the few persons indispensable to the progress of the action; on the contrary, it offers inner entanglements which result from given conditions and from the interplay of variously constituted characters and in which not only the milieu but even the landscape, even the spirits of the dead and other supernatural beings participate. And the role of these participants often contributes nothing at all or at least very little to the progress of the action, but instead consists in a sympathetic counterpoint—a parallel or contrary motion on various levels of style. There is an abundance of secondary actions and secondary characters which, in terms of the economy of the principal action, could be entirely dispensed with or at least greatly reduced. Instances are the Gloucester episode in *Lear*, the scene between Pompey and Menas in *Antony and Cleopatra* (2, 7), many scenes and characters in *Hamlet*—everybody can add to the list. Naturally, such actions and characters are not completely useless in the dramatic economy. Even a minor character like Osric in *Hamlet* is rendered so fully because he releases a significant reflex of Hamlet's temperament and momentary state of mind. Yet for the progress of the action, Osric need not have been fully rendered. Shakespeare's dramatic economy is prodigally lavish; it bears witness to his delight in rendering the most varied phenomena of life, and this delight in turn is inspired by the concept that the cosmos is everywhere interdependent, so that every chord of human destiny arouses a multitude of voices to parallel or contrary motion. The storm into which Regan drives her old father, the king, is not an accident; it is contrived by magic powers which are mobilized to bring the event to a crisis, and the fool's speeches, and Poor Tom's later, are voices from the same cosmic orchestra, although their function within the purely rational structure of the action is very slight. But they bring with them a rich scale of stylistic levels, which, within the prevailing key—the sublime—descends to farce and sheer nonsense.

This stylistic situation is characteristically Elizabethan and Shakespearean, but it is rooted in popular tradition, and indeed first of all in the cosmic drama of the story of Christ. There are intermediate steps and it is also true that a variety of folkloristic motifs not of Christian origin have forced their way in. But the creatural view of man, the loose construction with its numerous accessory actions and characters, and the mixture of the sublime with the low cannot in the last analysis come from any other source than the medieval Christian theater, in which all these things were necessary and essential. Even the participation of the elements in a great destiny has its best-known model in the earthquake at the time of Christ's death (Matthew 27: 51ff.), and this model had remained very influential during the Middle Ages (cf. *Chanson de Roland*, 1423ff. or *Vita Nova*, 23). Yet now, in the drama of the Elizabethans, the superstructure of the whole has been lost; the drama of Christ is no longer the general drama, is no longer the point of confluence of all the streams of human destiny. The new dramatized history has a specific human action as its center, derives its unity from that center, and the road has been opened for an autonomously human tragedy. The great order of the past—Fall, Divine Sacrifice, Last Judgment—recedes, the human drama finds its order within itself; and it is at this point that antique precedent intervenes with plot-complication, crisis, and tragic resolution; the division of the action into acts is from the same source. But the freedom of tragedy, and the realm of man generally, no longer acknowledge the limits of antiquity. The dissolution of medieval Christianity, running its course through a series of great crises, brings out a dynamic need for self-orientation, a will to trace the secret forces of life. Through this need and will, magic and science, the elemental sphere and the moral and human sphere, become mutually related. An immense system of sympathy seems to pervade the universe. Furthermore Christianity had conceived the problems of humanity (good and evil, guilt and destiny) more excitingly, antithetically, and even paradoxically than had antiquity. Even after the solution contained in the drama of original sin and salvation began to lose its validity, the more deeply stirring conception of the problem and the related ideas of the nature of man long remained influential. In Shakespeare's work the liberated forces show themselves as fully developed yet still permeated with the entire ethical wealth of the past. Not much later the restrictive countermovements gained the upper hand. Protestantism and the Counter Reformation, absolutistic ordering of society and intellectual life, academic and puristic imitation of antiquity, rationalism and scientific empiricism, all operated together to prevent Shakespeare's freedom in the tragic from continuing to develop after him.

Thus Shakespeare's ethical and intellectual world is much more agitated, multilayered, and, apart from any specific dramatic action, in itself more dramatic than that of antiquity. The very ground on which men move and actions take their course is more unsteady and seems shaken by inner disturbances. There is no stable world as background, but a world which is perpetually reengendering itself out of the most varied forces. No reader or spectator can fail to sense this; but it may not be superfluous to describe the dynamism of Shakespeare's thought in somewhat greater detail and give an example of it. In antique tragedy the philosophizing is generally undramatic; it is sententious, aphoristic, is abstracted from the action and generalized, is detached from the personage and his fate. In Shakespeare's plays it becomes personal; it grows directly out of the speaker's immediate situation and remains connected with it. It is not a result of the experience gained in the action, nor an effective rejoinder in the stychomythia; it is dramatic self-scrutiny seeking the right mode and moment for action or doubting the possibility of finding them. When the most revolutionary of the Greek tragic poets, Euripides, attacks the class distinctions between men, he does so in a sententiously constructed verse to the effect that only the name dishonors the slave; otherwise a noble slave is nowise inferior to a free man. Shakespeare does not attack class distinctions, and it would seem that he had no views of social revolutionary import. Yet when one of his characters expresses such ideas out of his own situation it is done with an immediacy, a dramatic force, which give the ideas something arresting and incisive: Let your slaves live as you live; give them the same food and quarters; marry them to your children! You say your slaves are your property? Very well, just so do I answer you: this pound of flesh is mine, I bought it. . . . The pariah Shylock does not appeal to natural right but to customary wrong. What a dynamic immediacy there is in such bitter, tragic irony!

The great number of moral phenomena which the constant renewal of the world as a whole produces, and which themselves constantly contribute to its renewal, engenders an abundance of stylistic levels such as antique tragedy was never able to produce. I open a volume of Shakespeare at random and come upon *Macbeth*, act 3, scene 6, where Lennox, a Scottish nobleman, tells a friend what he thinks of the most recent events:

> My former speeches have but hit your thoughts,
> Which can interpret further: only, I say,
> Things have been strangely borne. The gracious Duncan
> Was pitied of Macbeth:—marry, he was dead:—
> And the right-valiant Banquo walk'd too late;
> Whom, you might say, if't please you, Fleance kill'd,
> For Fleance fled. Men must not walk too late.
> Who cannot want the thought, how monstrous
> It was for Malcolm and for Donalbain
> To kill their gracious father? damned fact!
> How did it grieve Macbeth! did he not straight,
> In pious rage, the two delinquents tear,
> That were the slaves of drinks and thralls of sleep?
> Was not that nobly done? Ay, and wisely too;
> For 'twould have anger'd any heart alive,
> To hear the men deny't. . . .

The form of discourse employed in this passage—a form in which something is insidiously implied or "insinuated" without being stated —was well known in antiquity. Quintilian treats of it in his ninth book, where he discusses the *controversiae figuratae*, and the great orators offer examples of it. But that it should be used so completely unrhetorically, in the course of a private conversation, and yet entirely within the somberly tragic atmosphere, is a mixture which is foreign to antiquity. I turn a few pages and come to the lines in which, immediately before his last battle, Macbeth receives the news of his wife's death:

Seyton: The queen, my lord, is dead.
Macbeth: She should have died hereafter;
There would have been a time for such a word . . .
To-morrow, and to-morrow, and to-morrow
Creeps in this petty pace from day to day
To the last syllable of recorded time;
And all our yesterdays have lighted fools
The way to dusty death. Out, out, brief candle!
Life's but a walking shadow; a poor player,
That struts and frets his hour upon the stage,
And then is heard no more: it is a tale
Told by an idiot, full of sound and fury,
Signifying nothing. (Enter a Messenger.)
Thou com'st to use thy tongue; thy story quickly . . .

All the terrible things which Macbeth has done and which he has suffered because of what he has done, have made him hard and fearless. He is no longer easily affrighted ("I have supp'd full with horrors"). Furthermore all his strength is concentrated for a last stand. At this moment comes the news of the death of his wife—the companion who first drove him into crime and yet in whom the strength to live has failed before it has in him—and plunges him, though only for a moment, into somber brooding; it is a slackening of the tension, but one which can only lead to hopelessness, heaviness, and despair; yet it is heavy with humanity and wisdom too. Macbeth has become heavy with a self-acquired wisdom which has arisen for him from his own destiny, he has grown ripe for knowledge and death. This final ripeness he now attains, at the moment when his last and only human companion leaves him. As here from horror and tragedy, so, in another instance, it is from the grotesque and ridiculous that the man in all his purity arises, the man as he was really intended to be and as in fortunate moments he may possibly have realized himself. Polonius is a fool, he is silly and senile; but when he gives his blessing and final advice to his departing son (1, 3), he has the wisdom and the dignity of age.

But something else is to be noted here besides the great variety of phenomena to which we referred above and the ever-varied nuances of the profoundly human mixture of high and low, sublime and trivial, tragic and comic. It is the conception, so difficult to formulate in clear terms although everywhere to be observed in its effects, of a basic fabric of the world, perpetually weaving itself, renewing itself, and connected in all its parts, from which all this arises and which makes it impossible to isolate any one event or level of style. Dante's general, clearly delimited figurality, in which everything is resolved in the beyond, in God's ultimate kingdom, and in which all characters attain their full realization only in the beyond, is no more. Tragic characters attain their final completion here below when, heavy with destiny, they become ripe like Hamlet, Macbeth, and Lear. Yet they are not simply caught in the destiny allotted to each of them; they are all connected as players in a play written by the unknown and unfathomable Cosmic Poet; a play on which He is still at work, and the meaning and reality of which is as unknown to them as it is to us. Let me adduce in this connection a few lines from *The Tempest* (4, 1):

> . . . these our actors,
> As I foretold you, were all spirits, and
> Are melted into air, into thin air;
> And, like the baseless fabric of this vision
> The cloud-capp'd towers, the gorgeous palaces,
> The solemn temples, the great globe itself,
> Yea, all which it inherit, shall dissolve,
> And like this unsubstantial pageant faded,
> Leave not a rack behind; we are such stuff
> As dreams are made of, and our little life
> Is rounded with a sleep.

This says two things: that Shakespeare includes earthly reality, and even its most trivial forms, in a thousand refractions and mixtures, but that his purpose goes far beyond the representation of reality in its merely earthly coherence; he embraces reality but he transcends it. This is already apparent in the presence of ghosts and witches in his plays, and in the often unrealistic style in which the influences of Seneca, of Petrarchism, and of other fashions of the day are fused in a characteristically concrete but only erratically realistic manner. It is still more significantly revealed in the inner structure of the action, which is often—and especially in the most important plays—only erratically and sporadically realistic and often shows a tendency to break through into the realm of the fairy tale, of playful fancy, or of the supernatural and demonic.

From another viewpoint too the tragic in Shakespeare is not completely realistic. We alluded to it at the beginning of this chapter. He does not take ordinary everyday reality seriously or tragically. He treats only noblemen, princes and kings, statesmen, commanders, and antique heroes tragically. When common people or soldiers or other representatives of the middle or lower classes appear, it is always in the low style, in one of the many variations of the comic which he commands. This separation of styles in accordance with class appears more consistently in him than in medieval works of literature and art, particularly those of Christian inspiration, and it is doubtless a reflection of the antique conception of the tragic. It is true, as we have said, that in him tragic personages of the higher classes exhibit frequent stylistic lapses into the corporeal-creatural, the grotesque, and the ambiguous; but the reverse is hardly so. Shylock would seem to be the only figure which might be cited as an exception, and we have seen that in his case too the tragic motifs are dropped at the end. Shakespeare's world-spirit is in no way a popular spirit—a point which distinguishes him basically from his admirers and imitators in the *Sturm und Drang* period and the romantic period. The dynamic throbbing of elemental forces which we feel in his works has nothing to do with the depths of the popular soul with which those men of a later age connected it. From this point of view it is instructive to compare Shakespeare's and Goethe's populace scenes. The first scene in *Romeo and Juliet*, where the servants of the Montagues and Capulets meet, has much in common with the meeting of peasant leaders with troopers from Bamberg at the beginning of *Götz von Berlichingen*. But how much more serious, more human, and more intelligently interested in the events are Goethe's characters! And if in this case it might be objected that the problems developed in *Götz* concern the people directly, no such objection can be sustained in a comparison of the populace scenes in the Roman plays, in *Julius Caesar* or *Coriolanus*, with those in *Egmont*. It is not only any such sympathetic penetration of the popular soul which is foreign to Shakespeare; he shows nothing precursory of the Enlightenment, of bourgeois morality, and of the cultivation of sentiment. In his works, whose author remains almost anonymously aloof, there is a very different atmosphere from that in the products of the era of Germany's literary awakening, in which one always hears the voice of a deeply sensitive, richly emotional personality enthusiastically declaiming upon freedom and greatness in an austere bourgeois study. Consider how impossible a *Klärchen* or *Gretchen*, or a tragedy like *Luise Millerin*, would be in Shakespeare's world; a tragic situation revolving about the virginity of a middle-class girl is an absurdity within the frame of Elizabethan literature.

In this context we should recall the famous interpretation of Hamlet in Goethe's *Wilhelm Meister's Lehrjahre* (book 4, chapters 3 and 13). It is profound and beautiful; it has been admired with good reason not only by the Romanticists but also by many later readers, both in Germany and in England. There is convincing force in Goethe's explanation of Hamlet's tragedy as resulting from the sudden collapse of the external and ethical security of his early years, from the break-down of his trust in the ethical order represented for him by the bond—now cruelly disrupted—which previously united his parents, whom he loved and revered. But Goethe's interpretation is at the same time a stylistic mirror of his own time, the age of Goethe. Hamlet appears as a tender, emotional, modest young man, ideally striving for the highest good but insufficiently endowed with inner force. What happens—in Goethe's words—is that "a great deed is laid upon a soul not equal to it"; or—as he puts it a little later—"a beautiful, pure, noble, and highly moral being, devoid of the physical strength which makes the hero, is crushed by a burden which it can neither bear nor cast off. . . ." Must we assume that Goethe failed to sense Hamlet's native force, which continues to grow throughout the course of the play, his cutting wit, which makes all those about him tremble and flee, the cunning and boldness of his strategems, his savage harshness toward Ophelia, the energy with which he faces his mother, the icy calm with which he removes the courtiers who cross his path, the elasticity and boldness of all his words and thoughts? Despite the fact that he again and again puts off the decisive deed, he is by far the strongest character in the play. There is a demonic aura about him which inspires respect, awe, and often fear. Whenever he does move into action, it is quick, bold, and at times malicious, and it strikes the mark with assured power. True enough, it is precisely the events that summon him to vengeance which paralyze his power of decision. But can that be explained from a lack of vitality, a lack of that "physical strength which makes the hero"? Is it not rather that in a strong and almost demonically gifted nature, doubt and weariness of life must assert themselves, that the entire weight of his existence must be displaced in this direction? That it is precisely because of the passion with which a strong nature abandons itself to its emotions that they become so overwhelming that the duty to live and to act becomes a burden and a torture? Our intention here is not to set up another interpretation of Hamlet in opposition to Goethe's; we merely wish to indicate the direction in which Goethe and his age were moving when they undertook to assimilate Shakespeare to their own attitudes. In passing I might observe that more recent research has become very skeptical in regard to such homogeneously psychological interpretations of Shakespeare's characters—indeed, to my mind, rather too skeptical.

The wealth of stylistic levels contained in Shakespeare's tragedy goes beyond actual realism. At the same time it is freer, harder, more unqualified, more godlike in its nonpartisan objectivity than the realism of his admirers about 1800. On the other hand, as we attempted to show above, it is conditioned by the possibilities of the mixture of styles which the Christian Middle Ages had created. Only this Christian mixture of styles could realize the prophecy which Plato formulates at the end of the *Symposium*, when in the gray light of dawn Socrates explains to the only two revelers who have not yet succumbed to sleep, Agathon and Aristophanes, that one and the same poet should master both comedy and tragedy, and that the true tragic poet is also a comic poet. That this Platonic anticipation or demand could mature only by way of the Christian-medieval conception of man, that it could be realized only after that conception had been transcended, is an observation which has been made and formulated, at least in general terms, by a number of writers, among them Goethe. I shall quote a passage in which he expresses it—a passage which, again, is a stylistic self-mirroring. It combines keen insight with a certain critical shortsightedness, which in this case appears as an old-bourgeois humanism without sympathy for the Middle Ages. The passage occurs in his notes on his translation of Diderot's *Neveu de Rameau*, toward the end of the section on taste, which is remarkable in other respects too. It was written in 1805 and runs as follows:

> In the Greeks and many Romans there is to be found a very tasteful distinguishing and purifying of the various forms of literary composition, but we Northerners cannot be exclusively

> referred to their example. We have other ancestors to be proud of and many other models to bear in mind. If the romantic trend of ignorant centuries had not brought the monstrous and the insipid together, whence should we have a *Hamlet*, a *Lear*, a *Devoción de la Cruz*, a *Principe Constante?*
>
> To maintain ourselves at the height of these barbarous advantages—since we shall never attain the superiorities of Antiquity—and to do so with courage is our duty. . . .

The two plays which Goethe cites after the two by Shakespeare are by Calderón; and this brings us to the literature of the Spanish *siglo de oro,* in which, notwithstanding its very different premises and atmosphere, there is a treatment of the reality of life quite similar to that of the Elizabethans, both in regard to the mixture of stylistic levels and to the general intent which, while including the representation of everyday reality, does not stop there, but goes on beyond it. The constant endeavor to poeticize and sublimate reality is still more clearly noticeable than in Shakespeare. Even in regard to separation of styles in terms of class, certain parallels can be traced. But they are quite superficial; the Spanish national pride makes it possible for every Spaniard to be treated in the elevated style, not merely the Spaniard of noble descent; for the motif of woman's honor, which is so important and actually central in Spanish literature, occasions tragic complications even among peasants, and in this way popular dramas of a tragic character come into existence, as for example Lope de Vega's *Fuente Ovejuna* or Calderón's *El Alcalde de Zalamea.* In this sense Spanish realism is more decidedly popular, more filled with the life of the people, than English realism of the same period. In general it gives much more of contemporary everyday reality. While in the majority of the countries of Europe, especially in France, absolutism silenced the people so that its voice was hardly heard for two centuries, Spanish absolutism was so intimately connected with the very essence of the national tradition that under it the people attained the most variegated and lively literary expression.

Yet in the history of the literary conquest of modern reality, the literature of Spain's great century is not particularly important—much less so than Shakespeare, or even Dante, Rabelais, or Montaigne. To be sure, it too had a strong influence on the romantic movement from which, as we hope to show later, modern realism developed; but within romanticism it stimulated the fanciful, adventurous, and theatrical far more than it did the trend toward reality. Spanish medieval literature had been realistic in a peculiarly genuine and concrete fashion. But the realism of the *siglo de oro* is itself something like an adventure and seems almost exotic. Even when it depicts the lower spheres of life, it is extremely colorful, poetic, and illusionistic. It brightens everyday reality with ceremonious forms of social intercourse, with choice and precious turns of phrase, with the emotional force of chivalric ideals, and with all the inner and outer enchantment of Baroque and Counter-Reformation piety. It turns the world into a magic stage. And on that magic stage—this again is very significant for its relation to modern realism—a fixed order reigns, despite all the elements of adventure and miracle. In the world, it is true, everything is a dream, but nothing is a riddle demanding to be solved. There are passions and conflicts but there are no problems. God, King, honor and love, class and class decorum are immutable and undoubted, and the figures neither of tragedy nor comedy present us with questions difficult to answer. Among the Spanish authors of the golden age whom I know, Cervantes is certainly the one whose characters come nearest to being problematic. But if we want to understand the difference, we need only compare the bewildered, easily interpreted, and ultimately curable madness of Don Quixote with Hamlet's fundamental and many-faceted insanity which can never be cured in this world. Since the pattern of life is so fixed and secure, no matter how much that is wrong may occur within it, we feel in the Spanish works, despite all their colorful and lively bustle, nothing of a movement in the depths of life, or even of a will to explore it in principle and recast it in practice. The actions of the persons in these works predominantly serve to let their ethical attitudes, whatever they are, whether tragic or comic or a mixture of both, strikingly demonstrate and prove themselves. Whether or not the actions produce, promote, or initiate anything, is of lesser importance. In any case, the order of the world is as immutably fixed afterward as it was before. It is only within that order that one can prove oneself or go astray. How much more important ethical attitude and intention are than the success of an action is parodied by Cervantes in chapter 19 of book 1 of *Don Quixote*. When the knight is informed by the wounded *bachiller* Alonso Lopez of the harm he has done by his attack on the funeral procession, he feels nowise mortified or abashed. He had taken the procession for a satanic apparition, and so it was his duty to attack it. He is satisfied that he has done his duty and feels proud of it. Seldom, indeed, has a subject suggested the problematic study of contemporary reality as insistently as does Don Quixote. The ideal conceptions of a past epoch, and of a class which has lost its functions, in conflict with the reality of the contemporary present ought to have led to a critical and problematic portrayal of the latter, the more so since the mad Don Quixote is often superior to his normal opponents by virtue of his moral steadfastness and native wit. But Cervantes did not elaborate his work in this direction. His representation of Spanish reality is dispersed in many individual adventures and sketches; the bases of that reality remain untouched and unmoved.

14

THE ENCHANTED DULCINEA

—Yo no veo, Sancho, dijo Don Quijote, sino a tres labradoras sobre tres borricos.

—Ahora me libre Dios del diablo, respondió Sancho; ¿y es posible que tres hacaneas, o como se llaman, blancas como el ampo de la nieve, le parezcan a vuesa merced borricos? Vive el Señor, que me pele estas barbas si tal fuese verdad.

—Pues yo te digo, Sancho amigo, dijo Don Quijote, que es tan verdad que son borricos o borricas, como yo soy Don Quijote, y tú Sancho Panza: a lo menos a mí tales me parecen.

—Calle, señor, dijo Sancho, no diga la tal palabra, sino despabile esos ojos, y venga a hacer reverencia a la señora de sus pensamientos, que ya llega cerca: y diciendo esto se adelantó a recebir a las tres aldeanas, y apeándose del rucio tuvo del cabestro al jumento de una de las tres labradoras, y hincando ambas rodillas en el suelo, dijo:

—Reina y princesa y duquesa de la hermosura, vuestra altivez y grandeza sea servida de recebir en su gracia y buen talante al cautivo caballero vuestro, que allí está hecho piedra mármol, todo turbado y sin pulsos de verse ante vuesa magnífica presencia. Yo soy Sancho su escudero, y él es el asendereado caballero Don Quijote de la Mancha, llamado por otro nombre el Caballero de la Triste Figura.

A esta sazón ya se había puesto Don Quijote de hinojos junto a Sancho, y miraba con ojos desencajados y vista turbada a la que Sancho llamaba reina y señora; y como no descubría en ella sino una moza aldeana y no de muy buen rostro, porque era carirredonda y chata, estaba suspenso y admirabo, sin osar desplegar los labios. Las labradoras estaban asimismo atónitas viendo a aquellos dos hombres tan diferentes hincados de rodillas, que no dejaban pasar adelante a su compañera; pero rompiendo el silencio la detenida, toda desgradiada y mohina, dijo:

—Apártense nora en tal del camino, y dejenmos pasar, que vamos de priesa.

A lo que respondió Sancho:

—Oh princesa y señora universal del Toboso, ¿cómo vuestro magnífico corazón no se enternece viendo arrodillado ante vuestra sublimada presencia a la coluna y sustento de la andante caballería?

Oyendo lo cual otra de las dos dijo:

—Mas yo que te estrego burra de mi suegro: mirad con qué se vienen los señoritos ahora a hacer burlas de las aldeanas, como si aquí no supiésemos echar pullos como ellos: vayan su camino, y déjenmos hacer el nueso, y serles ha sano.

—Levántate, Sancho, dijo a este punto Don Quijote, que ya veo que la fortuna, de mi mal no harta, tiene tomados los caminos todos por donde pueda venir algún contento a esta ánima mezquina que tengo en las carnes. Y tú, oh extremo valor que puede desearse, término de la humana gentileza, único remedio de este afligido corazón que te adora, ya que el maligno encantador me persigue, y ha puesto nubes y cataratas en mis ojos, y para sólo ellos y no para otros ha mudado y transformando tu sin igual hermosura y rostro en el de una labradora pobre, si ya también el mío no le ha cambiado en el de algún vestiglo para hacerle aborrecible a tus ojos, no dejes de mirarme blanda y amorosamente, echando de ver en esta sumisión y arrodillamiento que a tu contrahecha hermosura hago, la humildad con que mi alma te adora.

—Toma que me agüelo, respondió la aldeana, amiguita soy yo de oír resquebrajos. Apártense y déjenmos ir, y agradecérselo hemos.

Apartóse Sancho y déjola ir, contentísimo de haber salido bien de su enredo. Apenas se vió libre la aldeana que había hecho la figura de Dulcinea cuando picando a su hacanea con un aguijón que en un palo traía, dió a correr por el prado adelante; y como la borrica sentía la punta del aguijón, que le fatigaba más de lo ordinario, comenzó a dar corcovos, de manera que dió con la señora Dulcinea en tierra: lo cual visto por Don Quijote, acudió a levantarla, y Sancho a componer y cinchar el albarda, que también vino a la barriga de la pollina. Acomodada pues el albarda, y queriendo Don Quijote levantar a su encantada señora en los brazos sobre la jumenta, la señora levantándose del suelo le quitó de aquel trabajo, porque haciéndose algún tanto atrás tomó una corridica, y puestas ambas manos sobre las ancas de la pollina dió con su cuerpo más ligero que un halcón sobre la albarda, y quedó a horcajadas como si fuera hombre, y entonces dijo Sancho:

—¡Vive Roque, que es la señora nuestra ama más ligera que un alcotán, y que puede enseñar a subir de la jineta al más diestro cordobés o mejicano; el arzón trasero de la silla pasó de un salto, y sin espuelas hace correr la hacanea como una cebra, y no le van en zaga sus doncellas, que todas corren como el viento!

Y así era la verdad, porque en viéndose a caballo Dulcinea todas picaron tras ella y dispararon a correr, sin volver la cabeza atrás por espacio de más de media legua. Siguiólas Don Quijote con las vista, y cuando vió que no parecían, volviéndose a Sancho le dijo:

—Sancho, ¿qué te parece, cuán mal quisto soy de encantadores? . . .

("I see nothing," declared Don Quixote, "except three farm girls on three jackasses."

"Then God deliver me from the devil!" exclaimed Sancho. "Is it possible that those three hackneys, or whatever you call them, white as the driven snow, look like jackasses to your Grace? By the living God, I would tear out this beard of mine if that were true!"

"But I tell you, friend Sancho, it is as true that those are jackasses, or she-asses, as it is that I am Don Quixote and you Sancho Panza. At least, that is the way they look to me."

"Be quiet, sir," Sancho admonished him, "you must not say such a thing as that. Open those eyes of yours and come do reverence to the lady of your affections, for she draws near."

Saying this, he rode on to meet the village maids and, slipping down off his donkey, seized one of their beasts by the halter and fell on his knees in front of its rider.

"O queen and princess and duchess of beauty," he said, "may your Highness and Majesty be pleased to receive and show favor to your captive knight, who stands there as if turned to marble, overwhelmed and breathless at finding himself in your magnificent presence. I am Sancho Panza, his squire, and he is the world-weary knight Don Quixote, otherwise known as the Knight of the Mournful Countenance."

By this time Don Quixote was down on his knees beside Sancho. His eyes were fairly starting from their sockets and there was a deeply troubled look in them as he stared up at the one whom Sancho had called queen and lady; all that he could see in her was a village wench, and not a very pretty one at that, for she was round-faced and snub-nosed. He was astounded and perplexed and did not dare open his mouth. The girls were also very much astonished to behold these two men, so different in appearance, kneeling in front of one of them so that she could not pass. It was this one who most ungraciously broke the silence.

"Get out of my way," she said peevishly, "and let me pass. And bad luck go with you. For we are in a hurry."

"O princess and universal lady of El Toboso!" cried Sancho. "How can your magnanimous heart fail to melt as you behold kneeling before your sublimated presence the one who is the very pillar and support of knight-errantry?"

Hearing this, one of the others spoke up. "Whoa, there, she-ass of my father!" she said. "Wait until I curry you down. Just look at the small-fry gentry, will you, who've come to make sport of us country girls! Just as if we couldn't give them tit for tat. Be on your way and get out of ours, if you know what's good for you."

"Arise, Sancho," said Don Quixote, "for I perceive that fortune has not had her fill of evil done to me but has taken possession of all the roads by which some happiness may come to what little soul is left within me. And thou, who art all that could be desired, the sum of human gentleness and sole remedy for this afflicted heart that doth adore thee! The malign enchanter who doth persecute me hath placed clouds and cataracts upon my eyes, and for them and them alone hath transformed thy peerless beauty into the face of a lowly peasant maid; and I can only hope that he has not likewise changed my face into that of some monster by way of rendering it abhorrent in thy sight. But for all of that, hesitate not to gaze upon me tenderly and lovingly, beholding in this act of submission as I kneel before thee a tribute to thy metamorphosed beauty from this humbly worshiping heart of mine."

"Just listen to him run on, will you? My grandmother!" cried the lass. "Enough of such gibberish. We'll thank you to let us go our way."

Sancho fell back and let her pass, being very thankful to get out of it so easily.

No sooner did she find herself free than the girl who was supposed to have Dulcinea's face began spurring her "cackney" with a spike on the end of a long stick that she carried with her, whereupon the beast set off at top speed across the meadow. Feeling the prick, which appeared to annoy it more than was ordinarily the case, the ass started cutting such capers that the lady Dulcinea was thrown to the ground. When he saw this, Don Quixote hastened to lift her up while Sancho busied himself with tightening the girths and adjusting the packsaddle, which had slipped down under the animal's belly. This having been accomplished, Don Quixote was about to take his enchanted lady in his arms to place her upon the she-ass when the girl saved him the trouble by jumping up from the ground, stepping back a few paces, and taking a run for it. Placing both hands upon the crupper of the ass, she landed more lightly than a falcon upon the packsaddle and remained sitting there astride it like a man.

"In the name of Roque!" exclaimed Sancho, "our lady is like a lanner, only lighter, and can teach the cleverest Cordovan or Mexican how to mount. She cleared the back of the saddle in one jump, and without any spurs she makes her hackney run like a zebra, and her damsels are not far behind, for they all of them go like the wind."

This was the truth. Seeing Dulcinea in the saddle, the other two prodded their beasts and followed her on the run, without so much as turning their heads to look back for a distance of half a league. Don Quixote stood gazing after them, and when they were no longer visible he turned to Sancho and spoke.

"Sancho," he said, "you can see now, can you not, how the enchanters hate me?") *Don Quixote,* by Miguel de Cervantes Saavedra. Translated by Samuel Putnam. The Viking Press. 1949.

This is a passage from chapter 10 of part 2 of Cervantes' *Don Quijote.* The knight has sent Sancho Panza to the hamlet of El Toboso to call on Dulcinea and announce his intention of paying her a visit. Sancho, entangled in his earlier lies, and not knowing how to find the imaginary lady, decides to deceive his master. He waits outside the hamlet for a time, long enough to make Don Quijote believe that he has done his errand. Then, seeing three peasant women on donkeys riding toward him, he hurries back and tells his master that Dulcinea and two of her ladies are coming to greet him. The knight is overwhelmed with surprise and joy, and Sancho leads him toward the peasant women, describing their beauty and splendid gear in glowing colors. But for once Don Quijote sees nothing except the actual reality, that is, three peasant women on donkeys—and this leads to the scene we have quoted.

Among the many episodes which represent a clash between Don Quijote's illusion and an ordinary reality which contradicts it, this one holds a special place. First because it is concerned with Dulcinea herself, the ideal and incomparable mistress of his heart. This is the climax of his illusion and disillusionment: and although this time too he manages to find a solution, a way to save his illusion, the solution (Dulcinea is under an enchantment) is so intolerable that henceforth all his thoughts are concentrated upon one goal: to save her and break the enchantment. In the last chapters of the book, his recognition or foreboding that he will never achieve this is the direct preparation for his illness, his deliverance from his illusion, and his death. In the second place the scene is distinguished by the fact that here for the first time the roles appear exchanged. Until now it had been Don Quijote who, encountering everyday phenomena, spontaneously saw and transformed them in terms of the romances of chivalry, while Sancho was generally in doubt and often tried to contradict and prevent his master's absurdities. Now it is the other way round. Sancho improvises a scene after the fashion of the romances of chivalry, while Don Quijote's ability to transform events to harmonize with his illusion breaks down before the crude vulgarity of the sight of the peasant women. All this seems most significant. As we have here (intentionally) presented it, it sounds sad, bitter, and almost tragic.

But if we merely read Cervantes' text, we have a farce, and a farce which is overwhelmingly comic. Many illustrators have rendered the scene: Don Quijote on his knees beside Sancho, staring in wide-eyed bewilderment at the repellent spectacle before him. But only the stylistic contrast in the speeches, and the grotesque movement at the end (Dulcinea's fall and remounting), afford the fullest enjoyment of what is going on. The stylistic contrast in the speeches develops only slowly, because at first the peasant women are much too astonished. Dulcinea's first utterance (her request to be allowed to pass) is still moderate. It is only in their later speeches that the peasant women display the pearls of their eloquence. The first representative of the chivalric style is Sancho, and it is amusing and surprising to see how well he plays his part. He jumps off his donkey, throws himself at the women's feet, and speaks as though he had never heard anything in all his life but the jargon of romances of chivalry. Forms of address, syntax, metaphors, epithets, the description of his master's posture, and his supplication to be heard—it all comes out most successfully, although Sancho cannot read and owes his education wholly to the example set him by Don Quijote. His performance is successful, at least insofar as he gets his master to follow suit: Don Quijote kneels down beside him.

It might be supposed that all this would bring on a terrible crisis. Dulcinea is really *la señora de sus pensamientos*, the paragon of beauty, the goal and meaning of his life. Arousing his expectations in this way, and then disappointing them so greatly, is no harmless experiment. It could produce a shock which in turn could bring on much deeper insanity. But there is also the possibility that the shock might bring about a cure, instantaneous liberation from his idée fixe. Neither of these things happens. Don Quijote surmounts the shock. In his idée fixe itself he finds a solution which prevents him both from falling into despair and from recovering his sanity: Dulcinea is enchanted. This solution appears each time the exterior situation establishes itself as in insuperable contrast to the illusion. It makes it possible for Don Quijote to persist in the attitude of the noble and invincible hero persecuted by a powerful magician who envies his glory. In this particular case—the case of Dulcinea—the idea of so repellent and base an enchantment is certainly hard to endure. Still, it is possible to meet the situation by means available within the realm of the illusion itself, that is, by means of the knightly virtues of unalterable loyalty, devoted self-sacrifice, and unhesitating courage. And then there is the established fact that virtue will win in the end. The happy ending is a foregone conclusion. Thus both tragedy and cure are circumvented. And so, after a brief pause of disconcerted silence, Don Quijote begins to speak. He turns to Sancho first. His words show that he has recovered his bearings, that he has interpreted the situation in terms of his illusion. This interpretation has become so firmly crystallized in him that even the earthy colloquialisms in the directly preceding speech of one of the peasant women—however sharply they may contrast with the elevated style of knightly refinement—can no longer make him doubtful of his attitude. Sancho's stratagem has succeeded. Don Quijote's second sentence is addressed to Dulcinea.

It is a very beautiful sentence. A moment ago we pointed out how cleverly and amusingly Sancho handles the style of the romances of chivalry which he has picked up from his master. Now we see what sort of a master he had. The sentence begins, like a prayer, with an imploring apostrophe (*invocatio*). This has three gradations (*extremo del valor . . . , término . . . , único remedio . . .*), and they are very carefully considered and arranged, for it first emphasizes an absolute perfection, then a perfection in human terms, and finally the special personal devotion of the speaker. The threefold structure is held together by the initial words *y tú*, and ends, in its third, sweepingly constructed division, with the rhythmically conventional but magnificently integrated *corazón que te adora*. Here, in content, choice of words, and rhythm, the theme which appears at the end is already alluded to. Thus a transition is established from the *invocatio* to its obligatory complement, the *supplicatio*, for which the optative principal clause is reserved (*no dejes de mirarme . . .*), although it is still some time before we are allowed to reach it. First we have the multiple gradation—dramatically contrasting with both *invocatio* and *supplicatio*—of the concessive complex, *ya que . . . , y . . . y . . . , si ya también. . . .* Its sense is "and even though," and its rhythmic climax is reached in the middle of the first (*ya que*) part, in the strongly emphasized words *y para sólo ellos*. Only after this entire wonderful and dramatic melody of the concessive clause has run its course, is the long-restrained principal clause of the *supplicatio* allowed to appear, but it too holds back and piles up paraphrases and pleonasms until finally the main motif, which constitutes the goal and purpose of the entire period, is sounded: the words which are to symbolize Don Quijote's present attitude and his entire life, *la humildad con que mi alma te adora*. This is the style so greatly admired by Sancho in part 1, chapter 25, where Don Quijote reads his letter to Dulcinea aloud to him: *¡y como que le dice vuestra merced ahí todo cuanto quiere, y qué bien que encaja en la firma El Caballero de la Triste Figura!* But the present speech is incomparably more beautiful; with all its art it shows less pedantic preciosity than the letter. Cervantes is very fond of such rhythmically and pictorially rich, such beautifully articulated and musical bravura pieces of chivalric rhetoric (which are nevertheless rooted in the tradition of antiquity). And he is a master in the field. Here again he is not merely a destructive critic but a continuer and consummator of the great epico-rhetorical tradition for which prose too is an art. As soon as great emotions and passions or sublime events are involved, this elevated style with all its devices appears. To be sure, its being so long a convention has shifted it slightly from the sphere of high tragedy toward that of the smoothly pleasant, which is capable of at least a trace of self-irony. Yet it is still dominant in the serious sphere. One has only to read Dorotea's speech to her unfaithful lover (part 1, chapter 36), with its numerous figures, similes, and rhythmic clauses, in order to sense that this style is still alive even in the serious and the tragic.

Here, however, in Dulcinea's presence, it simply serves the effect of contrast. The peasant girl's crude, contemptuous reply gives it its real significance; we are in the realm of the low style, and Don Quijote's elevated rhetoric only serves to make the comedy of the stylistic anticlimax fully effective. But even this is not enough to satisfy Cervantes. To the stylistic anticlimax he adds an extreme anticlimax in the action by having Dulcinea fall off her donkey and jump on again with grotesque dexterity, while Don Quijote still tries to maintain the chivalric style. His being so firmly fixed in his illusion that neither Dulcinea's reply nor the scene with the donkey can shake him is the acme of farce. Even Sancho's exuberant gaiety (*Vive Roque*), which after all is nothing short of impertinent, cannot make him lose his bearings. He looks after the peasant women as they ride away, and when they have disappeared he turns to Sancho with words expressive much less of sadness or despair than of a sort of triumphant satisfaction over the fact that he has become the target of the evil magician's darkest arts. This makes it possible for him to feel that he is elect, unique, and in a way which tallies perfectly with the conventions of the knight-errant: *yo nací para ejemplo de desdichados, y para ser blanco y terrero donde tomen la mira y asesten las flechas de la mala fortuna.* And the observation he now makes, to the effect that the evil enchantment affects even Dulcinea's aura—for her breath had not been pleasant—can disturb his illusion as little as Sancho's grotesque description of details of her beauty. Encouraged by the complete success of his trick, Sancho has now really warmed up and begins to play with his master's madness purely for his own amusement.

In our study we are looking for representations of everyday life in which that life is treated seriously, in terms of its human and social problems or even of its tragic complications. The scene from Don Quijote with which we are dealing is certainly realistic. All the participants are presented in their true reality, their living everyday existence. Not only the peasant women but Sancho too, not only Sancho but also Don Quijote, appear as persons representative of contemporary Spanish life. For the fact that Sancho is playing a rogue's game and that Don Quijote is enmeshed in his illusion does not raise either of them out of his everyday existence. Sancho is a peasant from La Mancha, and Don Quijote is no Amadis or Roland, but a little country squire who has lost his mind. At best we might say that the hidalgo's madness translates him into another, imaginary sphere of life; but even so the everyday character of our scene and others similar to it remains unharmed, because the persons and events of everyday life are constantly colliding with his madness and come out in stronger relief through the contrast.

It is much more difficult to determine the position of the scene, and of the novel as a whole, on the scale of levels between tragic and comic. As presented, the story of the encounter with the three peasant women is nothing if not comic. The idea of having Don Quijote encounter a concrete Dulcinea must certainly have come to Cervantes even when he was writing the first part of the novel. The idea of building up such a scene on the basis of a deceitful trick played by Sancho, so that the roles appear interchanged, is a stroke of genius, and it is so magnificently carried out that the farce presents itself to the reader as something perfectly natural and even bound to take place, despite the complex absurdity of all its presuppositions and relations. But it remains pure farce. We have tried to show above that, in the case of the only one of the participants with whom the possibility of a shift into the tragic and problematic exists, that is, in the case of Don Quijote, such a shift is definitely avoided. The fact that he almost instantaneously and as it were automatically takes refuge in the interpretation that Dulcinea is under an enchantment excludes everything tragic. He is taken in, and this time even by Sancho; he kneels down and orates in a lofty emotional style before a group of ugly peasant women; and then he takes pride in his sublime misfortune.

But Don Quijote's feelings are genuine and profound. Dulcinea is really the mistress of his thoughts; he is truly filled with the spirit of a mission which he regards as man's highest duty. He is really true, brave, and ready to sacrifice everything. So unconditional a feeling and so unconditional a determination impose admiration even though they are based on a foolish illusion, and this admiration has been accorded to Don Quijote by almost all readers. There are probably few lovers of literature who do not associate the concept of ideal greatness with Don Quijote. It may be absurd, fantastic, grotesque; but it is still ideal, unconditional, heroic. It is especially since the Romantic period that this conception has become almost universal, and it withstands all attempts on the part of philological criticism to show that Cervantes' intention was not to produce such an impression.

The difficulty lies in the fact that in Don Quijote's idée fixe we have a combination of the noble, immaculate, and redeeming with absolute nonsense. A tragic struggle for the ideal and desirable cannot at first blush be imagined in any way but as intervening meaningfully in the actual state of things, stirring it up, pressing it hard; with the result that the meaningful ideal encounters an equally meaningful resistance which proceeds either from inertia, petty malice, and envy, or possibly from a more conservative view. The will working for an ideal must accord with existing reality at least to such an extent that it meets it, so that the two interlock and a real conflict arises. Don Quijote's idealism is not of this kind. It is not based on an understanding of actual conditions in this world. Don Quijote does have such an understanding but it deserts him as soon as the idealism of his idée fixe takes hold of him. Everything he does in that state is completely senseless and so incompatible with the existing world that it produces only comic confusion there. It not only has no chance of success, it actually has no point of contact with reality; it expends itself in a vacuum.

The same idea can be developed in another way, so that further consequences become clear. The theme of the noble and brave fool who sets forth to realize his ideal and improve the world, might be treated in such a way that the problems and conflicts in the world are presented and worked out in the process. Indeed, the purity and ingenuousness of the fool could be such that, even in the absence of any concrete purpose to produce effects, wherever he appears he unwittingly goes to the heart of things, so that the conflicts which are pending and hidden are rendered acute. One might think here of Dostoevski's *Idiot*. Thus the fool could be involved in responsibility and guilt and assume the role of a tragic figure. Nothing of the sort takes place in Cervantes' novel.

Don Quijote's encounter with Dulcinea is not a good illustration of his relationship to concrete reality, inasmuch as here he does not, as elsewhere, impose his ideal will in conflict with that reality; here he beholds and worships the incarnation of his ideal. Yet this encounter too is symbolic of the mad knight's relationship to the phenomena of this world. The reader should recall what traditional concepts were contained in the Dulcinea motif and how they are echoed in Sancho's and Don Quijote's grotesquely sublime words. *La señora de sus pensamientos, extremo del valor que puede desearse, término de la humana gentileza,* and so forth—alive in all this are Plato's idea of beauty, courtly love, the *donna gentile* of the *dolce stil nuovo*, Beatrice, *la gloriosa donna della mia mente*. And all this ammunition is expended on three ugly and vulgar peasant women. It is poured into a void. Don Quijote can neither be graciously received nor graciously rejected. There is nothing but amusingly senseless confusion. To find anything serious, or a concealed deeper meaning in this scene, one must violently overinterpret it.

The three women are flabbergasted; they get away as fast as they can. This is an effect frequently produced by Don Quijote's appearance. Often disputes result and the participants come to blows. People are apt to lose their temper when Don Quijote interferes in their business with his nonsense. Very often too they humor him in his idée fixe in order to get some fun from it. The innkeeper and the whores at the time of his first departure react in this way. The same thing happens again later with the company at the second inn, with the priest and the barber, Dorotea and Don Fernando, and even with Maritornes. Some of these, it is true, mean to use their game as a way of getting the knight safely back home, but they carry it much further than their practical purpose would require. In part 2 the *bachiller* Sansón Carrasco bases his therapeutic plan on playing along with Don Quijote's idée fixe; later, at the duke's palace and in Barcelona, his madness is methodically exploited as a pastime, so that hardly any of his adventures are genuine; they are simply staged, that is, they have been especially prepared to suit the hidalgo's madness, for the amusement of those who get them up. Among all these reactions, both in part 1 and part 2, one thing is completely lacking: tragic complications and serious consequences. Even the element of contemporary satire and criticism is very weak. If we leave out of consideration the purely literary criticism, there is almost none at all. It is limited to brief remarks or occasional caricatures of types (for example the priest at the duke's court). It never goes to the roots of things and is moderate in attitude. Above all, Don Quijote's adventures never reveal any of the basic problems of the society of the time. His activity reveals nothing at all. It affords an opportunity to present Spanish life in its color and fullness. In the resulting clashes between Don Quijote and reality no situation ever results which puts in question that reality's right to be what it is. It is always right and he wrong; and after a bit of amusing confusion it flows calmly on, untouched. There is one scene where this might seem doubtful. It is the freeing of the galley slaves in part 1, chapter 22. Here Don Quijote intervenes in the established legal order, and some critics will be found to uphold the opinion that he does so in the name of a higher morality. This view is natural, for what Don Quijote says: *allá se lo haya cada uno con su pecado; Dios hay en el cielo que no se descuida de castigar al malo ni de premiar al bueno, y no es bien que los hombres honrados sean verdugos do los otros hombres, no yéndoles nada en ello*—such a statement is certainly on a higher level than any positive law. But a "higher morality" of the kind here envisaged must be consistent and methodical if it is to be taken seriously. We know, however, that Don Quijote has no idea of making a basic attack on the established legal order. He is neither an anarchist nor a prophet of the Kingdom of God. On the contrary, it is apparent again and again that whenever his idée fixe happens not to be involved he is willing to conform, that it is only through his idée fixe that he claims a special position for the knight-errant. The beautiful words, *alla se lo haya*, etc., are deeply rooted, to be sure, in the kindly wisdom of his real nature (this is a point to which we shall return), but in their context they are still merely an improvisation. It is his idée fixe which determines him to free the prisoners. It alone forces him to conceive of everything he encounters as the subject of a knightly adventure. It supplies him with the motifs "help the distressed" or "free the victims of force," and he acts accordingly. I think it wholly erroneous to look for a matter of principle here, for anything like a conflict between natural Christian and positive law. For such a conflict, moreover, an opponent would have to appear, someone like the Grand Inquisitor in Dostoevski, who would be authorized and willing to represent the cause of positive law against Don Quijote. His Majesty's commissary who is in charge of the convoy of prisoners is neither suited for the role nor prepared to play it. Personally he may very well be ready to accept the argument, "judge not that ye be not judged." But he has passed no judgment; he is no representative of positive law. He has his instructions and is quite justified in appealing to them.

Everything comes out all right, and time and again the damage done or suffered by Don Quijote is treated with stoic humor as a matter of comic confusion. Even the *bachiller* Alonso Lopez, as he lies on the ground, badly mauled and with one leg pinned under his mule, consoles himself with mocking puns. This scene occurs in chapter 19 of book 1. It also shows that Don Quijote's idée fixe saves him from feeling responsible for the harm he does, so that in his conscience too every form of tragic conflict and somber seriousness is obviated. He has acted in accordance with the rules of knight-errantry, and so he is justified. To be sure, he hastens to assist the *bachiller*, for he is a kind and helpful soul; but it does not occur to him to feel guilty. Nor does he feel any guiltier when at the beginning of chapter 30 the priest puts him to the test by telling him what evil effects his freeing of the prisoners had produced. He angrily exclaims that it is the duty of a knight-errant to help those in distress but not to judge whether their plight is deserved or not. And that settles the question as far as he is concerned. In part 2, where the gaiety is even more relaxed and elegant, such complications no longer occur at all.

There is, then, very little of problem and tragedy in Cervantes' book —and yet it belongs among the literary masterpieces of an epoch during which the modern problematic and tragic conception of things arose in the European mind. Don Quijote's madness reveals nothing of the sort. The whole book is a comedy in which well-founded reality holds madness up to ridicule.

And yet Don Quijote is not only ridiculous. He is not like the bragging soldier or the comic old man or the pedantic and ignorant doctor. In our scene Don Quijote is taken in by Sancho. But does Sancho despise him and deceive him all the way through? Not at all. He deceives him only because he sees no other way out. He loves and reveres him, although he is half conscious (and sometimes fully conscious) of his madness. He learns from him and refuses to part with him. In Don Quijote's company he becomes cleverer and better than he was before. With all his madness, Don Quijote preserves a natural dignity and superiority which his many miserable failures cannot harm. He is not vulgar, as the above-mentioned comic types normally are. Actually he is not a "type" at all in this sense, for on the whole he is no automaton producing comic effects. He even develops, and grows kinder and wiser while his madness persists. But would it be true to say that his is a wise madness in the ironical sense of the romanticists? Does wisdom come to him through his madness? Does his madness give him an understanding he could not have attained in soundness of mind, and do we hear wisdom speak through madness in his case as we do with Shakespeare's fools or with Charlie Chaplin? No, that is not it either. As soon as his madness, that is, the idée fixe of knight-errantry, takes hold of him, he acts unwisely, he acts like an automaton in the manner of the comic types mentioned above. He is wise and kind independently of his madness. A madness like this, it is true, can arise only in a pure and noble soul, and it is also true that wisdom, kindness, and decency shine through his madness and make it appear lovable. Yet his wisdom and his madness are clearly separated—in direct contrast to what we find in Shakespeare, the fools of Romanticism, and Charlie Chaplin. The priest says it as early as chapter 30 of part 1, and later it comes out again and again: he is mad only when his idée fixe comes into play; otherwise he is a perfectly normal and very intelligent individual. His madness is not such that it represents his whole nature and is completely identical with it. At a specific moment an idée fixe laid hold on him; but even so it leaves parts of his being unaffected, so that in many instances he acts and speaks like a person of sound mind; and one day, shortly before his death, it leaves him again. He was some fifty years of age when, under the influence of his excessive reading of romances of chivalry, he conceived his absurd plan. This is strange. An overwrought state of mind resulting from solitary reading might rather be expected in a youthful person (Julien Sorel, Madame Bovary), and one is tempted to look for a specific psychological explanation. How is it possible that a man in his fifties who leads a normal life and whose intelligence is well-developed in many ways and not at all unbalanced, should embark upon so absurd a venture? In the opening sentences of his novel Cervantes supplies some details of his hero's social position. From them we may at best infer that it was burdensome to him, for it offered no possibility of an active life commensurate with his abilities. He was as it were paralyzed by the limitations imposed upon him on the one hand by his class and on the other by his poverty. Thus one might suppose that his mad decision represents a flight from a situation which has become unbearable, a violent attempt to emancipate himself from it. This sociological and psychological interpretation has been advocated by various writers on the subject. I myself advanced it in an earlier passage of this book, and I leave it there because in the context of that passage it is justified. But as an interpretation of Cervantes' artistic purpose it is unsatisfactory, for it is not likely that he intended his brief observations on Don Quijote's social position and habits of life to imply anything like a psychological motivation of the knight's idée fixe. He would have had to state it more clearly and elaborate it in greater detail. A modern psychologist might find still other explanations of Don Quijote's strange madness. But this sort of approach to the problem has no place in Cervantes' thinking. Confronted with the question of the causes of Don Quijote's madness, he has only one answer: Don Quijote read too many romances of chivalry and they deranged his mind. That this should happen to a man in his fifties can be explained —from within the work—only in aesthetic terms, that is, through the comic vision which came to Cervantes when he conceived the novel: a tall, elderly man, dressed in old-fashioned and shabby armor, a picture which is beautifully expressive not only of madness but also of asceticism and the fanatic pursuit of an ideal. We simply have to accept the fact that this cultured and intelligent country gentleman goes suddenly mad—not, like Ajax or Hamlet, because of a terrible shock—but simply because he has read too many romances of chivalry. Here again there is nothing tragic. In the analysis of his madness we have to do without the concept of the tragic, just as we have to do without the specifically Shakespearean and romantic combination of wisdom and madness in which one cannot be conceived without the other.

Don Quijote's wisdom is not the wisdom of a fool. It is the intelligence, the nobility, the civility, and the dignity of a gifted and well-balanced man—a man neither demonic nor paradoxical, not beset by doubt and indecision nor by any feeling of not being at home in this world, but even-tempered, able to weigh and ponder, receptive, and lovable and modest even in his irony. Furthermore he is a conservative, or at least essentially in accord with the order of things as it is. This comes out wherever and whenever he deals with people—especially with Sancho Panza—in the longer or shorter intervals during which his idée fixe is quiescent. From the very beginning—although more in part 2 than in part 1—the kindly, intelligent, and amiable figure, Alsonso Quijano el bueno, whose most distinguishing characteristic is his naturally superior dignity, coexists with the mad adventurer. We need only read with what kindly and merry irony he treats Sancho in part 2 chapter 7, when the latter, on the advice of his wife Teresa, begins to present his request for a fixed salary. His madness intervenes only when he justifies his refusal by referring to the customs of knights-errant. Passages of this kind abound. There is evidence everywhere that we have to do with an intelligent Don Quijote and a mad one, side by side, and that his intelligence is in no way dialectically inspired by his madness but is a normal and, as it were, average intelligence.

That in itself yields an unusual combination. There are levels of tone represented here which one is not accustomed to finding in purely comic contexts. A fool is a fool. We are used to seeing him represented on a single plane, that of the comic and foolish, with which, at least in earlier literature, baseness and stupidity, and at times underhanded malice, were connected as well. But what are we to say of a fool who is at the same time wise, with that wisdom which seems the least compatible with folly, that is, the wisdom of intelligent moderation? This very fact, this combination of intelligent moderation with absurd excesses results in a multiplicity which cannot be made to accord altogether with the purely comic. But that is by no means all. It is on the very wings of his madness that his wisdom soars upward, that it roams the world and becomes richer there. For if Don Quijote had not gone mad, he would not have left his house. And then Sancho too would have stayed home, and he could never have drawn from his innate being the things which—as we find in delighted amazement—were potentially contained in it. The multifarious play of action and reaction between the two and their joint play in the world would not have taken place.

This play, as we think we have been able to show, is never tragic; and never are human problems, whether personal or social, represented in such a way that we tremble and are moved to compassion. We always remain in the realm of gaiety. But the levels of gaiety are multiplied as never before. Let us return once more to the text from which we set out. Don Quijote speaks to the peasant women in a style which is genuinely the elevated style of courtly love and which in itself is by no means grotesque. His sentences are not at all ridiculous (though they may seem so to many readers in our day), they are in the tradition of the period and represent a masterpiece of elevated expression in the form in which it was then alive. If it was Cervantes' purpose to attack the romances of chivalry (and there can be no doubt that it was), he nevertheless did not attack the elevated style of chivalric expression. On the contrary, he reproaches the romances of chivalry with not mastering the style, with being stylistically wooden and dry. And so it comes about that in the middle of a parody against the knightly ideology of love we find one of the most beautiful prose passages which the late form of the tradition of courtly love produced. The peasant women answer with characteristic coarseness. Such a rustically boorish style had long been employed in comic literature (although possibly never with the same balance between moderation and verve), but what had certainly never happened before was that it should follow directly upon a speech like Don Quijote's—a speech which, taken by itself, could never make us suspect that it occurs in a grotesque context. The motif of a knight begging a peasant woman to hear his love—a motif which produces a comparable situation—is age old. It is the motif of the *pastourelle*; it was in favor with the early Provençal poets, and, as we shall see when we come to Voltaire, it was remarkably long-lived. However, in the *pastourelle* the two partners have adapted themselves to each other; they understand each other; and the result is a homogeneous level of style on the borderline between the idyllic and the everyday. In Cervantes' case, the two realms of life and style clash by reason of Don Quijote's madness. There is no possibility of a transition; each is closed in itself; and the only link that holds them together is the merry neutrality of the playful scheme of puppet-master Sancho—the awkward bumpkin, who but a short time before believed almost everything his master said, who will never get over believing some of it, and who always acts in accordance with the momentary situation. In our passage the dilemma of the moment has inspired him to deceive his master; and he adapts himself to the position of puppet-master with as much gusto and elasticity as he later will to the position of governor of an island. He starts the play in the elevated style, then switches to the low—not, however, in the manner of the peasant women. He maintains his superiority and remains master of the situation which he has himself created under the pressure of necessity but which he now enjoys to the full.

What Sancho does in this case—assuming a role, transforming himself, and playing with his master's madness—other characters in the book are perpetually doing. Don Quijote's madness gives rise to an inexhaustible series of disguises and histrionics: Dorotea in the role of Princess Micomicona, the barber as her page, Sansón Carrasco as knight-errant, Ginés de Pasamonte as puppet-master—these are but a few examples. Such metamorphoses make reality become a perpetual stage without ever ceasing to be reality. And when the characters do not submit to the metamorphosis of their own free will, Don Quijote's madness forces them into their roles—as happens time and again, beginning with the innkeeper and the whores in the first tavern. Reality willingly cooperates with a play which dresses it up differently every moment. It never spoils the gaiety of the play by bringing in the serious weight of its troubles, cares, and passions. All that is resolved in Don Quijote's madness; it transforms the real everyday world into a gay stage. Here one should recall the various adventures with women which occur in the course of the narrative in addition to the encounter with Dulcinea: Maritornes struggling in Don Quijote's arms, Dorotea as Princess Micomicona, the lovelorn Altisidora's serenade, the nocturnal encounter with Doña Rodriguez (a scene which Cide Hamete Benengeli says that he would have given his best coat to see)—each of these stories is in a different style; each contains a shift in stylistic level; all of them are resolved by Don Quijote's madness, and all of them remain within the realm of gaiety. And yet there are several which need not necessarily have been thus restricted. The description of Maritornes and her muleteer is coarsely realistic; Dorotea is unhappy; and Doña Rodriguez is in great distress of mind because her daughter has been seduced. Don Quijote's intervention changes nothing of this—neither Maritornes' loose life nor the sad plight of Doña Rodriguez' daughter. But what happens is that we are not concerned over these things, that we see the lot and the life of these women through the prism of gaiety, and that our consciences do not feel troubled over them. As God lets the sun shine and the rain fall on the just and the unjust alike, so Don Quijote's madness, in its bright equanimity, illumines everything that crosses his path and leaves it in a state of gay confusion.

The most varied suspense and wisest gaiety of the book are revealed in a relationship which Don Quijote maintains throughout: his relationship with Sancho Panza. It is not at all as easy to describe in unambiguous terms as the relationship between Rocinante and Sancho's donkey or that between the donkey and Sancho himself. They are not always united in unfailing loyalty and love. It frequently happens that Don Quijote becomes so angry with Sancho that he abuses and maltreats him; at times he is ashamed of him; and once—in part 2, chapter 27—he actually deserts him in danger. Sancho, for his part, originally accompanies Don Quijote because he is stupid and for the selfishly materialistic reason that he expects fantastic advantages from the venture, and also because, despite all its hardships, he prefers a vagabond life to the regular working hours and monotony of life at home. Before long he begins to sense that something must be wrong with Don Quijote's mind, and then he sometimes deceives him, makes fun of him, and speaks of him disrespectfully. At times, even in part 2, he is so disgusted and disillusioned that he is all but ready to leave Don Quijote. Again and again the reader is made to see how variable and composite our human relationships are, how capricious and dependent on the moment even the most intimate of them. In the passage which was our point of departure Sancho deceives his master and plays almost cruelly on his madness. But what painstaking humoring of Don Quijote's madness, what sympathetic penetration of his world, must have preceded Sancho's conceiving such a plan and his being able to act his role so well! Only a few months earlier he had not the slightest inkling of all this. Now he lives, after his own fashion, in the world of knightly adventure; he is fascinated by it. He has fallen in love with his master's madness and with his own role. His development is most amazing. Yet withal, he is and remains Sancho, of the Panza family, a Christian of the old stock, well known in his village. He remains all that even in the role of a wise governor and also—and indeed especially—when he insists on Sanchica's marrying nothing less than a count. He remains Sancho; and all that happens to him could happen only to Sancho. But the fact that these things do happen, that his body and his mind are put in such violent commotion and emerge from the ordeal in all their unshakable and idiosyncratic genuineness—this he owes to Don Quijote, *su amo y natural señor*. The experience of Don Quijote's personality is not received by anyone as completely as it is by Sancho; it is not assimilated pure and whole by anyone as it is by him. The others all wonder about him, are amused or angered by him, or try to cure him. Sancho lives himself into Don Quijote, whose madness and wisdom become productive in him. Although he has far too little critical reasoning power to form and express a synthetic judgment upon him, it still is he, in all his reactions, through whom we best understand Don Quijote. And this in turn binds Don Quijote to him. Sancho is his consolation and his direct opposite, his creature and yet an independent fellow being who holds out against him and prevents his madness from locking him up as though in solitary confinement. Two partners who appear together as contrasting comic or semi-comic figures represent a very old motif which has retained its effectiveness even today in farce, caricature, the circus, and the film: the tall thin man and the short fat one; the clever man and his stupid companion; master and servant; the refined aristocrat and the simple-minded peasants; and whatever other combinations and variants there may be in different countries and under different cultural conditions. What Cervantes made of it is magnificent and unique.

Perhaps it is not quite correct to speak of what Cervantes made of it. It may be more exact to say "what became of the motif in his hands." For centuries—and especially since the romanticists—many things have been read into him which he hardly foreboded, let alone intended. Such transforming and transcendent interpretations are often fertile. A book like *Don Quijote* dissociates itself from its author's intention and leads a life of its own. Don Quijote shows a new face to every age which enjoys him. Yet the historian—whose task it is to define the place of a given work in a historical continuity—must endeavor insofar as that is still possible, to attain a clear understanding of what the work meant to its author and his contemporaries. I have tried to interpret as little as possible. In particular, I have pointed out time and again how little there is in the text which can be called tragic and problematic. I take it as merry play on many levels, including in particular the level of everyday realism. The latter differentiates it from the equally unproblematic gaiety of let us say Ariosto; but even so it remains play. This means that no matter how painstakingly I have tried to do as little interpreting as possible, I yet cannot help feeling that my thoughts about the book often go far beyond Cervantes' aesthetic intention. Whatever that intention may have been (we shall not here take up the problems presented by the aesthetics of his time), it most certainly did not consciously and from the beginning propose to create a relationship like that between Don Quijote and Sancho Panza as we see it after having read the novel. Rather, the two figures were first a single vision, and what finally developed from them—singly and together—arose gradually, as the result of hundreds of individual ideas, as the result of hundreds of situations in which Cervantes puts them and to which they react on the spur of the moment, as the result of the inexhaustible, ever-fresh power of the poetic imagination. Now and again there are actual incongruities and contradictions, not only in matters of fact (which has often been noted) but also in psychology: developments which do not fit into the total picture of the two heroes—which indicates how much Cervantes allowed himself to be guided by the momentary situation, by the demands of the adventure in hand. This is still the case—more frequently even—in part 2. Gradually and without any preconceived plan, the two personages evolve, each in himself and also in their relation to each other. To be sure, this is the very thing which allows what is peculiarly Cervantean, the sum of Cervantes' experience of life and the wealth of his imagination, to enter the episodes and speeches all the more richly and spontaneously. The "peculiarly Cervantean" cannot be described in words. And yet I shall attempt to say something *about* it in order to clarify its power and its limits. First of all it is something spontaneously sensory: a vigorous capacity for the vivid visualization of very different people in very varied situations, for the vivid realization and expression of what thoughts enter their minds, what emotions fill their hearts, and what words come to their lips. This capacity he possesses so directly and strongly, and in a manner so independent of any sort of ulterior motive, that almost everything realistic written before him appears limited, conventional, or propagandistic in comparison. And just as sensory is his capacity to think up or hit upon ever new combinations of people and events. Here, to be sure, we have to consider the older tradition of the romance of adventure and its renewal through Boiardo and Ariosto, but no one before him had infused the element of genuine everyday reality into that brilliant and purposeless play of combinations. And finally he has a "something" which organizes the whole and makes it appear in a definite "Cervantean" light. Here things begin to be very difficult. One might avoid the difficulty and say that this "something" is merely contained in the subject matter, in the idea of the country gentleman who loses his mind and convinces himself that it is his duty to revive knight-errantry, that it is this theme which gives the book its unity and its attitude. But the theme (which Cervantes, by the way, took over from the minor and in itself totally uninteresting contemporary work, the *Entremés de los romances*) could have been treated quite differently too. The hero might have looked very different; it was not necessary that there should be a Dulcinea and particularly a Sancho. But above all, what was it that so attracted Cervantes in the idea? What attracted him was the possibilities it offered for multifariousness and effects of perspective, the mixture of fanciful and everyday elements in the subject, its malleability, elasticity, adaptability. It was ready to absorb all forms of style and art. It permitted the presentation of the most variegated picture of the world in a light congenial to his own nature. And here we have come back to the difficult question we asked before: what is the "something" which orders the whole and makes it appear in a definite, "Cervantean" light?

It is not a philosophy; it is no didactic purpose; it is not even a being stirred by the uncertainty of human existence or by the power of destiny, as in the case of Montaigne and Shakespeare. It is an attitude—an attitude toward the world, and hence also toward the subject matter of his art—in which bravery and equanimity play a major part. Together with the delight he takes in the multifariousness of his sensory play there is in him a certain Southern reticence and pride. This prevents him from taking the play very seriously. He looks at it; he shapes it; he finds it diverting; it is also intended to afford the reader refined intellectual diversion.

But he does not take sides (except against badly written books); he remains neutral. It is not enough to say that he does not judge and draws no conclusions: the case is not even called, the questions are not even asked. No one and nothing (except bad books and plays) is condemned in the book: neither Ginés de Pasamonte nor Roque Guinart, neither Maritornes nor Zoraida. For us Zoraida's behavior toward her father becomes a moral problem which we cannot help pondering; but Cervantes tells the story without giving a hint of his thoughts on the subject. Or rather, it is not Cervantes himself who tells the story, but the prisoner—who naturally finds Zoraida's behavior commendable. And that settles the matter. There are a few caricatures in the book—the Biscayan, the priest at the duke's castle, Doña Rodriguez; but these raise no ethical problems and imply no basic judgments.

On the other hand no one is praised as exemplary either. Here one might think of the Knight of the Green Caftan, Don Diego de Miranda, who in part 2, chapter 16, gives a description of his temperate style of life and thereby makes such a profound impression upon Sancho. He is temperate and inclined to rational deliberation; in dealing with both Don Quijote and Sancho he finds the right tone of benevolent, modest, and yet self-assured politeness. His attempts to confute or mitigate Don Quijote's madness are friendly and understanding. He must not be put with the narrow-minded and intolerant priest at the duke's court (as has been done by the distinguished Spanish scholar, Américo Castro). Don Diego is a paragon of his class, the Spanish variety of the humanist nobleman: *otium cum dignitate*. But he certainly is no more than that. He is no absolute model. For that, after all, he is too cautious and too mediocre, and it is quite possible (so far Castro may be right) that there is a shade of irony in the manner in which Cervantes describes his style of life, his manner of hunting, and his views on his son's literary inclinations.

Cervantes' attitude is such that his world becomes play in which every participating figure is justified by the simple fact of living in a given place. Only Don Quijote in his madness is not justified, is wrong. He is also wrong, absolutely speaking, as against the temperate and peaceable Don Diego, whom Cervantes—"with inspired perversity," as Castro puts it—makes the witness of the adventure with the lion. It would be forcing things if one sought to see here a glorification of adventurous heroism as against calculating, petty, and mediocre caution. If there is possibly an undertone of irony in the portrait of Don Diego, Don Quijote is not possibly but unqualifiedly conceived not with an undertone of ridicule but as ridiculous through and through. The chapter is introduced by a description of the absurd pride he takes in his victory over Carrasco (disguised as a knight) and a conversation on this theme with Sancho. The passage bears rereading for the sake of the realization it affords that there is hardly another instance in the entire book where Don Quijote is ridiculed—also in ethical terms—as he is here. The description of himself with which he introduces himself to Don Diego is foolish and turgid. It is in this state of mind that he takes on the adventure with the lion. And the lion does nothing but turn its back on Don Quijote! This is pure parody. And the additional details are fit for parody too: Don Quijote's request that the guard should give him a written testimonial to his heroism; the way he receives Sancho; his decision to change his name (henceforth he will be the Knight of the Lion), and many others.

Don Quijote alone is wrong as long as he is mad. He alone is wrong in a well-ordered world in which everybody else has his right place. He himself comes to see this in the end when, dying, he finds his way back into the order of the world. But is it true that the world is well-ordered? The question is not raised. Certain it is that in the light of Don Quijote's madness and confronted with it, the world appears well-ordered and even as merry play. There may be a great deal of wretchedness, injustice, and disorder in it. We meet harlots, criminals as galley slaves, seduced girls, hanged bandits, and much more of the same sort. But all that does not perturb us. Don Quijote's appearance, which corrects nothing and helps no one, changes good and bad fortune into play.

The theme of the mad country gentleman who undertakes to revive knight-errantry gave Cervantes an opportunity to present the world as play in that spirit of multiple, perspective, non-judging, and even non-questioning neutrality which is a brave form of wisdom. It could very simply be expressed in the words of Don Quijote which have already been quoted: *allá se lo haya cada uno con su pecado, Dios hay en el cielo que no se descuida de castigar al malo, ni de premiar al bueno.* Or else in the words which he addresses to Sancho in part 2, chapter 8, at the end of the conversation about monks and knights: *muchos son los caminos por donde lleva Dios a los suyos al cielo.* This is as much as to say that in the last analysis it is a devout wisdom. It is not unrelated to the neutral attitude which Gustave Flaubert strove so hard to attain, and yet it is very different from it: Flaubert wanted to transform reality through style; transform it so that it would appear as God sees it, so that the divine order—insofar as it concerns the fragment of reality treated in a particular work—would perforce be incarnated in the author's style. For Cervantes, a good novel serves no other purpose than to afford refined recreation, *honesto entretenimiento*. No one has expressed this more convincingly in recent times than W. J. Entwistle in his book on Cervantes (1940) where he speaks of recreation and connects it very beautifully with re-creation. It would never have occurred to Cervantes that the style of a novel—be it the best of novels—could reveal the order of the universe. On the other hand, for him too the phenomena of reality had come to be difficult to survey and no longer possible to arrange in an unambiguous and traditional manner. Elsewhere in Europe men had long since begun to question and to doubt, and even to begin building anew with their own materials. But that was in keeping neither with the spirit of his country nor with his own temperament, nor finally with his conception of the office of a writer. He found the order of reality in play. It is no longer the play of Everyman, which provides fixed norms for the judgment of good and evil. That was still so in *La Celestina*. Now things are no longer so simple. Cervantes undertakes to pass judgment only in matters concerning his profession as a writer. So far as the secular world is concerned, we are all sinners; God will see to it that evil is punished and good rewarded. Here on earth the order of the unsurveyable is to be found in play. However arduous it may be to survey and judge phenomena, before the mad knight of La Mancha they turn into a dance of gay and diverting confusion.

This, it seems to me, is the function of Don Quijote's madness. When the theme—the mad hidalgo who sets forth to realize the ideal of the *caballero andante*—began to kindle Cervantes' imagination, he also perceived a vision of how, confronted with such madness, contemporary reality might be portrayed. And the vision pleased him, both by reason of its multifariousness and by reason of the neutral gaiety which the knight's madness spreads over everything which comes in contact with it. That it is a heroic and idealized form of madness, that it leaves room for wisdom and humanity, was no doubt equally pleasing to him. But to conceive of Don Quijote's madness in symbolic and tragic terms seems to me forced. That can be read into the text; it is not there of itself. So universal and multilayered, so noncritical and nonproblematic a gaiety in the portrayal of everyday reality has not been attempted again in European letters. I cannot imagine where and when it might have been attempted.

15

THE FAUX DEVOT

The portrait of the *faux dévot* in the chapter *De la mode* in La Bruyère's *Caractères* contains a number of polemic allusions to Molière's *Tartuffe.* The *faux dévot,* La Bruyère says at once, does not speak of "*my hair shirt and my scourge*; on the contrary; he would pass for what he is, for a hypocrite, and he wants to pass for what he is not, for a devout man: it is true that he behaves in a way which makes people believe, without his saying so, that he wears a hair shirt and scourges himself." Later he criticizes Tartuffe's behavior in Orgon's house:

> S'il se trouve bien d'un homme opulent, à qui il a su imposer, dont il est le parasite, et dont il peut tirer de grands secours, il ne cajole point sa femme, il ne lui fait du moins ni avance ni déclaration; il s'enfuira, il lui laissera son manteau, s'il n'est aussi sûr d'elle que de lui-même. Il est encore plus éloigné d'employer pour la flatter et pour la séduire le jargon de la dévotion; ce n'est point par habitude qu'il le parle, mais avec dessin, et selon qu'il lui est utile, et jamais quand il ne serviroit qu'à la rendre très-ridicule. . . . Il ne pense point à profiter de toute sa succession, ni s'attirer une donation générale de tous ses biens, s'il s'agit surtout de les enlever à un fils, le légitime héritier: un homme dévot n'est ni avare, ni violent, ni injuste, ni même intéressé; Onuphre n'est pas dévot, mais il veut être cru tel, et par une parfaite, quoique fausse imitation de la piété, ménager sourdement ses intérêts: aussi ne se joue-t-il pas à la ligne directe, et il ne s'insinue jamais dans une famille où se trouvent tout à la fois une fille à pourvoir et un fils à établir; il y a là des droits trop forts et trop inviolables: on ne les traverse point sans faire de l'éclat (et il l'appréhende), sans qu'une pareille entreprise vienne aux oreilles du Prince, à qui il dérobe sa marche, par la crainte qu'il a d'être découvert et de paroître ce qu'il est. Il en veut à la ligne collatérale: on l'attaque plus impunément; il est la terreur des cousins et des cousines, du neveu et de la nièce, le flatteur et l'ami déclaré de tous les oncles qui ont fait fortune; il se donne pour l'héritier légitime de tout vieillard qui meurt riche et sans enfants. . . .

(If he finds himself on a good footing with a wealthy man, whom he has been able to take in, whose parasite he is, and from whom he can draw great assistance, he does not cajole his wife, at least he does not make advances nor a declaration to her; he will run away, he will leave his cloak in her hands, if he is not as sure of her as of himself. Still less will he employ the jargon of devotion to flatter her and seduce her; he does not speak it from habit, but from design and according as it is useful to him, and never when it would serve only to make him extremely ridiculous. . . . He has no idea of becoming his sole heir, nor of getting him to give him his entire estate, especially if it is a case of taking it away from a son, the legitimate heir: a devout man is neither avaricious nor violent nor unjust nor even interested: Onuphre is not devout, but he wants to be thought so and, by a perfect, though false, imitation of piety, to take care of his interests secretly: hence he never ventures to confront the direct line and he never insinuates himself into a family where there are both a daughter to be provided for and a son to be set up in the world; such rights are too strong and too inviolable: they cannot be infringed without scandal (and he dreads scandal), without such an attempt coming to the ears of the Prince, from whom he hides his course because he fears to be exposed and to appear as what he is. He has designs on the collateral line: it is more safely to be attacked; he is the terror of cousins male and female, of nephew and niece, the flatterer and declared friend of all uncles who have acquired fortunes; he claims to be the legitimate heir of every old man who dies wealthy and childless. . . .)

Here La Bruyère is apparently thinking of the perfect, one might say, the ideal, type of the *faux dévot,* who is nothing but a hypocrite and who, without any human weakness or inconsistency, constantly vigilant, constantly rational, steadily pursues the coolly premeditated plan which goes with his part. But Molière cannot possibly have intended to bring a perfect incarnation of the term *faux dévot* on the stage. He needed strong comic effects for the stage, and he found them, most ingeniously, by contrasting the part played by his Tartuffe with the man's natural character. This strong, healthy fellow (*gros et gras, le teint frais, et la bouche vermeille*), with his big appetite (*deux perdrix avec une moitié de gigot en hachis* for supper) and his other no less strongly developed physical needs, has not the slightest talent for piety, not even for a feigned piety. Everywhere the ass looks out from under the lion's skin. He plays his part execrably by exaggerating it beyond all reason; and he loses control over himself as soon as his senses are aroused. His intrigues are crude and simple-minded, and no one except Orgon and his mother can be taken in by him even for a moment—neither the other actors in the play nor the audience. Tartuffe is not at all the embodiment of an intelligent self-disciplined hypocrite, but a coarse-grained fellow with strong, crude instincts who tries to assume the attitude of a bigot because it seems to promise results and despite the fact that it is not becoming to him at all and clashes with his inner nature and outward appearance. And this is precisely what impresses us as overwhelmingly comic. The critics of the seventeenth century who, like La Bruyère, accepted only the rationally plausible as probable would naturally wonder how it was possible that even Orgon and Madame Pernelle should be taken in by him. However, experience teaches us that even the crudest deception and the silliest temptation will succeed at times if they flatter the habits and instincts of their victims and satisfy their secret cravings. Orgon's most deeply instinctive and secret craving, which he can indulge precisely by selling himself and his soul to Tartuffe, is the sadism of a family tyrant. What he would never dare to do without piety making it legitimate, for he is as sentimental and uncertain of himself as he is choleric, he can now give himself up to with a clear conscience: *faire enrager le monde est ma plus grande joie!* (3, 7; cf. also 4, 3: *je porte en ce contrat de quoi vous faire rire*). He loves Tartuffe and lets himself be duped by him because Tartuffe makes it possible for him to satisfy his instinctive urge to tyrannize over and torment his family. This further weakens his power of judgment, which in itself is not too highly developed. A very similar psychological process takes place in Madame Pernelle. And again it is extremely ingenious how Molière makes use of piety itself to remove the obstacles which impede the free development of Orgon's sadism.

Here, as in many of his other plays, Molière is much less concerned with character types, he is much more intent upon rendering the individual reality, than the majority of the moralists of his century. He did not present "the miser" but a perfectly specific coughing old monomaniac; not "the misanthropist" but a young man of the best society, an unyielding fanatic of sincerity, who is steeped in his own opinions, sits in judgment upon the world, and finds it unworthy of himself; not "the hypochondriac" but a wealthy, extremely robust, healthy, and choleric family tyrant who keeps forgetting his role of invalid. And yet no one can help feeling that Molière fits perfectly into his moralizing and typifying century, for he seeks the individually real only for the sake of its ridiculousness, and to him ridiculousness means deviation from the normal and customary. For him too a character taken seriously would be "typical." He wants stage effects; his genius is livelier and requires freer play. The short-winded and finicky technique of La Bruyère, who builds up the abstractly moral type from a mass of traits and anecdotes, is unsuited to the stage; for the stage requires striking effects and greater homogeneity in the realm of the concrete and individual than in that of the abstract and typical. But the moralistic attitude is essentially the same.

Another and no less informative criticism leveled at Molière is to be found in some celebrated lines from Boileau's *Art poétique* (3, 391-405):

> Etudiez la Cour, et connoissez la Ville;
> L'une et l'autre est toujours en modèles fertile.
> C'est par là que Molière, illustrant ses écrits,
> Peut-être de son art eût remporté le prix,
> Si, moins ami du peuple, en ses doctes peintures,
> Il n'eût point fait souvent grimacer ses figures,
> Quitté, pour le bouffon, l'agréable et le fin,
> Et sans honte à Térence allié Tabarin.
> Dans ce sac ridicule, où Scapin s'enveloppe,
> Je ne reconnois plus l'auteur du Misanthrope.
> Le Comique, ennemi des soupirs et des pleurs,
> N'admet point en ses vers de tragiques douleurs;
> Mais son emploi n'est pas d'aller dans une place
> De mots sales et bas charmer la populace.
> Il faut que ses acteurs badinent noblement . . .

(Study the Court and know the City; both are always fertile in models. It is thus that Molière, shedding luster on his works, would perhaps have borne away the prize of his art if, less inclined toward the people, he had not, in his learned portrayals, often made his faces grimace, had not forsaken the pleasing and subtle for buffoonery, and shamelessly allied Terence with Tabarin. In the absurd sack in which Scapin cloaks himself, I do not recognize the author of the *Misanthrope*. Comedy, enemy of sighs and tears, does not admit tragic woes into its verses; but its use is not to go to a public square and delight the populace with foul and vulgar witticisms. Its actors must trifle nobly . . .)

In its way this criticism is entirely justified; and since Boileau after all was a great admirer of Molière it turned out to be rather mild and reserved. For the farcical gestures, expressions, and stage tricks occur not only in the farces proper (which include the *Fourberies de Scapin* cited by Boileau), they also make their way into the comedy of society. In *Tartuffe* for instance we have an effect of straight farce in the trio scene Orgon-Dorine-Marianne (2, 2) where Orgon gets himself into position to box Dorine's ears if she interrupts him again; and the same is even more true of the scene where both Orgon and Tartuffe go down on their knees (3, 6). Even *le Misanthrope,* which Boileau referred to as the model of a comedy of society, and which in fact is the comedy of Molière's which is most uniformly attuned to the key of polite social usage, contains a short farcical scene: the appearance of Alceste's servant Dubois (4, 4). Molière never renounced the effects which his mastery of the technique of the farce put within his reach, and perhaps his most inspired ideas are those which enabled him to work such originally quite mechanical clownish situations into the very essence and significance of his conflicts. The aim, *de faire rire les honnêtes gens sans personnages ridicules,* which had been the ambition of the French comic theater ever since Corneille's first comedies, never made Molière a stylistic purist. Anyone who has seen good performances of his plays, or has imagination enough to visualize them on the stage as he reads, knows that grotesquely farcical effects are scattered all through them, even in the comedies of society, even in *le Misanthrope.* Actors with verve and an eye for the stage everywhere find opportunity to exploit and indeed to improvise such possibilities. Molière himself, who was an outstanding comedian, missed no chance in his acting to carry a point to grotesque exaggeration. To be sure, the farcical effects are by no means limited to characters representing the lower classes, although that is all Boileau has in mind. Those whom Molière makes the subjects of such *lazzi* include persons from all classes, and in the controversy over the *École des femmes* he specifically prides himself on having introduced the *marquis ridicule* and indeed with having assigned to him the part which had previously been the prerogative of the clownish figure of the comic servant:

Le marquis aujourd'hui est le plaisant de la comédie; et comme, dans toutes les comédies anciennes, on voit toujours un valet bouffon qui fait rire les auditeurs, de même, dans toutes nos pièces de maintenant, il faut toujours un marquis ridicule qui divertisse la compagnie. (*L'Impromptu de Versailles,* scene 1.)

(Today the marquis is the droll of comedy; and as, in all the old comedies, we always find a buffoon of a valet who makes the audience laugh, so, in all our plays nowadays, there must always be an absurd marquis to divert the company.)

This is clearly an aggressive exaggeration born of the polemic mood of the moment, but it does reveal Molière's intent—which he put into actual practice—of carrying everyone's ridiculous traits to grotesque extremes, without limiting himself to comic types from the lower classes. Boileau in his criticism, on the other hand, calls for a strict tripartite distinction of stylistic levels inspired by antique models. He recognizes first the elevated, sublime style of tragedy; then the intermediate style of the comedy of society, which must treat of *honnêtes gens* and be intended for *honnêtes gens* and in which the actors *badinent noblement*; and finally the low style of popular farce, in whose action and language *le bouffon* prevails and for which Boileau has the most profound contempt if only because of its *mots sales et bas* which are the delight of the mob. He chides Molière—very mildly as we have seen—for having mixed the intermediate with the low style.

What especially interests us in this criticism of Boileau's is the conception of the people that is reflected in it. It is apparent that Boileau cannot imagine any popular types except the grotesque and comic, at least not as subjects worthy of artistic representation. In the seventeenth century, *la cour et la ville* signifies roughly what we should call the educated or simply the public. It consisted of the court nobility, the sphere whose center was the king (*la cour*) and the Parisian higher bourgeoisie (*la ville*), which in many cases already belonged to the nobility of office (*noblesse de robe*) or was attempting to enter it through the purchase of offices. This is the social stratum to which Boileau himself and the great majority of the leading minds of the century belonged. *La cour et la ville* is the most commonly used expression for the leading circles of the nation immediately before and during the reign of Louis XIV; in particular, it is the most commonly used designation for those to whom literary works were addressed, and not only in the present passage, but also, for example, in discussions of good usage in matters of language, it is very frequently employed in contrast with *le peuple. La cour et la ville,* says Boileau, are to be studied by those who wish to cultivate the intermediate style, the level of the comedy of society; and they must avoid the *bouffon*, the grimaces of the people. It seems that Boileau cannot conceive of any other pictures of the people and its life. And here we clearly discern the limits of his opposition to Molière, just as we did above the limits of the opposition between Molière and La Bruyère. To be sure Molière used farcical effects even in his fashionable comedies, he even caricatured with grotesquely farcical exaggeration personages representing educated society; but he too knew the people only as *personnages ridicules*.

One can see in Molière's art the greatest measure of realism which could still please in the fully developed classical literature of the France of Louis XIV. Molière staked out the limits of what was possible at the time. He did not conform completely to the prevailing trend toward psychological types; yet with him too the peculiar and characteristic is always ridiculous and extravagant. He did not avoid the farcical and the grotesque, yet with him too any real representation of the life of the popular classes, even in such a spirit of aristocratic contempt as Shakespeare's, is as completely out of the question as it is with Boileau. All his chambermaids and servingmen, his peasants and peasants' wives, even his merchants, lawyers, physicians, and apothecaries, are merely comic adjuncts; and it is only within the frame of an upper bourgeois or aristocratic household that servants—especially women—at times represent the voice of down-to-earth common sense. But their functions are always concerned with their masters' problems, never with those of their own lives. Not the slightest trace of politics, of social or economic criticism, or of an analysis of the political, social, and economic bases of life is to be found. Molière's criticism is entirely moralistic; that is to say, it accepts the prevailing structure of society, takes for granted its justification, permanence, and general validity, and castigates the excesses occurring within its limits as ridiculous. In this respect he actually falls behind La Bruyère, whose representational talent is more restricted but who is much more serious and ethical; who likewise refrains from criticizing the structure of society; but who, writing as he did toward the end of the century when the royal sun had lost some of its brilliance, grew aware of this limitation of the literary art and even expressed his awareness in some passages of his work—all the more strikingly since one senses that more is left unsaid than is actually stated. *Un homme né Chrétien et François*—he writes toward the end of his chapter, *Des ouvrages de l'es-*

prit—se trouve contraint dans la satire; les grands sujets lui sont défendus . . . (a man born a Christian and a Frenchman is under a constraint in satire; the great subjects are forbidden him). And in this context I should also like to quote the well-known and strangely arresting passage on the peasantry, which occurs in the chapter *De l'homme* (section 128 in the *Grands Écrivains* edition):

> L'on voit certains animaux farouches, des mâles et des femelles, répandus par la campagne, noirs, livides et tout brûlés du soleil, attachés à la terre qu'ils fouillent et qu'ils remuent avec une opiniâtreté invincible; ils ont comme une voix articulée, et quand ils se lèvent sur leurs pieds, ils montrent une face humaine, et en effet ils sont des hommes. Ils se retirent la nuit dans des tanières, où ils vivent de pain noir, d'eau et de racines; ils épargnent aux autres hommes la peine de semer, de labourer et de recueillir pour vivre, et méritent ainsi de ne pas manquer de ce pain qu'ils ont semé.

> (One sees certain ferocious animals, male and female, scattered over the countryside, black, livid, and burned by the sun, bound to the soil which they dig and turn over with unconquerable stubbornness; they have a sort of articulate voice, and when they stand up they exhibit a human face, and in fact they are men. They retire at night into dens, where they live on black bread, water, and roots; they spare other men the toil of sowing, tilling, and harvesting in order to live, and thus deserve not to be without the bread which they have sown.)

Although this important passage is clearly of its century through its moralizing emphasis, it yet would seem to stand alone in the belles-lettres of the time. Thoughts of this kind occur to Molière as little as they do to Boileau, and the one would be no less reluctant than the other to put them into words. They exceed the limits of what Boileau calls *l'agréable et le fin*; but not because they are great themes, *de grands sujets* (for according to the views of the times they were nothing of the sort) but because their concrete and serious treatment would attribute to an everyday contemporary subject greater weight than is aesthetically its due. The satirist and the moralist in general are not really excluded from treating great subjects. La Bruyère himself wrote chapters dealing with the monarch, the state, man, free thought; for this reason critics have tried to see in the above passage (*un homme né Chrétien et François*) no basic awareness of the limits of this manner of writing but only a discreet criticism of his friend and patron Boileau, an interpretation which deserves attention and is not difficult to defend, but which I nevertheless consider one-sided. On the basis of what we know about La Bruyère's nature and temperament, which was by no means revolutionary but at least more deeply critical and inclined to go to the root of the problems of society than was the wont of his time, I prefer to assume that he was also thinking of himself and of the general political and aesthetic situation; a situation which did permit him to treat great subjects, but only up to a point where he reaches a wall which may not be passed (*il les entame parfois et se détourne ensuite* . . .). He could deal with them only in elevated moralizing generalities. Treating their concrete contemporary structure with complete freedom remained inadmissible for both political and aesthetic reasons, and political reasons and aesthetic reasons are interrelated.

With Molière contemporary political allusions are extremely rare, and when they do occur they are intimated as discreetly as an impropriety, as something to be mentioned with caution or, better, paraphrased. In *Tartuffe* Orgon had apparently sided with the court during the insurrection of the Fronde:

> Nos troubles l'avaient mis sur le pied d'homme sage,
> Et pour servir son prince, il montra du courage . . . (1, 2).

> (Our troubles brought him out in the character of a sensible man, and, to serve his prince, he showed courage . . .)

It is no less discreetly intimated that he nevertheless received and concealed the personal documents of an acquaintance who had been compromised and was forced to flee. An equally discreet treatment is given to everything to do with professional and economic matters. We observed before that in Molière (as everywhere else in the literature of the time) not only peasants and other characters from the lowest classes but also merchants, lawyers, physicians, and apothecaries appear exclusively as comic adjuncts. This is connected with the fact that the social ideal of the time required the most general development and attitude possible from the *honnête homme*. The trend was away from any kind of specialization, even that of the poet or the scholar. Anyone who wanted to be socially unexceptionable must not allow the economic basis of his life to be conspicuous, nor his professional specialty if he had one. Failing that, he was considered pedantic, extravagant, and ridiculous. Only such abilities could be shown as might also pass as an elegant dilettantism and which contributed to easy and pleasant social intercourse. As a result—if we may interpolate this observation here—even difficult and important things were sometimes rendered in an exemplarily simple, elegant, and unpedantic way, and French, as we know, developed a linguistic expression of incomparable clarity and general validity. But professional specialization thus came to be socially and aesthetically impossible; only in the category of the grotesque could it appear as the subject of literary imitation. In this the tradition of the farce certainly played a part, but this is still not enough to explain why the grotesque conception of the professional man was maintained so generally and consistently in the new genre of the elegant social comedy in the intermediate style.

Let us try the opposite tack. Not a few of Molière's comedies have an upper bourgeois setting, for example *l'Avare, le Bourgeois gentilhomme, les Femmes savantes, le Malade imaginaire.* The people in all these households are well-to-do, but no one ever mentions any sort of professional work or productive economic activity. We are not even told how Harpagon, the miser, came by his money (perhaps he inherited it); and the only business transaction mentioned, the usurious loan, is grotesque, timelessly generalized, and furthermore not productive but the investment of a *rentier.* Of none of these middle-class people do we learn what they do for a living; apparently they are all *rentiers.* In only one instance is the origin of a man's fortune referred to: in *le Bourgeois gentilhomme,* where Mme Jourdain reminds her husband: *Descendons-nous tous deux que de bonne bourgeoisie?* . . . *Et votre père n'était-il pas marchand aussi bien que le mien?* . . . And with reference to her daughter she says: . . . *ses deux grands-pères vendaient du drap auprès de la porte Saint-Innocent.* But these bits of information only serve to bring out her husband's grotesque foolishness more strongly. M. Jourdain is an uneducated parvenu who fails to understand the social ideal of his age and attempts to engineer his social rise by unsuitable means. Instead of trying to become an educated *honnête homme* of the upper bourgeoisie, he commits the gravest social error that could be committed at the time: he pretends to be what he is not, a nobleman, *un gentilhomme.* This comes out very clearly when we think of his intended son-in-law, Cléonte, whom Molière contrasts with M. Jourdain as the model of an *honnête homme* of bourgeois background. When Cléonte asks to marry Jourdain's daughter, Jourdain asks him if he is a *gentilhomme,* and gets the following reply:

Monsieur, la plupart des gens, sur cette question, n'hésitent pas beaucoup; on tranche le mot aisément. Ce nom ne fait aucun scrupule à prendre, et l'usage aujourd'hui semble en autoriser le vol. Pour moi, je vous l'avoue, j'ai les sentiments, sur cette matière, un peu plus délicats. Je trouve que toute imposture est indigne d'un honnête homme, et qu'il y a de la lâcheté à déguiser ce que le ciel nous a fait naître, à se parer au monde d'un titre dérobé, à se vouloir donner pour ce qu'on n'est pas. Je suis né de parents, sans doute, qui ont tenu des charges honorables; je me suis acquis, dans les armes, l'honneur de six ans de service, et je me trouve assez de bien pour tenir dans le monde un rang assez passable; mais, avec tout cela, je ne veux point me donner un nom où d'autres, en ma place, croiraient pouvoir prétendre; et je vous dirai franchement que je ne suis point gentilhomme.

(Sir, on this subject most people show little hesitation; they do not boggle over the word. Taking the name causes no qualms, and custom today seems to authorize the theft of it. For my part, I will admit to you, my feelings in the matter are a little more scrupulous. I consider that any imposture is unworthy of an honorable man, and that there is cowardice in concealing what Heaven made us by our birth, in parading a filched title before society, in trying to make oneself out to be what one is not. I was born, certainly, of a family which has held honorable offices; I gained, in the army, the honor of six years of service, and I have fortune enough to hold a rather passable rank in society; but, with all that, I do not wish to give myself a designation to which others, in my place, would think they could lay claim; and I shall tell you frankly that I am not of gentle birth.)

Such, then, is the picture of a class-conscious young bourgeois, an *honnête homme,* who knows his place in society. The desire to push themselves into the nobility which afflicts parvenus like M. Jourdain (parvenus whose wealth goes back only two generations and whose fathers were still cloth-mongers) is something which Cléonte is as far from feeling as he is from condoning. But he is equally far from the people and a concrete profession. Not a word to tell us that his family's name is respected in the silk industry or among wine merchants, for example. Rather *ils ont tenu des charges honorables,* which means that they bought themselves offices through which they rose to membership in the intermediate estate of the robe. He himself was an army officer for six years and is wealthy enough *pour tenir dans le monde un rang assez passable.* There is no economic-mindedness, no idea of a productive bourgeoisie, in this young man. On the contrary, he turns away from such things. To him his bourgeoisie is simply *un rang qu'on tient dans le monde,* just as his nobility is to a young nobleman. Like his ancestors and relatives he will buy or inherit a *charge honorable.* (These last observations are taken almost verbatim from my earlier essay, *La cour et la ville,* last published in my *Vier Untersuchungen zur Geschichte der französischen Bildung,* Bern, 1951, pp. 46-48. I shall make further use of it elsewhere in this chapter.)

As we have seen, Molière does not hesitate to employ farcical elements in his comedies of society, but he consistently avoids any realistic concretizing, or even any penetrating criticism, of the political and economic aspects of the milieu in which his characters move. He is far more inclined to admit the grotesque into the intermediate level of style than the serious and basic reality of economic and political life. His realism, insofar as it has a serious and problematic side, is limited to the psychological and moral realm. To see this with the greatest clarity one should call to mind the description of the accumulation of Grandet's fortune which Honoré de Balzac gives at the beginning of his novel *Eugénie Grandet,* a description into which all of French history from 1789 to the Restoration is interwoven, and compare it with the absolute generality and ahistoricity of Harpagon's economic situation. Nor should it be objected that Molière had no room within the limits of a comedy for a description like Balzac's. Even on the stage it would have been possible to show, instead of Harpagon, a contemporary merchant or revenue farmer conducting his business. But this sort of thing does not appear until after the classical period, in Dancourt for instance or in Lesage, and even then without serious problems rooted in contemporary economy.

The observations on the limitations of realism which we have presented so far are entirely concerned with the intermediate style of comedy and satire. The limitations are much stricter in the realm of the elevated style, in tragedy. In that realm the separation of the tragic from the occurrences of everyday and human-creatural life was carried out in such a radical way as never before, not even during the period whose style served as the model, that is, Greco-Roman antiquity. At least Corneille was at times still aware of how much further the taste of his time went in this direction than the antique tradition demanded.

Neither the everyday aspects of its actions nor the creatural characteristics of its personages are allowed to appear on the French tragic stage. A type of tragic personage unknown to antiquity develops. To convey a concrete understanding of this type, I shall assemble a few characteristic stylistic effects. They are taken from Racine's tragedies *Bérénice* and *Esther*. But similar ones are to be found all through the tragic drama of the time, though not in so perfected a form as in Racine.

At the beginning of *Bérénice* we are taken to a room in the Emperor's palace:

> . . . La pompe de ces lieux,
> Je le vois bien, Arsace, est nouvelle à tes yeux.
> Souvent ce cabinet, superbe et solitaire,
> Des secrets de Titus est le dépositaire.
> C'est ici quelquefois qu'il se cache à sa cour. . . .

(The pomp of these chambers, I well see, Arsaces, is new to your eyes. This sumptuous and solitary room is often the repository of Titus's secrets. It is here that he sometimes hides from his court. . . .)

In keeping with this is the Emperor's manner of expressing himself when he wants to be alone: *Paulin, qu'on vous laisse avec moi* (2, 1); or *Que l'on me laisse* (4, 3); or when he wishes to speak to someone:

> Titus A-t-on vu de ma part le roi de Comagène?
> Sait-il que je l'attends?
>
> Paulin . . .
> De vos ordres, seigneur, j'ai dit qu'on l'avertisse.
>
> Titus Il suffit . . . (2, 1).

(*Titus*: Has the King of Commagene been given my message? Does he know that I am awaiting him: *Paulinus*: . . . I said that he was to be informed of your orders. *Titus*: Enough.)

When Titus charges King Antiochus to accompany Queen Bérénice on her journey, we get this:

> Vous, que l'amitié seule attache sur ses pas,
> Prince, dans son malheur ne l'abandonnez pas:
> Que l'Orient vous voie arriver à sa suite;
> Que ce soit un triomphe, et non pas une fuite;

Qu'une amitié si belle ait d'éternels liens;
Que mon nom soit toujours dans tous vos entretiens.
Pour rendre vos Etats plus voisins l'un de l'autre,
L'Euphrate bornera son empire et le vôtre.
Je sais que le sénat, tout plein de votre nom,
D'une commune voix confirmera ce don.
Je joins la Cilicie à votre Comagène. . . .

(You, whom friendship alone binds to her steps, Prince, forsake her not in her unhappiness: let the East see you arrive in her train; let it be a triumph, not a flight; let so fair a friendship have eternal bonds; let my name ever be in your conversations. To make your States closer to one another, the Euphrates shall bound her empire and yours. I know that the Senate, full of your name, will confirm this gift with a common voice. I join Cilicia to your Commagene. . . .)

From Antiochus' words I quote:

Titus m'accable ici du poids de sa grandeur:
Tout disparaît dans Rome auprès de sa splendeur;
Mais, quoique l'Orient soit plein de sa mémoire,
Bérénice y verra des traces de ma gloire (3, 1 and 2).

(Here Titus overwhelms me with the weight of his greatness: everything vanishes in Rome beside his splendor: but, though the East is full of his memory, there Berenice will see traces of my glory.)

The representation of the king in the prologue to *Esther* is too long to be quoted here, and the description of the search for a queen and the king's choice, which Esther gives in the first scene, can only be illustrated by a few samples:

De l'Inde à l'Hellespont ses esclaves coururent:
Les filles de l'Egypte à Suse comparurent;
Celles même du Parthe et du Scythe indompté
Y briguèrent le sceptre offert à la beauté.

(From India to the Hellespont his slaves ran: the daughters of Egypt, summoned, appeared at Susa; even those of Parthia and unconquered Scythia intrigued there for the scepter offered to beauty.)

And later:

Il m'observa longtemps dans un sombre silence;
Et le ciel qui pour moi fit pencher la balance,
Dans ce temps-là, sans doute, agissait sur son cœur.
Enfin, avec des yeux où régnait la douceur,
Soyez reine, dit-il. . . .

(For long he observed me in a somber silence; and Heaven, which caused the scale to tip for me, no doubt during that time acted upon his heart. At last, with eyes in which gentleness reigned, "Be queen," he said. . . .)

What Racine made of the scene where Esther appears unsummoned before the King is remembered by every reader:

Assuérus — Sans mon ordre on porte ici ses pas!
Quel mortel insolent vient chercher le trépas?
Gardes . . . C'est vous, Esther? Quoi! sans être attendue?
Esther — Mes filles, soutenez votre reine éperdue:
Je me meurs . . . (Elle tombe évanouie).
Assuérus — Dieux puissants! quelle étrange pâleur
De son teint tout à coup efface la couleur!
Esther, que craignez-vous? Suis-je pas votre frère?
Est-ce pour vous qu'est fait un ordre si sévère?
Vivez: le sceptre d'or que vous tend cette main
Pour vous de ma clémence est un gage certain.
. . .
Esther — Seigneur, je n'ai jamais contemplé qu'avec crainte
L'auguste majesté sur votre front empreinte;
Jugez comment ce front irrité contre moi
Dans mon âme troublée a dû jeter d'effroi:
Sur ce trône sacré qu'environne la foudre
J'ai cru vous voir tout prêt à me réduire en poudre.
Hélas! sans frissonner, quel cœur audacieux
Soutiendrait les éclairs qui partaient de vos yeux?
Ainsi du Dieu vivant la colère étincelle. . .
Assuérus — . . .
Calmez, reine, calmez la frayeur qui vous presse.
Du cœur d'Assuérus souveraine maîtresse,
Eprouvez seulement son ardente amitié.
Faut-il de mes Etats vous donner la moitié?

(*Ahasuerus*: One enters here without my orders! What insolent mortal comes seeking death? Guards! . . . Is it you, Esther? What! without being expected? *Esther*: My handmaids, sustain your distracted queen. I die . . . (She falls in a faint.) *Ahasuerus*: Mighty gods! what strange pallor suddenly blots out the color of her complexion! Esther, what do you fear? Am I not your brother? Is such a stern order made for you? Live: the golden scepter which this hand holds forth to you is a sure pledge to you of my clemency. . . . *Esther*: My lord, never but with fear have I beheld the august majesty imprinted on your brow; judge how that brow, angered against me, must have cast terror into my troubled soul: on that sacred throne, which thunderbolts surround, I thought that I saw you ready to reduce me to dust. Alas! without shuddering, what audacious heart would bear the lightnings which leaped from your eyes? Thus flashes the wrath of the living God. . . . *Ahasuerus*: . . . Calm, O queen, calm the terror which assails you. Sovereign mistress of Ahasuerus' heart, feel only his ardent friendship. Shall I give you half of my States?)

The text of the Book of Esther—not at this point, it is true, but a little later, during the banquet—accompanies the offer of half the King's realm with the "sober" remark *postquam vinum biberat abundanter*. In Racine we read nothing of the sort. And before this he similarly suppresses a realistic detail from the Book of Esther although it casts a clearer light on Esther's courage than the mere rule which prohibits her appearance before the king without having been summoned: *Ego igitur quo modo ad regem intrare potero, quae triginta iam diebus non sum vocata ad eum*? (Then how can I go in to the king, who have not been summoned to him for thirty days?)

What all these quotations bring out is the extreme exaltation of the tragic personage. Be it a prince who abandons himself to his love in his cabinet *superbe et solitaire* after saying to his retinue, *que l'on me laisse*; or be it a princess going aboard a ship which awaits her, *souveraine des mers qui vous doivent porter* (*Mithridate*, 1, 3)—the tragic personage is always in a sublime posture, in the foreground, surrounded by utensils, retinue, people, landscape, and universe, as by so many trophies of victory which serve it or are at its disposal. In this posture the tragic personage abandons itself to its princely passions. And the most impressive stylistic effects of this sort are those in which whole countries, continents, or even the universe appear as spectator, witness, background, or echo of the princely emotion. For this special case too I shall cite a few examples. In *Andromaque* (2, 2) Hermione says:

> Pensez-vous avoir seul éprouvé des alarmes;
> Que l'Epire jamais n'ait vu couler mes larmes?

(Think you that you alone have undergone alarms; that Epirus has never seen my tears flow?)

Far more famous is the marvelous verse from Antiochus' declaration of love, *Bérénice*, 1, 4, which I shall quote in its immediate context and in which the Baroque tendency toward exaltation appears to meet romanticism:

> Rome vous vit, madame, arriver avec lui.
> *Dans l'Orient désert quel devint mon ennui!*
> Je demeurai longtemps errant dans Césarée,
> Lieux charmants où mon cœur vous avait adorée,
> Je vous redemandais à vos tristes Etats;
> Je cherchais en pleurant les traces de vos pas. . . .

(Rome saw you, madam, arrive with him. In the desert East what did not my hopelessness become! For long I remained wandering in Caesarea, charming sites where my heart had adored you, I conjured your forlorn realms to give you back to me; weeping I sought the traces of your steps. . . .)

And finally another illustration from *Bérénice*:

> Aidez-moi, s'il se peut, à vaincre ma faiblesse,
> A retenir des pleurs qui m'échappent sans cesse;
> Ou, si nous ne pouvons commander à nos pleurs,
> Que la gloire du moins soutienne nos douleurs;
> Et que tout l'univers reconnaisse sans peine
> Les pleurs d'un empereur et les pleurs d'une reine. (4, 5).

(Aid me, if possible, to conquer my weakness, to hold back tears which constantly escape me; or, if we cannot command our tears, may glory at least sustain our griefs; and may the whole universe easily recognize the tears of an emperor and the tears of a queen.)

The tragic personage has so strong an awareness of its princely rank that it can never be without it. In the deepest misfortune and the most extreme passion Racine's tragic personages identify themselves by their rank. They do not say "I wretched," but "I, wretched prince!" Hermione calls herself *une triste princesse* (*Andromaque*, 2, 2), and Bérénice, in the most dreadful confusion, implores Antiochus in these words:

> O ciel! quel discours! Demeurez!
> Prince, c'est trop cacher mon trouble à votre vue:
> Vous voyez devant vous une reine éperdue,
> Qui, la mort dans le sein, vous demande deux mots . . . (3, 3).

(O Heaven! what words! Remain! Prince, it is too much to hide my trouble from your eyes: you see before you a distracted queen, who, with death in her heart, asks brief speech with you . . .)

Titus constantly calls himself *un prince malheureux*; and in the dramatic moment when Athalie, suddenly seeing herself betrayed and lost, breaks out in despair, she exclaims:

> Où suis-je? O trahison! ô reine infortunée!
> D'armes et d'ennemis je suis environnée! (5, 5).

(Where am I? O treachery! O unfortunate queen! By arms and enemies I am surrounded!)

We have already mentioned the passage where Esther, as she falls into a faint, exclaims: *Mes filles, soutenez votre reine éperdue. . . .* The princely rank of these tragic personages and their concomitant exaltation have become part of their natural being, inseparable from their substance, and they appear before even God or death in the princely posture which is theirs by right; quite in contrast to the "creatural" conception which we attempted to describe in our chapter on the fifteenth century (p. 249f.). Yet it would be quite wrong if, as the romanticists sometimes did, we were to deny them everything natural and human, immediate and simple. At least in the case of Racine such a judgment betrays an utter lack of understanding. His characters are completely and exemplarily natural and human—only their emotion-charged and exemplarily human lives are lived on an exalted level, which to them has become normal. And indeed, at times it occurs that their very exaltation yields the most enchanting and profoundly human effects. By way of example I might refer to many passages in *Phèdre*, but instead I shall limit myself to the speech of Bérénice when, in her unsuspecting happiness, she almost rapturously describes the majesty of her beloved Titus at the nocturnal ceremony in the Senate, to end with something which only a person in love could say:

> Parle: peut-on le voir sans penser, comme moi,
> Qu'en quelque obscurité que le sort l'eût fait naître,
> Le monde en le voyant eût reconnu son maître?

(Speak: can one see him, without thinking, as I do, that in whatever obscurity fate had caused him to be born, the world, seeing him, would have recognized its master?)

Now while the tragic personage, as we have seen, is pervaded in its very substance by its consciousness of princely rank, the actual function of rulership—that is, the tragic personage's practical activity—is not made apparent except through the most general allusions. Being a prince is much rather a posture, an "attitude," than a practical function. In the earliest plays, especially in *Alexandre,* the prince's political and military activity is made completely subservient to his love. Alexander conquers the world only in order to lay it at the feet of his beloved, and the whole play is full of Baroque stylistic effects in the manner of the following:

> Alexandre . . .
> Maintenant que mon bras, engagé sous vos lois,
> Doit soutenir mon nom et le vôtre à la fois,
> J'irai rendre fameux, par l'éclat de la guerre,
> Des peuples inconnus au reste de la terre,
> Et vous faire dresser des autels en des lieux
> Où leurs sauvages mains en refusaient aux dieux.
> Cléophile Oui, vous y traînerez la victoire captive;
> Mais je doute, seigneur, que l'amour vous y suive.
> Tant d'Etats, tant de mers, qui vont nous désunir
> M'effaceront bientôt de votre souvenir.
> Quand l'Océan troublé vous verra sur son onde
> Achever quelque jour la conquête du monde;
> Quand vous verrez les rois tomber à vos genoux,
> Et la terre en tremblant se taire devant vous,
> Songerez-vous, seigneur, qu'une jeune princesse,
> Au fond de ses Etats, vous regrette sans cesse
> Et rappelle en son cœur les moments bienheureux
> Où ce grand conquérant l'assurait de ses feux?

Alexandre Et quoi! vous croyez donc qu'à moi-même barbare
J'abandonne en ces lieux une beauté si rare?
Mais vous-même plutôt voulez-vous renoncer
Au trône de l'Asie où je vous veux placer? (3, 6)

(*Alexander*: . . . Now that my arm, enlisted under your laws, must maintain my name and yours together, I shall go and, by the splendor of war, bring fame to peoples unknown to the rest of the earth, cause altars to be raised to you in realms where their savage hands refused them to the gods. *Cléophile*: Yes, you will drag victory captive there; but there I doubt if love will follow you. So many States, so many seas, which will separate us, will soon blot me from your memory. When troubled Ocean shall one day see you on his flood achieving the conquest of the world; when you shall see kings fall at your knees, and the earth tremble and keep silent before you, will you remember, my Lord, that a young princess, in the depths of her States, regrets you without ceasing and recalls in her heart the blessed moments when that great conqueror assured her of his fires? *Alexander*: What! You think, then, that, barbarous to myself, I shall abandon so rare a beauty in these realms? Do you not rather wish to renounce the throne of Asia upon which I would set you?)

This fictitious order of things, which stems directly from the *romans galants* and indirectly from the courtly epic (cf. page 141), is still very pronounced in *Andromaque*, where Pyrrhus says to the heroine:

Mais, parmi ces périls où je cours pour vous plaire,
Me refuserez-vous un regard moins sévère? (1, 4)

(But, among these dangers into which I run to please you, will you refuse me a less severe look?)

or later, in a classical example of Baroque hyperbole, comparing the torment of his love with the torments he inflicted on the Trojans:

Je souffre tous les maux que j'ai faits devant Troie:
Vaincu, chargé de fers, de regrets consumé,
Brûlé de plus de feux que je n'en allumai
. . .
Hélas! fus-je jamais si cruel que vous l'êtes?

(I suffer all the ills which I caused before Troy: conquered, loaded with irons, devoured with regrets, burned with more fires than I kindled . . . alas! was I ever as cruel as you are?)

Quite comparable are Orestes' utterances in regard to his vain search for death among the Scythians as an escape from the torment of his love:

> Enfin, je viens à vous, et je me vois réduit
> A chercher dans vos yeux une mort qui me fuit.
> . . .
> Madame, c'est à vous de prendre une victime
> Que les Scythes auraient dérobée à vos coups,
> Si j'en avais trouvé d'aussi cruels que vous (2, 2).

(Now at last I come to you, and I see myself reduced to seeking in your eyes a death which flees me . . . Madam, it is for you to take a victim whom the Scythians would have snatched from your assaults, had I found any of them to be as cruel as you.)

In the later plays such motifs appear more rarely. An example is *Bérénice*, 2, 2:

> . . . et de si belles mains
> Semblent vous demander l'empire des humains. . . .

(. . . and such fair hands seem to demand that you give them the empire of the human race. . . .)

On the whole there is later a change in the conception of the ruler's business and of the political order of things, but it remains a loftily general conception, far removed from the practical and the factual. It is always a matter of court intrigues and struggles for power which do not go beyond the highest social spheres, the monarch's immediate entourage; and this allows the poet to confine everything entirely to the realm of the personal-psychological and to a small number of personages who are treated moralistically. What lies behind or beneath is either not expressed at all or only in the most general way. This latter procedure obtains for instance in the case of the *loi qui ne se peut changer* which prevents the Emperor Titus (*Bérénice*) from marrying a foreign queen. When in this conflict Titus asks what the mood of the people is, we get this:

> Que dit-on des soupirs que je pousse pour elle?

This completely moralistic view of the political order of things, which excludes every possibility of a factually problematic approach and every concern with the concrete and practical elements in the business of the ruler, may be best studied in *Britannicus*, *Bérénice*, and *Esther*.

In all these plays the good or evil of the state is exclusively dependent upon the moral qualities of the monarch, who either controls his passions and puts his omnipotence at the service of virtue and hence of the common weal, or succumbs to his passions and allows the flatterers in his entourage to mislead him and support him in his evil desires. His omnipotence is never challenged, encounters no resistance; and all the factual problems and obstacles which in the reality of life oppose both good and evil wills are completely disregarded; all that lies far below us. From this point of view the picture is everywhere the same, be it in the allusions to Nero's early years of virtuous rule:

Depuis trois ans entiers, qu'a-t-il dit, qu'a-t-il fait
Qui ne promette à Rome un empereur parfait?
Rome, depuis trois ans, par ses soins gouvernée,
Au temps de ses consuls croit être retournée;
Il la gouverne en père... (*Britannicus*, 1, 1);

(For three whole years what has he said, what has he done, which does not promise Rome a perfect emperor? Governed for these three years by his watchful care, Rome believes that she has returned to the days of her consuls; he rules her like a father...)

be it in the manner in which Titus's ambition to be a good ruler is expressed:

J'entrepris le bonheur de mille malheureux:
On vit de toutes parts mes bontés se répandre... (*Bérénice*, 2, 2);

(I undertook the happiness of a thousand who were unhappy; my benevolences were seen distributed everywhere...)

or

Où sont ces heureux jours que je faisais attendre?
Quels pleurs ai-je séchés? Dans quels yeux satisfaits
Ai-je déjà goûté le fruit de mes bienfaits?
L'univers a-t-il vu changer ses destinées? (*ibid.*, 4, 4);

(Where are those happy days of which I awakened expectation? What tears have I dried? In what satisfied eyes have I savored the fruit of my good deeds? Has the universe seen its destinies changed?)

be it in the description of the good king:

J'admire un roi victorieux,
Que sa valeur conduit triomphant en tous lieux:

Mais un roi sage et qui hait l'injustice,
Qui sous la loi du riche impérieux
Ne souffre pas que le pauvre gémisse
Est le plus beau présent des cieux.
La veuve en sa défense espère.
De l'orphelin il est le père.
Et les larmes du juste implorant son appui
Sont précieuses devant lui. (*Esther*, 3, 3);

(I admire a victorious king whose valor leads him to triumph everywhere: but a wise king, a king who hates injustice, who does not permit the poor man to groan under the law of the imperious rich, is the fairest gift of heaven. The widow trusts in his protection. He is the orphan's father. And the tears of the just man imploring his support are precious before him.)

be it, finally, in the description of court flatterers:

De l'absolu pouvoir vous ignorez l'ivresse,
Et des lâches flatteurs la voix enchanteresse.
Bientôt ils vous diront que les plus saintes lois,
Maîtresses du vil peuple, obéissent aux rois:
Qu'un roi n'a d'autre frein que sa volonté même;
Qu'il doit immoler tout à sa grandeur suprême. . . (*Athalie*, 4, 3).

(You do not know the intoxication of absolute power, nor the bewitching voice of unmanly flatterers. Soon they will tell you that the most sacred laws, mistresses of the vile people, are obedient to kings; that a king has no bridle but his own will; that he must sacrifice everything to his supreme greatness. . .)

As we have seen, this exclusively moralistic view of political matters, with its extreme simplification and neat distinction of black and white, is to be found not only in the plays destined for the young ladies of Saint-Cyr (in which it could be accounted for by their special purpose) but in the others too. In the Saint-Cyr tragedies it is more the moralism of the Bible, in the earlier tragedies more the moralism of late antiquity, which inspired this conception of things. But in both cases there is one outstanding motif which is either not voiced at all, or at least only much more faintly, in these sources: the motif of the ruler's omnipotence, which is a leading motif of Baroque absolutism. On earth the prince is like God. We have already found them compared in the passage from *Esther* quoted above (page 373). Correspondingly, we find God represented as a moralistic king of kings:

> L'Eternel est son nom, le monde est son ouvrage;
> Il entend les soupirs de l'humble qu'on outrage,
> Juge tous les mortels avec d'égales lois,
> Et du haut de son trône interroge les rois. . . . (*Esther*, 3, 4)

> (The Eternal is his name, the world is his work; he hears the sighs of the humble when they are outraged, judges all mortals by equal laws, and, high on his throne, interrogates kings. . . .)

Similar ideas are found in the concluding chorus of the first act of *Athalie*, for example, and in connection with them one cannot help recalling Bossuet's magnificently rolling periods at the beginning of his funeral oration for the Queen of England, Henriette-Marie de France, which close with a verse from the Psalms: *Et nunc, reges, intelligite; erudimini, qui iudicatis terram.* This oration was delivered in 1669, when both the King and Racine were in their first brilliance, twenty years before *Esther*.

In the tragedies of French classicism, as will be self-evident after all that has been said, the strictest seclusion of the tragic personages and the tragic action from everything below them prevails. Even the prince's immediate entourage is drawn upon only for a few figures indispensable to the action, or confidants; everyone else is *on*. The people are referred to but rarely and only in the most general terms. Details of everyday living, references to sleeping, eating and drinking, the weather, landscape, and time of day are almost completely absent; and when they do occur they are fused into the sublime style. The fact that no common word, no current term for any object of daily use, is permitted, is generally known as a result of the violent polemic with which the Romanticists attacked this style and of which the most vigorous and witty expression is probably found in Victor Hugo's poem, *Réponse à un acte d'accusation* (in the *Contemplations*). From the almost too eloquent verses in which Hugo describes his revolt against the classical ideal of the sublime I have always remembered one as especially characteristic:

> On entendit un roi dire: Quelle heure est-il?

Anything of the sort (it happens in Hugo's *Hernani*) would in fact be completely incompatible with the sublime style of Racine.

In this sublimity which secludes and isolates them the tragic princes and princesses abandon themselves to their passions. Only the most important considerations, freed from the turmoil of everyday life, cleansed of its odor and flavor, penetrate their souls, which are thus wholly free for the greatest and strongest emotions. The tremendous impact of the passions in Racine's works, and in Corneille's before him, is largely dependent upon the above-described atmospheric isolation of the action; it is comparable with the isolating procedure used in modern scientific experiments to create the most favorable conditions; the phenomenon is observed with no disturbing factors and in unbroken continuity. In the moral realm the trend toward a separation of styles in terms of class is carried so far that the practical considerations and reservations suggested by a given situation come from personages comparatively inferior in station. The princely heroes and heroines remain aloof from such things; their passionate sublimity scorns every kind of practical concern. In *Bérénice* it is the confidante Phénice who advises the queen not to discourage Antiochus completely because Titus has not yet fully declared himself (1, 5). In the same play it is Antiochus' confidant Arsace who draws his king's attention to the advantageous implications of the straits in which Bérénice finds herself; with Titus abandoning her—Arsace reasons—she must marry Antiochus (3, 2). Such considerations (one might fairly say, calculations), which view and judge a given situation in terms of its practical requirements, are too base to find room in the soul of a prince in the throes of sublime passions, and as a matter of fact they prove fallacious. The same sense of style induced Racine not to put the accusation against Hippolyte in Phèdre's own mouth, as his source, Euripides' *Hippolytos*, does, but in her nurse Oenone's. He explains this point in his *Préface*:

> J'ai même pris soin de la rendre un peu moins odieuse qu'elle n'est dans les tragédies des anciens, où elle se résout d'elle-même à accuser Hippolyte. J'ai cru que la calomnie avait quelque chose de trop bas et de trop noir pour la mettre dans la bouche d'une princesse qui a d'ailleurs des sentiments si nobles et si vertueux. Cette bassesse m'a paru plus convenable à une nourrice, qui pouvait avoir des inclinations plus serviles. . .

> (I have even been careful to make her a little less odious than she is in the tragedies of the ancients, where she herself resolves to accuse Hippolytus. I considered that calumny had something too base and too dark about it for me to put it in the mouth of a

princess who elsewhere has such noble and virtuous feelings. This baseness appeared to me more suitable to a nurse, whose inclinations could be more servile. . .)

But it seems to me that in this passage, where he is trying to defend the moral value of his tragedy against attacks made upon it in the name of Christian piety, Racine gives his thought too "virtuous" a turn; what is incompatible with the sublimity of his princely heroes is not so much the morally evil but rather the vulgar concern with practical advantages.

Another very essential and distinguishing characteristic of the sublimity of the tragic personages is their physical integrity: everything that happens to their bodies must happen in elevated style, and everything base and creatural must be omitted. Corneille still felt how far his age's conception of style outdid all tradition in this respect, even that of the ancients. When his *Théodore* failed, its failure was partly ascribed to the circumstance that the threatened prostitution of the heroine is mentioned in the play. He says in his *Examen* (*Œuvres, Grands Écrivains* edition, volume 5, page 11):

> Dans cette disgrace j'ai de quoi congratuler à la pureté de notre scène, de voir qu'une histoire qui fait le plus bel ornement du second livre de Saint-Ambroise, se trouve trop licencieuse pour y être supportée. Qu'eût-on dit, si, comme ce grand Docteur de l'Eglise, j'eusse fait voir cette vierge dans le lieu infâme. . . .

> (In this disfavor, I have reason to congratulate the purity of our stage, since I see that a story which forms the fairest ornament of St. Ambrose's second book proves too licentious to be tolerated there. What would people have said if, like that great Doctor of the Church, I had exhibited the virgin in the place of infamy. . . .)

Indeed every token of bodily-creatural infirmity is incompatible with the conception of the sublime entertained by French classicism. Only death, as pertaining to the elevated style, cannot be dispensed with. But no tragic hero may be old, ill, infirm, or disfigured. On this stage neither Lear nor Oedipus appears, or else they submit to adjust themselves to the prevailing sense of style. In the preface to his *Œdipe* Corneille says of his model Sophocles:

> Je n'ai pas laissé de trembler quand je l'ai envisagé de près, et un peu plus à loisir que je n'avais fait en le choisissant. J'ai connu

> que ce qui avait passé pour miraculeux dans ces siècles éloignés, pourrait sembler horrible au nôtre, et que cette éloquente et curieuse description de la manière dont ce malheureux prince se crève les yeux, et le spectacle de ces mêmes yeux crevés, dont le sang lui distille sur le visage, qui occupe tout le cinquième acte chez ces incomparables originaux, ferait soulever la délicatesse de nos dames . . . j'ai tâché de rémédier à ces désordres . . . (*Œuvres*, 6, 126).
>
> (Yet I could not but tremble when I looked at him closely and with somewhat more leisure than I had done when I chose him. I understood that what had passed for miraculous in those distant ages might seem horrible to our own age, and that the eloquent and meticulous description of the way in which that unfortunate prince puts out his eyes, and the spectacle of those eyes themselves, gouged out, with their blood trickling over his face, which takes up the whole fifth act in the work of those incomparable originals, would provoke the fastidiousness of our ladies . . . I attempted to remedy these disorders. . . .)

The tone of both these quotations makes one feel that Corneille regarded the sense of style of the age Louis XIV not entirely without inner reservations. In his first and by far his most effective masterpiece, *le Cid*, we have Don Diègue, who gets slapped in the face and at least for a moment is a helpless old man; and in *Attila*, written in Boileau's and Racine's time, the hero dies of a nose-bleed (which was considered shocking in many quarters). In Racine's tragedies such things are inconceivable. For his generation it went without saying that everything bodily and natural or even creatural could be tolerated only on the comic stage, and even there only within certain limits. In Racine's tragedies we find an aged hero too, Mithridate. But he is a thoroughly sublime figure, and his age occasions stylistic effects in the manner of the following:

> Ce cœur nourri de sang, et de guerre affamé,
> Malgré le faix des ans et du sort qui m'opprime
> Traîne partout l'amour qui l'attache à Monime. . . (2, 3).
>
> (This heart, nourished on blood and hungry for war, despite the burden of years and of fate which oppresses me, everywhere bears the love which binds it to Monimia. . . .)

Finally, there is also a sense of physical propriety which (although from a modern point of view it contrasts strangely with the boundless fury of the all-pervading passion of love) caused Racine to tone down the accusation against Hippolyte (in *Phèdre*). In his preface he says:

> Hippolyte est accusé, dans Euripide et dans Sénèque, d'avoir en effet violé sa belle-mère: vim corpus tulit. Mais il n'est ici accusé que d'en avoir eu le dessein. J'ai voulu épargner à Thésée une confusion qui l'aurait pu rendre moins agréable aux spectateurs.
>
> (In Euripides and Seneca, Hippolytus is accused of having actually ravished his mother-in-law: "he took her by force." But here he is accused of no more than having had that intention. I wished to spare Theseus a confusion which might have made him less agreeable to the audience.)

Here we may observe a very general contrast to the practice of antiquity. In the works of the ancients love is but rarely a subject for the elevated style; with them it occurs as the major theme—that is, not in conjunction with other motifs, divine or fatal—only in works on the intermediate level; but whenever it does appear—even though in a sublime epic or tragic work—its physical aspects are mentioned without qualms. In the case of French tragedy, the situation is exactly reversed. French tragedy took over the sublime conception of love which the Middle Ages had developed in courtly culture, not without the collaboration of mysticism, and which Petrarchism had carried still further. Already in Corneille it is a tragic and sublime motif. Under the influence of the *romans galants* it displaces almost all other higher themes, and Racine gives it the overwhelming power which precipitates men from their courses and annihilates them. But in all this there is hardly a trace of the physical and sexual, which the taste of the time considered base and improper.

The seclusion and isolation of the tragic process to which we have referred was also considerably enhanced by the rules of unity. These reduce the contacts of the action with its milieu to a minimum. When the place remains one and the same, when the time is restricted to a brief span of twenty-four hours, while the action is completely detached from its secondary implications, it becomes impossible to do more than allude in the most general way to the historical, social, economic, and regional determinants of the occurrence. It is marvelous how Racine nevertheless succeeds—with the most meager devices and entirely by means of the action proper—in creating an atmosphere.

However, his most felicitous achievements in this respect are *Phèdre* and *Athalie*, in which place and time—in the latter case Old Testament, and in the former from Greek mythology—come close to being absolute and extrahistorical. Scenes in which a specific moment reveals its identity in terms of time of day and landscape are very rare. One might cite the passage in *Britannicus* (2, 2) where Nero describes Junie's arrival at night. It is masterly and proves—as does another passage to which we shall come in a moment—that it was no poetic poverty which caused Racine to produce so few pictures of this kind, expressing the content of a moment; but it is fully incorporated into the psychological structure of the principal action and bears the stamp of the generalizing and periphrasing style of the times, especially in the lines which describe Junie's nightgown:

> Belle sans ornement, dans le simple appareil
> D'une beauté qu'on vient d'arracher au sommeil. . . .

The other passage I have in mind is the landscape at dawn, modeled after Euripides, in the first scene of *Iphigénie*. It contains the magnificent line:

> Mais tout dort, et l'armée, et les vents, et Neptune,

and is unique in its kind by virtue of its realistic "content of the moment": the king waking a sleeping servant. But it too is entirely grounded in the psychological development of the principal action; its content of atmosphere and color is not an end in itself; and its verbal expression contains no trace of realistic spontaneity. The language is sublime and full of metaphors. On the whole it is possible to say that the unity of time and place lifts the action out of time and place. The reader or listener has the impression of an absolute, mythical, and geographically unidentifiable locality. It is no longer the adventurous nowhere of the *romans galants* with its pedantic and ridiculous abundance of lovers. From that Racine had early emancipated himself. It is an exalted and isolated locality in which tragic personages, raised high above all everyday occurrences and speaking in sublime stylization, abandon themselves to their passionate emotions.

The classic tragedy of the French represents the ultimate extreme in the separation of styles, in the severance of the tragic from the everyday and real, attained by European literature. Its conception of the tragic individual and its linguistic expression are the product of a special aesthetic refinement which is rooted in a very complicated and multilayered tradition and remains aloof from the average life of any period whatever. This, however, is a modern interpretation, even though not a very recent one. The aesthetic theory of Racine's era did not know it. To justify, praise, or defend the tragedies of Racine and similar works, it used such terms as nature, reason, common sense, and probability. In Racine's works, his own and the following centuries saw the realization of *le naturel, la raison, le bon sens,* and *la vraisemblance,* together with *la bienséance* and the most perfect imitation of antiquity, at times indeed going beyond its models. Such a judgment requires interpretation, because it fails to strike us as immediately admissible. Is it reasonable and natural to exalt human beings in so extreme a fashion and to make them speak in so extremely stylized a language? Is it probable that crises mature in so short a time and with so little disturbance; and can we admit as probable that all their momentous phases shall occur in the same room? The impartial observer, that is, anyone who has not grown up with these masterpieces from childhood and early school days, so that he accepts even their most astonishing peculiarities as a matter of course, will answer in the negative.

The fact that the seventeenth century considered Racine's art not only masterly and overpoweringly effective but also reasonable, in accord with common sense, natural, and probable, can only be understood in terms of the period's own perspective. It had other standards than ours for the reasonable and natural. Judging Racine's art implied comparing it with that of the immediately preceding generation. This led to the observation that Racine's tragedy consists of a few simple and clearly interrelated events, while his predecessors had piled up an excessive number of extraordinary and adventurous occurrences; that, further, the psychological situations and conflicts in which Racine's characters are involved possess an exemplary and generally valid simplicity, whereas during the immediately preceding generation the fashion was for excessively heroic, subtle, and improbable conflicts (this through the influence of Corneille) and, through the influence of the Précieux, for the extravagances of a sentimental and pedantic gallantry. The echo of the revolt against these earlier trends is still perceptible in Boileau's polemics, in Molière's first comedies, and in Racine's prefaces, especially those he wrote for *Andromaque, Britannicus,* and *Bérénice*; and from Boileau and Racine we may also learn to what extent and in what way the poets of antiquity were revered as models. It is the simplicity of action and the polish of expression in the drama of the Greeks which charmed the elite among Racine's contemporaries. Several decades earlier, when Corneille was young and the court and the better circles of urban society were becoming interested in the theater, the rules of the three unities had been adopted, principally because of a conception of probability which is no longer current with us: it was felt to be improbable that during the few hours required to perform a play, and on a spatially limited stage only a few steps away from the spectator, occurrences far removed from one another in space and time should take place. This sort of probability, then, is not concerned with the occurrences themselves but with their rendition on the stage; it is concerned with the possibility of stage illusion. And indeed the technical situation of the French theater, especially during the first half of the century, was such that important changes of scene could hardly be suggested convincingly. But once these considerations and the endeavor to imitate the ancients had brought about the acceptance of the unity of place and the twenty-four-hour convention, the events of a play had to be organized in subservience to these premises, and this is precisely the realm in which Racine is a master. With him the action falls smoothly and naturally into the fixed pattern. And if he went further than anyone else in isolating the scene and secluding the action from everything low, extrinsic, and accessory, there is no doubt that, under the given conditions of the rules of unity, his doing so promotes the naturalness of the resulting effect.

In addition—and this may well be the most important point—we must realize that Racine's period had a conception of what is natural different from that held by later epochs. The concept of the natural was not contrasted with that of civilization; it was not associated with ideas of primitive culture, pure folkdom, or free and open countrysides; instead it was identified with a well-developed and well-educated type of human being, decorous in conduct and able to adjust with ease to the most exacting situations of social living; just as today we sometimes praise the naturalness of a person of great culture. To call something natural was almost tantamout to calling it reasonable and seemly. In this respect the age, rightly or wrongly, felt itself to be in accord with the golden ages of antique civilization, which were supposed to have possessed these qualities of a harmonious, rational, natural culture in exemplary measure. Under Louis XIV the French had the courage to consider their own culture a valid model on a par with that of the ancients, and they imposed this view upon the rest of Europe.

Building on the basis of this conception, which interprets the natural as a product of culture and intensive training, it became possible to consider natural what at all times and under all conditions move men's hearts: their feelings and passions. The natural was at the same time the eternally human. It seemed the highest mission of the art of literature to render a pure expression of the eternally human. And it was thought that the eternally human appeared clearer and less contaminated on isolated heights of life than in the base and confused turmoil of history. But this at the same time implied a restriction within the concept of the eternally human: only the "great" passions remained as possible subjects, and love too could be represented only in those forms which were in keeping with the contemporary concepts of the highest seemliness.

In any event the natural in the age of Louis XIV is something purely psychological, and within the limits of the psychological it is an immutable datum; it is the quintessence of what is immutably human. In expressing it in the forms of its own civilization, the age meant to stamp the latter as a valid model, a civilization exemplarily representing the eternally human, so that no other age except the golden ages of the cultures of antiquity could have greater or equal validity. Another characteristic of the civilization of the time was the Baroque exaltation of princely personages. From the sixteenth century on, the metaphorics of antiquity and of medieval courtly culture promoted the spread of absolutistic trends, and during the era of the Baroque the superman of the Renaissance crystallized in the current idea of the monarch. The court of Louis XIV marks the climax in the development of absolutism in essence as well as in external form. The person of the king, surrounded by the carefully hierarchized society of the former feudal nobility which, deprived of its power and original function, has come to be nothing but the King's entourage, is the perfect picture of the absolute ruler in Baroque exaltation. And indeed, the court was continued by the "town," for the *grande bourgeoisie* of Paris also considered the king its social center, and the line of demarcation between "court" and "town" was not clearly drawn. The exaltation also affected the princes and princesses of the royal family and to a lesser extent the king's representatives in the highest military and administrative positions. As an ideal model to be emulated in less distinguished spheres, the king and his court gained general validity both in France and outside it. The unintermitting publicness of the king's life, the perpetual observance of his exalted position in every word and every gesture, the fixed rules which governed the relations between the king and his entourage and which custom and training had made so natural, constitute a social work of art which is mirrored in numerous contemporary documents and which has often been excellently described, especially in Taine's article on Racine (*Nouveaux Essais de critique et d'histoire*, 109-163). The important and impressive aspect of it all is the correspondence between inner and exterior dignity which is always demanded of the persons concerned and always displayed by them, although they possess but a very limited degree of freedom. A perfect self-discipline, an unerring appraisal of every situation and the part one is to take in it, a subtly studied and yet spontaneous demeanor in every word and every gesture—these qualities have hardly ever been developed to such perfection as in the second half of the seventeenth century at the French court; and it is these qualities which manifested themselves in forms of style and life which in the late Baroque once again appeared in all their luster, at the same time attaining an elegance and warmth they had not possessed before. Such, then, is the society, such are the late Baroque forms filled with a new elegance, and such, above all, is the exaltation of princely figures, which are reflected in Racine's tragedies. A gloria of dignity radiates from all his heroes. *Ma gloire* is a term they often use to refer to the inviolability of their physical or spiritual dignity; for their dignity is not merely something outward but an integral element of their being —a fact of which Racine's women in particular (Monime for example) are the most admirable expression. All this has been well formulated by Taine in his penetrating way, although it seems to me that the verdict on Racine at which he arrives from such considerations is one-sided. In any case, he was the first to employ the sociological method, which is indispensable for an appreciation of the literature of the great century in its historical perspective. Without taking into consideration the social situation it would not be possible for us to explain how the exalted level of style, and the Baroque flourishes of expression which characterize it, could acquire such validity as models at a period which, in so many respects and in so many domains—in philosophy, science, politics, economy, and even in social relations—has a character of modern rationalism and which actually laid the foundations for modern rationalistic methods in more than one instance. Nor could we explain how it is possible that the criticism of the period judges such Baroque and hyperbolic forms in terms of reason and common sense, admires some and condemns others, displaying in the process a great deal of taste and artistic acumen without ever being aware of the discrepancy between the world of Baroque forms in general and a purely rational critique. This world of forms is the expression of a specific portion of society living under very special conditions, and the functional importance of this portion of society was far less than the prestige it enjoyed would lead one to suppose. It would not seem to have been the historical mission of complete absolutism to establish an exalted monarch surrounded by a great court. Its mission was rather to gather together the energies of the nation, to destroy centrifugal trends, and to impose a uniform organization upon politics, administration, and economy. The court is, as it were, a mere by-product of this process. It did not owe its existence to a function which had to be performed; on the contrary, the nobles gathered about the king because there was no longer any function for them to fulfill elsewhere. It was only from their new way of life as the king's entourage that the function of serving at court developed for them. Even if, as is certainly necessary, we consider not only the court but also *la ville* as the support and medium of classical French culture, we are again dealing with a small minority which to be sure was not without a diversifying influence upon the taste of the times but which nevertheless possessed no positive bourgeois consciousness either in politics or in aesthetics. In two very important features *la ville* and *la cour* coincide: their members were cultivated—that is, they were neither learned like professionals nor crude and ignorant like the people, but well-bred and equipped with the fund of knowledge required to make judgments in matters of taste; and secondly, they strove after the unspecialized, nonprofessional ideal of the *honnête homme*, they regarded bourgeois descent too as *un rang qu'on tient dans le monde*—we discussed this at the beginning of the present chapter (pp. 367-370).

Through the special character of the minority to which classical French literature was addressed, and particularly through its social ideal, we can understand or at least view with sympathy the fashion of Baroque and exalted forms and also their being combined with rational categories of taste. It is, further, exclusively on the basis of the taste of the elite, the cultivated society of the inner or more peripheral circles of the court, that it is possible to explain the radical separation of the tragic from the realistic, of which the Baroque forms with their tendency to exalt the tragic personage are only a particularly striking symptom. The separation of styles in French classicism is far more than mere imitation of the ancients as the sixteenth century humanists meant it. The antique model is transcended, and the result is a sharp break with the millennial popular and Christian tradition of mixed styles. The exaggerated tragic character (*ma gloire*) and the extreme cult of the passions are actually anti-Christian. This is a point which the theologians of the age who condemned the theater had understood very clearly, especially Nicole and Bossuet. Let us quote a few words from Bossuet's *Maximes et Réflexions sur la Comédie,* written in 1694:

> Ainsi tout le dessin d'un poète, toute la fin de son travail, c'est qu'on soit, comme son héros, épris des belles personnes, qu'on les serve comme des divinités; en un mot, qu'on leur sacrifie tout, si ce n'est peut-être la gloire, dont l'amour est plus dangereux que celui de la beauté même. (ch. 4.)

> (Thus a poet's entire design, the entire aim of his labors, is that we, like his hero, should be in love with beautiful women, that we should serve them as if they were divinities; in a word, that we should sacrifice all to them, unless perhaps it be honor, the love of which is even more dangerous than love of beauty.)

That is perfectly true, at least from the standpoint of the theologian. The passion of love as represented in Racine's tragedies is overwhelming; despite the tragic outcome, it tempts the auditor to admire and imitate so great and sublime a fate. This holds true most strongly in Phèdre's case. Although, as has often been observed and as Racine himself felt, she has something of the Christian woman to whom God refuses grace, the general effect is certainly not Christian at all. Every young and feeling heart is overpowered with admiration for her great all-forgetting and all-scorning passion. Equally pertinent and still more penetrating are Bossuet's remarks on *la gloire*: they strike at the exaltation of the tragic personage which, in Christian terms, is nothing but *superbia.*

But neither could Bossuet and Nicole have approved the popular mixed-style Christian theater whose performances had been forbidden a century earlier by the Paris parliament. Their ethico-aesthetic sense of style would have rebelled against it. They were themselves inevitably imbued with the style-separating taste of the age. The great and significant Christian literature of the French seventeenth century (which, compared with the religious crises of the sixteenth century and the Enlightenment of the eighteenth, is rightly considered an age of orthodox Christianity) is consistently elevated and sublime in tone, and becomes increasingly so as the century advances. It shuns every "base" expression, every type of concrete realism. It too takes part in the exaltation of princely personages, and almost all its productions sound as though they had been written for an elite, for *la cour et la ville*.

We know how great was the power of the classical French style throughout all Europe. It was only much later and under completely changed conditions that tragic seriousness and everyday reality could again meet.

16

THE INTERRUPTED SUPPER

On nous servit à souper. Je me mis à table d'un air fort gai; mais, à la lumière de la chandelle qui était entre elle et moi, je crus apercevoir de la tristesse sur le visage et dans les yeux de ma chère maîtresse. Cette pensée m'en inspira aussi. Je remarquai que ses regards s'attachaient sur moi d'une autre façon qu'ils n'avaient accoutumé. Je ne pouvais démêler si c'était de l'amour ou de la compassion, quoiqu'il me parût que c'était un sentiment doux et languissant. Je la regardai avec la même attention; et peut-être n'avait-elle pas moins de peine à juger de la situation de mon cœur par mes regards. Nous ne pensions ni à parler ni à manger. Enfin, je vis tomber des larmes de ses beaux yeux: perfides larmes!

"Ah Dieu!", m'écriai-je, "vous pleurez, ma chère Manon; vous êtes affligée jusqu'à pleurer, et vous ne me dites pas un seul mot de vos peines!" Elle ne me répondit que par quelques soupirs qui augmentèrent mon inquiétude. Je me levai en tremblant; je la conjurai, avec tous les empressements de l'amour, de me découvrir le sujet de ses pleurs; j'en versai moi-même en essuyant les siens; j'étais plus mort que vif. Un barbare aurait été attendri des témoignages de ma douleur et de ma crainte.

Dans le temps que j'étais ainsi tout occupé d'elle, j'entendis le bruit de plusieurs personnes qui montaient l'escalier. On frappa doucement à la porte. Manon me donna un baiser, et, s'échappant de mes bras, elle entra rapidement dans le cabinet, qu'elle ferma aussitôt sur elle. Je me figurai qu'étant un peu en désordre, elle voulait se cacher aux yeux des étrangers qui avaient frappé. J'allai leur ouvrir moi-même.

A peine avais-je ouvert, que je me vis saisir par trois hommes que je reconnus pour les laquais de mon père. . . .

(We were served supper. I sat down at table with an air of great gaiety; but, by the light of the candle which was between her and me, I thought that I saw a sadness on the face and in the eyes of my dear mistress. The thought aroused sadness in me. I noticed that her eyes fixed on me in an unaccustomed way. I could not make out whether it was love or compassion, although it seemed to me to be a tender and languishing feeling. I looked at her with the same attention; and perhaps she found it not less difficult to judge the situation of my heart by my eyes. We had no thought either of speaking or eating. At last, I saw tears fall from her beautiful eyes: perfidious tears!

"Oh God," I exclaimed, "you weep, my dear Manon; you are saddened to the point of tears, and you do not tell me one word of your griefs!" She answered only with a few sighs which increased my disquiet. I rose, trembling; I conjured her, with all the urgencies of love, to disclose the occasion of her tears to me; I shed tears myself as I dried hers; I was more dead than alive. A savage would have been softened by these evidences of my grief and my fear.

While I was thus absorbed in her, I heard the noise of several persons mounting the stairs. There was a soft knocking at the door. Manon gave me a kiss; and, slipping out of my arms, she hurried into the next room and at once shut herself in. I imagined that, being a trifle disordered, she wished to conceal herself from the eyes of the strangers who had knocked. I went to let them in myself.

I had hardly opened the door before I found myself seized by three men, whom I recognized as lackeys of my father's. . . .)

This text is from the story of Manon Lescaut by the Abbé Prévost. The little novel first appeared in 1731, that is, not long before Voltaire's *Lettres anglaises* and Montesquieu's work on the Romans.

The situation in which the two characters, Manon and the Chevalier des Grieux, find themselves at the beginning of the scene is as follows: the Chevalier, a lad of seventeen from a good family, who has just finished school, and Manon, still younger and on her way to enter a convent, had met by chance a few weeks earlier at the posthouse in Amiens and eloped to Paris. There the two had been living merrily and idyllically together until their money threatened to run out. In this predicament Manon has entered into relations with a very rich neighbor, a revenue farmer, who in turn has notified the Chevalier's family. On the morning of the very day when he is to be abducted, the Chevalier chances to learn of Manon's connection with the revenue farmer. He is greatly upset, but his naive trust and his love for Manon gain the upper hand. He thinks up a harmless explanation (namely, that Manon has used the revenue farmer as an intermediary to obtain money from her family, and intends to surprise him with it). When he returns that night, he does not question her, because he expects that she will bring up the subject herself. In this happily expectant though not quite confident mood he sits down to supper. Since the whole novel is in the form of a first-person narrative by the Chevalier, it is he himself who describes the scene.

It is a lively, dramatic scene, almost suitable for the stage in structure, and full of feeling. Three subdivisons can be distinguished in it. The first part contains the mute tension between the two lovers as they sit at table, with a candle between them, furtively watching each other and not eating. He senses that she is oppressed, and this quickly dampens his high spirits. He tries to analyze her sadness; he becomes uneasy, yet in his uneasiness there is far more loving sympathy with her depression than mistrust. The way in which he tries to interpret her emotions, his tenderly loving description of her, and even the reproaches which, as the narrator who already knows the further development of the action, he interjects here and in later passages (*perfides larmes!*) reflect his touching and guileless love, which ignores any grounds for suspicion. In Manon's easily influenced heart we may suppose pain over the imminent separation (for she does love him in her own way), perhaps a little remorse, and perhaps fear that he will discover her treachery. For she notices too that he is not his usual self. The instinctive contact between two people so young and so close to each other is admirably expressed in this mute scene; it is steeped in sensuality, although actually erotic subjects are not mentioned. And even though he is looking back upon events long past, upon an almost farcical scene in which he is taken in by mean and ridiculous devices, the narrator still treats it with pathos and emotion.

The mute tension ceases when Manon bursts into tears. And a second and violently agitated scene begins. He cannot bear to see her weep, and when she has nothing but sighs in answer to his insistent questions, which are touching in their loving reproachfulness, he loses all self-control. He jumps up; he trembles; and, as he assails her with questions and tries to dry her tears, he begins to weep himself. Even this scene he takes seriously and emotionally in retrospect (*un barbare aurait été attendri . . .*). In the literature of the eighteenth century tears begin to assume an importance which they had not previously possessed as an independent motif. Their effectiveness in the border region between the soul and the senses is exploited and found to be especially suited to produce the then fashionable thrill of mingled sentiment and eroticism. It is especially tears flowing singly from the eyes of a beautiful, easily moved, and easily inflamed woman, or rolling down her cheeks, which become increasingly popular in art and literature. They are seen and savored one by one as it were, *on les voit tomber des beaux yeux,* and are almost valued quantitatively in the frequent expression (though it does not occur here) *quelques larmes,* which it is hard to interpret without pedantry but which most strikingly characterizes the stylistic and emotional tenor of the age. It undoubtedly stems from the *Précieux.* I was struck by it for the first time in the dedication of *Andromaque* to Madame (Henriette-Anne d'Angleterre, who died very young), where Racine writes: . . . *on savait enfin que vous l'aviez* [that is, my tragedy] *honorée de quelques larmes.* . . . In this case the quantitative limitation expresses the high rank of the princess, who does Racine's tragedy great honor merely by consecrating "a few" tears to it. In the eighteenth century, however, *quelques larmes* betoken a brief erotic confusion which demands consolation: these tears, *qu'on verse, qu'on fait tomber,* or *qu'on cache,* are waiting to be dried.

Now begins the third scene. People are heard coming up the stairs, there is a knocking at the door. Manon kisses him quickly once again (years later he still remembers that kiss); then she slips from his arms and disappears into the next room. The Chevalier is still entirely without suspicion; she is *un peu en désordre,* perhaps because she had come to supper in *négligé,* perhaps because the preceding, violently emotional scene has been a little hard on her appearance—it is only natural that she prefers not to be seen by the unknown visitors. The Chevalier opens the door himself; the callers are lackeys of his father's; they seize him; for the moment the lovers' idyll has come to an end. At this point I should like to say a few words about *désordre* in the feminine toilette. This too is more emphasized during the eighteenth century than in earlier times. We have already come across it, in decorous periphrasis, in a scene from *Britannicus* (*dans le simple appareil / d'une beauté qu'on vient d'arracher au sommeil*); now such motifs are sought out and exploited. The intimately erotic in descriptions and allusions becomes very much the fashion from the Regency on. All through the century we find motifs of this kind in literature (and not only in erotic literature in the strict sense): a disturbed idyll, a gust of wind, a fall, a jump, through which normally covered parts of the female body are revealed or which produce a generally "charming disorder." During the classical epoch, in the days of Louis XIV, this form of eroticism does not even exist in comedy. Molière is never lewd. Now erotic and sentimental intimacy are fused and the erotic element appears even in the anecdotes produced by the philosophic and scientific Enlightenment.

The whole course of action in our text reminds us, in its intimacy, of the "domestic frames" of numerous late medieval descriptions; but it is completely lacking in the creatural element which is so significant for the latter. Rather, it is characterized by a smooth and coquettish elegance. Both the subject and its presentation are far removed from every kind of penetration to the depths of existence. Like the book illustrations of the famous etchers who attained masterly perfection at about the same time, it presents us with a neatly framed, vivid, intimate picture for which one might use the term *intérieur*. *Manon Lescaut* and many other works of the same and a somewhat later period are rich in such *intérieurs*, whose polished elegance, tearful sentimentality, and erotic and ethical frivolity represent a mixture unique in its kind. The subject matter is supplied by scenes of love and family life in which now the erotic, now the sentimental is more strongly emphasized, but in which neither element is rarely completely absent. When the occasion permits, clothes, utensils, furnishings are described or evoked with coquettish meticulousness and great delight in movement and color. There is no question of any strict separation of styles in these works. Secondary characters from all classes, commercial transactions, and a variety of pictures of contemporary culture in general are woven into the action. The *intérieurs* are at the same time *Sittenbilder*, pictures of contemporary mores. In *Manon Lescaut* we hear a great deal about money; there are lackeys, inns, prisons; officials appear; a scene outside a theater is carefully delineated, even to the name of the street; a convoy of prostitutes on their way to be transported to America passes by; there is realism everywhere. On the other hand, the author wants us to take his story seriously; he endeavors to make it in the highest degree moral and tragic. As for its moral aspects, we hear a great deal about honor and virtue, and although the Chevalier becomes a sharper, a cheat, and almost a pander, he yet never gives up his habit of expressing noble feelings and of allowing himself the pleasure of making moralizing observations which, to be sure, are extremely trite and sometimes rather dubious but which the author evidently takes quite seriously. Indeed, even Manon is to his mind "really" virtuous; only unfortunately her nature is such that she loves pleasure above everything. The *Avis de l'auteur* puts it this way:

> Elle connaît la vertu, elle la goûte même, et cependant elle commet les actions les plus indignes. Elle aime le Chevalier des Grieux avec une passion extrême; cependant le désir de vivre dans l'abondance et de briller lui fait trahir ses sentiments pour le Chevalier, auquel elle préfère un riche financier. Quel art n'a-t-il pas fallu pour intéresser le lecteur et lui inspirer de la compassion par rapport aux funestes disgrâces qui arrivent à cette fille corrompue!

> (She knows virtue, she even relishes it, and yet she commits the most shameful acts. She loves the Chevalier des Grieux with an extreme passion; yet her desire to enjoy a life of wealth and to shine makes her betray her feelings for the Chevalier, to whom she prefers a rich financier. What art did it not require to interest the reader and inspire him with compassion in regard to the fatal disgraces which come to this corrupted girl!)

This is an undistinguished sort of corruption; it lacks all greatness and dignity; but the author does not seem to feel this. There is something exemplary about the Chevalier's frenzied sexual thraldom and Manon's almost ingenuous amorality, precisely by virtue of their lack of distinction; and because of its representative character the little novel is justly famous. But the Abbé Prévost wants at all costs to make heroes of the two characters, insisting that they are "really" good and as different from ordinary ne'er-do-wells as night from day. The lively feeling of shame which overcomes the Chevalier when he suddenly finds himself and all his falsehoods exposed gives him an opportunity to declare himself a very special and distinguished character with emotions deeper and richer than those of *le commun des hommes,* and it is evident that Prévost takes the Chevalier's childish and overemotional interpretation of his moral "morning after" quite seriously. His conception of his heroes is consistently sentimental and high-flown. *Adieu, fils ingrat et rebelle!* exclaims the Chevalier's father. *Adieu, père barbare et dénaturé!* the son replies. This is the tone of the *comédie larmoyante,* which came into vogue at the time. With the lack of distinction in vice goes an equally undistinguished conception of virtue. It is concerned entirely with sex, with order or disorder in conducting one's sex life, and hence is itself steeped in eroticism. What is meant by virtue in this instance cannot be imagined detached from the whole apparatus of erotic sensations. The pleasure which the author endeavors to evoke in his readers by his representation of his lovers' childishly playful and unprincipled corruption, is in the last analysis a sexual titillation, which is constantly interpreted in sentimental and ethical terms while the warmth it evokes is abused to produce a sentimental ethics. This mixture is often found in the eighteenth century. Diderot's ethical attitudes are still rooted in an enthusiastic sentimentality in which the erotic plays a part; and even Rousseau still shows traces of it. The increasingly bourgeois cast of society, the stability (maintained throughout the greater part of the century) of political and economic conditions, the settled security of life in the intermediate and well-to-do strata of society, the consequent absence of professional and political worry for the younger generation in those strata—all this contributed to the development of the moral and aesthetic forms which can be gathered from our text and from many similar ones. And even when the prevailing order of society revealed its problematic nature to all eyes, when it began to rock and finally collapsed, the newly formed revolutionary concepts absorbed much bourgeois sentimentality, which survived into the nineteenth century.

Thus we may say that our text exemplifies a sort of intermediate style in which the realistic mixes with the serious—the story even ends tragically. This mixture is most appealing, but both its ingredients—realism as well as serious tragedy—are nonchalantly superficial. The realistic representation is colorful, varied, lively, and graphic; there is no lack of portrayals of the basest vice; yet the language always remains charming and elegant. There is not a trace of the problematic. The social milieu is an established frame of reference, which is accepted as it happens to be.

Quite different is the stylistic level of the realistic texts which serve the propaganda purposes of the Enlightenment. Examples are to be found from the Regency on, and in the course of the century they become more frequent and increasingly aggressive polemically. The master of the game is Voltaire. As a first example we choose a fairly early piece, from the sixth of the Philosophical Letters, which deal with his impressions of England.

Entrez dans la bourse de Londres, cette place plus respectable que bien des cours; vous y voyez rassemblés les députés de toutes les nations pour l'utilité des hommes. Là, le juif, le mahométan et le chrétien traitent l'un avec l'autre comme s'ils étaient de la même religion, et ne donnent le nom d'infidèles qu'à ceux qui font banqueroute; là, le presbytérien se fie à l'anabaptiste, et l'anglican reçoit la promesse du quaker. Au sortir de ces pacifiques et libres assemblées, les uns vont à la synagogue, les autres vont boire; celui-ci va se faire baptiser dans une grande cuve au nom du Père, par le Fils, au Saint-Esprit; celui-là fait couper le prépuce de son fils et fait marmotter sur l'enfant des paroles hébraiques qu'il n'entend point; ces autres vont dans leurs églises attendre l'inspiration de Dieu leur chapeau sur la tête, et tous sont contents.

(Enter the London stock exchange, that more respectable place than many a court; you will see the deputies of all nations gathered there for the service of mankind. There the Jew, the Mohammedan, and the Christian deal together as if they were of the same religion, and apply the name of infidel only to those who go bankrupt; there the Presbyterian trusts the Anabaptist, and the Anglican accepts the Quaker's promise. On leaving these peaceful and free assemblies, some go to the synagogue, others go to drink; one goes to have himself baptized in the name of the Father, through the Son, to the Holy Ghost; another has his son's foreskin cut off and Hebrew words mumbled over him which he does not understand; others go to their church to await the inspiration of God with their hats on their heads; and all are content.)

This description of the London exchange was not really written for a realistic purpose. What goes on there, we are told only in a general way. The purpose is much rather to insinuate certain ideas, which in their crudest and driest form would run as follows: "Free international business as dictated by the egotism of individuals is beneficial to human society; it unites men in common pacific activities. Religions, on the other hand, are absurd. Their absurdity needs no proof beyond the observation that they are very numerous while each claims to be the only true one, and that their dogmas and ceremonies are nonsensical. However, in a country where they are very many and very different, so that they are forced to put up with one another, they do not do much harm and can be regarded as an innocuous form of madness. It is only when they fight and persecute one another that things get really bad." But even in this dry formulation of the idea there is a rhetorical trick which, however, I find it impossible to eliminate because it is contained in Voltaire's conception itself. It is the unexpected contrast of religion and business, in which business is placed higher, practically and morally, than religion. The very device of coupling the two, as though they were forms of human endeavor on the same plane and to be judged from the same viewpoint, is not only an impertinence; it is a specific approach or, if one prefers, an experimental set-up, in which religion is ipso facto deprived of what constitutes its essence and its value. It is presented in a position in which it appears ridiculous from the start. This is a technique which sophists and propagandists of all times have employed with success, and Voltaire is a master of it. It is for precisely this reason that here, where he wants to demonstrate the blessings of productive work, he chooses neither a farm nor a business office nor a factory but the stock exchange, where people of all faiths and backgrounds congregate.

The way he invites us to enter the stock exchange is almost solemn. He calls it a place deserving of greater respect than many a court, and its frequenters deputies of all nations foregathered in the interests of humanity. Then he turns to a more detailed description of its frequenters and observes them first in their activity at the exchange, then in their private life; in both cases he emphasizes their differing in religion. As long as they are at the exchange, the difference has no importance. It does not interfere with business. This gives him the opportunity to introduce his play on the word *infidèle*. But as soon as they leave the exchange—that peaceful and free assembly, in contrast to the assemblies of battling clerics—the disparateness of their religious views comes to the fore. What was just now a harmonious whole—a symbol as it were of the ideal cooperation of all human society—now falls asunder into numerous unrelated and indeed incompatible parts. The remainder of the passage is given over to a lively description of a number of these. Leaving the exchange, the merchants disperse. Some go to a synagogue, others go to have a drink. The syntactic parallel presents the two as equally worthy ways of passing the time. Then we get a characterization of three groups of pious frequenters of the exchange: Anabaptists, Jews, and Quakers. In each case Voltaire emphasizes a purely external detail which differs from and is in no way related to the next but which in every instance is intrinsically absurd and comic. What comes out is not really the true nature of Jews or Quakers, not the grounds and the specific form of their convictions, but the external aspect of their religious ceremonial, which, especially to the uninitiated, looks strangely comic. This again is an example of a favorite propaganda device which is often used far more crudely and maliciously than in this case. It might be called the searchlight device. It consists in overilluminating one small part of an extensive complex, while everything else which might explain, derive, and possibly counterbalance the thing emphasized is left in the dark; so that apparently the truth is stated, for what is said cannot be denied; and yet everything is falsified, for truth requires the whole truth and the proper interrelation of its elements. Especially in times of excited passions, the public is again and again taken in by such tricks, and everybody knows more than enough examples from the very recent past. And yet in most cases the trick is not at all hard to see through; in tense periods, however, the people or the public lack the serious desire to do so. Whenever a specific form of life or a social group has run its course, or has only lost favor and support, every injustice which the propagandists perpetrate against it is half consciously felt to be what it actually is, yet people welcome it with sadistic delight. Gottfried Keller describes this psychological situation very finely in one of the novellas in his Seldwyla cycle, the story of lost laughter, in which a campaign of defamation in Switzerland is discussed. It is true, the things he describes compare with what we have seen in our time as a slight turbidity in the clear water of a brook would compare with an ocean of filth and blood. Gottfried Keller discusses the matter with his calm clarity and lack of prejudice, without softening the least detail, without the slightest attempt to whitewash the injustice or to speak of it as a "higher" form of justice; and yet he seems to sense in such things an element that is natural and at times beneficial, because after all "more than once a change of government and the expansion of freedom have resulted from an unjust cause or untrue pretense." Keller was fortunate in that he could not imagine an important change of government which would not entail an expansion of freedom. We have been shown otherwise.

Voltaire concludes with an unexpected turn: *et tous sont contents.* With the swiftness of a prestidigitator he has, in three sharp phrases, parodied three creeds or sects, and the four concluding words are sprung at us just as swiftly, surprisingly, and merrily. They are extremely rich in content. Why is everybody satisfied? Because everybody is allowed to do business and grow wealthy in peace; and because everybody is no less peacefully allowed to cling to his religious madness, with the result that no one persecutes or is persecuted. Long live tolerance! It lets everybody have his business and his fun, whether the latter is taking a drink or persisting in some absurd form of worship.

The method of posing the problem so that the desired solution is contained in the very way in which the problem is posed, and the searchlight technique, which overilluminates the ridiculous, the absurd, or the repulsive in one's opponent, were both in use long before Voltaire. But he has a particular way of handling them which is all his own. Especially his own is his tempo. His rapid, keen summary of the development, his quick shifting of scenes, his surprisingly sudden confronting of things which are not usually seen together—in all this he comes close to being unique and incomparable; and it is in this tempo that a good part of his wit lies. As one reads his marvelous rococo sketches, the point becomes strikingly clear. For example:

> Comme il était assez près de Lutèce,
> Au coin d'un bois qui borde Charenton,
> Il aperçut la fringante Marton
> Dont un ruban nouait la blonde tresse;
> Sa taille est leste, et son petit jupon
> Laisse entrevoir sa jambe blanche et fine.
> Robert avance; il lui trouve une mine
> Qui tenterait les saints du paradis;
> Un beau bouquet de roses et de lis
> Est au milieu de deux pommes d'albâtre
> Qu'on ne voit point sans en être idolâtre;
> Et de son teint la fleur et l'incarnat
> De son bouquet auraient terni l'éclat.
> Pour dire tout, cette jeune merveille
> A son giron portait une corbeille,
> Et s'en allait avec tous ses attraits
> Vendre au marché du beurre et des œufs frais.
> Sire Robert, ému de convoitise,
> Descend d'un saut, l'accole avec franchise:
> "J'ai vingt écus, dit-il, dans ma valise;
> C'est tout mon bien; prenez encor mon cœur:
> Tout est à vous.—C'est pour moi trop d'honneur,"
> Lui dit Marton. . . .

(Not far from Paris, at the corner of a wood which borders Charenton, he saw the dashing Marton, with her blond hair bound by a ribbon. Her waist is trim and her little skirt permits a glimpse of her slim white leg. Robert approaches: he finds a face which would tempt the saints in Paradise; a beautiful bouquet of roses and lilies lies between two alabaster apples which none can see without adoring; and the freshness and bloom of her complexion would have dulled the brightness of her bouquet. To speak plainly, the young miracle of beauty was carrying a basket in her arms and, with all her attractions, was on her way to market to sell butter and fresh eggs. Sir Robert, shaken with unholy desire, dismounted at one jump and frankly embraced her. Said he: "I have twenty crowns in my valise; it is my entire fortune; take my heart to boot: the whole is yours." "The honor is too great," Marton replied. . . .)

This passage is from a fairly late narrative in verse: *Ce qui plaît aux dames*. It is composed with great care, as may be inferred from the successive impressions the knight receives of Marton's beauty as he admires it first from afar and then from nearer and nearer. A great part of its charm lies in its tempo. If it were drawn out longer, it would lose its freshness and become trite. And the tempo determines the wit of the piece too. The declaration of love is so comical only because it states the essential data with such astounding brevity. Here as everywhere else, Voltaire's tempo is part of his philosophy. In this instance he uses it to set in sharp relief the essential motives of human actions as he sees them, to unmask them as it were and show their extreme materialism, without ever permitting himself anything crude. This little love scene contains nothing sublime or spiritual, all that comes out in it is physical lust and the profit motive. The declaration of love begins with an unrhetorical statement of the business side of the transaction, and yet it is charming, elegant, and far from pedestrian. Everybody knows—and Robert and Marton are no exception—that the words, *prenez encor mon cœur, tout est à vous,* are nothing but a flourish to express the desire for instantaneous sexual gratification. And yet they have all the charm and bloom which Voltaire and his time inherited from classicism (in this case specifically from La Fontaine) and which he presses into the service of the materialistic Enlightenment. The content has changed completely, but the pleasing clarity, *l'agréable et le fin,* of the classics has remained. It is present in every word, in every phrase, in every rhythmic movement. A specifically Voltairian feature is the swift tempo, which never becomes unaesthetic despite the author's boldness, not to say unscrupulousness, in moral matters and his technique of sophistic surprise attacks. He is completely free from the half-erotic and hence somewhat hazy sentimentality which we have tried to demonstrate in our analysis of the text from *Manon Lescaut.* His unmaskings in the spirit of the Enlightenment are never crude and clumsy; on the contrary they are light, agile, and as it were appetizing. And above all, he is free from the cloudy, contour-blurring, overemotional rhetoric, equally destructive of clear thinking and pure feeling, which came to the fore in the authors of the Enlightenment during the second half of the century and in the literature of the Revolution, which had a still more luxuriant growth in the nineteenth century through the influence of romanticism, and which has continued to produce its loathsome flowers down to our day.

Closely related to rapidity of tempo, but more generally in use as a propaganda device, is the extreme simplification of all problems. In Voltaire's case the rapidity, one feels almost tempted to say the alertness, of the tempo is made to serve the purpose of simplification. This simplification is almost always achieved by reducing the problem to an antithesis which is then exhibited in a giddy, swift, high-spirited narrative in which black and white, theory and practice, etc., are set in clear and simple opposition. We can observe this point in our passage on the London stock exchange, where the contrast business versus religion (the one useful and advancing human cooperation, the other senseless and raising barriers between men) is displayed in a vivid sketch which vigorously simplifies the problem in terms of a partisan approach; with this, and no less simplified, the contrast tolerance versus intolerance appears. Even in the little love story, if not a problem, at least the subject of the occurrence is reduced to a simplified antithetical formula (pleasure versus business). Let us consider yet another example. The novel *Candide* contains a polemic attack upon the metaphysical optimism of Leibnitz's idea of the best of all possible worlds. In chapter 8 of *Candide,* Cunégonde—who was lost and has been found again—begins her relation of the adventures she has undergone since Candide's expulsion from her father's castle:

> J'étais dans mon lit et je dormais profondément, quand il plut au ciel d'envoyer les Bulgares dans notre beau château de Thunder-ten-tronckh; ils égorgèrent mon père et mon frère, et coupèrent ma mère par morceaux. Un grand Bulgare, haut de six pieds, voyant qu'à ce spectacle j'avais perdu connaissance, se mit à me violer; cela me fit revenir, je repris mes sens, je criai, je me débattis,

je mordis, j'égratignai, je voulais arracher les yeux à ce grand Bulgare, ne sachant pas que tout ce qui arrivait dans le château de mon père était une chose d'usage: le brutal me donna un coup de couteau dans le flanc gauche dont je porte encore la marque. —Hélas, j'espère bien la voir, dit le naïf Candide.—Vous la verrez, dit Cunégonde; mais continuons.—Continuez, dit Candide.

(I was in my bed, in a deep sleep, when it pleased Heaven to send the Bulgarians into our fair castle of Thunder-ten-tronckh; they cut my father's throat and my brother's, and chopped my mother to pieces. A huge Bulgarian, six feet tall, observing that I had fainted at the sight, began to rape me; that brought me to, I recovered consciousness, I screamed, I struggled, I bit, I scratched, I tried to tear out the big Bulgarian's eyes, not knowing that everything that was happening in my father's castle was perfectly customary: the brute gave me a knife-thrust in my left side, of which I still bear the scar. "Alas! I hope that I shall see it," said the simple Candide. "You shall see it," said Cunégonde; "but let us go on." "Go on," said Candide.)

These dreadful incidents appear comic because they come hammering down with almost slapstick speed and because they are represented as willed by God and everywhere prevalent—which is in comic contrast to their dreadfulness and to the aims of their victims. On top of all this comes the erotic quip at the end. Antithetical simplification of the problem and its reduction to anecdotal dimensions, together with dizzying speed of tempo, prevail throughout the novel. Misfortune follows upon misfortune, and again and again they are interpreted as necessary, proceeding from sound causes, reasonable, and worthy of the best of all possible worlds—which is obviously absurd. In this way calm reflection is drowned in laughter, and the amused reader either never observes, or observes only with difficulty, that Voltaire in no way does justice to Leibnitz's argument and in general to the idea of a metaphysical harmony of the universe, especially since so entertaining a piece as Voltaire's novel finds many more readers than the difficult essays of his philosophical opponents, which cannot be understood without serious study. Indeed, even the observation that the supposed reality of experience which Voltaire builds up does not correspond to experience at all, that it has been artfully adjusted to his polemic purpose, must have escaped most contemporary readers, or if not, they would hardly have made much of it. The rhythm of the adventures which befall

Candide and his companions is to be nowhere observed in the reality of experience. Such a relentless, unrelated torrent of mishaps pouring down from a clear sky on the heads of perfectly innocent and unprepared people whom it involves by mere chance, simply does not exist. It is much more like the mishaps of a comic figure in a farce or a clown in a circus. Even apart from this excessive concentration of mishaps and the fact that in all too many cases they bear no inner relation whatever to their victims, Voltaire falsifies reality by an extreme simplification of the causes of events. The causes of human destinies which appear in his realistic propaganda pieces for the Enlightenment are either natural phenomena or accidents or—insofar as human behavior is admitted as a cause—the promptings of instinct, maliciousness, and especially stupidity. He never pursues historical conditions as determinants of human destinies, convictions, and institutions. This applies both to the history of individuals and to that of states, religions, and human society in general. Just as in our first example (the London exchange) Anabaptism, Judaism, and Quakerism are made to appear meaningless, stupid, and accidental, so in *Candide* the wars, troop-levies, religious persecutions, and the views of the nobility or the clergy are made to appear equally meaningless, stupid, and accidental. For Voltaire, it is a perfectly self-evident premise that no one in his senses can believe in an inner order of things or an inner justification for views. With equal assurance he assumes as a demonstrated premise that any individual in his personal history may encounter any destiny which is in accordance with the laws of nature, regardless of the possibility of a connection between destiny and character; and he sometimes amuses himself by putting together causal chains in which he explains only the factors which are phenomena of nature and purposely omits anything to do with morals or the history of the individuals concerned. By way of example we may turn to the fourth chapter of *Candide*, where Pangloss discusses the origin of his syphilis:

> . . . vous avez connu Paquette, cette jolie suivante de notre auguste baronne; j'ai goûté dans ses bras les délices du paradis, qui ont produit ces tourmens d'enfer dont vous me voyez dévoré; elle en était infectée, elle en est peut-être morte. Paquette tenait ce présent d'un cordelier très savant, qui avait remonté à la source; car il l'avait eue d'une vieille comtesse, qui l'avait reçue d'un capitaine de cavalerie, qui la devait à une marquise, qui la tenait d'un

page, qui l'avait reçue d'un jésuite qui, étant novice, l'avait eue en droite ligne d'un des compagnons de Christophe Colomb. . . .

(. . . you knew Paquette, our august Baroness's pretty attendant; in her arms I tasted the joys of Paradise which produced the infernal tortures which you see devouring me; she was infected with them; perhaps she has died of them. Paquette had received the gift from a most learned Franciscan, who himself had gone back to the source; for he had got it from an old countess, who had received it from a cavalry captain, who owed it to a marquise, who had it from a page, who had received it from a Jesuit, who, as a novice, had received it in the direct line from one of the companions of Christopher Columbus. . . .)

Such an account, which regards only natural causes, and on the moral plane merely lays a satirical emphasis on the mores of the clergy (including their homosexuality), at the same time merrily whisking out of sight and suppressing all details of the personal history of the individuals concerned, although it is these details which brought about the various love affairs—such an account insinuates a very specific conception of the concatenation of events, in which there is room neither for the individual's responsibility for acts he commits in obedience to his natural instincts nor for anything else in his particular nature or his particular inner and outer development which leads to particular acts. It is not often that Voltaire goes as far as he does in this instance and in *Candide* in general. Basically he is a moralist; and, especially in his historical writings, there are human portraits in which the individuality comes out clearly. But he is always inclined to simplify, and his simplification is always handled in such a way that the role of sole standard of judgment is assigned to sound, practical common sense (the type of enlightened reason which began to come to the fore during his time and under his influence) and that from among the conditions which determine the course of human lives none but the material and natural are given serious consideration. Everything historical and spiritual he despises and neglects. This has to do with the active and courageous spirit with which the protagonists of Enlightenment were filled. They set out to rid human society of everything that impeded the progress of reason. Such impediments were obviously to be seen in the religious, political, and economic actualities which had grown up historically, irrationally, in contradiction to common sense, and had finally become an inextricable maze. What seemed required was not to understand and justify them but to discredit them.

Voltaire arranges reality so that he can use it for his purposes. There is no denying the presence, in many of his works, of colorful, vivid, everyday reality. But it is incomplete, consciously simplified, and hence —despite the serious didactic purpose—nonchalant and superficial. As for the stylistic level, a lowering of man's position is implied in the attitude prevailing in the writings of the Enlightenment, even when they are not as impertinently witty as Voltaire's. The tragic exaltation of the classical hero loses ground from the beginning of the eighteenth century. Tragedy itself becomes more colorful and clever with Voltaire, but it loses weight. But in its stead the intermediate genres, such as the novel and the narrative in verse, begin to flourish, and between tragedy and comedy we now have the intermediate *comédie larmoyante.* The taste of the age does not favor the sublime; it seeks out the graceful, elegant, clever, sentimental, rational, and useful, all of which is more properly intermediate. In its intermediate level the erotic and sentimental style of *Manon Lescaut* coincides with Voltaire's style in propaganda. In both instances the people introduced are no sublime heroes detached from the context of everyday life but individuals embedded in circumstances which are usually intermediate, on which they are dependent, and in which they are enmeshed materially and even spiritually. A certain seriousness in all this cannot be overlooked, not even in Voltaire, who after all takes his ideas perfectly seriously. And so we must conclude that, in contrast to classicism, a mixing of styles now occurs once again. But it does not go far or very deep either in its everyday realism or its seriousness. It continues the aesthetic tradition of classicism inasmuch as its realism remains always pleasant. Tragic and creatural penetration and historical involvement are avoided. The realistic elements, however colorful and amusing they may be, remain mere froth. With Voltaire the pleasantness and frothiness of the realism, which is present only to serve the ends of Enlightenment ideology, have developed into such an art that he is able to use even the "creatural" premonitions of his own decrepitude and death which come to him during his last years, as material for an amiably jocular introduction to a popular philosophical disquisition. In this connection I will cite an example which has already been analyzed by L. Spitzer (*Romanische Stil- und Literaturstudien,* Marburg, 1931, 2, 238ff.). It is a letter which the gaunt seventy-six-year old patriarch with the fleshless mask, whom everybody remembers, wrote to Mme Necker when the sculptor Pigalle had come to Ferney to do a bust of him. It reads:

> A Madame Necker. Ferney, 19 juin 1770
>
> Quand les gens de mon village ont vu Pigalle déployer quelques instruments de son art: Tiens, tiens, disaient-ils, on va le disséquer; cela sera drôle. C'est ainsi, madame, vous le savez, que tout spectacle amuse les hommes; on va également aux marionnettes, au feu de la Saint-Jean, à l'Opéra-Comique, à la grand'messe, à un enterrement. Ma statue fera sourire quelques philosophes, et renfrognera les sourcils éprouvés de quelque coquin d'hypocrite ou de quelque polisson de folliculaire: vanité des vanités!
>
> Mais tout n'est pas vanité; ma tendre reconnaissance pour mes amis et surtout pour vous, madame, n'est pas vanité.
>
> Mille tendres obéissances à M. Necker.
>
> (When the people of my village saw Pigalle lay out some of the instruments of his art: "Why, look," said they, "he's going to be dissected; that will be curious." So it is, Madame, as you well know, that any spectacle amuses mankind; people go indifferently to a marionette-show, to a Midsummer Eve bonfire, to high mass, to a funeral. My statue will make a few philosophers smile, and knit the practiced brows of some villainous hypocrite or some depraved hack: vanity of vanities! But all is not vanity; my fond gratitude for my friends and above all for you, Madame, is not vanity. A thousand fond homages to Monsieur Necker.)

I refer the reader to Spitzer's excellent analysis, which pursues and interprets every shade of expression throughout the text, and shall limit myself to adding or summarizing what is essential for the problem of style here under discussion. The realistic anecdote which serves as point of departure is either invented or at least rearranged for the purpose. It is not at all likely that peasants about the year 1770 should have been more familiar with anatomical dissection than with the sculptor's craft. Who Pigalle was must have been widely discussed; and that portraits should be made of the famous châtelain who had lived among them for a decade must have seemed more natural to them than the idea of dissecting a person who had quite recently still been seen alive. That some half-educated wit among them could have made a remark of this sort is of course not entirely impossible, but I imagine most readers confronted with this question will find it much more probable that Voltaire himself was the wit. However that may be, whether he arranged the setting himself (as I suppose he did) or whether chance supplied him with it exactly as he describes it, in either case, it is an extraordinary, much too pat, theatrical piece of reality, admirably and exclusively suited to what he appends to it: the trite bit of worldly wisdom, charmingly and amiably presented, the fireworks display of examples in which the sacred and profane are mixed together with the characteristic impertinence of the Enlightenment, the irony in regard to his own fame, the polemic allusions to his enemies, the summing up of the whole in the basic theme from Solomon, and finally the recourse to the word *vanité* to find the turn of expression which concludes the letter and which radiates all the charm of the still amiable and still lively old man, all the charm of the entire century in the formation of which he played so prominent a part. The whole thing is, as Spitzer puts it, a unique phenomenon, the *billet* of the Rococo Enlightenment. It is so much the more unique in that the texture of worldly wisdom and amiable wit is here linked to an anecdote which conjures up the creaturality of the old man's decrepit body, but a step from the grave. Yet even with such a subject Voltaire remains witty and pleasing. How many different elements this text contains: there is the artfully arranged realism; there is the perfection of charm in social relations, which combine great warmth of expression with a high degree of reserve; there is the superficiality of a creatural self-confrontation which is at the same time the exalted amiability which refuses to let one's own somber emotions become a burden to anyone else; there is the didactic ethos which characterized the great men of the Enlightenment and which made them able to use their last breath to formulate some new idea wittily and pleasingly.

I hope that the examples from Prévost and Voltaire have yielded us all the important characteristics of the peculiarly charming and peculiarly superficial intermediate level upon which realism and seriousness, after having been so strictly separated during the era of Louis XIV, began to approach each other again from the first years of the eighteenth century on. Some points will grow clearer as we look back and make comparisons in the course of discussing later texts.

But I still have to speak of a literary genre which, by its very nature, cannot separate realism and a serious approach, and which hence does not submit unconditionally to the aesthetic principle of the separation of styles, even during the French seventeenth century. I refer to the genre of memoirs and diaries. From the Renaissance on, interesting and significant works of this type are to be found in several countries of Europe. During the period of absolutism in the seventeenth and eighteenth centuries, their authors—especially in France and the countries strongly influenced by French example—come almost exclusively from court circles; they are often men of princely blood, and their subject matter is drawn from politics, court intrigues, and the life of the highest classes of society. It is a fact worthy of note (cf. Sainte-Beuve, *Causeries du Lundi*, 15, 425) that among the most gifted, individual, and famous writers of memoirs in France, not one belongs to the generation of Louis XIV. They belong either to the immediately preceding period (as Retz, La Rochefoucauld, Tallemant des Réaux) or to the following. During the King's own reign, and under the uncontested dominance of the taste represented by his name, the moralism to the influence of which French memoir writing had previously been subject turned to more general forms and themes and avoided the rendering of specific contemporary events.

If we have not treated of memoirs until now, in connection with the first half of the eighteenth century, it is simply because by far the most important author in this genre in our opinion, Louis, duc de Saint-Simon, seems to belong rather to the eighteenth century than to the seventeenth. He was born in 1675. He goes to court in 1691 and begins his record at the early age of nineteen, in July 1694, as he tells us himself. However the real work of putting together the book cannot have begun until much later, until after the death of the Regent in 1723, when Saint-Simon retired from the court. He lived on and continued writing for another 32 years. Occasional allusions to events in the thirties and forties show that he was at work in the middle of the eighteenth century. Thus, for example, in his memoirs for the year 1700, where he discusses the establishment of the Prussian kingdom, he refers to the death of Frederick William I and the coronation of his successor as very recent events, which proves that he wrote the passage shortly after May 1740. The editors of the critical edition (in the *Collection des Grands Ecrivains*) have come to the conclusion that the *Mémoires* were written between 1739 and 1749 (*Notes sur l'édition des Mémoires*, vol. 41, pp. 442ff.). Chronologically, then, the work undoubtedly belongs to the eighteenth century. It is more difficult to determine the Duke's position in terms of the history of ideas and his inner affinities. For he is really not to be compared with anything else, and the one thing which is obvious upon even the most superficial acquaintance is that, in any case, neither his manner of writing nor his views place him in the age of Louis XIV. His manner of writing shows no trace of the well-balanced *bienséance,* of the classical striving for harmony, of the exalted aloofness from things, which characterized the great decades. It suggests, if it can be compared with anything at all, the pre-classical prose of the beginning of the seventeenth century. In his views he is a vigorous opponent of centralizing absolutism. He would like to see the kingdom given an organization by estates, with much greater freedom for the estates and especially with the high nobility as the directing class. In religious matters—despite his great and undoubtedly genuine piety—he is quite free from prejudice and disapproves of all persecution and suppression of faiths. He sees the reign of Louis XIII as ideal—undoubtedly a misapprehension caused by his perspective, for it was Richelieu under Louis XIII who laid the foundation for complete absolutism and the political ruin of the nobility. What deceives him in this matter is the tradition of his family, for his father, who had reached the age of seventy when Saint-Simon was born, had in his youth been a favorite of Louis XIII, who raised him to the rank of *duc et pair.*

Saint-Simon may thus be called an anti-absolutistic reactionary; and when he talks about the dignity and importance of the highest nobility, of the *ducs et pairs,* his views are at times somewhat anachronistic and maniacal. Nevertheless, in political matters he displays a great deal of common sense, sound judgment, and keen perception. We must not forget that the opposition which began to crystallize, during Louis XIV's last decades, in the minds of several important men at court, was almost always concerned with the restoration of older institutions involving the hierarchy of the estates. These, and especially the reestablishment of the high nobility in its earlier position, were regarded as an effective device against absolutism and its tools, the royal ministers who were unqualifiedly the King's creatures. Ideas of this kind were combined with practical and comparatively liberalistic plans for a policy of peace, for the reorganization of the country's administration, its finances, and church affairs. The views of the opposition group at court might be described as estate-conscious, patriarchal, and liberalistic; its influence is still to be detected in Montesquieu. Saint-Simon was close to this group; its most important members were his friends; he shared many of their ideas and developed them further in his own fashion. In his political attitudes there is a mixture of reactionary trends rooted in the era before Louis XIV, with liberalistic trends of the kind fostered by the early eighteenth century. Politically too he is outside of the style of Louis XIV. From his youth he had been a friend of the Duc d'Orléans, who became Regent after the King's death. As a member of the Council of Regency, Saint-Simon acquired a position of great influence, but he never succeeded in making much of it. Apparently he was no statesman; he was too arrogant, too honorable, too temperamental, and too nervous for that; perhaps too his life at court and his secret literary activity had spoiled him for practical political work. And here again he did not fit into his age, whose easy and elegant nonchalance was something he could neither share nor master. Still, it was during the decades from about 1694 to 1723—the period, that is, of his secret opposition during the latter part of the reign of Louis XIV, and then of his participation in the administration of the Duc d'Orléans—that his personality reached full development. It is these decades too that form the subject matter of the most important portions of his memoirs, which he edited during the subsequent decades. In view of all this, I believe that he can best be classed as a man of the early eighteenth century, as a special and idiosyncratic case of the anti-absolutistic, aristocratic, estate-conscious, and liberalizing reformist attitude which immediately preceded the beginnings of the Enlightenment.

Much has been written about his literary activity and his style, but to my mind the most cogent observations are to be found in the fourth section of an essay by Taine, who precedes them by a brilliant but one-sided and essentially inadequate description of the seventeenth century (*Essais de Critique d'Histoire*, 1, 188ff.). All critics are agreed in their admiration for Saint-Simon's mastery in the representation of living individuals. The best and most famous portraits from earlier memoirs pale beside his, and in all European literature there have probably been only a very few writers capable of giving their readers such an abundance of human characters, each so patently specific and homogeneous, and each so fully revealing the very basis of the individual's life. Saint-Simon does not invent; he works with the random unselected material which his life presents to him. One might call it everyday material, although it comes exclusively from the sphere of the French court. The setting is so vast and so richly peopled that it contains a whole world of human beings; and Saint-Simon rejects nothing and no one. His literary activity, which has almost the hold of a vice over him, eagerly applies the tools of verbal expression to every subject. This fact alone represents a point of departure for a review of his style in the light of our present approach. But in this case again we prefer to build on the basis of textual analysis, though choosing examples from such an abundance is not easy. Let us begin something comparatively superficial.

One night in April 1711, the King's only legitimate son, Monseigneur or le grand Dauphin, as he was called at court, died of smallpox at his castle of Meudon. In the afternoon the reports on his condition had been favorable, and at Versailles it was believed that the danger was past. That night the news came that he was dying. The entire court was affected by the excitement; no one could think of sleep. The ladies and gentlemen, most of them already in night apparel, came from their apartments and gathered about the dying Dauphin's two sons, the Dukes of Burgundy and Berry, and their wives. Very soon the Duchess of Burgundy, who had absented herself for a few moments to meet the King's carriage upon his return from Meudon, brings the news that Monseigneur is dead. The various emotions mirrored in the faces and attitudes of the numerous assembly, whom the unexpected occurrence affects in the most varied ways, provide a rich and significant spectacle, dramatically emphasized by the nocturnal and as it were improvised setting. Saint-Simon, who in any case is in an elated mood (which his conscience and sense of decorum make him try hard to repress) because he considers the disappearance of Monseigneur a piece of good luck for France, his friends, and himself, enjoys the occasion to the full and draws from it an abundance of scenes, portrait sketches, self-analyses, and reflections. In these the contradictory and confused elements of such a moment, the mixture of awe, despair, embarrassment, stupefaction, and suppressed delight, the dignity of death and the grotesque details which contrast with it, are brought together to produce an impression which is, on the whole, completely unified. From the description, which fills many pages, we shall choose one little scene. It concerns Madame, the King's sister-in-law, dowager duchess of Orléans, the Palatine Elizabeth Charlotte, famous for her letters. After describing the group of weeping young princes and princesses and the Duc de Beauvilliers calmly and circumspectly pursuing his court function and trying to comfort them, Saint-Simon continues (21, 35):

> Madame, rhabillée en grand habit, arriva hurlante, ne sachant bonnement pourquoi ni l'un ni l'autre, les inonda tous de ses larmes en les embrassant, fit retentir le château d'un renouvellement de cris, et fournit le spectacle bizarre d'une princesse qui se remet en cérémonie, en pleine nuit, pour venir pleurer et crier parmi une foule de femmes en déshabillé de nuit, presque en mascarades.

(Madame, reclothed in full dress, arrived howling, not really knowing the reason for either, flooded them all with tears as she embraced them, made the castle echo with a renewed outbreak of cries, and provided the singular spectacle of a princess who resumes court dress, in the middle of the night, in order to weep and scream among a crowd of women in nocturnal undress, almost in masquerade costume.)

The sentence is built up of four coordinate members with their verbs in the past tense (*arriva, inonda, fit retentir*, and *fournit*), of which the first three represent the stages of a progressive action, which is summarized and interpreted in the drawn-out sweep of the fourth. However, the interpretation, which emphasizes the contrast between the intended and the actual effect of the action, insinuates itself into the first members too. At the very start, after the words *Madame, rhabillée en grand habit,* one expects something solemn and ceremonious, but this expectation gets a rude shock from *arriva hurlante*; the participial insert (*ne sachant* . . .) follows, and, in the subsequent members, *inonda* . . . and *fit retentir* . . . ; so that this continuous and coordinated periodic structure, which includes no single syntactic device of contrast or concession, embraces a whole series of antitheses of meaning. Madame has no good reason either to dress up or to howl. It is ludicrous to do the former for the purpose of the latter. And for the latter she has no reason, since Monseigneur and his followers were hostile to her son's and her own interests and since no friendly relations whatever existed between the two groups. On the other hand, her behavior exhibits all the contradictory elements which make up her character: her tactless, noisy, and temperamental goodheartedness, which at such a moment forgets all personal grudges and feels only the terror of death and sympathy with the grieving; and, in contrast to this, her somewhat awkward and German sense (after a residence of decades still basically different from that of the French court) of what she owes to her princely dignity, so that, although genuinely shaken and sincerely sobbing, she yet has herself laced into a robe of state before she comes on for her great scene. All this admirably supplements the information which Saint-Simon elsewhere supplies about her: the slap in the face which she administers to her son in the presence of the assembled court because he has agreed, against her wish and against his own, to marry one of the King's illegitimate daughters; her clumsy and unsociable disapproval of what goes on at her husband's court; her no less clumsy and crude hostility toward Madame de Maintenon, which eventually led to her being dreadfully humiliated herself; and finally it agrees admirably with the general picture of her which Saint-Simon presents at the time of her death (41, 117):

> . . . Elle était forte, courageuse, allemande au dernier point, franche, droite, bonne et bienfaisante, noble et grande en toutes ses manières, et petite au dernier point sur tout ce qui regardait ce qui lui était dû. Elle était sauvage, toujours enfermée à écrire, hors les courts temps de cour chez elle; du reste, seule avec ses dames; dure, rude, se prenant aisément d'aversion, et redoutable par ses sorties qu'elle faisait quelquefois, et sur quiconque; nulle complaisance, nul tour dans l'esprit, quoiqu'elle (ne) manquât pas d'esprit; nulle flexibilité, jalouse, comme on l'a dit, jusqu'à la dernière petitesse de tout ce qui lui était dû; la figure et le rustre d'un Suisse, capable avec cela d'une amitié tendre et inviolable. . . .
>
> (. . . She was strong, brave, German to the last degree, frank, upright, good and beneficent, noble and great in all her ways, and small to the last degree about everything concerning what was due to her. She was unsociable, always shut up writing, except for the brief periods of court at her establishment; otherwise, alone with her ladies; hard, rough, easily conceiving aversions, and to be feared for the attacks which she sometimes made, and upon anyone at all; no complaisance, no subtlety in wit, though she was not without wit; no flexibility, jealous, as has been said, to the last degree of pettiness, concerning everything that was due to her; the face and loutishness of a Swiss guard, withal capable of tender and inviolable friendship. . . .)

This passage, with its disorganized accumulation, its repetitions and syntactic short cuts, will serve to show that it is not the rule but rather the exception when Saint-Simon writes such long-drawn-out and even-toned periods as the one describing the nocturnal entrance of the Duchess. His sentence patterns change in keeping with the hold the subject matter has on him: as he puts it himself (41, 335), *emporté toujours par la matière, et peu ıttentif à la manière de la rendre, sinon pour la bien expliquer*. In the night piece we have quoted, his memory of the stormy incident carries him into the current of it, but not to such a degree that his critical observation and his emphasis on the grotesque suffer from it. He fits these things into the current of his sentence. However different the two passages may be—the nocturnal entrance of the Duchess and the portrait of her—they have many things in common, and above all the denseness and as it were overcrowding of their content. As Saint-Simon writes, memories of people and scenes come to him so urgently and with such an abundance of details that his pen seems hardly able to keep up with it all; and he is apparently quite convinced that everything that occurs to him is indispensable for the whole and that it will find its proper place there without his having to prepare for it in advance. He does not take the time to finish dealing with Madame's entrance first, and then go on, in new sentences, to say (1) that she has little cause to mourn and (2) that her court dress was out of place—which are really two quite unrelated things. Instead, since they both come to him simultaneously with his memory image of the princess's precipitate arrival, and since he feels too beset by ideas and inspirations, too afraid that, if he attempts a less hectic arrangement, postponing certain things for later treatment, something may escape him or be crowded out by new images and ideas, he has to put everything in at once. And then the necessity turns out to be a virtue; he discovers that the two things can be combined because they are equally inappropriate, instinctive, and touching, and because they both illuminate the depths of Madame's character. And so he quickly puts it down, and there it stands, not quite symmetrically related to what went before, but that only makes it the more striking: *ne sachant bonnement pourquoi ni l'un ni l'autre.* This overhasty and impatient procedure is responsible for the syntactic hybrids and short cuts which occur everywhere in his work and which almost always result in new syntheses; as for example the inspired *jamais à son aise ni nul avec lui* with reference to le Président Harlay, or *sachant de tout, parlant de tout, l'esprit orné, mais d'écorce,* with reference to the Duc de Noailles; or such logically absurd but, in point of meaning, perfectly clear formulations as these: . . . *pour la faire connaître et en donner l'idée qu'on doit avoir pour s'en former une qui soit véritable* (Madame des Ursins), or . . . *divers traits de ce portrait, plus fidèle que la gloire qu'il a dérobée et qu'à l'exemple du roi il a transmise à la postérité* (on Maréchal Villars; the rest of the sentence is also characteristic of his short-cut method of condensation). The same urgent haste prevails in the enumeration of Madame's characteristics in his portrait of her. Quite evidently Saint-Simon did not take the time to arrange them beforehand; he has not even the patience to eliminate repetitions in thought, expression, and sound (*courts-cour*); he starts out twice with *elle était*, and if he does not go on doing so, the reason is simply that he has not the time. He twice uses *au dernier point* as a means of emphasis, and thus unwittingly produces a rhetorical effect. He combines two short adjectives in the absolute position (*dure, rude*) with a nine-syllabled adjectival phrase, proceeds with another adjective, which he substantiates in detail (14 syllables), and appends to it the condensed, abrupt, and four-syllabled *et sur quiconque*, which falls completely out of the construction. From the next clause on, he simply piles up nouns. And the most astounding feature of the entire thing is, to my mind, the conclusion, in which one no longer knows where the physical ends and the moral begins, and in which, for the most striking and, because of its inner truth, the most affecting of all these contrasts he does not trouble to find any other connective than the *avec cela* which every reader of Saint-Simon knows so well and which is unforgettable by reason of its inexpressiveness in the midst of so much that is expressive. What a monument for a woman: *la figure et le rustre d'un Suisse, capable avec cela d'une amitié tendre et inviolable!*

This brings us to another peculiar characteristic, which is to be found in both of our texts and in Saint-Simon generally: just as he makes no effort to construct his sentences harmoniously, so it also does not occur to him to harmonize their content. He has no idea of organizing his material in accordance with any ethical or aesthetic conception of order, with some predetermined idea of what is proper to beauty and to ugliness, to virtue and to vice, to the body and to the soul. Everything that occurs to him in connection with his subject, he throws into his sentences just as it happens to come to mind, in full confidence that it will somehow fit together in unity and clearness. For has he not in his consciousness a homogeneous conception of the individual he is describing, a total picture of the scene he is depicting? He has no objection to coupling *la figure et le rustre d'un Suisse* (where *rustre* is beginning to shift from the physical into the ethical) with *amitié tendre et inviolable*; other and even more extreme instances are to be found everywhere in his work. Of Monseigneur he says: *L'épaisseur d'une part, la crainte de l'autre formaient en ce prince une retenue qui a peu d'exemples.* His wonderful description of the Duchess of Burgundy (whom, like almost everyone who knew her, he found enchanting) begins with the words: *Régulièrement laide, les joues pendantes, le front trop avancé, un nez qui ne disait rien, de grosses lèvres mordantes. . . .* One might suppose that he intentionally begins with her ugly features and will then give her beauties; perhaps for a moment this was his plan; but he does not adhere to it, for after *des yeux les plus parlants et les plus beaux du monde* comes *peu de dents et toutes pourries dont elle parlait et se moquait la première.* After all that we get, among other things: . . . *peu de gorge mais admirable, le cou long avec un soupçon de goître qui ne lui seyait point mal . . . une taille longue, ronde, menue, aisée, parfaitement coupée, une marche de déesse sur les nuées: elle plaisait au dernier point* (22, 280)—and even that is not the end. Of Villars he says: *C'était un assez grand homme, brun, bien fait, devenu gros en vieillissant, sans en être appesanti, avec une physionomie vive, ouverte, sortante, et véritablement un peu folle.* Who would be prepared for such a conclusion? This passage, which Proust cites admiringly, and similar passages, which can be found in great numbers, must not be judged by our modern literary experiences; unexpected combinations (though hardly of this cast) are nowadays within the reach of any halfway gifted journalist and even many an advertising copywriter. They are to be judged in terms of the ethical and aesthetic conceptions of French classicism and post-classicism, when crystallized categories had come to exist for things that do and things that do not go together, categories of *vraisemblance* and *bienséance* which did not tolerate even the merest reference to anything which deviated from them. Only on this basis can one appreciate the peculiar character, the incomparability, of Saint-Simon's perception and expression.

The most important point in connection with this lack of every kind of prearranged harmony (from which, however, the harmony of the *individuum ineffable* in its breathing reality is then built up) is the constant medley of physical and moral, outer and inner characteristics. The external characteristic is always expressive of character; the inner being is never or at least very seldom described without its sensory manifestations; and often the two are fused in a single word or image, as is the case in the example discussed above (*la figure et*) *le rustre d'un Suisse.* This intermingling persists even when it is Saint-Simon's purpose to present externals and internals as in contrast. Such a contrast can only be deceptive, can only rest upon a misinterpretation of externals. In connection with the Church Council of 1700, Saint-Simon describes the surprise of the clergy when the cardinal archbishop of Paris, Noailles, little known to most of them, is unexpectedly called upon to preside and, though his outer appearance seemed to justify no great expectations, proves to be an extremely erudite, capable, and clear-headed man: *un air de béatitude que sa physionomie présentait, avec un parler gras, lent, et nasillard, la faisait volontiers prendre pour niaise, et sa simplicité en tout pour bêtise* [note the short cuts]; *la surprise était grande quand. . . .* He does not oppose outer to inner characteristics; instead, he presents a misinterpretation (*la faisait volontiers prendre*) of the whole, a misinterpretation which is itself interlarded with moral elements (*air de béatitude, simplicité*). And when he gives the correct interpretation, it is done in such a way that the traits misread by superficial observers fall admirably into the whole. And the correct interpretation likewise mingles corporeal and spiritual, outer and inner elements: *avec son siège, sa pourpre, sa faveur, sa douceur, ses mœurs, sa piété et son savoir, il gouverna toute l'assemblée sans peine. . . .* By way of conclusion there is a description of his eating habits.

An intermingling of body and spirit which sometimes grasps the inmost essence of the whole; in conjunction with this—or rather, equally indissolubly intermingled with it—the political and social situation of the person under discussion (*son siège, sa pourpre, sa faveur, sa douceur, ses mœurs, sa piété et son savoir,* all these things presented on a par with one another); and finally each person as an entity fused into the unity of the political and historical climate of the French court so that each is perpetually involved in a complex tissue of relationships —all this is mastered by Saint-Simon's style. With it all, the author's personal attitude toward the persons described appears most accurately nuanced. The non-fictitious, non-precogitated quality of his material, its being drawn from immediate appearances, gives Saint-Simon a depth of life which even the great decades' most important portrayers of character, Molière for example or La Bruyère, could not achieve. Let us read a less well-known portrait, that of one of Saint-Simon's sisters-in-law, the duchesse de Lorge, the daughter of a once powerful minister who fell into disfavor, *ma grande biche,* as he once called her in a letter (24, 275-277):

> La duchesse de Lorge, troisième fille de Chamillart, mourut à Paris en couche de son second fils, le dernier mai, jour de la Fête-Dieu, dans sa vingt-huitième année. C'était une grande créature, très bien faite, d'un visage agréable, avec de l'esprit, et un naturel si simple, si vrai, si surnageant à tout, qu'il en était ravissant; la meilleure femme du monde et la plus folle de tout plaisir, surtout

du gros jeu. Elle n'avait quoi que ce soit des sottises de gloire et d'importances des enfants des ministres; mais, tout le reste, elle le possédait en plein. Gâtée dès sa première jeunesse par une cour prostituée à la faveur de son père, avec une mère incapable d'aucune éducation, elle ne crut jamais que la France ni le Roi pût se passer de son père. Elle ne connut aucun devoir, pas même de bienséance. La chute de son père ne put lui en apprendre aucun, ni émousser la passion du jeu et des plaisirs. Elle l'avouait tout le plus ingénuement du monde, et ajoutait après qu'elle ne pouvait se contraindre. Jamais personne si peu soigneuse d'elle-même, si dégingandée: coiffure de travers, habits qui traînaient d'un côté, et tout le reste de même, et tout cela avec une grâce qui réparait tout. Sa santé, elle n'en faisait aucun compte, et pour sa dépénse, elle ne croyait que terre pût jamais lui manquer. Elle était délicate, et sa poitrine s'altérait. On le lui disait; elle le sentait; mais, de se retenir sur rien, elle en était incapable. Elle acheva de se pousser à bout de jeu, de courses, de veilles en sa dernière grossesse. Toutes les nuits, elle revenait couchée en travers de son carrosse. On lui demandait en cet état quel plaisir elle prenait; elle répondait, d'une voix qui, de faiblesse, avait peine à se faire entendre, qu'elle avait bien du plaisir. Aussi finit-elle bientôt. Elle avait été fort bien avec Madame la Dauphine, et dans la plupart de ses confidences. J'étais fort bien avec elle; mais je lui disais toujours que, pour rien, je n'eusse voulu être son mari. Elle était très douce, et, pour qui n'avait que faire à elle, fort aimable. Son père et sa mère en furent fort affligés.

(The duchesse de Lorge, third daughter of Chamillart, died at Paris in childbed of her second son, the last of May, Corpus Christi day, in her twenty-eighth year. She was a big creature, very well built, with an agreeable face, with wit and a nature so simple, so true, so floating over everything, that it made it ravishing; the best woman in the world and the maddest after all pleasure, especially high play. She had nothing at all of the stupid glory-seeking and self-importance of ministers' children; but all the rest she had in full measure. Spoiled from her earliest youth by a court prostituted to her father's favor, with a mother incapable of any education, she never thought that France or the King could do without her father. She knew no duty, not even of decorum. Her father's fall did not succeed in teaching her any, nor in blunting her passion for gambling and pleasures. She admitted it with all the ingenuousness in the world, and added afterward that she could not restrain herself. Never anyone so little careful of herself, so slovenly: headdress awry, clothes dragging to one side, and all the rest likewise, and all this with a grace which made up for everything. Her health she regarded not at all, and as for her expenditure, she thought there would always be ground under her feet. She was delicate, and her chest went from bad to worse. She was told so; she felt it; but, as for restraining herself in anything, she could not. She finally drove herself to the breaking-point with gambling, running about, and staying up late, during her last pregnancy. Every night she came home lying crosswise in her carriage. In this state, someone asked her what pleasure she found; she answered, in a voice which, for weakness, could hardly make itself heard, that she had a great deal of pleasure. So it was soon over with her. She had been on very good terms with Madame la Dauphine and in her confidence in most things. I was on very good terms with her; but I always told her that I would not have wanted to be her husband for anything. She was very gentle, and, toward anyone who had no business with her, extremely amiable. Her father and mother were very much afflicted by it.)

In this portrait of *ma grande biche* there is the most heartfelt affection, indeed one almost senses that tears come to his eyes as he remembers her. What writer of Saint-Simon's time, let alone of the preceding period, would have been able to describe such a lady simply as a poor young thing, to introduce his description with the words *c'était une grande créature*, to invent the crescendo *si simple, si vrai, si surnageant à tout*, to append to the trite phrase *c'était la meilleure femme du monde* the incisive accent *et la plus folle de tout plaisir*, to take her carelessness in dress, in her manner of life, and of her health, and put them together to make so charming a picture of self-abandonment, and finally to preserve for us the scene where, stretched out in her carriage, she says, in a dying voice, *qu'elle avait bien du plaisir*? For all this, the passage is pervaded by a clear, calm objectivity which describes the social and general environmental climate in which so unique a plant could grow. We must wait until the late nineteenth century and indeed actually until the twentieth, before we again find in European literature a similar level of tone, a synthesis of a human being which is so entirely free from traditional harmonizing, which presses so unswervingly on from the random data of the phenomenon itself to the ultimate depths of existence.

We should like to cite a few more examples, which will go further than those we have as yet considered in casting light on matters of politics and history. In 1714 began the long-drawn-out struggle over the anti-Jansenist papal bull Unigenitus. Saint-Simon opposes the bull, in part because he detests every kind of intolerance and the use of force in matters of faith, and in part also because the bull contains provisions for excommunication which seem to him politically dangerous. The Jesuit priest Tellier, the King's confessor, who is trying all means to get the bull accepted, would like to win over Saint-Simon and finally asks him for a private meeting. Circumstances bring it about that the meeting takes place in a windowless back room lit only by candles (Saint-Simon's "boutique"), while in the adjoining salon visitors are expected who must not be allowed to know what is going on in this study. The conversation becomes animated; with astonishing frankness the old Jesuit reveals the plan, a mixture of deceit and brutality, which he has concocted to force the issue. He tries by all sorts of sophisms to overcome Saint-Simon's scruples and, as he senses his opposition, grows more and more excited. In an earlier passage Saint-Simon had already sketched a portrait of Père Tellier. Here are a few sentences from it (17, 60):

> Sa tête et sa santé étaient de fer, sa conduite en était aussi, son naturel cruel et farouche . . . il était profondément faux, trompeur, caché sous mille plis et replis, et quand il put se montrer et se faire craindre, exigeant tout, ne donnant rien, se moquant des paroles les plus expressément données lorsqu'il ne lui importait plus de les tenir, et poursuivant avec fureur ceux qui les avaient reçues. C'était un homme terrible. . . . Le prodigieux de cette fureur jamais interrompue d'un seul instant par rien, c'est qu'il ne se proposa jamais rien pour lui-même, qu'il n'avait ni parents ni amis, qu'il était né malfaisant, sans être touché d'aucun plaisir d'obliger, et qu'il était de la lie du peuple et ne s'en cachait pas; violent jusqu'à faire peur aux jésuites les plus sages. . . . Son extérieur ne promettait rien moins, et tint exactement parole; il eût fait peur au coin d'un bois. Sa physionomie était ténébreuse, fausse, terrible; les yeux ardents, méchants, extrêmement de travers; on était frappé en le voyant.

(His head and his health were of iron, so was his conduct, his nature cruel and fierce . . . he was profoundly false, deceitful, concealed under a thousand turns and twists, and, when he could show himself and make himself feared, demanding everything, giving nothing, caring nothing for the most express promises when it was no longer important to him to keep them, and furiously pursuing those which he had received. He was a terrible man. . . . The prodigious thing about this fury, never interrupted for an instant by anything, was that he never projected anything for himself, that he had neither relatives nor friends, that he was born maleficent, without ever being touched by any pleasure in being obliging, and that he came from the dregs of the people and did not conceal it; violent to the point of making the wisest Jesuits afraid. . . . His exterior promised no less, and kept its word precisely; he would have aroused fear at the corner of a wood. His physiognomy was somber, false, terrible; the eyes burning, malicious, extremely squinted; one was struck when one saw him.)

Now the two sit face to face in the "boutique" (24, 117):

Je le voyais bec à bec entre deux bougies, n'y ayant du tout que la largeur de la table entre deux. J'ai décrit ailleurs son horrible physionomie. Eperdu tout à coup par l'ouïe et par la vue, je fus saisi, tandis qu'il parlait, de ce que c'était qu'un jésuite, qui, par son néant personnel et avoué, ne pouvait rien espérer pour sa famille, ni, par son état et par ses vœux, pour soi-même, pas même une pomme ni un coup de vin plus que les autres; qui par son âge touchait au moment de rendre compte à Dieu, et qui, de propos délibéré et amené avec grand artifice, allait mettre l'Etat et la religion dans la plus terrible combustion, et ouvrir la persécution la plus affreuse pour des questions qui ne lui faisaient rien, et qui ne touchaient que l'honneur de leur école de Molina. Ses profondeurs, les violences qu'il me montra, tout cela me jeta en un tel (sic) extase, que tout à coup je me pris à lui dire en l'interrompant: "Mon Père, quel âge avez-vous?" Son extrême surprise, car je le regardais de tous mes yeux, qui la virent se peindre sur son visage, rappela mes sens. . . .

(I saw him face to face between two candles, having nothing but the width of the table between the two of us. I have elsewhere described his horrible physiognomy. Bewildered suddenly by hearing and sight, I was seized, while he talked, with what a Jesuit was, who, through his personal and avowed nothingness, could hope nothing for his family, nor, through his condition and his vows, for himself, not even an apple or a drink of wine more than the others; who, through his age, was close to the moment of rendering his account to God, and who, of deliberate purpose, and brought about with great artifice, was going to put the State and religion into the most terrible combustion, and inaugurate the most frightful persecution for questions which meant nothing to him and which affected only the honor of their school of Molina. His depths, the violences which he showed me, all this threw me into such an ecstasy that I suddenly found myself saying, interrupting him: "Father, how old are you?" His extreme surprise, for I was looking at him with all my eyes, which saw it painted on his face, called back my senses. . . .)

Saint-Simon succeeds in neutralizing the effect of his tactless question, and he learns that Père Tellier is 73 years old. The scene shows with the greatest clarity how Saint-Simon reacts to phenomena confronting him. He instinctively sees the individual whom he has *bec à bec* before him, as an entity comprising body, mind, station in life, and personal history. This gives him a power of penetration which goes through the individual into the political subject matter—so deeply, indeed, that at times, as in this instance, he loses sight of its pressing aspect of the moment, and much deeper and more general insights are revealed beneath it. As he looks at his interlocutor *de tous ses yeux*, he forgets about the present occasion, their disagreement over a specific article of the Constitutio Unigenitus, and sees, with the utmost vividness, the essential nature of the Jesuit Order and, beyond that, the essential nature of any strictly organized solidaritarian community. This is a manner of perception which his interlocutor, for all his acumen, was hardly capable of divining. Neither the seventeenth nor the eighteenth century furnishes other examples of it. People were too reasonably superficial, too discreet themselves, too respectful of the other man's personality, too intent upon maintaining their distance, so that they shrank from such a disclosure. At the same time the passage shows that Saint-Simon obtains his most profound insights not by rationally analyzing ideas and problems but by an empiricism applied to whatever sensory phenomenon happens to confront him and pursued to the point of penetrating to the existential. In contrast (to mention an obvious example) the Jesuit priest of the first *Lettres provinciales* was quite clearly stylized on the basis of a preceding rational study.

I shall take up one more passage. Saint-Simon knew the duc d'Orléans, the later Regent, from his early childhood. He knew him very well and had a very high opinion of his intelligence and abilities. He shows that only the duke's uncomfortable and as it were oblique position in respect to his uncle Louis XIV ruined his character and his powers, making him the indecisive, unreliable, cynically indifferent, and dissipated man he finally became. Not long before the Regent's death Saint-Simon realized that the end was not far off, and he describes how he reached his conclusion. The Regent had bestowed an important office on the duc d'Humières:

> Le duc d'Humières voulut que je le menasse à Versailles remercier M. le duc d'Orléans le matin. Nous le trouvâmes qu'il allait s'habiller, et qu'il était encore dans son caveau [a basement room which is often mentioned], dont il avait fait sa garderobe. Il y était sur sa chaise percée parmi ses valets et deux ou trois de ses premiers officiers. J'en fus effrayé. Je vis un homme la tête basse, d'un rouge pourpre, avec un air hébété, qui ne me vit seulement pas approcher. Ses gens le lui dirent. Il tourna la tête lentement vers moi, sans presque la lever, et me demanda d'une langue épaisse ce qui m'amenait. Je le luis dis. J'étais entré là pour le presser de venir dans le lieu où il s'habillait, pour ne pas faire attendre le duc d'Humières; mais je demeurai si étonné que je restai court. Je pris Simiane, premier gentilhomme de sa chambre, dans une fenêtre, à qui je témoignai ma surprise et ma crainte de l'état où je voyais M. le duc d'Orléans. Simiane me répondit qu'il était depuis fort longtemps ainsi les matins, qu'il n'y avait ce jour-là rien d'extraordinaire en lui, et que je n'en étais surpris que parce que je ne le voyais jamais à ces heures-là; qu'il n'y paraîtrait plus tant quand il se serait secoué en s'habillant. Il ne laissa pas d'y paraître encore beaucoup lorsqu'il vint s'habiller. Il reçut le remerciement du duc d'Humières d'un air étonné et pesant; et lui, qui était toujours gracieux et poli envers tout le monde, et qui savait si bien dire à propos et à point, à peine lui répondit-il. . . . Cet état de M. le duc d'Orléans me fit faire beaucoup de réflexions. . . . C'était le fruit de ses soupers . . . (41, 229).

(The duc d'Humières wanted me to take him to Versailles to thank M. le duc d'Orléans in the morning. We found him about to dress and that he was still in his basement, which he had made his wardrobe. He was on his close-stool among his valets and two or three of his principal officers. He terrified me. I saw a man with his head down, a purplish red, with a vacant look, who did not even see me approach. His attendants told him. He turned his head toward me slowly, almost without raising it, and asked me thickly what brought me. I told him. I had gone there to urge him to come to the place where he dressed, so as not to make the duc d'Humières wait; but I remained so astonished that I stopped short. I took Simiane, first gentleman of his bedchamber, into a window, to whom I expressed my surprise and my fear over the state in which I found M. le duc d'Orléans. Simiane answered that he had been like this in the morning for some time past, that there was nothing unusual about him that morning, and that I was only surprised because I never saw him at those hours; that it would not show so much when he had shaken himself up getting dressed. Nevertheless it still showed a good deal when he came to dress. He received the duc d'Humières' thanks with an astonished and heavy air; and he, who was always gracious and polite toward everyone, and who knew so well how to speak pertinently and pointedly, hardly answered him. . . . This state of M. le duc d'Orléans caused me to make many reflections. . . . It was the fruit of his suppers. . . .)

One should not be surprised to learn that the Regent is surrounded by servants and court officials while sitting on his *chaise percée* and that he even receives a high dignitary in that position. The princes of the seventeenth and eighteenth centuries were almost never alone. When Louvois, in a dramatic scene, rushes into the King's apartment to prevent him from publicly acknowledging his marriage to Madame de Maintenon, he finds him just risen from his *chaise percée* and in the act of arranging his clothes. And of the duchesse de Burgogne Saint-Simon relates that it was her custom to carry on the most intimate conversations with her ladies in waiting under the same circumstances. But none of these scenes has the gripping power of the one quoted above. I suppose that in all known literature, especially in earlier literature, there is hardly a text that treats such a topic dramatically and tragically. This one does. Saint-Simon's terror in the face of the picture of decline and imminent death before him has tragic weight. The picture is developed, slowly, gradually, and in precise detail, in two fairly long sentences (*Je vis un homme . . .* and *Il tourna la tête . . .*) set between three very brief ones (*j'en fus effrayé, ses gens le lui dirent, je le lui dis*), all of which refer to the surroundings and, in their abruptness and sharpness, give the effect of thrusts vainly trying to pierce the Regent's apathy. The picture itself Saint-Simon begins with the words, "I saw a man" (not, "I saw the Duke")—which expresses two things: that in the first moment he does not recognize, or refuses to believe, who the man before him is; secondly, that the unfortunate creature is hardly Monsieur le duc d'Orléans any longer but "only" a man. And the slow precision of the second sentence, with the laborious turning of the head and the heavy tongue, is on a level of style which is hardly to be found anywhere else in the eighteenth century, and even in the nineteenth not much before the Goncourts and Zola.

The point is not simply that we have here a ruthless representation of everyday events, of things that are ugly and, in terms of classical aesthetics, undignified. Such a radical realism occurs elsewhere too, even in the seventeenth and eighteenth centuries. The point is rather that these things are made to serve a completely serious character portrayal which explores the problematic and even transcends the purely moralistic in order to penetrate into the *profondeurs opaques* of our nature. Every reader is constrained to feel that the entire destiny, the entire tragedy, of the duc d'Orléans is contained in this scene on the *chaise percée*. In his level of style Saint-Simon is a precursor of modern and ultramodern forms of conceiving and representing life. He takes human beings in the midst of their everyday environment, with their background, their multifarious relations, their possessions, every particle of their bodies, their gestures, every nuance of their speech, their hopes, and their fears. Very often he expresses what we would nowadays call their inheritance, and here too he expresses both the physical and the spiritual factors. He notes the peculiarities of the milieu with absolute precision, scorning nothing. What author of his age could and would have emphasized a thing like the peculiar mentality and manner of speech of the Mortemart family, as he does time and again (in connection with Mme. de Montespan; her daughter, the duchesse d'Orléans; Mme. de Castries; etc.). And all this serves the portrayal of the *condition de l'homme*. The sphere of his experiences is certainly limited, for he is always dealing only with the French court. But in compensation it is a sphere of great homogeneity; as such it practically predetermines that the whole work will have unity of action. And the scene is vast enough to furnish a world of characters and the possibility of random, unselected, everyday occurrences.

We said earlier that, in other instances too, the memoir literature of the seventeenth and eighteenth centuries did not conform with the aesthetic rule that the everyday and low should be kept apart from the sublime and serious; on the contrary, it in many cases reveals and unmasks what is elsewhere represented in an exalted manner—princes and their courts. But with Saint-Simon all this is carried much further than with any other author; it is different in substance and degree. With the others, even when they are talented writers, the very fact that their material is personal, everyday, unselected, and rarely permitting a general view of a situation in its entirety, leads to their being valued chiefly because of their documentary and local-color content, while their literary qualities, if any, are enjoyed as a pleasant makeweight. Anecdotes, intrigues, apologies, in short, the purely personal, is far too predominant; political events, presented as it were on a minute-to-minute basis and selected on that of a limited horizon and interest, lay no claim to the highest human sympathy. Nobody reads Retz with the same readiness for sympathy and participation with which one reads Shakespeare or Montaigne. Saint-Simon has also, in my opinion, too often been judged by the same standards as these others, that is to say, he has too often been treated as mere documentation in the history of culture. To be sure, he is that, and he is so more perfectly than the others. But he is something more and something else as well. Precisely the factors which account for the limited human and aesthetic effect of the others—the anecdotal, the personal, the idiosyncratic, the frequent insignificance of their themes—are his strength, simply because he alone knows how to use the random and idiosyncratic, the unselected, the at times absurdly personal and prejudiced, as points of departure for sudden descents into the depths of human existence.

What a distance from the charming and superficial intermediate level of the texts from the first half of the eighteenth century discussed at the beginning of this chapter! What a contrast to their display of a pleasantly stylized reality designed for the reader's enjoyment or as propaganda for some enlightened ideology! And yet, Saint-Simon belongs far more to the period during which he composed his work than to the seventeenth century, where he has been placed time and again because he treats of Louis XIV's court. Yet it is not even the court of the sixties and seventies, but that of the last decades! And those last decades, into whose life he penetrated, were, at the time he wrote, already the distant past. The first half of the eighteenth century affords not a few other instances of individuals, ideas, and movements which seem to be harbingers of much later developments and are unique in their own epoch. Who would put Giambattista Vico in the seventeenth century? And Vico was born seven years before Saint-Simon and wrote his principal work a little earlier too. Vico was an anti-Cartesian; in the same way Saint-Simon was against the great King; and they both admired their opponents and were deeply impressed by them. But there are further, and less external, similarities between these so very different contemporaries. In their predilections and mentality they both hark back to a past which had ceased to be modern by their day. They both wrote works which at first sight seem amorphously chaotic in contrast to the elegantly polished and limited style of their contemporaries. In both the urgency of an inner impulse gives their language something unusual, at times something violent and immoderately expressive, which runs counter to the ease and pleasantness which appealed to the taste of the time; and above all, they both regard man—the one wholly instinctively, in the process of portraying his fellows; the other speculatively, in a vision of the course of history—as being profoundly embedded in the historical data of his existence, and in this they are both in complete contradiction to the rationalistic and ahistorical attitude of their age. Of a basic historical theory of the kind postulated by Historism, whose first faint manifestation began to be perceptible just at the time Saint-Simon was writing his memoirs, there is yet no trace in him. The individualism of his representation is limited to individual human beings; historical forces in a superindividual and yet personalized sense are not within his range of vision. What he means by living history (he explains this in his impressive *Considérations préliminaires*, 1, 5f.), is exclusively an insight into the distinctive psychologies of the acting individuals and into the resulting connections and oppositions. The purpose of the historian, as he formulates it, is entirely moralizing and didactic in the pre-historistic sense. But the multifariousness of the reality in which he lived and which inspired his genius made him go far beyond it.

17

MILLER THE MUSICIAN

Miller (schnell auf- und abgehend). Einmal für allemal! Der Handel wird ernsthaft. Meine Tochter kommt mit dem Baron ins Geschrei. Mein Haus wird verrufen. Der Präsident bekommt Wind, und kurz und gut, ich biete dem Junker aus.

Frau Du hast ihn nicht in dein Haus geschwatzt—hast ihm deine Tochter nicht nachgeworfen.

Miller Hab' ihn nicht in mein Haus geschwatzt—hab' ihm's Mädel nicht nachgeworfen; wer nimmt Notiz davon?—Ich war Herr im Haus. Ich hätt' meine Tochter mehr koram nehmen sollen. Ich hätt' dem Major besser auftrumpfen sollen—oder hätt' gleich alles Seiner Excellenz, dem Herrn Papa stecken sollen. Der junge Baron bringt's mit einem Wischer hinaus, das muss ich wissen, und alles Wetter kommt über den Geiger.

Frau (schlürft eine Tasse aus). Possen! Geschwätz! Was kann über dich kommen? Wer kann dir was anhaben? Du gehst deiner Profession nach und raffst Scholaren zusammen, wo sie zu kriegen sind.

Miller Aber, sag mir doch, was wird bei dem ganzen Commerz auch herauskommen?—Nehmen kann er das Mädel nicht—Vom Nehmen ist gar die Rede nicht, und zu einer—dass Gott erbarm?—Guten Morgen!—Gelt, wenn so ein Musje *von* sich da und dort, und dort und hier schon herumbeholfen hat, wenn er, der Henker weiss! was als? gelöst hat, schmeckt's meinem guten Schlucker freilich, einmal auf süss Wasser zu graben. Gib du Acht! Gib du Acht! und wenn du aus jedem Astloch ein Auge strecktest und vor jedem Blutstropfen Schildwache ständest, er wird sie, dir auf der Nase, beschwatzen, dem Mädel eins hinsetzen, und führt sich ab, und das Mädel ist verschimpfiert auf ihr Lebenlang, bleibt sitzen, oder hat's Handwerk verschmeckt, treibt's fort, (die Faust vor die Stirn) Jesus Christus!

Frau Gott behüt' uns in Gnaden!

Miller Es hat sich zu behüten. Worauf kann so ein Windfuss wohl sonst sein Absehen richten?—Das Mädel ist schön—schlank—führt seinen netten Fuss. Unterm Dach mag's aussehen, wie's will. Darüber guckt man bei euch Weibsleuten weg, wenn's nur der liebe Gott par terre nicht hat fehlen lassen—Stöbert mein Springinsfeld erst noch dieses Capitel aus—he da! geht ihm ein Licht auf, wie meinem Rodney, wenn er die Witterung eines Franzosen kriegt, und nun müssen alle Segel dran und drauf los,—und ich verdenk's ihm gar nicht. Mensch ist Mensch. Das muss ich wissen.

Frau . . .

(*Miller* (walking rapidly to and fro). Once and for all! This business is getting serious. They will start talking about my daughter and the Baron. Our home will lose its reputation. The President is bound to hear about it and—well and good, I am going to forbid the young man to come here any more.

Frau Millerin You didn't talk him into coming here. You didn't throw your daughter at his head.

Miller Didn't talk him into coming here! Didn't throw the girl at his head! They won't inquire into that!—I was the master of the house. I should have told the girl. I should have given the Major a piece of my mind—or put the whole thing up to His Excellency Senior. The young Baron will be let off with a warning. I know how that works. And the full storm breaks over the fiddler.

Frau Millerin (sips the last drop from her cup). Nonsense! Idle talk! What can break over you? Who can touch you? You are doing your work and must take students where you can get them.

Miller But tell me, if you can, what is going to come of the whole business?—Marry her . . . that he can't, that is out of the question. And a . . . O my God! Thank you, Madam! Of course, when such a Mr. Sir has helped himself in this place here and that place there, when he has cashed in on the devil knows how much, then it's only natural that my good man will find it to his taste to go for a change and dig for sweet water. You watch out! You watch out! And if you have an eye peeping out of every knothole and play at being sentry in front of every drop of blood, he will talk her into it right under your nose. He will let her have what it takes, and then he will clear out, and the girl is disgraced for the rest of her life; she is left on the shelf, or she gets to like the taste of it, goes on with it (his fist against his forehead) . . . Jesus Christ!

Frau Millerin God in his Grace protect us!

Miller And we need it! What else can such a windbag be driving at? The girl is pretty—slender—and dangles a good-looking leg. Let the upstairs be as the upstairs will. That's easily overlooked in women, as long as the dear Lord didn't forget anything on the ground floor. Let my young racer find out about this feature of the story—hey there! and he will catch on the way old Rodney does when he smells a Frenchman around, and it's "Set all sails, and off we go"—and I cannot even blame him for it. A man is a man. I know how that works.

Frau Millerin . . .)*

This opening of Schiller's "middle-class tragedy" *Luise Millerin*—written 1782-1783—takes place in a petty bourgeois setting, a room in the musician's home. The stage directions emphasize the point by specifying: Frau Millerin, still in her nightgown, sits at a table and drinks her coffee. In keeping with this is the language of the two speakers, especially of the husband, whose good-natured and blustering character cannot, in these excited moments, do enough in the way of flavorful and hearty petty-bourgeois colloquialisms. Despite his profession, he is by no means an "artist" but rather a better-than-average craftsman, and no violence would be done to the style if an actor made him speak in dialect (Swabian). He has a heart and a head, but his views are completely bourgeois. A few lines further on, in the continuation of the first scene, which we have not included in our quotation, he becomes even more excited at the thought that the Baron's love may have made his daughter so proud that in the end "she turns me down a fine upright son-in-law who would have fitted in with my clientele so nicely." This is the atmosphere in which the tragedy takes place. It is not only Miller's family and Secretary Wurm who breathe this petty-bourgeois air. The conflict as such is bourgeois, and even the

* For this new version the translator is indebted to his friend Dr. Alexander Gode v. Äsch, his gratitude to whom for admirable advice and unstinted assistance on this and other occasions he welcomes this opportunity of acknowledging.

two persons of rank, the President and his son, have nothing about them to remind us of the heroic exaltation, the aloofness from the everyday, which characterized the French tragedy of the great period. The son is noble, full of sentiment, and idealistic. The father is diabolic and imperious, and in the end sentimental too. Neither is sublime in the sense of French classicism. For that the locale—a small German town, the capital of an absolute ruler—is much too narrow.

Schiller was not the first to take such or similar settings and conflicts tragically. The sentimental middle-class novel and the middle-class tragedy (referred to in our preceding chapter as the *comédie larmoyante*) had evolved long before in England and France. In Germany, where the Christian-creatural mixture of styles had survived through the seventeenth century and where even later it had not been completely displaced by the influence of French classicism, the evolution of middle-class realism assumed exceptionally vigorous forms. The influence of Shakespeare joined forces with that of Diderot and Rousseau; the narrow and disrupted domestic conditions furnished arresting subjects; works were produced which were at once sentimental, narrowly middle-class, realistic, and revolutionary. The first German work in this genre, Lessing's youthful play, *Miss Sara Sampson* (1755), written under English influence and set in England, does not, it is true, contain elements of contemporary politics. But his *Minna von Barnhelm,* published twelve years later, plunges into the most contemporary events. In book 7 of part 2 of *Dichtung und Wahrheit* (*Jubiläumsausgabe,* 23, 80), Goethe calls the play "the first theatrical production drawn from meaningful life and having a specifically contemporary content." He also points out a particularly timely feature of the play, which a modern reader will hardly notice but which may be assumed to have contributed not a little to the stir which the play made in its time: "the bitter tension with which Prussians and Saxons faced each other during this [the Seven Years'] war," a tension which "could not be resolved through its [the war's] termination," so that Lessing's work "was to achieve in a picture" the restoration of peace among the people. Now *Minna von Barnhelm,* to be sure, is a comedy and not a middle-class tragedy; its subject matter is distinguished from that of middle-class tragedies by its design, by its setting, by the independence of the leading female character, and the noble rank of both hero and heroine. Nevertheless, in its sentimental seriousness, in the simple straightforwardness of its conception of honor, and in its language there is something middle class and sometimes almost homespun, so that one tends to think of the noble principals (often also of the German nobles of the time in general) as living in an environment of middle-class domesticity. There is no doubt that Goethe is right when (in accordance with his own direct impression when the work had appeared during his student days at Leipzig) he says in the same passage: "It was this production which successfully opened the prospect into a higher and more meaningful world beyond the literary and bourgeois world to which the art of writing had been confined." Yet this superior outlook, which sets contemporary history before the reader's or auditor's eyes, has by no means caused the abandonment of the simplicity, the almost bourgeois sentiment, of the human attitudes. It is precisely the direct connection of both spheres which gives the work its particular charm. In *Emilia Galotti* the political tone appears in an entirely different but not less significant way. Here the major theme of the middle-class tragedy—the seduction of an innocent victim—is linked to the political phenomenon of absolutism in a petty state. However, the element of contemporary politics in *Emilia Galotti* remains weak and not really revolutionary. The setting is not a German but an Italian principality, and although we are specifically told that the Galotti family has neither rank nor title, their position and behavior, especially in the case of Odoardo, the father, do not impress us as middle class but rather as pronouncedly military and noble.

The final connection of sentimental middle-class realism with idealistic politics and concern for human rights was not established until the *Sturm und Drang* period. Traces of it are to be found in almost all the authors of this latter generation: in Goethe, Heinrich Leopold Wagner, Lenz, Leisewitz, Klinger, and many others, even in Johann Heinrich Voss. Of the works which have remained alive to the present day, *Luise Millerin* is the most significant for our problem because it undertakes to apprehend the practical contemporary present directly and to base the particular case on the general conditions. The sentimentally bourgeois and robust or idyllic realism, which in other cases is often expressed in historical or fantastic or personal and unpolitical subjects, with the result that a basic and direct apprehension of the reality of the time is not achieved, is here applied, unequivocally and without restraint, to the author's own experience of the political present. A familiar milieu, a timely and indeed revolutionary political interest, distinguish this tragedy from Lessing's *Emilia Galotti*, as well as from the other middle-class dramas of the period insofar as they are known to me. In its day and age it represents an extreme case of the literary rendering of reality in terms of principles and problems.

The very first words take us forcefully into the practical situation. The son of the all-powerful minister of a German prince pays court to a girl of petty-bourgeois background. He often comes to the home of her parents. We are later told that he writes her letters which are full of feeling, that he is concerned about her education, and gives her presents. The mother, a woman of limited intelligence, is delighted with her daughter's aristocratic lover and takes such pride in him that she fails to recognize the danger inherent in the situation. The father does recognize it. He fears he may become involved with the minister; he fears the worst for his daughter's reputation, for her earthly happiness and eternal bliss; for "marry her . . . that he can't!" He can only seduce her. And then "the girl is disgraced for the rest of her life; she is left on the shelf, or she gets to like the taste of it. . . ." He knows how this sort of thing must end; he knows it by virtue of his homespun common sense. He does not blame the minister's son. "A man is a man." But he loves his daughter and wants to save her. He intends to go and see the minister and tell him the whole story, although to do so goes against his nature; he is not the sort of man who meddles in matters of love. But the danger is too great. However, he never takes the desperate step; things go too fast. In the very next scene he is forced to conclude that it is too late; his daughter is too deeply enmeshed.

The world here revealed to the spectator is desperately narrow, both spatially and ethically. A petty-bourgeois parlor; a duchy so small that (as we are repeatedly told) it is only an hour's drive to the border; and class dictation of propriety and ethics in its most unnatural and pernicious form. In the court circle everything is permissible—not, however, as a noble freedom but as impertinence, corruption, and hypocrisy. Among the people we find the most unenlightened conception of virtue; a girl who yields to a man who cannot marry her according to the rules of the prevailing order of society would be considered a whore and would be despised. The prevailing order of society is viewed by the duke's subjects—including Luise herself—as "a general and eternal order." Servile submission is everywhere a matter of Christian duty; and the powers that be take advantage of the situation, especially the minister, a miserable petty tyrant to whom, it is true, Schiller tries to give certain imposing traits, a certain grandeur of conduct; but there is no inner justification whatever for doing so, since his crimes and intrigues serve nothing but the most narrowly personal goal, namely that of attaining and keeping a position of power simply as such, not as the expression of any will to practical accomplishment or of any feeling of a practical vocation to fill such a position.

The situation of Miller and his family is, then, portrayed tragically, realistically, and in terms of contemporary history. Middle-class realism and tragedy, at least so it seems at first sight, is no longer merely a skimming of the froth from the surface of social life in view of rendering a sentimentally tragic private destiny; instead the whole sociopolitical depth of the age is stirred up. We seem to be dealing with a first attempt to make an individual destiny echo the fullness of contemporary reality. To understand Luise's tragic fate, the contemporary auditor must visualize the social structure within which he lives. And yet we feel that this tragic realism—compared with either the medieval and figural or the modern and practical type of realism—somehow falls short of genuine and total reality. *Luise Millerin* is much more a political and even a demagogic play than a truly realistic one.

A political play it certainly is. H. A. Korff (*Geist der Goethezeit*, 1, 209-211) has written some excellent pages on the point. I shall summarize his argument: Although the subject matter bears no necessary but only an accidental relation to the idea of political freedom, the play is nevertheless, more than any other, a dagger thrust to the heart of absolutism. A stark light is cast upon the criminal procedures of the tyrannical princely governments; subjects have no rights whatever; they depend upon the arbitrary favor or disfavor of the prince, his favorites, and his mistresses; and from the course of events we infer with dismay the inner bondage and dependence of the ruled and recognize in it the psychological explanation for the possibility of tyrannical princely government.

All this is undeniable, and we can only regret that Schiller knew much more clearly *against* what than *for* what he was fighting, and that one might easily conclude from the play that all would be well if only a few of the leading characters were decent fellows instead of dissipated scoundrels. As it stands, the play could not but exert a significant political influence. But it is precisely the strong and bold coloration of the revolutionary tendency which impairs the genuine character of the realism. By this I do not mean to say that the reality of life in the small absolutistic principalities was better than Schiller represents it to be. But it was different and it presented itself less melodramatically. At the time when Schiller wrote *Luise Millerin,* he had not yet attained his full stature and maturity in artistic creation. It is a tempestuous, an inspired and inspiring, a very effective, and yet—when we look a little more closely—a fairly bad play. It is a melodramatic hit written by a man of genius. For a serious work the action is too calculated, too full of intrigue, and it is often improbable. To keep it going, the characters (with the exception of Miller) had to be portrayed in an altogether too naive technique of black and white. Utterances and decisions are sometimes unexpected and insufficiently motivated; the dialogue is often excessively rhetorical and sentimental, and when it tries to be witty, pointed, and refined, it usually turns out to be stilted, hard to understand, and quite often unintentionally funny. A case in point is the great scene between the Lady and Luise (4, 7) in which almost every word is unnatural. Yet the fact that Schiller's artistic sense was not fully developed when the play was written is not the decisive factor. The inadequacy of the realism lies above all in the very genre of middle-class tragedy as it had developed during the eighteenth century. It was a genre wedded to the personal, the domestic, the touching, and the sentimental, and it could not relinquish them. And this, through the tone and level of style which it implied, was unfavorable to a broadening of the social setting and the inclusion of general political and social problems. And yet it was in just this way that the break-through to things political and generally social was achieved: for the touching and, in essence, wholly personal love-alliance now no longer clashed with the opposition of ill-willed relatives, parents, and guardians or with private moral obstacles, but instead with a public enemy, with the unnatural class structure of society. In earlier chapters we have described how, in French classicism of the seventeenth century, love rose to rank highest among tragic subjects withdrawn from everyday reality, and how subsequently, in the Western European beginnings of the novel of manners and of the *comédie larmoyante,* love reestablished contact with the ordinary reality of life, but lost some of its dignity in the process. It became clearly erotic and at the same time touching and sentimental. It was in this form that the revolutionaries of the *Sturm und Drang* seized upon it, and following in Rousseau's footsteps, again gave it the highest tragic dignity, without abandoning any of its bourgeois, realistic, and sentimental elements. As the most natural and the most immediate of all things, it came to be sublime, in any life and in any setting. Its simplest and purest form appeared to be a condition of natural virtue, and its freedom in the face of mere convention was considered an inalienable natural right.

In this way love, in Schiller's *Luise Millerin,* became the point of departure for the revolutionary in politics, for a politically founded realism. However, the basis furnished by a love story was too narrow, and the sentimentally touching style was unsuitable for the production of a genuine reality. The accidental, personal, and touching features of the specific case claim too much of our attention. To make the conflict sufficiently sharp, the minister and Wurm had to be portrayed as unmitigated scoundrels. If they were not, if, furthermore, the minister did not happen just at this time to be confronted with the necessity of making sure of the prince's mistress by marrying her to a member of his own family, a solution or at least a delay would be possible. As for conditions in general throughout the principality, we are given only isolated and not always clearly understandable details. These are always gruesome, whether they concern the sale of subjects of the principality as soldiers to be sent to America or conditions at court, as in the great discussion between Ferdinand and the Lady (2, 3). They are always presented with hair-raising rhetorical pathos; they always give the impression that the duke and his court have no function whatever, but simply bleed the people by their extravagance and abuse them for their vicious pleasures. We hear and sense practically nothing of inner problems, historical complications, the function of the ruling class, the causes of its moral decline, nor of practical conditions in the principality. This is not realism, it is melodrama; it is very well adapted to release a strong, emotionally political effect; but it is in no way an artistic statement of the reality of the time. It is a caricature even where it depicts real conditions and events, because it detaches them from their roots, deprives them of their inner essence, overilluminates them both as a result of enthusiasm and in the service of propaganda. And the one motif which is probably of cardinal importance for the comprehension of the social structure, a motif which is also stressed by H. A. Korff—the inner lack of freedom of the subjects of the principality, who, in their stuffy, narrow, and misguided attitude of piety toward the burden laid upon them, acknowledge it as an eternal right—this motif does not come out clearly enough. Luise's failure, which is due to her lack of inner freedom (3, 4), is misinterpreted by Ferdinand, because the involved action demands a fit of jealousy on his part, which is entirely improbable after all that has happened; and so the auditor's interest is immediately diverted from the motif underlying her failure—as in general Luise is represented as so touchingly innocent, so filled with noble sentiments, that her essential narrowness and pusillanimity are not spontaneously recognized by the auditor; only the analytical critic of her character and Schiller's art becomes conscious of them. For even in this scene she produces the impression of being a self-sacrificing heroine, and even when she is taken in by Wurm's absurd scheme, she is still "great and awe-inspiring."

Nevertheless, the play is highly important in connection with our study—if only because, among the better known works of German classicism and romanticism, it has remained the only one of its kind. In the age of Goethe no further attempts were made toward the tragic treatment of an average contemporary bourgeois milieu on the basis of its actual social situation. The excellent characterization of the musician Miller especially, so much more homogeneous and natural than that of his daughter, remained quite unapproached in its level of style. Schiller himself, and the trend of German literature in general, turned away from realism in the sense of a concrete portrayal of contemporary political and economic conditions, with its forceful mixing of styles. Mixing of styles, which had been enthusiastically taken up under the influence of Shakespeare, appears almost exclusively in subjects from history or the realm of poetic fantasy; when applied to the present, it remains within the narrowest, unpolitical sphere or, as idyl or irony, aims exclusively at the personal. The combination of a forceful realism with a tragic conception of the problems of the age simply does not occur. This is the more striking and, if you will, the more paradoxical since it was precisely the German intellectual development during the second half of the eighteenth century which laid the aesthetic foundation of modern realism. I refer to what is currently known as Historism.

Basically, the way in which we view human life and society is the same whether we are concerned with things of the past or things of the present. A change in our manner of viewing history will of necessity soon be transferred to our manner of viewing current conditions. When people realize that epochs and societies are not to be judged in terms of a pattern concept of what is desirable absolutely speaking but rather in every case in terms of their own premises; when people reckon among such premises not only natural factors like climate and soil but also the intellectual and historical factors; when, in other words, they come to develop a sense of historical dynamics, of the incomparability of historical phenomena and of their constant inner mobility; when they come to appreciate the vital unity of individual epochs, so that each epoch appears as a whole whose character is reflected in each of its manifestations; when, finally, they accept the conviction that the meaning of events cannot be grasped in abstract and general forms of cognition and that the material needed to understand it must not be sought exclusively in the upper strata of society and in major political events but also in art, economy, material and intellectual culture, in the depths of the workaday world and its men and women, because it is only there that one can grasp what is unique, what is animated by inner forces, and what, in both a more concrete and a more profound sense, is universally valid: then it is to be expected that those insights will also be transferred to the present and that, in consequence, the present too will be seen as incomparable and unique, as animated by inner forces and in a constant state of development; in other words, as a piece of history whose everyday depths and total inner structure lay claim to our interest both in their origins and in the direction taken by their development. Now we know that the insights which I have just enumerated and which, taken all together, represent the intellectual trend known as Historism, were fully developed during the second half of the eighteenth century in Germany. To be sure, elsewhere and earlier there were trends which prepared for Historism and affected the form under which it established itself; but the fact remains that it was thus formed and established in Germany during the age of Goethe. We need not elaborate this, because much excellent material has been published on the subject. Friedrich Meinecke's book on the origins of Historism (Munich and Berlin, 1936) is the finest and most mature treatment I know. In the Germany of those days the revolt against the classicistic and rationalistic taste of France was also carried further than anywhere else. In the process the thing we call separation of styles, the exclusion of realism from high tragedy, was overcome, and this is a basic prerequisite both for a historical and for a contemporary realism of tragic dimensions. And yet at least the second of these, a contemporary realism, did not achieve complete development. Even the literary treatment of historical subjects, which had been begun with so much sensory truth in Goethe's early works, relapsed through Schiller's later development into a kind of separation of styles. Schiller's dualistic genius, which made a sharp separation between ideas and the sensory, increasingly asserted itself, and in his later years his interest went much more to the workings of the moral sense in man and to the freedom which builds upon it than to man's individuality as embedded in the sensory and the historical.

However, we are here more immediately concerned with realism in the treatment of contemporary subjects, and we shall try to determine the causes which prevented its full development in what appears to be such a favorable aesthetic situation. These causes are to be sought in contemporary conditions themselves and in the relation to them of the leading German writers and, more generally, of the leading classes in Germany. In this connection we shall have to deal especially with Goethe, partly because of his dominant influence and partly too because no other writer was endowed with so much natural talent for grasping the sensory and real.

Contemporary conditions in Germany did not easily lend themselves to broad realistic treatment. The social picture was heterogeneous; the general life was conducted in the confused setting of a host of "historical territories," units which had come into existence through dynastic and political contingencies. In each of them the oppressive and at times choking atmosphere was counterbalanced by a certain pious submission and the sense of a historical solidity, all of which was more conducive to speculation, introspection, contemplation, and the development of local idiosyncrasies than to coming to grips with the practical and the real in a spirit of determination and with an awareness of greater contexts and more extensive territories. The origins of German Historism clearly show the impress of the conditions under which it was formed. Justus Möser based his ideas on his penetrating study of the historical development of a very restricted territory, that of the cathedral chapter of Osnabrück. Herder, on the other hand, saw the historical in its broadest and most general implications, yet at the same time in its profound particularity; but he represented it so little concretely that he is of no help toward a grasp of reality. The work of these men already announces the basic tendencies which German Historism was long to retain: local particularism and popular traditionalism on the one hand, and all-inclusive speculation on the other. Both these tendencies are far more concerned with the extra-temporal spirit of history and the completed evolution of what is in existence than with the presently visible germs of the concrete future. Such, in all essentials, the position remained, down to Karl Marx; and that it remained such was due in no small measure to the fact that concrete futurity, which, pressing in from abroad, announced itself more and more imperatively from the last decades of the eighteenth century, aroused horror and revulsion in the majority of outstanding Germans. The French Revolution with all its emanations, the upheavals in its wake, the germs of a new social structure which irresistibly developed from it in spite of all opposition, encountered a passive, defensive, and irresponsive Germany. And it was not only the imperiled powers of the past which met the Revolution in a hostile spirit, it was also the youthful German intellectual movement. And here we find Goethe.

Goethe's attitude toward the Revolution, the Napoleonic era, the wars of liberation, and the dawning tendencies of the nineteenth century is known. It resulted from his solid bourgeois background, from his deepest inclinations and instincts, and finally from his education, which led him ever more to respect slowly evolving forms and to abhor formless ferment and everything recalcitrant to orderly disposition. His political attitudes do not interest us here as such, but only indirectly insofar as they determined his manner of treating contemporary subjects in his literary works.

Those among his works which are wholly or in part and directly or indirectly concerned with events of the Revolution all have one thing in common: they avoid entering into the dynamic forces at work. They sometimes present individual symptoms in the most concrete fashion, as well as such reflections and consequences of the Revolution as are visible in the fates of emigrants, of border districts affected, and of other individuals, families, and groups; but as soon as the whole is at issue, Goethe turns to generalities and ethical principles, sometimes in a disgruntled mood, sometimes in a spirit of cheerfully pessimistic worldly and political wisdom. Thus he writes in his Annals for 1793: "It will be set to the credit of an active, productive mind, of a truly patriotic man intent upon furthering literature at home, if he is frightened by the upheaval of everything that exists, while not the slightest premonition of something better, or only of something else, which is to result from it finds voice in him. His reaction will be shared if he finds it vexatious that such influences extend to Germany, that addle-headed and indeed unworthy individuals usurp the leadership." It was precisely his "vexation" which prevented him from devoting to the social restratification an interest of so lovingly genetic a kind as he did to so many other subjects—an interest of a kind which alone (as he knew better than anyone else) leads to "premonitions finding voice." In a very fine passage of his book on Historism (2, 579), Meinecke explains what it was that appealed to Goethe in the historical: the slow emergence and growth of historical entities through inner urgencies, the development of what is individual from what is typical, and the intervention of unpredictable powers of destiny in such developments. The situation, Meinecke continues, is that Goethe was certainly always aware of the general and vital current of history but that he drew from it only those phenomena which—because he loved them—he could master directly by the cognitional principles which were most peculiarly his own. Here, Meinecke concludes, Goethe's selective principle in regard to history is clearly illuminated, in precisely the sense in which it is contained in the regretful epilogue, "Cursory Description of Conditions at Florence," in the appendix to his translation of Benvenuto Cellini. There Goethe says: "Had Lorenzo [the Magnificent] lived longer, and could a progressive, gradual development of the situation as laid down have taken place, the history of Florence would represent one of the most beautiful of phenomena; but it would seem that in the course of earthly things we shall but seldom experience the fulfillment of beautiful possibilities."

In these explanations, however, I think Meinecke fails to clarify one thing: it seems to me that those parts of history which Goethe ignored, he could have "mastered directly by the cognitional principles which were most peculiarly his own"—if he had loved those parts of history. His personal dislike prevented him from applying those principles, and that is why the phenomena did not reveal their secret to him. The dynamics of opposing social forces and the economic substratum of Florentine history, which he ignored or touched upon but lightly (I am paraphrasing Meinecke here), the civic unrest which he censured as proof of "the infirmities of a badly administered and badly policed state"—these are things which he dislikes, and therefore he turns his back on them. Or at least, when he felt compelled to take up such matters, he ceased to be an observer of the dialectically tragic, and became a classicistic moralist. At such moments, I believe, he no longer senses "the general and vital current of history." For him, the "fulfillment of beautiful possibilities" lies entirely in the flowering of aristocratic cultures in which significant individuals can develop unimpeded, and the principle of order which is present to his mind in such connections is comparatively eudemonistic. It is his aversion to everything violent and explosive—which after all is also a result of the general and vital current of history—that explains why when confronted with the explosive and violent he did not probe beyond the symptomatic, the personal, and the moralistic; why he ascribed so great an importance to the Affair of the Necklace, with its elements of anecdote and intrigue, though after all it was only a symptom of certain conditions in the highest circles and did not reveal anything at all essential about the historical forces at work in the revolutionary crisis; why he was long inclined to see in the remarkable figure of Napoleon a "conclusion" which solved "the riddle in so decisive and unexpected a fashion" (*Campaign in France*, near the end); why finally (to quote, from among many, a particularly emphatic utterance) he wrote in the *Wanderjahre* in connection with a polemic against "prevailing opinions" in the sciences: "State and Church may be able to show cause why they should declare themselves dominant, for they are dealing with the recalcitrant masses, and as long as order is maintained it does not matter by what means; but in the sciences the most absolute freedom is necessary. . . ." (*Wanderjahre*, book 3, chapter 14.) Such attitudes and utterances interest us in the present connection not so much immediately in that they illustrate Goethe's conservative, aristocratic, and anti-revolutionary views, but rather mediately because they explain how Goethe's views prevented him from grasping revolutionary occurrences with the genetico-realistic-sensory method peculiar to him on other occasions. He disliked them. He tried harder to get rid of them than to understand them, and ridding himself of them meant assuming toward them a moralistic attitude in part condemnatory and in part serenely philosophical. For him, they represented the vulgar which subdues us all, "the vile . . . [which] is in power, whatever else you may be told."

This agrees with the fact that his other works of a serious nature, insofar as they depict contemporary social conditions, present the destinies of their characters on a solid basis of bourgeois class-consciousness without giving us much of an impression of the underlying political and economic movements of the period. Time and place are often alluded to in the most general way, and the reader feels that in spite of the graphic concreteness of many details he is—as far as the political and economic whole is concerned—being conducted through an indeterminate and unidentifiable landscape. By far the most realistic is *Wilhelm Meisters Lehrjahre*. Jacobi—as Goethe tells us in his Annals for 1795—thought that in that work "the realism, pertaining as it does to an inferior social stratum, is not edifying." Other contemporaries and later readers were charmed by just that realism; but we must not let this blind us to the fact that it is confined to a very narrow domain. Concrete political and politico-economic conditions receive no expression. The contemporary reshuffling of social strata hardly appears. To be sure, it is mentioned in one place. The occasion is as follows: A group of upper-class people is taking precautionary measures against revolutionary disturbances. Since "at this time it is extremely inadvisable to own property in only one place, to invest one's money in only one locality," they scatter to all parts of the world, acquire holdings everywhere, and "guarantee each other's existence in case a state revolution should definitely drive one or another of them from his estates" (book 8, chapter 7). Such precautionary measures can hardly be understood in terms of the novel itself, for the other and especially the earlier parts give no inkling of a politico-social unrest which could justify a plan for security so unusual at the period. The middle-class world lies before the reader's eyes in an almost timeless calm. As we read of Wilhelm's father, his grandfather, the father of his friend Werner, their habits, their collections, their affairs, their views, we have the impression of a perfectly peaceful society which changes only very gradually, in the course of successive generations. It is a completely undisturbed and unshaken class structure which appears, for example, in the letter which young Wilhelm writes to his friend Werner to justify his intention of becoming an actor. There we read (book 5, chapter 3):

> . . . I do not know how it is in other countries, but here in Germany only the nobleman has the possibility of a certain generalized personal culture, if this term is permissible. A bourgeois can achieve great merit; at a pinch he can even cultivate his mind; but his personality will be lost, try as he may. . . .
>
> Since the nobleman in ordinary life knows no barriers, since he can be turned into a king or a kinglike figure, it follows that he can everywhere appear before his equals with a calm mind. He can press ahead in all spheres, whereas nothing is more becoming to the bourgeois than a pure and settled awareness of the limits set for him. He may not ask himself, "What are you?" but only, "What have you? What understanding, what knowledge, what skills, what fortune?" While the nobleman gives everything by presenting his person, the bourgeois gives nothing through his personality and is not supposed to. The former may and should "appear to be"; the latter must only "be" and what he attempts to "appear to be" is ridiculous or insipid. The former is expected to

act a part, perform a function, the latter must do his share and produce results; he must develop specific skills to make himself useful, and it is taken for granted beforehand that his nature is not and should not possess harmony, because, in order to make himself useful in *one* way, he must neglect everything else.

This differentiation is not the fault of the noblemen's arrogance or of the bourgeois' conformability, but results from the very structure of society. Whether or not this state of affairs is going to change and if so, what it is that is going to change, is of little interest to me. However that is, as things now stand I must think of myself and of how I can protect and realize what I feel as an irreplaceable need.

I happen to have an irresistible propensity for the very kind of harmonious development of my nature which is denied me by my birth. . . .

This too is a significant fragment of the great confession. Goethe too was a burgher's son in that class-conscious social order. He too was irresistibly inclined toward such a harmonious development of his nature. His ideal of personal development too was rooted in the class-conscious and aristocratic concept of a lofty and unspecialized universality and of "appearance," although in his hands it became an all-inclusive dedication to individual details. He too, like Wilhelm Meister, sought his own particular way out of his bourgeois class, without concerning himself with whether and how the constitution of society might one day change. And he found the way that corresponded to his desires much more quickly and surely than Wilhelm Meister, who hoped to attain his goal by becoming an actor; he found it when, in opposition to his father's instinctive mistrust, he obeyed the summons of the Duke to Weimar and there, within the narrowest frame, created for himself a universal position which was perfectly suited to him. When, seventeen years later, he was on his way back from the campaign in France—where he had most impressively been made aware that "from here and today a new epoch in the history of the world begins"—he received in Trier a letter from his mother: an uncle of his, who had been a magistrate (in consequence of which his closest relatives had not been eligible for the Frankfurt council), had died; and now the question was presented to him whether he would accept the position of a Frankfurt city councillor if he should be elected. There could be no doubt in his mind; he must refuse—he had long since decided otherwise about his life. It is instructive to read the arguments he presented on this occasion and the reasons he gave (*Kampagne in Frankreich*, Trier, October 29). The passage concludes with the following sentences:

> For how was I to prove myself actively effective in the very special circle for which—possibly more than for any other—a man must be trained loyally and step by step? For so many years I had accustomed myself to affairs commensurate with my talents and furthermore of a kind which were hardly likely to be demanded for urban needs and purposes. Indeed, I was justified in adding that, if only burghers are received into the Council, that condition was now so foreign to me that I had to consider myself essentially a non-native. . . .

The immobility of the social background in the *Wahlverwandtschaften* is even more pronounced than in *Wilhelm Meister*. In contrast, the most vivid contemporary movement is to be found in the autobiographical works. The most varied scenes, events, and conditions of public life are presented with sensory truth. But their succession is determined by the course of Goethe's own life and development, and each of them becomes a subject of representation less for its own sake than by virtue of its importance for Goethe. The real interest—manifest in dynamic and genetic treatment—attaches especially to personal matters and the intellectual movements in which Goethe participated, while public conditions are seen, though often graphically and vividly, as established and quiescent.

We are left with the conclusion that Goethe never represented the reality of contemporary social life dynamically, as the germ of developments in process and in the future. Where he deals with the trends of the nineteenth century, he does so in general reflections, and these are almost always value judgments: they are predominantly mistrustful and disapproving. The technical development of machinery, the progressively conscious participation of the masses in public life, were distasteful to him. He foresaw a shallowing of intellectual life; he saw nothing to make up for such a loss. He also, as we know, remained aloof from the political patriotism which, if conditions had been more favorable at the time, might well have led to a unification of the social situation in Germany. If that had happened then, perhaps too the integration of Germany into the emerging new reality of Europe and the world might have been prepared more calmly, have been accomplished with fewer uncertainties and less violence. He deplored the political condition of Germany, but he did so dispassionately and accepted it as a fact. In a polemic essay (*Literarischer Sansculottismus, Jubiläumsausgabe*, 36, 139) he explains that classical national works can arise only where the author "finds in the history of his nation great events and their consequences in a felicitous and significant union." In Germany, he continues, this is not the case. "One need but consider our position [i.e., the position of German writers] as it was and is, and examine the conditions under which German writers pursue their careers, one will then easily find the point of view from which they should be judged. Nowhere in Germany is there a center of social *savoir vivre* where authors might congregate and, in their several domains, develop in one common manner and in one common direction. Born in scattered places, subjected to most different forms of education, generally left only to themselves and the impressions of very different conditions. . . ." Yet his regret over this state of affairs is only half-hearted, for in a passage which occurs shortly before, he had said: "But on the other hand the German nation should not be blamed if its geographic situation holds it closely together while its political situation partitions it. We shall not wish for upheavals which might prepare classical works in Germany." This essay, it is true, was written before 1795, but in later years too he would not have "wished for upheavals" which might have been able to create "a center of social *savoir vivre*" in Germany.

It is utterly silly to wish that Goethe might have been different from what he was. His instincts, his inclinations, the social position which he created for himself, the limits which he imposed upon his activities, all these things are part of him. None of them can be thought away without disrupting the whole. But as we look back upon all that has happened since, we are yet tempted to imagine what effect might have been exerted upon German literature and German society, if Goethe, with his vigorous sensuality, his mastery of life, his far-reaching and untrammeled vision, had devoted more interest and constructive effort to the emerging modern structure of life.

The fragmentation and limitation in the realm of realism which we have noted remained the same in Goethe's younger contemporaries and in the following generations. Until toward the end of the nineteenth century the most important works which undertook to treat contemporary social subjects seriously at all remained in the genres of semi-fantasy or of idyl or at least in the narrow realm of the local. They portray the economic, the social, and the political as in a state of quiescence. This applies equally to such different and important writers as Jean Paul, E. T. A. Hoffmann, Jeremias Gotthelf, Adalbert Stifter, Hebbel, Storm—the social realism in Fontane still does not go very deep, and the political current in Gottfried Keller is pronouncedly Swiss. Perhaps Kleist, and Büchner later, might have been able to bring about a change in direction, but they had no opportunity to develop freely and they died too young.

18

IN THE HÔTEL DE LA MOLE

Julien Sorel, the hero of Stendhal's novel *Le Rouge et le Noir* (1830), an ambitious and passionate young man, son of an uneducated petty bourgeois from the Franche-Comté, is conducted by a series of circumstances from the seminary at Besançon, where he has been studying theology, to Paris and the position of secretary to a gentleman of rank, the Marquis de la Mole, whose confidence he gains. Mathilde, the Marquis's daughter, is a girl of nineteen, witty, spoiled, imaginative, and so arrogant that her own position and circle begin to bore her. The dawning of her passion for her father's *domestique* is one of Stendhal's masterpieces and has been greatly admired. One of the preparatory scenes, in which her interest in Julien begins to awaken, is the following, from volume 2, chapter 14:

> Un matin que l'abbé travaillait avec Julien, dans la bibliothèque du marquis, à l'éternel procès de Frilair:
>
> —Monsieur, dit Julien tout à coup, dîner tous les jours avec madame la marquise, est-ce un de mes devoirs, ou est-ce une bonté que l'on a pour moi?
>
> —C'est un honneur insigne! reprit l'abbé, scandalisé. Jamais M. N. . . l'académicien, qui, depuis quinze ans, fait une cour assidue, n'a pu l'obtenir pour son neveu M. Tanbeau.
>
> —C'est pour moi, monsieur, la partie la plus pénible de mon emploi. Je m'ennuyais moins au séminaire. Je vois bâiller quelquefois jusqu'à mademoiselle de La Mole, qui pourtant doit être accoutumée à l'amabilité des amis de la maison. J'ai peur de m'endormir. De grâce, obtenez-moi la permission d'aller dîner à quarante sous dans quelque auberge obscure.
>
> L'abbé, véritable parvenu, était fort sensible à l'honneur de dîner avec un grand seigneur. Pendant qu'il s'efforçait de faire comprendre ce sentiment par Julien, un léger bruit leur fit tourner la tête. Julien vit mademoiselle de La Mole qui écoutait. Il rougit. Elle était venue chercher un livre et avait tout entendu; elle prit quelque considération pour Julien. Celui-là n'est pas né à genoux, pensa-t-elle, comme ce vieil abbé. Dieu! qu'il est laid.

A dîner, Julien n'osait pas regarder mademoiselle de La Mole, mais elle eut la bonté de lui adresser la parole. Ce jour-là, on attendait beaucoup de monde, elle l'engagea à rester. . . .

(One morning while the Abbé was with Julien in the Marquis's library, working on the interminable Frilair suit:

"Monsieur," said Julien suddenly, "is dining with Madame la Marquise every day one of my duties, or is it a favor to me?"

"It is an extraordinary honor!" the Abbé corrected him, scandalized. "Monsieur N., the academician, who has been paying court here assiduously for fifteen years, was never able to manage it for his nephew, Monsieur Tanbeau."

"For me, Monsieur, it is the most painful part of my position. Nothing at the seminary bored me so much. I even see Mademoiselle de la Mole yawning sometimes, yet she must be well inured to the amiabilities of the guests of this house. I am in dread of falling asleep. Do me the favor of getting me permission to eat a forty-sou dinner at some inn."

The Abbé, a true parvenu, was extremely conscious of the honor of dining with a noble lord. While he was trying to inculcate this sentiment into Julien, a slight sound made them turn. Julien saw Mademoiselle de la Mole listening. He blushed. She had come for a book and had heard everything; she began to feel a certain esteem for Julien. He was not born on his knees, like that old Abbé, she thought. God, how ugly he is!

At dinner Julien did not dare to look at Mademoiselle de la Mole, but she condescended to speak to him. A number of guests were expected that day, she asked him to stay. . . .)

The scene, as I said, is designed to prepare for a passionate and extremely tragic love intrigue. Its function and its psychological value we shall not here discuss; they lie outside of our subject. What interests us in the scene is this: it would be almost incomprehensible without a most accurate and detailed knowledge of the political situation, the social stratification, and the economic circumstances of a perfectly definite historical moment, namely, that in which France found itself just before the July Revolution; accordingly, the novel bears the subtitle, *Chronique de 1830*. Even the boredom which reigns in the dining room and salon of this noble house is no ordinary boredom. It does not arise from the fortuitous personal dullness of the people who are brought together there; among them there are highly educated, witty, and sometimes important people, and the master of the house is intelligent and amiable. Rather, we are confronted, in their boredom, by a phenomenon politically and ideologically characteristic of the Restoration period. In the seventeenth century, and even more in the eighteenth, the corresponding salons were anything but boring. But the inadequately implemented attempt which the Bourbon regime made to restore conditions long since made obsolete by events, creates, among its adherents in the official and ruling classes, an atmosphere of pure convention, of limitation, of constraint and lack of freedom, against which the intelligence and good will of the persons involved are powerless. In these salons the things which interest everyone—the political and religious problems of the present, and consequently most of the subjects of its literature or of that of the very recent past—could not be discussed, or at best could be discussed only in official phrases so mendacious that a man of taste and tact would rather avoid them. How different from the intellectual daring of the famous eighteenth-century salons, which, to be sure, did not dream of the dangers to their own existence which they were unleashing! Now the dangers are known, and life is governed by the fear that the catastrophe of 1793 might be repeated. As these people are conscious that they no longer themselves believe in the thing they represent, and that they are bound to be defeated in any public argument, they choose to talk of nothing but the weather, music, and court gossip. In addition, they are obliged to accept as allies snobbish and corrupt people from among the newly-rich bourgeoisie, who, with the unashamed baseness of their ambition and with their fear for their ill-gotten wealth, completely vitiate the atmosphere of society. So much for the pervading boredom.

But Julien's reaction, too, and the very fact that he and the former director of his seminary, the Abbé Pirard, are present at all in the house of the Marquis de la Mole, are only to be understood in terms of the actual historical moment. Julien's passionate and imaginative nature has from his earliest youth been filled with enthusiasm for the great ideas of the Revolution and of Rousseau, for the great events of the Napoleonic period; from his earliest youth he has felt nothing but loathing and scorn for the piddling hypocrisy and the petty lying corruption of the classes in power since Napoleon's fall. He is too imaginative, too ambitious, and too fond of power, to be satisfied with a mediocre life within the bourgeoisie, such as his friend Fouquet proposes to him. Having observed that a man of petty-bourgeois origin can attain to a situation of command only through the all-powerful Church, he has consciously and deliberately become a hypocrite; and his great talents would assure him a brilliant intellectual career, were not his real personal and political feelings, the direct passionateness of his nature, prone to burst forth at decisive moments. One such moment of self-betrayal we have in the passage before us, when Julien confides his feelings in the Marquise's salon to the Abbé Pirard, his former teacher and protector; for the intellectual freedom to which it testifies is unthinkable without an admixture of intellectual arrogance and a sense of inner superiority hardly becoming in a young ecclesiastic and protégé of the house. (In this particular instance his frankness does him no harm; the Abbé Pirard is his friend, and upon Mathilde, who happens to overhear him, his words make an entirely different impression from that which he must expect and fear.) The Abbé is here described as a true parvenu, who knows how highly the honor of sitting at a great man's table should be esteemed and hence disapproves of Julien's remarks; as another motive for the Abbé's disapproval Stendhal could have cited the fact that uncritical submission to the evil of this world, in full consciousness that it is evil, is a typical attitude for strict Jansenists; and the Abbé Pirard is a Jansenist. We know from the previous part of the novel that as director of the seminary at Besançon he had had to endure much persecution and much chicanery on account of his Jansenism and his strict piety which no intrigues could touch; for the clergy of the province were under the influence of the Jesuits. When the Marquis de la Mole's most powerful opponent, the Abbé de Frilair, a vicar-general to the bishop, had brought a suit against him, the Marquis had made the Abbé Pirard his confidant and had thus learned to value his intelligence and uprightness; so that finally, to free him from his untenable position at Besançon, the Marquis had procured him a benefice in Paris and somewhat later had taken the Abbé's favorite pupil, Julien Sorel, into his household as private secretary.

The characters, attitudes, and relationships of the dramatis personae, then, are very closely connected with contemporary historical circumstances; contemporary political and social conditions are woven into the action in a manner more detailed and more real than had been exhibited in any earlier novel, and indeed in any works of literary art except those expressly purporting to be politico-satirical tracts. So logically and systematically to situate the tragically conceived life of a man of low social position (as here that of Julien Sorel) within the most concrete kind of contemporary history and to develop it therefrom—this is an entirely new and highly significant phenomenon. The other circles in which Julien Sorel moves—his father's family, the house of the mayor of Verrières, M. de Rênal, the seminary at Besançon—are sociologically defined in conformity with the historical moment with the same penetration as is the La Mole household; and not one of the minor characters—the old priest Chélan, for example, or the director of the *dépôt de mendicité,* Valenod—would be conceivable outside the particular historical situation of the Restoration period, in the manner in which they are set before us. The same laying of a contemporary foundation for events is to be found in Stendhal's other novels—still incomplete and too narrowly circumscribed in *Armance,* but fully developed in the later works: in the *Chartreuse de Parme* (which, however, since its setting is a place not yet greatly affected by modern development, sometimes gives the effect of being a historical novel), as also in *Lucien Leuwen,* a novel of the Louis Philippe period, which Stendhal left unfinished. In the latter, indeed, in the form in which it has come down to us, the element of current history and politics is too heavily emphasized: it is not always wholly integrated into the course of the action and is set forth in far too great detail in proportion to the principal theme; but perhaps in a final revision Stendhal would have achieved an organic articulation of the whole. Finally, his autobiographical works, despite the capricious and erratic "egotism" of their style and manner, are likewise far more closely, essentially, and concretely connected with the politics, sociology, and economics of the period than are, for example, the corresponding works of Rousseau or Goethe; one feels that the great events of contemporary history affected Stendhal much more directly than they did the other two; Rousseau did not live to see them, and Goethe had managed to keep aloof from them.

To have stated this is also to have stated what circumstance it was which, at that particular moment and in a man of that particular period, gave rise to modern tragic realism based on the contemporary; it was the first of the great movements of modern times in which large masses of men consciously took part—the French Revolution with all the consequent convulsions which spread from it over Europe. From the Reformation movement, which was no less powerful and which aroused the masses no less, it is distinguished by the much faster tempo of its spread, its mass effects, and the changes which it produced in practical daily life within a comparatively extensive territory; for the progress then achieved in transportation and communication, together with the spread of elementary education resulting from the trends of the Revolution itself, made it possible to mobilize the people far more rapidly and in a far more unified direction; everyone was reached by the same ideas and events far more quickly, more consciously, and more uniformly. For Europe there began that process of temporal concentration, both of historical events themselves and of everyone's knowledge of them, which has since made tremendous progress and which not only permits us to prophesy a unification of human life throughout the world but has in a certain sense already achieved it. Such a development abrogates or renders powerless the entire social structure of orders and categories previously held valid; the tempo of the changes demands a perpetual and extremely difficult effort toward inner adaptation and produces intense concomitant crises. He who would account to himself for his real life and his place in human society is obliged to do so upon a far wider practical foundation and in a far larger context than before, and to be continually conscious that the social base upon which he lives is not constant for a moment but is perpetually changing through convulsions of the most various kinds.

We may ask ourselves how it came about that modern consciousness of reality began to find literary form for the first time precisely in Henri Beyle of Grenoble. Beyle-Stendhal was a man of keen intelligence, quick and alive, mentally independent and courageous, but not quite a great figure. His ideas are often forceful and inspired, but they are erratic, arbitrarily advanced, and, despite all their show of boldness, lacking in inward certainty and continuity. There is something unsettled about his whole nature: his fluctuation between realistic candor in general and silly mystification in particulars, between cold self-control, rapturous abandonment to sensual pleasures, and insecure and sometimes sentimental vaingloriousness, is not always easy to put up with; his literary style is very impressive and unmistakably original, but it is short-winded, not uniformly successful, and only seldom wholly takes possession of and fixes the subject. But, such as he was, he offered himself to the moment; circumstances seized him, tossed him about, and laid upon him a unique and unexpected destiny; they formed him so that he was compelled to come to terms with reality in a way which no one had done before him.

When the Revolution broke out Stendhal was a boy of six; when he left his native city of Grenoble and his reactionary, solidly bourgeois family, who though glumly sulking at the new situation were still very wealthy, and went to Paris, he was sixteen. He arrived there immediately after Napoleon's *coup d'état*; one of his relatives, Pierre Daru, was an influential adherent of the First Consul; after some hesitations and interruptions, Stendhal made a brilliant career in the Napoleonic administration. He saw Europe on Napoleon's expeditions; he grew to be a man, and indeed an extremely elegant man of the world; he also became, it appears, a useful administrative official and a reliable, cold-blooded organizer who did not lose his calm even in danger. When Napoleon's fall threw Stendhal out of the saddle, he was in his thirty-second year. The first, active, successful, and brilliant part of his career was over. Thenceforth he has no profession and no place claims him. He can go where he pleases, so long as he has money enough and so long as the suspicious officials of the post-Napoleonic period have no objection to his sojourns. But his financial circumstances gradually become worse; in 1821 he is exiled from Milan, where he had first settled down, by Metternich's police; he goes to Paris, and there he lives for another nine years, without a profession, alone, and with very slender means. After the July Revolution his friends get him a post in the diplomatic service; since the Austrians refuse him an exequatur for Trieste, he has to go as consul to the little port of Cività Vecchia; it is a dreary place to live, and there are those who try to get him into trouble if he prolongs his visits to Rome unduly; to be sure, he is allowed to spend a few years in Paris on leave—so long, that is, as one of his protectors is Minister of Foreign Affairs. Finally he falls seriously ill in Cività Vecchia and is given another leave in Paris; he dies there in 1842, smitten by apoplexy in the street, not yet sixty. This is the second half of his life; during this period, he acquires the reputation of being a witty, eccentric, politically and morally unreliable man; during this period, he begins to write. He writes first on music, on Italy and Italian art, on love; it is not until he is forty-three and is in Paris during the first flowering of the Romantic movement (to which he contributed in his way) that he publishes his first novel.

From this sketch of his life it should appear that he first reached the point of accounting for himself, and the point of realistic writing, when he was seeking a haven in his "storm-tossed boat," and discovered that, for his boat, there was no fit and safe haven; when, though in no sense weary or discouraged, yet already a man of forty, whose early and successful career lay far behind him, alone and comparatively poor, he became aware, with all the sting of that knowledge, that he belonged nowhere. For the first time, the social world around him became a problem; his feeling that he was different from other men, until now borne easily and proudly, doubtless now first became the predominant concern of his consciousness and finally the recurring theme of his literary activity. Stendhal's realistic writing grew out of his discomfort in the post-Napoleonic world and his consciousness that he did not belong to it and had no place in it. Discomfort in the given world and inability to become part of it is, to be sure, characteristic of Rousseauan romanticism and it is probable that Stendhal had something of that even in his youth; there is something of it in his congenital disposition, and the course of his youth can only have strengthened such tendencies, which, so to speak, harmonized with the tenor of life of his generation; on the other hand, he did not write his recollections of his youth, the *Vie de Henri Brulard*, until he was in his thirties, and we must allow for the possibility that, from the viewpoint of his later development, from the viewpoint of 1832, he overstressed such motifs of individualistic isolation. It is, in any case, certain that the motifs and expressions of his isolation and his problematic relation to society are wholly different from the corresponding phenomena in Rousseau and his early romantic disciples.

Stendhal, in contrast to Rousseau, had a bent for practical affairs and the requisite ability; he aspired to sensual enjoyment of life as given; he did not withdraw from practical reality from the outset, did not entirely condemn it from the outset—instead he attempted, and successfully at first, to master it. Material success and material enjoyments were desirable to him; he admires energy and the ability to master life, and even his cherished dreams (*le silence du bonheur*) are more sensual, more concrete, more dependent upon human society and human creations (Cimarosa, Mozart, Shakespeare, Italian art) than those of the *Promeneur Solitaire*. Not until success and pleasure began to slip away from him, not until practical circumstances threatened to cut the ground from under his feet, did the society of his time become a problem and a subject to him. Rousseau did not find himself at home in the social world he encountered, which did not appreciably change during his lifetime; he rose in it without thereby becoming happier or more reconciled to it, while it appeared to remain unchanged. Stendhal lived while one earthquake after another shook the foundations of society; one of the earthquakes jarred him out of the everyday course of life prescribed for men of his station, flung him, like many of his contemporaries, into previously inconceivable adventures, events, responsibilities, tests of himself, and experiences of freedom and power; another flung him back into a new everyday which he thought more boring, more stupid, and less attractive than the old; the most interesting thing about it was that it too gave no promise of enduring; new upheavals were in the air, and indeed broke out here and there even though not with the power of the first.

Because Stendhal's interest arose out of the experiences of his own life, it was held not by the structure of a possible society but by the changes in the society actually given. Temporal perspective is a factor of which he never loses sight, the concept of incessantly changing forms and manners of life dominates his thoughts—the more so as it holds a hope for him: In 1880 or 1930 I shall find readers who understand me! I will cite a few examples. When he speaks of La Bruyère's *esprit* (*Henri Brulard*, chapter 30), it is apparent to him that this type of formative endeavor of the intellect has lost in validity since 1789: *L'esprit, si délicieux pour qui le sent, ne dure pas. Comme une pêche passe en quelques jours, l'esprit passe en deux cents ans, et bien plus vite, s'il y a révolution dans les rapports que les classes d'une société ont entre elles.* The *Souvenirs d'égotisme* contain an abundance of observations (for the most part truly prophetic) based on temporal perspective. He foresees (chapter 7, near the end) that "at the time when this chatter is read" it will have become a commonplace to make the ruling classes responsible for the crimes of thieves and murderers; he fears, at the beginning of chapter 9, that all his bold utterances, which he dares put forth only with fear and trembling, will have become platitudes ten years after his death, if heaven grants him a decent allowance of life, say eighty or ninety years; in the next chapter he speaks of one of his friends who pays an unusually high price for the favors of an *honnête femme du peuple*, and adds in explanation: *cinq cents francs en 1832, c'est comme mille en 1872*—that is, forty years after the time at which he is writing and thirty after his death.

It would be possible to quote many more passages of the same general import. But it is unnecessary, for the element of time-perspective is apparent everywhere in the presentation itself. In his realistic writings, Stendhal everywhere deals with the reality which presents itself to him: *Je prends au hasard ce qui se trouve sur ma route*, he says not far from the passage just quoted: in his effort to understand men, he does not pick and choose among them; this method, as Montaigne knew, is the best for eliminating the arbitrariness of one's own constructions, and for surrendering oneself to reality as given. But the reality which he encountered was so constituted that, without permanent reference to the immense changes of the immediate past and without a premonitory searching after the imminent changes of the future, one could not represent it; all the human figures and all the human events in his work appear upon a ground politically and socially disturbed. To bring the significance of this graphically before us, we have but to compare him with the best-known realistic writers of the pre-Revolutionary eighteenth century: with Lesage or the Abbé Prévost, with the preeminent Henry Fielding or with Goldsmith; we have but to consider how much more accurately and profoundly he enters into given contemporary reality than Voltaire, Rousseau, and the youthful realistic work of Schiller, and upon how much broader a basis than Saint-Simon, whom, though in the very incomplete edition then available, he read assiduously. Insofar as the serious realism of modern times cannot represent man otherwise than as embedded in a total reality, political, social, and economic, which is concrete and constantly evolving—as is the case today in any novel or film—Stendhal is its founder.

However, the attitude from which Stendhal apprehends the world of event and attempts to reproduce it with all its interconnections is as yet hardly influenced by Historism—which, though it penetrated into France in his time, had little effect upon him. For that very reason we have referred in the last few pages to time-perspective and to a constant consciousness of changes and cataclysms, but not to a comprehension of evolutions. It is not too easy to describe Stendhal's inner attitude toward social phenomena. It is his aim to seize their every nuance; he most accurately represents the particular structure of any given milieu, he has no preconceived rationalistic system concerning the general factors which determine social life, nor any pattern-concept of how the ideal society ought to look; but in particulars his representation of events is oriented, wholly in the spirit of classic ethical psychology, upon an *analyse du cœur humain*, not upon discovery or premonitions of historical forces; we find rationalistic, empirical, sensual motifs in him, but hardly those of romantic Historism. Absolutism, religion and the Church, the privileges of rank, he regards very much as would an average protagonist of the Enlightenment, that is as a web of superstition, deceit, and intrigue; in general, artfully contrived intrigue (together with passion) plays a decisive role in his plot construction, while the historical forces which are the basis of it hardly appear. Naturally all this can be explained by his political viewpoint, which was democratic-republican; this alone sufficed to render him immune to romantic Historism; besides which the emphatic manner of such writers as Chateaubriand displeased him in the extreme. On the other hand, he treats even the classes of society which, according to his views, should be closest to him, extremely critically and without a trace of the emotional values which romanticism attached to the word people. The practically active bourgeoisie with its respectable money-making, inspires him with unconquerable boredom, he shudders at the *vertu républicaine* of the United States, and despite his ostensible lack of sentimentality he regrets the fall of the social culture of the *ancien régime. Ma foi, l'esprit manque,* he writes in chapter 30 of *Henri Brulard, chacun réserve toutes ses forces pour un métier qui lui donne un rang dans le monde.* No longer is birth or intelligence or the self-cultivation of the *honnête homme* the deciding factor—it is ability in some profession. This is no world in which Stendhal-Dominique can live and breathe. Of course, like his heroes, he too can work and work efficiently, when that is what is called for. But how can one take anything like practical professional work seriously in the long run! Love, music, passion, intrigue, heroism—these are the things that make life worthwhile. . . .

Stendhal is an aristocratic son of the *ancien régime grande bourgeoisie,* he will and can be no nineteenth-century bourgeois. He says so himself time and again: My views were Republican even in my youth but my family handed down their aristocratic instincts to me (*Brulard,* ch. 14); since the Revolution theater audiences have become stupid (*Brulard,* ch. 22); I was a liberal myself (in 1821), and yet I found the liberals *outrageusement niais* (*Souvenirs d'égotisme,* ch. 6); to converse with a *gros marchand de province* makes me dull and unhappy all day (*Egotisme,* ch. 7 and *passim*)—these and similar remarks, which sometimes also refer to his physical constitution (*La nature m'a donné les nerfs délicats et la peau sensible d'une femme, Brulard,* ch. 32), occur plentifully. Sometimes he has pronounced accesses of socialism: in 1811, he writes, energy was to be found only in the class *qui est en lutte avec les vrais besoins* (*Brulard,* ch. 2). But he finds the smell and the noise of the masses unendurable, and in his books, outspokenly realistic though they are in other respects, we find no "people," either in the romantic "folk" sense or in the socialist sense—only petty bourgeois, and occasional accessory figures such as soldiers, domestic servants, and coffee-house mademoiselles. Finally, he sees the individual man far less as the product of his historical situation and as taking part in it, than as an atom within it; a man seems to have been thrown almost by chance into the milieu in which he lives; it is a resistance with which he can deal more or less successfully, not really a culture-medium with which he is organically connected. In addition, Stendhal's conception of mankind is on the whole preponderantly materialistic and sensualistic; an excellent illustration of this occurs in *Henri Brulard* (ch. 26): *J'appelle* caractère *d'un homme sa manière habituelle d'aller à la chasse du bonheur, en termes plus claires, mais moins qualificatifs,* l'ensemble de ses habitudes morales. But in Stendhal, happiness, even though highly organized human beings can find it only in the mind, in art, passion, or fame, always has a far more sensory and earthy coloring than in the romanticists. His aversion to philistine efficiency, to the type of bourgeois that was coming into existence, could be romantic too. But a romantic would hardly conclude a passage on his distaste for money-making with the words: *J'ai eu le rare plaisir de faire toute ma vie à peu près ce qui me plaisait* (*Brulard*, ch. 32). His conception of *esprit* and of freedom is still entirely that of the pre-Revolutionary eighteenth century, although it is only with effort and a little spasmodically that he succeeds in realizing it in his own person. For freedom he has to pay the price of poverty and loneliness and his *esprit* easily becomes paradox, bitter and wounding: *une gaité qui fait peur* (*Brulard*, ch. 6). His *esprit* no longer has the self-assurance of the Voltaire period; he manages neither his social life nor that particularly important part of it, his sexual relations, with the easy mastery of a gentleman of rank of the *ancien régime*; he even goes so far as to say that he cultivated *esprit* only to conceal his passion for a woman whom he did not possess—*cette peur, mille fois répétée, a été, dans le fait, le principe dirigeant de ma vie pendant dix ans* (*Égotisme*, ch. 1). Such traits make him appear a man born too late who tries in vain to realize the form of life of a past period; other elements of his character, the merciless objectivity of his realistic power, his courageous assertion of his personality against the triviality of the rising *juste milieu*, and much more, show him as the forerunner of certain later intellectual modes and forms of life; but he always feels and experiences the reality of his period as a resistance. That very thing makes his realism (though it proceeded, if at all, to only a very slight degree from a loving genetic comprehension of evolutions—that is, from the historistic attitude) so energetic and so closely connected with his own existence: the realism of this *cheval ombrageux* is a product of his fight for self-assertion. And this explains the fact that the stylistic level of his great realistic novels is much closer to the old great and heroic concept of tragedy than is that of most later realists—Julien Sorel is much more a "hero" than the characters of Balzac, to say nothing of Flaubert.

That the rule of style promulgated by classical aesthetics which excluded any material realism from serious tragic works was already giving way in the eighteenth century is well known; we have discussed the matter in the two preceding chapters. Even in France the relaxation of this rule can be observed as early as the first half of the eighteenth century; during the second half, it was Diderot particularly who propagated a more intermediate level of style both in theory and in practice, but he did not pass beyond the boundaries of the bourgeois and the pathetic. In his novels, especially in the *Neveu de Rameau*, characters from everyday life and of intermediate if not low station are portrayed with a certain seriousness; but the seriousness is more reminiscent of the moralistic and satirical attitudes of the Enlightenment than of nineteenth-century realism. In the figure and the work of Rousseau there is unmistakably a germ of the later evolution. Rousseau, as Meinecke says in his book on Historism (2, 390), was able "even though he did not attain to complete historical thinking, to help in awakening the new sense of the individual merely through the revelation of his own unique individuality." Meinecke is here speaking of historical thinking; but a corresponding statement may be made in respect to realism. Rousseau is not properly realistic; to his material—especially when it is his own life—he brings such a strongly apologetic and ethico-critical interest, his judgment of events is so influenced by his principles of natural law, that the reality of the social world does not become for him an immediate subject; yet the example of the *Confessions*, which attempts to represent his own existence in its true relation to contemporary life, is important as a stylistic model for writers who had more sense of reality as given than he. Perhaps even more important in its indirect influence upon serious realism is his politicizing of the idyllic concept of Nature. This created a wish-image for the design of life which, as we know, exercised an immense power of suggestion and which, it was believed, could be directly realized; the wish-image soon showed itself to be in absolute opposition to the established historical reality, and the contrast grew stronger and more tragic the more apparent it became that the realization of the wish-image was miscarrying. Thus practical historical reality became a problem in a way hitherto unknown—far more concretely and far more immediately.

In the first decades after Rousseau's death, in French pre-romanticism, the effect of that immense disillusionment was, to be sure, quite the opposite: it showed itself, among the most important writers, in a tendency to flee from contemporary reality. The Revolution, the Empire, and even the Restoration are poor in realistic literary works. The heroes of pre-romantic novels betray a sometimes almost morbid aversion to entering into contemporary life. The contradiction between the natural, which he desired, and the historically based reality which he encountered, had already become tragic for Rousseau; but the very contradiction had roused him to do battle for the natural. He was no longer alive when the Revolution and Napoleon created a situation which, though new, was, in his sense of the word, no more "natural" but instead again entangled historically. The next generation, deeply influenced by his ideas and hopes, experienced the victorious resistance of the real and the historical, and it was especially those who had fallen most deeply under Rousseau's fascination, who found themselves not at home in the new world which had utterly destroyed their hopes. They entered into opposition to it or they turned away from it. Of Rousseau they carried on only the inward rift, the tendency to flee from society, the need to retire and to be alone; the other side of Rousseau's nature, the revolutionary and fighting side, they had lost. The outward circumstances which destroyed the unity of intellectual life, and the dominating influence of literature in France, also contributed to this development; from the outbreak of the Revolution to the fall of Napoleon there is hardly a literary work of any consequence which did not exhibit symptoms of this flight from contemporary reality, and such symptoms are still very prevalent among the romantic groups after 1820. They appear most purely and most completely in Sénancour. But in its very negativeness the attitude of the majority of pre-romantics to the historical reality of their time is far more seriously problematic than is the attitude of the society of the Enlightenment. The Rousseauist movement and the great disillusionment it underwent was a prerequisite for the rise of the modern conception of reality. Rousseau, by passionately contrasting the natural condition of man with the existing reality of life determined by history, made the latter a practical problem; now for the first time the eighteenth-century style of historically unproblematic and unmoved presentation of life became valueless.

Romanticism, which had taken shape much earlier in Germany and

England, and whose historical and individualistic trends had been long in preparation in France, reached its full development after 1820; and, as we know, it was precisely the principle of a mixture of styles which Victor Hugo and his friends made the slogan of their movement; in that principle the contrast to the classical treatment of subjects and the classical literary language stood out most obviously. Yet in Hugo's formula there is something too pointedly antithetical; for him it is a matter of mixing the sublime and the grotesque. These are both extremes of style which give no consideration to reality. And in practice he did not aim at understandingly bestowing form upon reality as given; rather, in dealing both with historical and contemporary subjects, he elaborates the stylistic poles of the sublime and the grotesque, or other ethical and aesthetic antitheses, to the utmost, so that they clash; in this way very strong effects are produced, for Hugo's command of expression is powerful and suggestive; but the effects are improbable and, as a reflection of human life, untrue.

Another writer of the romantic generation, Balzac, who had as great a creative gift and far more closeness to reality, seized upon the representation of contemporary life as his own particular task and, together with Stendhal, can be regarded as the creator of modern realism. He was sixteen years younger than Stendhal, yet his first characteristic novels appeared at almost the same time as Stendhal's, that is, about 1830. To exemplify his method of presentation we shall first give his portrait of the pension-mistress Madame Vauquer at the beginning of *Le Père Goriot* (1834). It is preceded by a very detailed description of the quarter in which the pension is located, of the house itself, of the two rooms on the ground floor; all this produces an intense impression of cheerless poverty, shabbiness, and dilapidation, and with the physical description the moral atmosphere is suggested. After the furniture of the dining room is described, the mistress of the establishment herself finally appears:

> Cette pièce est dans tout son lustre au moment où, vers sept heures du matin, le chat de Mme Vauquer précède sa maîtresse, saute sur les buffets, y flaire le lait que contiennent plusieurs jattes couvertes d'assiettes et fait entendre son *ronron* matinal. Bientôt la veuve se montre, attifée de son bonnet de tulle sous lequel pend un tour de faux cheveux mal mis; elle marche en traînassant ses pantoufles grimacées. Sa face vieillotte, grassouillette, du milieu de laquelle sort un nez à bec de perroquet; ses petites mains

potelées, sa personne dodue comme un rat d'église, son corsage trop plein et qui flotte, sont en harmonie avec cette salle où suinte le malheur, où s'est blottie la spéculation, et dont Mme Vauquer respire l'air chaudement fétide sans en être écœurée. Sa figure fraîche comme une première gelée d'automne, ses yeux ridés, dont l'expression passe du sourire prescrit aux danseuses à l'amer renfrognement de l'escompteur, enfin toute sa personne explique la pension, comme la pension implique sa personne. Le bagne ne va pas sans l'argousin, vous n'imagineriez pas l'un sans l'autre. L'embonpoint blafard de cette petite femme est le produit de cette vie, comme le typhus est la conséquence des exhalaisons d'un hôpital. Son jupon de laine tricotée, qui dépasse sa première jupe faite avec une vieille robe, et dont la ouate s'échappe par les fentes de l'étoffe lézardée, résume le salon, la salle à manger, le jardinet, annonce la cuisine et fait pressentir les pensionnaires. Quand elle est là, ce spectacle est complet. Agée d'environ cinquante ans, Mme Vauquer ressemble à toutes les femmes *qui ont eu des malheurs.* Elle a l'œil vitreux, l'air innocent d'une entremetteuse qui va se gendarmer pour se faire payer plus cher, mais d'ailleurs prête à tout pour adoucir son sort, à livrer Georges ou Pichegru, si Georges ou Pichegru étaient encore à livrer. Néanmoins elle est *bonne femme au fond,* disent les pensionnaires, qui la croient sans fortune en l'entendant geindre et tousser comme eux. Qu'avait été M. Vauquer? Elle ne s'expliquait jamais sur le défunt. Comment avait-il perdu sa fortune? "Dans les malheurs," répondait-elle. Il s'était mal conduit envers elle, ne lui avait laissé que les yeux pour pleurer, cette maison pour vivre, et le droit de ne compatir à aucune infortune, parce que, disait-elle, elle avait souffert tout ce qu'il est possible de souffrir.

(The room is at its brilliant best when, about seven in the morning, Madame Vauquer's cat enters before its mistress, jumps up on the buffet, sniffs at the milk which stands there in a number of bowls covered over with plates, and emits its matutinal purring. Presently the widow appears, got up in her tulle bonnet, from beneath which hangs an ill-attached twist of false hair; as she walks, her wrinkled slippers drag. Her oldish, fattish face, from the middle of which juts a parrot-beak nose, her small, plump hands, her figure as well filled out as a churchwarden's, her loose, floppy bodice, are in harmony with the room, whose walls ooze misfortune, where speculation cowers, and whose warm and fetid air Madame Vauquer breathes without nausea. Her face, as chilly as a first fall frost, her wrinkled eyes, whose expression changes from the obligatory smile of a ballet-girl to the sour scowl of a sharper, her whole person, in short, explains the pension, as the pension implies her person. A prison requires a warder, you could not imagine the one without the other. The short-statured woman's blowsy *embonpoint* is the product of the life here, as typhoid is the consequence of the exhalations of a hospital. Her knitted wool petticoat, which is longer than her outer skirt (made of an old dress), and whose wadding is escaping by the gaps in the splitting material, sums up the drawing-room, the dining room, the little garden, announces the cooking and gives an inkling of the boarders. When she is there, the spectacle is complete. Some fifty years of age, Madame Vauquer resembles all women *who have had troubles.* She has the glassy eye, the innocent expression of a bawd who is about to make a scene in order to get a higher price, but who is at the same time ready for anything in order to soften her lot, to hand over Georges or Pichegru if Georges or Pichegru were still to be handed over. Nevertheless, she is *a good woman at heart,* the boarders say, and they believe, because they hear her moan and cough like themselves, that she has no money. What had Monsieur Vauquer been? She never gave any information about the deceased. How had he lost his money? "In troubles," she answered. He had acted badly toward her, had left her nothing but her eyes to weep with, this house for livelihood, and the right to be indulgent toward no manner of misfortune because, she said, she had suffered everything it is possible to suffer.)

The portrait of the hostess is connected with her morning appearance in the dining-room; she appears in this center of her influence, the cat jumping onto the buffet before her gives a touch of witchcraft to her entrance; and then Balzac immediately begins a detailed description of her person. The description is controlled by a leading motif, which is several times repeated—the motif of the harmony between Madame Vauquer's person on the one hand and the room in which she is present, the pension which she directs, and the life which she leads, on the other; in short, the harmony between her person and what we (and Balzac too, occasionally) call her milieu. This harmony is most impressively suggested: first through the dilapidation, the greasiness, the dirtiness and warmth, the sexual repulsiveness of her body and her clothes—all this being in harmony with the air of the room which she breathes without distaste; a little later, in connection with her face and its expressions, the motif is conceived somewhat more ethically, and with even greater emphasis upon the complementary relation between person and milieu: *sa personne explique la pension, comme la pension implique sa personne*; with this goes the comparison to a prison. There follows a more medical concept, in which Madame Vauquer's *embonpoint blafard* as a symptom of her life is compared to typhoid as the result of the exhalations in a hospital. Finally her petticoat is appraised as a sort of synthesis of the various rooms of the pension, as a foretaste of the products of the kitchen, and as a premonition of the guests; for a moment her petticoat becomes a symbol of the milieu, and then the whole is epitomized again in the sentence: *Quand elle est là, ce spectacle est complet*—one need, then, wait no longer for the breakfast and the guests, they are all included in her person. There seems to be no deliberate order for the various repetitions of the harmony-motif, nor does Balzac appear to have followed a systematic plan in describing Madame Vauquer's appearance; the series of things mentioned—headdress, false hair, slippers, face, hands, body, the face again, eyes, corpulence, petticoat—reveal no trace of composition; nor is there any separation of body and clothing, of physical characteristics and moral significance. The entire description, so far as we have yet considered it, is directed to the mimetic imagination of the reader, to his memory-pictures of similar persons and similar milieux which he may have seen; the thesis of the "stylistic unity" of the milieu, which includes the people in it, is not established rationally but is presented as a striking and immediately apprehended state of things, purely suggestively, without any proof. In such a statement as the following, *ses petites mains potelées, sa personne dodue comme un rat d'église . . . sont en harmonie avec cette salle où suinte le malheur . . . et dont Mme Vauquer respire l'air chaudement fétide . . .* the harmony-thesis, with all that it includes (sociological and ethical significance of furniture and clothing, the deducibility of the as yet unseen elements of the milieu from those already given, etc.) is presupposed; the mention of prison and typhoid too are merely suggestive comparisons, not proofs nor even beginnings of proofs. The lack of order and disregard for the rational in the text are consequences of the haste with which Balzac worked, but they are nevertheless no mere accident, for his haste is itself in large part a consequence of his obsession with suggestive pictures. The motif of the unity of a milieu has taken hold of him so powerfully that the things and the persons composing a milieu often acquire for him a sort of second significance which, though different from that which reason can comprehend, is far more essential—a significance which can best be defined by the adjective demonic. In the dining-room, with its furniture which, worn and shabby though it be, is perfectly harmless to a reason uninfluenced by imagination, "misfortune oozes, speculation cowers." In this trivial everyday scene allegorical witches lie hidden, and instead of the plump sloppily dressed widow one momentarily sees a rat appear. What confronts us, then, is the unity of a particular milieu, felt as a total concept of a demonic-organic nature and presented entirely by suggestive and sensory means.

The next part of our passage, in which the harmony-motif is not again mentioned, pursues Madame Vauquer's character and previous history. It would be a mistake, however, to see in this separation of appearance on the one hand and character and previous history on the other a deliberate principle of composition; there are physical characteristics in this second part too (*l'œil vitreux*), and Balzac very frequently makes a different disposition, or mingles the physical, moral, and historical elements of a portrait indiscriminately. In our case his pursuit of her character and previous history does not serve to clarify either of them but rather to set Madame Vauquer's darkness "in the right light," that is, in the twilight of a petty and trivial demonism. So far as her previous history goes, the pension-mistress belongs to the category of women of fifty or thereabouts *qui ont eu des malheurs* (plural!); Balzac enlightens us not at all concerning her previous life, but instead reproduces, partly in *erlebte Rede*, the formless, whining, mendaciously colloquial chatter with which she habitually answers sympathetic inquiries. But here again the suspicious plural occurs, again avoiding particulars—her late husband had lost his money *dans les malheurs*—just as, some pages later, another suspicious widow imparts, on the subject of her husband who had been a count and a general, that he had fallen on LES *champs de bataille*. This conforms to the vulgar demonism of Madame Vauquer's character; she seems *bonne femme au fond*, she seems poor, but, as we are later told, she has a very tidy little fortune and she is capable of any baseness in order to improve her own situation a little—the base and vulgar narrowness of the goal of her egoism, the mixture of stupidity, slyness, and concealed vitality, again gives the impression of something repulsively spectral; again there imposes itself the comparison with a rat, or with some other animal making a basely demonic impression on the human imagination. The second part of the description, then, is a supplement to the first; after Madame Vauquer is presented in the first as synthesizing the milieu she governs, the second deepens the impenetrability and baseness of her character, which is constrained to work itself out in this milieu.

In his entire work, as in this passage, Balzac feels his milieux, different though they are, as organic and indeed demonic unities, and seeks to convey this feeling to the reader. He not only, like Stendhal, places the human beings whose destiny he is seriously relating, in their precisely defined historical and social setting, but also conceives this connection as a necessary one: to him every milieu becomes a moral and physical atmosphere which impregnates the landscape, the dwelling, furniture, implements, clothing, physique, character, surroundings, ideas, activities, and fates of men, and at the same time the general historical situation reappears as a total atmosphere which envelops all its several milieux. It is worth noting that he did this best and most truthfully for the circle of the middle and lower Parisian bourgeoisie and for the provinces; while his representation of high society is often melodramatic, false, and even unintentionally comic. He is not free from melodramatic exaggeration elsewhere; but whereas in the middle and lower spheres this only occasionally impairs the truthfulness of the whole, he is unable to create the true atmosphere of the higher spheres—including those of the intellect.

Balzac's atmospheric realism is a product of his period, is itself a part and a result of an atmosphere. The same intellectual attitude—namely romanticism—which first felt the atmospheric unity-of-style of earlier periods so strongly and so sensorily, which discovered the Middle Ages and the Renaissance as well as the historical idiosyncrasy of foreign cultures (Spain, the Orient)—this same intellectual attitude also developed organic comprehension of the atmospheric uniqueness of its own period in all its manifold forms. Atmospheric Historism and atmospheric realism are closely connected; Michelet and Balzac are borne on the same stream. The events which occurred in France between 1789 and 1815, and their effects during the next decades, caused modern contemporaneous realism to develop first and most strongly there, and its political and cultural unity gave France, in this respect, a long start over Germany; French reality, in all its multifariousness, could be comprehended as a whole. Another romantic current which contributed, no less than did romantic penetration into the total atmosphere of a milieu, to the development of modern realism, was the mixture of styles to which we have so often referred; this made it possible for characters of any station, with all the practical everyday complications of their lives—Julien Sorel as well as old Goriot or Madame Vauquer—to become the subject of serious literary representation.

These general considerations appear to me cogent; it is far more difficult to describe with any accuracy the intellectual attitude which dominates Balzac's own particular manner of presentation. The statements which he himself makes on the subject are numerous and provide many clues, but they are confused and contradictory; the richer he is in ideas and inspirations, the less is he able to separate the various elements of his own attitude, to channel the influx of suggestive but vague images and comparisons into intellectual analyses, and especially to adopt a critical attitude toward the stream of his own inspiration. All his intellectual analyses, although full of isolated observations which are striking and original, come in the end to a fanciful macroscopy which suggests his contemporary Hugo; whereas what is needed to explain his realistic art is precisely a careful separation of the currents which mingle in it.

In the *Avant-propos* to the *Comédie humaine* (published 1842) Balzac begins his explanation of his work with a comparison between the animal kingdom and human society, in which he accepts the guidance of Geoffroy Saint-Hilaire's theories. This biologist, under the influence of contemporary German speculative natural philosophy, had upheld the principle of typal unity in organization, that is, the idea that in the organization of plants (and animals) there is a general plan; Balzac here refers to the systems of other mystics, philosophers, and biologists (Swedenborg, Saint-Martin, Leibnitz, Buffon, Bonnet, Needham) and finally arrives at the following formulation:

> Le créateur ne s'est servi que d'un seul et même patron pour tous les êtres organisés. L'animal est un principe qui prend sa forme extérieure, ou, pour parler plus exactement, les différences de sa forme, dans les milieux où il est appelé à se développer . . .

> (The creator used but one and the same pattern for all organized creatures. The animal is a principle which takes its external form, or, to put it more precisely, the differences of its form, from the milieux in which it is called upon to evolve . . .)

This principle is at once transferred to human society:

> La Société [with a capital, as Nature shortly before] ne fait-elle pas de l'homme, suivant les milieux où son action se déploie, autant d'hommes différents qu'il y a de variétés en zoologie?
>
> (Does not Society make of man, according to the milieux in which his activity takes places, as many different men as there are varieties in zoology?)

And then he compares the differences between a soldier, a workman, an administrative employee, an idler, a scholar, a statesman, a shopkeeper, a seaman, a poet, a pauper, a priest, with those between wolf, lion, ass, raven, shark, and so on.

Our first conclusion is that he is here attempting to establish his views of human society (typical man differentiated by his milieu) by biological analogies; the word milieu, which here appears for the first time in the sociological sense and which was to have such a successful career (Taine seems to have adopted it from Balzac), he learned from Geoffroy Saint-Hilaire, who for his part had transferred it from physical science to biology; now it makes its way from biology to sociology. The biologism present in Balzac's mind, as may be deduced from the names he cites, is mystical, speculative, and vitalistic; however, the model-concept, the principle "animal" or "man," is not taken as immanent but, so to speak, as a real Platonic idea. The various genera and species are only *formes extérieures*; furthermore, they are themselves given not as changing within the course of history but as fixed (a soldier, a workman, etc., like a lion, an ass). The particular meaning of the concept milieu, as he uses it in practice in his novels he here seems not to have fully realized. Not the word, but the thing—milieu in the social sense—existed long before him; Montesquieu unmistakably has the concept; but whereas Montesquieu gives much more consideration to natural conditions (climate, soil) than to those which spring from human history, and whereas he attempts to construe the different milieux as unchanging model-concepts to which the appropriate constitutional and legislative models can be applied, Balzac in practice remains entirely within the orbit of the historical and perpetually changing structural elements of his milieux; and no reader arrives unassisted at the idea which Balzac appears to maintain in his *Avant-propos*, that he is concerned only with the type "man" or with generic types ("soldier," "shopkeeper"); what we see is the concrete individual figure with its own physique and its own history, sprung from the immanence of the historical, social, physical, etc. situation;

not "the soldier" but, for example, Colonel Brideau, discharged after the fall of Napoleon, ruined and leading the life of an adventurer in Issoudun (*La Rabouilleuse*).

After his bold comparison of zoological with sociological differentiation, however, Balzac attempts to bring out the distinguishing characteristics of *la Société* as against *la Nature*; he sees them above all in the far greater multifariousness of human life and human customs, as well as in the possibility—nonexistent in the animal kingdom—of changing from one species to another ("the grocer . . . becomes a Peer of France, and the nobleman sometimes sinks to the lowest rank of society"); furthermore, different species mate ("the wife of a merchant is sometimes worthy to be the wife of a prince . . . ; in Society, a woman does not always happen to be the female of a male"); he also refers to dramatic conflicts in love, which seldom occur among animals, and the different degrees of intelligence in different men. The epitomizing sentence reads: "The social State has risks which Nature does not permit herself, for it is Nature plus Society." Inaccurate and macroscopic as this passage is, badly as it suffers from the *proton pseudos* of the underlying comparison, it yet contains an instinctive historical insight ("customs, clothing, modes of speech, houses . . . change in accordance with civilizations"); there is much, too, of dynamism and vitalism ("if some scientists do not yet admit that Animality floods over into Humanity by an immense current of life"). The particular possibilities of comprehension between man and man are not mentioned—not even in the negative formulation that, as compared with man, the animal lacks them; on the contrary, the relative simplicity of the social and psychological life of animals is presented as an objective fact, and only at the very end is there any indication of the subjective character of such judgments: "the habits of each animal are, to our eyes at least, constantly similar at all times."

After this transition from biology to human history, Balzac continues with a polemic against the prevailing type of historical writing and reproaches it with having long neglected the history of manners; this is the task he has set himself. He does not mention the attempts at a history of manners which had been made from the eighteenth century on (Voltaire); hence there is no analysis setting forth the distinction between his presentation of manners and that of his possible predecessors; only Petronius is named. Considering the difficulties of his task (a drama with three or four thousand characters), he feels encouraged by the example of Walter Scott's novels; so here we are completely within the world of romantic Historism. Here too clarity of thought is often impaired by striking and fanciful formulations; for example *faire concurrence à l'Etat-Civil* is equivocal, and the statement *le hasard est le plus grand romancier du monde* requires some explanation if it is to tally with its author's historical attitude. But a number of important and characteristic motifs emerge successfully: above all the concept of the novel of manners as philosophical history, and, in general, Balzac's conception (which he upholds energetically elsewhere) of his own activity as the writing of history, to which we shall later return; also his justification of all stylistic genres and levels in works of this nature; finally his design of going beyond Walter Scott by making all his novels compose a single whole, a general presentation of French society in the nineteenth century, which he here again calls a historical work.

But this does not exhaust his plan; he intends also to render a separate account of *les raisons ou la raison de ces effets sociaux*, and when he has succeeded in at least investigating *ce moteur social*, his final intention is "to meditate upon natural principles and see wherein Societies depart from or approach the eternal rule, the true, the beautiful." We need not here discuss the fact that it was not given to him to make a successful theoretical presentation outside the frame of a narrative, that hence he could only attempt to realize his theoretical plans in the form of novels; here it is only of interest to note that the "immanent" philosophy of his novels of manners did not satisfy him and that in the passage before us this dissatisfaction, after so many biological and historical expositions, induces him to employ classical model-concepts (*la règle éternelle, le vrai, le beau*)—categories which he can no longer utilize practically in his novels.

All these motifs—biological, historical, classically moralistic—are in fact scattered through his work. He has a great fondness for biological comparisons; he speaks of physiology or zoology in connection with social phenomena, of the *anatomie du cœur humain*; in the passage commented on above he compares the effect of a social milieu to the exhalations which produce typhoid, and in another passage from *Père Goriot* he says of Rastignac that he had given himself up to the lessons and the temptations of luxury "with the ardor which seizes the calix of a female date-palm for the fecundating dusts of its nuptials." It is needless to cite historical motifs, for the spirit of Historism with its emphasis upon ambient and individual atmospheres is the spirit of his entire work; I will, however, quote at least one of many passages to show that historical concepts were always in his mind. The passage is from the provincial novel *La vieille Fille*; it concerns two elderly gentlemen who live in Alençon, the one a typical *ci-devant*, the other a bankrupt Revolutionary profiteer:

> Les époques déteignent sur les hommes qui les traversent. Ces deux personnages prouvaient la vérité de cet axiome par l'opposition des teintes historiques empreintes dans leurs physionomies, dans leurs discours, dans leurs idées et leurs coutumes.

> (Periods rub off on the men who pass through them. These two personages proved the truth of this axiom by the contrast in the historical coloring imprinted upon their physiognomies, their talk, their ideas, and their clothes.)

And in another passage from the same novel, in reference to a house in Alençon, he speaks of the *archétype* which it represents; here we have not the archetype of a nonhistorical abstraction but that of the *maisons bourgeoises* of a large part of France; the house, whose piquant local character he has previously described, deserves its place in the novel all the more, he says, *qu'il explique des mœurs et représente des idées*. Despite many obscurities and exaggerations, biological and historical elements are successfully combined in Balzac's work because they are both consonant with its romantic-dynamic character, which occasionally passes over into the romantic-magical and the demonic; in both cases one feels the operation of irrational "forces." In contrast, the classically moralistic element very often gives the impression of being a foreign body. It finds expression more especially in Balzac's tendency to formulate generalized apophthegms of a moral cast. They are sometimes witty as individual observations, but for the most part they are far too generalized; sometimes too they are not even witty; and when they develop into long disquisitions, they are often—to use the language of the vulgar—plain "tripe." I will quote some brief moralizing dicta which occur in *Père Goriot*:

> Le bonheur est la poésie des femmes comme la toilette en est le fard.—(La science et l'amour. . .) sont des asymptotes qui ne peuvent jamais se rejoindre.—S'il est un sentiment inné dans le cœur de l'homme, n'est-ce pas l'orgueil de la protection exercé à tout moment en faveur d'un être faible?—Quand on connaît Paris, on ne croit à rien de ce qui s'y dit, et l'on ne dit rien de ce qui s'y fait.—Un sentiment, n'est-ce pas le monde dans une pensée?

(Happiness is the poetry of women as get-up is their rouge.—[Science and love . . .] are asymptotes which can never meet.—If there is a sentiment innate in the heart of man, is it not pride in protection perpetually exercised in behalf of a weak creature?—When one knows Paris, one believes nothing that is told there and tells nothing that is done there.—Is not a sentiment a world in a thought?)

At best one can say of such apophthegms that they do not deserve the honor bestowed upon them—that of being erected into generalizations. They are *aperçus* produced by the momentary situation, sometimes extremely cogent, sometimes absurd, not always in good taste. Balzac aspires to be a classical moralist, at times he even echoes La Bruyère (e.g., in a passage from *Père Goriot* where the physical and psychological effects of the possession of money are described in connection with the remittance Rastignac receives from his family). But this suits neither his style nor his temperament. His best formulations come to him in the midst of narrative, when he is not thinking about moralizing—for example when in *La vieille Fille* he says of Mademoiselle Cormon, directly out of the momentary situation: *Honteuse elle-même, elle ne devinait pas la honte d'autrui.*

On the subject of his plan for the entire work, which gradually took shape in him, he has other interesting statements, particularly from the period when he finally saw it whole—in his letters of ca. 1834. In this self-interpretation three motifs are especially to be remarked; all three occur together in a letter to the Countess Hanska (*Lettres à l'Etrangère*, Paris 1899, letter of Oct. 26, 1834, pp. 200-206), where (p. 205) we find:

Les Etudes de Mœurs représenteront tous les effets sociaux sans que ni une situation de la vie, ni une physionomie, ni un caractère d'homme ou de femme, ni une manière de vivre, ni une profession, ni une zone sociale, ni un pays français, ni quoi que ce soit de l'enfance, de la vieillesse, de l'âge mûr, de la politique, de la justice, de la guerre ait été oublié.

Cela posé, l'histoire du cœur humain tracée fil à fil, l'histoire sociale faite dans toutes ses parties, voilà la base. Ce ne seront pas des faits imaginaires; ce sera ce qui se passe partout.

(The Studies of Manners will represent all social effects, without forgetting a single situation in life, a physiognomy, a man's or woman's character, a way of life, a profession, a social zone, a part of France, or anything of childhood, old age, maturity, politics, law, war.

This established, the history of the human heart traced thread by thread, social history set down in all its parts—there is the foundation. It will not be imaginary facts; it will be what happens everywhere.)

Of the three motifs to which I have referred, two are immediately apparent; first, the universality of his plan, his concept of his work as an encyclopedia of life; no part of life is to be omitted. Second, the element of random reality—*ce qui se passe partout.* The third motif lies in the word *histoire.* This *histoire du cœur humain* or *histoire sociale* is not a matter of "history" in the usual sense—not of scientific investigation of transactions which have already occurred, but of comparatively free invention; not, in short, of *history* but of *fiction*; is not, above all, a matter of the past but of the contemporary present, reaching back at most only a few years or a few decades. If Balzac describes his *Études de Mœurs au dix-neuvième siècle* as history (just as Stendhal had already given his novel *Le Rouge et le Noir* the subtitle *Chronique du dix-neuvième siècle*), this means, first, that he regards his creative and artistic activity as equivalent to an activity of a historical-interpretative and even historical-philosophical nature, as his *Avant-propos* in itself makes it possible to deduce; secondly, that he conceives the present as history—the present is something in the process of resulting from history. And in practice his people and his atmospheres, contemporary as they may be, are always represented as phenomena sprung from historical events and forces; one has but to read over, say, the account of the origin of Grandet's wealth (*Eugénie Grandet*), or that of Du Bousquier's life (*La vieille Fille*) or old Goriot's, to be certain of this. Nothing of the sort so conscious and so detailed is to be found before the appearance of Stendhal and Balzac, and the latter far outdoes the former in organically connecting man and history. Such a conception and execution are thoroughly historistic.

We will now return to the second motif—*ce ne seront pas des faits imaginaires; ce sera ce qui se passe partout.* What is expressed here is that the source of his invention is not free imagination but real life, as it presents itself everywhere. Now, in respect to this manifold life, steeped in history, mercilessly represented with all its everyday triviality, practical preoccupations, ugliness, and vulgarity, Balzac has an attitude such as Stendhal had had before him: in the form determined by its actuality, its triviality, its inner historical laws, he takes it seriously and even tragically. This, since the rise of classical taste, had occurred nowhere—and even before then not in Balzac's practical and historical manner, oriented as it is upon a social self-accounting of man. Since French classicism and absolutism, not only had the treatment of everyday reality become much more limited and decorous, but in addition the attitude taken toward it renounced the tragic and problematic as it were in principle. We have attempted to analyze this in the preceding chapters: a subject from practical reality could be treated comically, satirically, or didactically and moralistically; certain subjects from definite and limited realms of contemporary everyday life attained to an intermediate style, the pathetic; but beyond that they might not go. The real everyday life of even the middle ranks of society belong to the low style; the profound and significant Henry Fielding, who touches upon so many moral, aesthetic, and social problems, keeps his presentation always within the satiric moralistic key and says in *Tom Jones* (book 14, chapter 1): ". . . that kind of novels which, like this I am writing, is of the comic class."

The entrance of existential and tragic seriousness into realism, as we observe it in Stendhal and Balzac, is indubitably closely connected with the great romantic agitation for the mixture of styles—the movement whose slogan was Shakespeare vs. Racine—and I consider Stendhal's and Balzac's form of it, the mixture of seriousness and everyday reality, far more important and genuine than the form it took in the Hugo group, which set out to unite the sublime and the grotesque.

The newness of this attitude, and the new type of subjects which were seriously, problematically, tragically treated, caused the gradual development of an entirely new kind of serious or, if one prefers, elevated style; neither the antique nor the Christian nor the Shakespearean nor the Racinian level of conception and expression could easily be transferred to the new subjects; at first there was some uncertainty in regard to the kind of serious attitude to be assumed.

Stendhal, whose realism had sprung from resistance to a present which he despised, preserved many eighteenth-century instincts in his attitude. In his heroes there are still haunting memories of figures like Romeo, Don Juan, Valmont (from the *Liaisons dangereuses*), and Saint-Preux; above all, the figure of Napoleon remains alive in him; the heroes of his novels think and feel in opposition to their time, only with contempt do they descend to the intrigues and machinations of the post-Napoleonic present. Although there is always an admixture of motifs which, according to the older view, would have the character of comedy, it remains true of Stendhal that a figure for whom he feels tragic sympathy, and for whom he demands it of the reader, must be a real hero, great and daring in his thoughts and passions. In Stendhal the freedom of the great heart, the freedom of passion, still has much of the aristocratic loftiness and of the playing with life which are more characteristic of the *ancien régime* than of the nineteenth-century bourgeoisie.

Balzac plunges his heroes far more deeply into time-conditioned dependency; he thereby loses the standards and limits of what had earlier been felt as tragic, and he does not yet possess the objective seriousness toward modern reality which later developed. He bombastically takes every entanglement as tragic, every urge as a great passion; he is always ready to declare every person in misfortune a hero or a saint; if it is a woman, he compares her to an angel or the Madonna; every energetic scoundrel, and above all every figure who is at all sinister, he converts into a demon; and he calls poor old Goriot *ce Christ de la paternité*. It was in conformity with his emotional, fiery, and uncritical temperament, as well as with the romantic way of life, to sense hidden demonic forces everywhere and to exaggerate expression to the point of melodrama.

In the next generation, which comes on the stage in the fifties, there is a strong reaction in this respect. In Flaubert realism becomes impartial, impersonal, and objective. In an earlier study, "Serious Imitation of Everyday Life," I analyzed a paragraph from *Madame Bovary* from this point of view, and will here, with slight changes and abridgements, reproduce the pages concerned, since they are in line with the present train of thought and since it is unlikely, in view of the time and place of their publication (Istanbul, 1937), that they have reached many readers. The paragraph concerned occurs in part 1, chapter 9, of *Madame Bovary*:

> Mais c'était surtout aux heures des repas qu'elle n'en pouvait plus, dans cette petite salle au rez-de-chaussée, avec le poêle qui fumait, la porte qui criait, les murs qui suintaient, les pavés humides; toute l'amertume de l'existence lui semblait servie sur son assiette, et, à la fumée du bouilli, il montait du fond de son âme comme d'autres bouffées d'affadissement. Charles était long à

manger; elle grignotait quelques noisettes, ou bien, appuyée du coude, s'amusait, avec la pointe de son couteau, de faire des raies sur la toile cirée.

(But it was above all at mealtimes that she could bear it no longer, in that little room on the ground floor, with the smoking stove, the creaking door, the oozing walls, the damp floor-tiles; all the bitterness of life seemed to be served to her on her plate, and, with the steam from the boiled beef, there rose from the depths of her soul other exhalations as it were of disgust. Charles was a slow eater; she would nibble a few hazel-nuts, or else, leaning on her elbow, would amuse herself making marks on the oilcloth with the point of her table-knife.)

The paragraph forms the climax of a presentation whose subject is Emma Bovary's dissatisfaction with her life in Tostes. She has long hoped for a sudden event which would give a new turn to it—to her life without elegance, adventure, and love, in the depths of the provinces, beside a mediocre and boring husband; she has even made preparations for such an event, has lavished care on herself and her house, as if to earn that turn of fate, to be worthy of it; when it does not come, she is seized with unrest and despair. All this Flaubert describes in several pictures which portray Emma's world as it now appears to her; its cheerlessness, unvaryingness, grayness, staleness, airlessness, and inescapability now first become clearly apparent to her when she has no more hope of fleeing from it. Our paragraph is the climax of the portrayal of her despair. After it we are told how she lets everything in the house go, neglects herself, and begins to fall ill, so that her husband decides to leave Tostes, thinking that the climate does not agree with her.

The paragraph itself presents a picture—man and wife together at mealtime. But the picture is not presented in and for itself; it is subordinated to the dominant subject, Emma's despair. Hence it is not put before the reader directly: here the two sit at table—there the reader stands watching them. Instead, the reader first sees Emma, who has been much in evidence in the preceding pages, and he sees the picture first through her; directly, he sees only Emma's inner state; he sees what goes on at the meal indirectly, from within her state, in the light of her perception. The first words of the paragraph, *Mais c'était surtout aux heures des repas qu'elle n'en pouvait plus* . . . state the theme, and all that follows is but a development of it. Not only are the phrases dependent upon *dans* and *avec*, which define the physical scene, a commentary on *elle n'en pouvait plus* in their piling up of the individual elements of discomfort, but the following clause too, which tells of the distaste aroused in her by the food, accords with the principal purpose both in sense and rhythm. When we read further, *Charles était long à manger*, this, though grammatically a new sentence and rhythmically a new movement, is still only a resumption, a variation, of the principal theme; not until we come to the contrast between his leisurely eating and her disgust and to the nervous gestures of her despair, which are described immediately afterward, does the sentence acquire its true significance. The husband, unconcernedly eating, becomes ludicrous and almost ghastly; when Emma looks at him and sees him sitting there eating, he becomes the actual cause of the *elle n'en pouvait plus*; because everything else that arouses her desperation—the gloomy room, the commonplace food, the lack of a tablecloth, the hopelessness of it all—appears to her, and through her to the reader also, as something that is connected with him, that emanates from him, and that would be entirely different if he were different from what he is.

The situation, then, is not presented simply as a picture, but we are first given Emma and then the situation through her. It is not, however, a matter—as it is in many first-person novels and other later works of a similar type—of a simple representation of the content of Emma's consciousness, of *what* she feels *as* she feels it. Though the light which illuminates the picture proceeds from her, she is yet herself part of the picture, she is situated within it. In this she recalls the speaker in the scene from Petronius discussed in our second chapter; but the means Flaubert employs are different. Here it is not Emma who speaks, but the writer. *Le poêle qui fumait, la porte qui criait, les murs qui suintaient, les pavés humides*—all this, of course, Emma sees and feels, but she would not be able to sum it all up in this way. *Toute l'amertume de l'existence lui semblait servie sur son assiette*—she doubtless has such a feeling; but if she wanted to express it, it would not come out like that; she has neither the intelligence nor the cold candor of self-accounting necessary for such a formulation. To be sure, there is nothing of Flaubert's life in these words, but only Emma's; Flaubert does nothing but bestow the power of mature expression upon the material which she affords, in its complete subjectivity. If Emma could do this herself, she would no longer be what she is, she would have outgrown herself and thereby saved herself. So she does not simply see, but is herself seen as one seeing, and is thus judged, simply through a plain description of her subjective life, out of her own feelings. Reading in a later passage (part 2, chapter 12): *jamais Charles ne lui paraissait aussi désagréable, avoir les doigts aussi carrés, l'esprit aussi lourd, les façons si communes* . . . , the reader perhaps thinks for a moment that this strange series is an emotional piling up of the causes that time and again bring Emma's aversion to her husband to the boiling point, and that she herself is, as it were, inwardly speaking these words; that this, then, is an example of *erlebte Rede.* But this would be a mistake. We have here, to be sure, a number of paradigmatic causes of Emma's aversion, but they are put together deliberately by the writer, not emotionally by Emma. For Emma feels much more, and much more confusedly; she sees other things than these—in his body, his manners, his dress; memories mix in, meanwhile she perhaps hears him speak, perhaps feels his hand, his breath, sees him walk about, good-hearted, limited, unappetizing, and unaware; she has countless confused impressions. The only thing that is clearly defined is the result of all this, her aversion to him, which she must hide. Flaubert transfers the clearness to the impressions; he selects three, apparently quite at random, but which are paradigmatically taken from Bovary's physique, his mentality, and his behavior; and he arranges them as if they were three shocks which Emma felt one after the other. This is not at all a naturalistic representation of consciousness. Natural shocks occur quite differently. The ordering hand of the writer is present here, deliberately summing up the confusion of the psychological situation in the direction toward which it tends of itself —the direction of "aversion to Charles Bovary." This ordering of the psychological situation does not, to be sure, derive its standards from without, but from the material of the situation itself. It is the type of ordering which must be employed if the situation itself is to be translated into language without admixture.

In a comparison of this type of presentation with those of Stendhal and Balzac, it is to be observed by way of introduction that here too the two distinguishing characteristics of modern realism are to be found; here too real everyday occurrences in a low social stratum, the provincial petty bourgeoisie, are taken very seriously (we shall discuss the particular character of this seriousness later); here too everyday occurrences are accurately and profoundly set in a definite period of contemporary history (the period of the bourgeois monarchy)—less obviously than in Stendhal or Balzac, but unmistakably. In these two basic characteristics the three writers are at one, in contradistinction to all earlier realism; but Flaubert's attitude toward his subject is entirely different. In Stendhal and Balzac we frequently and indeed almost constantly hear what the writer thinks of his characters and events; sometimes Balzac accompanies his narrative with a running commentary—emotional or ironic or ethical or historical or economic. We also very frequently hear what the characters themselves think and feel, and often in such a manner that, in the passage concerned, the writer identifies himself with the character. Both these things are almost wholly absent from Flaubert's work. His opinion of his characters and events remains unspoken; and when the characters express themselves it is never in such a manner that the writer identifies himself with their opinion, or seeks to make the reader identify himself with it. We hear the writer speak; but he expresses no opinion and makes no comment. His role is limited to selecting the events and translating them into language; and this is done in the conviction that every event, if one is able to express it purely and completely, interprets itself and the persons involved in it far better and more completely than any opinion or judgment appended to it could do. Upon this conviction—that is, upon a profound faith in the truth of language responsibly, candidly, and carefully employed—Flaubert's artistic practice rests.

This is a very old, classic French tradition. There is already something of it in Boileau's line concerning the power of the rightly used word (on Malherbe: *D'un mot mis en sa place enseigna le pouvoir*); there are similar statements in La Bruyère. Vauvenargues said: *Il n'y aurait point d'erreurs qui ne périssent d'elles-mêmes, exprimées clairement.* Flaubert's faith in language goes further than Vauvenargues's: he believes that the truth of the phenomenal world is also revealed in linguistic expression. Flaubert is a man who works extremely consciously and possesses a critical comprehension of art to a degree uncommon even in France; hence there occur in his letters, particularly of the years 1852-1854 during which he was writing *Madame Bovary* (*Troisième Série* in the *Nouvelle édition augmentée* of the *Correspondance,* 1927), many highly informative statements on the subject of his aim in art. They lead to a theory—mystical in the last analysis, but in practice, like all true mysticism, based upon reason, experience, and discipline—of a self-forgetful absorption in the subjects of reality which transforms them (*par une chimie merveilleuse*) and permits them to develop to mature expression. In this fashion subjects completely fill the writer; he forgets himself, his heart no longer serves him save to feel the hearts of others, and when, by fanatical patience, this condition is achieved, the perfect expression, which at once entirely comprehends the momentary subject and impartially judges it, comes of itself; subjects are seen as God sees them, in their true essence. With all this there goes a view of the mixture of styles which proceeds from the same mystical-realistic insight: there are no high and low subjects; the universe is a work of art produced without any taking of sides, the realistic artist must imitate the procedures of Creation, and every subject in its essence contains, before God's eyes, both the serious and the comic, both dignity and vulgarity; if it is rightly and surely reproduced, the level of style which is proper to it will be rightly and surely found; there is no need either for a general theory of levels, in which subjects are arranged according to their dignity, or for any analyses by the writer commenting upon the subject, after its presentation, with a view to better comprehension and more accurate classification; all this must result from the presentation of the subject itself.

It is illuminating to note the contrast between such a view and the grandiloquent and ostentatious parading of the writer's own feelings, and of the standards derived from them, of the type inaugurated by Rousseau and continued after him; a comparative interpretation of Flaubert's *Notre cœur ne doit être bon qu'à sentir celui des autres,* and Rousseau's statement at the beginning of the Confessions, *Je sens mon cœur, et je connais les hommes,* could effectually represent the change in attitude which had taken place. But it also becomes clear from Flaubert's letters how laboriously and with what tensity of application he had attained to his convictions. Great subjects, and the free, irresponsible rule of the creative imagination, still have a great attraction for him; from this point of view he sees Shakespeare, Cervantes, and even Hugo wholly through the eyes of a romanticist, and he sometimes curses his own narrow petty-bourgeois subject which constrains him to tiresome stylistic meticulousness (*dire à la fois simplement et proprement des choses vulgaires*); this sometimes goes so far that he says things which contradict his basic views: . . . *et ce qu'il y a de désolant, c'est de penser que, même réussi dans la perfection, cela* [*Madame Bovary*] *ne peut être que passable et ne sera jamais beau, à cause du fond même.* Withal, like so many important nineteenth-century artists, he hates his period; he sees its problems and the coming crises with great clarity; he sees the inner anarchy, the *manque de base théologique*, the beginning menace of the mob, the lazy eclectic Historism, the domination of phrases, but he sees no solution and no issue; his fanatical mysticism of art is almost like a substitute religion, to which he clings convulsively, and his candor very often becomes sullen, petty, choleric, and neurotic. But this sometimes perturbs his impartiality and that love of his subjects which is comparable to the Creator's love. The paragraph which we have analyzed, however, is untouched by such deficiencies and weaknesses in his nature; it permits us to observe the working of his artistic purpose in its purity.

The scene shows man and wife at table, the most everyday situation imaginable. Before Flaubert, it would have been conceivable as literature only as part of a comic tale, an idyl, or a satire. Here it is a picture of discomfort, and not a momentary and passing one, but a chronic discomfort, which completely rules an entire life, Emma Bovary's. To be sure, various things come later, among them love episodes; but no one could see the scene at table as part of the exposition for a love episode, just as no one would call *Madame Bovary* a love story in general. The novel is the representation of an entire human existence which has no issue; and our passage is a part of it, which, however, contains the whole. Nothing particular happens in the scene, nothing particular has happened just before it. It is a random moment from the regularly recurring hours at which the husband and wife eat together. They are not quarreling, there is no sort of tangible conflict. Emma is in complete despair, but her despair is not occasioned by any definite catastrophe; there is nothing purely concrete which she has lost or for which she has wished. Certainly she has many wishes, but they are entirely vague—elegance, love, a varied life; there must always have been such unconcrete despair, but no one ever thought of taking it seriously in literary works before; such formless tragedy, if it may be called tragedy, which is set in motion by the general situation itself, was first made conceivable as literature by romanticism; probably Flaubert was the first to have represented it in people of slight intellectual culture and fairly low social station; certainly he is the first who directly captures the chronic character of this psychological situation. Nothing happens, but that nothing has become a heavy, oppressive, threatening something. How he accomplishes this we have already seen; he organizes into compact and unequivocal discourse the confused impressions of discomfort which arise in Emma at sight of the room, the meal, her husband. Elsewhere too he seldom narrates events which carry the action quickly forward; in a series of pure pictures—pictures transforming the nothingness of listless and uniform days into an oppressive condition of repugnance, boredom, false hopes, paralyzing disappointments, and piteous fears—a gray and random human destiny moves toward its end.

The interpretation of the situation is contained in its description. The two are sitting at table together; the husband divines nothing of his wife's inner state; they have so little communion that things never even come to a quarrel, an argument, an open conflict. Each of them is so immersed in his own world—she in despair and vague wish-dreams, he in his stupid philistine self-complacency—that they are both entirely alone; they have nothing in common, and yet they have nothing of their own, for the sake of which it would be worthwhile to be lonely. For, privately, each of them has a silly, false world, which cannot be reconciled with the reality of his situation, and so they both miss the possibilities life offers them. What is true of these two, applies to almost all the other characters in the novel; each of the many mediocre people who act in it has his own world of mediocre and silly stupidity, a world of illusions, habits, instincts, and slogans; each is alone, none can understand another, or help another to insight; there is no common world of men, because it could only come into existence if many should find their way to their own proper reality, the reality which is given to the individual—which then would be also the true common reality. Though men come together for business and pleasure, their coming together has no note of united activity; it becomes one-sided, ridiculous, painful, and it is charged with misunderstanding, vanity, futility, falsehood, and stupid hatred. But what the world would really be, the world of the "intelligent," Flaubert never tells us; in his book the world consists of pure stupidity, which completely misses true reality, so that the latter should properly not be discoverable in it at all; yet it is there; it is in the writer's language, which unmasks the stupidity by pure statement; language, then, has criteria for stupidity and thus also has a part in that reality of the "intelligent" which otherwise never appears in the book.

Emma Bovary, too, the principal personage of the novel, is completely submerged in that false reality, in *la bêtise humaine*, as is the "hero" of Flaubert's other realistic novel, Frédéric Moreau in the *Éducation sentimentale*. How does Flaubert's manner of representing such personages fit into the traditional categories "tragic" and "comic"? Certainly Emma's existence is apprehended to its depths, certainly the earlier intermediate categories, such as the "sentimental" or the "satiric" or the "didactic," are inapplicable, and very often the reader is moved by her fate in a way that appears very like tragic pity. But a real tragic heroine she is not. The way in which language here lays bare the silliness, immaturity, and disorder of her life, the very wretchedness of that life, in which she remains immersed (*toute l'amertume de l'existence lui semblait servie sur son assiette*), excludes the idea of true tragedy, and the author and the reader can never feel as at one with her as must be the case with the tragic hero; she is always being tried, judged, and, together with the entire world in which she is caught, condemned. But neither is she comic; surely not; for that, she is understood far too deeply from within her fateful entanglement—though Flaubert never practices any "psychological understanding" but simply lets the state of the facts speak for itself. He has found an attitude toward the reality of contemporary life which is entirely different from earlier attitudes and stylistic levels, including—and especially—Balzac's and Stendhal's. It could be called, quite simply, "objective seriousness." This sounds strange as a designation of the style of a literary work. Objective seriousness, which seeks to penetrate to the depths of the passions and entanglements of a human life, but without itself becoming moved, or at least without betraying that it is moved—this is an attitude which one expects from a priest, a teacher, or a psychologist rather than from an artist. But priest, teacher, and psychologist wish to accomplish something direct and practical—which is far from Flaubert's mind. He wishes, by his attitude—*pas de cris, pas de convulsion, rien que la fixité d'un regard pensif*—to force language to render the truth concerning the subjects of his observation: "style itself and in its own right being an absolute manner of viewing things" (*Corr.* 2, 346). Yet this leads in the end to a didactic purpose: criticism of the contemporary world; and we must not hesitate to say so, much as Flaubert may insist that he is an artist and nothing but an artist. The more one studies Flaubert, the clearer it becomes how much insight into the problematic nature and the hollowness of nineteenth-century bourgeois culture is contained in his realistic works; and many important passages from his letters confirm this. The demonification of everyday social intercourse which is to be found in Balzac is certainly entirely lacking in Flaubert; life no longer surges and foams, it flows viscously and sluggishly. The essence of the happenings of ordinary contemporary life seemed to Flaubert to consist not in tempestuous actions and passions, not in demonic men and forces, but in the prolonged chronic state whose surface movement is mere empty bustle, while underneath it there is another movement, almost imperceptible but universal and unceasing, so that the political, economic, and social subsoil appears comparatively stable and at the same time intolerably charged with tension. Events seem to him hardly to change; but in the concretion of duration, which Flaubert is able to suggest both in the individual occurrence (as in our example) and in his total picture of the times, there appears something like a concealed threat: the period is charged with its stupid issuelessness as with an explosive.

Through his level of style, a systematic and objective seriousness, from which things themselves speak and, according to their value, classify themselves before the reader as tragic or comic, or in most cases quite unobtrusively as both, Flaubert overcame the romantic vehemence and uncertainty in the treatment of contemporary subjects; there is clearly something of the earlier positivism in his idea of art, although he sometimes speaks very derogatorily of Comte. On the basis of this objectivity, further developments became possible, with which we shall deal in later chapters. However, few of his successors conceived the task of representing contemporary reality with the same clarity and responsibility as he; though among them there were certainly freer, more spontaneous, and more richly endowed minds than his.

The serious treatment of everyday reality, the rise of more extensive and socially inferior human groups to the position of subject matter for problematic-existential representation, on the one hand; on the other, the embedding of random persons and events in the general course of contemporary history, the fluid historical background—these, we believe, are the foundations of modern realism, and it is natural that the broad and elastic form of the novel should increasingly impose itself for a rendering comprising so many elements. If our view is correct, throughout the nineteenth century France played the most important part in the rise and development of modern realism. What the situation was in Germany, we discussed at the end of the last chapter. In England, though the development was basically the same as in France, it came about more quietly and more gradually, without the sharp break between 1780 and 1830; it began much earlier and carried on traditional forms and viewpoints much longer, until far into the Victorian period. Fielding's art (*Tom Jones* appeared in 1749) already shows a far more energetic contemporary realism of life in all its departments than do the French novels of the same period; even the fluidity of the contemporary historical background is not entirely lacking; but the whole is conceived more moralistically and sheers away from any problematic and existential seriousness; on the other hand, even in Dickens, whose work began to appear in the thirties of the nineteenth century, there is, despite the strong social feeling and suggestive density of his milieux, almost no trace of the fluidity of the political and historical background. Meanwhile Thackeray, who places the events of *Vanity Fair* (1847-48) most concretely in contemporary history (the years before and after Waterloo), on the whole preserves the moralistic, half-satirical, half-sentimental viewpoint very much as it was handed down by the eighteenth century. We must, unfortunately, forego discussing the rise of modern Russian realism (Gogol's *Dead Souls* appeared in 1842, his short story "The Cloak" as early as 1835) even in the most general way; for our purpose, this is impossible when one cannot read the works in their original language. We shall have to rest content with discussing the influence which it later exercised.

19

GERMINIE LACERTEUX

IN 1864 Edmond and Jules de Goncourt published their novel *Germinie Lacerteux*, which describes the sexual involvements and the gradual ruin of a maidservant. They wrote the following preface for it:

Il nous faut demander pardon au public de lui donner ce livre, et l'avertir de ce qu'il y trouvera.

Le public aime les romans faux: ce roman est un roman vrai.

Il aime les livres qui font semblant d'aller dans le monde: ce livre vient de la rue.

Il aime les petites œuvres polissonnes, les mémoires de filles, les confessions d'alcôves, les saletés érotiques, le scandale qui se retrousse dans une image aux devantures des libraires: ce qu'il va lire est sévère et pur. Qu'il ne s'attende point à la photographie décolletée du Plaisir: l'étude qui suit est la clinique de l'amour.

Le public aime encore les lectures anodines et consolantes, les aventures qui finissent bien, les imaginations qui ne dérangent ni sa digestion ni sa sérénité: ce livre, avec sa triste et violente distraction, est fait pour contrarier ses habitudes et nuire à son hygiène.

Pourquoi donc l'avons-nous écrit? Est-ce simplement pour choquer le public et scandaliser ses goûts?

Non.

Vivant au XIXe siècle, dans un temps de suffrage universel, de démocratie, de libéralisme, nous nous sommes demandé si ce qu'on appelle "les basses classes" n'avait pas droit au Roman; si ce monde sous un monde, le peuple, devait rester sous le coup de l'interdit littéraire et des dédains d'auteurs, qui ont fait jusqu'ici le silence sur l'âme et le cœur qu'il peut avoir. Nous nous sommes demandé s'il y avait encore pour l'écrivain et pour le lecteur, en ces années d'égalité ou nous sommes, des classes indignes, des malheurs trop bas, des drames trop mal embouchés, des catastrophes d'une terreur trop peu noble. Il nous est venu la curiosité de savoir si cette forme conventionelle d'une littérature oubliée et d'une société disparue, la Tragédie, était définitivement morte; si dans un pays sans caste et sans aristocratie légale, les misères des petits et des pauvres parleraient à l'intérêt, à l'émotion, à la pitié, aussi haut que les misères des grands et des riches; si, en un mot, les larmes qu'on pleure en bas, pourraient faire pleurer comme celles qu'on pleure en haut.

Ces pensées nous avaient fait oser l'humble roman de Sœur Philomène, en 1861; elles nous font publier aujourd'hui Germinie Lacerteux.

Maintenant, que ce livre soit calomnié: peu lui importe. Aujourd'hui que le Roman s'élargit et grandit, qu'il commence à être la grande forme sérieuse, passionnée, vivante de l'étude littéraire et de l'enquête sociale, qu'il devient, par l'analyse et par la recherche psychologique, l'Histoire morale contemporaine; aujourd'hui que le Roman s'est imposé les études et les devoirs de la science, il peut en revendiquer les libertés et les franchises. Et qu'il cherche l'Art et la Vérité; qu'il montre des misères bonnes à ne pas laisser oublier aux heureux de Paris; qu'il fasse voir aux gens du monde ce que les dames de charité ont le courage de voir, ce que les Reines autrefois faisaient toucher de l'œil à leurs enfants dans les hospices: la souffrance humaine, présente et toute vive, qui apprend la charité; que le Roman ait cette religion que le siècle passé appelait de ce large et vaste nom: *Humanité*;—il lui suffit de cette conscience: son droit est là.

(We must ask the public's pardon for giving it this book, and for warning it of what it will find there.

The public likes false novels: this is a true novel.

It likes books which pretend to move in society: this book comes from the street.

It likes little smutty works, prostitutes' memoirs, alcove confessions, erotic trash, scandal pulling up its dress in a picture in a bookstore window: what it is about to read is severe and pure. Let it not expect the décolleté photograph of Pleasure: the following study is the clinical examination of love.

The public further likes innocuous and consoling reading, adventures which end happily, imaginings which upset neither its digestion nor its serenity: this book, with its sad and violent distraction, is so made as to go against its habits and be injurious to its hygiene.

Why, then, have we written it? Is it simply to shock the public and scandalize its tastes?

No.

Living in the nineteenth century, in a time of universal suffrage, of democracy, of liberalism, we asked ourselves if what is called "the lower classes" did not have a right to the Novel; if that world beneath a world, the people, must remain under the literary interdict and the disdain of authors who have so far kept silent upon the soul and the heart which it may have. We asked ourselves if, for the writer and the reader, there were still, in these years of equality in which we live, unworthy classes, troubles too base, dramas too foul-mouthed, catastrophes too little noble in their terror. We became curious to learn if that conventional form of a forgotten literature and a vanished society, Tragedy, was definitively dead; if in a country without caste and without a legal aristocracy, the troubles of the little and the poor could speak to interest, to emotion, to pity, as loudly as the troubles of the great and the rich; if, in a word, the tears which are wept below could cause weeping, as do those which are wept above.

These thoughts caused us to venture the humble novel of *Sœur Philomène* in 1861; today they make us publish *Germinie Lacerteux.*

Now, let this book be calumniated: it matters little to it. Today when the Novel is broadening and growing, when it is beginning to be the great, serious, impassioned, living form of literary study and social investigation, when, through analysis and psychological research, it is becoming contemporary moral History; today when the Novel has imposed upon itself the studies and the duties of science, it can demand the freedoms and immunities of science. And if it seek Art and Truth; if it disclose troubles which it were well the happy people of Paris should not forget; if it show people of fashion what district visitors have the courage to see, what Queens of old let their children's eyes rest upon in hospitals; human suffering, present and alive, which teaches charity; if the Novel have that religion to which the past century gave the broad and vast name: *Humanity*;—that consciousness suffices it: its right lies there.)

The violent polemic against the public with which this preface begins we shall take up later. We shall now deal with the program of artistic purpose expressed in the later paragraphs (beginning with the words *Vivant au* XIXe *siècle*). It corresponds exactly to what we mean by our term mixing of styles and it is based on political and sociological considerations. We live, say the Goncourts, in an age of universal suffrage, democracy, and liberalism (it may be noted that they were not by any means unqualifiedly in agreement with these institutions and phenomena). Hence it is not just to exclude from literary treatment the so-called lower classes of the population, as is still being done, and to preserve in literature an aristocraticism of subject matter which is no longer in keeping with our social picture. It should be admitted, they argue, that no form of unhappiness is too low for literary treatment. That the novel is the proper form for such a treatment is taken for granted in the words *avoir droit au roman*. A later sentence—*Il nous est venu la curiosité . . .*—suggests that the realistic novel has become the successor of classical tragedy. And the last paragraph contains a rhetorically enthusiastic survey of the functions of the new art form in the modern world, a survey which contains a special motif, that of the scientific attitude. It is a motif which had appeared in Balzac, but here it has become much more vigorous and programmatic. The novel, they insist, has grown in scope and significance. It is the serious, passionate, and living form of literary study and social inquiry (note the words *étude* and especially *enquête*), through its analyses and psychological investigations it will become *l'Histoire morale contemporaine*, it has taken over the methods and duties of science, hence it can also lay claim to the rights and freedoms of science. Here, then, the right to treat any subject, even the lowest, seriously, that is to say, the extreme in mixture of styles, is justified by both politico-social and scientific arguments. The work of the novelist is compared to scientific work, and it seems beyond doubt that here the Goncourts are thinking of the methods of experimental biology. We are here under the influence of the enthusiasm for science which marked the first decades of positivism, when all active intellects—insofar as they were consciously searching for new methods and values in accord with the times—strove to assimilate the experimental techniques of science. Here the Goncourts are in the extreme vanguard; it is, so to speak, their vocation to be in the extreme vanguard. The conclusion of the preface, it is true, introduces a less modern position, a turn toward ethics, charity, and humanitarianism. A number of motifs of very different origin enter into this. The reference to the *heureux de Paris* and the *gens du monde* who ought to think of the misery of their fellow-men belongs to the mid-century socialism of sentiment. The queens of old who cared for the sick and showed them to their children remind us of the Christian Middle Ages. And finally there is the religion of humanity of the Age of Enlightenment. There is a great deal of eclecticism and not a little arbitrariness in this rhetorical finale.

But however we may feel about the individual motifs in this preface and in general about the way in which the Goncourts plead their cause, there is no doubt that they were right, and the suit has long since been settled in their favor. With the first great realists of the century, with Stendhal, Balzac, and even with Flaubert, the lower strata of the people, and indeed the people as such in general, hardly appear. And when it appears, it is seen not on its own premises, within its own life, but from above. Even with Flaubert (whose *Cœur simple*, by the way, did not appear until a decade after *Germinie Lacerteux*, so that at the time of our preface almost nothing of *Madame Bovary* had been written except the scene of the awarding of prizes at the *Comices agricoles*) the people is on the whole represented by servants and background figures only. But the advance of the realistic mixture of styles which Stendhal and Balzac had brought about could not stop short of the fourth estate; it had to follow the social and political development of the time. Realism had to embrace the whole reality of contemporary civilization, in which to be sure the bourgeoisie played a dominant role, but in which the masses were beginning to press threateningly ahead as they became ever more conscious of their own function and power. The common people in all its ramifications had to be taken into the subject matter of serious realism: the Goncourts were right, and they were to be borne out in it. The development of realistic art has proved it.

The first defenders of the rights of the fourth estate—politically as well as in literature—almost all belonged not to it but to the bourgeoisie. This is also true of the Goncourts, who, by the way, had little sympathy with political socialism. They were half-aristocratic upper bourgeois, not only by birth but also in their attitude and way of life, in their views, concerns, and instincts. In addition they were endowed with hypersensitive nerves; they dedicated their lives to a search for aesthetic sense impressions. They were, more completely and exclusively than anyone else, aesthetes and eclecticists of literature. To find them in the role of champions of the fourth estate, even though only of the fourth estate as a source of literary subject matter, is a surprise. What was it that connected them with the fourth estate? What did they know about its life, its problems, and reactions? And was it really nothing but a sense of social and aesthetic justice which induced them to dare this experiment? It is not difficult to answer these questions. It can be done simply on the basis of the Goncourts' bibliography. They wrote a considerable number of novels, almost all of them based on their own experience and observation. In these novels, in addition to the milieu of the lower classes, other milieux appear—the upper bourgeoisie, the underworld of the metropolis, various types of artistic circles; but whatever the milieu, the subjects treated are always strange and unusual, often pathological. In addition they wrote books on their travels, on contemporary artists, on women and art in the eighteenth century, and on Japanese art. Then there is that mirror of their life, the Diary. Their bibliography alone, then, reveals the principle of their choice of subject matter. They were collectors and depicters of sensory impressions, especially of sensory impressions valuable for their strangeness or novelty. They were professional discoverers or rediscoverers of aesthetic, and particularly of morbidly aesthetic, experiences suited to satisfy an exacting taste surfeited with the usual. It was from this point of view that the common people appealed to them as a literary subject. Edmond de Goncourt expressed this excellently in a diary entry of December 3, 1871:

> Mais pourquoi . . . choisir ces milieux? Parce que c'est dans le bas que dans l'effacement d'une civilisation se conserve le caractère des choses, des personnes, de la langue, de tout . . . . Pourquoi encore? peut-être parce que je suis un littérateur bien né, et que le peuple, la canaille, si vous voulez, a pour moi l'attrait de populations inconnues, et non découvertes, quelque chose de *l'exotique* que les voyageurs vont chercher. . . .
>
> (But why . . . choose these milieux? Because it is at the bottom that, in the obliteration of a civilization, the character of things, of persons, of the language, of everything, is preserved. . . . Why again? perhaps because I am a well-born man of letters, and because the people, the mob, if you will, has for me the attraction of unknown and undiscovered populations, something of the *exoticism* which travelers go to seek. . . .)

As far as this impulse took them, they could understand the people. But no further. And that automatically excludes everything functionally essential, the people's work, its position within modern society, the political, social, and moral ferments which are alive in it and which point to the future. The very fact that *Germinie Lacerteux* is once again a novel about a maid, that is, about an appendage of the bourgeoisie, shows that the task of including the fourth estate in the subject matter of serious artistic representation is not centrally understood and approached. The thing that drew the Goncourts in the subject matter of *Germinie Lacerteux* was something quite different. It was the sensory fascination of the ugly, the repulsive, and the morbid. In this, to be sure, the Goncourts are not entirely original, for Baudelaire's *Fleurs du mal* had appeared as early as 1857. But they would seem to have been the first to import such motifs into the novel; and this was the fascination which the strange erotic adventures of an elderly maidservant had for them. For it is a true story, of which they learned after the woman's death and from which they built up their novel. In an unexpected fashion the inclusion of the common people connected itself in them (and not only in them) with the need for sensory representation of the ugly, repulsive, and pathological—a need which went far beyond the factually requisite, the typical and representative. There was in it a radical and bitter protest against the forms of an idealizing and palliating elevated style, whether of classical or romantic origin, which despite its decline continued to govern the average taste of the public; against the conception of literature (and the arts in general) as a pleasant and soothing form of recreation—a basic about-face in the interpretation of the *prodesse* and *delectare* which constitutes its goal. And with this we come to the first part of the preface, the polemic against the public.

It is astounding. Perhaps not so much for us today, for we have heard the like and worse from our authors on many occasions. But if we think of earlier periods, so outspoken an attack upon those to whom the work is addressed constitutes an amazing phenomenon. The writer is a producer; the public is his customer. We can formulate the relationship between the two in other terms, looking at it from another point of view. We can regard the writer as an educator, a guide, a representative and occasionally prophetic voice. But aside from and indeed before all that, our economic formulation of the relationship is perfectly justified, and the Goncourts recognized as much. Although they did not exactly depend on their literary income, since they had means, they were yet most keenly interested in the success and sale of their books. How can the producer attack his customer in so outspoken a fashion! During the centuries when the writer depended on a princely patron or a definite aristocratic minority, such a tone would have been quite impossible. In the sixties of the past century an author could risk such a thing because he faced an anonymous and not clearly defined public. It is obvious that in doing so he counted upon the sensation which such a preface would cause. For the worst danger for his work was neither opposition, nor ill will on the part of the critics, nor even suppression by the authorities—all these things could occasion annoyance, delay, and personal unpleasantness, but they were not insuperable and often resulted in making the work better known—the worst danger which threatened a work of art was indifference.

The Goncourts charge the public with corrupt and perverted taste; with preferring false values, pseudo-refinement, pruriency, reading as a comfortable and soporific pastime, books which end happily and make no serious demands on the reader. Instead, they continue, they offer the public a novel which is true, which found its subject in the street, which, in its serious and pure content, presents the pathology of love, which will upset the public's habits and prove harmful to its hygiene. The tone of the passage as a whole is one of irritation. It is apparent that the writers have long been aware how far their taste has moved away from that of the average public, that they are convinced of being right, that they are trying by every means to shake the public out of its comfortable security, and that, already a little embittered, they can hardly believe in any great success for their efforts.

The polemic of this preface is a symptom; it is characteristic of the relationship which had developed in the course of the nineteenth century between the public and almost all important poets and writers, as well as painters, sculptors, and musicians—and not only in France, although earlier and more sharply there than anywhere else. It can safely be said that, with few exceptions, the significant artists of the later nineteenth century encountered hostility, lack of comprehension, or indifference on the part of the public. They achieved general recognition only at the price of violent and prolonged struggles, many of them only posthumously, or, before their deaths, among but a small circle of followers. Inversely, and again with but few exceptions, it is observable that during the nineteenth century, especially during its second half, and on into the beginning of the twentieth, those artists who quickly and easily achieved general recognition had no real and lasting importance. On the basis of this experience many critics and artists became convinced that this was necessarily so: that the very originality of a significant new work had as its concomitant that the public, not yet accustomed to its style, found it confusing and disturbing and could become accustomed only gradually to the new language of form. Yet this phenomenon was never so general and so extreme in the past. Often, to be sure, public recognition of great artists was diminished by unfortunate circumstances or by envy; they were often put on a par with rivals whom we today regard as totally unworthy of the honor. But that, despite the most favorable facilities for dissemination, the mediocre should almost generally be preferred to the significant, that almost all important artists should, according to their individual temperaments, regard the average public with bitterness or contempt or simply as nonexistent—this is a special feature of the past century. It is a situation which began to develop during the romantic period. Thereafter it grew worse and worse. Toward the end of the century there were a few great poets whose behavior and manner made it clear that they renounced every kind of general dissemination and recognition from the outset.

By way of explanation the first point that comes to mind is the tremendous and ever increasing expansion of the reading public since the beginning of the century, and the concomitant coarsening of taste. Intelligence, choiceness of feeling, concern for the forms of life and expression deteriorated. Stendhal in his time lamented this loss, as we pointed out earlier. The lowering of all standards was further accelerated by the commercial exploitation of the tremendous demand for reading matter on the part of publishers of books and periodicals, the majority of whom (there were exceptions) followed the path of least resistance and easy profits, supplying the public with what it wanted and possibly even with worse than it would have demanded if left to its own devices. But who was the reading public? It consisted largely of the urban middle class, which had greatly increased in numbers and, in consequence of the spread of education, had become able and willing to read. Here we have the "bourgeois," the creature whose stupidity, intellectual inertia, conceit, hypocrisy, and cowardice were attacked and ridiculed by poets, writers, artists, and critics from the romantic period on. Can we simply subscribe to their verdict? Are not these bourgeois the same people who undertook the tremendous task, the bold adventure, of the economic, scientific, and technological civilization of the nineteenth century, and who also produced the leaders of the revolutionary movements which were the first to recognize the crises, dangers, and foci of corruption inherent in that civilization? Even the average bourgeois of the nineteenth century shared in the tremendous activity in life and labor which characterized the age. Day in and day out he led a life which was much more dynamic and exacting than the life of the élite, with their routine of idleness and their almost complete immunity from the pressure of time and duty, who represented the literary public of the *ancien régime.* His physical security and his property were better guarded than in former times; he had incomparably greater possibilities of rising in the world. But acquiring and preserving property, exploiting opportunities for advancement, adjusting to quickly changing conditions—all as part of the bitter competitive struggle for survival—made such great and ceaseless demands on his strength and his nerves as had never been known in earlier times. From the pages on the life of the Parisians which Balzac wrote at the beginning of his novel *la Fille aux yeux d'or,* and which, though imaginative, are full of realistic observation, we can infer how exhausting the life there was even during the early years of the bourgeois monarchy. It is not surprising that these people expected and insisted that literature, and art in general, should give them relaxation, recreation, and at best an easily attained intoxication, and that they objected to the *triste et violente distraction,* to use an expressive phrase of the Goncourts, which most of the important authors offered.

But there is something else. In France, the influence of religion had been more profoundly shaken than elsewhere. Political institutions were undergoing constant change and afforded no moral support. The great ideas of the Enlightenment and the Revolution had quickly staled and become mere phrases. What they had resulted in was a vigorous fight of ego against ego which was regarded as justified because free enterprise was taken to be a natural and self-regulatory prerequisite for general prosperity and progress. But the self-regulation did not operate so as to satisfy the demand for justice. The success and failure of individuals and of whole strata of society were not exclusively decided only by intelligence and industry but also by conditions at the start, personal relations, luck, and not infrequently by a robust callousness of conscience. To be sure, justice had never ruled supreme in this world. But now it was no longer seriously possible, as it had been in earlier times, to interpret and accept injustice as decreed by God. A strong feeling of moral discomfort very soon arose. But the impetus of the economic movement was too powerful to be stopped by purely moral attempts to apply the brakes. The will to economic expansion and the moral discomfort existed side by side. In course of time the real dangers threatening the economic development and the structure of bourgeois society began to become apparent: the struggle of the great powers for markets and the threat from the progressive organization of the fourth estate. It was the time of preparation for the tremendous crisis the outbreak of which we have seen and continue to see in our day. In the nineteenth century there were very few men endowed with the perspicacity correctly to evaluate the decisive danger areas. Least of all perhaps the statesmen. They were still involved in ideas, desires, and methods of a kind which made it impossible for them to understand the economic and basically human situation.

These conditions, which in recent times have been clearly recognized and often described, we have here attempted to present as briefly as possible, in order to reach a basis for an evaluation of the function which literature created for itself within the pattern of bourgeois, and first of all of French, culture in the nineteenth century. Did it display any interest, any understanding, any sense of responsibility, in the face of the problems which we recognize in retrospect as having been the decisive ones? In regard to the most important men of the romantic generation, to Victor Hugo and Balzac, that is, these questions must be answered in the affirmative. They had overcome the romantic tendency to flee reality (cf. page 467 above), for it was not in harmony with their powerful temperaments, and Balzac's instinct for diagnosing the times is truly admirable. But with the very next generation, whose works began to appear during the fifties, the situation changes completely. There now arose the conception and the ideal of a literary art which in no way intrudes into the practical events of the present, which avoids every tendency to affect the lives of men morally, politically, or otherwise practically, and whose sole duty it is to fulfill the requirements of style. These demand that the subjects treated (be they external phenomena, be they products of the author's apperception or imagination) be made manifest with sensory vigor and, further, in a new, not yet outworn form which will reveal the writer's distinctive character. In this attitude (which, by the way, admitted no hierarchy of subjects) the value of art, that is, of perfect and original expression, was assumed to be absolute, and every kind of participation in the clash of contending philosophies and doctrines was discredited, for it seemed that any such participation must necessarily lead to slogans and clichés. When the traditional antique concepts of *prodesse* and *delectare* were cited, the reaction was an absolute denial of every kind of useful function for literature because usefulness immediately suggested practical usefulness or dreary didacticism. Under date of February 8, 1866, an entry in the Goncourt diary ridicules the idea *de demander à une œuvre d'art qu'elle serve à quelque chose.* But this is not at all the modesty of a Malherbe, who is supposed to have said that a good poet is no more useful than a good bowler. It is to ascribe to literature and art in general the most absolute value, to make them the object of a cult, almost a religion. And thus so high a rank was assigned to pleasure—which was primarily a sensory enjoyment of expression—that the word "pleasure," *delectatio*, seemed no longer to suffice. The term seemed discredited because it stood for something altogether too trivial and easily achieved.

The attitude here described, first observable in some of the later romanticists, became prevalent in the generation born about 1820: Leconte de Lisle, Baudelaire, Flaubert, the Goncourts. It continued to prevail during the second half of the century, although of course from the beginning it appears very differently in different individuals, running the gamut of modifications from collecting impressions for the sake of aesthetic enjoyment to destructive self-torture in complete devotion to impressions and to their artistic reformulation. The sources of this attitude are to be sought in the aversion which precisely the most outstanding writers felt toward contemporary civilization and contemporary society. This aversion acted all the more strongly to make them turn away from all contemporary problems because there was a mixture of helplessness in it. After all they were themselves indissolubly connected with the bourgeois society. They were part of it by descent and training. They profited by the security and freedom of expression which it had evolved. After all it was only within it that they found their public, perhaps only a small group but still their readers and admirers. Within it too they found the almost unlimited spirit of enterprise and experimentation which supplied every literary trend, even the strangest and most out-of-the-way, with patrons and publishers. The frequent emphasis on the contrast between "artist" and "bourgeois" must not lead to the conclusion that nineteenth-century literature and art had any other soil to grow in than that of the bourgeoisie. There simply was no other. For it was only very gradually, as the century progressed, that the fourth estate attained to political and economic self-comprehension; as yet there was no indication of aesthetic autonomy on its part; its aesthetic needs were those of the petty bourgeoisie. In this dilemma of instinctive aversion and necessary implication, yet at the same time amid an almost anarchic freedom in the realms of opinion, choice of possible subject matter, and development of personal idiosyncrasies in respect to forms of life and expression, those writers who were too proud and whose talents were too personally distinctive to produce the mass merchandise for which there was a general demand and a profitable sale were driven into an almost stubborn isolation in the domain of pure aesthetics and into renouncing any practical intervention in the problems of the age through their works.

Mixed-style realism was caught and carried along in the same current, as may be seen most clearly when, as in the case of *Germinie Lacerteux,* it claims to be concerned with contemporary social problems. As soon as we examine the content carefully, we recognize the driving force to be an aesthetic and not a social impulse. The subject treated is not one which concerns the center of the social structure; it is a strange and individual marginal phenomenon. For the Goncourts it is a matter of the aesthetic attraction of the ugly and pathological. By this I do not mean to deny the value of the courageous experiment the Goncourts undertook when they wrote and published *Germinie Lacerteux.* Their example helped to inspire and encourage others who did not stop with the purely aesthetic. It is surprising but undeniable that the inclusion of the fourth estate in serious realism was decisively advanced by those who, in their quest for new aesthetic impressions, discovered the attraction of the ugly and pathological. With Zola and the German naturalists of the end of the century the connection is still unmistakable.

Flaubert too, who was almost of the same age as Edmond de Goncourt, belonged among those who isolated themselves entirely in the realm of the aesthetic. Indeed, he may well be the one among them all who carried furthest ascetic renunciation of a personal life insofar as it did not serve his style directly or indirectly. In the preceding chapter we attempted to describe his artistic attitude as something comparable to a mystic's theory of absorption, and we also tried to show how, through the unfaltering consistency and depth of his effort, it was he above all who penetrated to the existence of things, so that the problems of the age are made manifest although the author takes no stand in regard to them. He succeeded in this during his best years, but not thereafter. His aesthetic isolation and the treatment of reality exclusively as an object of literary representation proved in the long run no more of a boon to him than it did to most of his like-minded contemporaries. When we compare Stendhal's or even Balzac's world with the world of Flaubert or the two Goncourts, the latter seems strangely narrow and petty despite its wealth of impressions. Documents of the kind represented by Flaubert's correspondence and the Goncourt diary are indeed admirable in the purity and incorruptibility of their artistic ethics, the wealth of impressions elaborated in them, and their refinement of sensory culture. At the same time, however, we sense—because today we read with different eyes than we did only twenty or thirty years ago—something narrow, something oppressively close in these books. They are full of reality and intellect but poor in humor and inner poise. The purely literary, even on the highest level of artistic acumen and amid the greatest wealth of impressions, limits the power of judgment, reduces the wealth of life, and at times distorts the outlook upon the world of phenomena. And while the writers contemptuously avert their attention from the political and economic bustle, consistently value life only as literary subject matter, and remain arrogantly and bitterly aloof from its great practical problems, in order to achieve aesthetic isolation for their work, often at great and daily expense of effort, the practical world nevertheless besets them in a thousand petty ways. There is vexation with publishers and critics; hatred of the public, which is to be conquered despite the fact that there is no common basis of emotion and thought. Sometimes there are also financial worries, and almost always there are nervous hypertension and a morbid concern with health. But since on the whole they lead the lives of well-to-do bourgeois, since they are comfortably housed, eat exquisitely, and indulge every craving of refined sensuality, since their existence is never threatened by great upheavals and dangers, what finally emerges, despite all their intellectual culture and artistic incorruptibility, is a strangely petty total impression: that of an "upper bourgeois" egocentrically concerned over his aesthetic comfort, plagued by a thousand small vexations, nervous, obsessed by a mania—only in this case the mania is called "literature."

Emile Zola is twenty years younger than the generation of Flaubert and the Goncourts. There are connections between him and them; he is influenced by them; he stands on their shoulders; he has a great deal in common with them. He too would seem not to have been free from neurasthenia, but through his family background he is poorer in money, tradition, fastidiousness of sentiment. He stands out boldly from among the group of the aesthetic realists. We will again cite a text, to bring out this point as clearly as possible. We have chosen a passage from *Germinal* (1888), the novel which describes life in a coal-mining region of Northern France. It is the end of the second chapter of part 3. It is kermess time, a Sunday night in July. The workmen of the place have spent the afternoon going from one bar to another, drinking, bowling, looking at all sorts of shows. The day ends climactically with a ball, the *bal du Bon-Joyeux*, at the *estaminet* of the fat, fiftyish, but still lusty widow Désir. The ball has been going on for several hours; even the older women are coming to it now, bringing their small children.

Jusqu'à dix heures, on resta. Des femmes arrivaient toujours, pour rejoindre et emmener leurs hommes; des bandes d'enfants suivaient à la queue; et les mères ne se gênaient plus, sortaient des mamelles longues et blondes comme des sacs d'avoine, barbouillaient de lait les poupons joufflus; tandis que les petits qui marchaient déjà, gorgés de bière et à quatre pattes sous les tables, se soulageaient sans honte. C'était une mer montante de bière, les tonnes de la veuve Désir éventrées, la bière arrondissant les panses, coulant de partout, du nez, des yeux et d'ailleurs. On gonflait si fort, dans le tas, que chacun avait une épaule ou un genou qui entrait chez le voisin, tous égayés, épanouis de se sentir ainsi les coudes. Un rire continu tenait les bouches ouvertes, fendues jusqu'aux oreilles. Il faisait une chaleur de four, on cuisait, on se mettait à l'aise, la chair dehors, dorée dans l'épaisse fumée des pipes; et le seul inconvénient était de se déranger, une fille se levait de temps à autre, allait au fond, près de la pompe, se troussait, puis revenait. Sous les guirlandes de papier peint, les danseurs ne se voyaient plus, tellement ils suaient; ce qui encourageait les galibots à culbuter les herscheuses, au hasard des coups de reins. Mais lorsqu'une gaillarde tombait avec un homme par dessus elle, le piston couvrait leur chute de sa sonnerie enragée, le branle des pieds les roulait, comme si le bal se fût éboulé sur eux.

Quelqu'un, en passant, avertit Pierron que sa fille Lydie dormait à la porte, en travers du trottoir. Elle avait bu sa part de la bouteille volée, elle était soûle, et il dut l'emporter à son cou, pendant que Jeanlin et Bébert, plus solides, le suivaient de loin, trouvant ça très farce. Ce fut le signal du départ, des familles sortirent du Bon-Joyeux, les Maheu et les Levaque se décidèrent à retourner au coron. A ce moment, le père Bonnemort et le vieux Mouque quittaient aussi Montsou, du même pas de somnambules, entêtés dans le silence de leurs souvenirs. Et l'on rentra tous ensemble, on traversa une dernière fois la ducasse, les poêles de friture qui se figeaient, les estaminats d'où les dernières chopes coulaient en ruisseaux, jusqu'au milieu de la route. L'orage menaçait toujours, des rires montèrent, dès qu'on eut quitté les maisons éclairées, pour se perdre dans la campagne noire. Un souffle ardent sortait des blés mûrs, il dut se faire beaucoup d'enfants, cette nuit-là. On arriva débandé au coron. Ni les Levaque ni les Maheu ne soupèrent avec appétit, et ceux-ci dormaient en achevant leur bouilli du matin.

Etienne avait emmené Chaval boire encore chez Rasseneur.

—"J'en suis!" dit Chaval, quand le camarade lui eut expliqué l'affaire de la caisse de prévoyance. Tape là-dedans, tu es un bon!

Un commencement d'ivresse faisait flamber les yeux d'Etienne. Il cria:—Oui, soyons d'accord. . . Vois-tu, moi, pour la justice je donnerais tout, la boisson et les filles. Il n'y a qu'une chose qui me chauffe le cœur, c'est l'idée que nous allons balayer les bourgeois.

(It was ten o'clock before anyone left. Women kept arriving, to find and take away their men; bands of children followed at their heels; and the mothers no longer troubled about appearances, took out long blond breasts like bags of oats, smeared their fat-cheeked babies with milk; while the children who could already walk, gorged with beer and on all fours under the tables, relieved themselves without shame. It was a rising sea of beer, Widow Désir's casks broached, beer swelling out bellies, flowing from all sides, from noses, from eyes, and from elsewhere. People swelled up so, in the press, that everyone had a shoulder or a knee digging into his neighbor, all were made cheerful, at ease, by feeling one another's elbows in this way. A continuous laugh kept mouths open, gaping to the ears. It was as hot as an oven, everyone was roasting, all made themselves comfortable, their flesh exposed, gilded in the thick smoke of the pipes; and the only difficulty was to move, a girl got up from time to time, went to the back, near the pump, tucked up her skirts, then returned. Under the garlands of colored paper the dancers no longer saw each other, they were sweating so—which encouraged the pit-boys to knock over the haulage-girls by promiscuous thrusts of their haunches. But when a strapping girl fell with a man on top of her, the cornet covered their fall with its furious sounds, the swing of feet rolled them, as if the dance had collapsed on them.

Someone passing by told Pierron that his daughter Lydie was sleeping at the door, across the sidewalk. She had swallowed her share of the stolen bottle, she was drunk, and he had to carry her in his arms, while Jeanlin and Bébert, more resistant, followed him at a distance, finding it very funny. This was the signal for departure, the families left the Bon-Joyeux, the Maheus and the Levaques decided to return to the mining village. At that moment, Père Bonnemort and old Mouque also left Montsou, both with the same sleep-walking gait, stubbornly maintaining the silence of their memories. And they all went home together, for the last time they passed through the carnival, the solidifying pans of fried stuff, the bars from which the last mugs were pouring in streams, even to the middle of the road. There was still a storm threatening, laughter rose as soon as they had left the lighted houses to lose themselves in the dark countryside. A hot breath poured from the ripe wheat, many children must have been conceived that night. When they reached the village, they felt let down. Neither the Levaques nor the Maheus supped with appetite, and the latter fell asleep finishing their morning boiled beef.

Etienne had taken Chaval to drink some more at Rasseneur's.

"I'm on!" said Chaval, when his comrade had explained the matter of the reserve fund to him. "Shake! You're all right!"

A touch of drunkenness made Etienne's eyes flame. He cried, "Yes, let's be together . . . As for me, I tell you, for justice I would give everything, drink and women. There's only one thing that warms my heart, it's the idea that we are going to get rid of the bosses.")

The passage is one of those which, when Zola's work first appeared during the last thirty years of the past century, aroused disgust and horror, but also, on the part of a not inconsiderable minority, great admiration. Many of his novels attained high sales figures immediately upon publication, and a strong movement set in for and against the justification of this kind of art. A reader who, knowing nothing of all this, should read nothing of Zola's except the first paragraph of the passage cited above, could believe for a moment that he had before him a literary form of the coarse realism which is so well known from the Flemish and especially the Dutch painting of the seventeenth century. He might take it as nothing but a lower-class orgy of dancing and drinking, of the kind to be found or imagined in Rubens or Jordaens, in Brouwer or Ostade. To be sure, these are not peasants drinking and dancing but factory workers; and there is also a difference in the effect produced, in that the especially brutal details impress us, for the length of time it takes to utter them or read them, as more disagreeable and painful than they would as elements in a painting. But these are not basic differences. We might add that Zola apparently attributed great importance to the purely sensory aspects of his "literary portrait" of a mob orgy, that in this paragraph his genius reveals a decidedly pictorial vein, for example in his details of flesh painting (. . . *les mères . . . sortaient des mamelles longues et blondes comme des sacs d'avoine* . . . ; and later . . . *la chair dehors, dorée dans l'épaisse fumée des pipes*). The flowing beer, the haze of sweat, the grinning and wide-open mouths likewise become visual impressions; acoustic and other sensory effects are also produced. In short, for a moment we might be tempted to think that what is set before us is nothing but an unusually robust action on the lowest level of style, sheer rowdyism. Especially the last part of the paragraph, the furious blowing of cornets and the ferocious dancing which muffles and swallows up the fall of one couple, supplies the orgiastic note which such farcical creations require.

But all that alone would not have caused so much excitement among Zola's contemporaries. Among his enemies, who worked themselves into a fury over what they called the repulsiveness, the filth, and the obscenity of his art, there were doubtless many who accepted the grotesque or comic realism of earlier epochs, even in its crudest or most indecent representations, with equanimity and even with delight. What excited them so was rather the fact that Zola by no means put forth his art as "of the low style," still less as comic. Almost every line he wrote showed that all this was meant in the highest degree seriously and morally; that the sum total of it was not a pastime or an artistic parlor game but the true portrait of contemporary society as he —Zola—saw it and as the public was being urged in his works to see it too.

This could hardly be surmised from the first paragraph of our text taken by itself. The one aspect of it which could give us pause is the matter-of-factness of the presentation. It is almost like a *procès-verbal*; despite the sensory immediacy it achieves, there is a certain dryness, excessive clarity, almost inhumanity in it. This is not the style of a writer who aims at nothing but comic or grotesque effects. The first sentence—*Jusqu'à dix heures, on resta*—would be inconceivable in a grotesque mob orgy. Why are we told of the end of the orgy at the start? For a purely amusing or grotesque purpose, that would be much too sobering. And why such an early hour? What sort of an orgy is it which reaches its end so early? The coal-miners have to be out of bed early on Monday morning, some of them at four o'clock. . . . And once we have paused, there are many other things that strike us. An orgy, even among the lowest classes, calls for plenty. And plenty there is, but it is poor and frugal—nothing but beer. The whole thing shows how desolate and miserable the joys of these people are.

The real purport of the passage grows clearer in the second paragraph, which describes the various participants' departure and home-going. The daughter of the miner Pierron, Lydie, is found in the street outside the estaminet, asleep and very drunk. Lydie is a girl of twelve who has spent the evening running around with two neighborhood boys of the same age, Jeanlin and Bébert. The three of them already work as haulers in the mine. They are prematurely depraved children, especially the wily and vicious Jeanlin. This time he has talked the other two into stealing a bottle of gin from one of the kermess stalls. They have emptied it together, but the girl's share proved too much for her. Now she is being carried home by her father. The two boys follow at a distance, *trouvant cela très farce. . . .* Meanwhile the Maheu and Levaque families, who are neighbors, are getting ready to leave. They are joined by two old, worn-out pitmen, Bonnemort and Mouque, who have spent the day together as they usually do. They are hardly sixty years old but they are already the last of their generation—used up and apathetic and no longer employable in the mine except with the horses. During their free hours they stay together constantly, almost without talking. Now once again they drag themselves through the ebbing bustle of the kermess in the direction of the village where they all live. As soon as they get beyond the rows of lighted houses to where the open countryside begins, laughter rises, a hot vapor flows from the darkness of the ripe fields: many children are being begotten that night. Finally they arrive at their hut where, already half asleep, they eat the left-overs of their noonday meal.

Meanwhile two younger men have gone to another tavern. In general they are not on very good terms, because of a girl; but today they have something important to discuss. Etienne wants to win over Chaval for his plan of a workmen's fund, so that their crew will not be without means when a strike is called. Chaval goes in on it. Warmed by their revolutionary hopes and some liquor, they forget their enmity (not for long, to be sure) and unite in their common hatred of the bourgeois.

Crude and miserable pleasures; early depravity and rapid wearing out of human material; a dissolute sex life, and a birth-rate too high for such living conditions, since intercourse is the only amusement that costs nothing; behind all this, at least among the most energetic and intelligent, revolutionary hatred on the verge of breaking out—these are the motifs of our text. They are unreservedly translated into sensory terms, with no hesitation before the most unambiguous words and the ugliest scenes. The art of style has wholly renounced producing pleasing effects in the conventional sense of the term. Instead it serves unpleasant, depressing, desolate truth. But this truth is at the same time a summons to action in terms of a social reform. It is no longer, as it still was with the Goncourts, a matter of the sensory fascination of ugliness; what we have here is, beyond the shadow of a doubt, the core of the social problem of the age, the struggle between industrial capital and labor. The principle of *l'art pour l'art* has outlived its usefulness. It may be pointed out that Zola too felt and exploited the sensory power of suggestion of the ugly and the repulsive; it may even be held against him that his somewhat coarse-grained and powerful imagination led him to exaggerations, violent simplifications, and a far too materialistic psychology. But all that is not of decisive significance. Zola took the mixing of styles really seriously; he pushed on beyond the purely aesthetic realism of the preceding generation; he is one of the very few authors of the century who created their work out of the great problems of the age. In this respect only Balzac can be compared with him; but Balzac wrote at a time when much of what Zola saw had not yet developed or was not yet discernible. If Zola exaggerated, he did so in the direction which mattered; and if he had a predilection for the ugly, he used it most fruitfully. Even today, after half a century the last decades of which have brought us experiences such as Zola never dreamed of, *Germinal* is still a terrifying book. And even today it has lost none of its significance and indeed none of its timeliness. There are passages in it which deserve to become classic, which ought to be in anthologies, because they depict, with exemplary clarity and simplicity, the situation and the awakening of the fourth estate in an earlier phase of the same era of change in which we now find ourselves. I am thinking for example of the evening conversation at the miner Maheu's, in the third chapter of part 3. The theme is first the crowded living conditions in the small houses of the village, their deleterious effects upon health and morals; and then the passage continues as follows:

> "Dame!" répondait Maheu, "si l'on avait plus d'argent, on aurait plus d'aise. . Tout de même, c'est bien vrai que ça ne vaut

rien pour personne, de vivre les uns sur les autres. Ça finit toujours par des hommes soûls et par des filles pleines."

Et la famille partait de là, chacun disait son mot, pendant que le pétrole de la lampe viciait l'air de la salle, déjà empuantie d'oignon frit. Non, sûrement, la vie n'était pas drôle. On travaillait en vraies brutes à un travail qui était la punition des galériens autrefois, on y laissait sa peau plus souvent qu'à son tour, tout ça pour ne pas même avoir de la viande sur sa table, le soir. Sans doute, on avait sa pâtée quand même, on mangeait, mais si peu, juste de quoi souffrir sans crever, écrasé de dettes, poursuivi comme si l'on volait son pain. Quand arrivait le dimanche on dormait de fatigue. Les seuls plaisirs, c'était de se soûler ou de faire un enfant à sa femme; encore la bière vous engraissait trop le ventre, et l'enfant, plus tard, se foutait de vous. Non, non, ça n'avait rien de drôle.

Alors, la Maheude s'en mêlait.

"L'embêtant, voyez-vous, c'est lorsqu'on se dit que ça ne peut pas changer. . . Quand on est jeune, on s'imagine que le bonheur viendra, on espère des choses; et puis, la misère recommence toujours, on reste enfermé là-dedans. . . Moi, je ne veux du mal à personne, mais il y a des fois où cette injustice me révolte."

Un silence se faisait, tous soufflaient un instant, dans le malaise vague de cet horizon fermé. Seul, le père Bonnemort, s'il était là, ouvrait des yeux surpris, car de son temps on ne se tracassait pas de la sorte: on naissait dans le charbon, on tapait à la veine, sans en demander davantage; tandis que, maintenant, il passait un air qui donnait de l'ambition aux charbonniers.

"Faut cracher sur rien, murmurait-il. Une bonne chope est une bonne chope. . . Les chefs, c'est souvent de la canaille; mais il y aura toujours des chefs, pas vrai? Inutile de se casser la tête à réfléchir là-dessus."

Du coup, Etienne s'animait. Comment! la réflexion serait défendue à l'ouvrier! Eh! justement, les choses changeraient bientôt, parce que l'ouvrier réfléchissait à cette heure. . .

("Sure!" Maheu would answer, "if we had more money, we'd have things easier . . . Just the same, it's perfectly true that living on top of each other is no good for anybody. That always ends with the men drunk and the girls knocked up."

And the family would start from there, each saying his word, while the kerosene of the lamp fouled the air, already reeking with fried onion. No, indeed, life was not amusing. You toiled like beasts at work which was the punishment of criminals in earlier days, you lost your hide at it more often than your turn came, and all that and not even have meat on your table at night. Of course you had your rations after all, but so little, just enough to keep you suffering without dying, crushed under debts, persecuted as if you stole your bread. When Sunday came you slept from exhaustion. The only pleasures were to get drunk or make your wife a child; and even at that, beer gave you too big a belly, and the child, later on, said to hell with you. No, no, there was nothing amusing about it.

Then his wife would put in her word.

"The bad thing, I say, is when you tell yourself that it can't change. . . When you're young, you imagine that happiness will come, you hope for things; and then, it's always trouble beginning over again, you get caught in it. . . As for me, I don't wish anyone any harm, but there are times when this injustice sickens me."

There would be a silence, all would breathe heavily for a moment, in the vague uneasiness of that closed horizon. Only old Bonnemort, if he were present, would open surprised eyes, for in his day people didn't get into a fuss like this: you were born in coal, you hammered away at the vein, without asking for anything more; whereas today, there was a wind blowing which made coal-miners ambitious.

"Never belittle anything," he would murmur. "A good mug is a good mug. . . The bosses are often lice; but there'll always be bosses, won't there? No use breaking your brains thinking about it."

At once Etienne would become animated. What! the workman forbidden to think! Why, it was just because the workman was thinking these days, that things would soon change . . .)

This is not meant to be a specific conversation, but only an example, one of the many conversations which arise night after night at the Maheu's under the influence of their tenant Etienne Lantier. Hence too the imperfect tense. The slow transition from torpid resignation to conscious awareness of one's own situation, the budding of hopes and plans, the various attitudes of different generations; then too the somber poverty and the reeking atmosphere of the room, the densely packed bodies, the simple appositeness of the speeches: all this together gives a typical picture of labor during the early socialist epoch, and surely no one today will seriously attempt to deny that the subject has world-historical importance. What level of style should be ascribed to such a text? There is here, beyond all doubt, great historical tragedy, a mixture of *humile* and *sublime* in which, because of the content, the latter prevails. Statements like Maheu's (*si l'on avait plus d'argent on aurait plus d'aise*—or, *Ça finit toujours par des hommes soûls et par des filles pleines*), not to mention his wife's, have come to be part of the great style. A far cry from Boileau, who could imagine the people only as grimacing grotesquely in the lowest farce. Zola knows how these people thought and talked. He also knows every detail of the technical side of mining; he knows the psychology of the various classes of workers and of the administration, the functioning of the central management, the competition between the capitalist groups, the cooperation of the interests of capital with the government, the army. But he did not confine himself to writing novels about industrial workers. His purpose was to comprise—as Balzac had done, but much more methodically and painstakingly—the whole life of the period (the Second Empire): the people of Paris, the rural population, the theater, the department stores, the stock exchange, and very much more besides. He made himself an expert in all fields; everywhere he penetrated into social structure and technology. An unimaginable amount of intelligence and labor went into the *Rougon-Macquart*. Today we are surfeited with such impressions; Zola has had many successors, and scenes similar to that at Maheu's could be found in any piece of modern reporting. But Zola was the first, and his work is full of pictures of a similar kind and a similar value. Did anyone before him see a tenement house as he did in the second chapter of *l'Assommoir*? Hardly! And the picture he gives of it is not even seen from his point of view; it is the impression received by a young washerwomen who has recently come to Paris to live and who is waiting at the entrance. These pages too I should call classic. The errors in Zola's anthropological conception and the limits of his genius are patent; but they do not impair his artistic, ethical, and especially his historical importance, and I am inclined to think that his stature will increase as we attain distance from his age and its problems—the more so because he was the last of the great French realists. Even during the last decade of his life the "anti-naturalist" reaction was becoming very strong; and besides, there was no one left to vie with him in working capacity, in mastery of the life of the time, in determination and courage.

In its grasp of contemporary reality French literature is far ahead of the literature of other European countries in the nineteenth century. As for Germany, or rather, the territory where German is spoken, we have briefly referred to it in an earlier passage (page 452f.). If we consider that Jeremias Gotthelf (born 1797) was but two years older and Adalbert Stifter (1805) six years younger than Balzac; that the German contemporaries of Flaubert (1821) and Edmond de Goncourt (1822) are men like Freytag (1816), Storm (1817), Fontane and Keller (both 1819); that the (comparatively) most noteworthy prose-fiction writers born roughly contemporaneously with Emile Zola—that is, about 1840—are Anzengruber and Rosegger: these names alone are enough to show that in Germany life itself was much more provincial, much more old-fashioned, much less "contemporary." The regional sections of the German language territory lived each in its own way, and in none of them had consciousness of modern life and of imminent developments ripened into concrete form; even after 1871 that consciousness was slow in awakening, or at least a long time went by before it manifested itself vigorously in the literary representation of contemporary reality. Life itself long continued to be more firmly rooted in the individual, the idiosyncratic, the traditional than was the case in France. It yielded no subject matter for a realism so generally national, so materially modern, so intent upon an analysis of the emerging destiny of European society, as the realism of France. And among the German writers who came out as radical critics of conditions in their homelands—almost all of whom had undergone the influence of French public life—there was no important realistic talent. Those noteworthy German writers who concerned themselves with the literary treatment of contemporary reality all had one thing in common. They were immersed in the traditional attitudes of the particular corner of the land in which they were rooted. Which meant that their romanticism, poeticism, Jean-Paulism or on the other hand their old-fashioned solidly bourgeois common sense—or a combination of both—long excluded the possibility of so radical a mixture of styles as had been evolved quite early in France. Anything of that nature made itself accepted only toward the very end of the century and then only after a hard struggle. In compensation, in the work of the best of them there is an intense reverence for life, a pure conception of the vocation of man, such as is nowhere to be found in France. Men like Stifter and Keller can give their readers a much purer and more intense delight than Balzac or Flaubert, to say nothing of Zola. Nothing is more unjust than a remark in Edmond de Goncourt's diary for 1871 (though perhaps it might be explained through the natural bitterness of a Frenchman who was hard hit by the events of the Franco-Prussian war): he denies the Germans every kind of humanism and insists that they have neither novel nor drama! But it is true that the best German works of this period had no world-wide importance and could not, by their very nature, become accessible to a man like Edmond de Goncourt.

A few dates may give a general view of the situation. Let us begin with the forties. In 1843 the most significant realistic tragedy of the period, Hebbel's *Maria Magdalena,* appears. At about the same time Stifter makes himself known (first volume of the *Studien* in 1844, *Nachsommer* in 1857). The best-known narrative works of the somewhat older Gotthelf also fall in this decade. The following ten years witness the appearance of Storm (*Immensee* in 1852, but this writer achieves full maturity only much later), Keller (first edition of *Der Grüne Heinrich* in 1855, *Die Leute von Seldwyla*—first volume—in 1856), Freytag (*Soll und Haben* in 1855), Raabe (*Chronik der Sperlingsgasse* in 1856, *Der Hungerpastor* in 1864). During the decades before and after the foundation of the Empire nothing distinctively new appears in contemporary realism. There is to be sure the development of something like a modern novel of manners whose most popular representative at the time and on into the nineties was the now totally forgotten Friedrich Spielhagen. These decades are marked by a decline of language, content, and taste. Only a few members of the older generation, especially Keller, continue to write a prose which has cadence and weight. It is only after 1880 that Fontane, then already past the age of sixty, attains his full development as a delineator of contemporary subject matter. I am inclined to assign him a rank far below men like Gotthelf, Stifter, or Keller, but his clever and amiable art at any rate affords us the best picture we possess of the society of his period. Then too we can regard his art—despite its restriction to Berlin and the Prussian provinces east of the Elbe—as the transition to a freer, less secluded, more cosmopolitan realism. About 1890 foreign influences break in from all directions. As far as the portrayal of contemporary reality is concerned, this leads to the formation of a German naturalistic school whose most important figure by far is the dramatist Hauptmann. *Die Weber, Der Biberpelz, Fuhrmann Henschel* all belong to the nineteenth century. In the new century falls the first great realistic novel, which, despite its complete originality, corresponds in its level of style to the works of the French nineteenth-century realists: Thomas Mann's *Buddenbrooks*, which appeared in 1901. It must be emphasized that Hauptmann too, and even Thomas Mann in his beginnings, were much more solidly anchored in the soil of their native regions—the mountains of Lower Silesia and Lübeck—than any one of the great Frenchmen.

None of the men between 1840 and 1890—from Jeremias Gotthelf to Theodor Fontane—displays, fully developed, all of the major characteristics of French realism, that is, of the nascent European form of realism: namely, as has appeared from our analyses in the foregoing chapters, a serious representation of contemporary everyday social reality against the background of a constant historical movement. Two figures as basically different as the practical, sturdy Gotthelf, who—in the best tradition of the clergy—flinched from no reality, and the young, oppressed, and somber Hebbel, who wrote the unrelieved tragedy of the cabinet-maker Anton and his daughter, have this much in common: that the historical background of the events they represent appears completely immobile. The homesteads of the Bernese farmers seem destined to rest for centuries in a calm stirred only by the change of seasons and generations, as they have done for centuries past; and the horrible old-fashioned code of petty-bourgeois ethics which smothers the people in *Maria Magdalena* also appears to be completely without historical movement. Hebbel, by the way, does not let his characters speak as colloquially as Schiller does his musician Miller for example. He does not localize them, for his setting is "a medium-sized town." His dialogue—of which F. T. Vischer, even in his day, said that no housewife and no master cabinet-maker talked like that—contains, side by side with colloquial expressions, much forced poetic rhetoric, which at times affects us as unnatural and yet with as much terrifyingly suggestive power as would Seneca transposed into a petty-bourgeois key. In terms of our problem the situation is very much the same in the case of Adalbert Stifter, again a writer of a completely different genius. He too stylizes the language of his characters, making it so simple, pure, and noble that we never find a coarse expression, hardly ever even a hearty colloquialism. His language touches the common things of everyday life with delicate, innocent, and somewhat timid refinement. This has a direct bearing on the fact that his characters too live in a world with hardly a trace of historical movement. Everything which forces its way in from the bustle of contemporary history, from the modern life of the world, politics, business, money matters, professional concerns (unless it is in the domain of agriculture or the crafts), he expresses in simple and noble, extremely general, allusive, and cautious terms, so that nothing proceeding from that ugly and impure confusion shall reach him and his reader. Much more politically inclined is Gottfried Keller, more modern too, yet only within the specialized and narrow frame of Switzerland. The democratic-liberal optimism which is the breath of life to him and which still permits the individual personality to seek its way in unhampered freedom, is for us today a fairytale from an earlier age. Then too he remains upon an intermediate level of seriousness. Indeed, the most compelling charm of his genius is his characteristic serene cheerfulness, which is able to play its game of benign irony with the most incongruous and repulsive things.

The successful wars which culminated in the establishment of the Empire had the most disastrous consequences morally and aesthetically. The noble purity of a regionalism which had kept apart from the rush of the modern world could no longer assert itself in public and literary life. And the modern trends which imposed themselves in literature were unworthy of the German tradition, false, blind both to their own falseness and to the problems of the times. To be sure, there were a few writers whose eyes saw more keenly—the aging Vischer for example, and Jacob Burckhardt (who was really not German but Swiss), and above all Nietzsche, who, in addition, was the first to experience the conflict between author and public which is to be observed very much earlier in France (see pages 499ff.). But Nietzsche was not concerned with the realistic portrayal of contemporary reality. Among those who were—that is, among the authors of novels and plays—there would seem, from 1870 to 1890, to have been no single new figure of weight and rank, no one capable of providing a serious creative expression for any part of the structure of contemporary life. Only in the case of Fontane, who was already getting on in years—and even with him only in his last and finest novels, those written after 1890—is it possible to discern the rudiments of a genuine contemporary realism. But they do not develop fully because his tone after all never goes beyond the half-seriousness of pleasant, partly optimistic, partly resigned conversation. To reproach him with this would be unjust, for he never claimed to be an essentially critical realist in respect to his age, in the sense in which Balzac or Zola were. On the contrary, it is to his honor that his name is the only one which nevertheless imposes itself when we discuss his generation from the point of view of serious realism.

Nor in the other countries of Western and Southern Europe does realism during the second half of the century attain the independent power and consistency which it achieved in France. Not even in England, although there are important realists among the English novelists. The quieter development of public life during the Victorian period is reflected in the comparative immobility of the contemporary background against which the events of most of those novels occur. Traditional, religious, and ethical motifs exercise a counterbalancing effect, so that realism does not assume the extreme forms it has in France. At times, to be sure, and particularly toward the end of the century, there is an important French influence.

About this time, that is, from the eighties on, the Scandinavian countries and above all Russia enter the limelight of European public attention with realistic works of literature. Among the Scandinavians the most influential personality is the Norwegian dramatist Henrik Ibsen. His dramas of society are tendentious; they oppose the rigidity, restriction, and falseness of moral life among the upper classes of the bourgeoisie. Although they are all set in Norway and deal with pronouncedly Norwegian conditions, their problems nevertheless were pertinent to the Central European bourgeoisie in general. Ibsen's masterly dramatic technique, his unerring conduct of the action, and his sharp outlining of his characters—especially of some of his women—carried away the public. The impression he made was very great, especially in Germany, where the naturalistic movement of 1890 revered him as a master on an equality with Zola, where his plays were excellently produced by the best theaters, and where the remarkable renewal of the drama which took place at that time is in general linked to his name. Through the complete transformation of the social status of the bourgeoisie since 1914 and in general through the upheavals brought about by the current world crisis, his problems have lost their timeliness and we can now better see how calculated and contrived his art often is. Yet it remains to his credit that he accomplished the historic task of giving a style to the serious bourgeois drama: a problem which had been pending since the *comédie larmoyante* of the eighteenth century and which he was the first to solve. It is his misfortune, though perhaps it is also in a small degree due to him, that the bourgeoisie has since changed beyond recognition.

More lasting and important is the effect of the Russians. Gogol, it is true, had scarcely any influence in Europe, and Turgenev, who was on friendly terms with Flaubert and Edmond de Goncourt, would seem on the whole to have received more than he gave. From the eighties on, Tolstoi and Dostoevski begin to come into the picture. From 1887 we find them named and discussed in the Goncourt diary. But it seems that a real appreciation of their work, especially Dostoevski's, came about only very slowly. German translations of Dostoevski do not appear until the twentieth century. This is not the place to discuss the Russian writers in general, their roots and premises, their individual significance in Russian literature itself; we can only take up their influence upon the European way of seeing and representing reality.

It seems that the Russians were naturally endowed with the possibility of conceiving of everyday things in a serious vein; that a classicistic aesthetics which excludes a literary category of "the low" from serious treatment could never gain a firm foothold in Russia. Then too, as we think of Russian realism, remembering that it came into its own only during the nineteenth century and indeed only during the second half of it, we cannot escape the observation that it is based on a Christian and traditionally patriarchal concept of the creatural dignity of every human individual regardless of social rank and position, and hence that it is fundamentally related rather to old-Christian than to modern occidental realism. The enlightened, active bourgeoisie, with its assumption of economic and intellectual leadership, which everywhere else underlay modern culture in general and modern realism in particular, seems to have scarcely existed in Russia. At least it cannot be found in the novels, not even in Tolstoi or Dostoevski. There are in the realistic novels members of the higher aristocracy, noble landowners of various ranks and degrees of wealth, there are hierarchies of civil servants and of the clergy; then there are petty bourgeois and peasants, that is, the people in its most living multiplicity. But what lies between, the wealthy upper bourgeoisie and the merchant class, is still generally split up into guilds and in any case is completely patriarchal in attitudes and forms of life. We may think for example of the merchant Samsanov in Dostoevski's *Brothers Karamazov* or of the Rogoshin family and their house in the *Idiot*. This sort of thing has nothing whatever in common with the enlightened bourgeoisie of central and western Europe. The reformers, rebels, and conspirators —of whom there are many—come from the most varied classes, and the manner of their revolt, however different it may be in the individual instances, still everywhere shows a close connection with the

Christian and traditionally patriarchal world from which they manage to break away only through painful violence.

Another characteristic feature which strikes the western reader of Russian literature is the uniformity of the population and its life in that vast country, an obviously spontaneous or at least very long established unity of all that is Russian, so that it often seems superfluous to state in what particular region the action takes place. Even the character of the landscape is much more homogeneous than in any other European country. With the exception of the two principal cities, Moscow and Saint Petersburg, whose distinctly different characteristics are clearly to be recognized from literary sources, it is a rare occurrence if a city, hamlet, or province is identified. In Gogol's *Dead Souls* or in his famous comedy *The Inspector General* the place of the action is given simply as "the capital of a government" or "a provincial town," and the situation is very much the same in Dostoevski's *The Possessed* or *The Brothers Karamazov*. The landowners, civil servants, merchants, clergymen, petty bourgeois, and peasants seem everywhere to be "Russian" in much the same way. There are but rare instances where speech peculiarities are noted, and where it is done, it is not a matter of dialectal regionalisms but of personal idiosyncracies, or of social stigmata (as for instance the special pronunciation of the vowel 'o' which is current among the lower classes), or finally of peculiarities characteristic of the minorities domiciled in the country (Jews, Poles, Germans, Little Russians). As for the born Orthodox Russians, throughout the entire country, and regardless of class distinctions, they seem to form a single ancient patriarchal family. True, this sort of thing may be observed elsewhere in the nineteenth century, for example in individual German districts, but nowhere so pronouncedly and above all not over so vast a territory. Everywhere in this gigantic country the same Russian regional atmosphere seems to exist.

Now, within this great and homogeneous national family (which is differentiated from contemporary European society above all by the fact that an enlightened bourgeoisie, conscious of its value and working toward a definite end, has scarcely begun to exist) all through the nineteenth century an inner movement of the most powerful nature prevails. This is unmistakably recognized in the literary output of the time. Considerable movement prevails in the other European literatures of this period too, especially in French literature; but it is a different kind of movement. The most essential characteristic of the inner movement documented in Russian realism is the unqualified, unlimited, and passionate intensity of experience in the characters portrayed. That is the strongest impression which the western reader receives, before and above all else, especially in Dostoevski but also in Tolstoi and the others. It seems that the Russians have preserved an immediacy of experience which had become a rare phenomenon in western civilization of the nineteenth century. A strong practical, ethical, or intellectual shock immediately arouses them in the depths of their instincts, and in a moment they pass from a quiet and almost vegetative existence to the most monstrous excesses both in practical and spiritual matters. The pendulum of their vitality, of their actions, thoughts, and emotions seems to oscillate farther than elsewhere in Europe. This too reminds us of the Christian realism which we have tried to elaborate in the early chapters of this book. There is something truly monstrous—especially in Dostoevski but elsewhere too—in the change from love to hatred, from humble devotion to animal brutality, from a passionate love of truth to the most vulgar lust for pleasure, from pious simplicity to the most cruel cynicism. Such changes often occur in one person—almost without transition—in tremendous and unpredictable oscillations. And each time the person spends himself completely, so that his words and acts reveal chaotic instinctive depths of a kind which to be sure were not unknown in the countries of the west but which scientific detachment, sense of form, and respect for social proprieties prevented the writers there from expressing without restraint. When the great Russians, especially Dostoevski, became known in Central and Western Europe, the immense spiritual potential and the directness of expression which their amazed readers encountered in their works seemed like a revelation of how the mixture of realism and tragedy might at last attain its true fulfillment.

In addition one final point needs to be considered. If we ask what it was that released the powerful inner movement in the characters who people the Russian works of the nineteenth century, the answer must be as follows: In the first place, the infiltration of modern European and especially of German and French forms of life and thought. These in all their power collided in Russia with a society which, though frequently rotten, was wholly independent, which had its own will, and which above all was hardly yet prepared for such an encounter. For moral and practical reasons it was impossible to avoid coming to terms with modern European civilization, although the preparatory periods which had brought Europe to the position it then occupied had not nearly been lived through in Russia. The process of coming to terms was dramatic and confused. Observing it as it is reflected in Tolstoi or Dostoevski we clearly grasp the savage, tempestuous, and uncompromising nature of Russian acceptance or rejection of European culture. The very choice of the ideas and systems over which the struggle takes place is somehow accidental and arbitrary. Then too, nothing but their final result is extracted, as it were, and this is not evaluated in its relation to other ideas and systems, for example, as a more or less significant contribution within a rich and many-sided intellectual production, but is immediately evaluated as an absolute, which is true or false, an inspiration or a devilish delusion. Immense theoretical countersystems are improvised. The most complex phenomena, fraught with historical premises and very difficult to formulate in a clear synthesis—phenomena like "western culture," liberalism, socialism, the Catholic Church—are judged in a few words, in accordance with a particular and more often than not erroneous point of view. And always the points at issue are "ultimate" ethical, religious, and social questions. An extremely characteristic case in point is the postulate which Ivan Karamazov sets up and which represents the basic motif of the great novel: that there can be no morality without God and immortality, that indeed crime must be recognized as the unavoidable and rational way of escape from the position of every atheist—a postulate in which the radical passion for "Everything or Nothing" brings into the thinking something which is at once amateurish and disconcertingly magnificent. But Russian coming to terms with European civilization during the nineteenth century was significant not only for Russia. However confused and amateurish a process it often was, however much it was impaired by inadequate information, false perspectives, by prejudice and passion, there was at work in it an extremely sure instinct for the things that were unsound and critical in Europe. In this respect too the effect of Tolstoi and still more of Dostoevski in Europe was very great, and if, in many domains, among them that of realistic literature, the moral crisis became increasingly keen from the last decade before the first World War, and something like a premonition of the impending catastrophe was observable, the influence of the Russian realists was an essential contributing factor.

20

THE BROWN STOCKING

"And even if it isn't fine to-morrow," said Mrs. Ramsay, raising her eyes to glance at William Bankes and Lily Briscoe as they passed, "it will be another day. And now," she said, thinking that Lily's charm was her Chinese eyes, aslant in her white, puckered little face, but it would take a clever man to see it, "and now stand up, and let me measure your leg," for they might go to the Lighthouse after all, and she must see if the stocking did not need to be an inch or two longer in the leg.

Smiling, for an admirable idea had flashed upon her this very second—William and Lily should marry—she took the heather mixture stocking, with its criss-cross of steel needles at the mouth of it, and measured it against James's leg.

"My dear, stand still," she said, for in his jealousy, not liking to serve as measuring-block for the Lighthouse keeper's little boy, James fidgeted purposely; and if he did that, how could she see, was it too long, was it too short? she asked.

She looked up—what demon possessed him, her youngest, her cherished?—and saw the room, saw the chairs, thought them fearfully shabby. Their entrails, as Andrew said the other day, were all over the floor; but then what was the point, she asked herself, of buying good chairs to let them spoil up here all through the winter when the house, with only one old woman to see to it, positively dripped with wet? Never mind: the rent was precisely twopence halfpenny; the children loved it; it did her husband good to be three thousand, or if she must be accurate, three hundred miles from his library and his lectures and his disciples; and there was room for visitors. Mats, camp beds, crazy ghosts of chairs and tables whose London life of service was done—they did well enough here; and a photograph or two, and books. Books, she thought, grew of themselves. She never had time to read them. Alas! even the books that had been given her, and inscribed by the hand of the poet himself: "For her whose wishes must be obeyed . . ." "The happier Helen of our days. . ." disgraceful to say, she had never read them. And Croom on the Mind and Bates on the

Savage Customs of Polynesia ("My dear, stand still," she said) —neither of those could one send to the Lighthouse. At a certain moment, she supposed, the house would become so shabby that something must be done. If they could be taught to wipe their feet and not bring the beach in with them—that would be something. Crabs, she had to allow, if Andrew really wished to dissect them, or if Jasper believed that one could make soup from seaweed, one could not prevent it; or Rose's objects—shells, reeds, stones; for they were gifted, her children, but all in quite different ways. And the result of it was, she sighed, taking in the whole room from floor to ceiling, as she held the stocking against James's leg, that things got shabbier and got shabbier summer after summer. The mat was fading; the wall-paper was flapping. You couldn't tell any more that those were roses on it. Still, if every door in a house is left perpetually open, and no lockmaker in the whole of Scotland can mend a bolt, things must spoil. What was the use of flinging a green Cashmere shawl over the edge of a picture frame? In two weeks it would be the colour of pea soup. But it was the doors that annoyed her; every door was left open. She listened. The drawing-room door was open; the hall door was open; it sounded as if the bedroom doors were open; and certainly the window on the landing was open, for that she had opened herself. That windows should be open, and doors shut—simple as it was, could none of them remember it? She would go into the maids' bedrooms at night and find them sealed like ovens, except for Marie's, the Swiss girl, who would rather go without a bath than without fresh air, but then at home, she had said, "the mountains are so beautiful." She had said that last night looking out of the window with tears in her eyes. "The mountains are so beautiful." Her father was dying there, Mrs. Ramsay knew. He was leaving them fatherless. Scolding and demonstrating (how to make a bed, how to open a window, with hands that shut and spread like a Frenchwoman's) all had folded itself quietly about her, when the girl spoke, as, after a flight through the sunshine the wings of a bird fold themselves quietly and the blue of its plumage changes from bright steel to soft purple. She had stood there silent for there was nothing to be said. He had cancer of the throat. At the recollection—how she had stood there, how the girl had said "At home the mountains are so beautiful," and there was no hope, no hope whatever, she had a spasm of irritation, and speaking sharply, said to James:

"Stand still. Don't be tiresome," so that he knew instantly that her severity was real, and straightened his leg and she measured it.

The stocking was too short by half an inch at least, making allowance for the fact that Sorley's little boy would be less well grown than James.

"It's too short," she said, "ever so much too short."

Never did anybody look so sad. Bitter and black, half-way down, in the darkness, in the shaft which ran from the sunlight to the depths, perhaps a tear formed; a tear fell; the waters swayed this way and that, received it, and were at rest. Never did anybody look so sad.

But was it nothing but looks? people said. What was there behind it—her beauty, her splendour? Had he blown his brains out, they asked, had he died the week before they were married—some other, earlier lover, of whom rumours reached one? Or was there nothing? nothing but an incomparable beauty which she lived behind, and could do nothing to disturb? For easily though she might have said at some moment of intimacy when stories of great passion, of love foiled, of ambition thwarted came her way how she too had known or felt or been through it herself, she never spoke. She was silent always. She knew then—she knew without having learnt. Her simplicity fathomed what clever people falsified. Her singleness of mind made her drop plumb like a stone, alight exact as a bird, gave her, naturally, this swoop and fall of the spirit upon truth which delighted, eased, sustained—falsely perhaps.

("Nature has but little clay," said Mr. Bankes once, hearing her voice on the telephone, and much moved by it though she was only telling him a fact about a train, "like that of which she moulded you." He saw her at the end of the line, Greek, blue-eyed, straight-nosed. How incongruous it seemed to be telephoning to a woman like that. The Graces assembling seemed to have joined hands in meadows of asphodel to compose that face. Yes, he would catch the 10:30 at Euston.

"But she's no more aware of her beauty than a child," said Mr. Bankes, replacing the receiver and crossing the room to see what progress the workmen were making with an hotel which they were building at the back of his house. And he thought of Mrs.

Ramsay as he looked at that stir among the unfinished walls. For always, he thought, there was something incongruous to be worked into the harmony of her face. She clapped a deerstalker's hat on her head; she ran across the lawn in goloshes to snatch a child from mischief. So that if it was her beauty merely that one thought of, one must remember the quivering thing, the living thing (they were carrying bricks up a little plank as he watched them), and work it into the picture; or if one thought of her simply as a woman, one must endow her with some freak of idiosyncrasy; or suppose some latent desire to doff her royalty of form as if her beauty bored her and all that men say of beauty, and she wanted only to be like other people, insignificant. He did not know. He did not know. He must go to his work.)

Knitting her reddish-brown hairy stocking, with her head outlined absurdly by the gilt frame, the green shawl which she had tossed over the edge of the frame, and the authenticated masterpiece by Michael Angelo, Mrs. Ramsay smoothed out what had been harsh in her manner a moment before, raised his head, and kissed her little boy on the forehead. "Let's find another picture to cut out," she said.

This piece of narrative prose is the fifth section of part 1 in Virginia Woolf's novel, *To the Lighthouse*, which was first published in 1927. The situation in which the characters find themselves can be almost completely deduced from the text itself. Nowhere in the novel is it set forth systematically, by way of introduction or exposition, or in any other way than as it is here. I shall, however, briefly summarize what the situation is at the beginning of our passage. This will make it easier for the reader to understand the following analysis; it will also serve to bring out more clearly a number of important motifs from earlier sections which are here only alluded to.

Mrs. Ramsay is the wife of an eminent London professor of philosophy; she is very beautiful but definitely no longer young. With her youngest son James—he is six years old—she is sitting by the window in a good-sized summer house on one of the Hebrides islands. The professor has rented it for many years. In addition to the Ramsays, their eight children, and the servants, there are a number of guests in the house, friends on longer or shorter visits. Among them is a well-known botanist, William Bankes, an elderly widower, and Lily Briscoe, who is a painter. These two are just passing by the window. James is sitting on the floor busily cutting pictures from an illustrated catalogue. Shortly before, his mother had told him that, if the weather should be fine, they would sail to the lighthouse the next day. This is an expedition James has been looking forward to for a long time. The people at the lighthouse are to receive various presents; among these are stockings for the lighthouse-keeper's boy. The violent joy which James had felt when the trip was announced had been as violently cut short by his father's acid observation that the weather would not be fine the next day. One of the guests, with malicious emphasis, has added some corroborative meteorological details. After all the others have left the room, Mrs. Ramsay, to console James, speaks the words with which our passage opens.

The continuity of the section is established through an exterior occurrence involving Mrs. Ramsay and James: the measuring of the stocking. Immediately after her consoling words (if it isn't fine tomorrow, we'll go some other day), Mrs. Ramsay makes James stand up so that she can measure the stocking for the lighthouse-keeper's son against his leg. A little further on she rather absent-mindedly tells him to stand still—the boy is fidgeting because his jealousy makes him a little stubborn and perhaps also because he is still under the impression of the disappointment of a few moments ago. Many lines later, the warning to stand still is repeated more sharply. James obeys, the measuring takes place, and it is found that the stocking is still considerably too short. After another long interval the scene concludes with Mrs. Ramsay kissing the boy on the forehead (she thus makes up for the sharp tone of her second order to him to stand still) and her proposing to help him look for another picture to cut out. Here the section ends.

This entirely insignificant occurrence is constantly interspersed with other elements which, although they do not interrupt its progress, take up far more time in the narration than the whole scene can possibly have lasted. Most of these elements are inner processes, that is, movements within the consciousness of individual personages, and not necessarily of personages involved in the exterior occurrence but also of others who are not even present at the time: "people," or "Mr. Bankes." In addition other exterior occurrences which might be called secondary and which pertain to quite different times and places (the telephone conversation, the construction of the building, for example) are worked in and made to serve as the frame for what goes on in the consciousness of third persons. Let us examine this in detail.

Mrs. Ramsay's very first remark is twice interrupted: first by the visual impression she receives of William Bankes and Lily Briscoe passing by together, and then, after a few intervening words serving the progress of the exterior occurrence, by the impression which the two persons passing by have left in her: the charm of Lily's Chinese eyes, which it is not for every man to see—whereupon she finishes her sentence and also allows her consciousness to dwell for a moment on the measuring of the stocking: we may yet go to the lighthouse, and so I must make sure the stocking is long enough. At this point there flashes into her mind the idea which has been prepared by her reflection on Lily's Chinese eyes (William and Lily ought to marry)—an admirable idea, she loves making matches. Smiling, she begins measuring the stocking. But the boy, in his stubborn and jealous love of her, refuses to stand still. How can she see whether the stocking is the right length if the boy keeps fidgeting about? What is the matter with James, her youngest, her darling? She looks up. Her eye falls on the room—and a long parenthesis begins. From the shabby chairs of which Andrew, her eldest son, said the other day that their entrails were all over the floor, her thoughts wander on, probing the objects and the people of her environment. The shabby furniture . . . but still good enough for up here; the advantages of the summer place; so cheap, so good for the children, for her husband; easily fitted up with a few old pieces of furniture, some pictures and books. Books—it is ages since she has had time to read books, even the books which have been dedicated to her (here the lighthouse flashes in for a second, as a place where one can't send such erudite volumes as some of those lying about the room). Then the house again: if the family would only be a little more careful. But of course, Andrew brings in crabs he wants to dissect; the other children gather seaweed, shells, stones; and she has to let them. All the children are gifted, each in a different way. But naturally, the house gets shabbier as a result (here the parenthesis is interrupted for a moment; she holds the stocking against James's leg); everything goes to ruin. If only the doors weren't always left open. See, everything is getting spoiled, even that Cashmere shawl on the picture frame. The doors are always left open; they are open again now. She listens: Yes, they are all open. The window on the landing is open too; she opened it herself. Windows must be open, doors closed. Why is it that no one can get that into his head? If you go to the maids' rooms at night, you will find all the windows closed. Only the Swiss maid always keeps her window open. She needs fresh air. Yesterday she looked out of the window with tears in her eyes and said: At home the mountains are so beautiful. Mrs. Ramsay knew that "at home" the girl's father was dying. Mrs. Ramsay had just been trying to teach her how to make beds, how to open windows. She had been talking away and had scolded the girl too. But then she had stopped talking (comparison with a bird folding its wings after flying in sunlight). She had stopped talking, for there was nothing one could say; he has cancer of the throat. At this point, remembering how she had stood there, how the girl had said at home the mountains were so beautiful—and there was no hope left—a sudden tense exasperation arises in her (exasperation with the cruel meaninglessness of a life whose continuance she is nevertheless striving with all her powers to abet, support, and secure). Her exasperation flows out into the exterior action. The parenthesis suddenly closes (it cannot have taken up more than a few seconds; just now she was still smiling over the thought of a marriage between Mr. Bankes and Lily Briscoe), and she says sharply to James: Stand still. Don't be so tiresome.

This is the first major parenthesis. The second starts a little later, after the stocking has been measured and found to be still much too short. It starts with the paragraph which begins and ends with the motif, "never did anybody look so sad."

Who is speaking in this paragraph? Who is looking at Mrs. Ramsay here, who concludes that never did anybody look so sad? Who is expressing these doubtful, obscure suppositions?—about the tear which—perhaps—forms and falls in the dark, about the water swaying this way and that, receiving it, and then returning to rest? There is no one near the window in the room but Mrs. Ramsay and James. It cannot be either of them, nor the "people" who begin to speak in the next paragraph. Perhaps it is the author. However, if that be so, the author certainly does not speak like one who has a knowledge of his characters—in this case, of Mrs. Ramsay—and who, out of his knowledge, can describe their personality and momentary state of mind objectively and with certainty. Virginia Woolf wrote this paragraph. She did not identify it through grammatical and typographcal devices as the speech or thought of a third person. One is obliged to assume that it contains direct statements of her own. But she does not seem to bear in mind that she is the author and hence ought to know how matters stand with her characters. The person speaking here, whoever it is, acts the part of one who has only an impression of Mrs. Ramsay, who looks at her face and renders the impression received, but is doubtful of its proper interpretation. "Never did anybody look so sad" is not an objective statement. In rendering the shock received by one looking at Mrs. Ramsay's face, it verges upon a realm beyond reality. And in the ensuing passage the speakers no longer seem to be human beings at all but spirits between heaven and earth, nameless spirits capable of penetrating the depths of the human soul, capable too of knowing something about it, but not of attaining clarity as to what is in process there, with the result that what they report has a doubtful ring, comparable in a way to those "certain airs, detached from the body of the wind," which in a later passage (2, 2) move about the house at night, "questioning and wondering." However that may be, here too we are not dealing with objective utterances on the part of the author in respect to one of the characters. No one is certain of anything here: it is all mere supposition, glances cast by one person upon another whose enigma he cannot solve.

This continues in the following paragraph. Suppositions as to the meaning of Mrs. Ramsay's expression are made and discussed. But the level of tone descends slightly, from the poetic and non-real to the practical and earthly; and now a speaker is introduced: "People said." People wonder whether some recollection of an unhappy occurrence in her earlier life is hidden behind her radiant beauty. There have been rumors to that effect. But perhaps the rumors are wrong: nothing of this is to be learned directly from her; she is silent when such things come up in conversation. But supposing she has never experienced anything of the sort herself, she yet knows everything even without experience. The simplicity and genuineness of her being unfailingly light upon the truth of things, and, falsely perhaps, delight, ease, sustain.

Is it still "people" who are speaking here? We might almost be tempted to doubt it, for the last words sound almost too personal and thoughtful for the gossip of "people." And immediately afterward, suddenly and unexpectedly, an entirely new speaker, a new scene, and a new time are introduced. We find Mr. Bankes at the telephone talking to Mrs. Ramsay, who has called him to tell him about a train connection, evidently with reference to a journey they are planning to make together. The paragraph about the tear had already taken us out of the room where Mrs. Ramsay and James are sitting by the window; it had transported us to an undefinable scene beyond the realm of reality. The paragraph in which the rumors are discussed has a concretely earthly but not clearly identified scene. Now we find ourselves in a precisely determined place, but far away from the summer house —in London, in Mr. Bankes's house. The time is not stated ("once"), but apparently the telephone conversation took place long (perhaps as much as several years) before this particular sojourn in the house on the island. But what Mr. Bankes says over the telephone is in perfect continuity with the preceding paragraph. Again not objectively but in the form of the impression received by a specific person at a specific moment, it as it were sums up all that precedes—the scene with the Swiss maid, the hidden sadness in Mrs. Ramsay's beautiful face, what people think about her, and the impression she makes: Nature has but little clay like that of which she molded her. Did Mr. Bankes really say that to her over the telephone? Or did he only want to say it when he heard her voice, which moved him deeply, and it came into his mind how strange it was to be talking over the telephone with this wonderful woman, so like a Greek goddess? The sentence is enclosed in quotation marks, so one would suppose that he really spoke it. But this is not certain, for the first words of his soliloquy, which follows, are likewise enclosed in quotation marks. In any case, he quickly gets hold of himself, for he answers in a matter-of-fact way that he will catch the 10:30 at Euston.

But his emotion does not die away so quickly. As he puts down the receiver and walks across the room to the window in order to watch the work on a new building across the way—apparently his usual and characteristic procedure when he wants to relax and let his thoughts wander freely—he continues to be preoccupied with Mrs. Ramsay. There is always something strange about her, something that does not quite go with her beauty (as for instance telephoning); she has no awareness of her beauty, or at most only a childish awareness; her dress and her actions show that at times. She is constantly getting involved in everyday realities which are hard to reconcile with the harmony of her face. In his methodical way he tries to explain her incongruities to himself. He puts forward some conjectures but cannot make up his mind. Meanwhile his momentary impressions of the work on the new building keep crowding in. Finally he gives it up. With the somewhat impatient, determined matter-of-factness of a methodical and scientific worker (which he is) he shakes off the insoluble problem "Mrs. Ramsay." He knows no solution (the repetition of "he did not know" symbolizes his impatient shaking it off). He has to get back to his work.

Here the second long interruption comes to an end and we are taken back to the room where Mrs. Ramsay and James are. The exterior occurrence is brought to a close with the kiss on James's forehead and the resumption of the cutting out of pictures. But here too we have only an exterior change. A scene previously abandoned reappears, suddenly and with as little transition as if it had never been left, as though the long interruption were only a glance which someone (who?) has cast from it into the depths of time. But the theme (Mrs. Ramsay, her beauty, the enigma of her character, her absoluteness, which nevertheless always exercises itself in the relativity and ambiguity of life, in what does not become her beauty) carries over directly from the last phase of the interruption (that is, Mr. Bankes's fruitless reflections) into the situation in which we now find Mrs. Ramsay: "with her head outlined absurdly by the gilt frame" etc.—for once again what is around her is not suited to her, is "something incongruous." And the kiss she gives her little boy, the words she speaks to him, although they are a genuine gift of life, which James accepts as the most natural and simple truth, are yet heavy with unsolved mystery.

Our analysis of the passage yields a number of distinguishing stylistic characteristics, which we shall now attempt to formulate.

The writer as narrator of objective facts has almost completely vanished; almost everything stated appears by way of reflection in the consciousness of the dramatis personae. When it is a question of the house, for example, or of the Swiss maid, we are not given the objective information which Virginia Woolf possesses regarding these objects of her creative imagination but what Mrs. Ramsay thinks or feels about them at a particular moment. Similarly we are not taken into Virginia Woolf's confidence and allowed to share her knowledge of Mrs. Ramsay's character; we are given her character as it is reflected in and as it affects various figures in the novel: the nameless spirits which assume certain things about a tear, the people who wonder about her, and Mr. Bankes. In our passage this goes so far that there actually seems to be no viewpoint at all outside the novel from which the people and events within it are observed, any more than there seems to be an objective reality apart from what is in the consciousness of the characters. Remnants of such a reality survive at best in brief references to the exterior frame of the action, such as "said Mrs. Ramsay, raising her eyes . . ." or "said Mr. Bankes once, hearing her voice." The last paragraph ("Knitting her reddish-brown hairy stocking . . .") might perhaps also be mentioned in this connection. But this is already somewhat doubtful. The occurrence is described objectively, but as for its interpretation, the tone indicates that the author looks at Mrs. Ramsay not with knowing but with doubting and questioning eyes—even as some character in the novel would see her in the situation in which she is described, would hear her speak the words given.

The devices employed in this instance (and by a number of contemporary writers as well) to express the contents of the consciousness of the dramatis personae have been analyzed and described syntactically. Some of them have been named (*erlebte Rede*, stream of consciousness, *monologue intérieur* are examples). Yet these stylistic forms, especially the *erlebte Rede*, were used in literature much earlier too, but not for the same aesthetic purpose. And in addition to them there are other possibilities—hardly definable in terms of syntax—of obscuring and even obliterating the impression of an objective reality completely known to the author; possibilities, that is, dependent not on form but on intonation and context. A case in point is the passage under discussion, where the author at times achieves the intended effect by representing herself to be someone who doubts, wonders, hesitates, as though the truth about her characters were not better known to her than it is to them or to the reader. It is all, then, a matter of the author's attitude toward the reality of the world he represents. And this attitude differs entirely from that of authors who interpret the actions, situations, and characters of their personages with objective assurance, as was the general practice in earlier times. Goethe or Keller, Dickens or Meredith, Balzac or Zola told us out of their certain knowledge what their characters did, what they felt and thought while doing it, and how their actions and thoughts were to be interpreted. They knew everything about their characters. To be sure, in past periods too we were frequently told about the subjective reactions of the characters in a novel or story; at times even in the form of *erlebte Rede*, although more frequently as a monologue, and of course in most instances with an introductory phrase something like "it seemed to him that . . ." or "at this moment he felt that . . ." or the like. Yet in such cases there was hardly ever any attempt to render the flow and the play of consciousness adrift in the current of changing impressions (as is done in our text both for Mrs. Ramsay and for Mr. Bankes); instead, the content of the individual's consciousness was rationally limited to things connected with the particular incident being related or the particular situation being described—as is the case, for example, in the passage from *Madame Bovary* interpreted above (pp. 482ff.). And what is still more important: the author, with his knowledge of an objective truth, never abdicated his position as the final and governing authority. Again, earlier writers, especially from the end of the nineteenth century on, had produced narrative works which on the whole undertook to give us an extremely subjective, individualistic, and often eccentrically aberrant impression of reality, and which neither sought nor were able to ascertain anything objective or generally valid in regard to it. Sometimes such works took the form of first-person novels; sometimes they did not. As an example of the latter case I mention Huysmans's novel A *rebours*. But all that too is basically different from the modern procedure here described on the basis of Virginia Woolf's text, although the latter, it is true, evolved from the former. The essential characteristic of the technique represented by Virginia Woolf is that we are given not merely one person whose consciousness (that is, the impressions it receives) is rendered, but many persons, with frequent shifts from one to the other—in our text, Mrs. Ramsay, "people," Mr. Bankes, in brief interludes James, the Swiss maid in a flash-back, and the nameless ones who speculate over a tear. The multiplicity of persons suggests that we are here after all confronted with an endeavor to investigate an objective reality, that is, specifically, the "real" Mrs. Ramsay. She is, to be sure, an enigma and such she basically remains, but she is as it were encircled by the content of all the various consciousnesses directed upon her (including her own); there is an attempt to approach her from many sides as closely as human possibilities of perception and expression can succeed in doing. The design of a close approach to objective reality by means of numerous subjective impressions received by various individuals (and at various times) is important in the modern technique which we are here examining. It basically differentiates it from the unipersonal subjectivism which allows only a single and generally a very unusual person to make himself heard and admits only that one person's way of looking at reality. In terms of literary history, to be sure, there are close connections between the two methods of representing consciousness—the unipersonal subjective method and the multipersonal method with synthesis as its aim. The latter developed from the former, and there are works in which the two overlap, so that we can watch the development. This is especially the case in Marcel Proust's great novel. We shall return to it later.

Another stylistic peculiarity to be observed in our text—though one that is closely and necessarily connected with the "multipersonal representation of consciousness" just discussed—has to do with the treatment of time. That there is something peculiar about the treatment of time in modern narrative literature is nothing new; several studies have been published on the subject. These were primarily attempts to establish a connection between the pertinent phenomena and contemporary philosophical doctrines or trends—undoubtedly a justifiable undertaking and useful for an appreciation of the community of interests and inner purposes shown in the activity of many of our contemporaries. We shall begin by describing the procedure with reference to our present example. We remarked earlier that the act of measuring the length of the stocking and the speaking of the words related to it must have taken much less time than an attentive reader who tries not to miss anything will require to read the passage—even if we assume that a brief pause intervened between the measuring and the kiss of reconciliation on James's forehead. However, the time the narration takes is not devoted to the occurrence itself (which is rendered rather tersely) but to interludes. Two long excursuses are inserted, whose relations in time to the occurrence which frames them seem to be entirely different. The first excursus, a representation of what goes on in Mrs. Ramsay's mind while she measures the stocking (more precisely, between the first absent-minded and the second sharp order to James to hold his leg still) belongs in time to the framing occurrence, and it is only the representation of it which takes a greater number of seconds and even minutes than the measuring—the reason being that the road taken by consciousness is sometimes traversed far more quickly than language is able to render it, if we want to make ourselves intelligible to a third person, and that is the intention here. What goes on in Mrs. Ramsay's mind in itself contains nothing enigmatic; these are ideas which arise from her daily life and may well be called normal—her secret lies deeper, and it is only when the switch from the open windows to the Swiss maid's words comes, that something happens which lifts the veil a little. On the whole, however, the mirroring of Mrs. Ramsay's consciousness is much more easily comprehensible than the sort of thing we get in such cases from other authors (James Joyce, for example). But simple and trivial as are the ideas which arise one after the other in Mrs. Ramsay's consciousness, they are at the same time essential and significant. They amount to a synthesis of the intricacies of life in which her incomparable beauty has been caught, in which it at once manifests and conceals itself. Of course, writers of earlier periods too occasionally devoted some time and a few sentences to telling the reader what at a specific moment passed through their characters' minds—but for such a purpose they would hardly have chosen so accidental an occasion as Mrs. Ramsay's looking up, so that, quite involuntarily, her eyes fall on the furniture. Nor would it have occurred to them to render the continuous rumination of consciousness in its natural and purposeless freedom. And finally they would not have inserted the entire process between two exterior occurrences so close together in time as the two warnings to James to keep still (both of which, after all, take place while she is on the point of holding the unfinished stocking to his leg); so that, in a surprising fashion unknown to earlier periods, a sharp contrast results between the brief span of time occupied by the exterior event and the dreamlike wealth of a process of consciousness which traverses a whole subjective universe. These are the characteristic and distinctively new features of the technique: a chance occasion releasing processes of consciousness; a natural and even, if you will, a naturalistic rendering of those processes in their peculiar freedom, which is neither restrained by a purpose nor directed by a specific subject of thought; elaboration of the contrast between "exterior" and "interior" time. The three have in common what they reveal of the author's attitude: he submits, much more than was done in earlier realistic works, to the random contingency of real phenomena; and even though he winnows and stylizes the material of the real world—as of course he cannot help doing—he does not proceed rationalistically, nor with a view to bringing a continuity of exterior events to a planned conclusion. In Virginia Woolf's case the exterior events have actually lost their hegemony, they serve to release and interpret inner events, whereas before her time (and still today in many instances) inner movements preponderantly function to prepare and motivate significant exterior happenings. This too is apparent in the randomness and contingency of the exterior occasion (looking up because James does not keep his foot still), which releases the much more significant inner process.

The temporal relation between the second excursus and the framing occurrence is of a different sort: its content (the passage on the tear, the things people think about Mrs. Ramsay, the telephone conversation with Mr. Bankes and his reflections while watching the building of the new hotel) is not a part of the framing occurrence either in terms of time or of place. Other times and places are in question; it is an excursus of the same type as the story of the origin of Odysseus' scar, which was discussed in the first chapter of this book. Even from that, however, it is different in structure. In the Homer passage the excursus was linked to the scar which Euryclea touches with her hands, and although the moment at which the touching of the scar occurs is one of high and dramatic tension, the scene nevertheless immediately shifts to another clear and luminous present, and this present seems actually designed to cut off the dramatic tension and cause the entire footwashing scene to be temporarily forgotten. In Virginia Woolf's passage, there is no question of any tension. Nothing of importance in a dramatic sense takes place; the problem is the length of the stocking. The point of departure for the excursus is Mrs. Ramsay's facial expression: "never did anybody look so sad." In fact several excursuses start from here; three, to be exact. And all three differ in time and place, differ too in definiteness of time and place, the first being situated quite vaguely, the second somewhat more definitely, and the third with comparative precision. Yet none of them is so exactly situated in time as the successive episodes of the story of Odysseus' youth, for even in the case of the telephone scene we have only an inexact indication of when it occurred. As a result it becomes possible to accomplish the shifting of the scene away from the window-nook much more unnoticeably and smoothly than the changing of scene and time in the episode of the scar. In the passage on the tear the reader may still be in doubt as to whether there has been any shift at all. The nameless speakers may have entered the room and be looking at Mrs. Ramsay. In the second paragraph this interpretation is no longer possible, but the "people" whose gossip is reproduced are still looking at Mrs. Ramsay's face—not here and now, at the summer-house window, but it is still the same face and has the same expression. And even in the third part, where the face is no longer physically seen (for Mr. Bankes is talking to Mrs. Ramsay over the telephone), it is nonetheless present to his inner vision; so that not for an instant does the theme (the solution of the enigma Mrs. Ramsay), and even the moment when the problem is formulated (the expression of her face while she measures the length of the stocking), vanish from the reader's memory. In terms of the exterior event the three parts of the excursus have nothing to do with one another. They have no common and externally coherent development, as have the episodes of Odysseus' youth which are related with reference to the origin of the scar; they are connected only by the one thing they have in common—looking at Mrs. Ramsay, and more specifically at the Mrs. Ramsay who, with an unfathomable expression of sadness behind her radiant beauty, concludes that the stocking is still much too short. It is only this common focus which connects the otherwise totally different parts of the excursus; but the connection is strong enough to deprive them of the independent "present" which the episode of the scar possesses. They are nothing but attempts to interpret "never did anybody look so sad"; they carry on this theme, which itself carries on after they conclude: there has been no change of theme at all. In contrast, the scene in which Euryclea recognizes Odysseus is interrupted and divided into two parts by the excursus on the origin of the scar. In our passage, there is no such clear distinction between two exterior occurrences and between two presents. However insignificant as an exterior event the framing occurrence (the measuring of the stocking) may be, the picture of Mrs. Ramsay's face which arises from it remains present throughout the excursus; the excursus itself is nothing but a background for that picture, which seems as it were to open into the depths of time—just as the first excursus, released by Mrs. Ramsay's unintentional glance at the furniture, was an opening of the picture into the depths of consciousness.

The two excursuses, then, are not as different as they at first appeared. It is not so very important that the first, so far as time is concerned (and place too), runs its course within the framing occurrence, while the second conjures up other times and places. The times and places of the second are not independent; they serve only the polyphonic treatment of the image which releases it; as a matter of fact, they impress us (as does the interior time of the first excursus) like an occurrence in the consciousness of some observer (to be sure, he is not identified) who might see Mrs. Ramsay at the described moment and whose meditation upon the unsolved enigma of her personality might contain memories of what others (people, Mr. Bankes) say and think about her. In both excursuses we are dealing with attempts to fathom a more genuine, a deeper, and indeed a more real reality; in both cases the incident which releases the excursus appears accidental and is poor in content; in both cases it makes little difference whether the excursuses employ only the consciousness-content, and hence only interior time, or whether they also employ exterior shifts of time. After all, the process of consciousness in the first excursus likewise includes shifts of time and scene, especially the episode with the Swiss maid. The important point is that an insignificant exterior occurrence releases ideas and chains of ideas which cut loose from the present of the exterior occurrence and range freely through the depths of time. It is as though an apparently simple text revealed its proper content only in the commentary on it, a simple musical theme only in the development-section. This enables us also to understand the close relation between the treatment of time and the "multipersonal representation of consciousness" discussed earlier. The ideas arising in consciousness are not tied to the present of the exterior occurrence which releases them. Virginia Woolf's peculiar technique, as exemplified in our text, consists in the fact that the exterior objective reality of the momentary present which the author directly reports and which appears as established fact—in our instance the measuring of the stocking—is nothing but an occasion (although perhaps not an entirely accidental one). The stress is placed entirely on what the occasion releases, things which are not seen directly but by reflection, which are not tied to the present of the framing occurrence which releases them.

Here it is only natural that we should recall Proust's work. He was the first to carry this sort of thing through consistently; and his entire technique is bound up with a recovery of lost realities in remembrance, a recovery released by some externally insignificant and apparently accidental occurrence. Proust describes the procedure more than once. We have to wait until volume 2 of *Le Temps retrouvé* for a full description embracing the corresponding theory of art; but the first description, which occurs as early as section 1 of *Du Côté de chez Swann*, is impressive enough. Here, one unpleasant winter evening, the taste of a cake (*petite Madeleine*) dipped in tea arouses in the narrator an overwhelming though at first indefinite delight. By intense and repeated effort he attempts to fathom its nature and cause, and it develops that the delight is based on a recovery: the recovery of the taste of the *petite Madeleine* dipped in tea which his aunt would give him on Sundays when, still a little boy, he went into her room to wish her good morning, in the house in the old provincial town of Combray where she lived, hardly ever leaving her bed, and where he used to spend the summer months with his parents. And from this recovered remembrance, the world of his childhood emerges into light, becomes depictable, as more genuine and more real than any experienced present—and he begins to narrate. Now with Proust a narrating "I" is preserved throughout. It is not, to be sure, an author observing from without but a person involved in the action and pervading it with the distinctive flavor of his being, so that one might feel tempted to class Proust's novel among the products of the unipersonal subjectivism which we discussed earlier. So to class it would not be wrong but it would be inadequate. It would fail to account completely for the structure of Proust's novel. After all, it does not display the same strictly unipersonal approach to reality as Huysmans's *A Rebours* or Knut Hamsun's *Pan* (to mention two basically different examples which are yet comparable in this respect). Proust aims at objectivity, he wants to bring out the essence of events: he strives to attain this goal by accepting the guidance of his own consciousness—not, however, of his consciousness as it happens to be at any particular moment but as it remembers things. A consciousness in which remembrance causes past realities to arise, which has long since left behind the states in which it found itself when those realities occurred as a present, sees and arranges that content in a way very different from the purely individual and subjective. Freed from its various earlier involvements, consciousness views its own past layers and their content in perspective; it keeps confronting them with one another, emancipating them from their exterior temporal continuity as well as from the narrow meanings they seemed to have when they were bound to a particular present. There is to be noted in this a fusion of the modern concept of interior time with the neo-Platonic idea that the true prototype of a given subject is to be found in the soul of the artist; in this case, of an artist who, present in the subject itself, has detached himself from it as observer and thus comes face to face with his own past.

I shall here give a brief passage from Proust in order to illustrate this point. It deals with a moment in the narrator's childhood and occurs in volume 1, toward the end of the first section. It is, I must admit, too good and too clear an example of the layered structure of a consciousness engaged in recollection. That structure is not always as evident as it is in this instance; elsewhere it could be made clearly apparent only through an analysis of the way the subject matter is arranged, of the introduction, disappearance, and reappearance of the characters, and of the overlapping of the various presents and consciousness-contents. But every reader of Proust will admit that the whole work is written in accordance with the technique which our passage makes apparent without comment or analysis. The situation is this: One evening during his childhood the narrator could not go to sleep without the usual ceremony of being kissed good night by his mother. When he went to bed his mother could not come to his room because there was a guest for supper. In a state of nervous hypertension he decides to stay awake and catch his mother at the door when, after the guest's departure, she herself retires. This is a serious offense, because his parents are trying to correct his excessive sensitivity by sternly suppressing such cravings. He has to reckon with severe punishment; perhaps he will be banished from home and sent to a boarding school. Yet his need for momentary satisfaction is stronger than his fear of the consequences. Quite unexpectedly it happens that his father, who is usually far stricter and more authoritarian but at the same time less consistent than his mother, comes upstairs directly behind her. Seeing the boy, he is touched by the desperate expression in his face and advises his wife to spend the night in the child's room to calm him down. Proust continues:

> On ne pouvait pas remercier mon père; on l'eût agacé par ce qu'il appelait des sensibleries. Je restai sans oser faire un mouvement; il était encore devant nous, grand, dans sa robe de nuit blanche sous le cachemire de l'Inde violet et rose qu'il nouait autour de sa tête depuis qu'il avait des névralgies, avec le geste d'Abraham dans la gravure d'après Benozzo Gozzoli que m'avait donné M. Swann, disant à Hagar, qu'elle a à se départir du côté d'Isaac. Il y a bien des années de cela. La muraille de l'escalier, où je vis monter le reflet de sa bougie n'existe plus depuis longtemps. En moi aussi bien des choses ont été détruites que je croyais devoir durer toujours et de nouvelles se sont édifiées donnant naissance à des peines et à des joies nouvelles que je n'aurais pu prévoir alors, de même que les anciennes me sont devenues difficiles à comprendre. Il y a bien longtemps aussi que mon père a cessé de pouvoir dire à maman: "Va avec le petit." La possibilité de telles heures ne renaîtra jamais pour moi. Mais depuis peu de temps, je recommence à très bien percevoir si je prête l'oreille, les sanglots que j'eus la force de contenir devant mon père et qui n'éclatèrent que quand je me retrouvai seul avec maman. En réalité ils n'ont jamais cessé; et c'est seulement parce que la vie se tait maintenant davantage autour de moi que je les entends de nouveau, comme ces cloches de couvents que couvrent si bien les bruits de la ville pendant le jour qu'on les croirait arrêtées mais qui se remettent à sonner dans le silence du soir.

> (It was impossible for me to thank my father; what he called my sentimentality would have exasperated him. I stood there, not daring to move; he was still confronting us, an immense figure in his white nightshirt, crowned with the pink and violet scarf of Indian cashmere in which, since he had begun to suffer from

neuralgia, he used to tie up his head, standing like Abraham in the engraving after Benozzo Gozzoli which M. Swann had given me, telling Hagar that she must tear herself away from Isaac. Many years have passed since that night. The wall of the staircase, up which I had watched the light of his candle gradually climb, was long ago demolished. And in myself, too, many things have perished which, I imagined, would last for ever, and new structures have arisen, giving birth to new sorrows and new joys which in those days I could not have foreseen, just as now the old are difficult of comprehension. It is a long time, too, since my father has been able to tell Mamma to "Go with the child." Never again will such hours be possible for me. But of late I have been increasingly able to catch, if I listen attentively, the sound of the sobs which I had the strength to control in my father's presence, and which broke out only when I found myself alone with Mamma. Actually, their echo has never ceased: it is only because life is now growing more and more quiet round about me that I hear them afresh, like those convent bells which are so effectively drowned during the day by the noises of the streets that one would suppose them to have been stopped for ever, until they sound out again through the silent evening air.) *Remembrance of Things Past*, by Marcel Proust. Translated by C. K. Scott Moncrieff. Random House. 1934.

Through the temporal perspective we sense here an element of the symbolic omnitemporality of an event fixed in a remembering consciousness. Still clearer and more systematic (and also, to be sure, much more enigmatic) are the symbolic references in James Joyce's *Ulysses*, in which the technique of a multiple reflection of consciousness and of multiple time strata would seem to be employed more radically than anywhere else. The book unmistakably aims at a symbolic synthesis of the theme "Everyman." All the great motifs of the cultural history of Europe are contained in it, although its point of departure is very specific individuals and a clearly established present (Dublin, June 16, 1904). On sensitive readers it can produce a very strong immediate impression. Really to understand it, however, is not an easy matter, for it makes severe demands on the reader's patience and learning by its dizzying whirl of motifs, wealth of words and concepts, perpetual playing upon their countless associations, and the ever rearoused but never satified doubt as to what order is ultimately hidden behind so much apparent arbitrariness.

Few writers have made so consistent a use of reflected consciousness and time strata as those we have so far discussed. But the influence of the procedure and traces of it can be found almost everywhere—lately even in writers of the sort whom discriminating readers are not in the habit of regarding as fully competent. Many writers have invented their own methods—or at least have experimented in the direction—of making the reality which they adopt as their subject appear in changing lights and changing strata, or of abandoning the specific angle of observation of either a seemingly objective or purely subjective representation in favor of a more varied perspective. Among these writers we find older masters whose aesthetic individualities had long since been fully established but who were drawn into the movement in their years of maturity before and after the first World War, each in his own way turning to a disintegration and dissolution of external realities for a richer and more essential interpretation of them. Thomas Mann is an example, who, ever since his *Magic Mountain,* without in any way abandoning his level of tone (in which the narrating, commenting, objectivizing author addressing the reader is always present) has been more and more concerned with time perspectives and the symbolic omnitemporality of events. Another very different instance is André Gide, in whose *Faux-Monnayeurs* there is a constant shifting of the viewpoint from which the events (themselves multilayered) are surveyed, and who carries this procedure to such an extreme that the novel and the account of the genesis of the novel are interwoven in the ironic vein of the romanticists. Very different again, and much simpler, is the case of Knut Hamsun who, for example in his *Growth of the Soil,* employs a level of tone which blurs the dividing line between the direct or indirect discourse of the characters in the novel and the author's own utterances; as a result one is never quite certain that what one hears is being said by the author as he stands outside his novel; the statements sound as though they came from one of the persons involved in the action, or at least from a passer-by who observes the incident. Finally, we have still to mention certain further peculiarities of the kind of writing we are considering—those which concern the type of subject matter treated. In modern novels we frequently observe that it is not one person or a limited number of persons whose experiences are pursued as a continuum; indeed, often there is no strict continuum of events. Sometimes many individuals, or many fragments of events, are loosely joined so that the reader has no definite thread of action which he can always follow. There are novels which attempt to reconstruct a milieu from mere splinters of events, with constantly changing though occasionally reappearing characters. In this latter case one might feel inclined to assume that it was the writer's purpose to exploit the structural possibilities of the film in the interest of the novel. If so, it is a wrong direction: a concentration of space and time such as can be achieved by the film (for example the representation, within a few seconds and by means of a few pictures, of the situation of a widely dispersed group of people, of a great city, an army, a war, an entire country) can never be within the reach of the spoken or written word. To be sure, the novel possesses great freedom in its command of space and time—much more than the drama of pre-film days, even if we disregard the strict classical rules of unity. The novel in recent decades has made use of this freedom in a way for which earlier literary periods afford no models, with the possible exception of a few tentative efforts by the romanticists, especially in Germany, although they did not restrict themselves to the material of reality. At the same time, however, by virtue of the film's existence, the novel has come to be more clearly aware than ever before of the limitations in space and time imposed upon it by its instrument, language. As a result the situation has been reversed: the dramatic technique of the film now has far greater possibilities in the direction of condensing time and space than has the novel itself.

The distinctive characteristics of the realistic novel of the era between the two great wars, as they have appeared in the present chapter —multipersonal representation of consciousness, time strata, disintegration of the continuity of exterior events, shifting of the narrative viewpoint (all of which are interrelated and difficult to separate)—seem to us indicative of a striving for certain objectives, of certain tendencies and needs on the part of both authors and public. These objectives, tendencies, and needs are numerous; they seem in part to be mutually contradictory; yet they form so much one whole that when we undertake to describe them analytically, we are in constant danger of unwittingly passing from one to another.

Let us begin with a tendency which is particularly striking in our text from Virginia Woolf. She holds to minor, unimpressive, random events: measuring the stocking, a fragment of a conversation with the maid, a telephone call. Great changes, exterior turning points, let alone catastrophes, do not occur; and though elsewhere in *To the Lighthouse* such things are mentioned, it is hastily, without preparation or context, incidentally, and as it were only for the sake of information. The same tendency is to be observed in other and very different writers, such as Proust or Hamsun. In Thomas Mann's *Buddenbrooks* we still have a novel structure consisting of the chronological sequence of important exterior events which affect the Buddenbrook family; and if Flaubert —in many respects a precursor—lingers as a matter of principle over insignificant events and everyday circumstances which hardly advance the action, there is nevertheless to be sensed throughout *Madame Bovary* (though we may wonder how this would have worked out in *Bouvard et Pécuchet*) a constant slow-moving chronological approach first to partial crises and finally to the concluding catastrophe, and it is this approach which dominates the plan of the work as a whole. But a shift in emphasis followed; and now many writers present minor happenings, which are insignificant as exterior factors in a person's destiny, for their own sake or rather as points of departure for the development of motifs, for a penetration which opens up new perspectives into a milieu or a consciousness or the given historical setting. They have discarded presenting the story of their characters with any claim to exterior completeness, in chronological order, and with the emphasis on important exterior turning points of destiny. James Joyce's tremendous novel—an encyclopedic work, a mirror of Dublin, of Ireland, a mirror too of Europe and its millennia—has for its frame the externally insignificant course of a day in the lives of a schoolteacher and an advertising broker. It takes up less than twenty-four hours in their lives—just as *To the Lighthouse* describes portions of two days widely separated in time. (There is here also, as we must not fail to observe, a similarity to Dante's Comedy.) Proust presents individual days and hours from different periods, but the exterior events which are the determining factors in the destinies of the novel's characters during the intervening lapses of time are mentioned only incidentally, in retrospect or anticipation. The ends the narrator has in mind are not to be seen in them; often the reader has to supplement them. The way in which the father's death is brought up in the passage cited above—incidentally, allusively, and in anticipation—offers a good example. This shift of emphasis expresses something that we might call a transfer of confidence: the great exterior turning points and blows of fate are granted less importance; they are credited with less power of yielding decisive information concerning the subject; on the other hand there is confidence that in any random fragment plucked from the course of a life at any time the totality of its fate is contained and can be portrayed. There is greater confidence in syntheses gained through full exploitation of an everyday occurrence than in a chronologically well-ordered total treatment which accompanies the subject from beginning to end, attempts not to omit anything externally important, and emphasizes the great turning points of destiny. It is possible to compare this technique of modern writers with that of certain modern philologists who hold that the interpretation of a few passages from *Hamlet*, *Phèdre*, or *Faust* can be made to yield more, and more decisive, information about Shakespeare, Racine, or Goethe and their times than would a systematic and chronological treatment of their lives and works. Indeed, the present book may be cited as an illustration. I could never have written anything in the nature of a history of European realism; the material would have swamped me; I should have had to enter into hopeless discussions concerning the delimitation of the various periods and the allocation of the various writers to them, and above all concerning the definition of the concept realism. Furthermore, for the sake of completeness, I should have had to deal with some things of which I am but casually informed, and hence to become acquainted with them *ad hoc* by reading up on them (which, in my opinion, is a poor way of acquiring and using knowledge); and the motifs which direct my investigation, and for the sake of which it is written, would have been completely buried under a mass of factual information which has long been known and can easily be looked up in reference books. As opposed to this I see the possibility of success and profit in a method which consists in letting myself be guided by a few motifs which I have worked out gradually and without a specific purpose, and in trying them out on a series of texts which have become familiar and vital to me in the course of my philological activity; for I am convinced that these basic motifs in the history of the representation of reality—provided I have seen them correctly—must be demonstrable in any random realistic text. But to return to those modern writers who prefer the exploitation of random everyday events, contained within a few hours and days, to the complete and chronological representation of a total exterior continuum—they too (more or less consciously) are guided by the consideration that it is a hopeless venture to try to be really complete within the total exterior continuum and yet to make what is essential stand out. Then too they hesitate to impose upon life, which is their subject, an order which it does not possess in itself. He who represents the course of a human life, or a sequence of events extending over a prolonged period of time, and represents it from beginning to end, must prune and isolate arbitrarily. Life has always long since begun, and it is always still going on. And the people whose story the author is telling experience much more than he can ever hope to tell. But the things that happen to a few individuals in the course of a few minutes, hours, or possibly even days—these one can hope to report with reasonable completeness. And here, furthermore, one comes upon the order and the interpretation of life which arise from life itself: that is, those which grow up in the individuals themselves, which are to be discerned in their thoughts, their consciousness, and in a more concealed form in their words and actions. For there is always going on within us a process of formulation and interpretation whose subject matter is our own self. We are constantly endeavoring to give meaning and order to our lives in the past, the present, and the future, to our surroundings, the world in which we live; with the result that our lives appear in our own conception as total entities—which to be sure are always changing, more or less radically, more or less rapidly, depending on the extent to which we are obliged, inclined, and able to assimilate the onrush of new experience. These are the forms of order and interpretation which the modern writers here under discussion attempt to grasp in the random moment—not one order and one interpretation, but many, which may either be those of different persons or of the same person at different times; so that overlapping, complementing, and contradiction yield something that we might call a synthesized cosmic view or at least a challenge to the reader's will to interpretive synthesis.

Here we have returned once again to the reflection of multiple consciousnesses. It is easy to understand that such a technique had to develop gradually and that it did so precisely during the decades of the first World War period and after. The widening of man's horizon, and the increase of his experiences, knowledge, ideas, and possible forms of existence, which began in the sixteenth century, continued through the nineteenth at an ever faster tempo—with such a tremendous acceleration since the beginning of the twentieth that synthetic and objective attempts at interpretation are produced and demolished every instant. The tremendous tempo of the changes proved the more confusing because they could not be surveyed as a whole. They occurred simultaneously in many separate departments of science, technology, and economics, with the result that no one—not even those who were leaders in the separate departments—could foresee or evaluate the resulting overall situations. Furthermore, the changes did not produce the same effects in all places, so that the differences of attainment between the various social strata of one and the same people and between different peoples came to be—if not greater—at least more noticeable. The spread of publicity and the crowding of mankind on a shrinking globe sharpened awareness of the differences in ways of life and attitudes, and mobilized the interests and forms of existence which the new changes either furthered or threatened. In all parts of the world crises of adjustment arose; they increased in number and coalesced. They led to the upheavals which we have not weathered yet. In Europe this violent clash of the most heterogeneous ways of life and kinds of endeavor undermined not only those religious, philosophical, ethical, and economic principles which were part of the traditional heritage and which, despite many earlier shocks, had maintained their position of authority through slow adaptation and transformation; nor yet only the ideas of the Enlightenment, the ideas of democracy and liberalism which had been revolutionary in the eighteenth century and were still so during the first half of the nineteenth; it undermined even the new revolutionary forces of socialism, whose origins did not go back beyond the heyday of the capitalist system. These forces threatened to split up and disintegrate. They lost their unity and clear definition through the formation of numerous mutually hostile groups, through strange alliances which some of these groups effected with non-socialist ideologies, through the capitulation of most of them during the first World War, and finally through the propensity on the part of many of their most radical advocates for changing over into the camp of their most extreme enemies. Otherwise too there was an increasingly strong factionalism—at times crystallizing around important poets, philosophers, and scholars, but in the majority of cases pseudo-scientific, syncretistic, and primitive. The temptation to entrust oneself to a sect which solved all problems with a single formula, whose power of suggestion imposed solidarity, and which ostracized everything which would not fit in and submit—this temptation was so great that, with many people, fascism hardly had to employ force when the time came for it to spread through the countries of old European culture, absorbing the smaller sects.

As recently as the nineteenth century, and even at the beginning of the twentieth, so much clearly formulable and recognized community of thought and feeling remained in those countries that a writer engaged in representing reality had reliable criteria at hand by which to organize it. At least, within the range of contemporary movements, he could discern certain specific trends; he could delimit opposing attitudes and ways of life with a certain degree of clarity. To be sure, this had long since begun to grow increasingly difficult. Flaubert (to confine ourselves to realistic writers) already suffered from the lack of valid foundations for his work; and the subsequent increasing predilection for ruthlessly subjectivistic perspectives is another symptom. At the time of the first World War and after—in a Europe unsure of itself, overflowing with unsettled ideologies and ways of life, and pregnant with disaster—certain writers distinguished by instinct and insight find a method which dissolves reality into multiple and multivalent reflections of consciousness. That this method should have been developed at this time is not hard to understand.

But the method is not only a symptom of the confusion and helplessness, not only a mirror of the decline of our world. There is, to be sure, a good deal to be said for such a view. There is in all these works a certain atmosphere of universal doom: especially in *Ulysses*, with its mocking *odi-et-amo* hodgepodge of the European tradition, with its blatant and painful cynicism, and its uninterpretable symbolism—for even the most painstaking analysis can hardly emerge with anything more than an appreciation of the multiple enmeshment of the motifs but with nothing of the purpose and meaning of the work itself. And most of the other novels which employ multiple reflection of consciousness also leave the reader with an impression of hopelessness. There is often something confusing, something hazy about them, something hostile to the reality which they represent. We not infrequently find a turning away from the practical will to live, or delight in portraying it under its most brutal forms. There is hatred of culture and civilization, brought out by means of the subtlest stylistic devices which culture and civilization have developed, and often a radical and fanatical urge to destroy. Common to almost all of these novels is haziness, vague indefinability of meaning: precisely the kind of uninterpretable symbolism which is also to be encountered in other forms of art of the same period.

But something entirely different takes place here too. Let us turn again to the text which was our starting-point. It breathes an air of vague and hopeless sadness. We never come to learn what Mrs. Ramsay's situation really is. Only the sadness, the vanity of her beauty and vital force emerge from the depths of secrecy. Even when we have read the whole novel, the meaning of the relationship between the planned trip to the lighthouse and the actual trip many years later remains unexpressed, enigmatic, only dimly to be conjectured, as does the content of Lily Briscoe's concluding vision which enables her to finish her painting with one stroke of the brush. It is one of the few books of this type which are filled with good and genuine love but also, in its feminine way, with irony, amorphous sadness, and doubt of life. Yet what realistic depth is achieved in every individual occurrence, for example the measuring of the stocking! Aspects of the occurrence come to the fore, and links to other occurrences, which, before this time, had hardly been sensed, which had never been clearly seen and attended to, and yet they are determining factors in our real lives. What takes place here in Virginia Woolf's novel is precisely what was attempted everywhere in works of this kind (although not everywhere with the same insight and mastery)—that is, to put the emphasis on the random occurrence, to exploit it not in the service of a planned continuity of action but in itself. And in the process something new and elemental appeared: nothing less than the wealth of reality and depth of life in every moment to which we surrender ourselves without prejudice. To be sure, what happens in that moment—be it outer or inner processes—concerns in a very personal way the individuals who live in it, but it also (and for that very reason) concerns the elementary things which men in general have in common. It is precisely the random moment which is comparatively independent of the controversial and unstable orders over which men fight and despair; it passes unaffected by them, as daily life. The more it is exploited, the more the elementary things which our lives have in common come to light. The more numerous, varied, and simple the people are who appear as subjects of such random moments, the more effectively must what they have in common shine forth. In this unprejudiced and exploratory type of representation we cannot but see to what an extent—below the surface conflicts—the differences between men's ways of life and forms of thought have already lessened. The strata of societies and their different ways of life have become inextricably mingled. There are no longer even exotic peoples. A century ago (in Mérimée for example), Corsicans or Spaniards were still exotic; today the term would be quite unsuitable for Pearl Buck's Chinese peasants. Beneath the conflicts, and also through them, an economic and cultural leveling process is taking place. It is still a long way to a common life of mankind on earth, but the goal begins to be visible. And it is most concretely visible now in the unprejudiced, precise, interior and exterior representation of the random moment in the lives of different people. So the complicated process of dissolution which led to fragmentation of the exterior action, to reflection of consciousness, and to stratification of time seems to be tending toward a very simple solution. Perhaps it will be too simple to please those who, despite all its dangers and catastrophes, admire and love our epoch for the sake of its abundance of life and the incomparable historical vantage point which it affords. But they are few in number, and probably they will not live to see much more than the first forewarnings of the approaching unification and simplification.

EPILOGUE

THE subject of this book, the interpretation of reality through literary representation or "imitation," has occupied me for a long time. My original starting point was Plato's discussion in book 10 of the *Republic*—mimesis ranking third after truth—in conjunction with Dante's assertion that in the *Commedia* he presented true reality. As I studied the various methods of interpreting human events in the literature of Europe, I found my interest becoming more precise and focused. Some guiding ideas began to crystallize, and these I sought to pursue.

The first of these ideas concerns the doctrine of the ancients regarding the several levels of literary representation—a doctrine which was taken up again by every later classicistic movement. I came to understand that modern realism in the form it reached in France in the early nineteenth century is, as an aesthetic phenomenon, characterized by complete emancipation from that doctrine. This emancipation is more complete, and more significant for later literary forms of the imitation of life, than the mixture of *le sublime* with *le grotesque* proclaimed by the contemporary romanticists. When Stendhal and Balzac took random individuals from daily life in their dependence upon current historical circumstances and made them the subjects of serious, problematic, and even tragic representation, they broke with the classical rule of distinct levels of style, for according to this rule, everyday practical reality could find a place in literature only within the frame of a low or intermediate kind of style, that is to say, as either grotesquely comic or pleasant, light, colorful, and elegant entertainment. They thus completed a development which had long been in preparation (since the time of the novel of manners and the *comédie larmoyante* of the eighteenth century, and more pronouncedly since the *Sturm und Drang* and early romanticism). And they opened the way for modern realism, which has ever since developed in increasingly rich forms, in keeping with the constantly changing and expanding reality of modern life.

Looking at the problem in this fashion, I came to realize that the revolution early in the nineteenth century against the classical doctrine of levels of style could not possibly have been the first of its kind. The barriers which the romanticists and the contemporary realists tore down had been erected only toward the end of the sixteenth century and during the seventeenth by the advocates of a rigorous imitation of antique literature. Before that time, both during the Middle Ages and on through the Renaissance, a serious realism had existed. It had been possible in literature as well as in the visual arts to represent the most everyday phenomena of reality in a serious and significant context. The doctrine of the levels of style had no absolute validity. However different medieval and modern realism may be, they are at one in this basic attitude. And it had long been clear to me how this medieval conception of art had evolved, and when and how the first break with the classical theory had come about. It was the story of Christ, with its ruthless mixture of everyday reality and the highest and most sublime tragedy, which had conquered the classical rule of styles.

But if one compares the two breaks with the doctrine of stylistic levels, one cannot but see at once that they came about under completely different conditions and yielded completely different results. The view of reality expressed in the Christian works of late antiquity and the Middle Ages differs completely from that of modern realism. It is very difficult to formulate the specific character of the older Christian view in such a way that the essential points are brought out and all of the pertinent phenomena are included. A solution which struck me as on the whole satisfactory resulted from an investigation of the semantic history of the word *figura*. For this reason I use the term figural to identify the conception of reality in late antiquity and the Christian Middle Ages. What I mean by it is repeatedly explained in this book (for example, pp. 73ff.); a detailed presentation is to be found in my essay on *figura* (which has been reprinted in my *Neue Dante-Studien, Istanbuler Schriften* No. 5, Istanbul 1944, now Berne). In this conception, an occurrence on earth signifies not only itself but at the same time another, which it predicts or confirms, without prejudice to the power of its concrete reality here and now. The connection between occurrences is not regarded as primarily a chronological or causal development but as a oneness within the divine plan, of which all occurrences are parts and reflections. Their direct earthly connection is of secondary importance, and often their interpretation can altogether dispense with any knowledge of it.

These three closely related ideas, which gave the original problem form, though at the same time they narrowed its scope, are the base upon which the entire study is built. Naturally it involves a variety of other motifs and problems inherent in the abundance of historical phenomena which had to be treated. But most of these are in some way related to the ideas mentioned, and at any rate those ideas form the constant point of reference.

As for the methods employed, they have been discussed in an earlier context (p. 548). A systematic and complete history of realism would not only have been impossible, it would not have served my purpose. For the guiding ideas had delimited the subject matter in a very specific way. I was no longer concerned with realism in general, the question was to what degree and in what manner realistic subjects were treated seriously, problematically, or tragically. As a result, merely comic works, works which indubitably remained within the realm of the low style, were excluded. They could at most be referred to occasionally as contrasting illustrations, in the same sense in which completely unrealistic works in the elevated style were to be mentioned from time to time. The category of "realistic works of serious style and character" has never been treated or even conceived as such. I have not seen fit to analyze it theoretically and to describe it systematically. To do that would have necessitated an arduous and, from the reader's point of view, a tiresome search for definitions at the very beginning of my study. (Not even the term "realistic" is unambiguous.) And it is most probable that I could not have managed without an unusual and clumsy terminology. The procedure I have employed—that of citing for every epoch a number of texts and using these as test cases for my ideas—takes the reader directly into the subject and makes him sense what is at issue long before he is expected to cope with anything theoretical.

The method of textual interpretation gives the interpreter a certain leeway. He can choose and emphasize as he pleases. It must naturally be possible to find what he claims in the text. My interpretations are no doubt guided by a specific purpose. Yet this purpose assumed form only as I went along, playing as it were with my texts, and for long stretches of my way I have been guided only by the texts themselves. Furthermore, the great majority of the texts were chosen at random, on the basis of accidental acquaintance and personal preference rather than in view of a definite purpose. Studies of this kind do not deal with laws but with trends and tendencies, which cross and complement one another in the most varied ways. I was by no means interested merely in presenting what would serve my purpose in the narrowest sense; on the contrary, it was my endeavor to accommodate multiplex data and to make my formulations correspondingly elastic.

The individual chapters treat individual epochs, in some cases comparatively short ones, as little as half a century, in others much longer. There are frequent gaps—that is to say, periods which have not been treated at all: antiquity for example, which I use only by way of introduction, or the early Middle Ages, from which but too little has been preserved. Additional chapters could have been inserted later to deal with English, German, and Spanish texts. I should have liked to treat the *siglo de oro* more extensively; I should especially have liked to add a special chapter on German realism of the seventeenth century. But the difficulties were too great. As it was, I had to deal with texts ranging over three thousand years, and I was often obliged to go beyond the confines of my own field, that of the romance literatures. I may also mention that the book was written during the war and at Istanbul, where the libraries are not well equipped for European studies. International communications were impeded; I had to dispense with almost all periodicals, with almost all the more recent investigations, and in some cases with reliable critical editions of my texts. Hence it is possible and even probable that I overlooked things which I ought to have considered and that I occasionally assert something which modern research has disproved or modified. I trust that these probable errors include none which affect the core of my argument. The lack of technical literature and periodicals may also serve to explain that my book has no notes. Aside from the texts, I quote comparatively little, and that little it was easy to include in the body of the book. On the other hand it is quite possible that the book owes its existence to just this lack of a rich and specialized library. If it had been possible for me to acquaint myself with all the work that has been done on so many subjects, I might never have reached the point of writing.

With this I have said all that I thought the reader would wish me to explain. Nothing now remains but to find him—to find the reader, that is. I hope that my study will reach its readers—both my friends of former years, if they are still alive, as well as all the others for whom it was intended. And may it contribute to bringing together again those whose love for our western history has serenely persevered.

APPENDIX: "EPILEGOMENA TO *MIMESIS*"*

by Erich Auerbach

Translated by Jan M. Ziolkowski

SINCE the publication of the book more than six years have passed; numerous reviews have appeared, among which many have been very extensive. It can be assumed that most of the critical ideas that *Mimesis* can prompt have been expressed in them. For that reason I would like now to say something in reply to some of these ideas. Only to some: it would be wholly impossible to give due recognition to everything instructive and interesting that has been presented by so many commentators, mostly well informed and understanding. I have selected topics that are especially close to my heart—either because I have something to concede or because I believe that I am obliged to defend my views against misunderstandings.

I expected that the most serious objections against the train of thought in the book would come from the direction of classical philology, for ancient literature is treated in my book above all as a counter-example. According to the statement of the basic theme, I had to show what ancient literature does not possess. The one-sidedness that results from this can disturb and perhaps even offend a reader who is a philologist of ancient literature, and it could be moderated, but not altogether avoided. I was gratified that both of the reviews by classical philologists—Otto Regenbogen [1891-1966][1] and Ludwig Edelstein [1902-1965][2]—formulated their objections with much understanding and consideration for the overall intent of the book.

The two reviews have much in common: both try to contest or to weaken my view on the limits of ancient realism, both offer examples in opposition, and both engage in polemic against one passage (*Mimesis*, pp. 38-39) where I turn to speaking of the limits of ancient historiography. The much more extensive review by Regenbogen (which is most especially interesting for me) introduces, in addition, a criticism of my handling of Homer and Augustine.[3]

* First published in *Romanische Forschungen* 65 (1953) 1-18.

1 *Mimesis. Eine Rezension*. Den Mitgliedern von Svenska Klassikerförbundet . . . überreicht. Uppsala: Privately Printed, 1949, 23 pp. Rept. in Otto Regenbogen, *Kleine Schriften*, ed. Franz Dirlmeier (Munich: C. H. Beck, 1961), pp. 600-617.

2 *Modern Language Notes* 55 (1950) 426-431.

3 I will not here delve into the questions relating to Augustine; they have been dealt with in the meantime in this journal [*Romanische Forschungen*], 64 (1952) 309ff.

Here I have to admit, first of all, that the themes of Homer's lack of tension and "foregrounding" were emphasized all too strongly in the initial chapter, and that I am on the whole not entirely satisfied with my first chapter. On many points I am in agreement with what Regenbogen says, especially on pages 12 and 13 of his review; this first chapter might have dealt with other literary documents of archaic Greece (to bring into consideration ones from Homer himself, from Aeschylus, perhaps from Hesiod, and even perhaps the art of the sixth century) in which something very closely related to existential realism is sometimes expressed. However, that would have given the book an entirely new dimension, so to speak, into early antiquity, and I recoiled from that. I considered for a moment letting the Homer chapter fall entirely by the wayside. For my purposes it would have sufficed to begin with the time around the birth of Christ. But it proved not to be feasible to find an introduction that would have been able to measure up to the Homer chapter in clarity and effectiveness for presenting the problem, and so I let it stand, somewhat toned down in regard to the first draft. It seemed to me justified to stress themes that matter in the context of the book and that have been properly viewed, even if developed in a one-sided way. But I emphasize the one-sidedness of the presentation here expressly because, time and again, there are readers who especially praise the first chapter in particular.

Perhaps I should also have refrained, in the second chapter, from the remarks about ancient historiography; perhaps then it would have been possible to avoid this complex of problems. For an undertaking like my book, it is advisable to confine oneself to what is absolutely necessary for the development of one's thoughts; and it is always difficult to choose one's expressions, in the treatment of a problem as broadly layered as is the problem of ancient historical writing, so that they characterize adequately the totality of the phenomena—as in this case, for example, Herodotus, Thucydides, Polybius, and the later historians. For instance, Herodotus is not comprehended in my terminology (rhetorically and moralistically), even if one understands the expression "moralistically" as it is meant in the context of my thought (in opposition to "historically"). But I can make no further concession. In the decade that has passed since the editing of the Petronius chapter, my views on the difference between ancient and modern historiography have become stronger in relation to the presentation of the problem and the shaping of the idea. To explain them again here would go beyond the framework of an essay; *vita comite* ("if I live so long"), as a Carolingian author was accustomed to say, I will return once again to the topic.[4] Yet I wish to remind readers that I did not compare Thucydides or Tacitus with figures like them in modern times (it would be difficult even to find figures like them there!) but rather with a modern, albeit prominent, professor of history—just to show how the bases for the presentation of the problem and the shaping of the idea have changed.[5] I wish also to remind readers that the modern perspectival and "historicist" examination of history has been fully developed for just barely a century and a half. And finally I wish to state that the word "limits" of ancient historical writing contains no negative value judgment at all. Quite the contrary. The unity, drama, plasticity, and humanity, which come into being through the restriction to a narrow circle of people acting with and against one another, have become unattainable.

In regard to the "stylistic differentiation" in later (thus, for example, "post-Socratic") ancient literature, I was sure of my facts from the beginning; but I still read with satisfaction which counterexamples were adduced by my reviewers who were classical philologists. Edelstein cites Aristophanes' assertion that he pursues serious intentions, as well as Plato's, Cratinus', and Cicero's remarks that tend in the same direction. He brings up Middle Comedy and Menander (is it justified to exclude the latter from an analysis of realism?); he speaks of Milesian fable, of Theocritus and Herondas (I never claimed that these were to be excluded from the category considered by me because they wrote in verse!), of mime and of epigrams; and he mentions later also Xenophon's *Oeconomicus*. People can adduce such counterexamples only if they have lost sight of the concept of realism as I meant it, and consequently assume that I intended to characterize the whole of ancient realism as "a vaudeville show" or as "poking fun." That, however, I neither intended nor did. I call the realism that is alien to antiquity serious, problematic, or tragic; I set it in express opposition to the "moralistic." Perhaps I would have done better to call it "existential realism," but I hesitated to use this all too contemporary term for phenomena of the distant past. And what I meant, it seemed to me, was to be inferred with unmistakable, even overpowering clarity from the passage about Peter and my analysis of it [*Mimesis*, pp. 40-49]. But Regenbogen, too, mentions Xenophon (*Oeconomicus* and *Socratic Memoirs*), where "the

[4] [The phrases *vita comes* and *vita comitante* are frequent in Carolingian poetry: see Otto Schumann, *Lateinisches Hexameter-Lexikon. Dichterisches Formelgut von Ennius bis zum Archipoeta*, vol. 5 (Munich: Monumenta Germaniae Historica, 1982), p. 680.]

[5] [Auerbach compared the self-expression and thinking of the ancient authors with that of [Michael Ivanovitch] Rostovtzeff [1870-1952] (*Mimesis*, p. 39).]

description of everyday life turns up in a sense not at all comic or idyllic." Does Regenbogen believe that these examples of "serious" realism have something to do with what the temptation of Peter contains, that they anticipate or even just announce the world-historical change in stylistic feeling that is proclaimed there? Edelstein writes toward the end of his review: "Yet, in my opinion, it is not only the contrast, it is also the similarities (between ancient and modern concepts) that need to be emphasized." Of course. It is quite clear to me with what great justification, for example, early Christianity can be regarded as the product of late antiquity. I have read many significant investigations that have been written from this point of view, and I have learned from them. In *Mimesis* I also took account, partly expressly, partly implicitly, of this approach. But the task that my theme imposed on me was a different one: I had to show not the transition but rather the complete change.

Only much later, six years after the book had appeared, did E[rnst] R[obert] Curtius [1886-1956] publish his objections to it. He sees in the book a theoretical construct, from which he seeks to extract theses in order to refute them. But the book is no theoretical construct; it aims to offer a view, and the very elastic thoughts or ideas that hold it together cannot be grasped and proven wrong in single, isolated phrases. I will return to this later. First it is necessary here to enter into the details of Curtius' refutations. He considers as the theses of the book the doctrine of stylistic differentiation and mingling (which for its part rests on the concept of the three ancient types of style) and the doctrine of the figural view of reality of Christian late antiquity and the Middle Ages.

[Curtius] deals with the doctrine of the three styles in this periodical (*Romanische Forschungen* 64 [1952] 57ff.).[6] He begins with an enumeration of the expert opinions on the types of style that have been preserved to our day, from the *Rhetoric to Herennius* down to Meinhard of Bamberg (eleventh century), so as to reach the conclusion "that the ancient rule of stylistic differentiation is neither so unified nor so absolute as it might seem according to Auerbach." The compilation of expert opinions is useful,[7] but it contributes nothing to the criticism of *Mimesis*.

[6] What is said there occasionally about the questions, which were also dealt with by Edelstein and Regenbogen, will not be discussed again here. That the "rustic, serious, and sober" Hesiod has nothing to do with the realism of the Gospels is perfectly clear. And that alone matters, not words that have been taken out of context and that can be interpreted variously.

[7] Some observations about this: I do not find a mention of the especially poetic theory of three styles of Heracleides of Pontos ([as transmitted by] Philodemos), which is to be

Mimesis is an attempt at the history of the matter itself, not of the expert opinions on it; to write the latter with the resources that were at my disposal in Istanbul would have been altogether impossible. The conceptual pair "stylistic differentiation/stylistic mixing" is one of the themes of my book and always has the same significance throughout the twenty chapters, from Genesis all the way to Virginia Woolf. Thus it does not conform to changes in expert opinions. It has to do with a version of the thought, which was formed by me around 1940. In particular, the idea of realism, which is present in *Mimesis*, was dealt with previously only rarely—and even then in another context. It has nothing to do with "Jest and Earnest in the Middle Ages" or "Kitchen Humor."[8] Incidentally, in the extant ancient opinions on the three styles (most of which relate to oratory) very little is said about realism.

It is an entirely different question, whether my pair of concepts covers the tradition adequately, whether it is applicable, whether, therefore, stylistic differentiation was really a characteristic element of ancient stylistic feeling. On the last two pages of his essay (and already in note 3 on page 60) Curtius tries to contest this also, and specifically he thinks:

1. I advocated the thesis that ancient comedy had been classed in the humble style.[9] Presumably I let myself be misled to this end by Dante's

---

regarded as a source of Horace, as presented by Christian Jensen ("Herakleides vom Pontos bei Philodem und Horaz," *Sitzungsberichte der Preussischen Akademie der Wissenschaften* [Berlin: Akademie der Wissenschaften, 1936], Phil.-Hist. Klasse 23, pp. 292ff.; pp. 304ff. on the three styles)—a significant work, of which I was made aware by Curtius himself (*European Literature and the Latin Middle Ages*, p. 439, note 14).

The concept of the *prepon* appears for the first time not in Theophrastus but instead already in Aristotle (*Rhetoric* 3.2.1404 b).

"Good taste" and "neatness" are however probably too general translations of *elegantia* and *munditia* in Cicero, *Orator* 23.79; it has to do with linguistic purity in a puristic sense, as emerges from what follows: "sermo purus erit et latinus" ("the language will be pure Latin"). Compare Quintilian 8.3.87 and also many passages in Cicero himself, for example the one cited by Curtius later, *De optimo genere oratorum* 4. On the significance of *elegantia*, see George Lincoln Hendrickson, "The Origin and Meaning of the Ancient Characters of Style," *American Journal of Philology* 26 (1905) 249-290; on *elegantia*, pp. 263-264. I hope later to return to some medieval material.

It might also be noted as far as method is concerned that an assembly of rhetorical expert opinions is a somewhat single-track way to clarify the situation. A picture of the truly living ideas can be gained only through the study of terms, as for example *altus, gravis, sublimis, suavis, dulcis, subtilis, planus, tenuis, privatus, humilis, remissus, pedester, comicus*, and so forth; this can now be done with the help of the *Thesaurus Linguae Latinae* [Leipzig: B. G. Teubner, 1900-].

[8] [These two phrases refer pointedly to the title and subtitle of an excursus in *European Literature and the Latin Middle Ages*. In the handling of these two phrases and in all page references, I follow the English translation as found in *European Literature and the Latin Middle Ages*, trans. Willard R. Trask, Bollingen Series 36 (Princeton, New Jersey: Princeton University Press, 1953; rept. 1990).]

[9] As witness (so says Curtius ironically, but inaccurately) I cited Montaigne. It would

statements in *De vulgari eloquentia* 2.4 and *Epistola* 10.10. But [according to Curtius] this theory surfaces for the first time, as Paget Toynbee [1855-1932] has demonstrated (*Dante Studies and Researches* [London: Methuen and Co., 1902] p. 103), in Uguccione of Pisa [often known by his Latin name, Hugutio] (ca. 1200).

2. I seemed generally to accept that for ancient theory a conscious correspondence existed between the types of style and the genres of poetry. This is [according to Curtius] false. At the beginning of *De optimo genere oratorum* Cicero denies the equation of the types of style with the genres of poetry. While there should be no transition between the genres of poetry, there must be between the types of style. Curtius cites verbatim: "oratorem genere non divido, optimum enim quaero" ("I do not divide up the orator by class, for I seek the best"). This would be an express denial of stylistic differentiation. In *Institutio oratoria* 10.2.22 Quintilian reproduces Cicero's train of thought in a way true to its meaning.

I advocated absolutely no "thesis" on the ascription of genres of poetry to set levels of stylistic elevation. But to be sure, tragedy is always assigned to the high style,[10] comedy—ever in accord with its character—to the middle or humbler style,[11] as Boileau still does (and, by the way, Dante, too, in *De vulgari eloquentia*, loc. cit.). Paget Toynbee takes care not to claim that Dante's characterization of comedy surfaces first in Uguccione. He contents himself with the reference to Uguccione as Dante's direct source. A. Philip McMahon, whom Curtius, for reasons beyond my comprehension, likewise cites, references even older sources of Uguccione: Papias and Isidore ("Seven Questions on Aristotelian Definitions of Tragedy and Comedy," *Harvard Studies in Classical Philology* 40 [1929] 97-198, here: 140). It is hard to understand how the author of the book *European Literature and the Latin Middle Ages* can believe that Uguccione, or another medieval author whom Uguccione could have used, created a new definition of comedy. Uguccione's and Dante's definition derives, in the final analysis, from one of the oldest

not be so wrong, if I had done it. Montaigne, after all, was traveling on the road from Rome.

[10] Curtius maybe still remembers the passage cited by him (*European Literature and the Latin Middle Ages*, p. 417) from Wilhelm Schmid, *Geschichte der griechischen Literature*, vol. 1/2 (Munich: C. H. Beck, 1934), p. 85.

[11] The special situation of Old Comedy (Aristophanic comedy) in ancient theory, for which Curtius cites Quintilian 10.1.65, is a subject that has concerned me for a long time because it plays a role in Dante criticism from the sixteenth up to the eighteenth century, in Vico too. But there was no room for it in *Mimesis*.

definitions we know, and the one that became far and away the most influential: that of Theophrastus. It developed as follows in the glosses of Placidus (fifth-sixth century: *Placidus liber glossarum. Glossaria reliqua*, ed. Georg Goetz, Corpus *glossariorum Latinorum* 5 [Leipzig: B. G. Teubner, 1894], p. 56): "Comoedia est quae res privatarum et humilium personarum comprehendit, non tam alto ut tragoedia stilo, sed mediocri et dulci" ("Comedy is that which comprehends the affairs of ordinary and humble individuals, not in so high a style as tragedy but in a humble and engaging one"). Although the words *privatarum et humilium* point rather to the lower style, this gloss rates comedy as belonging to the middle style, to which Menander and Terence particularly gave impetus. The contrast to the level of tragedy is essential and permanent. A scholium on Terence (*Scholia Terentiana*, ed. Friedrich H. Schlee [Leipzig: B. G. Teubner, 1893], p. 163, l. 12) counts comedy as belonging to the lower style: "comoedia villanus cantus, ut qui sit affinis cotidianae locutioni" ("Comedy is lower-class song, the kind related to everyday speech"). Note the agreement with Uguccione and Dante: it is a late-antique topos![12] And why does Curtius reject the Horace passage, *Ars poetica* 93-98, Dante's true source—and one cited by him? Because it has to do with the connection of *lexis* ["language"] to the *prepon* ["the apt (the virtue of parts that fit harmoniously into a whole: decorum)"]. But the doctrine of the types of style is nothing other than the expression of that will to style that connects *lexis* to the *prepon*. From its earliest beginnings, ever since Aristotle, the *prepon* has been the basis for the doctrine of the types of style.

That is the heart of the argument. I never claimed a precise connection of the genres of poetry to the types of style; except for tragedy, the epic in Virgil's or Lucan's style, and on the other hand for the various forms of humbler realism, the classification is uncertain. But I claim the differentiation of style, which is based on the *prepon*; a hierarchy of forms of expression corresponds to a hierarchy of topics. Every offense against it is *cacozelia* ["affectation of style"] ("aut magnarum rerum humilis dictio aut minimarum oratio tumens" ["either humble diction for great topics or bombastic speech for the least important"]: Marius Plotius Sacerdos, *Artes grammaticae*, in Heinrich Keil, ed. *Grammatici*

[12] A selection of additional, infrequently cited testimonies: Seneca, *Epist.* 100.10; Donatus, *Commentum Terenti*, ed. Paul Wessner (Leipzig: B. G. Teubner, 1902-1908), passim (e.g., *Adelphoe* 638, *Hecyra* 611); *Anthologia latina*, ed. Franz Buecheler and Alexander Riese, vol. 1/2 (Leipzig: B. G. Teubner, 1894-1926), nos. 664 and 664a; quite similarly Ausonius, *Opuscula*, ed. Rudolf Peiper (Leipzig: B. G. Teubner, 1886), p. 412, no. 367, ll. 2-3.

latini, vol. 6 [Leipzig: B. G. Teubner, 1874], p. 455, ll. 12-13). Curtius' polemic against this truism of classical philology rests upon a misunderstanding of the texts. He mistakes the mingling of the types of styles or the levels of stylistic elevation with Cicero's challenge that the ideal orator must command them all. The latter appears in the passages of Cicero and Quintilian that he adduces, but there is nothing about a rejection of stylistic differentiation. That Cicero demands the command of all levels of stylistic elevation only from the orator and not from the poet has only a very remote connection with the subject treated in *Mimesis* (of the differentiation between the high style and everyday realism), but I would like nonetheless to present here briefly the thinking of Cicero. He thinks—and this corresponded to the actual situation—[that] there are genres of poetry in which, under all circumstances, a loftiness prevails, namely, tragedy or grand epic on the one hand, comedy on the other.[13] In each of them, individual poets (Cicero names Homer and Menander) distinguished themselves as specialists, as it were. In contrast, there is, for the most part, in one and the same judicial or political speech a motivation for the application of many levels; yet that does not mean such application must happen all at once, but rather in alternation according to an intention (*docere* "to show," *delectare* "to delight," *commovere* "to move"). Cicero and Quintilian never taught that one ought to present (*docere*) the facts in the high style or excite and rouse the audience in the matter-of-fact, lower one. That would amount to a rejection of stylistic differentiation for oratory; but it would appear to them as *cacozelia* ["affectation of style"] or *tapeinosis* ["lowness of style"]. A greater authority than Cicero and Quintilian demanded, by the way, or so it seems, the same from the poet as they did from the orator. At the end of Plato's *Symposium* it is related how at daybreak, among the many people sleeping, Socrates explained to Agathon and Aristophanes, who were still drinking with him but who were also already half asleep, that one and the same person must know how to compose tragedies and comedies.

I believe that one can have confidence in my idea of ancient stylistic differentiation without fear of being misled. The idea is not incautious.

The second of my "theses," that of the figuralism of the Christian view of reality, Curtius briefly "repudiated," as he puts it, in another place.

[13] In the process Cicero (and likewise Quintilian) gives an exact formulation of stylistic differentiation: "in tragoedia comicum vitiosum est, et in comoedia turpe tragicum" ["in tragedy the comic is faulty, and in comedy the tragic is indecent"].

The repudiation, which is directed against my essay on *figura* (first in *Archivum Romanicum* 22 [1938], reprinted in *Neue Dantestudien*, Istanbuler Schriften, no. 5 [Istanbul, 1944]),[14] is found somewhat irrelevantly in a footnote of his work on [Gustav] Gröber [1844-1911] (*Zeitschrift für romanische Philologie* 67 (1951) 276-277) and consists substantially of an enumeration of book and essay titles. [He charges] that I had not taken into consideration the research results contained in these writings [and that] if I had done so, my thesis would have become worth discussing. Among the works enumerated are found only two (by [Jean] Daniélou [1905-1974] and [Rudolf Karl] Bultmann [1884-1976]) of the specialized theological investigations of typology, which have recently become very numerous. All of these works appeared long after *figura*; the two specialized works did not appear until four years after *Mimesis*. What is more, they would not have been accessible to me in Istanbul.[15] It is also astounding that Curtius mentions among the witnesses against me the work of Bultmann, which makes reference to my work.[16] More important, however, is that the theological writings on typology—both those named by Curtius and other more recent ones—give me no cause to change anything substantive in my views.[17] This is because, among

[14] Now reprinted by Francke in Bern. ["Figura" is available in English, translated by Ralph Manheim, in Erich Auerbach, *Scenes from the Drama of European Literature: Six Essays* (New York: Meridian Books, Inc., 1959; rept. Gloucester, Mass.: Peter Smith, 1973), pp. 11-76.]

[15] Compare *Mimesis*, p. 557. I was able to write the works on *figura* and *passio* because an entire set of Migne's *Patrologia* was located in an attic-level library room of the Dominican monastery of San Pietro di Galata. The monastery library was not public, but the apostolic delegate, Monsignor Roncalli (now papal nuncio in Paris and a cardinal), had the kindness to grant me use of it. [Born Angelo Giuseppe Roncalli in 1881, the man to whom Auerbach referred as Monsignor Roncalli was apostolic delegate in Turkey and Greece from 1934 to 1944, when he was promoted to new—and difficult—duties as papal nuncio to occupied Paris. In 1953 he was created a cardinal. Later, in 1958, Roncalli was elected to the papacy, as Pope John XXIII. The Second Vatican Council (1962-1965) was the achievement for which he is best known. He died on 3 June 1963.]

[16] "Ursprung und Sinn der Typologie als hermeneutischer Method," in *Pro regno, pro sanctuario: een bundel studies en bijdragen van vrienden en vereerders bij de zestsigste verjaardag van Prof. Dr. G. Van der Leeuw*, ed. W. J. Kooiman and J. M. Van Veen (Nijkerk: G. F. Callenbach, 1950), pp. 89-100, also in *Theologische Literaturzeitung*, (1950) 205ff. I have been in contact with Bultmann for over two decades—contact that was interrupted only by the war; I owe much to his counsel, as well as recently to that of Erich Dinkler.

So as to mention a Catholic point of view on the topic as well, compare William F. Lynch in *Thought* (New York) 25 (1951) 44-47.

[17] I will take this occasion to communicate to the readers of this periodical, most of whom are not theologians, those points in my presentation that could give rise to controversies. Both of them relate to the early Christian period.

1. In my presentation of the beginnings of Christian typology, the role of Paul is

other things, far and away most of them concern themselves with individual questions of sources and with restricted segments of time, whereas my efforts rest upon collections of motifs that I began seventeen years ago and that extend from Paul up into the seventeenth century.

What Curtius understands by typological allegoresis, about which I am supposed to have refrained from informing myself, is unfathomable; typological allegoresis is, after all, the subject of my investigations. Whether one calls it so or calls it figural explication is irrelevant. My original terminology came into being naturally through the fact that I proceeded from a semantic history of the word *figura*. I spoke there extensively about the fluctuation of the terminology in late antiquity and the Middle Ages. The terminology that I first preferred is so practical, and was alive so long in the tradition, that a separate *Index figurarum* and *Index de allegoriis* are still found in the second volume of indices in Migne's *Patrologia*.[18] But the terminology does not matter, so

---

perhaps emphasized too exclusively. Of course people in the Middle Ages were of my view. Compare, for example, such representations as the one of "St. Paul Grinding the Corn of the Doctrine of the Prophets in His Mill" on a capital in Vézelay, in Joan Evans, *Cluniac Art of the Romanesque Period* (Cambridge: Cambridge University Press, 1950), fig. 175b. [Abbot] Suger had the same representation painted on a window of Saint-Denis and had the following verses placed there (Erwin Panofsky, *Abbot Suger on the Abbey Church of St.-Denis and Its Art Treasures* [Princeton, New Jersey: Princeton University Press, 1946]; 2d. ed. by Gerda Panofsky-Soergel [Princeton, New Jersey: Princeton University Press, 1979], pp. 74-75):

> Tollis agendo molam de furfure, Paule, farinam.
> Mosaicae legis intima nota facis.
> Fit de tot granis verus sine furfure panis,
> Perpetuusque cibus noster et angelicus.
> [By working the mill, you, Paul, take the flour out of the bran.
> You make known the inmost meaning of the Law of Moses.
> From so many grains is made the true bread without bran,
> our and the angels' perpetual food.]

On the same window is found a representation, on which the veil has been taken from Moses' face, with this distich:

> Quod Moyses velat, Christi doctrina revelat;
> Denudant legem, qui spoilant Moysen.
> [What Moses veils the doctrine of Christ unveils;
> They who despoil Moses bare the Law.]

2. Furthermore, there appears sometimes in more recent, specialized works the tendency to ascribe to Origen a significant role for typology, whereas I counted him among the abstract-allegorical interpreters. That is a decisive problem for the conception of typology. I believe that I am right without any alteration of my view, but I must leave the clarification of the question to theologians.

[18] [The reference is to *Patrologiae cursus completus; series latina*, ed. J.-P. Migne, 221 vols. (Paris: J.-P. Migne, 1844-1864).]

long as one distinguishes clearly between abstract/allegorical and real/prophetic methods of explication.

I have often heard the reproach that I generalize the meaning of the figural or typological principle more than is appropriate, but even so, I had never heard it yet from a medievalist or a historical theologian, apart from Curtius. Unfortunately Curtius has occupied himself little with the subject; earlier researchers of the Middle Ages of the same level possessed great experience in it—not only liturgists and hymnologists, but also figures such as [Konrad] Burdach [1859-1936] or [Karl] Strecker [1861-1945], whose notes on the poems of Walter of Châtillon are a trove of typological information. Among contemporaries, apart from some art historians, it would be fitting to name as an example Ernst H. Kantorowicz [1895-1963].[19] The effect of typology is most certainly just as important and permanent a phenomenon for the medieval structure of expression as is the survival of ancient rhetorical *topoi* of form and content; it has strengthened in me ever more the conviction, and that conviction has been confirmed through discussions with experts in the material, that typology is the real vital element of Bible poetry and hymns, or, even more, of almost the whole Christian literature of late antiquity and the Middle Ages, as also of Christian art, from the sarcophagi down to the end of the Middle Ages—and sometimes beyond. Politically, too, to establish or deny claims to power, it played a significant role over many centuries. Curtius certainly has the right, in his synthetic researches into the Middle Ages, in so monumental a subject, to limit himself to the points of view that interest him particularly; but the neglect and inadequate treatment of the problem of allegory (in the broadest sense) must be emphasized. In this context I have stated that Curtius' claim is misleading and substantially incorrect that "in his study of the sacred text [Augustine] persisted in the antiquarianizing and allegorizing method which Macrobius had applied to Cicero and Virgil" (*European Literature and the Latin Middle Ages*, p. 74).[20] In opposition to that, Curtius refers me to the fifth chapter of the third part of [Henri Irénée] Marrou's book on Augustine. This chapter bears the heading "La Bible et les lettrés de la décadence." But a person can get better instruction about Augustine's exegesis from Augustine than from

[19] [For a study, see Yakov Malkiel, "Ernst H. Kantorowicz," in *On Four Modern Humanists: Hofmannsthal, Gundolf, Curtius, Kantorowicz*, ed. Arthur R. Evans, Jr. (Princeton, New Jersey: Princeton University Press, 1970), pp. 146-219.]

[20] [By translating the German phrase "antiquarisch spielenden" (which Auerbach quotes) as "antiquarianizing," Trask loses a nuance of playfulness.]

Marrou. His posing of the problem motivated him to an overly sharp development of the influence on Augustine of late-antique erudition, an influence that is incontestable in itself. Yet even in his significant, but one-sided and not always insightful book, Marrou did not and would not ever have used a formulation such as that of Curtius. Later he published an addition to the book, entitled *Saint Augustin et la fin de la culture antique: Retractatio* (Paris: E. De Boccard, 1949). There one can read on page 646: "If there is a chapter the inadequacy of which I deplore today, it is in fact the one I dared to entitle 'La Bible et les lettrés de la décadence.'"

Many reviewers have ascribed to the book, in praise or blame, tendencies that were far removed from me: that the method of the book is sociological, even that the tendency was socialist; that it is focused all too much on the Middle Ages, but also the opposite: it is antimedieval and anti-Christian; that it is wholly pro-Romance, especially pro-French, neglects German, [and] is unjust toward German literature. But there have also been patriotic readers who have congratulated me on the observation that the tragic in the *Hildebrandslied* and in the *Nibelungenlied* is deeper than that of Roland. One reviewer concluded on the basis of the first paragraph of the Roland chapter that I am an enlightened pacifist.

Here I will go into only one of these questions, namely, the relation of the book to German literature and culture, and in fact chiefly because in that context one misunderstanding can be dispelled. World history has made it so that one in my situation can scarcely speak on this topic without hurting someone's feelings. I will take the risk anyway.

The preponderance of Romance material in *Mimesis* is to be explained not only because of the fact that I am a Romanist, but rather above all because in most periods the Romance literatures are more representative of Europe than are, for example, the German. In the twelfth and thirteenth centuries France took unquestionably the leading role; in the fourteenth and fifteenth centuries Italy took it over; it fell again to France in the seventeenth, remained there also during the greater part of the eighteenth, partly still in the nineteenth, and precisely for the origin and development of modern realism (just as for painting). It would be erroneous to read between the lines of my selection [any] preferences or aversions of a fundamental kind—and equally wrong to see estrangement or aversion in the regret or criticism that occasionally comes to be expressed about certain limitations of outlook in German literature of the nineteenth century. The opposite would be more accurate. The criticism comes out of sorrow over missed possibilities to give a different direction to European history. The great French novelists are, for the posing of the problem in *Mimesis*, of crucial significance; my admiration for them is great. But for pleasure and relaxation I prefer to read Goethe, Stifter, and Keller.

It has been said that I acquired my category of stylistic mingling from modern French realism, and indeed one could deduce that from the epilogue of *Mimesis*. However, the arrangement of this is chronologically misleading. The motif of a stylistic break became apparent to me first in the story of Christ, during my Dante studies in the 1920s; one finds it in *Dante als Dichter der irdischen Welt* (which appeared at the end of 1928), pages 18-23.[21] Shortly after the appearance of this book I began to teach in Marburg, and the teaching activity led me back to French, which I had rather neglected during my years as a librarian, in which I worked on Vico and Dante.[22] While preparing a course of lectures in Marburg, the thought came to me that one could present the principle of modern realism in corresponding fashion; it was then published in two essays that appeared in 1933 and 1937.[23]

There is yet another side to the matter: *Mimesis* attempts to comprehend Europe, but it is a German book not only on account of its language. Anyone who is a little familiar with the structure of the humanities in various countries sees that at once. It arose from the themes and methods of German intellectual history and philology; it would be conceivable in no other tradition than in that of German romanticism and Hegel. It would have never been written without the influences that I experienced in my youth in Germany.[24]

[21] [Translated into English by Ralph Manheim, *Dante, Poet of the Secular World* (Chicago: University of Chicago Press, 1961).]

[22] [After passing the *Staatsexamen* in 1922, Auerbach acquired training in library science. From 1924 to 1929 he was salaried as a librarian at the Prussian State Library in Berlin. After completing an abridged translation of Giambattista Vico's *The New Science* in 1924, a collaborative translation of Benedetto Croce's introductory study of Vico in 1927, and a book of his own on Dante in 1929, Auerbach was transferred to the University Library in Marburg. In 1920 he was appointed to a professorship in Romance philology at the University of Marburg.]

[23] "Romantik und Realismus," in *Neue Jahrbücher für Wissenschaft und Jugendbildung* 9 (1933) 143ff., and "Über die ernste Nachahmung des Alltäglichen," in *Travaux du Séminaire de Philologie Romane*, vol. 1 (İstanbul: İstanbul Üniversitesi Edebiyat Fakültesi, 1937), 262ff.

[24] An unfriendly and also unpleasant review begins with the claim that *Mimesis* has been greatly discussed and praised especially abroad [outside German-speaking countries]. That gives a false impression. Of the reviews and other extensive assessments that

It has often been said that my conceptualization is not unambiguous and that the expressions that I use for organizational categories required a sharper definition. It is true that I do not define these terms, in fact even that I am not consistent throughout in using them. That happened intentionally and methodically. My effort for exactitude relates to the individual and the concrete. In contrast, the general, which compares, compiles, or differentiates phenomena, ought to be elastic and flexible; to the utmost that is possible, it ought to fall into line with what is feasible from case to case, and it is to be understood from case to case only from the context. There is not in intellectual history identity and strict conformity to laws, and abstract, reductive concepts falsify or destroy the phenomena. The arranging must happen in such a way that it allows the individual phenomenon to live and unfold freely. Were it possible, I would not have used any generalizing expressions at all, but instead I would have suggested the thought to the reader purely by presenting a sequence of particulars. That is not possible; accordingly I used some much-used terms, like realism and moralism, and, compelled by my subject, I even introduced two little-used ones: stylistic differentiation and stylistic mingling. That they all, but especially the much-used words, signify all and nothing was perfectly clear to me; they should acquire their meaning only from the context, and in fact from the particular context. That has obviously not always worked out. Almost all misunderstandings have arisen because, all the same, the reader has precisely the possibility to release the schema of a concept from the context and to hold fast pedantically to it; and thus, to give an example that has not been mentioned yet, he can hold against me that he finds *Phèdre* more realistic than *Madame Bovary*. A good writer must write in such a way that one infers from the text what he intended to express. That is not easy. Earlier I believed that one could devise words and collocations that comprehend the general in the historically intellectual more exactly than do the usual ones, and I tried it with "popular spiritualism," "dialectic of feeling" ([Karl] Vossler [1872-1949]), and "serious imitation of the everyday." But that only leads to new misunderstandings and, what is more, sounds pretentious and pedantic. It is in

I have seen up until now, over half appeared in Germany or in German-speaking Switzerland; of the remaining foreign ones, once again almost half (mostly in the U.S.A.) were composed by such individuals who had spent their youth in Germany and received their education there. The rest are distributed among Scandinavia, Holland, Belgium, the Spanish-speaking world, and Turkey. Only a few remarks have come to my attention from France, not a single one from England.

the nature of our subject that our general concepts are poorly differentiable and are undefinable. Their worth—the worth of concepts such as classic, Renaissance, mannerism, baroque, enlightenment, Romanticism, realism, symbolism, and so forth, most of which originally designate literary epochs or groups, but which are also applicable far beyond those—accordingly, their worth consists in that they elicit in readers or hearers a series of ideas that facilitate for them an understanding of what is meant in the particular context. They are not exact. The attempts to define them, or even only to collect completely and without contradiction those characteristics that compose them, can never lead to the desired result—even though they are often interesting, for the reason that someone produces in the discussion a new point of view and thereby assists in the enrichment of our ideas. One must beware, it seems to me, of regarding the exact sciences as our model; our precision relates to the particular. The progress of the historical arts in the last two centuries consists above all, apart from the opening up of new material and in a great refinement of methods in individual research, in a perspectival formation of judgment, which makes it possible to accord the various epochs and cultures their own presuppositions and views, to strive to the utmost toward the discovery of those, and to dismiss as unhistorical and dilettantish every absolute assessment of the phenomena that is brought in from outside. This historical perspectivism was founded by the pre-Romantic and Romantic critics; since then it has turned out to be very refined and ever more complicated, through insight into a great number of previously unknown or unheeded developments, influences, and relationships. A person with a classificatory taxonomy that works with exact and set conceptions of order cannot succeed in drawing together the aspects that intersect multiply into a synthesis that does justice to the subjects.

Another objection that people have made is this: that my presentation is all too time-bound and all too much determined by the present. That is also intentional. I tried to make myself thoroughly conversant with the many subjects and periods that are treated in *Mimesis*. With a deliberate extravagance of time I studied not only the phenomena that had direct significance for the aim of the book, but I read around widely in the various periods. But in the end I asked: How do matters look in the European context? No one today can see such a context from anywhere else today than precisely from the present, and specifically from the present that is determined by the personal origin, history, and education of the viewer. It is better to be consciously than unconsciously time-bound. In many learned writings one finds a kind of objectivity in which, entirely unbeknownst to the composer, modern judgments and prejudices (often not even today's but instead yesterday's or those of the day before yesterday) cry out from every word, every rhetorical flourish, every phrase. *Mimesis* is quite consciously a book that a particular person, in a particular situation, wrote at the beginning of the 1940s.

INDEX